駿台

東大 入試詳解 25年
英語 第2版
2019〜1995

問題編

駿台文庫

目　次

	問題	解答・解説
2019 年度	4	20
2018 年度	18	46
2017 年度	32	72
2016 年度	46	96
2015 年度	62	120
2014 年度	76	144
2013 年度	90	166
2012 年度	104	186
2011 年度	118	206
2010 年度	134	228
2009 年度	150	250
2008 年度	164	272
2007 年度	180	294
2006 年度	196	316
2005 年度	210	336
2004 年度	224	358
2003 年度	238	378
2002 年度	252	400
2001 年度	266	420
2000 年度	276	438
1999 年度	290	456
1998 年度	302	472
1997 年度	312	488
1996 年度	324	504
1995 年度	334	518

※各年度の解答時間と配点は，リスニング問題の放送時間（約30分）と配点
　を含むものです。

入試問題

解答時間：120分
配　　点：120点

1 **(A)** 以下の英文を読み，ヨーロッパで生じたとされる変化の内容を70〜80字の日本語で要約せよ。句読点も字数に含める。

　　In pre-industrial Europe, child labor was a widespread phenomenon and a significant part of the economic system. Until and during the nineteenth century, children beyond six years of age were required to contribute to society according to their abilities. From about the age of seven, they began a slow entry into the world of work, a world inhabited by both adults and children. The concepts of education, schooling, and protection against hazards were rare or entirely absent. In the early nineteenth century, children were also mostly viewed as the personal property of their parents, with few or no legal rights. Parents, mainly fathers, were given unlimited power and control over them and were allowed to treat them as they wished; physical punishment was almost universal and socially accepted.

　　This situation began to change as the nineteenth century progressed. Particularly in the half-century from 1870 to 1920, the rights of children in relation to parents, employers, and others expanded in the form of legal protection. Gradually, children began to be perceived as a separate category and not simply as the property of adults. The view that children have no more than economic value began to change and be replaced by the perception that they are a unique group that society has the responsibility to support and protect from the various dangers they face.

　　Another change in this period was the protection of children from parental abuse and neglect, which were subjected to intense scrutiny and challenged increasingly by government authorities. In 1889, both France and

Great Britain passed laws against cruelty to children, including that caused by their parents. The nation became the defender of children's rights. The child's right to protection then led to the right to provision of various sorts, with the national government responsible for providing services. Health care, acceptable housing, and playgrounds — together with freedom from work and access to public schooling — emerged as elements of children's rights.

(B) 以下の英文を読み，(ア)，(イ)の問いに答えよ。なお，文章中の linguistic という単語は「言語の」，linguist は「言語学者」を意味する。

　　Music is a universal language. Or so musicians like to claim. "With music," they'll say, "you can communicate across cultural and linguistic boundaries in ways that you can't with ordinary languages like English or French." On one level, this statement is obviously true. You don't have to speak French to enjoy a piece of music written by the French composer Claude Debussy. ⎢ (1) ⎢ That depends on what you mean by "universal" and what you mean by "language."

　　Every human culture has music, just as each has language. So it's true that music is a universal feature of the human experience. At the same time, both music and language systems vary widely from culture to culture. Nevertheless, no matter how strange a foreign musical system may seem, studies show that people are pretty good at detecting the emotions conveyed in unfamiliar forms of music — that is, at least the two basic emotions of happiness and sadness. ⎢ (2) ⎢ For example, higher pitch, more variations in pitch and rhythm, and faster tempo convey happiness, while the opposite conveys sadness.

　　Perhaps, then, we are born with a musical sense. But language also has melody, which linguists call prosody. Exactly these same features — pitch, rhythm, and tempo — are used to convey emotion in speech in a way that appears to be universal across languages. Listen in on a conversation in French or Japanese or some other language you don't speak. You won't understand the content, but you will understand the shifting emotional states of the speakers. She's upset, and he's getting defensive. Now she's really angry, and he's backing off. He pleads with her, but she isn't convinced. . . . We understand this exchange in a foreign language because we know what it sounds like in our own language. Likewise, when we listen to a piece of music, either from our culture or from another, we recognize emotion on the basis of melodic features that mirror universal prosodic features. (3)

But is music a kind of language? Again, we have to define our terms. (4) Biologists talk about the "language of bees," which is a way to tell fellow bees about the location of a new source of food. People talk about the "language of flowers," through which they can express their intentions. "Red roses mean . . . Pink carnations mean . . . White lilies mean . . ." And then there's "body language." By this we mean the gestures, movements, and facial expressions we use to convey emotions, social status, and so on. Although we often use body language when we speak, linguists don't consider it a true form of language. Instead, it's a communication system, just as are the so-called languages of bees and flowers.

By definition, language is a communication system consisting of a set of meaningful symbols (words) and a set of rules (syntax) for combining those symbols into larger meaningful units (sentences). While many species have communication systems, none of these counts as language because they lack one or the other component. The alarm and food calls of many species consist of a set of meaningful symbols, but they don't combine those symbols productively according to rules. Likewise, bird song and whale song have rules for combining elements, but these elements aren't meaningful symbols. Only the song as a whole has (ア).

2019年　入試問題

Like language, music has syntax — rules for ordering elements, such as notes, chords, and intervals, into complex structures. 　(5)　 Rather, it's the larger structure — the melody — that conveys emotional meaning. And it does that by mirroring the prosody of speech.

Since music and language share features in common, it's not surprising that many of the brain areas that process language also process music. 　(6)　 We tend to think that specific areas of the brain are tied exclusively to specific functions, but any complex behavior, whether language or music or driving a car, will recruit contributions from many different brain areas.

Music certainly isn't a universal language in the sense that you could use it to express any thought to any person on the planet. But music does have the power to evoke basic feelings at the core of the shared human experience. It not only crosses cultures, but it also reaches deep into our evolutionary past. And in that sense, music truly is a universal language.

(ア)　空所 (ア) に入れるのに最も適切な単語 1 語を同じページの本文中から抜き出し，その単語を記述解答用紙の 1 (B) に記入せよ。

（**編集注**：実際の試験問題での範囲は第 4 段落（But is music...）から第 7 段落 3 行目（...brain are tied）まで。）

(イ)　空所 (1) ～ (6) に入れるのに最も適切な文を以下の a) ～ h) より一つずつ選び，マークシートの (1) ～ (6) にその記号をマークせよ。ただし，同じ記号を複数回用いてはならない。

a)　But is music really a universal language?

b)　But is the opposite true, that is, is language a universal music?

c)　But this doesn't mean that music is language.

— 7 —

2019年　入試問題

d) In this sense, music really is a universal system for communicating emotion.

e) Specific features of music contribute to the expression of these emotions.

f) We, including scientists, often use "language" to mean "communication system."

g) We usually do not define "language" as "communication."

h) Yet none of these elements has significance on its own.

2 (A) 新たに祝日を設けるとしたら，あなたはどのような祝日を提案したいか。その祝日の意義は何か。また，なぜそのような祝日が望ましいと考えるのか。60〜80 語の英語で説明しなさい。なお，この場合の祝日は，国民のための祝日でもよいし，国内外の特定の地域，もしくは全世界で祝うようなものでもかまわない。

(B) 以下の下線部を英訳せよ。

　世界中でプラスチックごみを減らす動きが活発だ。食品などのプラスチック製容器や包装をなくしたり，レジ袋を有料化したりするのはもっとも容易にできることだろう。それらを紙製品や生分解性の素材に変えたりする動きも目立つ。しかし，もっとも重要なのは，プラスチックごみによってかけがえのない自然環境を汚染しているのは私たち自身であると，私たちひとりひとりが日々の暮らしのなかで自覚することである。とはいえ，そうした意識改革が難しいことも確かで，先日もペットボトルの水を買った際に，水滴で本が濡れてはいけないと，ついレジ袋をもらってしまった。

— 8 —

2019年　入試問題

4 (A) 以下の英文の段落 (22) ～ (26) にはそれぞれ誤りがある。修正が必要な下線部を各段落から一つずつ選び，マークシートの (22) ～ (26) にその記号をマークせよ。

(22) The old-fashioned stereotype that women are (a)not suited by nature at mathematical study (b)suffered a major blow in 2014, when Maryam Mirzakhani became the first woman to receive the Fields Medal, math's most prestigious award.　An equally important blow was struck by an Italian mathematician, Maria Gaetana Agnesi, born three hundred years ago.　Agnesi was the first woman to write a mathematics textbook and to be (c)appointed to a university chair in math, (d)yet her life was marked by paradox. (e)Though brilliant, rich and famous, she eventually chose a life of poverty and service to the poor.

(23) Born May 16, 1718, in Milan, Agnesi was the eldest of her wealthy father's twenty-one children.　As she grew up, her talents shone, particularly in the study of languages.　(a)In part to give her the best education possible, her father invited (b)leading intellectuals of the day to the family's home. When Agnesi was nine, she repeated from memory a Latin speech, (c)likely composed by one of her tutors, in front of her father's guests.　The speech condemned the widespread prejudice against educating women in the arts and sciences, (d)which had either been grounded in the view that a life of managing a household would require no such learning.　Agnesi presented a clear and convincing argument that women should be free to pursue (e)any kind of knowledge available to men.

(24) Agnesi eventually became (a)tired of displaying her intellectual abilities in public and (b)expressed a desire to retire from the world and to (c)dedicate her to a religious life.　When her father's second wife died, however, she (d)assumed responsibility for his household and the education of her many younger brothers and sisters.　Through this role, she (e)recognized the need for a comprehensive mathematics textbook to introduce Italian

— 9 —

2019 年　　入試問題

students to basic methods that summarized recent mathematical discoveries.

(25) Agnesi found a special appeal in mathematics. Most knowledge acquired from experience, she believed, is prone to error and open to dispute. From mathematics, however, (a)come truths that are wholly certain. (b)Published in two volumes in 1748, Agnesi's work was titled the *Basic Principles of Analysis*. It was composed not in Latin, (c)as was the custom for great mathematicians such as Newton and Euler, but in Italian, to (d)make it more accessible to students. Agnesi's textbook was praised in 1749 by the French Academy: "It took much skill and good judgment to (e)reduce almost uniform methods to discoveries scattered among the works of many mathematicians very different from each other."

(26) (a)A passionate advocate for the education of women and the poor, Agnesi believed that the natural sciences and math should play an important role in an educational curriculum. As a person of deep religious faith, however, she also believed that scientific and mathematical studies must be (b)viewed in the larger context of God's plan for creation. When her father died in 1752, she was free to answer a religious calling and devote the rest of her life to her other great passion: service to the poor. Although few remember Agnesi today, her pioneering role in the history of mathematics serves as (c)an inspiring story of triumph over gender stereotypes. She helped to clear a path for women in math (d)for generations to follow. Agnesi excelled at math, but she also loved it, perceiving (e)in its mastery of an opportunity to serve both her fellow human beings and a higher order.

— 10 —

<u>2019 年　　入試問題</u>

(B)　以下の英文を読み，下線部 (ア)，(イ)，(ウ) を和訳せよ。なお，文章中の Fred は，著者の両親が飼っている大型のリクガメの名前である。

　　Last July, I went to Honolulu to meet Fred and to spend the summer with my parents. My parents and I have a warm relationship, even though, or perhaps because, I don't speak to or visit them frequently; until my most recent trip there, the previous July, I hadn't seen them in six years. I live in New York, and they live in Hawaii, and (ア)<u>while it is true that traveling to the islands requires a certain commitment of time, the real reason I stayed away is that there were other places I wanted to visit.</u> Of all the gifts and advantages my parents have given me, one of the greatest is their conviction that it is the duty of children to leave and do what they want, and the duty of parents not just to accept this but to encourage it. When I was 14 and first leaving my parents — then living in East Texas — to attend high school in Honolulu, my father told me that any parent who expected anything from his child was bound to be disappointed, because (イ)<u>it was foolish and selfish to raise children in the hope that they might someday pay back the debt of their existence;</u> he has maintained this ever since.

　　(ウ)<u>This philosophy explains their love for a pet that, in many ways, contradicts what we generally believe a pet should be.</u> Those of us with animals in our lives don't like to think of ourselves as having expectations for them, but we do. We want their loyalty and affection, and we want these things to be expressed in a way that we can understand. Fred, however, provides none of these things. Although he is, in his way, friendly, he is not a creature who, you feel, has any particular fondness for you.

— 11 —

2019年 入試問題

5 以下の文章を読み, (A) ~ (D) の問いに答えよ。なお, 文章中の stratocumulus という単語は「層積雲」を意味する。

Gavin Pretor-Pinney decided to take a break. It was the summer of 2003, and for the last 10 years, in addition to his graphic-design business in London, he and a friend had been running a magazine called *The Idler*. This title suggests "literature for the lazy." It argues against busyness and careerism and for the value of aimlessness, of letting the imagination quietly run free. Pretor-Pinney anticipated all the jokes: that (A)he'd burned out running a magazine devoted to doing nothing, and so on. But it was true. Getting the magazine out was tiring, and after a decade, it seemed appropriate to stop for a while and live without a plan — to be an idler himself in a positive sense and make space for fresh ideas. So he exchanged his apartment in London for one in Rome, where everything would be new and anything could happen.

Pretor-Pinney is 47, tall and warm, with a grey beard and pale blue eyes. His face is often bright, as if he's being told a story and can feel some terrific surprise coming. He stayed in Rome for seven months and loved it, especially all the religious art. One thing he noticed: the paintings he encountered were crowded with clouds. They were everywhere, he told me recently, "these soft clouds, like the sofas of the saints." But outside, when Pretor-Pinney looked up, the real Roman sky was usually cloudless. He wasn't accustomed to such endless, blue emptiness. He was an Englishman; he was accustomed to clouds. He remembered, as a child, being charmed by them and deciding that people must climb long ladders to harvest cotton from them. Now, in Rome, he couldn't stop thinking about clouds. "I found myself ア(27) them," he told me.

Clouds. They were a strange obsession, perhaps even a silly one, but he didn't resist it. He went with it, as he often does, despite not having a specific goal or even a general direction in mind; he likes to see where things go. When Pretor-Pinney returned to London, he talked about clouds constantly. He walked around ア(28) them, learned their scientific names, like "stratocumulus," and

— 12 —

the weather conditions that shape them and argued with friends who complained they were gloomy or dull. He was realizing, as he later put it, that "clouds are not something to complain about. They are, in fact, the most dynamic and poetic aspect of nature."

Slowing down to appreciate clouds enriched his life and sharpened his ability to appreciate other pockets of beauty ｜ ア(29) ｜ in plain sight. At the same time, Pretor-Pinney couldn't help noting, (B) we were entering an era in which we were losing a sense of wonder. New, supposedly amazing things bounced around the internet so quickly that, as he put it, we can now all walk around with an attitude like, "Well, I've just seen a panda doing something unusual online — what's going to amaze me now?" His passion for clouds was teaching him that "it's much better for our souls to realize we can be amazed and delighted by what's around us."

At the end of 2004, a friend invited Pretor-Pinney to give a talk about clouds at a small literary festival in South West England. The previous year, there were more speakers than people in the audience, so Pretor-Pinney wanted an interesting title for his talk, to draw a crowd. "Wouldn't it be funny," he thought, "to have a society that defends clouds against the bad reputation they get — that stands up for clouds?" So he called it "The First Annual Lecture of the Cloud Appreciation Society." And it worked. Standing room only! Afterward, people came up to him and asked for more information about the Cloud Appreciation Society. They wanted to join the society. "And I had to tell them, well, I haven't really got a society," Pretor-Pinney said. So he set about ｜ ア(30) ｜ one.

He created a simple website with a gallery for posting photographs of clouds, a membership form and a bold manifesto. ("We believe that clouds are unjustly insulted and that life would be infinitely poorer without them," it began.) He also decided to charge a membership fee and issue a certificate in the mail. He did these things because he recognized that joining an online Cloud Appreciation Society that existed in name only might appear ridiculous, and he wanted to make sure that it did not seem (イ).

— 13 —

<u>2019 年　　入試問題</u>

Within a couple of months, the society had 2,000 　ア(31)　 members. Pretor-Pinney was surprised and delighted.　Then, Yahoo placed the Cloud Appreciation Society first on its 2005 list of Britain's "Wild and Wonderful Websites." People kept clicking on that link, which wasn't necessarily surprising, but thousands of them also clicked through to Pretor-Pinney's own website, then paid for memberships.　Other news sites noticed.　They did their own articles about the Cloud Appreciation Society, and people followed the links in those articles too.　Previously, Pretor-Pinney had proposed writing a book about clouds and had been rejected by 28 editors.　Now he was an internet sensation with a large online following; he got a deal to write a book about clouds.

The writing process was 　ア(32)　 .　On top of not actually having written a book before, he demanded perfection of himself, so the work went slowly.　But *The Cloudspotter's Guide*, published in 2006, is full of joy and wonder.　Pretor-Pinney surveys clouds in art history, poetry, and modern photography.　In the middle of the book, there's a cloud quiz.　Question No. 5 asks of a particular photograph, "(C)＿＿＿＿ stratocumulus?" The answer Pretor-Pinney supplies is, "It is pleasing for whatever reason you find it to be."

The book became a bestseller.

(A)　下線部 (A) に関して，"all the jokes" の例であることがわかるように，その内容を日本語で説明せよ。

(B)　下線部 (B) の内容を本文に即して日本語で説明せよ。

(C)　下に与えられた語を正しい順に並べ替え，下線部 (C) を埋めるのに最も適切な表現を完成させよ。

about　　is　　it　　layer　　of　　pleasing　　so　　that's　　this　　what

— 14 —

2019 年　　入試問題

(D)　以下の問いに解答し，その答えとなる記号をマークシートにマークせよ。

(ア)　空所 (27) ~ (32) には単語が一つずつ入る。それぞれに文脈上最も適切な
語を次のうちから一つずつ選び，マークシートの (27) ~ (32) にその記号を
マークせよ。ただし，同じ記号を複数回用いてはならない。

a)　admiring　　　b)　disturbing　　　c)　exhausting　　　d)　hating

e)　hiding　　　　f)　ignoring　　　　g)　inventing　　　　h)　missing

i)　paying　　　　j)　recovering

(イ)　空所 (イ) に入れるのに最も適切な単語を次のうちから一つ選び，マーク
シートの (33) にその記号をマークせよ。

a)　cloudy　　　　　　b)　expensive　　　　　c)　lazy

d)　pointless　　　　　e)　serious

(ウ)　本文の内容と合致しないものはどれか。一つ選び，マークシートの (34)
にその記号をマークせよ。

a)　It was not until he went to Rome that Pretor-Pinney found clouds
attractive.

b)　Pretor-Pinney learned a lot about clouds after he came back to London,
which helped him write *The Cloudspotter's Guide*.

c)　Pretor-Pinney's Cloud Appreciation Society drew people's attention
quickly.

d)　Pretor-Pinney's talk about clouds at a small literary festival turned out to
be exceptionally successful.

e)　Pretor-Pinney was busy both when co-editor of *The Idler* and when
founder of the Cloud Appreciation Society.

入試問題

解答時間：120分
配　点：120点

1　(A)　次の英文の要旨を70〜80字の日本語にまとめよ。句読点も字数に含める。

Rumours spread by two different but overlapping processes: popular confirmation and in-group momentum. The first occurs because each of us tends to rely on what others think and do. Once a certain number of people appear to believe a rumour, others will believe it too, unless they have good reason to think it is false. Most rumours involve topics on which people lack direct or personal knowledge, and so most of us often simply trust the crowd. As more people accept the crowd view, the crowd grows larger, creating a real risk that large groups of people will believe rumours even though they are completely false.

In-group momentum refers to the fact that when like-minded people get together, they often end up believing a more extreme version of what they thought before. Suppose that members of a certain group are inclined to accept a rumour about, say, the evil intentions of a certain nation. In all likelihood, they will become more committed to that rumour after they have spoken to each other. Indeed, they may move from being tentative believers to being absolutely certain, even though their only new evidence is what other members of the group believe. Consider the role of the internet here: when people see many tweets or posts from like-minded people, they are strongly inclined to accept a rumour as true.

What can be done to reduce the risk that these two processes will lead us to accept false rumours? The most obvious answer, and the standard one, involves the system of free expression: people should be exposed to balanced

— 18 —

information and to corrections from those who know the truth. Freedom usually works, but in some contexts it is an incomplete remedy. People do not process information in a neutral way, and emotions often get in the way of truth. People take in new information in a very uneven way, and those who have accepted false rumours do not easily give up their beliefs, especially when there are strong emotional commitments involved. It can be extremely hard to change what people think, even by presenting them with facts.

(B) 以下の英文を読み, (ア), (イ) の問いに答えよ。

When we think back on emotional events from the past, our memories tend to be distorted by internal influences. One way this can happen is through sharing our memories with others, something that most of us are likely to do after important life events — whether it's calling our family to tell them some exciting news, reporting back to our boss about a big problem at work, or even giving a statement to police. In these kinds of situations we are transferring information that was originally received visually (or indeed through other senses) into verbal information. We are turning inputs from our five senses into words. | (1) | ; every time we take images, sounds, or smells and verbalise them, we potentially alter or lose information. There is a limit to the amount of detail we are able to communicate through language, so we have to cut corners. We simplify. This is a process known as "verbal overshadowing," a term invented by psychologist Jonathan Schooler.

Schooler, a researcher at the University of Pittsburgh, published the first set of studies on verbal overshadowing in 1990 with his colleague Tonya Engstler-Schooler. Their main study involved participants watching a video of a bank robbery for 30 seconds. After then doing an unrelated task for 20 minutes, half of the participants spent five minutes writing down a description of the bank robber's face, while the other half undertook a task naming countries and their capitals. After this, all the participants were presented with a line-up of eight faces that were, as the researchers put it, "verbally similar," meaning that the faces matched the same kind of description — such as "blonde hair, green eyes, medium nose, small ears, narrow lips." This is different from matching photos purely on visual similarity, which may focus on things that are harder to put into words, such as mathematical distances between facial features.

We would expect that the more often we verbally describe and reinforce the appearance of a face, the better we should retain the image of it in our memory. (2) . The researchers found that those who wrote down the description of the robber's face actually performed significantly worse at identifying the correct person out of the line-up than those who did not. In one experiment, for example, of those participants who had written down a description of the criminal, only 27 percent picked the correct person out of the line-up, while 61 percent of those who had not written a description managed to do so. That's a huge difference. By stating only details that could be readily put into words, the participants had overlooked some of the details of their original visual memory.

(3) , as indicated by the outcome of possibly the biggest effort ever to reproduce the result of an experiment in psychology. This was a massive project by 33 labs and almost 100 scholars, including Jonathan Schooler and Daniel Simons, published in 2014. All researchers followed the same methods, and they found that even when the experiment was conducted by different researchers, in different countries, and with different participants, the verbal overshadowing effect was constant. Putting pictures into words always makes our memories of those pictures worse.

Further research by Schooler and others has suggested that this effect may also transfer to other situations and senses. It seems that whenever something is difficult to put into words, verbalisation of it generally diminishes recall. Try to describe a colour, taste, or melody, and you make your memory of it worse. Try describing a map, a decision, or an emotional judgement, and it becomes harder to remember all the details of the original situation.   (4)   . If we hear someone else's description of something we have seen, our memory of it is weakened in that case too. Our friends may be trying to help us when they give their verbal account of something that happened, but they may instead be overshadowing our own original memories.

According to Schooler, besides losing details, verbalising non-verbal things makes us generate competing memories. We put ourselves into a situation where we have both a memory of the time we described the event and a memory of the time we actually experienced the event. This memory of the verbalisation seems to overwhelm our original memory fragment, and we may subsequently remember the verbalisation as the best account of what happened. When faced with an identification task where we need all the original details back, such as a photo line-up, it then becomes difficult to think past our verbal description. In short, it appears our memories can be negatively affected by our own attempts to improve them.

   (5)   . Schooler's research also shows that verbalising our memories does not diminish performance — and may even improve it — for information that was originally in word form: word lists, spoken statements, or facts, for example.

2018 年　入試問題

(ア)　空所 (1) ～ (5) に入れるのに最も適切な文を以下の a) ～ h) より選び,
マークシートの (1) ～ (5) にその記号をマークせよ。ただし, 同じ記号を複数
回用いてはならない。

a)　All this is not surprising

b)　But this process is imperfect

c)　This effect is incredibly robust

d)　However, it seems that the opposite is true

e)　This is without doubt a highly sensitive area

f)　This is also true when others verbalise things for us

g)　This effect extends to more complex memories as well

h)　This does not mean that verbalising is always a bad idea

(イ)　Jonathan Schooler らが発見したと言われていることの内容を, 15～20 語
程度の英語で要約せよ。文章から答えを抜き出すのではなく, できるだけ自分
の英語で答えよ。

2　(A)　次の, シェイクスピアの戯曲『ジュリアス・シーザー』からの引用を読み,
二人の対話の内容について思うことを 40～60 語の英語で述べよ。

引用

CASSIUS　Tell me, good Brutus, can you see your face?

BRUTUS　No, Cassius; for the eye sees not itself,

But by reflection, by some other things.

………

CASSIUS　I, your glass,

Will modestly discover to yourself

That of yourself which you yet know not of.

— 22 —

2018年　入試問題

引用の和訳

キャシアス　どうだ、ブルータス、きみは自分の顔が見えるか？

ブルータス　いや、キャシアス、見えない。目は、反射によってしか、つまり他のものを通してしか自分自身を見ることができないから。

(中略)

キャシアス　私が、きみの鏡として、

きみ自身もまだ知らないきみの姿を、

あるがままにきみに見せてやろう。

(B)　以下の下線部を英訳せよ。

　「現在の行動にばかりかまけていては、生きるという意味が逃げてしまう」と小林秀雄は語った。それは恐らく、自分が日常生活においてすべきだと思い込んでいることをやってそれでよしとしているようでは、人生などいつのまにか終わってしまうという意味であろう。

4　(A)　次の英文の空所 (21-22), (23-24), (25-26), (27-28) それぞれについて、最も自然な英語となるように与えられた語を並べ替えて、その3番目と6番目に来る単語の記号をマークシートの (21) 〜 (28) にマークせよ。3番目の単語の記号と6番目の単語の記号を、それぞれその順にマークすること。ただし、それぞれ不要な語が一つずつ入っている。

　　The roots of the detective story go as far back as Shakespeare. But Edgar Allan Poe's tales of rational crime-solving created an important genre. His stories revolve around solving the puzzle of who committed the crime, (21-22)　too.

<u>2018 年</u>　　入試問題

The key figure in such a story is the detective. Poe's detective, Auguste Dupin, is a gentleman of leisure. He has no need to work. Instead, he keeps himself occupied by using "analysis" to help the real police solve crimes.

Even Arthur Conan Doyle, creator of Sherlock Holmes, had to acknowledge Poe's influence. Dupin, like Sherlock, smokes a pipe. He's also unnaturally smart and rational, a kind of superhero (23-24) great feats of crime-solving. And in both cases, the story's narrator, who is literally following the detective around, is his roommate.

Poe's formula appealed to the scientific spirit of the 19th century. That's because detective stories promised that (25-26) question. The detective story caught on because it promised that intelligence will triumph. The crime will be solved by the rational detective. Science will track down the (27-28) at night.

(21-22)

a)	inviting	b)	puzzle	c)	readers
d)	solve	e)	the	f)	them
g)	to				

(23-24)

a)	accomplish	b)	is	c)	of
d)	powers	e)	thinking	f)	to
g)	uses	h)	who		

(25-26)

a)	answer	b)	any	c)	could
d)	hold	e)	in	f)	reasoning
g)	the	h)	to		

— 24 —

2018年　入試問題

(27-28)

a) and   b) honest   c) let

d) nor   e) sleep   f) souls

g) troublemakers

(B)　次の英文を読み，下線部(ア)，(イ)，(ウ)を和訳せよ。なお，文章中の mammal という単語は「哺乳動物」を意味する。

  As a class, birds have been around for more than 100 million years. They are one of nature's great success stories, inventing new strategies for survival, using their own distinctive brands of intelligence, which, in some respects at least, seem to far exceed our own.

  Somewhere in the mists of deep time lived the common ancestor of all birds. Now there are some 10, 400 different bird species — more than double the number of mammal species. In the late 1990s, scientists estimated the total number of wild birds on the planet. They came up with 200 to 400 billion individual birds. (ア)That's roughly 30 to 60 live birds per person. To say that humans are more successful or advanced really depends on how you define those terms. After all, evolution isn't about advancement; it's about survival. It's about learning to solve the problems of your environment, something birds have done surprisingly well for a long, long time. (イ)This, to my mind, makes it all the more surprising that many of us have found it hard to swallow the idea that birds may be bright in ways we can't imagine.

  Birds learn. They solve new problems and invent novel solutions to old ones. They make and use tools. They count. They copy behaviors from one another. They remember where they put things. (ウ)Even when their mental powers don't quite match or mirror our own complex thinking, they

— 25 —

often contain the seeds of it — insight, for instance, which has been defined as the sudden emergence of a complete solution without trial-and-error learning.

5 次の文章を読み，問いに答えよ。なお，文章の中で使われている sign language という表現は「手話」を意味する。

"Janey, this is Mr. Clark. He's going to take a look at the room under the stairs." Her mother spoke too slowly and carefully, so that Janey could be sure to read each word. She had told her mother many times that she didn't have to do this, but her mother almost always did, even in front of people, to her embarrassment.

Mr. Clark kept looking at Janey intently. Maybe, because of the way her mother had spoken, he suspected she was deaf. (A)It would be like her mother not to have mentioned it. Perhaps he was waiting to see if she'd speak so that he could confirm his suspicion. She simply left her silence open to interpretation.

"Will you show him the room?" her mother said.

She nodded again, and turned so that he would follow her. Directly ahead and beneath a portion of the stairs was a single bedroom. She opened the door and he walked past her into the room, turned, and looked at her. She grew uncomfortable under his gaze, though she didn't feel as if he were looking at her as a woman, the way she might once have wanted if it were the right man. She felt she'd gone past the age for romance. It was a passing she'd lamented, then gotten over.

"I like the room," he spelled out in sign language. "⬚(B29)⬚"

That was all. No conversation, no explanation about how he'd known for certain that she was deaf or how he'd learned to speak with his hands.

— 26 —

2018 年　　入試問題

Janey came back to her mother and signed a question.

"He is a photographer," she said, again speaking too slowly.　"Travels around the world taking pictures, he says."

"　(B30)　"

"Buildings."

＊　　　　　　　　　＊

Music was her entry into silence.　She'd been only ten years old, sitting on the end of the porch above the steps, listening to the church choir.　Then she began to feel dizzy, and suddenly fell backwards into the music.

She woke into silence nights later, there in her room, in her bed.　She'd called out from her confusion as any child would, and her mother was there instantly.　But something　(C)　wrong, or had not　(C)　, except inside her where illness and confusion grew.　She hadn't heard herself, hadn't heard the call she'd made — *Mama*.　And though her mother was already gripping her tightly, she'd called out again, but only into silence, which is where she lived now, had been living for so many years that she didn't feel uncomfortable inside its invisibility.　Sometimes she thought it saved her, gave her a separate place to withdraw into as far as she might need at any given moment — and (D)there were moments.

The floor had always carried her mother's anger.　She'd learned this first as a little girl when her mother and father argued.　Their words might not have existed as sound for her, but anger always caused its own vibration.

She hadn't been exactly sure why they argued all those years ago, but sensed, the way a child will, that it was usually about her.　One day her mother found her playing in the woods behind their house, and when she wouldn't follow her mother home, her mother grabbed her by the arm and dragged her through the trees. She finally pulled back and shouted at her mother, not in words but in a scream that expressed all she felt in one great vibration. Her mother slapped her hard across her face. She saw her mother shaking and knew her mother loved her, but love was sometimes like silence, beautiful but hard to bear. Her father told her, (E)"She can't help herself."

　　　　　　　＊　　　　　　　　　　＊

Weeks later, Mr. Clark said to Janey, "You might be able to help me."

"If I can," she spelled with her fingers.

"I'll need to 　(F)　 tomorrow. Maybe you can tell me some history about them."

She nodded and felt glad to be needed, useful in some small way. Then Mr. Clark asked her to accompany him to the old house at the top of Oakhill. "You might enjoy that. Some time away from here."

She looked toward the kitchen door, not aware at first why she turned that way. Perhaps she understood, on some unconscious level, what she hadn't a moment before. Her mother was standing there. She'd been listening to him.

When Janey turned back to him, she read his lips. "Why don't you go with me tomorrow?"

She felt the quick vibration of her mother's approach. She turned to her mother, and saw her mother's anger and fear, the way she'd always seen them. Janey drew in her breath and forced the two breath-filled words out in a harsh whisper that might have 　(C)　 , for all she knew, like a sick child or someone dying: she said, " 　(B31)　 "

Her mother stared at her in surprise, and Janey wasn't sure if her mother was more shocked that she had used what was left of her voice, or at what she'd said.

"You can't. You just can't," her mother said. "I need you to help me with

— 28 —

2018年　　入試問題

some things around the house tomorrow."

　　"No," she signed, then shook her head. "　(B32)　"

　　"You know good and well I do. There's cleaning to be done."

　　"It will　(G)　," she said and walked out before her mother could reply.

(A)　下線部 (A) を，文末の it の内容がわかるように訳せ。

(B)　空所 (B29) ~ (B32) を埋めるのに最も適切な表現を次のうちから選び，そ
　　れぞれの記号をマークシートの (29) ~ (32) にマークせよ。同じ記号を複数回
　　用いてはならない。

　　a)　I'll go.

　　b)　I can't.

　　c)　I won't.

　　d)　Of what?

　　e)　I'll take it.

　　f)　You don't.

　　g)　Don't you dare.

(C)　本文中に 3 か所ある空所 (C) にはいずれも同じ単語が入る。最も適切な単
　　語を次のうちから一つ選び，その記号をマークシートの (33) にマークせよ。

　　a)　ended

　　b)　gone

　　c)　seemed

　　d)　sounded

　　e)　went

— 29 —

2018 年　　入試問題

(D)　下線部(D)の後にさらに言葉を続けるとしたら，以下のもののうちどれが最も適切か。一つ選び，その記号を<u>マークシートの (34)</u> にマークせよ。

　a)　given her when needed

　b)　when she didn't feel uncomfortable

　c)　when her mother would not let her go

　d)　when she needed to retreat into silence

(E)　下線部 (E) の内容を，She が誰を指すか，また，She のどのような行動を指して言っているのかわかるように説明せよ。

(F)　下に与えられた語を正しい順に並べ替え，空所 (F) を埋めるのに最も適切な表現を完成させよ。ただし，すべての語を用い，どこか 1 か所にコンマを入れること。

about　　buildings　　I　　know　　ones　　photograph　　something

the　　　the　　　will

(G)　空所 (G) を埋めるのに最も適切な単語を次のうちから一つ選び，その記号を<u>マークシートの (35)</u> にマークせよ。

　a)　do

　b)　not

　c)　postpone

　d)　wait

— 30 —

1 (A)　次の英文の要旨を，70 ～ 80 字の日本語にまとめよ。句読点も字数に含める。

According to one widely held view, culture and country are more or less interchangeable. For example, there is supposed to be a "Japanese way" of doing business (indirect and polite), which is different from the "American way" (direct and aggressive) or the "German way" (no-nonsense and efficient), and to be successful, we have to adapt to the business culture of the country we are doing business with.

A recent study has challenged this approach, however. Using data from 558 previous studies over a period of 35 years, this new research analyzed four work-related attitudes: the individual versus the group; the importance of hierarchy and status; avoiding risk and uncertainty; and competition versus group harmony. If the traditional view is correct, differences between countries ought to be much greater than differences within countries. But, in fact, over 80% of the differences in these four attitudes were found within countries, and less than 20% of the differences correlated with country.

It's dangerous, therefore, to talk simplistically about Brazilian culture or Russian culture, at least in a business context. There are, of course, shared histories and languages, shared foods and fashions, and many other shared country-specific customs and values. But thanks to the many effects of globalization — both in human migration and the exchange of technologies and ideas — it's no longer acceptable to generalize from country to business culture. A French businessperson in Thailand may well have more in common with his or her Thai

— 32 —

counterparts than with people back in France.

In fact, occupation and socioeconomic status are much better predictors of work values than country of origin. A hundred doctors from different countries, for example, are much more likely to share attitudes than a hundred Britons from different walks of life. Language aside, a truck driver in Australia is likely to find an Indonesian truck driver more familiar company than an Australian lawyer.

Successful negotiation depends on being able to predict the actions of the other party. In an international context, to the extent that our judgments arise from ideas about national characteristics, we are likely to make the wrong predictions and respond inappropriately. Cultural stereotyping by country is just bad business.

(B)　次の空所(1)〜(5)に入れるのに最も適切な文を後の a 〜 f より選び，マークシートの(1)〜(5)にその記号をマークせよ。ただし，同じ記号を複数回用いてはならない。また，空所（　ア　）に入るべき "v" で始まる単語1語を記述解答用紙の 1(B)に記入せよ。

Cycling one morning, Professor Dacher Keltner had a near-death experience. "I was riding my bike to campus," he recalls, "and I came to a crossing. I had the right of way, but this big luxury car just didn't slow down." With only about one metre to spare before impact, the driver finally stopped. "He seemed both surprised and contemptuous, as if I was in his more important way." Keltner's first response was a mixture of anger and relief: his university had not lost a psychology professor that day. His second was more academic. Was there, he wondered, a measurable difference between the behaviour of owners of luxury cars and that of other drivers?

The professor sent a group of psychology students to monitor driving

— 33 —

etiquette and keep notes on car models. They noted which drivers allowed pedestrians their right of way at street crossings, and which drivers pretended not to see them and sped straight past. The results couldn't have been clearer. People driving luxury cars were a quarter as likely to stop at a crossing and four times more likely to cut in front of another car than drivers of less expensive cars. The more luxurious the vehicle, the more entitled its owner felt to (　ア　) the traffic laws.

(　1　) In some experiments Keltner and his collaborators put participants from a variety of income levels to the test; in others, they tried to make participants feel less powerful or more powerful by asking them to think about people more or less powerful than themselves, or to think about times when they felt strong or weak. The results all pointed in the same direction. People who felt powerful were less likely to be considerate; wealthy participants were more likely to cheat in games involving small cash rewards and to dip their hands into a jar of sweets marked for the use of visiting children. When watching a video about childhood cancer their faces showed fewer signs of sympathy.

(　2　) When Keltner and his colleagues published an influential paper on the subject in 2010, three European academics, Martin Korndörfer, Stefan Schmukle and Boris Egloff, wondered if it would be possible to reproduce the findings of small lab-based experiments using much larger sets of data from surveys carried out by the German state. The idea was to see whether this information, which documented what people said they did in everyday life, would offer the same picture of human behaviour as results produced in the lab. "We simply wanted to reproduce their results," says Boris Egloff, "which seemed very believable to us." The numbers they obtained, however, did not fit the expected patterns. Taken as a whole, they suggested the opposite. Privileged individuals, the data suggested, were proportionally more

— 34 —

generous to charity than their poorer fellow citizens, more likely to volunteer, more likely to help a traveller struggling with a suitcase or to look after a neighbour's cat.

Who, then, is right? Are powerful people nicer or nastier than powerless ones? How can we explain the conflicting answers yielded by these two sets of data? (3) If being generous in public brings rewards, then rich people might be more inclined to help old ladies across roads. Drivers, invisible in their cars, need not worry about aggressive driving damaging their reputations. And Keltner points out that the data come from people's accounts of their own generosity, and not from actually observing their good actions. "We know from other studies that the wealthy are more likely to lie and exaggerate about ethical matters," he says. "Self-reported data in economics and face-to-face data in psychology capture different processes. What I say I do in society may not be how I behave with actual people."

(4) In August 2015, the journal Science reported that a group of 270 academics, led by Brian Nosek, a respected professor of psychology at the University of Virginia, had attempted to reproduce the results of 100 similar psychological studies. Ninety-seven of the original studies had produced results consistent with the hypotheses being tested. Only 36 of the Nosek group's experiments did the same. Those numbers threatened to undermine the entire discipline of experimental psychology, for if a result cannot be reproduced it must be in doubt. (5)

a) Not everyone accepts this conclusion, however.

b) What happened on the road also happened in the lab.

c) The connection between privilege and selfishness, then, is still unproved.

d) It may be that rich people are better at disguising their selfishness than poor people.

e) This idea, however, created a considerable sensation outside the academic world.

f) But it is also possible that the problem lies not with the survey data but with the psychological experiments.

2 (A) あなたがいま試験を受けているキャンパスに関して，気づいたことを一つ選び，それについて 60 ～ 80 語の英語で説明しなさい。

(B) 以下は手紙とそれに対する返事である。返事の空所に入る文章を，あなたが Jun だと仮定して 60 ～ 80 語の英語で書きなさい。

Dear Jun,

You will not remember me. I am your grandfather and I left the country when you were only three years old. But — though I have only a few weeks to live — I have made a success of my life, and you will inherit all my vast wealth if you convince me that you will use it well. Tell me *what* you would use my money for, and *why*. I am looking forward to your reply.

Your grandfather,
Marley

2017 年　入試問題

Dear Grandfather Marley,

Your grandchild,

Jun

4 (A)　次の英文の段落(21)～(25)にはそれぞれ誤りが一つある。誤った箇所を含む下線部を段落から選び，マークシートの(21)～(25)にその記号をマークせよ。

(21) The term "documentary" <u>emerged awkwardly out of early</u>_(a) practice. When entrepreneurs in the late nineteenth century first began to record moving pictures of real-life events, <u>some called what they were making</u>_(b) "documentaries." The term did not stabilize for decades, however. Other people called their films "educationals," "actualities," "interest films," <u>or perhaps referred to their subject matter</u>_(c) — "travel films," for example. John Grierson, a Scot, decided to use this new form in the service of the British government and invented the term "documentary" <u>by applying to a work</u>_(d) of the great American filmmaker Robert Flaherty. He defined documentary as the "artistic representation of actuality" — a definition that has proven durable probably <u>because it is so very flexible.</u>_(e)

(22) Documentary film began in the last years of the nineteenth century <u>with the first films ever projected</u>_(a), and it can take many forms. It can be a trip to exotic lands and lifestyles, as was *Nanook of the North* (1922). It can be a visual poem, such as Joris Ivens's *Rain* (1929) — a

— 37 —

story about a rainy day, is set to a piece of classical music, in which the
(b)
storm echoes the structure of the music. It can be an artful piece of
(c)
propaganda. Soviet filmmaker Dziga Vertov, who proclaimed that fiction
cinema was poisonous and dying and that documentary film was the
(d)
future, made *Man with a Movie Camera* (1929) as propaganda both for a
(e)
political regime and for a film style.

(23) What is a documentary? A simple answer might be: a movie *about*
real life. And that is precisely the problem: documentaries are about
real life; they are not real life. They are not even windows onto real
(a)
life. They are portraits of real life, using real life as their raw material,
(b)
constructed by artists and technicians who make numerous decisions
about what story to tell to whom and for what purpose. You might
(c)
then say: a movie that does its best to represent real life and that it
(d)
doesn't manipulate it. And yet, there is no way to make a film without
(e)
manipulating the information. Selection of topic, editing, and mixing
sound are all manipulations. Broadcast journalist Edword R. Murrow
once said, "Anyone who believes that every individual film must represent
a 'balanced' picture knows nothing about either balance or pictures."

(24) The problem of deciding how much to manipulate is as old
(a)
as the form. *Nanook of the North* is considered one of the first great
documentaries, but its subjects, the Inuit, assumed roles at filmmaker
Robert Flaherty's direction, much like actors in a fiction film. Flaherty
(b)
asked them to do things they no longer did, such as hunt for walrus*
(c)
with a spear, and he represented them as ignorant about things they
(d)
understood. At the same time, Flaherty built his story from his own
(e)
experience of years into living with the Inuit, who happily participated in
his project and gave him plenty of ideas for the plot.

*注：walrus　セイウチ

(25) The importance of documentaries is linked to a notion of the
(a)

public as a social phenomenon. The philosopher John Dewey argued persuasively that the public — so crucial to the health of a democratic society — is not just individuals added up. A public is a group of people who can act together for the public good and so can challenge the deep — seated power of business and government. It is an informal body that can come together in a crisis if necessary. There are as many publics as there are occasions and issues to call them forth. We can all be members of any particular public — if we have a way to communicate each other about the shared problems we face. Communication, therefore, is the soul of the public.

(B) 次の英文を読み，下線部(ア)，(イ)，(ウ)を和訳せよ。ただし，下線部(ア)の it と，下線部(イ)の this が，それぞれ何を意味するのかを明らかにすること。

How can the capacity for solitude be cultivated? With attention and respectful conversation.

Children develop the capacity for solitude in the presence of an attentive other. Imagine a mother giving her two-year-old daughter a bath, allowing the girl to daydream with her bath toys as she makes up stories and learns to be alone with her thoughts, all the while knowing her mother is present and available to her. Gradually, the bath, taken alone, becomes a time when the child is comfortable with her imagination. Attachment enables solitude.

One philosopher has a beautiful formulation: "Language ... has created the word 'loneliness' to express the pain of being alone. And it has created the word 'solitude' to express the glory of being alone."

Loneliness is emotionally and even physically painful, born from a lack of warmth in early childhood, when we need it most. Solitude — the capacity to be contentedly and constructively alone — is built

— 39 —

from successful human connection at just that time. But if we don't have experience with solitude — and this is often the case today — we start to equate loneliness and solitude. This reflects the poverty of our experience. If we don't know the satisfaction of solitude, we only know the panic of loneliness.

Recently, while I was working on my computer during a train ride from Boston to New York, we passed through a magnificent snowy landscape. I wouldn't have known this but for the fact that I happened to look outside on my way to get a coffee. Then I noticed that every other adult on the train was staring at a computer. We deny ourselves the benefits of solitude because we see the time it requires as a resource to use more profitably. These days, instead of using time alone to think (or not think), we hurry to fill it with some digital connection.

5 次の文章を読み，(A)〜(D)の問いに答えよ。

When she died last year at the age of ninety-four, I'd known Doris* for fifty years. In all that time, I've never managed to figure out a (26) for her that properly and briefly describes her role in my life, let alone my role in hers. We have a handy set of words to describe our nearest relations: mother, father, daughter, son, uncle, aunt, cousin, although that's as far as it goes usually in contemporary Western society.

Doris wasn't my mother. I didn't meet her until she opened the door of her house after I had knocked on it to be allowed in to live with her. What should I call her to others? For several months I lived with Doris, worked in the office of a friend of hers and learned typing. Then, after some effort, she persuaded my father to allow me to go back to school. As a (27), he had turned down further schooling after I was expelled — for climbing

— 40 —

out of the first-floor bathroom window to go to a party in the town — from the progressive, co-ed boarding school** that I had been sent to some years before when I was eleven. My father gave in and Doris sent me to my new school.

At the new school, teenagers constantly referred to and complained about their parents, using the regular words for them. Could I refer to Doris as my adoptive mother? She hadn't adopted me, although she'd suggested it. My mother had had one of her screaming fits and threatened to sue Doris if she tried to adopt me. So that was quietly dropped. I sometimes said 'adoptive mother' anyway, as an easy though inexact solution. It mattered how I referred to her; whenever I was called on to say 'Doris, my er... sort of, adoptive mother... my er... Doris...' to refer to my adult-in-charge, I was aware of giving the wrong impression.

For some reason, being precise, finding a simple possessive phrase that covered my circumstances, was very important. I didn't want to lie and I did want to find some way of summing up my (　28　) accurately to others. But I hadn't been an adopted child. Both my parents were still alive and (regrettably, in my view) in contact with me.

After I was expelled from my old school, I ran away from my father in Banbury and went to stay with my mother in Hove, in her very small flat. That had lasted only a few days before the wisest (　29　) seemed to be to roll up in a corner and refuse to eat or talk. 'How can you do this to me? Why can't you be decent, like other children?' she screamed.

It was considered a good idea to keep me away from my parents, so after the authorities had fed me, they put me into the Lady Chichester Hospital in Hove. It was a small psychiatric unit in a large detached house. I became the official bady of the place, and both staff and patients looked after me and tried to shield me from the worst of the other people's problems. I was fascinated and felt quite at home and well cared for at last.

I developed a secret (30) that I was mysteriously pregnant and the doctor was waiting for me to come to terms with it. Apart from that, I wasn't mentally ill at all and they weren't trying to treat me. I stayed there for four months, without medication, spending long periods sitting on the beach in Hove, staring at the sea — it was a winter of unprecedented ice and snow — while they tried to figure out what to do with me.

Then, all of a sudden, I received a letter from Doris, saying that although I didn't know her, she knew about me from her son, who had been in my class at school. Much over-excited gossip, you can imagine, had been going on there about the wicked Jennifer who'd got expelled and was now in a madhouse.

In his letter to Doris, her son Peter wondered, in all innocent generosity (since we had by no means got on with each other at school), if, since I was 'quite intelligent', they might not be able to help me somehow. Doris said in her letter to me that she had just moved into her first house, that it had central heating (she was particularly proud of that) and a spare room, so I might like to stay there, and perhaps, in spite of my father's reluctance, go back to school to get my exams and go to university. It wasn't clear in the letter how long I was invited to stay for, but the notion of going to university suggested something long-term.

I read the letter many times. The first time <u>with a kind of shrug</u>: 'Ah, I see. That's what's going to happen to me next.' Unexpected things had happened to me so frequently and increasingly during my childhood that they seemed normal. I came to expect them with a detached passivity. Then I read the letter again with astonishment that I had a guardian angel. Then fear. Then a certain amount of disappointment, and some real thought about whether to accept or not. And finally all these responses ware mixed, and I had no idea how to respond either to my own fears and expectations, or to this stranger for her invitation.

2017 年　入試問題

So Doris was not my mother. And aside from <u>awkward social moments,</u>
what she was to me was laid aside along with other questions best left
unthought.

注　*Doris　イギリスのノーベル賞作家ドリス・レッシング（1919 ~ 2013）
のこと
**co-ed boarding school　男女共学の全寮制の学校

(A)　下線部(A)を前後関係をふまえて次のように言い換える場合，空所に入る最も
適切な単語1語を書きなさい。

that's（　　）we usually use

(B)　下線部(B)で筆者はなぜこのような反応をしたのか，日本語で説明せよ。

(C)　下線部(C)の具体的な内容を日本語で説明せよ。

(D)　以下の問いに答え，<u>解答の記号をマークシートにマークせよ。</u>

(ア)　空所⒄~㈽には単語が一つずつ入る。それぞれに文脈上最も適切な語を次
のうちから一つずつ選び，マークシートの⒄~㈽にその記号をマークせよ。
同じ記号を複数回用いてはならない。
a)　designation　b)　disease　　c)　fear　　　d)　generosity
e)　move　　　　f)　participation　g)　punishment　h)　result
i)　rush　　　　j)　situation

(イ)　本文の内容と<u>合致しない</u>ものはどれか。一つ選び，マークシートの㉛にそ
の記号をマークせよ。

— 43 —

2017 年　　入試問題

a) The author struggled to define her relationship with Doris.

b) The author's mother did not want her to be adopted by Doris.

c) A bad rumour about the author was spreading at her new school.

d) Doris's son wanted to help the author because she was very smart.

e) The author was staying at a hospital when she received a letter from Doris.

(ウ)　Doris と筆者の関係を表現するのに最も適切なものを一つ選び，マークシートの(32)にその記号をマークせよ。

a) disastrous　　　b) illegal　　　c) passionate

d) unconventional　　e) unstable

— 44 —

入試問題

解答時間：120 分
配　　点：120 点

1 (A)　次の英文の要旨を，100 〜 120 字の日本語にまとめよ。句読点も字数に含める。

　　The notion of "imagined family" helps us to understand how group feelings can be extended beyond real family. Because humans evolved in small groups whose members were closely related, evolution favored a psychology designed to help out members of our close families. However, as human societies developed, cooperation between different groups became more important. By extending the language and sentiments of family to non-family, humans were able to create "imagined families" — political and social communities able to undertake large-scale projects such as trade, self-government, and defense.

　　By itself, though, this concept still can't explain why we consider all member of such a community to be equal. Imagined family differs from real family not only by the lack of genetic ties, but also by the lack of distinction between near and distant relatives. In general, all members of a brotherhood or motherland have equal status, at least in terms of group membership, whereas real family members have different degrees of relatedness and there is no fixed or firm way of defining family membership or boundaries. We need to search for a more fundamental factor that unites people and creates a strong bond among them.

　　At a deeper level, human communities are united by a well-known psychological bias which is believed to be universal. Studies of childhood development across cultures indicate that people everywhere tend to attribute certain essential qualities to human social categories such as race, ethnicity, or dress. This mental attitude has been used to generate notions of "in-group" versus "out-group", and to give coherence to a group where initially there was none, dramatically enhancing the group's chance of survival. However, this can also lead us to see an "out-group" as a different biological species, increasing the risk of hostility and conflict. Throughout history, and likely through human prehistory, people have routinely organized themselves to fight or dominate others by seeing them as belonging to different species.

(B) 次の空所(1)〜(5)に入れるのに最も適した段落を後のa〜eより選び，マークシートの(1)〜(5)にその記号をマークせよ。ただし，同じ記号を複数回用いてはならない。

Is free speech merely a symbolic thing, like a national flag or motto? Is it just one of many values that we balance against each other? Or is free speech fundamental — a right which, if not absolute, should be given up only in carefully defined cases?

The answer is that free speech is indeed fundamental. It's important to remind ourselves why, and to have the reasons ready when that right is called into question.

The first reason is that the very thing we're doing when we ask whether free speech is fundamental — exchanging and evaluating ideas — assumes that we have the right to exchange and evaluate ideas. When talking about free speech (or anything else), we're *talking*. We're not settling our disagreement by force or by tossing a coin. Unless you're willing to declare, in the words of Nat Hentoff, "free speech for me but not for you," then as soon as you show up to a debate to argue against free speech, you've lost. It doesn't make sense to use free speech to argue against it.

<u>2016年　入試問題</u>

(1)

Perhaps the greatest discovery in modern history — one that was necessary for every later discovery — is that we cannot trust the pre-scientific sources of belief. Faith, miracle, authority, fortune-telling, sixth sense, conventional wisdom, and subjective certainty are generators of error and should be dismissed.

(2)

Once this scientific approach began to take hold early in the modern age, the classical understanding of the world was turned upside down. Experiment and debate began to replace authority as the source of truth.

(3)

A third reason that free speech is fundamental to human flourishing is that it is essential to democracy and a guard against dictatorship. How did the monstrous regimes of the 20th century gain and hold power? The answer is that violent groups silenced their critics and opponents. And once in power, the dictatorship punished any criticism of the regime. This is still true of the governments of today known for mass killing and other brutal acts.

(4)

Common knowledge is created by public information. The story of "The Emperor's New Clothes" illustrates this logic. When the little boy shouted that the emperor was naked, he was not telling others anything they didn't already know, anything they couldn't see with their own eyes. But he was changing their knowledge nonetheless, because now everyone knew that everyone else knew that the emperor was naked. And that common knowledge encouraged them to challenge the emperor's authority with their laughter.

(5)

It's true that free speech has limits. We may pass laws to prevent

— 48 —

people from making dishonest personal attacks, leaking military secrets, and encouraging others to violence. But these exceptions must be strictly defined and individually justified; they are not an excuse to treat free speech as one replaceable good among many.

And if you object to these arguments — if you want to expose a flaw in my logic or an error in my ideas — it's the right of free speech that allows you to do so.

a) We also use speech as a weapon to undermine not just those who are in power but bullies in everyday life: the demanding boss, the boastful teacher, the neighbors who strongly enforce trivial rules.

b) Those who are unconvinced by this purely logical reasoning can turn to an argument from human history. History tells us that those who claim exclusive possession of truths on religious or political grounds have often been shown to be mistaken — often comically so.

c) How, then, can we acquire knowledge? The answer is the process called hypothesis and testing. We come up with ideas about the nature of reality, and test them against that reality, allowing the world to falsify the mistaken ones. The hypothesis part of this procedure, of course, depends upon the exercise of free speech. It is only by seeing which ideas survive attempts to test them that we avoid mistaken beliefs.

d) Why do these regimes allow absolutely no expression of criticism? In fact, if tens of millions of suffering people act together, no regime has the power to resist them. The reason that citizens don't unite against their dictators is that they lack common knowledge — the awareness that everyone shares their knowledge and knows they share it. People will expose themselves to a risk only if they know that others are exposing themselves to that risk at the same time.

e) One important step along this path was Galileo's demonstration that the Earth revolves around the sun, a claim that had to overcome fierce resistance. But the Copernican revolution was just the first in a series of events that would make our current understanding of the world unrecognizable to our ancestors. We now understand that the widely held convictions of every time and culture may be decisively falsified, doubtless including some we hold today, and for this reason we depend on the free exchange of new ideas.

2016 年　　入試問題

2 (A) 下の画像について，あなたが思うことを述べよ。全体で 60 〜 80 語の英語で答えること。

(B) 次の文章を読んで，そこから導かれる結論を第三段落として書きなさい。全体で 50 〜 70 語の英語で答えること。

　　In order to study animal intelligence, scientists offered animals a long stick to get food outside their reach. It was discovered that primates such as chimpanzees used the stick, but elephants didn't. An elephant

— 51 —

can hold a stick with its trunk, but doesn't use it to get food. Thus it was concluded that elephants are not as smart as chimpanzees.

However, Kandula, a young elephant in the National Zoo in Washington, has recently challenged that belief. The elephant was given not just sticks but a big square box and some other objects, while some fruit was placed just out of reach above him. He ignored the sticks but, after a while, began kicking the box with his foot, until it was right underneath the fruit. He then stood on the box with his front legs, which enabled him to reach the food with his trunk.

注：trunk　ゾウの鼻

4 (A)　次の英文の段落(21)～(25)にはそれぞれ誤りが一つある。誤った箇所を含む下線部を各段落から選び，マークシートの(21)～(25)にその記号をマークせよ。

(21) Knowledge is our most important business. The success of <u>almost all our other business</u>_(a) depends on it, but its value is not only economic. The pursuit, production, spread, application, and preservation of knowledge are the <u>central activities of a civilization</u>_(b). Knowledge is social memory, a connection to the past; and it is social hope, an investment in the future. The ability to create knowledge and <u>put use to it</u>_(c) is the key characteristic of humans. It is how we <u>reproduce ourselves</u>_(d) as social beings and how we change — how we keep <u>our feet on the ground</u>_(e) and our heads in the clouds.

(22) Knowledge is a form of capital <u>that is always unevenly distributed</u>_(a), and people who have more knowledge, or greater access to knowledge, enjoy <u>advantages</u>_(b) <u>over people who have less.</u>_(c) This means that knowledge stands in a close relation to power. We speak of <u>"knowledge for their own sake,"</u>_(d) but there is nothing we learn <u>that</u>_(e)

— 52 —

does not put us into a different relation with the world — usually, we hope a better relation.

(23) As a society, we are committed to the principle that the production of the knowledge should be unrestricted and access it should be (a) universal. This is a democratic ideal. We think that where knowledge is concerned, more is always better. (b) We don't believe that there are things that we would rather not know, (c) or things that only some of us (d) should know — just as we don't believe that there are points of view that should not be expressed, or citizens who are too ignorant to vote. (e)

(24) We believe that the more information and ideas we produce, (a) and the more people we make them available, (b) the better our chances of making good decisions. We therefore make a large social investment in institutions whose purpose is (c) simply the production and spread of knowledge — that is, research and teaching. We grant these (d) institutions all kinds of protections, and we become worried, sometimes angry, when we suspect that they are not working the way we want (e) them to.

(25) Some of our expectations about colleges and universities are unrealistic (and so some are of (a) our expectations about democracy). Teaching is a messy process, an area in which success can be hard to measure or even to define. (b) Research is messy, too. The price for every good idea or scientific claim is a lot of not-so-good ones. (c) We can't reasonably expect that every student will be well educated, or that every piece of scholarship or research will be worthwhile. But we want to believe that the system, as large and diverse as it is, (d) is working for us and not against us , and that it is enabling us (e) to do the kind of research and teaching that we want to do.

— 53 —

2016年　入試問題

(B) 下の英文を読み，下線部(ア), (イ), (ウ)を和訳せよ。

　　News reports from Afghanistan in the 1990s tended to portray little more than a ruined place, destroyed by extremist military groups. Such images were rarely balanced by insights into ordinary life. Countries at war are described by reporters who tend, especially in dangerous places, to stay together, reporting only on isolated events. <u>In Kabul, visiting television crews invariably asked to be taken to the worst-hit parts of the city</u>; one reporter even described Kabul as "ninety percent destroyed".

　　Wars complicate matters; there is a terrible fascination to war which tends to overshadow less dramatic news. Conflict is a notoriously difficult thing to convey accurately. Fighting comes and goes, and modern conflicts move with an unpredictable will of their own. Key battles are fought overnight and absorbed into the landscape. <u>Even a so-called war zone is not necessarily a dangerous place: seldom is a war as comprehensive as the majority of reports suggest.</u>

　　Yet there was a deeper obstacle to describing the place: Afghanistan was, to outsiders, a broken mirror, yielding an image as broad or narrow as the observer's gaze. <u>Even in peacetime Afghanistan had been open to outsiders for only a brief interval, a forgotten period from the 1960s until the 1970s.</u> It had never been a single nation but a historically improbable mixture of races and cultures, each with its own treasures of customs, languages and visions of the world.

5　次の文章を読み，(A)〜(D)の問いに答えよ。

　　Last year, there was great public protest against the use of "anti-homeless" spikes outside a London residential complex, not far from where I live. The

— 54 —

spikes were sharp pieces of metal stuck in concrete to keep people from sitting or lying on the ground. Social media were filled with anger, a petition was signed, a sleep-in protest undertaken, and within a few days the spikes were removed. But the phenomenon of "defensive" or "hostile" architecture, as it is known, remains common.

From bus-shelter seats that lean forward, to water sprinklers, hard tube-like rests, and park benches with solid dividers, urban spaces are aggressively (26) soft, human bodies.

We see these measures all the time within our urban environments, whether in London or Tokyo, but we fail to grasp their true intent. I hardly noticed them before I became homeless in 2009. An economic crisis, a death in the family, a sudden divorce and an even more sudden mental breakdown were all it took for me to go from a more than decent income to being homeless in the space of a year. It was only then, when I started looking around my surroundings with the distinct purpose of (27) shelter, that the city's cruelty became clear.

I learned to love London Underground's Circle Line back then. To others it was just a rather inefficient line on the subway network. To me — and many homeless people — it was a safe, dry, warm container, continually travelling sometimes above the surface, sometimes below, like a giant needle stitching London's center into place. Nobody bothered you or made you move. You were allowed to take your poverty on tour. But engineering work put a stop to that.

Next was a bench in a smallish park just off a main road. It was an old, wooden bench, made smooth by thousands of sitters, underneath a tree with leaves so thick that only the most persistent rain could penetrate it. Sheltered and warm, this was prime property. Then, one morning, it was gone. In its place stood an uncomfortable metal perch, with three solid armrests. I felt such loss that day. The message was clear: I was not a member of the public, at least not of the public that is welcome here. I had to find somewhere else to go.

There is a wider problem, too. These measures do not and cannot distinguish the homeless from others considered more (28). When we make it impossible for the poor to rest their weary bodies at a bus shelter, we also make it impossible for the elderly, for the handicapped, for the pregnant woman who needs rest. By making the city less (29) of the human body, we make it less welcoming to all humans.

Hostile architecture is (30) on a number of levels, because it is not the product of accident or thoughtlessness, but a thought process. It is a sort of unkindness that is considered, designed, approved, funded and made real with the explicit motive to threaten and exclude.

Recently, as I walked into my local bakery, a homeless man (who I had seen a few times before) asked whether I could get him something to eat. When I asked Ruth — one of the young women who work behind the counter — to put a couple of meat pies in a separate bag and explained why, her remark was severe: "He probably makes more money than you from begging, you know," she said coldly.
(B)

He probably didn't. Half his face was covered with sores. A blackened, badly injured toe stuck out of a hole in his ancient shoe. His left hand was covered in dry blood from some recent accident or fight. I pointed this out. Ruth was unmoved by my protest. "I don't care," she said. "They foul the green area. They're dangerous. Animals."

It's precisely this viewpoint that hostile architecture upholds: that the homeless are a different species altogether, inferior and responsible for their fall. Like pigeons to be chased away, or urban foxes disturbing our sleep with their screams. "You should be ashamed," jumped in Libby, the older lady who works at the bakery. "That is someone's son you're talking about."
(C)

Poverty exists as a parallel, but separate, reality. City planners work

— 56 —

very hard to keep it outside our field of vision. It is too miserable, too discouraging, too painful to look at someone sleeping in a doorway and think of him as "someone's son." It is easier to see him and only ask the question: "How does his homelessness affect me?" So we cooperate with urban design and work very hard at not seeing, because we do not want to see. We silently agree to this apartheid.

Defensive architecture keeps poverty unseen. It conceals any guilt about leading a comfortable life. It brutally reveals out attitude to poverty in general and homelessness in particular. It is the concrete, spiked expression of a collective lack of generosity of spirit.

And, of course, it doesn't even achieve its basic goal of making us feel safer. There is no way of locking others out that doesn't also lock us in. Making our urban environment hostile breeds hardness and isolation. It makes life a little uglier for all of us.

Spikes outside an office building in London

(A) 下線部(A)は具体的にどのような内容を表すか，日本語で述べよ。

2016 年　入試問題

(B)　下線部(B)で，語り手は具体的に何が何のためであったと説明したか，日本語で述べよ。

(C)　下線部(C)で言われていることを次のように言い換える場合，空所に入る最も適切な一語を本文中からそのまま形を変えずに選んで書きなさい。なお，空所(26)〜(30)の選択肢を書いてはならない。

The man you're talking about is no less (　　　) than you are.

(D)　以下の問いに答え，解答の記号をマークシートにマークせよ。

(ア)　空所(26)〜(30)には単語が一つずつ入る。それぞれに文脈上最も適切な語を次のうちから一つずつ選び，マークシートの(26)〜(30)にその記号をマークせよ。同じ記号を複数回用いてはならない。

a)　accepting　b)　depriving　c)　deserving　d)　finding

e)　forcing　　f)　implying　　g)　raising　　h)　rejecting

i)　revealing　　j)　satisfying

(イ)　下線部(31)はどのような考えを表しているのか，最も適切なものを一つ選び，マークシートの(31)にその記号をマークせよ。

a)　Seeing this homeless person upsets me.

b)　His homelessness has an impact on everyone.

c)　I wonder how I can offer help to this homeless person.

d)　This homeless person has no right to sleep in the doorway.

e)　I wonder whether this homeless person has any relevance to my life at all.

— 58 —

2016 年　　入試問題

(ウ)　下線部(32)はどのような考えを表しているのか，最も適切なものを一つ選び，
マークシートの(32)にその記号をマークせよ。

　　a)　Defensive architecture harms us all.

　　b)　Ignoring homelessness won't make it go away.

　　c)　Restrictions on the homeless are for their own good.

　　d)　Homeless people will always be visible whatever we do.

　　e)　For security, we have to keep homeless people out of sight.

入試問題

解答時間：120 分
配　点：120 点

1 (A)　次の英文の内容を，70 〜 80 字の日本語に要約せよ。句読点も字数に含める。

We like to think that humans are supremely logical, making decisions on the basis of hard data and not on impulse. But this vision of *homo economicus* — a person who acts in his or her best interest when given accurate information — has been shaken, especially by discoveries in the emerging field of risk perception. It has been found that humans have great difficulty in accurately gauging risk. We have a system that gives us conflicting advice from two powerful sources — logic and instinct, or the head and the gut.

Our instinctive gut reactions developed in a world full of hungry wild animals and warring tribes, where they served important functions. Letting the amygdala (in the brain's emotional core) take over at the first sign of danger, milliseconds before the neo-cortex (the thinking part of the brain) was aware that a spear was headed for our chest, was probably a very useful adaptation. Even today those gut responses save us from getting flattened by buses or dropping a brick on our toes. But our amygdala is not suited for a world where risks are measured by clicks on a radiation detector.

A risk-perception apparatus designed for avoiding wild animals makes it unlikely that we will ever run screaming from fatty food. "People are likely to react with little fear to certain types of objectively dangerous risk that evolution has not prepared them for, such as hamburgers, automobiles, and smoking, even when they recognize the threat at a conscious level," says one researcher. Even Charles Darwin failed to break the amygdala's iron grip on risk perception. As an experiment, he placed his face up against the rattlesnake cage at the London Zoo and tried to keep himself calm and unmoved when the snake struck the plate glass. He failed.

A whole industry has developed around conquering the fear of flying, but while we pray not to be one of the roughly five hundred annual airline casualties around the world, we give little thought to driving to the grocery store, even though more than one million people die in automobile accidents each year.

(B) 次の空所(1)～(5)に入れるのに最も適したものを後の a ～ h より選び, マークシートの(1)～(5)にその記号をマークせよ。ただし, 同じ記号を複数回用いてはならない。また, 最後の段落の空所 (ア) に入れるべき単語 1 語を記述解答用紙の 1 (B)に記入せよ。

"Decision fatigue" may help explain why ordinary, sensible people get angry at colleagues and families, waste money, and make decisions they would not normally make. No matter how rational you try to be, you can't make decision after decision without paying a biological price. It's different from ordinary physical fatigue — you're low on mental energy, but you're not consciously aware of being tired. And the more choices you make throughout the day, it seems, the harder each one becomes for your brain.

(1) Afterward, all the participants were given one of the classic tests of self-control: holding your hand in ice water for as long as you can. The impulse is to pull your hand out, and the deciders gave up much sooner.

(2) The researchers interviewed shoppers after shopping and asked them to solve as many arithmetic problems as possible but said they could quit at any time. Sure enough, the shoppers who had already made the most decisions in the stores gave up the quickest on the math problems.

Any decision can be broken down into what is called the Rubicon model of action phases, in honor of the Rubicon river that separated Italy from the Roman province of Gaul. When Caesar reached it in 49 B.C., on his way home after conquering the Gauls, he knew that a general returning to Rome was forbidden to take his army across the river with him, lest it be considered an invasion of Rome. Waiting on the Gaul side of the river, in the "predecisional phase," he contemplated the risks and benefits of starting a civil war. Then he stopped calculating, made his decision, and crossed the Rubicon with his army, reaching the "postdecisional phase."

(3) Researchers have shown that crossing the Rubicon is moretiring than anything that happens on either bank — whether sitting on the Gaul side contemplating your options or advancing towards Rome.

Once you're mentally exhausted, you become reluctant to make particularly demanding decisions. This decision fatigue makes you easy prey for sales staff who know how to time their offers. One experiment was conducted at German car dealerships, where customers ordered options for their new vehicles. They had to choose, for instance, among thirteen kinds of wheel rims, twenty-five arrangements of the engine, and fifty-six colors for the interior.

At first, customers would carefully weigh the choices, but as decision fatigue set in, they would start taking whatever was recommended. (4) By manipulating the order of the car buyers' choices, the researchers found that the customers would end up settling for different kinds of options, and the average difference totaled more than 1,500 euros per car (about $2,000 at the time). Whether the customers paid a little extra or a lot extra depended on when the choices were offered and how much willpower was left in the customer.

Shopping can be especially tiring for the poor. Some researchers argue that decision fatigue could be a major — and often ignored — factor in trapping people in poverty. Because their financial situation forces them to make so many difficult decisions, they have less willpower to devote to school, work, and other activities that might get them into the middle class. (　5　)

It is also known that when the poor and the rich go shopping, the poor are much more likely to (　ア　) during the shopping trip. This might seem like confirmation of their weak character — after all, they could presumably improve their nutrition by cooking meals at home instead of consuming ready-to-eat snacks which contribute to their higher rate of health problems. But if a trip to the supermarket causes more decision fatigue in the poor than in the rich, by the time they reach the cash register, they'll have less willpower left to resist chocolate bars. Not for nothing are these items called impulse purchases.

a)　But why is crossing the Rubicon so risky?

b)　The whole process can exhaust anyone's willpower, but which phase of the decision-making process is most exhausting?

c)　For a more realistic test of their theory, the researchers went into that great modern arena of decision-making: the suburban shopping center.

d)　In other words, because the financially poor have so little willpower, they cannot even decide to blame society for making their life difficult.

e) And the more tough choices they encountered early in the process, the quicker they became tired and settled for the path of least resistance by taking a proposed option.

f) In one experiment conducted by researchers at Florida State University, shoppers' awareness of their mental exhaustion was confirmed through a simple test of their calculating ability.

g) This is significant because study after study has shown that low self-control is associated with low income as well as a large number of other problems, including poor achievement in school, divorce, crime, alcoholism and poor health.

h) Researchers at Florida State University conducted an experiment to test this theory. A group of students were asked to make a series of choices. Would they prefer a pen or a candle? A candle or a T-shirt? They were not actually given the chosen items — they just decided which they preferred. Another group, meanwhile — let's call them the nondeciders — spent an equally long period contemplating all these same products without having to make any choices.

2015年　　入試問題

2 (A) 下の絵に描かれた状況を簡単に説明したうえで，それについてあなたが思ったことを述べよ。全体で 60 〜 80 語の英語で答えること。

(B) "Look before you leap" と "He who hesitates is lost" という，内容の相反することわざがある。どのように相反するか説明したうえで，あなたにとってどちらがよい助言と思われるか，理由とともに答えよ。全体で 60 〜 80 語の英語で答えること。

4 (A) 次の英文の(ア)，(イ)，(ウ)の括弧内の語を並べ替えて，文脈上意味が通るように文を完成させ，2番目と5番目にくる語の記号をマークシートにマークせよ。(ア)は(21)と(22)に，(イ)は(23)と(24)に，(ウ)は(25)と(26)に，順にマークせよ。ただし，それぞれ不要な語が1語ずつ混じっている。

2015年　入試問題

Biologist Christina Riehl is studying the odd cooperative breeding behaviors of certain tropical birds called "anis." Groups of anis raise their young together in a single nest, every adult sharing in the work. Remarkably, however, the birds in these groups aren't necessarily blood relatives.

For half a century, the study of animal cooperation has been largely dominated by the theory of "kin selection": animals help each other only if they stand to gain something — if not for themselves, then for their kin (family and relatives). This ensures that they always pass along some of their genetic material to the next generation. But [a) comes, b) has, c) it, d) raising, e) their, f) to, g) when, h) young], anis behave in ways that cannot be explained by kin selection alone.

Riehl has learned that, although anis work together cooperatively, some work much harder than others. In every group, one male [a) all, b) ends, c) much, d) labor, e) performing, f) the, g) tiring, h) up] of sitting on the eggs in the nest. While other group members sleep, the bird on the night shift performs extra work for no apparent additional gain in the fitness or survival of his own young — again, breaking the rules of kin selection.

The anis aren't totally unselfish. Although females cooperate in tending the nest, they simultaneously improve their young's chances for survival by pushing other females' eggs out of it. Here, too, their behavior is odd: of ten thousand species of birds in the world, only a half-dozen engage in this wasteful practice of destroying eggs — strengthening Riehl's assertion that "this is one of [a) except, b) existence, c) for, d) in, e) interesting, f) most, g) species, h) the] animal social behavior."

2015 年　　入試問題

(B)　ナバホ語 (Navajo) に関する次の英文を読み，下線部(ア), (イ), (ウ)を和訳せよ。

Eugene Crawford is a Navajo, a Native American; he cannot forget the day he and his friends were recruited for the United States military. Upon arrival at Camp Elliott, they were led to a classroom, which reminded him of the ones he had entered in boarding schools as a child. Those memories were far from pleasant. He could almost taste the harsh brown soap the teachers had forced him to use to wash his mouth out when he was caught speaking Navajo. His thoughts were interrupted when the door suddenly opened and an officer entered. The new recruits stood to attention. "At ease, gentlemen. Please be seated."

The first hour they spent in that building changed their lives forever, and the shock of what occurred is still felt by them to this day. They could never have imagined the project the military had recruited them for. Some of them believed that, had they known beforehand, they might not have joined up so eagerly. Navajo had been chosen as a code for secret messages because unless you were a Navajo, you'd never understand a word of it. Navajo is a complex language and a slight change in pronunciation can completely change the meaning of a message. The government's decision was wise — it turned out to be the only code the enemy never managed to break — but for the young Navajo soldiers, it was a nightmare. At no time under any circumstances were they to leave the building without permission or alone. They were forbidden to tell anyone about the project, even their families, until it was finally made public in 1968.

Many of these men had been punished, sometimes brutally, for speaking Navajo in classrooms similar to this, classrooms in schools run by the same government. Now this government that had punished them in the past for speaking their own language was asking them to use

— 69 —

it to help win the war. White people were stranger than the Navajos had imagined.

5 次の文章を読み，問いに答えよ。

Rebecca was getting ready to start her bookstore, making a business plan, applying for loans. "A bookstore?" Harriet, her mother, said. "With your education you want to start a store, and one that doesn't even have a hope of making money? What is your life adding up to?"

Rebecca was hurt, furious. They had one of their old fights, made worse by the fact that Rebecca hadn't realized these old fights were still possible. The recent long peace since the beginning of Harriet's illness had given Rebecca a false sense of safety. She felt deceived.

Then Harriet sent Rebecca a check, for quite a lot of money. To help with the bookstore, she wrote on the card.

"You can't (27) this," Rebecca said.

"It's what I want to do," Harriet said.

Then she got sick again.

Pneumonia*— not life-threatening, but it took a long time to get over. Rebecca drove down and made Harriet chicken soup and vanilla custard, and lay across the foot of Harriet's bed.

So this has been going on for years and years. Harriet getting sick and recovering. Rebecca showing up and withdrawing. Living her life between interruptions.

Rebecca is tired. Harriet has been sick on and off for more than a decade. Rebecca has just driven four hours from Boston to get to the Connecticut nursing home where Harriet now lives. She is taking two days off from the

— 70 —

small bookstore she (28), paying her part-time assistant extra to cover for her. She's brought a shopping bag full of things Harriet likes. She has walked into the room, and Harriet has barely looked away from the TV to say hello. Rebecca pulls over a chair and sits facing her mother. Harriet is in a wheelchair, paralyzed again — it has happened before; she has some rare back disease, but this time the doctor says it is permanent.

Rebecca feels guilty about not coming down to see her mother more often. Harriet is always mentioning something she needs — lavender bath powder, or socks, or a blanket to put over her legs when they wheel her outside. Rebecca mails what she can, sometimes (29) by but at other times annoyed by the many requests.

The last time Rebecca visited, on the day Harriet moved to the nursing home, the nurse put an enormous plastic napkin on Harriet's front before bringing in her dinner tray. Harriet allowed it, looking at Rebecca with a kind of stunned sadness; of all the insults received on that day, this was the one that undid her. "She doesn't need that," Rebecca told the nurse.

"We do it for everybody."

"Right, but my mother doesn't need it."

So that was one small battle that Rebecca was there to win for Harriet. (A) Without Rebecca, Harriet could have won it just fine for herself. Both of them knew this — and yet, between them, love has always had to be proved. It is there; and it gets proved, over and over. Some of their worst fights, confusingly, seem to both prove and disprove it: two people who didn't love each other couldn't fight like that — certainly not repeatedly.
(B)

Nearly fifteen years ago, Harriet seemed to be dying. She had stage four colon cancer.** Rebecca believed that her mother was dying, and for the first time, she began to feel close to her. She sometimes lay in bed at night and cried, alone, or with Peter Bigelow, who taught architectural history at

Harvard. He held her and listened while she talked about how hard it was to be (30) her mother and yet losing her at the same time.

Incredibly, Harriet didn't die. The operation was successful, and she kept having more surgeries. Rebecca kept driving down and spending time with her mother. But she couldn't keep it up: the attention, the sympathy, the friendship, the aimless joy of just hanging around with her mother, watching the TV news. She had burned herself out.

Harriet started feeling that Rebecca wasn't visiting often enough. It was true, she was coming down less often. But oh, that "enough." That tricky guilty-sounding word that doesn't even need to be spoken between a mother and daughter because both of them can see it lying there between them, injured and complaining, <u>a big violent-colored wound.</u>
(31)

Peter asked Rebecca how she would feel about getting married. That was how he did it: not a proposal, but an introduction of a topic for discussion. She said she wasn't sure. The truth was that when he said it, she got a cold, sick feeling in her stomach. This lovely, good, thoughtful man: what was the matter with her? She was nervous, and also irritated that he seemed so calm about the whole thing, that he wasn't desperate for her, that he wasn't knocking her over with forceful demands that she belong to him. On the other hand, she wasn't knocking him over either.

Then his book was finished and published. He brought over a copy one night, and she had a bottle of champagne waiting. "Peter, I'm so happy for you," and she kissed him. She turned the pages, and her own name jumped out at her: "... and to Rebecca Hunt, who has given me so many pleasant hours."

It was understatement, wasn't it? The kind of understatement that can exist between two people who understand each other? What did she want, a dedication that said, "For Rebecca, whom I love with all my heart and would

2015年　　入試問題

die for"?

Here was something she suddenly saw and disliked in herself, something she might have inherited from Harriet: a raw belief that love had to be declared and proved — intensely, loudly, explicitly.

注　*pneumonia　肺炎　**colon cancer　結腸癌

(A)　下線部(A)を，指示代名詞 that の内容を明らかにして和訳せよ。

(B)　下線部(B)を，省略されている部分を補って和訳せよ。

(C)　以下の問いに答え，解答の記号をマークシートにマークせよ。

　問　空所(27)〜(30)には単語が一つずつ入る。それぞれに文脈上最も適切な語を次のうちから一つずつ選び，マークシートの(27)〜(30)にその記号をマークせよ。ただし，動詞の原形で示してあるので，空所に入れる際に形を変える必要があるものもある。また，同じ記号を複数回用いてはならない。

a)　afford　　b)　anticipate　　c)　complain　　d)　find

e)　own　　f)　participate　　g)　prevent　　h)　talk

i)　touch　　j)　walk

　問　下線部(31)で，a big violent-colored wound と呼ばれているものは何か。最も適切なものを次のうちから一つ選び，マークシートの(31)にその記号をマークせよ。

a)　Harriet's illness.

b)　The nurse's insult.

c)　Rebecca's tiredness.

d)　The word "enough."

e)　Peter's unenthusiastic proposal.

— 73 —

2015年　入試問題

問　本文の最後で Rebecca はどのような認識に至ったか。正しいものを一つ選び，マークシートの⑫にその記号をマークせよ。

a) She is more like Peter than she thought.

b) She is more like Harriet than she thought.

c) She doesn't really like her mother, Harriet.

d) She doesn't really like her boyfriend, Peter.

e) She doesn't really have the capacity to love.

問　本文の内容と合致しないものはどれか。一つ選び，マークシートの⑬にその記号をマークせよ。

a) Harriet didn't want Rebecca to run a bookstore, which she thought would be unprofitable.

b) Rebecca was angry when she found that the nurse was treating her mother as if she were a baby.

c) Rebecca was so happy about the publication of Peter's book that she kissed him, grateful to him for mentioning her in it.

d) Relations between Rebecca and her mother improved when the latter was hospitalized for a serious illness about fifteen years ago.

e) Although Peter is a fine man that Rebecca should be happy to marry, she felt irritated when he didn't declare his love to her strongly enough.

— 74 —

1 (A)　次の英文の内容を，80～100字の日本語に要約せよ。句読点も字数に含める。

I live in a nice old apartment building in Edinburgh: several floors of individual flats, all connected by an internal staircase made of sandstone. The building is at least a century old, and nowadays each of those sandstone steps is looking a little worn.

This wear is the result of a century of people walking up and down from their flats. As they have left for and returned from work, as they have gone out to the shops or for dinner, many times a day the feet of the people living here have fallen upon each stair.

As every geologist knows, even a small force, repeated over a large enough stretch of time, can add up to some very large effects indeed. A century of footsteps is quite a lot. If each of thirty-five residents travelled up and down the staircase four times a day on average, then each step has been struck by at least ten million feet since it was laid down.

When I climb this staircase to my flat, I enjoy the daily reminder that humans are a geological force. If ten million people were all sent up this staircase one by one, it would take less than eight months for their feet to wear away a centimeter of sandstone.

And then, consider that ten million people is but a small fraction of the seven billion people currently in the world. If you could somehow use the feet of all of those people at once, then you could grind meters of rock away in a few moments. A few more repetitions and you'd have an impressive hole. Keep going for a few hours, and you could produce a new valley.

2014年　入試問題

This might seem like a rather unrealistic thought experiment, but it does highlight, in a rather literal way, the idea of a carbon footprint, which is a measure of the environmental impact of human actions. When it comes to our carbon footprints, the entire planet is the staircase. Our individual contribution — the energy we consume, the waste we produce — may seem insignificant, hardly something that is going to affect the planet. But when you multiply by seven billion, the small environmental impact of any one person becomes a very weighty footstep indeed. It's not surprising that Earth is as worn down as my old staircase.

注：geologist, geological < geology　地質学

(B)　次の空所(1)〜(5)に入れるのに最も適切なものを下に記したア〜クより選び，その記号を記せ。ただし，同じ記号を複数回用いてはならない。

　　One of the best measures for judging the true complexity of a job is how easily it can be replaced by a machine. In the early days of the automation revolution, most people thought that technology would cause jobs to (　1　). The factory, it seemed, would be the place this reduction would happen first. Assembly-line workers tightening the same few bolts would be swept away by machines doing the job faster, more efficiently and without complaint. Mid-level supervisors would fare better, since no robot would be able to manage the remaining workforce. Fewer manual laborers, however, would mean the loss of at least some managers. It would only be at the top ranks of the organization that jobs would be safe from machines.

　　To a degree that happened. Robots did replace many bolt-turners, but the losses went only so far. No machine could bring the multiple senses to the job that a human can, feeling the way a car door just doesn't click properly in its frame or noticing a small flaw in a half-finished product. Robots might perform truly automatic, repetitive tasks, but jobs that required complex human skills and the ability to think independently were safe.

Meanwhile, one level above the manual workers, the mid-level management jobs started to (2). However, at the top of the ladder, the bosses and executives, whose jobs often called for subtle anticipation of markets and expert reactions to changing demands and trends, did, for the most part, keep their positions.

The computer revolution had even greater impact on the workforce by automating the handling of information. This caused the mid-level job loss that started in the factory to (3). While such a development may have caught a lot of hard-working employees by surprise, it was in fact a very predictable result.

The vast range of jobs and professions follows a U-shaped complexity curve. At its left peak are the bluest of the blue-collar jobs, the ones often held in the least esteem and usually the most poorly paid. At the right peak are the whitest of the white-collar jobs — very highly regarded and equally highly paid. Most people, however, work in the middle — in the valley of the U — where the jobs are the simplest.

Nothing better illustrates how the complexity U-curve works than airline ticketing clerks, low-status workers once thought likely to be replaced by automated kiosks. The next time you're in an airport, you will see just as many clerks as there ever were. While a kiosk might be fine for the individual traveler with a single suitcase, it's no good at all to a disabled passenger who needs help boarding a plane, or to anxious parents trying to arrange care for a young child flying alone. Often, human assistance is the only way to solve a problem, particularly if it requires a little creativity or includes an emotional aspect that calls for a personal touch.

The jobs at the other end of the U-curve (4). It's here that you find the lawyer reading through documents to construct a legal argument; the biochemist gathering test results and making an intuitive leap that leads to a new cure; the psychologist responding to facial, vocal and physical gestures that reveal more than words can.

It's only in the lower parts of the complexity U-curve that things are a bit simpler. There, the jobs most often (5). In industrialized parts of the world, the growing ability of computers to do this kind of work has led to a hollowing-out of the workforce, with many office clerks and bookkeepers losing their jobs.

ア　disappear from the bottom up

イ　give great personal satisfaction to the worker

ウ　involve collecting and transmitting information

エ　provide secure foundations for future prosperity

オ　vanish, as employees required less direct instruction

カ　spread to office tasks like evaluating loan applications

キ　determine what we can take of value from our experiences

ク　rely even more heavily on intellectual and instinctive skills

<u>2014 年　入試問題</u>

2.(A)　下に示す写真の左側の人物を X，右側の人物を Y として，二人のあいだの会話を自由に想像し，英語で書け。分量は全体で 50 〜 70 語程度とする。どちらが話しているかわかるように，下記のように記せ。X と Y のどちらから始めてもよいし，それぞれ何度発言してもよい。

X:-------------------- 　Y:-------------------- 　X:--------------------
Y:--------------------

(B) 以下のような有名な言葉がある。これについてどう考えるか。50 〜 70 語の英語で記せ。ただし，下の文をそのままの形で用いてはならない。

People only see what they are prepared to see.

4 (A) 次の下線部(1)〜(5)には，文法上あるいは文脈上，取り除かなければならない語が一語ずつある。解答用紙の所定欄に，該当する語とその直後の一語，合わせて二語をその順に記せ。文の最後の語を取り除かなければならない場合は，該当する語と×（バツ）を記せ。カンマやピリオドは語に含めない。

(1) Of all the institutions that have come down to us from the past none is in the present day so damaged and unstable as the family has.

(2) Affection of parents for children and of children for parents is capable of being one of the greatest sources of happiness, but in fact at the present day the relations of parents and children are that, in nine cases out of ten, a source of unhappiness to both parties. (3) This failure of the family to provide the fundamental satisfaction for which in principle it is capable of yielding is one of the most deeply rooted causes of the discontent which is widespread in our age.

For my own part, speaking personally, I have found the happiness of parenthood greater than any other that I have experienced. (4) I believe that when circumstances lead men or women to go without this happiness, a very deep need for remains unfulfilled, and that this produces dissatisfaction and anxiety the cause of which may remain quite unknown.

It is true that some parents feel little or no parental affection, and it is also true that some parents are capable of feeling an affection for children not their own almost as strong as that which they feel for their own.

2014年　入試問題

Nevertheless, the broad fact remains that parental affection is a special (5) kind of feeling which the normal human being experiences towards his or her own children but not towards any of other human being.

(B)　次の英文の下線部(1), (2), (3)を和訳せよ。ただし，下線部(1)については either approach が何を意味するかを明らかにすること。

　　If a welfare state is acting on behalf of the community at large, it can distribute resources on the same basis to every member of that community, or it may operate selectively, providing resources only to those who need or deserve help.　A case can be made on grounds of efficiency for either approach. (1) If sufficient benefits and services are available on the same basis to everybody, then　all are guaranteed the minimum level of help to secure their basic needs. (2) Because everybody gets the same, no shame can be attached to receiving that help and nobody need be discouraged from seeking it.　Those people who do not need the help they receive will, if the system is funded by progressive taxation, be able to pay back what they have received, as well as contribute to the help received by other members of the community.　If, on the other hand, benefits and services are made available only to those who need or deserve them, then those resources will be put to the most effective use; more generous levels of help may be given to those in the greatest need; and　those people who do not require help will not be made to feel unfairly treated by high levels of taxation. (3)

— 82 —

2014 年　入試問題

5 次の文章はアフリカ系アメリカ人の著者が妻と息子とともにパリに滞在したとき
に記したブログの記事である。これを読み，以下の問いに答えよ。

　　I went out this early July morning for a quick run along the Seine. That was fun. There were very few people out, which made it easier. Paris is a city for strollers, not runners.

　　Women pedal their bikes up the streets, without helmets, in long white dresses; or they dash past in pink cut-off shorts and matching roller skates. Men wear orange pants and white linen shirts. They chat un petit peu (a little) and then disappear around corners. When I next see them they are driving Porsches slowly up the Boulevard Saint-Germain, loving their lives. In this small section of the city, <u>everyone seems to be offering a variation on the phrase "I wasn't even trying."</u>
₍₁₎

　　Couples sit next to each other in the cafés, watching the street. There are rows of them assembled as though in fashion photographs from Vogue or like a stylish display of mannequins. Everyone smokes. They know what awaits them — horrible deaths, wild parties, <u>in no particular order.</u>
₍₂₎

　　I came home. I showered. I dressed. I walked across the way and bought some bread and milk. My wife brewed coffee. We had breakfast. Then a powerful fatigue came over me and I slept till noon. When I woke, my son was dressed. My wife was wearing a Great Gatsby tee-shirt, sunglasses, earrings and jeans. Her hair was pulled back and blown out into a big beautiful Afro. We walked out and headed for a train to the suburbs. My son was bearing luggage. <u>This was the last we'll see of him for six weeks.</u>
₍₃₎

　　It was on the train that I realized I'd gone mad. Back in Boston, I had started studying French through a workbook and some old language tapes. I then moved on to classes at a French language school. Next I hired a personal tutor. We would meet at a café in my neighborhood. Sometimes my son would stop by. I noticed he liked to linger around. One day he asked

— 83 —

if he could be tutored in French. It struck me as weird, but I went (4) it. In May, before coming to France, he did a two-week class — eight hours a day. He woke up at six a.m. to get to class on time and didn't get back until twelve hours later. He would eat dinner and then sleep like a construction worker. But he liked it. Now he and my wife and I had just come to Paris for the summer, and I was sending him off to an immersion sleep-away camp — *français tous les jours* (French every day).

It is insane. I am trying to display the discipline of my childhood home, the sense of constant, unending challenge, without the violence. <u>A lot of us who came up hard</u> respect the lessons we learned, even if they were given by the belt or the boot. How do we pass those lessons on without subjecting our children to those forces? How do we toughen them for a world that will bring war to them, without subjecting them to abuse? My only answer is to put them in strange and different places, where no one cares that someone somewhere once told them they were smart. My only answer is to try to copy the style of learning I have experienced as an adult and adapt it for childhood.

But I am afraid for my beautiful brown boy.

Three weeks ago, back in America, I was sitting with my dad telling him how I had to crack down on my own son for some misbehavior. I told my dad that the one thing I (6a) for about fatherhood was how much it hurt me to be the bad guy, how much I wanted to let him loose, how much I (6b) whenever I (6c). I felt it because I remembered when I was my son's age, and how much I had hated being twelve. I was shocked to see my dad nodding in agreement. My dad was a tough father. I didn't think he was joyous in his toughness, but it never occurred to me that he had to force himself to discipline us. He never let us see that part of him. His rule was "Love your mother. Fear your father." And so he wore a mask. As it happens, I feared them both.

I told my son this story yesterday. I told him that I would never force

— 84 —

him to take up something he wasn't interested in (like piano). But once he declared his interests, there was no other way to be, except to push him to do it to the very end. How very un-Parisian. But I told him that pain in this life is inevitable, and that he could only choose whether it would be the pain of acting or the pain of being acted upon. *C'est tout* (That's all).

We signed in. He took a test. We saw his room and met his roommate. We told him we loved him. And then we left.

"When I e-mail you," he said, "be sure to e-mail back so that I know you're OK."

So that he knows that we are OK.
(7)
When we left my wife began to cry. On the train we talked about the madness of this all, that we — insignificant and crazy — should be here right now. First you leave your block. Then you leave your neighborhood. Then you leave your high school. Then your city, your college and, finally, your country. At every step you are leaving another world, and at every step you feel a warm gravity, a large love, pulling you back home. And you feel crazy for leaving. And you feel that it is ridiculous to do this to yourself. And you wonder who would do this to a child.
(8)

注：the Seine　セーヌ川

Porsches　ポルシェ（高級スポーツカー）

the Boulevard Saint-Germain　サン＝ジェルマン大通り

Vogue　『ヴォーグ』（ファッション雑誌）

(1)　下線部(1)から筆者はパリの人びとのことをどのように考えていることがうかがえるか。その思いに最も近いものを次のうちから一つ選び，その記号を記せ。

　ア　Aimless and self-destructive.

　イ　Health-conscious and diligent.

　ウ　Self-disciplined and free from vice.

— 85 —

2014 年　　入試問題

エ　Escaping from reality and longing for the past.

オ　Devoted to effortless pleasure and ease of living.

(2)　下線部(2)の order の意味と最も近いものを次のうちから一つ選び，その記号
を記せ。

ア　Her room is always kept in good order.

イ　The police failed to restore public order.

ウ　The words are listed in alphabetical order.

エ　He gave a strict order for the students to line up.

オ　I will place a quick order for fifty copies of this book.

(3)　下線部(3)を和訳せよ。

(4)　空所(4)を埋めるのに最も適切な単語を次のうちから一つ選び，その記号を記せ。

ア　against　　イ　around　　ウ　in　　エ　through　　オ　with

(5)　下線部(5)が意味しているのはどのような人びとか。最も適切なものを次のう
ちから一つ選び，その記号を記せ。

ア　一所懸命に努力を重ねてきた人びと

イ　子どものときから病弱だった人びと

ウ　他人に対して冷たくしてきた人びと

エ　親から厳しいしつけを受けた人びと

オ　苦労して現在の地位を築いた人びと

(6)　空所(6a)，(6b)，(6c)を埋めるのに最も適切な語句を次のうちから一つずつ
選び，その記号を記せ。ただし，同じ記号を複数回用いてはならない。

ア　disciplined him

イ　felt his pain

ウ　hated being a kid

— 86 —

エ　was looking

オ　wasn't prepared

カ　was thrilled

(7)　下線部(7)には息子に対する筆者のさまざまな思いが表されている。その思いとして最も可能性の低いものを次のうちから一つ選び，その記号を記せ。

ア　The author is astonished by his son's rudeness.

イ　The author is moved by his son's consideration.

ウ　The author is struck by his son taking a parent's role.

エ　The author is surprised by his son making the first move.

オ　The author is impressed to see how rapidly his son is maturing.

(8)　下線部(8)の do this が意味することは何か。日本語で説明せよ。

(9)　次のア〜キはそれぞれ問題文で語られている出来事について述べたものである。これらを出来事の起きた順に並べたとき，2番目と6番目にくる文の記号を記せ。

ア　The author ran along the Seine.

イ　The author's wife began to cry.

ウ　The author sat and talked with his father.

エ　The author's son took a two-week French course.

オ　The author told his son that pain in this life is inevitable.

カ　The author, his wife and his son took a train to the suburbs.

キ　The author and his wife met his son's roommate in the language-immersion camp.

1 (A) 次の英文の内容を，70 〜 80 字の日本語に要約せよ。句読点も字数に含める。

The silk that spiders use to build their webs, trap their prey, and hang from the ceiling is one of the strongest materials known. But it turns out it's not just the material's exceptional strength that makes spiderwebs so durable.

Markus Buehler, an associate professor of civil and environmental engineering, previously analyzed the complex structure of spider silk, which gains strength from different kinds of molecular interactions at different scales. He now says a key property of the material that helps make webs strong is the way it can soften at first when pulled and then stiffen again as the force increases. Its tendency to soften under stress was previously considered a weakness.

Buehler and his team analyzed how materials with different properties, arranged in the same web pattern, respond to localized stresses. They found that materials with simpler responses perform much less effectively.

Damage to spiderwebs tends to be localized, affecting just a few threads — the place where a bug got caught and struggled around, for example. This localized damage can be repaired easily or just left alone if the web continues to function adequately. "Even if it has a lot of defects, the web still functions mechanically virtually the same way," Buehler says.

To test the findings, he and his team literally went into the field, pushing and pulling at spiderwebs. In all cases, damage was limited to

— 90 —

the immediate area they disturbed.

This suggests that there could be important advantages to materials whose responses are complex. The principle of permitting localized damage so that an overall structure can survive, Buehler says, could end up guiding structural engineers. For example, earthquake-resistant buildings might bend up to a point, but if the shaking continued or intensified, specific structural elements could break first to contain the damage.

That principle might also be used in the design of networked systems: a computer experiencing a virus attack could shut down instantly, before its problems spread. So the World Wide Web may someday grow more secure thanks to lessons learned from the spidery construction that inspired its name.

注：molecular = molecule（分子）の形容詞形

(B) 次の空所(1)〜(5)に入れるのに最も適切なものを後のア〜クより選び，その記号を記せ。ただし，同じ記号を複数回用いてはならない。

It's sometimes said that human beings live two lives, one before the age of five and another one after, and this idea probably stems from the enormous amount of time which those first five years of our lives contain. It's possible that we experience as much time during those years as we do during the seventy or more years which come after them.

It seems that during the first months of our lives we don't experience any time at all. According to the research of the psychologist Jean Piaget, during the first months of our lives we live in a state of 'spacelessness', unable to distinguish between different objects or between objects and ourselves. We are fused together with the world, and we don't know where we end and where it begins. We also experience a state of timelessness, since — in the same way that we can't distinguish between objects — we can't distinguish one moment from the next. We (1).

We only begin to emerge from this timeless realm as our sense of separation begins to develop. According to Piaget, this begins at around seven months. We start to become aware of ourselves as separate entities, apart from the world, and also to perceive the separation between different objects. Along with this, we begin to be aware of separation between different events. We (2), encouraged by the development of language, with its past, present, and future tenses. According to Piaget, this process follows four stages. First, we recognise that people arrive and events begin; second, we recognise that people leave and events end; third, we recognise that people or objects cover distances when they move; fourth, we become able to measure the distance between different moving objects or people — and at this point we have developed a sense of sequential time.

After this point of 'falling' into time, we (3). If the sense of sequence is the result of our development of a separate sense of self, we can probably assume that the more developed our sense of self becomes, the more developed the sense of sequence will be. As a result, time will seem to move faster. This sense of time speeding up isn't something that we just experience as adults; it probably happens from early childhood onwards. Time may pass for a two-year-old child, but probably only at an incredibly slow speed. But as the child's sense of self becomes more developed, the speed of time increases, too. Time probably moves faster to a child of four than it does to a child of three, and faster to a child of seven than it does to a child of six.

However, even at this age time passes many times more slowly than it does for adults. This is why, as any parent knows, young children

(4). Primary-school teachers should be mindful of this when their pupils' attention starts to wander — what seems to be a fairly short 40-minute lesson to them is stretched many times longer to the children.

Young children's sense of time is not yet fully developed in other ways, too. They can't accurately guess how long events last — in fact, they only become able to do this in terms of seconds at the age of six or seven. They (5). When children between the age of two and four talk about what they have done, or retell the story of something that's happened to them, they almost always mix up the order of the events, usually grouping them together in terms of association rather than sequence.

ア　can only speak in the present tense

イ　become more and more subject to it

ウ　begin to rank the importance of events

エ　don't know when an event begins or when it ends

オ　don't have a clear sense of the sequence of past events, either

カ　develop a sense of sequential time, a sense of the past and future

キ　encounter many new things every minute but still retain a sense that each event is unique

ク　always think that more time has gone by than actually has, and often complain that things are taking too long

2013年　入試問題

2 (A) 次に示す写真の左側の人物をX，右側の人物をYとして，二人のあいだの会話を自由に想像し，英語で書け。分量は全体で60〜70語程度とする。どちらが話しているかわかるように，以下のように記せ。XとYのどちらから始めてもよいし，それぞれ何度発言してもよい。

X:......................　Y:......................　X:......................
Y:......................

(B) これまで学校や学校以外の場で学んできたことのなかで，あなたが最も大切だと思うことは何か，またそれはなぜか。50〜60語の英語で答えよ。ただし，英語に関すること以外について述べること。

2013 年　　入試問題

4 (A)　次の英文の(1)～(3)の括弧内の単語を並べ替えて，文脈上意味が通るように文を完成させ，2番目と4番目にくる語の記号を記せ。

　　Personal　(ア fuel，イ information，ウ is，エ powers，オ that，カ the) online social networks, attracting users and advertisers alike, and operators of such networks have had a largely free hand in how they handle it. But a close look is now being　(ア all，イ at，ウ taken，エ that，オ the，カ way) information is collected, used, and protected, and it has been found that operators have repeatedly left personal data unprotected, exposing users to all sorts of risks. Not surprisingly, the claim of many operators is that they are following existing laws and that more regulation is unnecessary, even counterproductive. They argue, for example, that users who face a lot of detailed questions about　(ア access，イ how，ウ their，エ they，オ to，カ want) information controlled before they even start using a service may become confused and make poor privacy choices. Nevertheless, it seems likely that the industry's management of private data will have to change before long.

(B)　次の英文の下線部(1)と(2)を和訳せよ。ただし，(1)については their current ones の内容がわかるように訳せ。また下線部(3)について，そこで使われているたとえは具体的に何を言おうとしているのか，その内容をわかりやすく30～40字で説明せよ。句読点も字数に含める。

　　A general limitation of the human mind is its imperfect ability to reconstruct past states of knowledge or beliefs that have changed. Once you adopt a new view of the world (or of any part of it), you immediately lose much of your ability to recall what you used to believe before your mind changed.

　　Many psychologists have studied what happens when people

— 95 —

change their minds. Choosing a topic on which people's minds are not completely made up — say, the death penalty — the experimenter carefully measures the subjects' attitudes. Next, the participants see or hear a persuasive message either for or against it. Then the experimenter measures their attitudes again; those attitudes usually are closer to the persuasive message that the subjects were exposed to. Finally, the participants report the opinion they held beforehand. This task turns out to be surprisingly difficult. <u>Asked to reconstruct their former beliefs, people repeat their current ones instead</u> — an instance of substitution — and many cannot believe that they ever felt differently. <u>Your inability to reconstruct past beliefs will inevitably cause you to underestimate the extent to which you were surprised by past events.</u>

Because of this "I-knew-it-all-along" effect, we are prone to blame decision-makers for good decisions that worked out badly and to give them too little credit for successful moves that appear obvious only after the fact. When the outcomes are bad, people blame their decision-makers for not seeing the signs, forgetting that <u>they were written in invisible ink that became visible only afterward.</u>

5 次の文章を読み，以下の問いに答えよ。

When I was eleven, I took violin lessons once a week from <u>a Miss Katie McIntyre.</u> She had a big sunny fourth-floor studio in a building in the city, which was occupied below by dentists, paper suppliers, and cheap photographers. It was approached by an old-fashioned lift that swayed dangerously as it rose to the fourth floor, which she shared with the only (2a) occupant, Miss E. Sampson, a spiritualist who could communicate with the dead.

<u>2013 年　　入試問題</u>

I knew about Miss Sampson from gossip I had heard among my mother's friends. The daughter of a well-known doctor, she had gone to Clayfield College and been clever and popular. But then her gift appeared — that is how my mother's friends put it, just declared itself out of the blue, without in (2b) way changing her cleverness or good humour.

She came to speak in the voices of the dead: little girls who had been murdered in suburban parks, soldiers killed in one of the wars, lost sons and brothers. Sometimes, if I was early for my lesson, I would find myself riding up with her. Holding my violin case tightly, I pushed myself hard against the wall of the lift to make room for <u>the presences</u> she might have brought into the lift with her.
₍₃₎

It was odd to see her name listed so boldly — "E. Sampson, Spiritualist" — in the entrance hall beside the lift, among the dentists, photographers, and my own Miss McIntyre. It seemed appropriate, in those days, that music should be separated from the everyday business that was being carried on below — the whizzing of dentists' drills and the making of passport photos for people going overseas. But I thought of Miss Sampson, for (2c) her sensible shoes and businesslike suits, as a kind of fake doctor, and was sorry that <u>Miss McIntyre and classical music should be associated</u>
₍₄₎
<u>with Miss Sampson</u> and with the troops of sad-eyed women (they were mostly women) who came all the way to her room and shared the last stages of the lift with us: women whose husbands might have been bank managers — wearing smart hats and gloves and tilting their chins a little in defiance of their having at last reached this point; other women who worked in hospital kitchens or offices, all decently gloved and hatted now, but <u>looking scared of the company they were in and the heights to which the</u>
₍₅₎
<u>lift brought them.</u> They tried to hang apart, using their elbows in a ladylike way, but using them, and saying politely "Pardon," or "I'm so sorry," when the crush brought them too close.

— 97 —

On such occasions the lift, loaded to capacity, made heavy work of it. And it wasn't, I thought, simply the weight of bodies (eight persons only, a notice warned) that made the old mechanism grind in its shaft, but the weight of all that sorrow, all that hopelessness and last hope, all that dignity in the privacy of grief. We went up slowly.

Sometimes, in the way of idle curiosity (if she could have had such a thing), Miss Sampson would let her eyes for a moment rest on me, and I wondered hotly what she might be seeing beyond a small eleven-year-old. Like most boys of that age I had much to conceal. But she appeared to be looking at me, not through me. She would smile, I would respond, and, clearing my throat to find a voice, I would say in a well-brought-up manner that I hoped might fool her and <u>leave me alone with my secrets</u>, "Good
₍₆₎
afternoon, Miss Sampson." Her own voice was as unremarkable as an aunt's: "Good afternoon, dear."

It was therefore <u>all the more</u> alarming, as I sat waiting on one of the
₍₇₎
chairs just outside Miss McIntyre's studio, while Ben Steinberg, her star pupil, played the Max Bruch, to hear the same voice, oddly changed, coming through the half-open door of Miss Sampson's office. Though much above the breathing of all those women, it had stepped down a tone — no, several — and sounded as if it were coming from another continent. It was an Indian, speaking through her.

It was a being I could no longer think of as the woman in the lift, and I was reminded of something I had once seen from the window of a railway carriage as my train sat steaming on the line: three old men behind the glass of a waiting room and the enclosed space shining with their breathing like a jar full of fireflies. It was entirely real, but the way I saw them changed that reality, making me so impressionably aware that <u>I could recall details I could</u>
₍₈₎
<u>not possibly have seen at that distance or with the naked eye</u>: the greenish-grey of one old man's eyes, and a stain near a shirt collar. Looking through

— 98 —

2013 年　　入試問題

into Miss Sampson's room was like that.　I saw too much.　I felt dizzy and began to sweat.

　　There is no story, no set of events that leads anywhere or proves anything — no middle, no end.　Just a glimpse through a half-open door.

(1)　下線部(1)にある不定冠詞の a の用法と同じものを次のうちから一つ選び，その記号を記せ。

　ア　The car in the driveway looked like a Ford.

　イ　All who knew him thought he was an Edison.

　ウ　A Johnson came to see you while you were out.

　エ　At that museum I saw a Picasso for the first time.

　オ　She was an Adams before she married John Smith.

(2)　空所(2a)，(2b)，(2c)を埋めるのに最も適切な単語を次のうちから一つずつ選び，その記号を記せ。

　ア　all　　　イ　another　　ウ　any　　　エ　different　　オ　every

　カ　no　　　キ　none　　　ク　other　　ケ　same　　　コ　some

　サ　that　　シ　those　　　ス　what　　セ　which

(3)　下線部(3)と最も意味が近い，2語からなる別の表現を文中から抜き出して記せ。

(4)　下線部(4)の意味に最も近いものを次のうちから一つ選び，その記号を記せ。

　ア　Miss McIntyre and classical music should be involved in Miss Sampson's business

　イ　Miss McIntyre and classical music should be influenced by someone like Miss Sampson

　ウ　Miss McIntyre and classical music should be looked down on even more than Miss Sampson was

エ Miss McIntyre and classical music should be coupled with someone as unrespectable as Miss Sampson

オ Miss McIntyre and classical music should be considered to be as unprofessional as Miss Sampson

⑸ 下線部⑸の意味に最も近いものを次のうちから一つ選び，その記号を記せ。

ア seeming frightened of the other women in the lift and of how high the lift was rising

イ looking fearfully at the other women in the lift, which went up to the fourth floor

ウ showing their fear of the unfamiliar women in the lift, which brought them to a high floor

エ looking anxiously at the other passengers in the lift, frightened because the lift seemed to go up forever

オ apparently feeling frightened of the company which employed them and the heights to which the unsteady lift rose

⑹ 下線部⑹の意味として，最も適切なものを次のうちから一つ選び，その記号を記せ。

ア hide my feeling of guilt

イ let me enjoy being alone

ウ assure her of my good manners

エ keep her from reading my mind

オ prevent her from telling others my secrets

⑺ 下線部⑺の表現がここで用いられている理由として，最も適切なものを次のうちから一つ選び，その記号を記せ。

ア Because Miss Sampson usually spoke in a mild voice.

イ Because Ben Steinberg heard the same voice oddly changed.

ウ Because more and more people were afraid of Miss Sampson's voice.

エ Because the piano in Miss McIntyre's studio sounded as if it were far away.

オ Because Miss Sampson could be heard more easily than all the other women.

(8) 下線部(8)を和訳せよ。

1 (A) 次の英文の内容を，70〜80字の日本語に要約せよ。句読点も字数に含める。

As many developed countries become the destination for immigrants — people coming from other lands in search of better opportunities — the ethnic mix is changing and with this has come the fear of the loss of national identity as represented in a shared national language and common values. Anxiety is growing about what appears to be the increasing separateness of some ethnic communities. Surveys in the USA, for example, have found that immigrants who have little or no mastery of English and who primarily rely on Spanish in their homes and work lives have strikingly different opinions from English speakers about controversial social issues such as divorce and homosexuality.

There is, however, another side to such separate, parallel lives. We now live in a world in which immigrants do not have to break connections with friends and family to begin the generations-long process of adopting a new identity. Not only is it possible to retain close contact with the 'home' community on a daily basis via email and telephone, but it is also possible for people to read the same newspapers as those being read in the community they have left, watch the same television programmes on satellite television, or borrow the same films on DVD.

Social network ties which were broken in previous generations are everywhere becoming reconnected. Families and communities which were separated generations ago are finding each other once again. Ties are being reconnected, helping to create a different type of society: one which is more spread out and less dependent on geographic closeness.

2012 年　　入試問題

(B)　次の英文を読み，以下の問いに答えよ。

　　On that morning the bus was standing-room-only as we squeezed on at our regular stop.　Several blocks later, my son, Nick, found a free seat halfway back on one side of the bus and his little sister, Lizzie, and I took seats on the other.

　　I was listening to Lizzie chatter on about something when I was surprised to see Nick get up.　<u>　ア　</u>　I watched as he spoke politely to an older, not quite grandmotherly woman who didn't look familiar to me.　<u>　イ　</u>　A little thing, but still I was flooded with appreciation. <u>　ウ　</u>　For all the times we have talked about what to do and what not to do on the bus — say "Excuse me," cover your mouth when you cough, don't point, don't stare at people who look unusual — this wasn't something I had trained him to do.　<u>　エ　</u>　It was a small act of kindness, and it was entirely his idea.　<u>　オ　</u>

　　For all we try to show our kids and tell them how we believe people should act, how we hope they will act, it still comes as a shock and a pleasure — a relief, frankly — when they do something that suggests they understand.　All the more so because in the world in which Nick is growing up, the rules that govern social interaction are so much vaguer than they were when we were his age.　Kids are exposed to a complex confusion of competing signals about what's (　2　), let alone what's admirable.　It's hard to know what good manners are anymore.

(a)

— 105 —

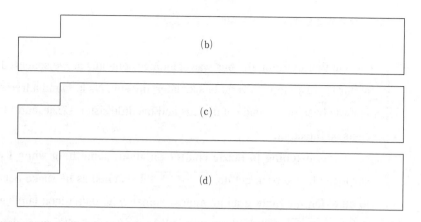

　　Under the circumstances, good manners require a good deal more imagination than they once did, if only because it's so much harder to know what the person sitting across from you — whether stranger or friend — expects, needs, wants from you. When you don't have an official rulebook, you have to listen harder, be more sensitive, be ready to play it by ear.

(1) 以下の文は，第二段落のア〜オのどの位置に補うのが最も適切か。その記号を記せ。

　　Suddenly I understood: he was offering her his seat.

(2) 第三段落の空所（　2　）に入れる語として最も適切なものはどれか。その記号を記せ。
　　ア　acceptable
　　イ　achievable
　　ウ　avoidable
　　エ　inevitable
　　オ　predictable

2012 年　入試問題

(3) 上の文章で空白になっている(a)から(d)には，次のア〜オのうち四つの段落が入る。それらを最も適切な順に並べた場合に，不要となる段落，(a)に来る段落，(c)に来る段落はどれか。それぞれの記号を記せ。

ア　Of course, this sort of confusion is about much more than etiquette on public transportation. It's about what we should do for each other, and expect of each other, now that our roles are no longer closely dictated by whether we are male or female, young or old.

イ　I was reminded of this incident on the train the other day, on another crowded morning, as I watched a young man in an expensive suit slip into an open seat without so much as losing his place in the New York Times, smoothly beating out a silver-haired gentleman and a group of young women in trendy clothes.

ウ　Not for a minute do I regret the passing of the social contract that gave men most of the power and opportunity, and women most of the seats on the bus. But operating without a contract can be uncomfortable, too. It's as if nobody quite knows how to behave anymore; the lack of predictability on all fronts has left our nerve endings exposed. And the confusion extends to everything from deciding who goes through the door first to who pays for dates.

エ　I was taking my kids to school when I had another of those experiences particular to parents. Just as when a child first plays outside alone, comes home talking excitedly about what has happened at school, or eats with pleasure a food previously rejected, it is a moment that nobody else sees but that we replay over and over because in it we notice something new about our children. This time,

— 107 —

though, the experience was played out in public, making it all the more meaningful to me.

オ My first thought was that his mother would be ashamed of him. And then I thought, with some amusement, that I am hopelessly behind the times. For all I know, the older man would've been insulted to be offered a seat by someone two or three decades his junior. And the women, I suppose, might consider polite behavior toward themselves discrimination. Besides, our young executive or investment banker probably had to compete with women for a job; why would he want to offer a potential competitor a seat?

(4) この文章全体のまとめとして最も適切なものを一つ選び, その記号を記せ。

ア The author thinks that times change but good manners remain the same.

イ The author complains that good manners are dead in the modern world.

ウ The author argues that the next generation will find new rules for social behavior.

エ The author believes that good manners in today's world demand much thought and effort.

オ The author recommends that we continue to behave according to established social rules.

— 108 —

<u>2012 年　　入試問題</u>

2 (A)　次の(1)〜(5)について，以下の例に従って，括弧内の語句とほぼ同じ意味となるよう，指定した文字で始まる一語で空欄を埋めよ。

（例1）　The wind was so strong that I was b＿＿＿＿ able to remain standing. **[almost not]**

解答例　barely

（例2）　At yesterday's public meeting, many citizens c＿＿＿＿ about the recent tax increases. **[expressed disapproval]**

解答例　complained

(1)　The rich s＿＿＿＿ in the area makes farming very profitable.
　[the surface layer of ground in which plants grow]

(2)　No one could have a＿＿＿＿ such a rapid increase in prices.
　[expected that something would happen]

(3)　The three sisters i＿＿＿＿ their mother's house after she passed away. **[received as property from a person who had died]**

(4)　The police stopped and questioned several youths who were b＿＿＿＿ suspiciously. **[conducting themselves]**

(5)　Many people with special health needs have to check the list of i＿＿＿＿ on all of the packages of food that they buy.
　[materials used to make food]

— 109 —

2012年　　入試問題

(B)　もし他人の心が読めたらどうなるか，考えられる結果について 50 ～ 60 語
の英語で記せ。複数の文を用いてかまわない。

4 (A)　次の下線部(1)～(5)には，文法上あるいは文脈上，取り除かなければならな
い語が一語ずつある。解答用紙の所定欄に，該当する語を記せ。

　　　　Every so often I read an article on how to survive when is lost in the
(1)
wilds, and I have to laugh.　　The experts who write these pieces know
(2)
everything about survival but next to it nothing about getting lost.　I am
an expert on getting lost.　　I have been lost in nine different countries,
(3)
forty-three cities, seven national forests, four national parks, countless
of parking lots, and one passenger train.　My wife claims I once got lost
riding an elevator in a tall building.　But that is an exaggeration based on
my confusion over the absence of a thirteenth floor.　(If you are a person
with a fear of heights, you want to make certain that the floors are right
where they are supposed to be.　　And you're not all about to listen to a
(4)
lot of excuses for any empty space between the twelfth and fourteenth
floors.)　　Ever since I have survived all of these experiences of being
(5)
lost, it follows that I am also something of an expert on survival.

(B)　次の英文は，ある作家が小説家 Kazuo Ishiguro (＝Ish) にインタビューし
たあとで書いた文章の一部である。下線部(1)，(2)，(3)を和訳せよ。ただし，
下線部(2)については，it が何を指すか明らかにすること。

　　It's perhaps not much known that Ish has a musical side.　I was only
vaguely aware of it, if at all, when I interviewed him, though I'd known
him by then for several years — a good example of how he doesn't give
(1)
much away.　Ish plays the piano and the guitar, both well.　I'm not sure

－　110　－

how many different guitars he now actually possesses, but I wouldn't be surprised if it's in double figures. His wife, Lorna, sings and plays; so does his daughter. Evenings of musical entertainment in the Ishiguro household can't be at all uncommon.

One of the few regrets of my life is that I have no formal grounding in music. I never had a musical education or came from the sort of 'musical home' that would have made this possible or probable, and always rather readily assumed that music was what those other, 'musical' people did.

I've never felt, on the other hand, though a great many people who didn't grow up reading books have perhaps felt it, that writing is what those other, 'writerly' people do.
(2)

This contrast between writing and music is strange, however, since I increasingly feel that a lot of my instincts about writing are in fact musical, and I don't think that writing and music are fundamentally so far apart. The basic elements of narrative — timing, pacing, flow, tension and release, repetition of themes — are musical ones too. And where would writing be without rhythm, the large rhythms that shape a story, or the small ones that shape a paragraph?
(3)

5 次の文章を読み，以下の問いに答えよ。

A sari for a month. It shouldn't have been a big deal but it was. After all, I had grown up around women wearing saris in India. My mother even slept in one.

In India, saris are adult clothes. After I turned eighteen, I occasionally wore a beautiful sari for weddings and holidays and to the temple. But wearing a silk sari to an Indian party was one thing. Deciding to wear a sari every day while living in New York, especially after ten years in Western

clothes, seemed outrageous, even to me.
(1)

The sari is six yards of fabric folded into a graceful yet impractical garment. It is fragile and can fall apart at any moment. When worn right, it is supremely elegant and feminine.

It requires (2a), however. No longer could I spring across the street just before the light changed. The sari forced me to shorten my strides. I had to throw my shoulders (3a) and pay attention to my posture. I couldn't squeeze (3b) a crowded subway car for fear that someone would accidentally pull my sari. I couldn't balance four bags from the supermarket in one hand and pull out my house keys from a convenient pocket (3c) the other. By the end of the first week, I was feeling frustrated and angry with myself. What was I trying to (4a)?

The notion of wearing a sari every day was relatively new for me. During my college years — the age when most girls in India begin wearing saris regularly — I was studying in America as an art student and I wore casual clothes just as other students did. After getting married, I became a housewife experimenting with more fashionable clothes. Over the years, in short, I tried to talk, walk, and act like an American.

Then I moved to New York and became a mother. I wanted to teach my three-year-old daughter Indian values and traditions because I knew she would be profoundly different from the children she would play with in religion (we are Hindus), eating habits (we are vegetarians), and the festivals we celebrated. Wearing a sari every day was my way of showing her that she could melt into the pot while keeping her individual flavor.

It wasn't just for my daughter's sake that I decided to wear a sari. I was tired of trying to (4b). No American singers had ever spoken to me as deeply as my favorite Indian singers. Nor could I sing popular American songs as easily as I could my favorite Indian tunes. Much as I enjoyed American food, I couldn't last four days without an Indian meal. It was time

— 112 —

to show my ethnicity with a sari and a bright red bindi. I was going to be an
(5a), but on my own terms. It was America's turn to adjust to me.

Slowly, I eased into wearing the garment. I owned it and it owned me.
Strangers stared at me as I walked proudly across a crowded bookstore.
Some of them caught my eye and smiled. At first, I resented being an (5b).
Then I wondered: perhaps I reminded them of a wonderful holiday in India
or a favorite Indian cookbook. Shop assistants pronounced their words
clearly when they spoke to me. Everywhere, I was stopped with questions
about India as if wearing a sari had made me an (5c). One Japanese lady
near Times Square asked to have her picture taken with me.   A tourist had
thought that I was one, too, just steps from my home. (6)

But there were unexpected (2b). Indian taxi drivers raced across
lanes and stopped in front of me just as I stepped into the street to hail a
cab. When my daughter climbed high up the jungle gym in Central Park, I
gathered my sari and prepared to follow, hoping it wouldn't balloon out like
Marilyn Monroe's dress. One of the dads standing nearby saw that I was in
trouble and volunteered to climb after her.   A knight in New York? Was it
me? Or was it my sari? (7)

Best of all, my family approved. My husband praised me. My parents
were proud of me. My daughter gave out a sigh of admiration when I pulled
out my colorful saris. When I hugged her tenderly in my arms, scents from
the small bag of sweet-smelling herbs that I used to freshen my sari at night
escaped from the folds of cloth and calmed her to sleep. I felt part of a long
line of Indian mothers who had rocked their babies this way.

Soon, the month was over. My self-imposed (2c) was coming to an
end. Instead of feeling liberated, I felt a sharp pain of unease. I had started to
(4c) my sari.

Saris were impractical for America, I told myself. I would continue to
wear them (8). It was time to go back to my sensible casual clothes.

— 113 —

<u>2012 年</u>　　入試問題

注：bindi　ヒンドゥー教徒の女性が額につける印

(1)　下線部(1)の言い換えとして最も適切なものを次のうちから選び，その記号を
記せ。

ア　extreme

イ　gorgeous

ウ　hostile

エ　precious

オ　serious

(2)　空所（　2a　）～（　2c　）を埋めるのに最も適切なものを次のうちから一つず
つ選び，それぞれの記号を記せ。同じ記号を複数回使ってはならない。

ア　advantages　　　イ　assistance　　　ウ　attempts

エ　convenience　　　オ　feelings　　　カ　helplessness

キ　information　　　ク　obligation　　　ケ　opportunity

コ　sacrifices

(3)　空所（　3a　）～（　3c　）を埋めるのに最も適切なものを次のうちから一つず
つ選び，それぞれの記号を記せ。同じ記号を複数回使ってはならない。

ア　above　　イ　at　　　ウ　back　　エ　beyond　　オ　for

カ　from　　キ　into　　　ク　under　　ケ　with

(4)　空所（　4a　）～（　4c　）を埋めるのに最も適切なものを次のうちから一つず
つ選び，それぞれの記号を記せ。同じ記号を複数回使ってはならない。

ア　avoid　　　　　イ　enjoy　　　　ウ　fit in

エ　insist　　　　　オ　prove　　　　カ　put on

(5)　空所（　5a　）～（　5c　）を埋めるのに最も適切な組み合わせを次のうちから
選び，その記号を記せ。

－　114　－

2012 年　　入試問題

ア　authority / exhibit / immigrant

イ　authority / immigrant / exhibit

ウ　exhibit / authority / immigrant

エ　exhibit / immigrant / authority

オ　immigrant / authority / exhibit

カ　immigrant / exhibit / authority

(6)　下線部(6)を和訳せよ。ただし，one が何を指すか明らかにすること。

(7)　下線部(7)の説明として最も適切なものを次のうちから一つ選び，その記号を記せ。

　ア　She is amazed that a man would be kind enough to help a stranger in New York.

　イ　She is surprised that a man of noble birth would act so bravely in New York.

　ウ　She wonders if men have many opportunities to help beautiful women in New York.

　エ　She is confused by a father putting her daughter before his own children in New York.

　オ　She is shocked at a man's eagerness to get to know someone who looks so different in New York.

(8)　空所(　8　)を埋めるのに最も適切なものを次のうちから一つ選び，その記号を記せ。

　ア　but not every day

　イ　in order to feel liberated

　ウ　no matter how inconvenient

　エ　and enjoy their sweet herb smell

　オ　only to show I am an Indian mother

— 115 —

2012 年　　入試問題

(9)　本文の内容と一致するものを次のうちから一つ選び，その記号を記せ。

ア　The writer decided to wear saris because she wanted to express her Indian identity.

イ　The sari was so elegant and feminine that the writer naturally behaved gracefully.

ウ　Despite her initial reluctance to wear saris, the writer gradually became an expert on India.

エ　Shop assistants spoke to the writer very politely because they saw her in a sari and thought she should be treated with respect.

入試問題

解答時間：120 分
配　　点：120 点

1 (A)　次の英文の内容を，70 〜 80 字の日本語に要約せよ。句読点も字数に含める。

　　Familiarity with basic science is more important than ever, but conventional introductory courses in science do not always provide the necessary understanding. Though knowledge itself increasingly ignores boundaries between fields, professors are apt to organize their teaching around the methods and history of their academic subject rather than some topic in the world. Science courses should instead be organized around content rather than academic field: the physical universe, rather than physics or astronomy or chemistry, and living things, rather than biology.

　　Psychology has shown that the mind best understands facts when they are woven together into a conceptual fabric, such as a story, a mental map, or a theory. Facts which are not connected together in the mind are like unlinked pages on the Web: they might as well not exist. Science has to be taught in a way that knowledge is organized, one hopes permanently, in the minds of students.

　　One possibility is to use time as a framework for organizing teaching. The big bang which started the universe marks the origin of the subject matter of physics; the formation of the solar system and the earth was the beginning of earth sciences such as geology; biology came into being with the emergence of life. And if we begin to teach in this way, a science curriculum organized in terms of time could naturally lead into teaching world history and the history of civilizations and ideas, thus potentially unifying an entire general education curriculum.

(B) 次の文章で空白になっている(a)から(e)には，次のア～カのうち五つの段落が入る。それらを最も適切な順に並べ替えた場合に，不要となる段落，(b)に来る段落，(d)に来る段落はどれか。それぞれの記号を記せ。

　I'm sixteen. The other night, while I was busy thinking about important social issues, like what to do over the weekend and who to do it with, I happened to hear my parents talking in the kitchen about the future. My dad was upset — not the usual stuff that he and Mom and, I guess, a lot of parents worry about, like which college I'm going to go to, how far away it is from home, and how much it's going to cost. Instead, he was upset about the world his generation is turning over to mine, a world he fears has a dark and difficult future — if it has a future at all.

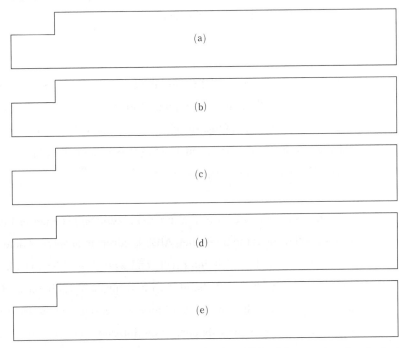

　As I listened to my dad that night describing his worries about what the future holds for me and my generation, I wanted to put my arm around him and tell him what he always told me, "Don't worry, Dad. Tomorrow will be a better day."

ア　"There will be a widespread disease that kills millions," he said, "a devastating energy crisis, a horrible worldwide depression, and a nuclear explosion set off in anger."

イ　Ever since I was a little kid, whenever I've had a bad day, my dad would put his arm around me and promise me that "tomorrow will be a better day." I challenged my father once: "How do you know that?" He said, "I just do." I believed him. My great-grandparents believed that, and my grandparents, and so do I. And now, I suddenly realized that it was my turn to make him feel better.

ウ　I considered some of the awful things my grandparents and great-grandparents had seen in their lifetimes: two world wars, epidemics, racial discrimination, nuclear bombs. But they saw other things, too, better things: the end of two world wars, new medicines, the passing of the civil rights laws. They even saw the Boston Red Sox win the World Series baseball championship — twice.

エ　In the same way, I believe that my generation will see better things, too: we will witness the time when AIDS is cured and cancer is defeated, when the Middle East will find peace, and when the Chicago Cubs win the World Series baseball championship — probably only once. I will see things as unbelievable to me today as a moon rocket was to my grandfather when he was sixteen, or the Internet to my father when he was sixteen.

2011年　入試問題

オ　One of the most awful of those things was the First World War. My great-grandparents originally came from Sweden, which was not involved in that war. Within a few years of his arrival in America, my great-grandfather had been called up for military service and sent to fight in France. Although he later recovered to some extent — partly because of the great pleasure he took in baseball — the experiences he underwent on the battlefields of France permanently threw a dark shadow over his life.

カ　As I lay on the living room couch, hearing what was being said, starting to worry about the future my father was describing, I found myself looking at some old family photos. There was a picture of my grandfather in his military college uniform. He was a member of the class of 1942, the war class. Next to his picture were photos of my great-grandparents, immigrants from Europe. Seeing those pictures made me feel a lot better. I believe tomorrow will be better than today — that the world my generation grows into is going to get better, not worse. Those pictures helped me understand why.

(C)　次の英文を読み，以下の問いに答えよ。

　　Caffeine is the most widely used drug in the world, and the value of the coffee traded on international commodity markets is exceeded only by oil. Yet for most of human history, coffee was unknown outside a small region of the Ethiopian highlands. After initially being recognised in the late sixteenth century by a few travellers in the Ottoman Empire, coffee established itself in Europe among curious scientists and merchants. The first coffee-house in the Christian world finally opened in the early 1650s in London.

　　A coffee-house exists to sell coffee, but the coffee-house cannot

— 121 —

simply be reduced to this basic commercial activity. In his famous dictionary, Samuel Johnson defined a coffee-house^(a) as 'a house of entertainment where coffee is sold, and the guests are supplied with newspapers'. More than a place that sells coffee, Johnson suggests, a coffee-house^(b) is also an idea, a way of life, a mode of socialising, a philosophy. Yet the coffee-house does have a vital relationship with coffee, which^(c) remains its governing symbol. The success of the coffee-house made coffee a popular commercial product.^(d) The associations with alertness, and thus with seriousness and with lively^(e) discussion, grant the coffee-house a unique place in modern urban life and manners, in sharp contrast to its alcoholic competitors.

The history of the coffee-house is not business history. The early coffee-house has left very few commercial records. But historians have made much use of the other kinds of evidence that do exist. Government documents are full of reports by state spies about conversations heard in coffee-houses. Further evidence is found in early newspapers, both in their advertisements and in news reports. The well-known diaries of the seventeenth and eighteenth centuries also indicate that the coffee-house was central to the social life of the period.

In describing the life-world of coffee-houses, however, much of the most compelling evidence is literary. 　ア　 The variety and nature of the coffee-house experience have made it the subject of a huge body of satirical jokes and humour. 　イ　 Considered as literature, this body of writing is rich and exciting, made lively by currents of enthusiasm and anger, full of references to particular and local disputes. 　ウ　 In representing the coffee-house, these literary materials, more than anything else, established and confirmed the place of coffee in modern urban life. 　エ　 It is in the nature of satire to exaggerate what it describes, to heighten foolishness and vice, and to portray its material

— 122 —

in the most colourful language. オ The coffee-house satires can nevertheless be considered not only as works of literature but also as historical evidence: these low and crude satires are not a simple criticism of coffee-house life, but part of their conversation, one voice in the ongoing discussion of the social life of the city.

satirical：風刺的な

satire：風刺文学

(1) 第二段落の文(a)〜(e)のうち，取り除いてもその段落の展開に最も影響の小さいものを選び，その記号を記せ。

(2) 以下の文は，第四段落のア〜オのどの位置に補うのが最も適切か。その記号を記せ。

Using this evidence, however, is not straightforward and has long troubled historians.

(3) 上の文章全体の趣旨として最も適切なものを選び，その記号を記せ。

ア　After the mid-seventeenth century, the coffee-house became a social centre of modern city life in Europe.

イ　The culture of the coffee-house can be seen in government documents and other publications during the seventeenth and eighteenth centuries.

ウ　After coffee reached Europe in the late sixteenth century, the coffee-house became a central topic in literature, particularly satirical literature.

エ　Although coffee did not reach Europe till the late sixteenth century, the coffee-house soon established coffee as an internationally traded commodity.

2011年　入試問題

2 (A)　次の Kiyoshi と Helen の会話を読み，空所(1)と(2)をそれぞれ 15 ～ 20 語の英語で埋めよ。(1)と(2)のそれぞれが複数の文になってもかまわない。

Kiyoshi:　Have you read today's newspaper?　Apparently, in England, it's illegal to sell pets — even goldfish! — to children under the age of sixteen because they may not be able to take proper care of them.　Offenders can be put in prison for one year.

Helen:　Wow! (1)＿＿＿＿＿＿＿＿＿

Kiyoshi:　Yes, that's true.　But (2)＿＿＿＿＿＿＿＿＿

Helen:　I guess you're right.

(B)　次の英文を読み，その内容について思うところを 50 ～ 60 語の英語で記せ。ただし，understand と pain は，それぞれ一回しか用いてはならない。

It is not possible to understand other people's pain.

4 (A)　次の英文(1)～(5)には，文法上取り除かなければならない語が一語ずつある。解答用紙の所定欄に，該当する語とその直後の一語，合わせて二語をその順に記せ。文の最後の語を取り除かなければならない場合は，該当する語と × (バツ) を記せ。

(1)　Among the many consequences of those political developments was for one that in the end turned out to be too complicated for the government to handle.

(2)　The sacrifices that the two countries have been told they must make are to restore stability to the world economy are almost if not completely the opposite of each other.

— 124 —

2011年　入試問題

(3) Not only did the country become economically successful, but its citizens achieved some level of psychological unity as a people, despite the fact that they became consisted of several distinct ethnic groups.

(4) Science sometimes simplifies things by producing theories that reduce to the same law phenomena previously considered were unrelated — thus clarifying our understanding of the apparent complexity of the universe.

(5) However hard it may have had been to justify the prime minister's support for those groups, she proved herself to be a person of principle by continuing to hold this position despite considerable opposition during the next decade.

(B)　次の英文の下線部(1), (2), (3)を和訳せよ。

　　The processes of change in early twentieth-century life are most commonly presented in terms of technological inventions such as those in motorized transport, aviation, and radio, or sometimes by reference to new theoretical models such as Relativity and Psychoanalysis. But there were innovations in the sphere of language as well. Although now scarcely remembered as an event of any cultural significance, the arrival of the crossword puzzle in 1924 may be seen as marking a new kind of relationship between the educated public and the vocabulary of the English language. It started as a newspaper trend, promoted by the offer of cash prizes, but it soon established itself as a national tradition, confirmed by the introduction of the first daily crossword in *The Times*, a British newspaper, in 1930. By this time, crossword fans were beginning to appear in fiction, too.　Whether there is a connection between

— 125 —

2011年　入試問題

enthusiasm for the crossword and the 1930s boom in detective fiction, with its obvious puzzle-solving appeal, can only be guessed at. More certainly, the crossword encouraged a widespread interest in words.

(3)From their newspapers, readers were thus sent hurrying to dictionaries, which libraries complained they had repeatedly to replace because they were being roughly handled or even stolen by crossword lovers. The crossword, after all, relies strongly upon prior language regulation, including standard spellings, and the availability of widely respected dictionaries.

5 次の文章を読み，以下の問いに答えよ。

One morning there was a knock on the front door. The knocking continued, and someone called out: '(1a)' It was Mrs. Brodie, a neighbour who lived a few houses away. She first saw the unfortunate child whose (2a) name she could never remember. Then she saw her mother, and put her hand over her mouth: 'Oh, my goodness!' She arranged an ambulance (2b) to take her to hospital. Meanwhile, Perdita was taken in by the Ramsays, (2c) Flora and Ted, who were both in their sixties and had their own grown-up children somewhere. They were sensitive and considerate people.

Perdita often wondered where her mother was and if she was eating and recovering her strength, but it was almost a liberation; the Ramsays' understanding and easy concern enabled her to breathe freely again. Both (3) Flora and Ted took trouble to make Perdita feel at home. Less than a month after Perdita joined them, Flora Ramsay announced to her that she was to see a doctor. Perdita consented, but she was afraid of having her speech examined by a stranger. '(1b)' said Flora, without offering any details. So Perdita arrived at a clinic building attached to the children's hospital.

— 126 —

2011年　入試問題

Perdita decided that she must be brave. But although the nurse at the reception desk smiled at her as she asked her to spell her name, courage was not, after all, so easy to <u>come by</u>. Once again, her attempt to spell her own name disclosed her condition. So Flora, who was a sensible woman, did all the talking.

Here, in a small office behind the clinic in which Perdita felt so afraid, she met her doctor, Doctor Viktor Oblov. A native of Novosibirsk, in Russia, he had come to Australia on a merchant ship at the end of the First World War, in which he had served as a doctor, treating soldiers who had psychological problems. Although he was introducing himself to Flora, Perdita also listened closely. He sounded like an exciting and interesting person. He had thinning grey hair, unfashionably long, and wore a pair of glasses with gold frames. The sleeves of his shirt were rolled, as if he were (5). Perdita was immediately charmed. When he spoke his voice was soft and low, an excellent thing in a doctor.

'Very pleased to meet you,' he said, as if he meant it. His office was untidy and unmedical, his manner a pleasant surprise.

Doctor Oblov had glass objects — paperweights — resting on his desk, which he took up from time to time, turned in his delicate hands, and set down again. One of the objects was a solid, perfectly round piece of glass containing a strange flower of brilliant blue, a kind of flower that could not (6) exist in nature. There was a second one containing a tiny ship sailing through stormy waves, and a third that held a butterfly of bright yellow. As a child who had rarely been given gifts, who possessed a piece of pearl shell but little else that might be considered as treasure, Perdita found these objects delightfully attractive.

At this first meeting, there were a few questions, but very little else, and Perdita hardly believed that Doctor Oblov was a doctor at all. He saw her looking at the three glass objects as he played with them, and asked her if she

— 127 —

would like to choose one to hold while he asked her some questions. It would make talking easier, he said. Perdita thought this was a silly suggestion, but agreed in order to please him, and because the invitation to hold one of the paperweights was what she had (7) for. She chose the one that contained the unnatural flower.

'When you speak to me,' said Doctor Oblov, 'imagine that your voice is projected beyond you, into the paperweight, and coming, like magic, out of the centre of the blue flower.'

Again Perdita thought this was a foolish suggestion — he was treating her as a little girl, she felt — but so beautiful was the object that <u>it somehow allowed her to overcome that feeling.</u> She held the paperweight, which was cold and perfect, which was, she had to admit, one of the most beautiful things she had ever seen, and responded to <u>the doctor's simple questions,</u> asked in a voice so low she could hardly hear him.

Yes, the problem started about two years ago, after she had witnessed her father's death. Yes, it was getting worse, she spoke less and less. Yes, there were occasions when she spoke without difficulty; she could recite whole verses of Shakespeare, which she had learned from her mother.

<u>At this</u> Doctor Oblov leaned back in his chair, knitting his fingers. 'Shakespeare?'

'(1c)' Flora interrupted loudly.

Perdita looked up at her and smiled, and then resumed looking into the complex beauty of the glass paperweight.

'(1d)' asked the doctor. 'Just a verse or two?'

It did not need effort; Perdita recited Hamlet's famous speech, which was her easiest piece. She heard the words flowing easily off her tongue with a sense of pride.

Doctor Oblov looked impressed. A happy smile spread across Flora's face, and she held her handbag close like a girl thrilled to meet a famous actor.

'I see,' said the doctor.

He stretched out his open palm. She placed the paperweight carefully in his hand. It caught the light, and shone like a jewel.

'One day,' he said to her, 'when your words come easily again, you can take it home.'

Perdita was thrilled for a moment, but then she began to doubt him. It was hardly a promise he would be required to keep. But Doctor Oblov smiled at her, and reached to shake her hand, as though he considered her not a child after all, but another adult. She took the doctor's hand earnestly, shook it like a grown-up, and was pleased she had come.

(1) 空所(1a)〜(1d)を埋めるのに最も適切な表現を次のうちから選び，それぞれの記号を記せ。同じ記号を複数回使ってはならない。

ア　Who was it?

イ　Just to check!

ウ　Anyone there?

エ　That's a pity ...

オ　Would you mind?

カ　That's what she said!

(2) 下線部 (2a)〜(2c) は誰を指すと考えられるか，それぞれの記号を記せ。同じ記号を複数回使ってはならない。

ア　Perdita

イ　Mrs. Brodie

ウ　Flora's child

エ　Flora Ramsay

オ　Perdita's mother

2011 年　　入試問題

(3) 下線部(3)の意味として最も適切なものを次のうちから一つ選び，その記号を記せ。

ア　She was able to get over her cold.

イ　She was able to express her opinion.

ウ　She was able to share her excitement.

エ　She was able to recover her peace of mind.

(4) 下線部(4)の意味として最も適切なものを次のうちから一つ選び，その記号を記せ。

ア　lose

イ　obtain

ウ　require

エ　display

(5) 下に与えられた語を正しい順に並べ替え，空所(　5　)を埋めるのに最も適切な表現を完成させよ。ただし，下の語群には，不要な語が二つ含まれている。

about　　engage　　find　　in　　interested　　labour　　physical　　to

(6) 空所(　6　)を埋めるのに最も適切な単語を次のうちから一つ選び，その記号を記せ。

ア　only

イ　openly

ウ　possibly

エ　completely

— 130 —

2011 年　　入試問題

(7)　空所(　7　)を埋めるのに最も適切な単語を次のうちから一つ選び，その記号を記せ。

ア　lived

イ　asked

ウ　hoped

エ　prepared

(8)　下線部(8)を和訳せよ。ただし，it と that feeling が意味する内容を明らかにすること。

(9)　下線部(9)の質問内容と合致しないものを次のうちから一つ選び，その記号を記せ。

ア　Is it becoming more severe?

イ　Did the trouble start long ago?

ウ　Does holding the paperweight help?

エ　Are there any times when it doesn't happen?

(10)　下線部(10)の言い換えとして最も適切なものを次のうちから一つ選び，その記号を記せ。

ア　Hearing what she said,

イ　Seeing how she said it,

ウ　Guessing what she said,

エ　Trying to repeat what she said,

入試問題

解答時間：120分
配　点：120点

1 (A)　次の英文の内容を，挙げられた例にも触れながら，90 〜 100字の日本語に
要約せよ。ただし，句読点も字数に含め，"science fiction" は「SF」（2字）
と表記せよ。英文は次ページまで続いているので注意すること。

Science fiction not only is good fun but also serves a serious purpose,
that of expanding the human imagination.　We can explore how the
human spirit might respond to future developments in science, and we
can imagine what those developments might be.

There is a two-way trade between science fiction and science.
Science fiction suggests ideas that scientists include in their theories, but
sometimes science turns up notions that are stranger than any science
fiction.　Black holes are an example, greatly assisted by the inspired
name that the physicist John Archibald Wheeler gave them.　Had they
continued with their original names of "frozen stars" or "gravitationally
completely collapsed objects," there wouldn't have been half so much
written about them.

One thing that science fiction has focused attention on is travel faster
than light.　If a spaceship were restricted to flying just under the speed
of light, it might seem to the crew that the round trip to the center of
the galaxy took only a few years, but 80,000 years would have passed on
Earth before the spaceship's return.　So much for going back to see your
family!

Fortunately, Einstein's general theory of relativity allows the
possibility for a way around this difficulty: one might be able to bend,
or warp, space and time and create a shortcut between the places

— 134 —

one wanted to visit. It seems that such warping might be within our capabilities in the future. There has not been much serious scientific research along these lines, however, partly, I think, because it sounds too much like science fiction. One of the consequences of rapid space travel would be that one could also travel back in time. Imagine the complaint about the waste of taxpayers' money if it were known that the government were supporting research on time travel. For this reason, scientists working in this field have to hide their real interest by using technical terms like "closed timelike curves" that really mean time travel. Nevertheless, today's science fiction is often tomorrow's science fact. The science behind science fiction is surely worth investigating.

(B) 次の英文を読み，以下の問いに答えよ。

First proposed early in the 20th century, the idea of obtaining (a) resources from asteroids continues to attract attention. The basic (b) notion is to get material from near-earth asteroids, that is, those having orbits that come close to our planet. This group is distinct from the (c) main belt asteroids, which orbit between the planets Mars and Jupiter.

Materials from the asteroids could be used in space to support space (d) flight, space stations, or even a moon base. The resources could also be (e) brought back to earth for use here.

☐ ア ☐ The first resource of interest is likely to be water from the near-earth asteroids that are either C-type (carbon-rich) asteroids or the cores of dead comets. ☐ イ ☐ Together these probably make up half or more of the near-earth asteroid population. ☐ ウ ☐ That water would be used to make hydrogen and oxygen for rocket fuel. ☐ エ ☐ Of course, that water and oxygen would also then be available to support human life in space. ☐ オ ☐ These substances are very common not only on earth but

— 135 —

in asteroids as well, and they could be used as structural materials in space.

Whether the resources sought in space are materials or energy, technology for obtaining them still needs to be developed. While the technology needed to travel to near-earth asteroids is now available — in fact, the amount of rocket power and fuel needed to visit some of these bodies is less than it takes to go to the moon — the technology necessary to mine them and either process or bring back the asteroids' resources has not been developed. It is also not clear how difficult and costly this would be, nor is it known if the task could be done by robots or would require human supervision. Although some space agencies have explored asteroids with robots and the possibility of human missions has been discussed as well, no specific plans for mining asteroids have yet been made.

注：asteroid 小惑星
　　cobalt コバルト

2010年　入試問題

　　helium-3　ヘリウムの同位体の一つ

　　to mine, mining　鉱石などを採掘する（こと）

　　nuclear fusion　核融合

　　orbit　軌道（を回る）

　　platinum　プラチナ，白金

(1)　第一段落の文(a)〜(e)のうち，取り除いても大意に影響を与えないものを
　　一つ選び，その記号を記せ。

(2)　以下の文は，第二段落のア〜オのどの位置に補うのが最も適切か。その記
　　号を記せ。

Another resource that could be used in space is almost certainly metals
such as iron and cobalt.

(3)　上の文章で空白になっている第三段落から第六段落には，次のア〜オのう
　　ちの四つの段落が入る。それらを最も適切な順に並べた場合に，不要となる
　　段落，一番目に来る段落，三番目に来る段落はどれか。それぞれの記号を記せ。

　ア　Most early asteroid-mining concepts required humans to visit the
　　asteroids and mine them, but some of the newer ideas involve strictly
　　robotic missions.　One option would be simply to bring pieces of
　　the asteroid back to the earth and crash them in some remote area
　　where a processing plant would be set up.　Another possibility would
　　be processing the materials on the asteroid itself.

　イ　Yet another potential resource would be precious metals that could
　　be brought back to the earth.　The most promising metals to obtain
　　from asteroids would include the platinum-group metals, which are
　　rare and costly on earth and could be used here for many industrial

－　137　－

applications. Planetary astronomers believe the average asteroid should have much higher amounts of these metals than typical rocks on the earth or even on the moon.

ウ   But while it might be too expensive to bring back materials from space, economists also point to some very interesting opportunities associated with the generation of electrical power in space for use on earth. For example, solar-power satellites could be placed in high earth orbits to beam solar power down to the ground in the form of microwave energy. Helium-3 taken from the surface of the moon might also be economically attractive for nuclear fusion on the moon with the power beamed down to the earth.

エ   Similarly, solar collectors may be built on the moon out of native materials to send their power back to the earth. The construction of solar-power plants in space could in principle be made much cheaper if the high-mass, low-tech components of the plants are made in space using materials made from asteroids or even the moon. Farther away, the supply of helium-3 in the giant planets (especially Uranus and Neptune) is so vast that schemes for obtaining fuel for nuclear fusion from their atmospheres could power the earth until the sun dies of old age.

オ   Some economists, however, question whether asteroid materials could be brought back to the earth profitably. A sudden increase on earth in the supply of platinum-group metals from space, for example, without a similar increase in demand could cause the price of the metals to drop drastically, thereby eliminating profits and discouraging further investment. Another possible import—

rare substances used in laboratory analysis—not only has a limited
market, but demand for such substances is expected to decrease in
the future as analytical techniques improve.

(4) 上の文章全体との関係を考えて，最後の段落の要点として最も適切なもの
を一つ選び，その記号を記せ。

ア　The challenges of space travel

イ　A dream still waiting to be realized

ウ　The costs and benefits of asteroid-mining

エ　The risks to our planet posed by near-earth asteroids

オ　Obtaining asteroid resources: By humans or by robots?

2 (A)　現在，全世界で約3,000から8,000の言語が話されていると言われている。
もしそうではなく，全世界の人々がみな同じ一つの言語を使用しているとした
ら，我々の社会や生活はどのようになっていたと思うか。空所を50～60語
の英語で埋める形で答えよ。答えが複数の文になってもかまわない。

If there were only one language in the world, ＿＿＿＿＿＿＿＿＿＿

＿＿＿＿＿＿＿＿＿＿＿＿＿＿＿＿＿＿＿＿＿＿

＿＿＿＿＿＿＿＿＿＿＿＿＿＿＿＿＿＿＿＿＿＿

＿＿＿＿＿＿＿＿＿＿＿＿＿＿＿＿＿＿＿＿＿＿

(B)　以下の例に従って，次の(1)～(8)の括弧内の単語の形を変え，文脈に合うよ
うに空所を一語で埋めよ。

(例)　The organization issues three publications every week: a
magazine, a newspaper, and a catalog. **(publish)**

2010年　入試問題

(例)　Our new neighbors seemed <u>unfriendly</u> at first, but they turned out to be very nice. **(friend)**

(1)　The bridge was _____ by the earthquake and had to be closed for repairs. **(weak)**

(2)　The witnesses _____ yesterday about how the accident occurred, so the police are still investigating it. **(agree)**

(3)　She had to cancel her _____ in the gym after she injured herself. **(member)**

(4)　The composer's new symphony is a unique _____ of cheerful melodies and sad harmonies. **(combine)**

(5)　Because the residents of the neighborhood worked together very _____ they were able to reduce crime in the area. **(effect)**

(6)　For the past month, the leader of the opposition party has been _____ the prime minister for wasting government money. **(critic)**

(7)　On Tuesday, the country celebrated the 50th anniversary of the day it became _____ from Britain. **(depend)**

(8)　It may be necessary to consult a _____ who can show us how to interpret the data correctly. **(special)**

— 140 —

2010 年　　入試問題

4 (A) 次の英文(1)～(5)には，文法上，取り除かなければならない語が一語ずつある。解答用紙の所定欄に該当する語を記せ。

⑴　Discovery is not the sort of process about finding which the question "Who discovered it?" is appropriately asked.

⑵　Discovering a new phenomenon is necessarily a complex event, one of which involves recognizing both that something is and what it is.

⑶　Science does and must continually try to bring theory and in fact into closer agreement, and that activity can be seen as testing or as a search for confirmation or disconfirmation.

⑷　Discovery makes it possible for scientists to account for a wider range of natural phenomena or to account with greater precision for some of those were previously unknown.

⑸　Newton's second law of motion, though it took centuries of difficult factual and theoretical research to achieve, behaves for those committed to Newton's theory seem very much like a purely logical statement that no amount of observation could prove wrong.

(B)　次の英文の下線部(1)，(2)，(3)を和訳せよ。(2)については，**They** が何を指すか明らかになるように訳すこと。

　　Stars are made for profit. In terms of the market, stars are part of the way films are sold.　The star's presence in a film is a promise of what you will see if you go to see the film.　In the same way, stars sell newspapers and magazines, and are used to sell food, fashions, cars and

— 141 —

2010年　入試問題

almost anything else.

This market function of stars is only one aspect of their economic importance. They are also property on the strength of whose name money can be raised to make a film; they are an asset to the stars themselves, to the studios and agents who control them; they are a major part of the cost of a film. Above all, they are part of the labour that produces films as commercial products that can be sold for profit on the market.

Stars are involved in making themselves into commercial products; they are both labour and the thing that labour produces. They do not produce themselves alone. The person is a body, a psychology, a set of skills that have to be worked up into a star image. This work of making the star out of the raw material of the person depends on how much the essential qualities of that material are respected; make-up, hairstyle, clothing, dieting, and bodybuilding can make use of the original body features to a variety of degrees, skills can be learned, and even personality can be changed. The people who do this labour include the stars themselves as well as make-up artists, hairdressers, dress designers, dieticians, personal trainers, acting, dancing and other teachers, photographers, gossip columnists, and so on.

5 次の文章は，William Porter という人物の伝記の一部である。これを読んで以下の問いに答えよ。

When William Porter left Houston, never to return, he left because he was ordered to come immediately to Austin and stand trial for stealing funds while working at the First National Bank of Austin.

Had he gone he would certainly have been declared innocent. "A (　1　)

－ 142 －

of circumstances" is the judgment of the people in Austin who followed the trial most closely. Not one of them, so far as I could learn after many interviews, believed him guilty of doing anything wrong. It was well known that the bank, <u>long since closed</u>, was terribly managed. Its customers, (2) following an old practice, used to enter, go behind the counter, take out one hundred or two hundred dollars, and say a week later: "Porter, I took out two hundred dollars last week. See if I left a note about it. <u>I meant to.</u>" It was (3) impossible to keep track of the bank's money. The affairs of the bank were managed so loosely that Porter's predecessor was driven to retirement, his successor to attempted suicide.

There can be no doubt that Porter boarded the train at Houston with the intention of going to Austin. I imagine that he even felt a certain sense of relief that the trial, which had hung as a heavy weight around his neck, was at last to take place, and his innocence publicly declared. His friends were confident of his innocence. <u>If even one of them had been with Porter, all</u> (4) <u>would have been different.</u> But when the train reached Hempstead, about a third of the way to Austin, Porter had had time to imagine the scenes of the trial, to picture himself a prisoner, to look into the future and see himself marked with suspicion. <u>His imagination outran his reason</u>, and when the (5) night train passed Hempstead on the way to New Orleans, Porter was on it.

His mind seems to have been fully made up. He was not merely saving himself and his family from a public shame, he was going to start life over again in a new place. His knowledge of Spanish and his ignorance of Honduras made the little Central American republic seem just the place to escape to. His letters to his wife from Honduras show that he had determined to make Central America their home, and that a school had already been selected for the education of their daughter.

How long Porter remained in New Orleans, on his way to Honduras, is not known. It is probable that he merely passed through New Orleans on his way

to Honduras and took the first available boat for the Honduran coast, arriving at Puerto Cortez or Trujillo. At any rate, he was in Trujillo and was standing at the dock when he saw a man in a worn dress suit step from a newly arrived boat. "Why did you leave so hurriedly?" asked Porter. "Perhaps for the same reason as yourself," replied the stranger. "What is your destination?" inquired Porter. "I left America to keep away from <u>my destination</u>" was the reply.
₍₆₎

The stranger was Al Jennings, the leader of one of the worst gangs of train robbers that ever existed in the American Southwest. He and his brother Frank had chartered a boat in Galveston, and the departure had been so (7) their dress suits and high hats for plainer clothing. Jennings and his brother had no thought of continuing their career of (8) in Latin America. They were merely putting distance between them and the detectives already on their trail. Porter joined them and together they circled the entire coast of South America. This was Porter's longest voyage and certainly the strangest.

In these wanderings together Jennings probably saw deeper into one side of Porter's life than anyone else had ever seen. In a letter to a friend, he writes: "Porter was to most men a difficult character but when men have gone hungry together, eaten together, and looked death in the face and laughed, it may be said they have (9) each other. Again, there is no period in a man's life that shows his unique characteristics so much as terrible hunger. I have known that with our friend and could find no fault. If the world could only know him as I knew him, the searchlight of investigation could be turned on his beautiful soul and find it as spotless as a beam of sunlight after the storm-cloud had passed."

Porter's letters to his wife came regularly after the first three weeks. The letters were enclosed in envelopes directed to Mr. Louis Kreisle, in Austin, who handed them to Porter's wife. "Mrs. Porter used to read me selections from her husband's letters," said Mrs. Kreisle. "They told of his plans to

— 144 —

2010年　入試問題

bring Mrs. Porter and Margaret to him as soon as he was settled. He had a hard time but his letters were cheerful and hopeful and full of (10a) for his wife. Mrs. Porter's parents were, of course, willing to provide for her and Margaret but she did not want to be dependent. She said she did not know how long they would be separated, so she planned to do something to earn some money. She began taking a course in a business college but (10b) interfered. When Christmas came she made a lace handkerchief, sold it for twenty-five dollars, and sent her husband a box containing his overcoat, fine perfumes, and many other delicacies. I never saw such (10c). The only day she remained in bed was the day she died."

　　Porter did not know till a month later that this box was packed by Mrs. Porter when her temperature was 104°F (40℃). As soon as he learned it, he gave up all (10d) of a Latin American home and started for Austin, determined to give himself up and to take whatever punishment fate or the courts had in store for him.

(1)　空所(1)を埋めるのに最も適切な単語を次のうちから一つ選び，その記号を記せ。

　ア　victim

　イ　nature

　ウ　creature

　エ　punishment

(2)　下線部(2)の言い換えとして最も適切な表現を次のうちから一つ選び，その記号を記せ。

　ア　as long as it was closed

　イ　which had been closed at long last

　ウ　which had been closed for a long time

　エ　because it had been closed a long time ago

— 145 —

2010年　　入試問題

(3)　下線部(3)の意味として最も適切なものを次のうちから一つ選び，その記号を記せ。

ア　確かな記憶がある。

イ　よく調べてもらいたい。

ウ　そのつもりだったが，忘れたかもしれない。

エ　そういう意味だったので，誤解しないでほしい。

(4)　下線部(4)を和訳せよ。ただし，them と all が意味する内容を明らかにすること。

(5)　下線部(5)に描かれている Porter の心理について，最もよく当てはまるものを一つ選び，その記号を記せ。

ア　He was afraid of the trial even though he thought that he was likely to be declared innocent.

イ　He was afraid of the trial because he had reason to believe that his guilt would be apparent.

ウ　He was afraid of the trial even though he couldn't remember why he had stolen funds from the bank.

エ　He was afraid of the trial because people wouldn't understand his reasons for stealing funds from the bank.

(6)　下線部(6)は具体的に何を指すと考えられるか。最も適切なものを次のうちから一つ選び，その記号を記せ。

ア　prison

イ　robbery

ウ　the bank

エ　his home

— 146 —

2010 年　　入試問題

(7)　下に与えられた語を正しい順に並べ替え，空所(　7　)を埋めるのに最も適切な表現を完成させよ。ただし，下の語群には，不要な語が一つ含まれている。

exchange,　had,　had,　not,　sudden,　they,　time,　to,　with

(8)　空所(　8　)を埋めるのに最も適切な単語を次のうちから一つ選び，その記号を記せ。

ア　crime

イ　travel

ウ　escape

エ　finance

(9)　空所(　9　)を埋めるのに最も適切な表現を次のうちから一つ選び，その記号を記せ。

ア　no use for

イ　knowledge of

ウ　despaired for

エ　worried about

(10)　空所(　10a　)〜(　10d　)を埋めるのに最も適切な表現を次のうちから選び，それぞれの記号を記せ。同じ記号は一度しか使えない。

ア　hope

イ　affection

ウ　ill health

エ　willpower

— 147 —

入試問題

解答時間：120分
配　　点：120点

1 (A) 次の英文の趣旨を，70〜80字の日本語でまとめよ。句読点も字数に含める。

When I was six or seven years old, I used to take a small coin of my own, usually a penny, and hide it for someone else to find. For some reason I always "hid" the penny along the same stretch of sidewalk. I would place it at the roots of a huge tree, say, or in a hole in the sidewalk. Then I would take a piece of chalk, and, starting at either end of the block, draw huge arrows leading up to the penny from both directions. After I learned to write I labeled the arrows: SURPRISE AHEAD or MONEY THIS WAY. I was greatly excited, during all this arrow-drawing, at the thought of the first lucky passer-by who would receive in this way, regardless of merit, a free gift from the universe.

Now, as an adult, I recall these memories because I've been thinking recently about seeing. There are lots of things to see, there are many free surprises: the world is full of pennies thrown here and there by a generous hand. But — and this is the point — what grown-up gets excited over a mere penny? If you follow one arrow, if you crouch motionless at a roadside to watch a moving branch and are rewarded by the sight of a deer shyly looking out, will you count that sight something cheap, and continue on your way? It is dreadful poverty indeed to be too tired or busy to stop and pick up a penny. But if you cultivate a healthy poverty and simplicity of mind, so that finding a penny will have real meaning for you, then, since the world is in fact planted with pennies, you have with your poverty bought a lifetime of discoveries.

— 150 —

2009 年　　入試問題

(B)　次の英文を読み，以下の問いに答えよ。

　　Collecting has long been a popular hobby, be it for the usual stamps, coins, and buttons, or more recently for Pokemon trading cards. But some kinds of collecting require more than an amateur's knowledge; in this category we find fountain pens. Widely replaced by more affordable and convenient ballpoint and rollerball pens, today fountain pens as everyday writing tools are rarely seen. Precisely for this reason, they have caught the eye of collectors.

　　　ア　　For collectors, an item's value is increased not only by how rare it is but also by how many colorful stories are told about it, and the long history of the fountain pen contains many.　　イ　　The fascinating origins of the pen, for example, are inseparable from the development of writing itself.　　ウ　　We all know about China's crucial invention of paper around 104 A.D. for brush-writing with "India ink."　　エ　　But consider the Egyptians' earlier use of hollow reed pens to write on papyrus some 4,000 years ago.　　オ　　What is this if not the basic principle of the modern fountain pen, the ideal pen whose "fountain" would not run dry?

　　From the Middle Ages, writers in Europe and elsewhere used a goose quill, or other bird's feather, that held berry juice or ink. Although feather quills appear romantic when we see them in movies, and we might well imagine Shakespeare composing his masterpieces with them, in reality, the quill pen was often unattractive and messy. It had to be constantly dipped in ink and sharpened with a knife. It quickly became worn down just by writing and handling.

— 151 —

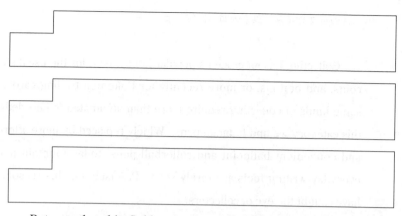

But now that this Golden Age is giving way to a new era of writing technologies, from rollerball pens to computers, it rests with the ordinary collector, like me, to keep the fountain pen and its stories alive. Indeed, I confess to having recently purchased my first collectable pen.(a) The De La Rue Company of Great Britain was founded as a paper and printing(b) company in 1821. Even today, it is De La Rue's high-security paper on which Bank of England(c) money is printed. But for some time in the early 20th century it also used to manufacture pens,(d) such as the one I now own; in fact, it created quite a name for itself with them. Before I can explain why I wanted this particular De La Rue pen, I must first(e) tell you the story of the writer who led me to it.

A 19th-century novelist, Onoto Watanna, once wrote enormously popular stories in English about the West and Japan. She wanted to tell her English readers about Japan's language, culture, and customs. While she never revealed her actual name, she once acknowledged "Onoto Watanna" was just a pen name. Quite literally, it turns out, for "Onoto" was also the name of the De La Rue Company's fountain pen!

The actual identity of Onoto Watanna, I already knew: Winnifred Eaton was half-Chinese, half-English, and raised in Canada and the US. She spoke no Japanese and had never been to Japan. The pen caught my attention later, by chance, when I saw a 1920s Japanese advertisement for "Onoto, the Pen." Immediately, I assumed the pen was Japanese-made, and the clever origin of Onoto's pen name. But the Onoto pen was born in Britain in 1905 after "Onoto Watanna"; that is, just as had Winnifred Eaton before them, the De La Rue Company too followed the global fashion for things Japanese, even borrowing Eaton's fake Japanese name. Sparking my search for the truth about pen and writer, this misunderstanding led to a new passion for collecting unusual fountain pens with unexpected stories.

注 : reed　葦

(1)　以下の文は，第二段落のア～オのどの位置に補うのが最も適切か。その記号を記せ。

Historians suggest that even these very early writing instruments can be seen as having a sort of internal tank which could supply ink steadily to the writing tip.

(2)　上の文章で空白になっている第四段落から第七段落には，次のア～オのうちの四つの段落が入る。それらを最も適切な順に並べた場合に，不要となる段落，一番目に来る段落，三番目に来る段落はどれか。その記号を記せ。

ア　In his case, truly, "necessity was the mother of invention." Determined to avoid the same thing happening again, he got to work. His new feeder system caused the ink to move safely down from storage inside the pen body to the specially designed pen tip, or "nib."

イ　During the 19th century, scientific advances made many inventions possible. One of these was Charles Goodyear's discovery of the

— 153 —

chemical process by which soft rubber was made harder, making it ideal for shaping a stronger body for the fountain pen or making boots and coats waterproof.

ウ Once technology and design made the fountain pen more reliable, attention could turn to beauty and not just usefulness. Pen companies the world over competed for quality and status, creating pens specifically marketed to powerful world leaders, famous people, soldiers in the field, and everyday consumers.

エ Ironically, it was an accident that solved all these problems and led to the technological improvement of the fountain pen. In 1883, the businessman Lewis Waterman needed a contract signed. He gave his fountain pen to a customer to do just that but, without warning, the pen flooded ink all over their documents! Waterman lost his business deal, and then his temper.

オ Throughout its long development, the pen had always faced similar problems: how to hold the ink inside and then get it to flow steadily to the paper, without requiring constant cutting or dipping in the ink bottle, and without either going dry or leaking. Many of us have had the unpleasant experience of the bad pen that suddenly leaks ink all over our hands. Such occurrences were common in the early days of the pen.

(3) 第八段落の文(a)～(e)のうち，取り除いてもその段落の展開に最も影響の小さいものを選び，その記号を記せ。

— 154 —

2009年　入試問題

(4) 上の文章全体との関係において，最後の三段落の趣旨として最も適切なものを選び，その記号を記せ。

ア　Uncovering the true identity of Onoto Watanna

イ　Explaining why I began to collect fountain pens

ウ　Giving the most recent history of the fountain pen

エ　Introducing a product made by the De La Rue Company

オ　Revealing why the De La Rue Company named its pen "Onoto"

2 (A)　次のような質問を受けたと仮定し，空所(1)，(2)をそれぞれ20〜30語の英語で埋める形で答えを完成させよ。(1)，(2)のそれぞれが複数の文になってもかまわない。

Question:　Do you think reading books will help you acquire the knowledge you need to live in today's world?

Answer:　My answer is both yes and no.

Yes, because (1)

No, because (2)

(B)　以下の例に従って，次の(1)〜(5)について，(a)と(b)の文が同じ意味になるよう，括弧内の単語をそのままの形で用いて，空所を2〜5語の英語で埋めよ。

— 155 —

2009年　入試問題

(例)　(a)　"Can I go to the party?" Susan asked. **(she)**

　　(b)　Susan asked *if she could go* to the party.

(1)　(a)　It's extremely rare for her to miss class. **(almost)**

　　(b)　She ＿＿＿＿＿＿＿＿＿＿＿＿ class.

(2)　(a)　His eyesight is so poor that he can hardly read. **(such)**

　　(b)　He ＿＿＿＿＿＿＿＿＿＿＿＿ he can hardly read.

(3)　(a)　Because the weather was bad, the trains were late. **(to)**

　　(b)　The trains were late ＿＿＿＿＿＿＿＿＿＿＿＿ weather.

(4)　(a)　That's the nicest compliment anyone has ever paid me. **(a)**

　　(b)　No one has ever ＿＿＿＿＿＿＿＿＿＿＿＿ nice compliment.

(5)　(a)　We can't afford that car. **(us)**

　　(b)　That car is ＿＿＿＿＿＿＿＿＿＿＿＿ buy.

4 (A)　次の英文(1)〜(5)には，文法上あるいは文脈上，取り除かなければならない語が一語ずつある。所定欄に該当する語を記せ。

　　　If you were asked to fall backward into the arms of a stranger, would you have trust the other person to catch you?　Such an exercise, which is sometimes used in psychology, is a bit extreme, but every day most people put on some degree of trust in individuals they do not know.

　　　Unlike other animals, we humans tend to spend a great deal of time around all others who are unknown to us.　Those who live in cities, for example, regularly find their way through a sea of strangers, deciding to

— 156 —

2009年　入試問題

avoid certain familiar individuals they feel are not safe.　They are equally good at identifying others who will, say, give accurate directions to some destination or other who will, at the very least, not actually attack them.

(B)　次の英文の下線部(1)，(2)，(3)を和訳せよ。

　　How she loved her mother! Still perfectly beautiful at eighty-six. The only concession she'd made to her age was a pair of hearing aids. "My ears," she called them. Everything her mother touched she touched carefully, and left a little smoother, a little finer for her touch. Everything about her mother reminded her of trees changing with the seasons, each garment some variety of leaf color: the light green of spring with a hint of yellow, the dark green of full summer, occasionally a detail of bright autumn — an orange scarf, a red ribbon in her hair. Wool in winter, cotton in summer; never an artificial fiber next to her skin. What she didn't understand, she often said, was　the kind of laziness which, in the name of convenience, in the end made more work and deprived one of the small but real joys. The smell of a warm iron against damp cloth, the comfort of something that was once alive against your body. She was a great believer in not removing yourself from the kind of labor she considered natural. She wouldn't own an electric food processor or have a credit card. She liked, she said, chopping vegetables, and　when she paid for something, she wanted to feel, on the tips of her fingers, on the palms of her hands, the cost.

— 157 —

2009 年　　入試問題

5 次の文章を読み，以下の問いに答えよ。

When people hear that I'm writing an article about the way human beings deceive each other, they're quick to tell me how to catch a liar. Liars always look to the left, several friends say; liars always cover their mouths, says a man sitting next to me on a plane. Beliefs about (　1　) are numerous and often contradictory. Liars can be detected because they move a lot, keep very still, cross their legs, cross their arms, look up, look down, make eye contact or fail to make eye contact. Freud thought anyone could spot people who are lying by paying close enough attention to the way they move their fingers. Nietzsche wrote that "the mouth may lie, but the face it makes nonetheless tells the truth."

Most people think they're good at spotting liars, but studies show otherwise. It is wrong to expect that professionally trained people will have the ability to detect liars with accuracy. In general, even professional lie-catchers, like judges and customs officials, perform, when tested, (　2　). In other words, even the experts would have been right almost as often if they had just tossed a coin.

Just as it is hard to decide who is lying and who is not, it is also much more difficult (　3　) tell what is a lie and what is not. "Everybody lies," Mark Twain wrote, "every day; every hour; awake; asleep; in his dreams; in his joy; in his grief."

First, there are the lies which consist of not saying something. You go out to dinner with your sister and her handsome boyfriend, and you find him utterly unpleasant. When you and your sister discuss the evening later, isn't it a lie for you to talk about the restaurant and not about the boyfriend? What if you talk about his good looks and not about his offensive personality?

Then there are lies which consist of saying something you know to be false. Many of these are harmless lies that allow us to get along with one

— 158 —

another. When you receive a gift you can't use, or are invited to lunch with a co-worker you dislike, you're likely to say, "Thank you, it's perfect" or "I wish I could, but I have a dentist's appointment," rather than speak the harsher truth. These are the lies we teach our children to tell; we call them manners. Even our automatic response of "Fine" to a neighbor's equally mechanical "How are you?" is often, when you get right down to it, a lie.

More serious lies can have a range of motives and implications; for example, lying about a rival's behavior in order to get him fired. But in other cases, not every lie is one that needs to be uncovered. We humans are active, creative animals who can represent what exists as if it did not, and what doesn't exist as if it did. Concealment, indirectness, silence, outright lying — all contribute to the peace-keeping of the human community.

Learning to lie is an important part of growing up. What makes children able to start telling lies, usually at about age three or four, is that they have begun developing a theory of mind, the idea that what goes on in their heads is different from what goes on in other people's heads. With their first lie to their parents, the power balance shifts a little: they now know something their parents don't know. With each new lie they gain a bit more power over the people who believe them. After a while, the ability to lie becomes just another part of their emotional landscape.

Lying is just so ordinary, so much a part of our everyday lives and everyday conversations, that we hardly notice it. The fact is that in many cases it would be more difficult, challenging and stressful for people to tell the truth than to lie. Can't we say that deceiving is, (7), one characteristic associated with the evolution of higher intelligence?

At present, attempts are being made by the US Federal Government to develop an efficient machine for "credibility assessment," (8), a perfect lie detector, as a means to improve the nation's security level in its "war on terrorism." This quest to make the country safer, however, may

— 159 —

2009年　入試問題

have implications for our everyday lives in the most unexpected ways. How will the newly developed device be able to tell which are truly dangerous lies and which are lies that are harmless and kind-hearted, or <u>self-serving without being dangerous</u>? What happens if one day we find ourselves₍₉₎ with instruments that can detect untruth not only in the struggle against terrorism but also in situations that have little to do with national security: job interviews, tax inspections, classrooms, bedrooms?

　　A perfect lie-detection device would turn our lives upside down. Before long, we would stop speaking to each other, television would be abolished, politicians would be arrested and civilization would come to a halt. It would be a mistake to bring such a device too rapidly to market, before considering what might happen not only if it didn't work — <u>which is the kind of risk we're accustomed to thinking about</u> — but also what₍₁₀₎ might happen if it did. Worse than living in a world filled with uncertainty, in which we can never know for sure who is lying to whom, might be to live in a world filled with certainty about where the lies are, thus forcing us to tell one another nothing but the truth.

(1)　空所（　1　）を埋めるのに最も適切な表現を次のうちから一つ選び，その記号を記せ。

　ア　why people lie

　イ　the timing of lying

　ウ　what lying looks like

　エ　the kinds of lies people tell

(2)　空所（　2　）を埋めるのに最も適切な表現を次のうちから一つ選び，その記号を記せ。

　ア　as accurately as expected

　イ　not much better than chance

— 160 —

2009 年　　入試問題

ウ　somewhat worse than average

エ　far better than non-professionals

(3)　下に与えられた語を正しい順に並べ替え，空所(　3　)を埋めるのに最も適切
な表現を完成させよ。ただし，下の語群には，不要な語が一つ含まれている。

look　　　tend　　　than　　　think　　　to　　　to　　　we

(4)　下線部(4)の意味内容として最も近いものを次のうちから一つ選び，その記号
を記せ。

ア　how you really feel

イ　the lies children tell

ウ　a visit to the dentist

エ　why you don't like lunch

(5)　下線部(5)を和訳せよ。

(6)　下線部(6)の意味内容として最も近いものを次のうちから一つ選び，その記号
を記せ。

ア　They become less dependent on others.

イ　They learn more clearly to tell right from wrong.

ウ　They realize that their parents are just like other people.

エ　They understand that they are being encouraged to learn how to lie.

(7)　空所(　7　)を埋めるのに最も適切な表現を次のうちから一つ選び，その記号
を記せ。

ア　in vain

イ　after all

ウ　in no way

エ　by contrast

― 161 ―

2009 年　　入試問題

(8)　空所（　8　）を埋めるのに最も適切な表現を次のうちから一つ選び，その記号を記せ。

　　ア　all the same
　　イ　by all means
　　ウ　in other words
　　エ　on the other hand

(9)　下線部(9)で説明されている lies はこの文脈では何を意味するか。次のうちから最も適切なものを一つ選び，その記号を記せ。

　　ア　自分にとっては安全で使いやすい嘘
　　イ　自動的に出てくる，たわいのない嘘
　　ウ　自己犠牲を必要とする割に無難な嘘
　　エ　利己的だが，国家にとって安全な嘘

(10)　下線部(10)で説明されている risk とは，この場合どのようなものか。15 〜 20字の日本語で具体的に説明せよ。

(11)　以下は筆者の見解をまとめたものである。空所（　a　）〜（　d　）を埋めるのに最も適切な語を下の語群から選び，必要に応じて適切な形にして記せ。同じ語は一度しか使えない。

　　As human beings, we cannot （　a　） lying at times. Indeed, sometimes lying （　b　） people from unnecessary confrontation. In many cases, peace in human society is （　c　） because not all the truth is （　d　）.

　　avoid　　invite　　maintain　　protect　　reveal　　struggle

— 162 —

入試問題

解答時間：120分
配　　点：120点

1 (A) 次の英文の内容を，70 〜 80 字の日本語に要約せよ。句読点も字数に含める。

One serious question about faces is whether we can find attractive or even pleas-ant-looking someone of whom we cannot approve. We generally give more weight to moral judgments than to judgments about how people look, or at least most of us do most of the time. So when confronted by a person one has a low moral opinion of, perhaps the best that one can say is that he or she *looks* nice — and one is likely to add that this is only a surface impression. What we in fact seem to be doing is reading backward, from knowledge of a person's past behavior to evidence of that behavior in his or her face.

We need to be cautious in assuming that outer appearance and inner self have any immediate relation to each other. It is in fact extremely difficult to draw any conclusions we can trust from our judgments of a person's appearance alone, and often, as we gain more knowledge of the person, we can discover how wrong our initial judgments were. During Hitler's rise and early years in power, hardly anyone detected the inhumanity that we now see so clearly in his face. There is nothing necessarily evil about the appearance of a small man with a mustache and exaggerated bodily movements. The description would apply equally well to the famous comedian Charlie Chaplin, whose gestures and mustache provoke laughter and sympathy. Indeed, in a well-known film Chaplin plays the roles of both ordinary man and wicked political leader in so similar a way that it is impossible to tell them apart.

2008 年　入試問題

(B) 次の英文を読み，以下の問いに答えよ。

　　As the human mind evolved, at some point we began to consider the possibility of life beyond our planet.　Perhaps it was a starry evening, thousands of years ago, when some primitive human being stepped outside of his or her cave, gazed at the sky, and was the first to ask that profound question: Are we alone?　It has kept us wondering ever since. No one could have guessed, until just a few years ago, that an important clue as to where to search for life beyond our planet might be right here on Earth, beneath our feet.

　　In our recent search for the origin of life on Earth, we have made a series of fascinating discoveries of microbes that thrive thousands of meters beneath the surface, at extremely high temperatures and pressures.　[ア]　Within the rocks and clays, these microbes have access to water but often little else that we would consider necessities.　[イ]　For example, many have been cut off from sunlight for hundreds of millions of years.　[ウ]　They form the base of an underground food chain, just as plants do on the surface, and the proven existence of these underground communities has completely changed our thinking about life on our planet and elsewhere.　[エ]　It contradicts the lesson many of us learned in high school biology — that all life is ultimately dependent on solar energy.　[オ]　Some scientists now believe that these underground microbes may directly descend from Earth's first life forms.

　　Astronomers and other scientists agree that many of the planets in the universe are likely to have subsurface environments very similar to Earth's.　The temperature and pressure conditions within the interiors of some of these planets could even maintain water.　The deep interiors may also contain valuable natural resources that would be very useful to our society in both the near and distant future.　Since there are life

(a)

(b)

— 165 —

forms that survive in the extreme conditions of deep Earth, why not the deep subsurface of Mars? And if, as some suspect, life originated within Earth's underground, couldn't life also have arisen in one of the many similar environments elsewhere in the solar system, or in the wider universe? In our narrow-minded view that only solar-powered life is possible, we have presumed that if any planet could support life it would be in a zone where the surface conditions are similar to ours.

It now appears, however, that this widely held assumption was wrong and that the zone where life can be sustained, within our own planet and throughout the universe, has been substantially underesti-mated.

For the investigators of Earth's underground, the area of most interest is in some ways just as remote as a distant planet. Unable to visit the area themselves, they have had to be satisfied working in the laboratory with the soil or pieces of rock brought up from the depths.

Recently, however, a small team of scientists found a way to live out their fantasy by going down into one of the deepest mines in the world — South Africa's East Driefontein gold mine. Here a series of tunnels have been dug to reach more than three kilometers deep into the Earth's underground. The mine has taken decades to construct and is an engineering wonder by any standard. During a typical production shift, more than five thousand workers are underground, creating new tunnels, building support structures, and digging up rocks that contain gold.

In the fall of 1998, Tullis Onstott, a scientist from Princeton University, along with a carefully selected team of scholars, joined the workers in the underground gold mine for several weeks. On the first day, the researchers decided to head immediately to the deepest area that had been dug most recently, where the contamination from surface microbes would presumably be minimal. On their way down, the researchers could feel the pressure build and the temperature rise as they went deep into the Earth. By the time they reached the deepest area, they were sweating so much that they had to reach for their water bottles. At this three-kilometer depth, the rock surface temperature was 60℃.

注：microbes　微生物

(1) 以下の文は，第二段落のア〜オのどの位置に補うのが最も適切か。その記号を記せ。

　In spite of all this, these microbes have an importance very much out of proportion to their size.

(2) 第三段落の文(a)〜(e)のうち，段落の論旨と最も関係のうすいものはどれか。その記号を記せ。

(3) 前の文章の末尾には，次のア〜エの四つの段落が入る。それらを適切な順に並べ替えて，解答欄に記号を記せ。

<u>2008 年　　入試問題</u>

ア　It was not until months later that they were able to complete the laboratory analysis of their samples. They found that some samples contained much higher populations of microbes than expected — between 100,000 and 1 million per gram. Many of these microbes did indeed have unusual ways of sustaining their lives.

イ　The discovery of the strange microbes in the South African gold mine convinced the scientists that further study of the underground world is absolutely necessary if we are to understand how life has evolved on Earth. They are now paying as much attention to the deep interior of the earth as to the outer universe in their investigation into the question of life beyond our planet.

ウ　The whole area was busy with activity. The researchers had to shout to hear each other over the sounds of drills and other equipment used for digging. The lamps attached to the workers' helmets could be seen here and there through the dust-filled darkness, and the smell of explosive was in the air. Ignoring the noise, the physical discomfort, and the very real danger of accidents, the researchers got to work.

エ　When all of their sample bags were full, they spent some time looking around. Although they were planning to return the next day, they were so excited that they felt reluctant to leave. Eventually, when their energy began to fade, they hiked back to the elevator for the ride to the surface.

(4)　この文章の表題として，最も適切なものを次のうちから選び，その記号を記せ。

ア　Looking for Life on Other Planets

— 168 —

2008 年　　入試問題

イ　How Microbes Survive Underground

ウ　New Understandings of the Basis of Life

エ　Scientists Investigate an Engineering Wonder

オ　The Significance of the East Driefontein Gold Mine

2 (A)　次の英文は，授業でグループ発表をすることになった生徒同士の電子メール
でのやり取りである。空所(1)，(2)をそれぞれ 15 ～ 20 語の英語で埋めて，全
体として意味の通った文章にせよ。

From: Ken O'Hare

To: Yoshiko Abe, John Carter

Date: Thursday, January 31, 2008, 8:23 PM

Subject: Our group presentation

Dear Yoshiko and John,

I'm writing this e-mail in order to ask you two if you have any idea
about how we should cooperate in our group presentation for Ms.
Talbot's class next week.　Can I suggest that one of us should do
some basic research into a contemporary issue such as global
warming, the aging society, environmental pollution, etc., another
write a short paper on it, and the third give a presentation based on
the paper, representing the team?　What do you think about my plan?

All the best,

Ken

2008 年　　入試問題

From: Yoshiko Abe

To: Ken O' Hare

Cc: John Carter

Date: Thursday, January 31, 2008, 9:12 PM

Subject: Re: Our group presentation

Dear Ken,

Thank you for your message. Your suggestion sounds very interesting, but (1) _____

_____ . So, I would rather suggest that (2) _____ .

Best wishes,

Yoshiko

From: John Carter

To: Ken O'Hare

Cc: Yoshiko Abe

Date: Thursday, January 31, 2008, 10:31 PM

Subject: Re: Our group presentation

Dear Ken,

I am happy with Yoshiko's suggestion about the presentation. Let's talk about it more tomorrow.

— 170 —

2008 年　　入試問題

Best wishes,

John

(B)　今から 50 年の間に起こる交通手段の変化と，それが人々の生活に与える影
響を想像し，50 〜 60 語の英語で具体的に記せ。

4　(A)　次の英文の下線部(1)〜(5)には，文法上あるいは文脈上，取り除かなければ
ならない語が一語ずつある。所定欄に該当する語を記せ。

　　I have had a hard time explaining what it means for me to "speak"
three languages. I don't think of it as "speaking" them — it feels more
like I live in them, breathe them.　<u>There was a time in my life when I</u>
<u>was trying to explain that I was not really multilingual, but rather than</u>
<u>monolingual in three languages.</u> That's how it felt for those years when
my life was really split between three worlds.　<u>Today I hardly seem to</u>
<u>have settled into a more integrated lifestyle, one in which I weave in and</u>
<u>out of my three languages and the various worlds they are attached to.</u> I
keep track of my relation to them, a complex relation, never stable, always
powerful, sometimes frightening or embarrassing, sometimes exciting,
but never neutral.

　　<u>I can see my life as a set of relations to languages, those that</u>
<u>surrounded me, those I refused to learn, those I badly wanted to learn,</u>
<u>those I studied professionally, those — the intimate ones — I think in, write</u>
<u>in, am funny in, work in them.</u>　<u>Sometimes I catch myself envying</u>
<u>intensely at those monolinguals who were born, grew up, have lived</u>
<u>all their adult life in one language.</u>　I miss the feeling of comfort, of

— 171 —

2008年　　入試問題

certainty, of control I imagine they have, unaware as they usually are that it could not be otherwise.

(B)　次の英文の下線部(1), (2), (3)を和訳せよ。

　　There is no arguing that we are currently undergoing a profound change in our approach to communication. The two most obvious symbols of that change are the mobile phone and e-mail. Looking at the impact of the emergence of these communication tools on our social landscape, the change occurring in telephonic communication may seem the greater of the two because it is so obvious, on the street, in the elevator, in the restaurant. But this is only a technological change. (1)A phone without wires, so small that it fits in a pocket, containing such miracles of technology that one can call home from the back seat of a London taxi without thinking twice, is still just a phone.

　　In contrast, (2)the shift in the nature of mail is by far the more profound, and its implications are nothing less than revolutionary. E-mail is, apparently, merely letter writing by a different means. Looking at it more closely, however, we find that this new medium of communication is bringing about significant changes in the nature of human contact as well as in our ability to process information. The apparent simplicity of its use may lead us to think that we know everything that we need to know about it, but in fact (3)e-mail has overtaken us without our really understanding what it is.

— 172 —

2008年　入試問題

5 次の短編小説の一節を読み，以下の問いに答えよ。

Jackie leant idly against the window frame, staring out at the beach in front of the house. In the distance down the beach she could see the familiar figure in the blue dress slowly coming towards the house. She loved these moments when she could watch her daughter in secret. Toni was growing up fast.　It seemed no time since she and the confused little seven-year-old had arrived here. How Toni had adored her father! When she was still only five or six years old, they would all make the long trip from the city to the beach every weekend, and Toni would go out with him into the wildest waves, bravely holding on to his back, screaming in pleasure as they played in the waves together. She had trusted him entirely. And then he had left them. No message, no anything. Just like that.

She could make (　2　) Toni's figure quite clearly now. She saw her put her shoes onto the rocks near the water's edge and walk into the wet sand, then just stand there, hand on hip, head on an angle, staring down. What was she thinking? Jackie felt a surge of love that was almost shocking in its intensity. "I'd do anything for her," she found herself saying aloud, "anything."

It was for Toni that she had moved from the city to this house eight years ago, wanting to put the (　3　). Surely, up here it would be simpler, safer, more pleasant to bring up a child. And indeed, it had been. Toni had been able to ride her bicycle to school, run in and out of her friends' homes, take a walk around the beach, in safety. There had never been a lack of places for her to go after school while Jackie was at work. They had a comfortable relationship, and Toni had given her (　4　) whatsoever. So, only three years to go and then she, Jackie, planned to return to the city, move in with Tim, marry, maybe.

She glanced up at the clock. Four o'clock. He'd be here at seven, just like every Friday. Besides Toni, he was the person she loved best in the world.

— 173 —

2008 年　入試問題

Every weekend he came and they lived together like a family. He never put pressure on her to go and live in the city with him. He understood that she wanted to see Toni through school first. He said he was prepared to wait until she was ready. Jackie loved the arrangement. Not seeing each other through the week had kept their relationship fresh. They had so much to tell each other each Friday. Getting ready — shampooing her hair, blow-drying it, putting on her favourite clothes, looking pretty — was such fun. Jackie thanked God for Toni and Tim.

＊＊＊

Toni pressed her feet further into the wet sand. She didn't want to go home yet — she had too much to think about. At home Mum would be rushing about, singing, cleaning, getting ready for Tim, all excited. Someone her Mum's age behaving like that! Toni thought it was a bit too much, really — it was almost a bit pitiful. Although Tim was great — she had to admit that. One part of her was really pleased for Mum, that she had a partner; the other part was embarrassed. No, she wouldn't go home just yet.

She looked up and down the beach. She was relieved it was empty. She'd hate to be seen in this dress — it was so fancy and girlish. She had just applied for a Saturday job and Mum had made her wear this. "It's lovely, darling, and you look so pretty in it. It's important to make a good impression," she'd said. Well, she'd got the job. Mum would be waiting now, wanting to hear the news, and she'd get all excited as if she'd won a prize or something. She wished sometimes that Mum didn't get so carried away with things. There was one good thing, though. She'd have some money of her own for once, and would be able to buy some of the clothes she wanted for a change.

One thing was for sure. She wasn't going to wear this dress tonight!

— 174 —

2008 年　　入試問題

She'd wear it as she left the house to make sure Mum let her go, but then she'd change at Chrissy's place. It had all been a bit complicated — she'd never had to do this before. Just getting Mum to give her permission to go to the dance had been hard enough.

"Will there be supervision there?" "Will there be alcohol?" "What time does it finish?" On and on — like a police investigation. Other kids' parents didn't go on like Mum. But at least she'd been allowed to go. It was her first time to the beach club!

Chrissy had told her not to even ask. "Just get out of the window when your Mum and her boyfriend have gone to bed," had been her advice. "Things don't get started until late anyway." But Toni couldn't do that, not this first time. Anyway, Mum had said okay after Toni had done some pretty fast talking; she'd had to tell a few lies, but in the end Mum had swallowed them. "Chrissy's parents are taking us. Five parents will be supervising. Alcohol's not allowed. I'll be home by eleven-thirty."

She was especially embarrassed by the last one. Eleven-thirty — no chance! Still, once she got out of the house, Mum wouldn't know. Toni twisted her feet deeper into the sand. She was just a tiny bit uneasy about all the lies. But, why should she worry? Everyone had to do it. She'd never go anywhere if she didn't. Look at Chrissy. Look at what she had been getting away with for a year now.

(1) 下線部(1)の言い換えとして最も適切な表現を次のうちから一つ選び，その記号を記せ。

　ア　It appeared to be so long ago that

　イ　It seemed like only yesterday that

　ウ　It had always been such a rush since

　エ　It allowed her little time to think since

2008 年　　入試問題

(2)　空所（　2　）を埋めるのに最も適切な一語を記せ。

(3)　次に与えられた語を適切な順に並べ替えて空所（　3　）を埋め，その2番目と
　　　5番目にくる単語を記せ。ただし，以下の語群には，不要な語が一つ含まれている。

again　　　and　　　behind　　　child　　　past　　　start　　　them

(4)　空所（　4　）を埋めるのに最も適切な表現を次のうちから一つ選び，その記号
　　　を記せ。

　　ア　no joy

　　イ　little joy

　　ウ　no trouble

　　エ　little trouble

(5)　下線部(5)とほぼ同じ意味の表現を次のうちから一つ選び，その記号を記せ。

　　ア　see Toni off to school

　　イ　help Toni come first in school

　　ウ　wait until Toni finished school

　　エ　enjoy watching Toni go to school

(6)　下線部(6)の a bit too much という Toni の思いは，母親のどのような態度に
　　　対するものか。20 ～ 30 字の日本語で述べよ。

(7)　(7)の段落に描かれている Toni の心理について当てはまるものを次のうちから
　　　一つ選び，その記号を記せ。

　　ア　She is looking forward to receiving the prize she has won.

　　イ　She is looking forward to spending her wages on new clothes.

　　ウ　She is looking forward to hearing her mother's news about the job.

　　エ　She is looking forward to making a good impression on her employers.

2008 年　　入試問題

(8)　下線部(8)の this が表す内容を次のうちから一つ選び，その記号を記せ。

　　ア　buy a dress

　　イ　stay with her friend

　　ウ　be dishonest with her mother

　　エ　leave the house through the window

(9)　下線部(9)を和訳せよ。ただし，she が誰を指すかを明らかにすること。

(10)　この文章の前半で描かれている Toni の子供時代について，正しいものを一つ次のうちから選び，その記号を記せ。

　　ア　Toni's father moved to the city to live by himself when Toni was seven.

　　イ　Toni and her parents lived in a house by the beach until she was seven.

　　ウ　Toni and her mother moved to a house by the beach when Toni was seven.

　　エ　Toni's father came to the beach to see her on the weekend until she was seven.

(11)　次は，この文章で表現されている Jackie と Toni の心情について述べたものである。空所（　a　）～（　d　）を埋めるのに最も適切な動詞を以下の語群から選び，その記号を記せ。語群の動詞は原形で記されている。同じ記号は一度しか使えない。

　　Jackie doesn't （　a　） that her daughter is quickly growing up, more quickly, perhaps, than she would like. She （　b　） to see that Toni now has her own thoughts and ideas. Toni still （　c　） her mother but feels a little uncomfortable with the rela-tionship and wants to （　d　） more independent.

　　ア　become　　イ　fail　　ウ　live　　エ　love

　　オ　realize　　カ　succeed　　キ　wish

— 177 —

入試問題

解答時間：120分
配　点：120点

1 (A)　次の英文の内容を，80〜100字の日本語に要約せよ。句読点も字数に含める。

　　We usually think of the meaning of a poem — or any other literary work — as having been created and fixed by the writer; all we readers have to do is find out what the author intended to say. However, although it is indeed the poet who gives verbal form to his or her idea or vision, it is the reader who translates this verbal shape into meaning and personal response. Reading is in reality a creative process affected by the attitudes, memories, and past reading experiences of each individual reader. It is this feature of reading which allows for the possibility of any poem having more than one interpretation.

　　This emphasis on the reader as the source of meaning can, however, be problematic since it is sometimes difficult to draw the line between what we can all agree is a reasonable interpretation and one that appears wild and unjustifiable. Readers often seem eager to produce their own meanings out of their encounters with poems, meanings which, however reasonable or satisfying they are to the readers themselves, may not have been intended by the poet and may not be shared by other readers.

　　So who actually has the authority to determine meaning? Any strict distinction made between the reader and the writer as the source of meaning is not helpful. Of course, it is in some ways useful to think about and to discuss the differences in the contributions of reader and writer, but this does not alter the fundamental fact that reading is a kind of interaction. It would be misleading to think that the meaning or value of a poem was under the exclusive control of one or the other.

2007 年　　入試問題

(B)　次の英文を読み，以下の問いに答えよ。

　　　Far away from the beautiful lawns of New Delhi lies West Delhi's Swaran Park Industrial Area. Plastic is everywhere in the park: it covers the ground, blows in the wind, and is sorted, melted, and cut into pieces. Heavy trucks drive in and out, transporting huge sacks that are loaded and unloaded by strong men, while other men make complex deals in a specialised language that outsiders cannot understand.

　　　Swaran Park is Asia's biggest market for plastic recycling. On four square kilometres of land, there are hundreds of small open-air warehouses piled high with plastic. Business runs round the clock, with plastic being purchased from small traders and passed on to the many recycling mills.

　　　In India, waste collection, recycling, and disposal are conducted by government agencies, informal groups, and private companies. Until recently, only government agencies were supposed to collect, recycle, and dispose of all solid waste, but they are often inefficient. One result is that in Delhi, for example, almost all recycling has been handled informally — as at Swaran Park — by groups without official recognition. But now waste management is being transferred to regular private companies, and the jobs of the informal workers may be in danger.

　　　　ア　The waste management process involves, first, collection from streets, houses, offices, and factories; second, sorting, during which materials are separated; and finally, recycling itself.　イ　In Delhi, waste collection has traditionally been carried out by an informal network of *pheriwallahs, binnewallahs, khattewallahs,* and *thiawallahs.*　ウ　*Pheriwallahs* are often seen around the city carrying large plastic sacks. Their job is to search the streets for usable *maal. Maal* is anything that is of some value, whether paper, plastic, glass, or metal. *Binnewallahs* pick

— 181 —

maal only from city bins in specific areas, while *khattewallahs* collect only office waste. *Thiawallahs* buy *maal* from offices or households, and they can usually charge higher prices for their material, as it is of much higher quality. ☐ エ ☐ After the waste has been collected, it is sorted into more than 40 categories. ☐ オ ☐ The sorting process in effect makes the waste more valuable and easier to recycle.

This informal economy, with its recycling-based business model, seems$^{(a)}$ to be doing the city a great service. However, informal waste collection is probably not even legal, and there$^{(b)}$ is almost no government recognition for the service. Some informal workers feel that stronger government recognition of the$^{(c)}$ industry would result in an increase in their low daily wages. At present, an average *pheriwallah* makes about 70 rupees, or about 180$^{(d)}$ yen, a day. Those supporting government recognition also hope that it would improve$^{(e)}$ their working conditions, which can be dirty and dangerous.

Government recognition, however, would bring its own challenges. A major reason for the success of this informal industry has been its low cost of production and its flexible standards — a flexibility that would be lost if government regulations came into effect. Government recognition is also unlikely to benefit those who most need protection, as licensing might merely create a privileged group that would make large amounts of money just because of their licences.

2007年　入試問題

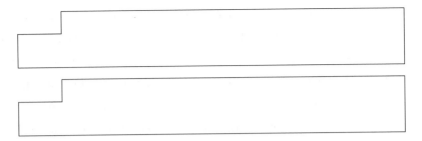

(1) 以下の文は，第四段落のア〜オのどの位置に補うのが最も適切か。その記号を記せ。

Each category has a specific task.

(2) 第五段落の文(a)〜(e)のうち，取り除いても大意に影響を与えないものはどれか。その文の記号を記せ。

(3) 上の文章の末尾には，次の四段落が入る。その最も適切な順番をア〜エから選び，その記号を記せ。

(i) Another source of conflict comes from new regulations which require that all urban waste be sorted according to complex rules. These rules are difficult for the informal processors to follow, so many neighbourhoods are handing over waste collection and separation to private waste management companies.

(ii) In the case of waste collection, private waste companies in Delhi are paid on a weight basis. This puts the private companies in direct conflict with the existing informal system, as one kilogram of waste collected by the informal collectors is one less kilogram for which the private companies would otherwise be paid.

2007年　入試問題

(iii) If big business becomes even more involved in waste management, the present informal economy will be at risk. Soon private companies could be building sorting stations, warehouses, and finally recycling factories. Eventually they might drive the informal collectors, transporters, and traders out of business, and the huge recycling system of Swaran Park — a unique and colourful part of Delhi life — would no longer exist.

(iv) Something like that happened as a result of the Supreme Court ruling in 2000 to close all polluting industries in Delhi. The decision caused a number of factories to move to the neighbouring state of Haryana. But the transfer of any material across the state border was impossible without a trader's licence. Few possessed this, resulting in the rise of dealers who make huge profits simply by carrying raw materials across the border.

ア　(i) — (iii) — (ii) — (iv)

イ　(ii) — (iv) — (iii) — (i)

ウ　(iii) — (i) — (iv) — (ii)

エ　(iv) — (ii) — (i) — (iii)

(4) この文章の表題として，最も適切なものを次のうちから選び，その記号を記せ。

ア　Informal Workers Find New Careers

イ　The Importance of Recycling in India

ウ　The Worsening Pollution of Swaran Park

エ　Competing Systems of Waste Management

オ　West Delhi Resists Government Regulation

— 184 —

2007 年　　入試問題

2 (A)　次の会話は，英語学習について悩んでいる男子生徒と，その相談を受けた英語教師との会話である。生徒がどのような悩みを持っているか，生徒の英語学習のどこが間違っていたのか，教師はどのようなアドバイスをしたか，の三つの内容を盛り込んだ形で，この会話の要点を 50 〜 60 語の英語で述べよ。

生徒：先生，いくら練習しても英語の聴き取りがうまくできるようにならないんですけど，どうすればいいでしょうか？

先生：どうすればいいと言われても，やっぱり地道に勉強するしかないよね。自分ではどんな勉強をしているの？

生徒：ケーブル・テレビやインターネットで英語のニュースを見たり聴いたりしてはいるんですけど……。

先生：え？　いきなりそんな難しい英語を聴いても分からないでしょう。

生徒：分からないです。まったく。

先生：そりゃ駄目だよ。意味の分からないものをいくら聴いたって，雑音を聴いているのと同じだからね。聴いて，ある程度中身が理解できるくらいの教材を選ばないと。

生徒：とにかくたくさん英語を聴けばいいんだと思っていました。そうか，そこが間違っていたんですね。

先生：そう。それに，聴き取りが苦手といったって，英語の音声に慣れていないことだけが問題じゃないんだ。語彙を知らなかったり，知っていても間違った発音で覚えていたり，あるいは構文が取れなかったりしている場合のほうが多いわけだよ。内容を理解する力も必要になってくるしね。毎日やさしめの英文の聴き取りをやって，それと同時に，内容的に関連する読み物を，辞書を引きながら丁寧に読んでごらん。そういう総合的な勉強をすれば，聴き取りの力も伸びると思うよ。

生徒：はい，わかりました。

— 185 —

2007年　入試問題

(B) 下の絵に描かれた状況を自由に解釈し，40〜50語の英語で説明せよ。

4 (A) 次の英文の下線部(1)〜(5)には，文法上取り除かなければならない語が一語ずつある。解答用紙の所定欄に該当する語を記せ。

　　Deep below the ground in California and Wyoming are two huge but silent volcanoes. Scientists believe that, were they to explode, these supervolcanoes would have set off terrible earthquakes and put the western United States under a thick blanket of ash. As evidence in uncovered ash deposits from old eruptions shows, they have done so for at least three times over the past two million years. Researchers are eagerly looking for an information about what causes these giants to erupt; when they could become destructive again, and how much damage might result. Recent analyses focusing on extremely small crystals

2007 年　　入試問題

5　次の短編小説を読み，以下の問いに答えよ。

BACK HOME

Rebecca's mother was standing outside the bus station when the bus arrived. It was seven thirty-five on Sunday morning. She looked tired. "How was the ride?" she asked.

"I didn't fall asleep until we got to Ohio," Rebecca replied. She had come by overnight bus from New York City. The familiar smells of the early Michigan summer filled the air as they walked to her mother's car. "But I'm okay."

Rebecca looked out the window as her mother drove the dozen blocks back to the house. The town was nearly deserted. Along Main Street, a discount shoe store stood where the department store used to be, and the drugstore had become a laundry. But on Lincoln Ave., the fast-food places — Bonus Burger, Pizza Delight, Taco Time — were (　1　), as were the houses on Willow, the street where Rebecca had grown up. Only the house t   doors down from her mother's looked different.

"What happened to the Wilsons' house?" Rebecca asked. "Did they paint it or something?"

"They moved to Kentucky," her mother replied.

There was a long pause. Rebecca realized that her mother had still not (　2　) her former cheerfulness.

"Somebody else moved in." Her mother parked the car in the driveway, and they got out.

The house was empty when they entered. Henry, Rebecca's stepfather, was working the early shift at the chemical plant; he wouldn't be home until midafternoon. As Rebecca carried her suitcase through the dining room, she tried not to look at the pictures of Tracy — her twin brother — on the wall.

— 188 —

found in the ash deposits have pointed to some of answers.   These
discoveries are making scientists more confident that it will ever be
possible to see warning signs well before the next big eruption happens.

(B) 次の英文の下線部(1)，(2)，(3)を和訳せよ。(2)については，it が何を指すか
　　明らかになるように訳すこと。

　　The nature and function of medicine has gradually changed over the
past century.   What was once a largely communicative activity aimed
at looking after the sick has become a technical enterprise able to treat
them with increasing success.   While few would want to give up these
technical advances and go back to the past, medicine's traditional caring
functions have been left behind as the practices of curing have become
more established, and   it is criticized now for losing the human touch
that made it so helpful to patients even before it knew how to cure them.
　　The issue looks simple: human communication versus technique.
However, we all know that in medicine it is never easy to separate the two.
Research on medical practice shows that a patient's physical condition is
often affected by the quality of communication between the doctor and
the patient.   Even such an elementary form of consideration for the
patient as explaining the likely effects of a treatment can have an impact
on the outcome.   We are also aware that in the cases where medicine still
does not offer effective cures the need for old-style care is particularly
strong.   Hence it is important to remember the communicative dimension
of modern medicine.

2007 年　　入試問題

"I have to go to church," her mother said. "I'll be back by noon, if you want to use the car later."

The bedroom where she had slept as a child was transformed. The bed was new, the carpet was gray instead of green, and hanging from the ceiling was Henry's collection of model airplanes.　<u>Down the hall</u>, the door of Tracy's old room was still shut, as it had been for years.
(3)

Rebecca left her suitcase next to the bed and went into the kitchen. She made herself a cup of coffee, switched on the television, and sat down to watch a quiz show.

＊ ＊ ＊

That afternoon, Rebecca drove her mother's car to the shopping mall outside town. The mall had opened before Rebecca was born. When she was in high school, it had been the most exciting place in town, and she and her friends would hang out there in the evenings until it closed. Years of living in Brooklyn and working in Manhattan, though, had given Rebecca a new (　4　), and the mall looked plain and uninteresting. Even on a Sunday afternoon, the stores had few customers.

She bought some shampoo and conditioner — her mother didn't have the kind Rebecca used — and sat at a table in the food court and sipped on a soda. Some children were running around the tables as their mothers chatted nearby. She thought about the coffee shop in New York where she went almost every evening after work. It was on 35th Street, just east of Broadway, between a Swedish bakery and a shop that sold circus equipment. One of the servers, a boy of eighteen or nineteen, always remembered her order and gave her a big smile when she came in. She would sit at a corner table and watch the customers — every age, every nationality, every kind of clothing and hairstyle — come and go.　<u>It gave her a thrill to feel she was one thread in such a rich cultural fabric.</u>
(5)

Rebecca was getting up to leave when one of the mothers came over to

— 189 —

her.

"Rebecca?" she said.

Rebecca hesitated for a moment. Then she cried, "Julia!" She stood, and they embraced each other. "I didn't (6) you at first!"

"It's been a long time."

Since Tracy's memorial service, Rebecca thought.

Julia sat down. "Are you still living in New York?"

"Yeah," Rebecca replied. "I'm just here for a couple of days. But I'm thinking of moving back to Michigan."

"(7a) I thought you liked New York."

"Well, my roommate is getting married and moving out, so I have to either find a new roommate or move. Rent is really expensive there."

"(7b)"

"My stepfather says he can get me an office job at the chemical plant. I have an interview there tomorrow."

"(7c)" Julia paused. "Have you been dating anybody?"

"Not really." Then Rebecca asked, "How's Jerry?"

"(7d) Still working for his father. He's gone fishing today, so I brought the kids to the mall to let them run around."

Rebecca and Julia had been friends in high school. Julia had dated Tracy pretty seriously, but they broke up after high school. Julia was already married to Jerry when Tracy was killed in Afghanistan.

* * *

At dinner that evening, Henry talked about an accident that had happened at the plant: "... and then the cracker overheated, and we had to deal with that, too, while we were flushing out the reflux line ...." Even (8) a teenager, Rebecca was embarrassed not to understand what Henry said. Neither she nor her mother said much. Later, Rebecca helped Henry wash and put away the dishes. He had married Rebecca's mother and moved in when Rebecca

— 190 —

and Tracy were eleven. Their real father had left three years earlier. Rebecca hadn't seen him for twenty years.

"I told my boss that you'd come in to the office tomorrow at eleven," Henry said. "I'll take your mother to work, so you can drive her car."

"Thanks."

"He just wants to meet you before he hires you. I didn't ask about the pay, but it should be okay. The girl who had the job before you didn't (9)."

Fatigue from the bus trip hit Rebecca early in the evening, so she said goodnight to her mother and Henry and went to bed. She fell asleep quickly and slept soundly. Around four in the morning, while it was still dim and silent outside, she woke up. She stayed in bed and gazed at the model airplanes hanging from the ceiling. She thought about Julia spending Sunday afternoon with her kids at the mall and about how she couldn't imagine doing that herself. She thought about the chemical plant where Henry worked, and the call center outside of town where her mother spent her days talking to faraway voices about their credit card problems. She thought about New York City — the noisy streets, the crowded sidewalks, the tiny Korean restaurant near her apartment, the boy in the coffee shop on 35th Street.

Then she thought about Tracy, who would never grow older than twenty-three. She remembered how they had quarreled when they were small, when their mother had been a good-natured referee, and how they had stopped quarreling when their father left. Why had they stopped? And why had her mother become so silent towards her after Tracy's death? Rebecca felt a surge of helplessness wash over her.

It was not yet five o'clock, the house still silent, when she got out of bed and quietly packed her bag. What had made her decide? She wasn't sure. But she wrote a note to her mother and Henry: "I've decided to <u>go back</u> <u>home</u>. I'm sorry." (10)

She put the note on the kitchen table and slipped out the front door. She

2007 年 入試問題

walked the twelve blocks downtown to catch the first bus to Detroit, from where she would take another bus back to New York.

(1) 空所（ 1 ）を埋めるのに最も適切な表現を次のうちから一つ選び，その記号を記せ。

ア as she left

イ as her childhood

ウ as she was a child

エ as she remembered

(2) 空所（ 2 ）を埋めるのに最も適切な単語を次のうちから一つ選び，その記号を記せ。

ア recovered　　イ reformed　　ウ replaced　　エ revised

(3) 下線部(3)を和訳せよ。

(4) 空所（ 4 ）を埋めるのに最も適切な単語を次のうちから一つ選び，その記号を記せ。

ア perspective　　イ sight　　ウ transformation　　エ way

(5) 下線部(5)は，主人公のどのような心情を表現しているか。最も適切なものを次のうちから一つ選び，その記号を記せ。

ア 大都会の多彩な文化に参加している喜び

イ 都市文化の中で地に足がつかない不安感

ウ 最新の都市文化を目の当たりにした興奮

エ 巨大な都市の文化に入り込めない無力感

— 192 —

2007年　入試問題

⑹　空所(　6　)を埋めるのに最も適切な単語を次のうちから一つ選び，その記号を記せ。

　　ア　appreciate　　イ　confirm　　ウ　foresee　　エ　recognize

⑺　空所(　7a　)～(　7d　)を埋めるのに最も適切な文をそれぞれ次のうちから一つ選び，その記号を記せ。同じ記号は一度しか使えない。

　　ア　Why not?
　　イ　He's okay.
　　ウ　Here he is.
　　エ　How come?
　　オ　That's great.
　　カ　That's what I hear.

⑻　下に与えられた語を適切な順に並べ替えて空所(　8　)を埋め，その2番目と5番目にくる単語を記せ。ただし，下の語群には，不要な語が一つ含まれている。

　　as　　　been　　　had　　　more　　　she　　　than　　　would

⑼　文脈から考えて空所(　9　)を埋めるのに最も適切な単語を次のうちから一つ選び，その記号を記せ。

　　ア　claim　　イ　complain　　ウ　demand　　エ　insist

⑽　下線部⑽の go back home という表現から，実家滞在中の Rebecca に大きな心境の変化があったことが読み取れる。その心境の変化とはどのようなものか。40～50字の日本語で説明せよ。

⑾　物語中の記述から，主人公 Rebecca は現在何歳くらいだと考えられるか。最も適切なものを次のうちから一つ選び，その記号を記せ。

　　ア　22歳　　イ　24歳　　ウ　26歳　　エ　28歳

― 193 ―

1 (A) 次の英文の内容を，65 〜 75 字の日本語に要約せよ。句読点も字数に含める。

Democracy is unthinkable without the ability of citizens to participate freely in the governing process. Through their activity citizens in a democracy seek to control who will hold public office and to influence what the government does. Political participation provides the mechanism by which citizens can communicate information about their interests, goals, and needs, and create pressure to respond.

Voice and equality are central to democratic participation. In a meaningful democracy, the people's voice must be clear and loud — clear so that policymakers understand citizen concerns and loud so that they have to pay attention to what is said. Since democracy implies not only governmental action in response to citizen interests but also equal consideration of the interests of each citizen, democratic participation also must be equal.

No democratic nation — certainly not the United States — lives up to the ideal of participatory equality. Some citizens vote or engage in more active forms of participation. Others do not. In fact, a majority of Americans undertake no other political activity aside from voting. In addition, those who do take part are in important ways not representative of the citizenry as a whole. They differ in their social characteristics and in their needs and goals. Citizen activists tend to be drawn more from more advantaged groups — to be well-educated and wealthy and to be white and male. The voice of the people as expressed through participation thus comes from a limited and unrepresentative set of citizens.

(B) 次の英文はアメリカのある行事について述べたものであるが、一つおきに段落が抜けている。空所 1 ～ 4 を埋めるのに最も適切な段落を、以下のア～カよりそれぞれ一つ選んでその記号を記せ。ただし不要な選択肢が二つ含まれている。

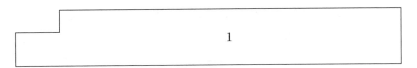

Although sheep and pony festivals had been held on the islands since the early eighteenth century as part of the regular control of animals, today's version of Pony Day began in 1924. At that time, the Volunteer Fire Department on Chincoteague began selling ponies during the annual festival to raise money for fire-fighting equipment. By selling ponies each year, the Fire Department has been able to support its operations and maintain the population of ponies at a suitable size for the balance of nature on the island. The Volunteer Fire Department's Pony Day was, surprisingly, just the first step in the direction of putting two tiny islands on the world map.

Before Pony Day became an international tourist attraction, very few people, even in the United States, knew these islands by name. After all, Chincoteague and Assateague are tiny islands where there used to be more wild birds and ponies than people. For centuries, the ponies lived mostly free of human contact; gradual human settlement on Chincoteague, however, resulted in their being only on Assateague where even today no people live. The ponies had been on the islands long before such things as Volunteer Fire Departments, carnivals, or tourism existed there, and their story is the one that continues to draw the most visitors.

3

It was difficult environmental conditions and isolation over centuries that created the "Chincoteague pony," which was originally a horse. Indeed, if taken off the islands while young and raised with standard food and shelter, the ponies are known sometimes to grow to horse size, taller than fifty-eight inches. Yet, on the islands, where the weather and insects are severe, and their food mostly tough beach grasses, these horses have been quite literally downsized by their environment.

4

Thousands of visitors from all parts of the globe attend the festival, and selling the ponies, especially to families with children, is far from difficult. Children come to the festival trying to find ponies that look like Misty, and adults come to learn about simple island life and the history of Chincoteague and Assateague. It is a fact of modern times that global tourism is the best way to preserve local customs; without their popularity with huge crowds of tourists each summer, it is likely that the wild ponies would not be allowed to survive. Although Pony Day has become necessary to the local economy, the fishermen and residents of Chincoteague as well as the ponies must be relieved to return to their quiet lives after Pony Day is over. The tourists, on the other hand, return to their busy modern lives from brief summer vacations, refreshed somehow by the sight of wild ponies swimming to freedom.

ア　Despite their hard lives, however, the ponies are not thin or ugly like so many wild mustangs in the American West; on the contrary, because they eat mostly salty sea grasses, wetland plants, and seaweed, the ponies drink a lot more water than average horses, which gives them a "fat" and healthy appearance. Once under human control, they are known to become gentle animals, too. Indeed, it is just their small size, intelligence, and good looks that have made these ponies such desirable pets for children.

イ　Fame truly came, however, with the 1947 publication of *Misty of Chincoteague*, a best-selling children's book translated into languages all over the world. In this story, author Marguerite Henry describes not only how the Beebe family adopted a clever little Chincoteague pony named Misty, but also the island people's customs and lifestyles seemingly untouched by the mad rush of modern life in cities. The qualities of small island life that today's tourists find so appealing in Chincoteague — quiet, old-fashioned, and not at all convenient — are the very same qualities that kept these islands unknown to so many for so long.

ウ　It is a cruel fact of American history that many such places as these islands, rich in the language and history of what was once a strong Native American presence, now have only their native names remaining. Chincoteague and Assateague, in fact, were first named by a group of Native Americans called the Gingo-Teague. "Chincoteague," for example, is said to mean "beautiful land across the water." English settlers kept these names when they began to come to the islands, long after Native Americans had been forced out of the area altogether or onto lands where only Native Americans could live, called "reservations."

エ　George Breeden runs a local gift store on Chincoteague. "I have lived here for almost eighty years now, and my people came to these islands centuries before I was born," says Breeden. "Some folks say that the first settlers sent here from the colonies were criminals, but I do not believe that was the case with my family. Where is the evidence?" Breeden and other island residents have organized an official list of the first families of Chincoteague. These families are proud of their long history on the island, but critics claim that they are more interested in making money on tourism today than in learning about the real history of times past.

オ　Every July, people from all over the world gather on an island off the mid-Atlantic coast of the United States for an event called "Pony Day": a carnival where the only remaining wild ponies east of the Rocky Mountains lose their freedom for a day. The ponies swim and splash, as people cheer and "water cowboys" guide them across a narrow channel of water separating two small islands named Chincoteague and Assateague. A mere five minutes later, the ponies reach land. Once on Chincoteague, the ponies receive health inspections and some are sold. The next day, the ponies swim back home to freedom on Assateague, marking the end of a local festival known around the world.

カ　Part of that appeal is the mystery of their origins; while the ponies have been on Chincoteague and Assateague for hundreds of years, how they got there is unknown. One tale has it that when a sixteenth-century Spanish ship sank nearby during a fierce storm, only the

— 200 —

horses survived by swimming to safety. Another legend claims that Spanish pirates hid their precious horses on these lonely islands. However, most historians insist that early settlers in the Virginia and Maryland colonies brought the horses from England, and later kept them on the remote islands to avoid taxes on animals. No matter which story one believes, however, the legends of the wild ponies' origins are rich with facts and fiction. No less interesting is their biology.

2 (A)　次の会話は，ある小学校の運動会 (sports day) の種目についての先生どうしの議論である。A 先生 (Mr. A) と B 先生 (Ms. B) の主張とその根拠を明確に伝えるような形で，議論の要点を 60 ～ 70 語の英語で述べよ。

A 先生：今回の運動会では，競争心をあおるような種目をやめてはどうでしょうか。

B 先生：そりゃまたどうしてですか？　それじゃやっていて面白くないでしよう。

A 先生：いやいや，競技の結果によって子供が一喜一憂したり，いらぬ敗北感を味わったりするのはよくないと思うんですよ。むしろ，みんなで協力することの大切さを教えるべきです。

B 先生：もちろん勝ち負けだけにこだわるのはまずいですけど，勉強においてもある程度の競争心が刺激になるということはありませんか。第一，やめるといっても，たとえばどんな種目をやめるんですか？　徒競走とか？

A 先生：徒競走なら，同じくらいのタイムの子たちを同時に走らせることにして，それで順位をつけなければ，さほど勝負の要素は強くありません

－ 201 －

2006年　　入試問題

が，綱引きとか，騎馬戦とか，玉入れとか，どれも勝つか負けるかの
どちらかでしょう。

B先生：だけど，そういうものを除いたら，出し物が大幅に減って，運動会に
ならないでしょう。

A先生：組み体操とか創作ダンスとか，出し物なんていくらでもあるじゃない
ですか。

B先生：そんな出し物ばかりで子供が喜びますかねえ。いい意味でのライバル
意識を育てるために，運動会でも普段の勉強でも，子供にはもっと競
争させるべきだと思いますよ。

(B)　あなたが今までに下した大きな決断について，60 ～ 70 語の英文で説明せよ。
ただし，

(1)　その時点でどのような選択肢があったか

(2)　そこで実際にどのような選択をしたか

(3)　そこで違う選択をしていたら，その後の人生がどのように変わっていたと
思われるか

という三つの内容を盛り込むこと。適宜創作をほどこしてかまわない。

4 (A)　次の(1)～(5)が最も自然な英語表現となるように（　　　）内の語を並べか
え，その２番目と３番目に来るものの記号を記せ。

Bats have a problem: how to find their way around in the dark. They
hunt at night, and therefore (1)(ア　cannot　イ　find　ウ　help　エ　light
オ　them　カ　to　キ　use) food and avoid obstacles. You might say
that if it is a problem it is one of their own making, which they could avoid

— 202 —

2006年　入試問題

simply by changing their habits and hunting by day. However, other creatures such as birds already take advantage of the daytime economy. Given that there is a living to be made at night, and given that alternative daytime trades are thoroughly occupied, natural selection has favoured bats that succeed at the night-hunting trade.

It is probable, by the way, that night-hunting (2)(ア back イ goes ウ history エ in オ of カ the キ way) all us mammals. In the time when the dinosaurs dominated the daytime economy, our ancestors probably only managed to survive at all because they found ways of making a living at night. Only after the mysterious disappearance of the dinosaurs about 65 million years ago (3)(ア able イ ancestors ウ come エ our オ out カ to キ were) into the daylight in any significant numbers.

In addition to bats, plenty of modern animals make their living in conditions where seeing is difficult or impossible. Given (4)(ア around イ how ウ move エ of オ question カ the キ to) in the dark, what solutions might an engineer consider? The first one that might occur to him is to use something like a searchlight. Some fish have the power to produce their own light, but the process seems to use a large amount of energy since the eyes have to detect the tiny bit of the light that returns from each part of the scene. The light source must therefore be a lot brighter if it is to be used as a headlight to light up the path, than if it is to be used as a signal to others. Anyway, (5)(ア is イ not ウ or エ reason オ the カ whether) the energy expense, it seems to be the case that, except perhaps for some deep-sea fish, no animal apart from man uses artificial light to find its way about.

注：mammal　ほ乳類

dinosaur　恐竜

― 203 ―

2006年　入試問題

(B)　次の英文の下線部(1), (2), (3)を和訳せよ。

　　Merely stating a proposal by no means requires listeners to accept it. (1)If you say, "We should spend money on highway construction," all you have done is to assert that such a step should be taken. From the audience's point of view, you have only raised the question, "Why should we?" No person in that audience has any reason to believe that the (2) proposal is good simply because you have voiced it. If, however, you are able to say, "Because ..." and list several reasons why each of your listeners should honestly make the same statement, you are likely to succeed in proving your point. You have achieved your purpose when (3) your audience would, if asked, lean towards agreement on the importance of highway spending.

5　次の英文を読み，以下の問いに答えよ。

　　A few months ago, as I was walking down the street in New York, I saw, at a distance, a man I knew very well heading in my direction. The trouble was that I couldn't remember his name or where I had met him. This is one of those feelings you have especially when, in a foreign city, you run into someone you met back home or the other way around. A face out of (　1a　) creates confusion. Still, that face was so familiar that, I felt, I should certainly stop, greet and talk to him; perhaps he would immediately respond, "My dear Umberto, how are you?" or even "Were you able to do that thing you were telling me about?" And I would be at a total loss. It was too late to (　2　) him. He was still looking at the opposite side of the street, but now he was beginning to turn his eyes towards me. I might as well make the first move; I would wave and then, from his voice, his first remarks, I would try to guess

― 204 ―

2006年　入試問題

his identity.

We were now only a few feet from each other, I was just about to break into a big, broad smile, when suddenly I recognized him. It was Anthony Quinn, the famous film star. Naturally, I had never met him in my life, (3). In a thousandth of a second I was able to check myself, and I walked past him, my eyes staring into (1b).

Afterwards, reflecting on this incident, I realized how totally (4) it was. Once before, in a restaurant, I had caught sight of Charlton Heston and had felt an impulse to say hello. These faces live in our memory; watching the screen, we spend so many hours with them that they are as familiar to us as our relatives', even more so. You can be a student of mass communication, discuss the effects of reality, or the confusion between the real and the imagined, and explain the way some people fall permanently into this confusion — but still you cannot escape the same confusion yourself.

My problems with film stars were all in my head, of course. But there is worse.

I have been told stories by people who, appearing fairly frequently on TV, have been involved with the mass media over a certain period of time. I'm not talking about the most famous media stars, but public figures, and experts who have participated in talk shows often enough to become recognizable. All of them complain of the same unpleasant experience. Now, (7), when we see someone we don't know personally, we don't stare into his or her face at length, we don't point out the person to the friend at our side, we don't speak of this person in a loud voice when he or she can hear us. Such behavior would be impolite, even offensive, (8). But the same people who would never point to a customer at a counter and remark to a friend that the man is wearing a smart tie behave quite differently with famous faces.

My own relatively famous friends insist that, at a newsstand, in a bookstore, as they are getting on a train or entering a restaurant toilet, they

— 205 —

2006年　入試問題

run into others who, among themselves, say aloud,

"Look, there's X."

"Are you sure?"

"Of course I'm sure. It's X, I tell you."

And they continue their conversation happily, <u>while X hears them</u>, and they don't care if he hears them: it's <u>as if he didn't exist</u>.
(9)　　　　　　　　　　　　　　　　　　　　(10a)

Such people are confused by the (1c) that a character in the mass media's imaginary world should unexpectedly enter real life, but at the same time they behave in the presence of the real person as if he still belonged to the world of images, as if he were on a screen, or in a weekly picture magazine. <u>As if they were speaking in his (10)</u>.
(10b)

I might as well have taken hold of Anthony Quinn by the arm, dragged him to a telephone box, and called a friend to say,

"Guess what! I'm with Anthony Quinn. And you know something? He seems real!" <u>After which I would throw Quinn aside and go on about my business.</u>
(11)

The mass media first convinced us that the (12a) was (12b), and now they are convincing us that the (12b) is (12a); and the more reality the TV screen shows us, the more movie-like our everyday world becomes — until, as certain philosophers have insisted, we think that we are alone in the world, and that everything else is the film that God or some evil spirit is projecting before our eyes.

⑴　空所(1a)〜(1c)を埋めるのに最も適切な単語をそれぞれ次のうちから一つ選び，その記号を記せ。

ア context　イ fact　ウ identity　エ sound　オ space

⑵　空所(2)を埋めるのに最も適切な表現を次のうちから選び，その記号を記せ。

— 206 —

2006 年 入試問題

ア catch up with

イ get away from

ウ take advantage of

エ make friends with

(3) 空所(3)を埋めるのに最も適切な表現を次のうちから選び, その記号を記せ。

ア nor he me

イ nor did he

ウ neither did I

エ neither had I

(4) 空所(4)を埋めるのに最も適切な単語を次のうちから選び, その記号を記せ。

ア foreign   イ lucky   ウ normal   エ useless

(5) 下線部(5)の "so" は何をさしているか。7語の英語で答えよ。

(6) 下線部(6)で "worse" とされていることは何か。25 ～ 35 字の日本語で述べよ。

(7) 空所(7)を埋めるのに最も適切な表現を次のうちから選び, その記号を記せ。

ア as a rule

イ for all that

ウ as is the case

エ for better or worse

(8) 空所(8)を埋めるのに最も適切な表現を次のうちから選び, その記号を記せ。

ア if carried too far

イ if noticed too soon

ウ if taken too seriously

エ if made too frequently

— 207 —

2006年　　入試問題

(9)　下線部(9)の場面で，X氏はどのように感じていたと考えられるか。最も適切なものを次のうちから選び，その記号を記せ。

ア　I wonder if they've taken me for somebody else.

イ　I can't believe they're talking like that in front of me!

ウ　I'm curious to know what they're going to say about me.

エ　I can't remember their names or where I met them.　What can I do?

(10)　空所（　10　）に一語を補うと，下線部(10a)と(10b)はほぼ同じ意味になる。その単語を記せ。

(11)　下線部(11)を和訳せよ。

(12)　空所（　12a　），（　12b　）を埋めるのに，最も適切な単語の組み合わせを次のうちから選び，その記号を記せ。

ア　(a)　confusion　　　(b)　real

イ　(a)　real　　　　　(b)　confusion

ウ　(a)　imaginary　　 (b)　real

エ　(a)　real　　　　　(b)　imaginary

オ　(a)　confusion　　　(b)　imaginary

カ　(a)　imaginary　　 (b)　confusion

— 208 —

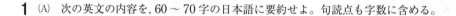

入試問題

解答時間：120 分
配　　点：120 点

1 (A) 次の英文の内容を，60～70 字の日本語に要約せよ。句読点も字数に含める。

　　We are only born with so much natural rhythm and harmony, and we have to search for and develop ways of maintaining both. My fifty years of experience in teaching and encouraging top sports people have made me realize that total harmony in movement should resemble a fish in water — one shake of its tail and off it goes, changing pace and direction with ease. Minimum effort is applied, but maximum results are achieved.

　　All the great heroes in the history of sport — Pele, Muhammad Ali, Bjorn Borg — started each movement with rhythm and fluency. They did not move suddenly from a dead stop: they were thinking sway-and-flow, not start-and-run. They had developed what might be called high-level awareness, which is an absolute necessity for any athlete who wants to reach the top of their profession.

　　We all know that nerves and tension can cause bad movements and errors, but these can be minimized by developing a lifestyle around this high-level awareness. You must focus the body and make it aware, as you would your fingers that were about to pick something up. Your whole body, like your fingers, must be sensitive to its position in space. Gradually, you will develop your own sense of rhythm, and this will show up in better and more consistent performance.

(B) 次の英文はエスペラントについて述べたものであるが，一つおきに段落が抜けている。空所 1～4 を埋めるのに最も適切な段落を，ア～カよりそれぞれ一つ選んでその記号を記せ。ただし不要な選択肢が二つ含まれている。

— 210 —

2005年　入試問題

Bialystok in the 1860s was a city torn apart by intolerance and fear. Located in the north-east of what is now Poland, and at the time under Russian rule, the city was home to four main communities: the Poles, the Russians, the Germans, and the Jews. These communities lived separately, had no shared language, and mistrusted each other deeply. Violence was an everyday event.

1

Zamenhof had been brought up by his parents to speak Polish, German, Russian, Yiddish, and Hebrew, and he also had a good knowledge of English and French, so he knew that no existing language would work. For one thing, the fact that all of these languages were associated with a particular country, race, or culture meant that they lacked the neutrality any international language would need in order to be accepted.

2

But inventing languages doesn't pay the bills, so Zamenhof needed a career. He studied medicine and became an eye doctor. By day he took care of people's eyes, and in the evenings he worked on his new language: Esperanto. Esperanto is a beautifully simple language with only 16 basic rules and not a single exception. It is probably the only language in the world to have no irregular verbs (French has more than 2,000, Spanish and German about 700 each) and, with just six verb endings to master, it is estimated that most beginners can begin speaking it after an hour.

3

— 211 —

Although Zamenhof's beautiful language is not associated with any one nation or culture, three-quarters of its root words have been taken from Latin, Greek, and modern European languages. The advantage to this is that about half the world's population is already familiar with much of the vocabulary. For an English speaker, Esperanto is reckoned to be 5 times as easy to learn as Spanish or French, 10 times as easy as Russian, and 20 times as easy as Arabic or Chinese.

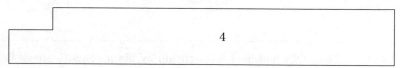

ア　At the same time, Johann Schleyer, a German minister, was working on his own new language, Volapuk, meaning "World Speech." Schleyer's language first appeared in Germany in 1878, and by 1890 more than 283 Volapuk-speaking associations had been formed. But generally, people found Schleyer's language strange and ugly — and no easier to learn than Latin.

イ　These existing languages also had complicated grammatical rules, each rule with its own exceptions, and this meant that they lacked another essential characteristic of a universal second language: they could not be easily learned by ordinary people. The difficulty factor also meant that neither Latin nor classical Greek had much potential as a universal language. Zamenhof was left with only one option: he would have to devise his own.

ウ　It was here, where lack of understanding created racial hatred, and racial hatred regularly exploded on the streets, that Ludovic Zamenhof was born in 1859. His mother was a language teacher and his father

2005 年　入試問題

was also a student of languages. By the time he was fifteen, young Ludovic had seen enough violence in his hometown to convince him of the need for a common language that would enable different communities to understand each other.

エ　The disadvantage, obviously, is that speakers of non-European languages have to work a little harder to get started with Esperanto. But Esperantists argue that the simplicity of Zamenhof's language scheme quickly makes up for any unfamiliarity with its root words. They proudly point to the popularity of Esperanto in Hungary, Finland, Japan, China, and Vietnam as the proof of Zamenhof's achievement in creating a global language for mutual communication and understanding.

オ　Esperanto vocabulary is also very simple. Instead of creating a huge list of words to learn, Zamenhof invented a system of very basic root words and simple ways to change their meanings. Putting "mal-" at the start of an Esperanto word, for example, changes that word into its opposite. Esperanto speakers easily make new words by putting two or more existing words together. This kind of word invention is regarded by Esperantists as a creative process which adds to the appeal of the language.

カ　The fact that Esperanto is so easy to learn has been the key to its success. Of course, English is even more important as a world language today than it was when Ludovic Zamenhof was alive. But while English may have become even more useful, it hasn't become any easier — and that's why Esperanto is still so popular. Whatever your native language, you start from the beginning with Esperanto.

— 213 —

2005年　入試問題

Not even speakers of European languages have an advantage. Truly, Esperanto is a language that offers everybody, equally, the chance to speak up and be heard in today's world.

2 (A)　下の絵に描かれた状況を自由に解釈し，30〜40語の英語で説明せよ。

(B)　次の文中の空所を埋め，意味のとおった英文にせよ。空所(1)〜(3)を合わせて 40〜50 語とすること。

Communication styles differ from person to person. For example, some people (1)＿＿＿＿＿＿＿＿＿＿＿＿＿＿＿＿＿＿＿＿, while others (2)＿＿＿＿＿＿＿＿＿＿＿＿＿＿＿＿＿＿＿＿＿＿. Therefore, the most important thing in human communication is (3)＿＿＿＿＿＿＿＿＿＿＿＿＿＿＿＿＿＿＿.

2005 年　入試問題

4 (A)　次の英文(1)〜(5)には，文法上取り除かなければならない語が一語ずつある。所定欄に該当する語を記せ。

(1)　In one of the earliest attempts at solar heating, energy from the sun was absorbed by and large metal sheets covered by double plates of glass.

(2)　The death of plants beside the roads led environmentalists to investigate further and to discover just how widespread the problem caused by the use of salt to prevent from ice on roads really is.

(3)　Some of the greatest advances in science have come about because some clever person saw a connection between a subject that was already understood, and another noticed still mysterious subject.

(4)　In the early years of the 21st century the trend toward the unisex look had reached so advanced from a state that it was almost impossible to distinguish males and females unless they were completely unclothed.

(5)　Librarians have meaningful disagreements with one another about the problem of how to classify books, but the criteria by themselves which arguments are won or lost will not include the "truth" or "correctness" of one classification system relative to another.

(B)　次の英文の下線部(1), (2), (3)を和訳せよ。

　　　The Scientific Revolution is the term traditionally used to describe the great intellectual triumphs of sixteenth- and seventeenth-century European astronomy and physical science. By around 1700 educated

— 215 —

men conceived of the universe as a mechanical structure like a clock, and the earth was regarded as a planet moving round the sun. The intellectual transformation associated with the Scientific Revolution led to a new confidence in the value of the investigation of nature and its control, a development which is fundamental to an understanding of the importance of science in modern society.

The seventeenth century was also characterized by a new optimism about the potential for human advancement through technological improvement and an understanding of the natural world. Hopes were expressed that the understanding and control of nature would improve techniques in industry and agriculture. There was, however, a large gap between intention and achievement in the application of scientific knowledge. While claims for the practical usefulness of natural knowledge and its future significance for technological improvement were common, the cultivation of science had little effect on the relationship between man and his environment. Nevertheless, the cultural values associated with the pursuit of natural knowledge were a significant characteristic of seventeenth-century society. Science expressed the values of technological progress, intellectual understanding and the celebration of God's wisdom in creating the world. The hostile and mysterious environment of the natural world would, people believed, yield its secrets to human investigation. The belief in the human capacity to dominate nature was justified by the argument that the study of God's book of nature went hand in hand with the study of the Bible, the book of God's word.

These important shifts in cultural outlook dramatically transformed the conception of the universe and of man's place in nature. The belief that the universe is a machine and that it might contain other worlds like the earth threatened traditional assumptions about the uniqueness of man, leading to a denial of the doctrine that the universe had been created for the benefit of man.

5 次の英文は，イギリスのウェールズ地方の灯台を舞台にした物語である。これを読み，以下の問いに答えよ。解答は所定欄に記せ。

The old lighthouse was white and round, with a little door, a circular window at the top, and the huge lamp. The door was usually half open, and one could see a spiral staircase. It was so inviting that one day I couldn't resist going inside, and, once inside, going up. I was thirteen, a cheerful, black-haired boy; I could enter places then that I can't enter now, slip into them lightly and (1a)(1b)(1c) my not (1d)(1e).

I climbed the spiral staircase and knocked on the door up at the top. A man came to open it who seemed the image of what a lighthouse-keeper ought to be. He smoked a pipe and had a gray-white beard.

"Come in, come in," he said, and immediately, with that strange power some people have to put you at ease, he made me feel at home. He seemed to consider it most natural that a boy should come and visit his lighthouse. Of course a boy my age would want to see it, his whole manner seemed to say — there should be more people interested in it, and more visits. He practically made me feel he was there to show the place to strangers, almost as if that lighthouse were a museum or a tower of historical importance.

Well, it was nothing of the sort. There were the boats, and they depended on it. Looking out, we could see the tops of their masts. Outside the harbor was the Bristol Channel, and opposite, barely visible, some thirty miles away, the coast of Somerset.

"And this," he said, "is a barometer. When the hand goes down, a storm is in the air. Small boats better watch out. Now it points to 'Variable.' That means it doesn't really know what is going to happen — just like us. And that," he added proudly, like someone who is leaving the (4a) thing for the (4b), "is the lamp."

I looked up at the enormous lens with its powerful bulb inside.

"And this is how I switch it on, at sunset." He went to a control box near the wall and put his hand on a lever.

(5), but he did, and the light came on, slowly and powerfully. I could feel its heat above me, like the sun's. I smiled delightedly, and he looked satisfied. "Beautiful! Lovely!" I cried.

"It stays on for three seconds, then off for two. One, two, three; one, two," he said, timing it, like a teacher giving a piano lesson, and the light seemed to obey. He certainly knew just how long it stayed lit. "One, two, three," he said, his hand went down, and the light went off. Then with both hands, like the Creator, he seemed to ask for light, and the light came.

I watched, thrilled.

"Where are you from?" he asked me.

"Italy."

"Well, all the lights in (6a) parts of the world have a (6b) rhythm. A ship's captain, seeing this one and timing it, would know which one it was."

I nodded.

"Now, would you like a cup of tea?" he said. He took out a blue-and-white cup and saucer and poured the tea. Then he gave me a biscuit. "You must come and see the light after dark sometime," he said.

Late one evening, I went there again. The lamp's flash lit up a vast stretch of the sea, the boats, the beach, and the dark that followed seemed more than ever dark — so dark that <u>the lamp's light, powerful as it was, seemed not much stronger than a match's, and almost as short-lived.</u>
⁽⁷⁾

At the end of the summer, I went home to Italy. For Christmas, I bought

— 218 —

a *panforte* — a sort of fruitcake, the specialty of the town I lived in — and sent it to the lighthouse-keeper. I didn't think I would see him again, but the very next year I was back in Wales — not on a holiday this time but running away from the war. One morning soon after I arrived, I went to the lighthouse, only to find that the old man had retired.

"He still comes, (8)," the much younger man who had taken over said. "You'll find him sitting outside here every afternoon, weather permitting."

I returned after lunch, and there, sitting on a bench beside the door of the lighthouse, smoking his pipe, was my lighthouse-keeper, with a little dog. He seemed heavier than the year before, not because he had gained weight but because he looked as though he had been put down on the bench and would not easily get off it without help.

"Hello," I said. "Do you remember me? I came to see you last year."

"Where are you from?"

"From Italy."

"Oh, I used to know a boy from Italy. An awfully nice boy. Sent me a fruitcake for Christmas."

"That was me."

"Oh, he was a fine boy."

"I was the one who sent it."

"Yes, he came from Italy — an awfully nice boy."

"Me, me, that was me," I insisted.
He looked straight into my eyes for a moment, then away. I felt like a thief, someone who was trying to take somebody else's place without having a right to it. "Ay, he was an awfully nice boy," he repeated, as though the visitor he saw now could never match last year's.

And seeing that he had such a nice memory of me, I didn't insist further; I didn't want to spoil the picture. I was at that time of life when suddenly boys

2005年　入試問題

turn awkward, lose what can never be regained — a certain early freshness — and enter a new stage in which a hundred things combine to spoil the grace of their performance. I couldn't see this change, this awkward period in myself, of course, but, standing before him, I felt I never could — never could possibly — be as nice as I had been a year before.

"Ay, he was an awfully nice boy," the lighthouse-keeper said again, and he looked lost in thought.

"Was he?" I said, as if I were talking of someone whom I didn't know.
(10b)

(1)　空所（　1a　）～（　1e　）を埋めるのに最も適切な単語をそれぞれ次のうちから選び，その記号を記せ。

　　ア　about　イ　being　ウ　welcome　エ　without　オ　worrying

(2)　下線部(2)を和訳せよ。

(3)　文脈から判断して，下線部(3)はどのようなことを意味していると考えられるか。最も適切なものを次のうちから選び，その記号を記せ。

　　ア　Thanks to the boats, the lighthouse was highly popular with visitors.

　　イ　The significance of the lighthouse was practical rather than historical.

　　ウ　The lighthouse was worthless compared to museums or historical towers.

　　エ　Although boats still depended on it, the lighthouse also functioned as a museum.

(4)　空所（　4a　），（　4b　）を埋めるのに最も適切な単語をそれぞれ次のうちから選び，その記号を記せ。

　　ア　best　イ　last　ウ　least　エ　most

－　220　－

2005 年　　入試問題

(5)　空所（　5　）を埋めるのに最も適切な表現を次のうちから選び，その記号を記せ。

　　ア　I was surprised to see the lever

　　イ　I was sure he'd wait until sunset

　　ウ　I asked him to show me how it worked

　　エ　I didn't think he'd switch it on just for me

(6)　空所（　6a　），（　6b　）には同じ一つの語が入る。その単語を記せ。

(7)　下線部(7)を和訳せよ。

(8)　空所（　8　）を埋めるのに最も適切な単語を次のうちから選び，その記号を記せ。

　　ア　maybe　　イ　then　　ウ　though　　エ　yet

(9)　下線部(9)から判断して，語り手はどのような印象を受けたと考えられるか。
　　最も適切なものを次のうちから選び，その記号を記せ。

　　ア　He looked old and tired.

　　イ　He looked eager to leave.

　　ウ　He looked as strong as ever.

　　エ　He looked less interesting than before.

(10)　下線部(10a)と(10b)の二つの発言の間で，語り手の老人への接し方にはどの
　　ような変化が見られるか。40～60字の日本語で答えよ。句読点も字数に含める。

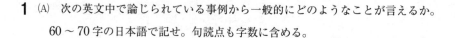

1 (A) 次の英文中で論じられている事例から一般的にどのようなことが言えるか。60〜70字の日本語で記せ。句読点も字数に含める。

　　Chess masters can exhibit remarkable memory for the location of chess pieces on a board. After just a single five-second exposure to a board from an actual game, international masters in one study remembered the locations of nearly all twenty-five pieces, whereas beginners could remember the locations of only about four pieces. Moreover, it did not matter whether the masters knew that their memory for the board would be tested later; they performed just as well when they glanced at a board with no intention to remember it. But when the masters were shown a board consisting of randomly arranged pieces that did not represent a meaningful game situation, they could remember no more than the beginners.

　　Experienced actors, too, have extraordinary memory within their field of specialized knowledge; they can remember lengthy scripts with relative ease, and the explanation for this is much the same as in the case of the chess masters. Recent studies have shown that rather than attempting word-by-word memorization, actors analyze scripts for clues to the motivations and goals of their characters, unconsciously relating the words in them to the whole of their knowledge, built up over many years of experience; memorization is a natural by-product of this process of searching for meaning. As one actor put it, "I don't really memorize. There's no effort involved ... it just happens. One day early on, I know the lines." An actor's attempt to make sense of a script often involves extended technical analyses of the exact words used by a character, which in turn encourages precise recall of what was said, not just the general sense of it.

(B)　次の英文はマダガスカルの開発と環境保全について述べたものであるが，1 つおきに段落が抜けている。空所1～4を埋めるのに最も適切な段落を，ア～オよりそれぞれ1つ選んでその記号を記せ。ただし不要な選択肢が1つ含まれている。

About the same size as France, or a bit larger than California, the tropical island of Madagascar has one of the most interesting and important collections of plant and animal life in the world today. But although Madagascar's ecological system is unique, the dangers it faces are not. Like many of the world's other valuably wild places, Madagascar today has a big problem with people.

1

In the relatively short time that people have been living on Madagascar, however, they have managed to cause serious damage to its biological system. In traditional Madagascar farming, the farmer cuts down and burns a part of the forest and then plants rice on the cleared land. After harvesting the rice, the farmer leaves the land alone again for up to twenty years in order to give the forest enough time to grow back. But if farmers return to the same area of land too soon, the soils become exhausted. Eventually this leads to large areas of forest becoming transformed into wastelands, upon which nothing can grow.

2004年　入試問題

2

This is a difficult balance to achieve. Although much of the destruction has been caused by individual farmers, the causes of Madagascar's environmental problems are deeply rooted in the island's social conditions and history. Madagascar is one of the world's poorest nations, with an average individual income of less than $250 per year. About 80 percent of the population are farmers who depend almost entirely on the land to support their way of life. Many farmers continue to practice traditional cut-and-burn agriculture because they know no other way, and have no other means to survive.

3

The key point has been to emphasize a combination of wildlife protection and local development. The idea is to make sure that local people living near the new parks benefit from them, so that they become active participants in the program. For example, if the parks attract tourists from abroad and bring economic benefits to a region, then local people will support the establishment of parks in areas that they would otherwise have been able to farm. Park projects are also now helping local people to grow rainforest butterflies and sell them to butterfly zoos around the world, while tourism in the park is also bringing many benefits to local communities.

4

<u>2004 年　　入試問題</u>

ア　Historically, the absence of a human population was one of the main reasons for the development of the island's unique ecological system. Madagascar's ecosystem was able to establish itself, in other words, not only because of the island's relatively large size, geographical isolation, and tropical location, but also because it was only about 2,000 years ago that a human population began to disturb the natural environment.

イ　Plants which once grew only in Madagascar are now being commercially grown in various regions worldwide, including the southern parts of the United States. The pink and white flowers of the Madagascar Rosy Periwinkle, for example, are grown for use in some highly effective medical treatments. Medicines made from the flowers are used to treat many serious conditions, including childhood cancers, high blood pressure, and high blood sugar levels.

ウ　Understanding that any program of wildlife protection would also have to pay attention to the needs and traditional way of life of the local population, the Madagascar government has developed a program called the National Environmental Action Plan. This plan is designed to break the cycle of environmental destruction, reduce poverty, develop management plans for natural resources, and protect biological variety. At the center of the plan is the creation of a system of national parks.

エ　Much of Madagascar has already been destroyed by the gradual action of small farmers. Human populations have grown beyond the point at which these activities can be practiced without permanent destruction. As the forest is destroyed, so is the home for Madagascar's unique plant and animal species. Today, only 10 percent of Madagascar's original forests remain. The biggest problem facing

－ 227 －

2004 年　　入試問題

Madagascar is the question of how to meet the needs of its human population while managing to protect its environment.

オ　Since Madagascar's Environmental Action Plan was first established in the 1980s, the government has created eight new protected areas totaling 6,809 square kilometers. Madagascar today is proud of its efforts to develop a realistic approach to "parks for wildlife and for people." A most encouraging beginning has been made in making sure that the parks will remain protected far into the future, to provide homes for Madagascar's wonderful variety of plant, bird, and animal life, and resources for Madagascar's people.

2 (A)　もし，あなたが自宅から電車で片道2時間の距離にある大学に通うことになったとしたら，あなたは自宅から通学しますか，それともアパートなどを借りて一人暮らしをしますか。いくつかの理由を挙げ，50語程度の英語で答えなさい。

(B)　次の文章は，ある大学の登山隊の隊長 (the team leader) が出発予定日の朝に隊員たちに向かって発した言葉である。この内容について英語圏から来た留学生の隊員に質問されたと仮定し，その要点を60語程度の英語で述べよ。

　　ちょっと聞いてください。えーとですね，出発の時間になりましたけれども，ご覧の通り，どうも雲行きが怪しくなってきました。それで，このまま出発すると途中で激しい雷雨に見舞われる危険性があるんですね。そこで，どうでしょう，ここでしばらく様子を見てですね，それで天気が回復するようなら出発，2時間ぐらいたってもまだぐずついているようなら，出発は明朝に延期ということにしたいと思います。

2004 年　入試問題

4 (A)　次の(1)〜(5)が最も自然な英文になるためには，それぞれア〜エの選択肢に
他の英語１語を補って空所を埋める必要がある。それぞれの空所に何を入れれ
ばよいか。解答欄には，補うべき単語および(c)と(e)に入るべき語句の記号を
記せ。なお，(c)と(e)にはア〜エに与えられている語句が入る。

㋄　The campaign started six months ago.　But only (　a　)(　b　)
(　c　)(　d　)(　e　) attract media attention.

　　ア　begun　　　イ　it　　　　ウ　recently　　　エ　to

例	補う単語	(c)	(e)
	has	イ	エ

(1)　I can't get into my room.　I was (　a　)(　b　) to (　c　)(　d　)
(　e　).

　　ア　enough　　　イ　lock　　　ウ　out　　　　エ　stupid

(2)　Let's not use any of these pictures for the poster.　They (　a　)(　b　)
(　c　) a lot (　d　)(　e　) he really is.

　　ア　him　　　イ　look　　　ウ　older　　　エ　than

(3)　She is intelligent, but she just doesn't have (　a　)(　b　)(　c　)
(　d　)(　e　) a good journalist.

　　ア　be　　　イ　takes　　　ウ　to　　　エ　what

(4)　I'm terribly sorry for saying what I said yesterday.　I shouldn't have
(　a　)(　b　) get (　c　)(　d　)(　e　) me.

　　ア　better　　　イ　my emotions　ウ　of　　　　エ　the

(5)　We've been waiting for you for over an hour.　How (　a　)(　b　) do
you think (　c　)(　d　)(　e　) to spend on your homework?

— 229 —

2004年　入試問題

ア longer　　イ need　　　ウ will　　　エ you

(B) 次の英文の下線部(1)，(2)，(3)を和訳せよ。

Why is the Mona Lisa the best-known painting in the entire world? (1)A simple glimpse at even some of her features — her silhouette, her eyes, perhaps just her hands — brings instant recognition even to those who have no taste or passion for painting. Its commercial use in advertising far exceeds that of any other work of art.

There are works of art that appear to be universal, in the sense that they are still loved and enjoyed centuries after their production. They awake instant recognition in millions throughout the world. They speak not only to their own time — the relatively small audience for whom they were originally produced — but to worlds beyond, to future generations, to (2)a mass society connected by international communications that their creators could not suspect would ever come into being.

It is precisely because such universal appeal cannot be separated from the system which makes them famous that one should question the idea that the success of artistic works lies within the works themselves. The Western origin of so many masterpieces suggests that they need, for their global development, appropriate political, ideological and technological support.

Mozart was, we know, greatly appreciated in his lifetime, but only in Europe. (3)He would not be as widely known as he is today throughout the world without the invention of recording equipment, film music, and plays and films about his life. Mozart would not be 'Mozart', the great universal artist, without adequate technical and marketing support.

— 230 —

2004年　入試問題

5 地図を参照しながら次の説明文（斜字体部分）と物語文を読み，以下の設問に答えよ。解答は解答用紙の所定欄に記せ。

The modern country of Bangladesh, with its capital in Dhaka, is the eastern half of the area traditionally known as Bengal; the western half, with its capital in Calcutta, is part of India. Although the people of the two halves of Bengal speak the same language, they are divided by religion, the majority of the population in the east being Muslim, and the majority in the west Hindu. When the whole of this part of the world was part of the British Empire, Bengal was a single province. In 1947, when the British left, the British Empire in India was divided into two independent countries: India, with a largely Hindu population, and Pakistan, with a largely Muslim population. The latter consisted of West Pakistan (now Pakistan), and East Pakistan (previously the eastern half of Bengal, now Bangladesh). As a result of this division — known as Partition — many Muslims fled from India into one of the two parts of Pakistan, and many Hindus fled from the two parts of Pakistan into India. This exchange of population was very violent; it has been estimated that about 500,000 people were killed. More than a million people moved from East Pakistan to the western half of Bengal in India; the grandmother in the passage below was one of those people. In 1971, East Pakistan gained its independence from Pakistan and became Bangladesh.

— 231 —

2004年　入試問題

A few weeks later, at dinner, my father, grinning hugely, pushed an envelope across the table to my grandmother. 'That's for you,' he said.

'What is it?' she said suspiciously.

'Go on,' he said. 'Have a look.'

She picked it up, opened it and had a look inside. 'I can't tell,' she said. 'What is it?'

My father burst into laughter. 'It's your plane ticket,' he said. 'For Dhaka — for the third of January.'

That night, for the first time in months, my grandmother seemed really excited. When I went up to see her, before going to bed, I found her pacing around the room, her face flushed, her eyes shining. I was delighted. It was the first time in my eleven-year-old life that she had presented me with a response that I could fully understand — since I had never been on a plane myself, it seemed the most (1) thing in the world to me that the prospect of her first flight should fill her with excitement. But I couldn't help worrying about her too, for I also knew that, unlike me, she was totally ignorant about aeroplanes, and before I fell asleep that night I made up my mind that (2a) that (2b) before (2c). But soon enough it was apparent to me that it wasn't going to be easy to educate her: I could tell from the direction of the questions she asked my father that, left to herself, she would learn nothing about aeroplanes.
₍₃₎

For instance, one evening when we were sitting out in the garden she wanted to know whether she would be able to see the border between India and East Pakistan from the plane. When my father laughed and said, why, did she really think the border was a long black line with green on one side and scarlet on the other, like it was in a schoolroom map, she was not so much offended as puzzled.
₍₄₎

'No, that wasn't what I meant,' she said. 'Of course not. But surely there's something — a fence perhaps, or soldiers, or guns pointing at each other, or

— 232 —

2004 年　　入試問題

even just strips of empty land. Don't they call it no-man's land?'

My father was already an experienced traveller. He burst out laughing and said, 'No, you won't be able to see anything except clouds and perhaps, if you're lucky, some green fields.'

His laughter irritated her. 'Be serious,' she said. 'Don't talk to me as though I were a secretary in your office.'

Now it was his (　5　) to be offended: it upset him when she spoke sharply to him within my hearing.

'That's all I can tell you,' he said. 'That's all there is.'

My grandmother thought this over for a while, and then she said, 'But if there isn't a fence or anything, how are people to know? I mean, where's the difference then? And if there's no difference, both sides will be the same; it'll be just like it used to be before, when we used to catch a train in Dhaka and get off in Calcutta the next day without anybody stopping us. What was it all for then — Partition and all the killing and everything — if there isn't something in between?'

'I don't know what you expect, Ma,' my father said. 'It's not as though you're flying over the Himalayas into China. This is the modern world. The border isn't on the frontier: it's right inside the airport. You'll see. You'll cross it when you have to fill in all those official forms and things.'

My grandmother shifted nervously in her chair. 'What forms?' she said. 'What do they want to know about on those forms?'

My father scratched his forehead. 'Let me see,' he said. 'They want your nationality, your date of birth, place of birth, that kind of thing.'

My grandmother's eyes widened and she sank back in her chair. 'What's the matter?' my father said in alarm.

With an effort she sat up straight again and smoothed back her hair. 'Nothing,' she said, shaking her head. 'Nothing at all.'

I could see then that she was going to (　9　) up in a hopeless mess, so

— 233 —

<u>2004 年　　入試問題</u>

I took it upon myself to ask my father for all the essential information about flying and aeroplanes that I thought she ought to have at her (　10　) — I was sure, for example, that she would roll the windows down in mid-air unless I warned her not to.

　It was not till many years later that I realised it had suddenly occurred to her then that she would have to fill in 'Dhaka' as her place of birth on that form, and that the prospect of this had worried her because she liked things to be neat and in place — and at that moment she had not been able quite to understand how her place of birth had come to fit so uncomfortably with her nationality.

(1)　空所(　1　)を埋めるのに最も適切な単語を次のうちから選び, その記号を記せ。
　ア　boring　　イ　natural　　ウ　unexpected　　エ　unusual

(2)　空所(　2a　)〜(　2c　)を埋めるのに最も適切な表現をそれぞれ次のうちから選び, その記号を記せ。
　ア　she left
　イ　I grew up
　ウ　she is ready to go
　エ　she should travel
　オ　I would make sure
　カ　she was properly prepared

(3)　下線部(3)を訳せ。

(4)　下線部(4)はどのような意味か。最も適切なものを次のうちから選び, その記号を記せ。
　ア　彼女はいらだちよりもむしろ困惑の表情を浮かべた。
　イ　彼女は怒りもしなければ困った顔一つ見せなかった。

— 234 —

2004 年　入試問題

ウ　彼女は当惑というよりはむしろ怒りの表情を見せた。

エ　彼女はどうしたらよいか分からずにムッとしていた。

(5)　空所(　5　)を埋めるのに最も適切な単語を次のうちから選び，その記号を記せ。

　　ア　order　　　イ　reason　　　ウ　round　　　エ　turn

(6)　下線部(6)の後にさらに言葉を続けるとしたら，どのような表現を加えるのが
　　最も適切か。次のうちから選び，その記号を記せ。

　　ア　where the border is

　　イ　how far they have come

　　ウ　which way they are going

　　エ　when to show their passport

(7)　下線部(7)を訳せ。ただし，it の内容がわかるように訳すこと。

(8)　下線部(8)には祖母のどのような気持ちが表現されているか。それを表す語と
　　して最も適切なものを次のうちから選び，その記号を記せ。

　　ア　angry　　　イ　excited　　　ウ　joyful　　　エ　troubled

(9)　空所(　9　)を埋めるのに最も適切な単語を次のうちから選び，その記号を記せ。

　　ア　catch　　　イ　end　　　ウ　hang　　　エ　put

(10)　空所(　10　)を埋めるのに最も適切な単語を次のうちから選び，その記号を
　　記せ。

　　ア　command　　　イ　feet　　　ウ　side　　　エ　understanding

2004年　　入試問題

⑾　説明文と物語文の記述から推測される祖母の出身都市 (city of birth)，宗教
　(religion)，国籍 (nationality) を，それぞれ1語の英語で答えよ。

city of birth : （　11a　）

religion 　　 : （　11b　）

nationality 　: （　11c　）

⑿　説明文と物語文の記述から，この物語の時代設定として可能な年はいつと考え
　られるか。次のうちから1つ選び，その記号を記せ。

ア　1946年

イ　1963年

ウ　1972年

エ　1989年

入試問題

解答時間：120分
配　点：120点

1 (A)　次の英文の内容を，60〜70字の日本語に要約せよ。句読点も字数に含める。

There are estimated to be about 5,000 languages currently spoken in the world today, depending on which you count as dialects and which as distinct languages.　To these, you can perhaps add a handful of 'dead' languages that are still taught in schools (ancient Greek and Latin) or used in religious services (Sanskrit and Ge'ez).　Linguists expect that well over half of all these languages will become extinct, in the sense of having no native speakers, within the next half-century.　They are mostly languages which currently have fewer than a thousand native speakers, most of whom are already elderly.　The time may come, it has even been suggested, when the world will be dominated by just two languages; on present performance, these will almost certainly be English and Chinese.　The loss of all these languages will, of course, be a pity.　As we lose them, we lose fragments of our past, for languages represent the history of peoples, the accumulation of their experiences, their migrations and the invasions they have suffered.

But this observation overlooks one curious feature of human behaviour: our tendency to generate new dialects as fast as we lose others.　English has spread around the globe to become the common language for trade, government and science, as well as the national language of countries on every continent; yet, at the same time, many local dialects have developed whose speakers can hardly understand each other.　Most linguists now recognize Pisin (the 'pidgin English' of New Guinea), Black English Vernacular (a form of English mainly spoken by blacks in the major cities of the US), Caribbean Creoles (the English of the various Caribbean islands) and Krio (the Creole of Sierra Leone in West Africa) and even Scots (the English spoken in the Scottish lowlands) as distinct languages.

(B) 次の英文はサーフィンとハワイ (Hawai'i) の文化の関係について述べたものである。空所 1 ～ 6 を埋めるのに最も適切なものを，ア～クよりそれぞれ 1 つ選んでその記号を記せ。ただし不要な選択肢が 2 つ含まれている。また，空白の長さは答えの長さとは無関係である。

The sport of riding on waves while lying down or standing up on long hardwood surfboards has been associated by Europeans with the Hawaiian Islands ever since the late 18th century, when a two-page description of surfing was included in the official journal of Captain James Cook's third expedition to the Pacific. The true beginnings of the sport can, however, be traced much further back than that, to the ancient history of the Polynesian peoples.

| 1 |

But while Tahitians are said to have occasionally stood on their boards, the art of surfing upright on long boards was certainly perfected, if not invented, in Hawai'i. By the end of the 18th century, when the first Europeans visited Hawai'i, surfing was already deeply rooted in many centuries of Hawaiian legend and culture.

| 2 |

| 3 |

Before the coming of the 'white-skinned people' almost every aspect of life on the islands, including surfing, was ruled by a code of taboo. Taboo rules decided where to eat, how to grow food, how to predict weather, how to build a surfboard, how to predict when the surf would be good, and even how to convince the Gods to make it good. Hawaiian society was distinctly divided into royal and common classes, and there were beaches where the chiefs surfed and beaches where the common people surfed. Common people generally rode waves lying down or standing on boards of up to 12 feet, while the chiefs rode waves on boards that were as long as 24 feet.

4

In 1819, less than 50 years after Captain Cook made contact with the Hawaiians, Liholiho, the son and successor of the ruler, Kamehameha I, publicly sat down to eat with his mother and other high-ranking females. Men eating with women had been taboo since the beginning of Hawaiian time, but Liholiho had been influenced by European culture. His refusal to obey a basic taboo sent a message throughout Hawai'i that the old system of laws was no longer to be followed.

5

By the start of the 20th century, surfing was all but gone from the Hawaiian islands. Most of the surfing took place on the south shore of Oahu, with a few surfers at spots on Maui, Kauai and the other islands. Honolulu had become Hawai'i's largest city, with one out of every four Hawaiians living there, but surfing was now a rarity there. There are some famous photos from this time of native surfers near Diamond Head, but these were solitary men, most likely posing for the camera, standing alone where at one time hundreds had surfed. The importance of surfing for Hawaiian people had almost completely disappeared.

6

Then, with the help of some dramatic photographs and famous supporters, it began its spread around the world, to the beaches of California and beyond. What had once been a lively and unique part of local Hawaiian culture started to grow into its current status

— 240 —

2003年　入試問題

as a highly popular part of world culture. Unlike many other aspects of ancient Hawaiian life, surfing has evolved and survived into modern times. Despite the commercialism that accompanied its popularization, surfing continues to provide enjoyment and a special connection with nature for millions of people around the world.

ア　There are few sports as dramatic and exciting as surfing.

イ　Surfing was also deeply connected to the social system of Hawaiian life.

ウ　As the taboo system declined, so did surfing's ritual significance within Hawaiian culture.

エ　Surfing was one of the only aspects of early Hawaiian life not strictly controlled by taboo rules.

オ　At the crucial moment, however, surfing attracted the attention of some curious and influential non-Hawaiians.

カ　After the culture of the 'white-skinned people' and Hawaiian culture were thrown together in collision at the end of the 18th century, Hawai'i was changed forever.

キ　The custom of playing in the surf on short 'body boards' was actually brought to Hawai'i by the Polynesians who came to the Hawaiian Islands from Tahiti in the 4th century.

ク　Some local Hawaiian place names, for example, recorded famous surfing incidents, and surfing experts sang special songs to celebrate the

— 241 —

first use of new surfboards, to bring the surf up, and to give courage to the men and women who challenged the big waves.

2 (A) 次の2つのグラフから何が言えるか。40語程度の英語で記しなさい。

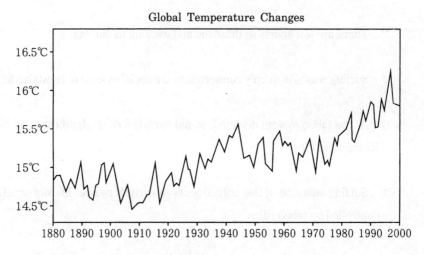

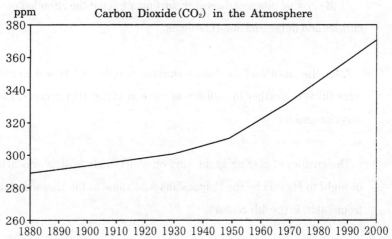

2003 年　　入試問題

(B)　次の文章は，あるアマチュア・スポーツチームの監督の訓話の一部である。この中の，「雨降って地固まる」という表現について，それが字義通りにはどういう意味か，諺としては一般的にどのような意味で用いられるか，さらにこの特定の文脈の中でどのような状況を言い表しているかの３点を盛り込んだ形で，60 語程度の英語で説明しなさい。

　　昨年は，マネージャーを採用すべきであるとかないとか，補欠にも出場の機会を与えるべきだとか，いやあくまで実力主義で行くべきであるとか，チームの運営の仕方をめぐってずいぶん色々とやり合いましたけれども，「雨降って地固まる」と申しまして，それで逆にチームの結束が固まったと思います。今年もみんなで力を合わせて頑張りましょう。

4　(A)　次の(1)から(5)が最も自然な英文となるように（　　　）内の語句を並べ換え，その２番目と６番目にくるものの記号をその順に記せ。ただし(3)と(5)については，文頭の大文字は考慮されていない。

(1)　I cannot imagine how anyone (ア　can　　イ　convince　　ウ　easy　エ　expect　　オ　Sue　　カ　to　　キ　to be). She never listens to anyone.

(2)　Look at the sign. It says, 'At no (ア　be　　イ　door　　ウ　left　エ　must　　オ　this　　カ　time　　キ　unlocked).' I wonder what's inside.

(3)　(ア　for　　イ　newspapers　　ウ　the　　エ　the last　　オ　they　カ　thing　　キ　wanted　　ク　was) to find out that they were soon to be married. They had not even told their friends or relatives about it.

(4)　No one (ア　any　　イ　as　　ウ　behaves　　エ　has　　オ　he does　カ　idea　　キ　John　　ク　why). He is so unusual.

— 243 —

2003年　入試問題

(5) (ア be　イ by　ウ close　エ investigation　オ owned
カ revealed　キ the store　ク to) terrorists, which shocked the
customers.

(B) 次の英文の下線部(1), (2), (3)を和訳せよ。ただし, (1)の that, (3)の it につ
いては, その内容がわかるように訳すこと。

　　Some people will find the hand of God behind everything that happens.
I visit a woman in the hospital whose car was run into by a drunken
driver driving through a red light.　Her vehicle was totally destroyed, but
miraculously she escaped with only a broken ankle.　She looks up at me
from her hospital bed and says, 'Now I know there is a God.　If I could
come out of that alive and in one piece, it must be because He is watching
over me up there.'　I smile and keep quiet,　running the risk of letting her
think that I agree with her — though I don't exactly.　My mind goes back
to a funeral I conducted two weeks earlier, for a young husband and father
who died in a similar drunk-driver collision.　The woman before me may
believe that she is alive because God wanted her to survive, and　I am not
inclined to talk her out of it, but what would she or I say to that other family?

5　次の英文を読み, 以下の設問に答えよ。解答は解答用紙の所定欄に記せ。

　　I am on a bus traveling through the desert between Kerman and Yazd
when we pull over to a checkpoint.　Checkpoints are common along Iranian
highways and I've grown accustomed to stopping every hundred miles or so
to watch the driver climb out, papers in hand.　Sometimes a guard in dark
green uniform enters the bus and walks up and down the aisle, eyes flicking
from side to side, pistol gleaming in the shadowed interior light.

— 244 —

2003年　入試問題

This is one of those times. The bus falls silent as a young guard enters, and we all determinedly stare straight ahead, as if by our pretending to ignore the guard, he will ignore us. We listen to his footfalls sound down the Persian carpet that lines the aisle, turn, and come back again. He reaches the front of the bus and makes a half-turn toward the door. But then, just as we begin a collective deep breath, he surprises us by (1) completing his turn and starting down the aisle again, this time to tap various passengers on the shoulder. They gather their belongings together and move slowly out of the bus and up the steps of a cement block building.

I sit frozen, hoping that the guard will not notice me and the blond hair sticking out of my *rusari*, or head scarf. I've seen guards pull passengers off buses before, and although it never seems to be anything serious — the passengers always return within five or ten minutes — I'd just as soon (2) remain in my seat.

The guard climbs out of the bus and I relax, wondering what, (3) anything, he is looking for. I've been told that these searches are usually about drugs and smuggling, but to me, they seem to be more about the (4) of power.

The guard is back, and instinctively, I know why. He points to me.

Me? I gesture, still not completely convinced that he wants me. After two months in Iran, I've learned that — contrary to what I had (5) expected — foreigners are seldom bothered here.

You, he nods.

Copying my fellow passengers, I gather my belongings together and stand up. Everyone is staring at me — as usual, I am the only foreigner on the bus.

I climb out, nearly falling over my long black raincoat — it or something (6) women in public in Iran. My heart is knocking against my chest. The guard and one of his colleagues are waiting for me on the

— 245 —

2003 年　　入試問題

steps of the guardhouse. At their feet is my bag, which they've dragged out
of the belly of the bus. It looks like a fat green watermelon.

'Passport,' the young guard barks in Persian.

I hand him my crisp, dark blue document, suddenly feeling that *United
States of America* is printed across the front much too boldly. I remember
someone back home （　7　） entering Iran. Too late now.

'Visa?'

I show him the appropriate page in my passport.

'Where are you coming from?' His Persian has a strange accent that I
haven't heard before.

'Kerman,' I say.

'Where are you going to?'

'Yazd'

'Tourist?'

I nod, thinking there's no need to complicate matters by telling him
that I'm here in Iran to write a *safarnameh*, the Persian word for travelogue
or, literally, 'travel letter.' But then immediately （　8　）. My visa says
Journalist.

Slowly, the young guard flips through the pages of my passport,
examining the immigration stamps and the rules and regulations listed
in the back. He （　9　） my picture long and hard, and then passes my
passport to his unsmiling colleague, who asks me the same questions I've
just been asked.

'Where are you coming from?'

'Kerman.'

'Where are you going to?'

'Yazd.'

'Tourist?'

I nod again. I can't change my answer now.

— 246 —

2003 年　　入試問題

The second guard hands my passport back to the first, who reluctantly hands it back to me. I look at his smooth boyish face and wonder if he's old enough to shave.

'Is this your suitcase?' he says, looking at my bag.

'Yes,' I say, and move to open it.

He shakes his head.

All of the other passengers are now back on the bus, and I wonder how much longer the guards will keep me. What will happen, I worry, (10)? We're out in the middle of the desert; there are no other buildings (11). Hardened dust-white plains, broken only by thin grass, stretch in all directions. The sky is a pale metallic dome sucking the color and moisture out of the landscape.

Clearing his throat, the first guard stares at me intently. His eyes are an unusual smoke blue, framed by long lashes. They're the same eyes I've noticed before on more than a few Iranians. He looks at his colleague and they whisper together. Sweat is slipping down their foreheads, and down mine.

Then the first guard straightens his shoulders, takes a deep breath, and blushes. 'Thank you,' he says carefully in stiff, self-conscious English. 'Nice to meet you.'

'Hello.' The second guard is now blushing as furiously as the first. 'How are you?' He falls back into Persian, only some of which I understand. 'We will never forget this day. You are the first American we have met. Welcome to the Islamic Republic of Iran. Go with Allah.'

(1)　下線部(1)を訳せ。

(2)　下線部(2)はどのような意味か。最も適切なものを次のうちから選び，その記号を記せ。

— 247 —

2003 年　　入試問題

ア　I hope I will be allowed to remain seated.

イ　In no time I take a seat and remain there.

ウ　I hope I will not be out of my seat for long.

エ　Quickly I make up my mind to remain seated.

(3)　空所（　3　）を埋めるのに最も適切な単語を次のうちから選び，その記号
を記せ。

　　ア　by　　　　　　イ　for　　　　　　ウ　if　　　　　　エ　or

(4)　空所（　4　）を埋めるのに最も適切な単語を次のうちから選び，その記号
を記せ。

　　ア　denial　　　　イ　display　　　　ウ　finding　　　　エ　lack

(5)　下線部(5)の内容を，10 ～ 20 字の日本語で説明せよ。

(6)　空所（　6　）に当てはまるように，次の語を並べかえよ。

　　（all　　　being　　　for　　　required　　　similar）

(7)　空所（　7　）を埋めるのに最も適切な表現を次のうちから選び，その記号
を記せ。

　　ア　warning me not to disobey the guards after

　　イ　advising me to learn some basic Persian before

　　ウ　warning me to put a cover on my passport before

　　エ　advising me not to forget to carry my passport after

(8)　空所（　8　）を埋めるのに最も適切な表現を次のうちから選び，その記号
を記せ。

　　ア　I wish I were a journalist

　　イ　I wonder if I've done the right thing

－　248　－

2003 年　　入試問題

ウ　I realize that I look too much like a tourist

エ　I realize I should have said 'tourist' in English

⑼　空所（　9　）を埋めるのに最も適切な単語を次のうちから選び，その記号を記せ。

ア　detects　　イ　gazes　　ウ　studies　　エ　watches

⑽　空所（　10　）を埋めるのに最も適切な表現を次のうちから選び，その記号を記せ。

ア　if the bus leaves without me

イ　if the weather suddenly changes

ウ　if the bus runs out of gas or breaks down

エ　if some other passengers are asked to get off the bus

⑾　空所（　11　）を埋めるのに最も適切な表現を次のうちから選び，その記号を記せ。

ア　in sight

イ　on vision

ウ　in my eyes

エ　to the view

⑿　下線部⑿の理由として考えられるものは何か。次の英文を完成させて答えよ。

It is the first time he _____

－ 249 －

1 (A) 次の英文は，日本のニュース番組についての，ある外国人の評論である。これを読んで次のページの設問に答えよ。

In Japanese television programs, we see a commentator at one side of the small screen and an assistant at the other. The commentator is usually male and middle-aged. The assistant is usually female, young and often pretty. He comments on various topics, and she assists. However, she assists so little that, to our eyes, she might as well not be there at all. She only nods at the camera when he makes his various statements, and says *So desu ne* when he makes an important point. She never presents an idea of her own. To many Americans watching these two, the situation might seem quite strange indeed. We are certainly used to double commentators, but usually each commentator really comments and both are equals. In this common style of Japanese television, the pretty girl seems absolutely unnecessary. We fail to understand her role. Yet she has a very important one.
(1)   (2)

A commentator is, by definition, giving his opinion. In the West this is quite enough. In Japan, however, to give an opinion in public is to appear too self-centered, and this is a fault in a society where unity of opinion is an important value. The attractive, nearly silent, young assistant emphasizes this value. Her nods and expressions of agreement indicate that he is not alone in his opinion and that therefore he is not merely self-centered. Rather, he is stating a truth, since at least one person agrees with what he says. At the same time she introduces harmony by indicating that we all agree — after all, it is to us that she is nodding — and the desired unity of opinion has already been reached.

2002 年　　入試問題

(1)　下線部(1)の理由を 5 〜 15 字の日本語で記せ。

(2)　下線部(2)の「重要な役割」とはどのような役割であると述べられているか。
日本の文化の特質という観点から 40 〜 50 字の日本語で記せ。

(B)　次の英文の空白部分(1)〜(6)のそれぞれを埋めるのに最も適切なものを，ア
〜クより 1 つ選んでその記号を記せ。ただし不要な選択肢が 2 つ含まれている。

"Snow" does not, at first sight, look like a topic for a cultural or social historian. As a subject of inquiry, one might think, it more obviously belongs to the geographer or the weather and climate specialist. What could be "cultural" about snow? What could be "social" about it? At first these questions may seem hard to answer.　(1)

Snow certainly existed before humans first invented words to describe it. It's a physical phenomenon. But it is also, at the same time, part of shared human experience. So the questions that a cultural or social historian would use in their approach to the topic of snow would focus on the *experience* of snow: What names have people given to snow? What questions have they asked about snow? What symbolic meanings have they found? How have they managed snow? These kinds of questions open up wide areas of useful historical inquiry.

There is a clear history of change in social ways of thinking about and living with snow in America. Snow has been a constant in American history, but its cultural meanings have not. According to one historian, we can divide this evolving history of snow in America into six periods. In the first period, Americans simply survived their snow. Then, in the next period, they gradually began to identify with snow, to think of it as a part of their

— 253 —

national identity, a symbol of something clean and pure.

(2) Snow became celebrated for its multiple meanings and its many faces. It started to represent the contradictions, differences, and variety in American life. There was a new interest in the endlessly changing appearance of American snow. It became both peaceful and dangerous, creative and destructive, passive and active, cold but full of life, and blank but beautiful.

(3) It could be measured and predicted. And this trend towards thinking of snow as something that could be understood, if not exactly controlled, encouraged people to organize the study of snow. In this next period, American snow became something to be investigated, described, and named. In this period, the National Weather Bureau grew in importance, and scientific interest in the North and South Poles increased the public consciousness of snow.

In the fifth period, winter sports started to become a major commercial activity, especially skiing. But then just when snow was for the first time beginning to look like fun, people also started to have to pay attention to it as a serious social problem. (4)

Finally, for many Americans today, snow might be most immediately associated with the safety of a lost past. This past might be the remembered winters of childhood, or it might be an imagined past America, a place and time in which life seemed somehow to have been cleaner and simpler. This way of seeing snow is almost certainly connected to growing social concern about pollution, the environment, and global climate changes, and it may also be interestingly connected to changes in the American sense of national identity and its position as a global power.

(5)

Looking at the history of a particular snowfall, they would probably focus on the "four Ds." What were the dates of its occurrence and its disappearance? To what depth did it accumulate? What was its density, or water content? And what was its duration — for how long did it snow? Answers to these questions would provide basic information about the impact of snow in a particular geographical region.

For the cultural historian, however, snow provides a window on the history of the interrelation of nature and culture in the United States. The majority of Americans experience some snow every year. Every year, for centuries, snow has changed the American landscape and challenged its people both physically and mentally in different ways. (6)

ア But of course snow was always more than an idea or a symbol; it was also weather.

イ Specialists studying weather and climate are interested in snowfalls as physical phenomena.

ウ Next, as creative writers and creative scientists started to look at snow in new ways, a more complicated version of snow in America began to appear.

— 255 —

2002年　入試問題

エ　With the start of the transportation revolution, snow became a major headache for the people responsible for the cities, the roads, and the railways.

オ　In the third period, as people started to have more leisure time, they learned how to experience snow as entertainment: it became enjoyable as well as troublesome.

カ　By examining how Americans know what they know about their snow, we can begin to understand a lot more than the truth about snow itself. We will also learn a great deal about American culture and society.

キ　But for a cultural historian, it isn't enough just to say that "snow is snow"— a physical thing, part of the weather, nothing to do with culture and society. For the cultural historian, there is much more to snow than that.

ク　Snow in America, though, has always been more significant as an idea than as a physical event, and as a subject of study it belongs to the historians, not to the scientists. It is all about the American imagination, not the American climate.

2 (A)　次の会話文を読み，話がつながるように空所(1)と(2)を英語で埋めよ。それぞれ 10 ～ 20 語程度とすること。

A : What are your plans for the coming vacation?

B : There are lots of things I'd like to do, but I'll probably have to spend most of my time doing part-time jobs.

— 256 —

2002年　　入試問題

A：Me, too. Say, if you had a month for vacation and enough money, what would you do? What's your ideal vacation?

B：Here's what I'd like to do. ⑴ _____

_____

A：I wouldn't like to do that at all!

B：Why not?

A：If I did that, ⑵ _____

_____

⒝　次の会話は，ある高校の授業に「能力別クラス編成」(ranking system) を導入するかどうかについての教師同士の議論である。このA先生 (Ms. A) とB先生 (Mr. B) のやりとりの内容について，日本語のわからない英会話の先生から質問されたと仮定し，2人の主張とその根拠を明確に伝えるような形で，議論の要点を 40 ～ 50 語の英語で述べなさい。

A先生：私は基本的に能力別クラス編成に賛成です。そのほうが生徒一人一人の能力に応じたきめ細かい指導ができると思いますよ。本校には英語圏からの帰国子女もたくさんおりますし，たとえば英語の授業でそういう生徒と普通の生徒を一緒にしてしまうと，結局，どちらに合わせればいいかわからなくなって，授業自体が中途半端になってしまいますからね。生徒主体の授業運営をするためにも，能力別にすべきだと思います。

B先生：そうは言ってもですね，能力別という発想自体，そもそも民主主義の原則に反する古い考え方ですよ。だって，英語にかぎらず，上級のクラスでは高度な教材を用いて高度な内容の授業が行われるわけだし，逆にそうでないクラスでは教材も内容もやさしくなるわけでしょう？それはやはり差別なんじゃないですか。成績自体はふるわなくたって，高度な内容を教えてほしいと言い出す生徒がいたらどうします？

2002 年　　入試問題

4 (A)　次の英文の(1)〜(10)の下線部には，文法上1語取り除かなければならないものが5つある。解答欄の該当する番号の下の欄に，取り除くべき語がある場合はその語を記し，ない場合は空欄のままにせよ。

Although thought and action tend to be considered two separate things, some researchers have suggested that it is not necessarily the case. Consider a jigsaw puzzle. One unlikely way to approach such a puzzle would be to look very hard at a piece and to try to decide by thinking let alone whether it will fit in a certain location. Our actual practice, however, employs a mixed method in itself which we make a rough guess and then physically try out the piece to see if it will fit. We do not, in general, picture the detailed shape of a piece well enough to know for certain even if it is going to fit in advance of such an action. Moreover, we may physically rotate as possible pieces even before we try to fit them, so as to simplify the mental task of guessing whether the piece will fit. Completing a jigsaw puzzle thus involves a complicated and repeated dance in which "pure thought" leads to actions which in turn change or simplify the problems facing to "pure thought". This is probably the simplest kind of example to show that thought and action do not always function separately.

(B)　次の英文の下線部(1), (2)を和訳せよ。

I was wondering how on earth I was going to get through the evening. Saturday. Saturday night and I was left alone with my grandmother.

The others had gone — my mother and my sister, both dating. Of course, I would have gone, too, if I had been able to get away first. Then I would not have had to think about the old woman, going through the routines that she would fill her evening with. I would have slipped away and left my mother and my sister to argue, not with each other but with my

— 258 —

2002 年　　入試問題

grandmother, each separately conducting a running battle as they prepared for the night out. One of them would lose and the loser would stay at home, angry and frustrated at being in on a Saturday night, the one night of all the week for pleasure. Well, some chance of pleasure.　There was hardly ever any real fulfillment of hopes but at least the act of going out brought with it a possibility and that was something to fight for.
₍₁₎

"Where are you going?" my grandmother would demand of her daughter, forty-six and a widow for fifteen years.

"I'm going out." My mother's reply would be calm and　she would look determined as I imagine she had done at sixteen, and always would do.
₍₂₎

5 次の英文を読み，以下の設問に答えよ。解答は解答用紙の所定欄に記せ。

"I shall never believe that God plays dice with the world," Einstein famously said. Whether or not he was right about the general theory of relativity and the universe, his statement is certainly not true of the games people play in their daily lives. Life is not chess but a game of backgammon, with a throw of the dice at every turn. As a result, it is hard to make (　1　). But in a world with any regularity at (　2　), decisions informed by the past are better than decisions made at random. That has always been true, and we would expect animals, especially humans, to have developed sharp intuitions about probability.
₍₃₎

However, people often seem to make illogical judgments of probability. One notorious example is the "gambler's fallacy." "Fallacy" means a false idea widely believed to be true, and you commit the gambler's fallacy if you expect that when a tossed coin has fallen on the same side, say, three times in a row, this increases the chance of it falling on the other side the next time, as if the coin had a memory and a desire to (　4　). I remember

— 259 —

(5) an incident during a family vacation when I was a teenager. My father mentioned that we had suffered through several days of rain (6). I corrected him, accusing him of the gambler's fallacy. But long-suffering Dad was right, and his know-it-all son was wrong. Cold fronts, which cause rain, aren't removed from the earth at day's end and replaced with new ones the next morning. A cloud must have some average size, speed, and direction, and it would not surprise me now if a week of clouds really did predict that the edge of the clouds was near and the sun was about to appear again, just as the (7) railroad car on a passing train suggests more strongly than the fifth one that the last one will be passing soon.

Many events (8) like that. They have a characteristic life history, a changing probability of occurring over time. A clever observer *should* commit the gambler's fallacy and try to predict the next occurrence of an event from its history (9) far. There is one exception: devices that are *designed* to make events occur independently of their history. What kind of devise would do that? We call them gambling machines. Their reason for being is to beat an observer who likes to turn (10). If our love of patterns were not sensible because randomness is everywhere, gambling machines should be easy to build and gamblers easy to beat. In fact, roulette wheels, slot machines, even dice must be made with extreme care and precision to produce random results.

So, in any world but a casino, the gambler's fallacy is rarely a fallacy. Indeed, <u>calling our intuitive predictions unreliable because they fail with gambling</u>₍₁₁₎ <u>devices is unreasonable.</u> A gambling device is an artificially invented machine which is, by definition, designed (12). It is like calling our hands badly designed because their shape makes it hard to get out of handcuffs.

2002 年　　入試問題

(1)　空所（　　1　　）を埋めるのに最も適切な表現を次のうちから選び，その記号
　　を記せ。

　　ア　progress

　　イ　predictions

　　ウ　random turns

　　エ　probable moves

(2)　空所（　　2　　）を埋めるのに最も適切な表現を次のうちから選び，その記号
　　を記せ。

　　ア　all　　　　　　イ　large　　　　　ウ　length　　　　エ　most

(3)　下線部(3)はどのような意味か。最も適切なものを次のうちから選び，その
　　記号を記せ。

　　ア　自然界の規則性に基づいて，いかなる場合にも的確な判断を下せる直感

　　イ　過去のできごとの経験から，次に何が起きそうであるかを判断する直感

　　ウ　自然界で起きる諸事象から，常に真となるような法則を抽象化する直感

　　エ　過去のできごとに基づいて，物事の本質について確実に理解できる直感

(4)　空所（　　4　　）を埋めるのに最も適切な表現を次のうちから選び，その記号
　　を記せ。

　　ア　be fair　　　　イ　cheat us　　　ウ　amuse us　　　エ　be repetitive

(5)　空所（　　5　　）を埋めるのに最も適切な表現を次のうちから選び，その記号
　　を記せ。

　　ア　in pride

　　イ　in despair

　　ウ　to my shame

　　エ　to my surprise

— 261 —

2002年　入試問題

⑹　空所（　6　）を埋めるのに最も適切な表現を次のうちから選び，その記号を記せ。

ア　but could only hope for a sunny day

イ　and were likely to have good weather

ウ　and the bad weather was likely to continue

エ　but couldn't tell when it would stop raining

⑺　空所（　7　）を埋めるのに最も適切な語を次のうちから選び，その記号を記せ。

ア　first　　　　イ　fourth　　　ウ　tenth　　　エ　final

⑻　空所（　8　）を埋めるのに最も適切な語を次のうちから選び，その記号を記せ。

ア　change　　　イ　follow　　　ウ　look　　　エ　work

⑼　空所（　9　）を埋めるのに最も適切な1語を記せ。

⑽　空所（　10　）を埋めるのに最も適切な表現を次のうちから選び，その記号を記せ。

ア　patterns into predictions

イ　predictions into patterns

ウ　patterns into randomness

エ　randomness into predictions

⑾　下線部⑾を和訳せよ。

⑿　空所（　12　）を埋めるのに最も適切な表現を次のうちから選び，その記号を記せ。

— 262 —

<u>2002 年　　入試問題</u>

ア　to follow the observed patterns

イ　to meet gamblers' requirements

ウ　to defeat our intuitive predictions

エ　to remind us of the regularity of nature

入試問題　　　解答時間：120 分
　　　　　　　　　配　　点：120 点

1 (A)　次の英文の内容を 30 〜 40 字の日本語に要約せよ。句読点も字数に含める。

　　The other day I happened to become aware for the first time that my
electric toothbrush was white with two upright blue stripes of rubber to
hold the handle.　The button to turn the toothbrush on and off was made
of the same blue rubber.　There was even a matching blue section of the
brush itself, and a colored ring of rubber at the base of the brush handle.
This was a far more carefully thought-out design than I had ever imagined.
The same was true of my plastic throwaway razor with its graceful bend
that made it seem as if the head was eagerly reaching out to do its job.　If
either my toothbrush or razor had been mounted on a base, it might well
have qualified as a sculpture.　Had they been presented as works of art,
I would have seen something more than an object, something deeper in
the way forms can take on a life of their own and create enduring values.
"Rightly viewed," Thomas Carlyle wrote in his book *Sartor Resartus*, "no
meanest object is insignificant; all objects are as windows, through which
the philosophic eye looks into Infinitude itself."

(B)　次の英文は，ある雑誌記事の一節であるが，第 2 〜第 4，第 6 〜第 8，第
　　10 段落が抜けている。それぞれの空所を埋めるのに最もふさわしいものを，
　　ア〜クから 1 つ選んでその記号を記せ。8 つの選択肢のうちから 7 つ選ぶこと。

(1)　A lonely seeker of truth fighting against overwhelming odds.　This is
　　the conventional image of "the scientist".　Just think of Galileo.　He had
　　to single-handedly discover the laws of falling bodies in a physical world

－ 266 －

all too reluctant to give up its secrets, improve the telescope and face the wrath of the Church, but his devotion to scientific truth changed history.

(2)

(3)

(4)

(5) I think the heroic model is being abandoned a bit too hastily. Just as individuals can change deeply-rooted national policies by taking on government or big business, so individual scientists can confront established scientific prejudices and change the course of science.

(6)

(7)

(8)

(9) So, the lonely scientist fighting against all odds can triumph. Purdey and Hooper can be seen as contemporary equivalents of Galileo. But who is the Church in this case? Not a religious establishment, but a scientific one. As far as the individual scientist working on his or her

own is concerned, the Church has been replaced by rigidly dogmatic institutions of science — large laboratories, academic research institutions and government ministries.

(10)

ア　Perhaps the real moral is that institutions of all kinds tend to suppress uncomfortable truths. And a lonely scientist armed with truth can still be a powerful force.

イ　Nowadays, however, major discoveries are seldom made by individual scientists. Much of contemporary science is corporate science, involving huge laboratories where large groups of scientists work on individual problems.

ウ　Worse: Purdey had his own theory, unacceptable to establishment science, which blamed legally required insecticides. Ten years of lonely research eventually linked BSE with an excess of the metal manganese, a connection recently confirmed by a research team in Cambridge.

エ　Not surprisingly, then, most philosophers and sociologists of science have given up the heroic model. The individual seeker of scientific truth, working alone, may occasionally discover a comet or two, but on the whole, the argument goes, he or she has little to contribute to science as such.

オ　On the other hand, Isaac Newton's *Principia Mathematica* is commonly thought to be the climax of the seventeenth century's

2001年　入試問題

scientific revolution, a great burst of systematic, ordered, and empirical science — though preceding Newton were great successes in physiology and astronomy.

カ　Of course, there are serious problems with this romantic picture. Galileo was not as innocent as we might think, and his observations have been shown to be less than strictly scientific. But Galileo does provide us with a heroic model of science where the heroes, the individual scientists working on their own, make major discoveries.

キ　We do not have to look very far to find another example of the heroic model in action. The most recent is Aids researcher Edward Hooper, who denies that HIV was caused by a chimpanzee virus. Instead he shows that most cases of Aids in Africa came from the same places where an experimental oral polio vaccine called Chat was used.

ク　Mark Purdey provides us with an example of how this can be done. Purdey is an organic farmer who was suspicious of the official version of the origins of BSE (so-called "mad cow disease"). He noticed that his cows never touched the "cattle cake" that contained the ground-up brains of sheep and cows, yet they became sick with BSE. Purdey's detailed records were available for inspection, but who would listen to a mere farmer?

— 269 —

2001 年　　入試問題

2 (A)　次の文章は，死に対して人間の抱く恐怖が動物の場合とどのように異なると
論じているか。50 〜 60 語程度の英語で述べよ。

　　死の恐怖を知るのは人間だけであると考えられる。もちろん，動物も死を避
けようとする。ライオンに追いかけられるシマウマは，殺されて食べられるの
を恐れて必死で逃げる。しかし，これと人間の死の恐怖は異なる。動物は目の
前に迫った死の危険を恐れるだけだが，人間は，遠い先のことであろうが，い
つの日か自分が死ぬと考えただけで怖い。人間は，自分の持ち時間が永遠でな
いことを恐れるのである。

(B)　次の会話文を読み，話がつながるように空所(1)〜(3)を英語で埋めよ。(2), (3)
については，それぞれ 10 〜 20 語程度とすること。

A : Say, what do you think was the greatest invention or discovery of the
　　twentieth century?

B : That's a hard question, because there were so many of them.　But if I
　　had to name only one, it would be (1)＿＿＿＿＿.

A : Why?

B : Because (2)＿＿＿＿＿＿＿＿＿＿＿＿＿＿＿＿＿＿＿＿＿＿＿＿
　　＿＿＿＿＿＿＿＿＿＿＿＿＿＿＿＿＿＿＿＿＿＿＿＿＿＿＿＿＿＿.

A : It may sound strange, but I take the opposite view.　I think that was
　　the worst because (3)＿＿＿＿＿＿＿＿＿＿＿＿＿＿＿＿＿＿＿＿

　　＿＿＿＿＿＿＿＿＿＿＿＿＿＿＿＿＿＿＿＿＿＿＿＿＿＿＿＿＿.

4 (A)　次の英文には，文法上あるいは文脈上，取り除かなければならない語が全部
で5語ある。それぞれどのセンテンスのどの語か。センテンス番号と，その語
を記せ。

— 270 —

2001年　入試問題

(1) Some of philosophers come to the conclusion that there is no such thing as philosophical progress, and that philosophy itself is nothing but its history. (2) This view has been proposed by more than one philosopher and it has been called "historicism". (3) This idea that philosophy consists not only of its history is a strange one, but it has been defended with apparently striking arguments. (4) However, we shall not find ourselves are compelled to take such a view. (5) I intend to take an entirely different in view of philosophy. (6) For example, all of you have probably read some of Plato's *Dialogues*. (7) There, Socrates asks questions and receives various answers. (8) He asks what it was meant by these answers, why a particular word was used in this way or that way. (9) In short, Socrates' philosophy tried to clarify thought by analyzing the meaning of our expressions.

(B)　次の英文の下線部(1),　(2)を和訳せよ。(1)については，it が何を指すか明らかになるように訳すこと。

　　Indeed, in the year 1000 there was no concept of an antiseptic at all. If a piece of food fell off your plate, the advice of one contemporary document was to pick it up, make the sign of the cross over it, salt it well — and then eat it. The sign of the cross was, so to speak, the antiseptic of the year 1000. The person who dropped his food on the floor knew that he was taking some sort of risk when he picked it up and put it in his mouth, but he trusted in his faith. Today we have faith in modern medicine, though <u>few of us can claim much personal knowledge of how it actually works.</u> (1) <u>We also know that the ability to combat quite major illnesses can be</u> (2) <u>affected by what we call "a positive state of mind"</u> — what the Middle Ages experienced as "faith".

— 271 —

5 次の英文を読み，以下の設問に答えよ。解答は解答用紙の所定欄に記せ。

She said to him. 'On your birthday, McCreedy, what do you want to do?' She always called him McCreedy. You would have thought by now, after being his wife for so long, she should have started to call him John, but she never did. He called her Hilda; she called him McCreedy, as if he was a (1), as if he was a footballer she had seen on the television.

'What would the kids like?' he said.

She lighted up a cigarette. Her twentieth or thirtieth that Sunday, he had stopped counting.

'Never mind the kids, McCreedy,' she said. 'It's your birthday.'

'Go back to Ireland,' he said. 'That's what I'd like. Go back there for (3).'

She put out the cigarette. Typical, he thought. She was always changing her mind about everything, minute to minute. 'When you've got a sensible answer,' she said, 'let me know what it is.'

He went out into the garden where his nine-year-old daughter, Katy, was playing on her own. Katy and the garden had something in common: they were both small and it looked as if they would never be beautiful no matter how hard anyone tried, because Katy (5) her dad. More's the pity.

Now the two of them were in the neglected garden together, with the North London September sun quite warm on them, and McCreedy said to the daughter he tried so hard to love, 'What'll we do on my birthday, then, Katy?'

She was playing with her showily stylish little dolls. She held them by their shapely legs and their golden hair waved around like flags. 'I don't know,' she said.

He sat on a plastic garden chair and she laid her nymphs side by side. 'Cindy and Barbie are getting stung,' she complained.

— 272 —

<u>2001 年　　入試問題</u>

'Who's stinging them, darling?'

'Those plants, of course.　Cut them down, can't you?'

'Oh, no.' he said, looking at where they grew so fiercely, crowding out the roses Hilda planted years ago.　'<u>Saving them</u>, sweetheart.'
₍₆₎

'Why?'

'For soup.　Nettle soup — to make you beautiful.'

She looked at him gravely.　For nine years, she had believed everything he had said.　<u>Now she was on a cliff-edge, almost ready to fly off.</u>
₍₇₎

'Will it?'

'Sure it will.　You wait and (　8　).'

Later in the day, when his son Michael came in, McCreedy stopped him before he went up to his room.　He was thirteen.

'Your mother was wondering what we might all do on my birthday.　If you had any thoughts about it ...?'

Michael shrugged.　It was as if he knew he was untouchable, unconquerable.　He was the future.　<u>He didn't have to give the present any</u>
₍₉₎
<u>attention</u>.　'No,' he said.　'Not specially.　How old are you anyway?'

'Forty-five.　Or it might be a year more.　I don't remember.'

'Come on, Dad.　Everyone remembers their age.'

'Well, I don't.　(　10　) since I left Ireland.　I used to know it then, but that's long ago.'

'Ask Mum, then.　She'll know.'

Michael went on up the stairs, scuffing the carpet with the smelly shoes he wore.　No thoughts.　No ideas.　Not specially.

And again McCreedy was alone.

⑴　空所（　1　）を埋めるのに最も適当な語を次のうちから選び，その記号を記せ。

　　ア　brother　　イ　father　　ウ　master　　エ　stranger

－ 273 －

2001年　　入試問題

(2)　下線部(2)を和訳せよ。

(3)　空所（　3　）を埋めるのに最も適当な語を次のうちから選び，その記号を
　　記せ。
　　ア　all　　　　　イ　dead　　　　ウ　good　　　　エ　granted

(4)　下線部(4)には誰のどのような気持ちが表われているか。最も適当なものを
　　次のうちから選び，その記号を記せ。
　　ア　妻の柔軟なものの考え方に対する夫の驚嘆が表われている。
　　イ　妻の日頃の生活態度に対する夫のいらだちが表われている。
　　ウ　夫の強い望郷の念に共感できない妻の不満が表われている。
　　エ　夫の非常識な発言を理解できない妻の困惑が表われている。

(5)　空所（　5　）を埋めるのに最も適当な語を次のうちから選び，その記号を
　　記せ。
　　ア　recognised　イ　represented　ウ　resembled　エ　respected

(6)　下線部(6)を，them が何を指すか明らかになるように和訳せよ。

(7)　下線部(7)は，彼女の中にどのような気持ちが芽生えたことを表わしている
　　か。10字以内で記せ。

(8)　空所（　8　）を埋めるのに最も適当な英語1語を記せ。

(9)　下線部(9)を和訳せよ。

(10)　次のうちから空所（　10　）を埋めることができない語を1つ選び，その記
　　号を記せ。
　　ア　Especially　イ　Ever　　　ウ　Lately　　　エ　Not

— 274 —

1 (A) 次の英文の内容を 40 〜 50 字の日本語に要約せよ。句読点も字数に含める。

What makes us specifically human? The complexity of our language? Our problem-solving strategies? You may be shocked by my suggestion that, in some very deep sense, language and some aspects of human problem solving are no more or less complex than the behaviors of other species. Complexity as such is not the issue. Spiders weave complex webs, bees transmit complex information about sources and quality of nectar, ants interact in complex colonies, beavers build complex dams, chimpanzees have complex problem-solving strategies, just as humans use complex language. Nor are our problem-solving skills so remarkable: there are human beings who have perfectly normal human mental abilities, but who nevertheless are unable to solve certain problems that a chimpanzee can solve. There is, however, one extremely important difference between human and non-human intelligence, a difference which distinguishes us from all other species. Unlike the spider, which stops at web weaving, the human child — and, I maintain, only the human child — has the potential to take its own representations as objects of cognitive attention. Normally, human children not only become efficient users of language; they also have the capacity to become little grammarians. By contrast, spiders, ants, beavers, and probably even chimpanzees do not have the potential to analyze their own knowledge.

— 276 —

<u>2000 年　　入試問題</u>

(B)　次の英文は第 2，第 3，第 5，第 6，第 8 段落が抜けている。それぞれの空
　　所を埋めるのに最もふさわしいものを，ア〜カから 1 つ選んでその記号を記せ。
　　6 つの選択肢のうち 5 つ選ぶこと。

(1)　Science and technology have improved our lives over the past 150
　　　years. And there is every possibility, given the correct regulatory
　　　framework, that they will do the same over the next 150. The growth of
　　　scientific knowledge has allowed us to control some of the risks of life
　　　and eliminate some of its worst evils. In particular, advances in medical
　　　science have reduced the threat of a great variety of diseases.

(2)

(3)

(4)　The benefits of science are thus enormous — and not only in the
　　　areas of life expectancy and health care. At present, one of the gravest
　　　problems we face is damage to the environment. The rush towards
　　　industrialisation has led to an unthinking approach to our natural
　　　resources. But, unless we want to go back to a pre-industrial world, we
　　　will not be able to protect the environment without the use of science.

(5)

(6)

— 277 —

2000 年　　入試問題

(7) To guard against such threats to human well-being, we must make certain that we have effective systems of regulation in place to ensure that future scientific progress is safe, ethical and environmentally sound. Openness in explaining the meanings and possible consequences of scientific advances is absolutely essential, both in government departments and in the scientific community.

(8)

ア　To take one simple example, it was the work of chemists in the USA and Germany that first showed that CFCs (chlorofluorocarbons, used in refrigerators and aerosols, for example) can cause the breakdown of ozone when they are released into the upper levels of the atmosphere. Then, in the 1980s, British scientists produced proof that the stratospheric ozone has partially disappeared over Antarctica. This observation and the known chemical mechanism were crucial pieces of evidence that together led in 1987 to the signing of the Montreal Protocol on reducing the use of CFCs. The replacement of CFCs has also relied on science to produce alternative methods of refrigeration.

イ　In Britain now we tend to take our good health for granted, but we should remember how common death at an early age would have been in the pre-industrial era, and that the reason why that is no longer so is mostly due to advances in science. As the historian J. H. Plumb once commented: 'No one in his senses would choose to have been born in a previous age unless he could be certain that he would have been born into a prosperous family, that he would have enjoyed extremely good health, and that he would have accepted stoically the death of the

－ 278 －

majority of his children.'

ウ　Information technology has already had an enormous effect on the availability and speed of transfer of information. It has literally shrunk the world — or at least the developed world. However, as the technology develops, and computers become cheaper, and thus affordable by more and more people in all parts of the world, this new global access to information will have profound and, in some cases, regrettable consequences.

エ　I am not arguing for the mindless pursuit of scientific change; I am arguing against a mindless opposition to it. Our lives in the coming century will inevitably be changed by the revolutions taking place in almost all scientific fields. However, it is only the existence of a properly regulated scientific framework that will ensure that these developments are put to use for our collective good. We cannot turn away from progress, but we can encourage it and guide it in such a way that people in all countries may enjoy its advantages.

オ　Thus, in the fields of both health care and the environment — as well as in other areas, such as transport, media, information technology and food — scientific progress is improving the quality of our lives. But we must never be arrogant about the advance of science: terrible medical tragedies, such as Thalidomide, and the development of weapons of mass destruction, have to be set against progress.

カ　The result has been an incredible increase in the quality and length of our lives over the past fifty years. If we take the world as a whole, life expectancy at birth rose from 46.4 years in 1950-55 to 64.4 years in

1990-95. And, equally significant, the gap in life expectancy between the more developed regions and the less developed ones fell from 26 years in 1950-55 to 12 years in 1990-95.

2 (A) 下のグラフは，海外における日本人の学齢期の子供の就学状況を，地域別に示したものである。これを参考にしながら，一貫した内容の会話となるように，(1)〜(7)の下線部を埋めよ。(1), (3), (5)にはそれぞれ地域名を入れよ。(2), (4)は15語以内，(6)は10語以内，(7)は15〜25語の英文を書け。

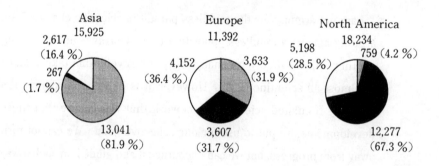

■ ① Japanese children enrolled in full-time Japanese schools only.

■ ② Japanese children enrolled in local schools or international schools, while also attending a part-time Japanese school.

□ ③ Japanese children enrolled only in local schools or international schools.

(注)
Full-time Japanese schools：日本人学校。日本国内と同等の教育を日本語で行う。
Local schools：現地校。現地の公立学校など。その国の言語で授業が行われる。
Part-time Japanese schools：日本語による補習授業校。

<u>2000 年　　入試問題</u>

This is a social studies class in a junior high school in Japan. The teacher is showing the graphs on the preceding page to the students.

Teacher： For the two graphs which are most different, how do the situations in those areas differ?

Miyako： In (1)＿＿＿＿＿ , (2)＿＿＿＿＿＿＿＿＿＿ . On the other hand, in (3)＿＿＿＿＿ , (4)＿＿＿＿＿＿＿＿＿＿ .

Teacher： Imagine you are eight years old. If you lived in one of the areas shown in the graphs, what type school would you prefer to go to, and why?

Kazuyuki： If I lived in (5)＿＿＿＿＿ , I'd want to (6)＿＿＿＿＿＿＿＿＿ , because (7)＿＿＿＿＿＿＿＿＿＿＿＿＿＿＿＿＿＿＿＿ .

(B)　次の手紙は，「クローン技術」を特集した雑誌の読者が編集者にあてた投書である。(1)のア，イのうちいずれかを選び，その記号を解答欄に記した上で，一貫した内容になるよう，(2)，(3)の下線部にそれぞれ5〜10語の英文を書け。

To the Editor:

　I read the article "Cloning: It Isn't Just for Sheep Anymore" with great interest. I think the government (1)［ア　should　　イ　should not］support research on cloning people because (2)＿＿＿＿＿ . Furthermore, (3)＿＿＿＿＿ .

Sincerely,

Taro Yamashita

2000 年　　入試問題

4 (A)　次の各文が意味の通った英文となるようにア〜オを並べ換え，その2番目と
4番目にくる語の記号を記せ。

(1)　I know how you feel about the mistake, but it is (ア　a　　イ　much
ウ　not　エ　of　オ　problem).

(2)　John will be late for the first game, so we'll just (ア　do　　イ　have
ウ　make　エ　to　　オ　with) ten players.

(3)　His official position hasn't changed, but actually he isn't (ア　as
イ　as　ウ　before　エ　in　オ　involved) our decision-making
processes.

(4)　She can't come to the phone. She is (ア　in　　イ　middle　　ウ　of
エ　right　　オ　the) her work.

(5)　You're not making any sense —— (ア　is　イ　it　ウ　that　エ　what
オ　you) want?

(B)　次の英文の下線部を和訳せよ。ただし，"it" の内容を明らかにすること。

Chance had been our ally too often.　We had grown complacent,
over-confident of its loyalty.　And so <u>the moment when it first chose to
betray us was also the moment when we were least likely to suspect that it
might</u>.

— 282 —

2000 年　　入試問題

5 次の英文を読み，以下の設問に答えよ。

I came home from school one day to find a strange man in the kitchen. He was making something on the stove, peering intently into a saucepan.

'Who are you? What are you doing here?' I asked him. It was a week since my father died.

The man said, 'Shh. Not now. Just a minute.' He had a strong foreign accent.

I recognised that he was concentrating and said, 'What's that you're making?'

This time he glanced at me. 'Polenta,' he said.

I went over to the stove and looked inside the saucepan. The stuff was yellowy, sticky, a thick semolina. 'That looks disgusting,' I told him, and then went in search of my mother.

I found her in the garden. 'Mum, there's a man in the kitchen. He's cooking. He says he's making polenta.'

'Yes, darling? Polenta?' said my mother. <u>I began to suspect she might not be much help</u>. I wished my father were here. 'I'm not exactly sure what that is,' my mother said vaguely.

'Mum, I don't care about the polenta. Who is he? What's he doing in our kitchen?'

'Ah!' exclaimed my mother. She was wearing a thin flowery summer dress, and I noticed suddenly how thin she was. *My Mother*, I thought.

<u>Everything seemed to pile on top of me</u> and I found myself unexpectedly crying. 'Don't cry, love,' said my mother. 'It's all right. He's our new lodger.' She hugged me.

I wiped my eyes, sniffing. 'Lodger?'

'With your father gone,' my mother explained, 'I'm afraid I'm having to (3) one of the spare rooms.' She turned and began to walk back

— 283 —

towards the house. We could see the lodger in the kitchen, moving about. I put my hand on my mother's arm to stop her going inside.

'Is he living here then?' I asked. 'With us? I mean, will he eat with us and (4)?'

'This is his home now,' said my mother. 'We must make him feel at home.' She added, as if it were an afterthought, 'His name's Konstantin. He's Russian.' Then she went inside.

I paused to take (5) this information. A Russian. This sounded exotic and interesting and made me inclined to forgive his rudeness. I watched my mother enter the kitchen. Konstantin the Russian looked up and a smile lighted up his face. 'Maria!' He opened his arms and she went up to him. They kissed on both cheeks. My mother looked around and beckoned to me.

'This is my daughter,' she said. There was a note in her voice that I couldn't identify. She stretched out her hand to me.

'Ah! You must be Anna,' the Russian said.

I was startled, not expecting him to have my name so readily on his lips. I looked at my mother. She was giving nothing away. The Russian held out his hands and said, 'Konstantin. I am very pleased to meet you. I have heard so much about you.'

We shook hands. I wanted to know how he had heard so much about me, but couldn't think of a way of asking, at least not with my mother there.

The Russian turned back to his cooking. He seemed familiar with our kitchen. He sprinkled salt and pepper over the top of the mass of semolina-like substance, and then carried it through to the living room. For some reason, my mother and I followed him. We all sat in armchairs and looked at one another. I thought I was the only one who felt any sense of (9).

When I got home late next evening, Konstantin and my mother were

— 284 —

deep in conversation over dinner. There were candles on the table.

'What's going on?' I asked.

'Are you hungry, darling?' said my mother. 'We've left you some. It's in the kitchen.'

I was starving. 'No thanks,' I said sullenly, 'I'm fine.'

Though it was early, I went upstairs to bed.

Later I heard my mother's footsteps on the stairs. She came into my room and leant over me. I kept my eyes closed and breathed deeply. 'Anna?' she said, 'Anna, are you awake?'

I remained silent.

'I know you're awake,' she said.

There was a pause. I was on the point of giving in when she spoke again. She said, 'Your father never loved me. You should not have had to know this. He did not love me.' She spoke each word with a terrible clarity, as if trying to burn it in my brain. I squeezed my eyes tight. Rigid in my bed, I waited for my mother to leave the room, wondering if I would get (11) all this with time.

(1) 下線部(1)の説明として最も適当なものはどれか。次のうちから１つ選び，その記号を記せ。

ア 母親は料理の知識が不足しているという落胆を表している。

イ 母親は驚いていないのではないかという懸念を表している。

ウ 母親は自分の質問を理解できないという失望を表している。

エ 母親だけでは家の管理ができないという不安を表している。

(2) 下線部(2)に示される語り手の気持ちの説明として最も適当なものはどれか。次のうちから１つ選び，その記号を記せ。

ア I was still in the depths of depression.

イ I suddenly realised how defenceless she was.

— 285 —

2000 年 入試問題

ウ My mother's arms felt heavy on my shoulders.

エ I suddenly felt that things were too much to bear.

(3) 空所(3)に入れるのに最も適当な語はどれか。次のうちから1つ選び，その記号を記せ。

ア close イ decorate ウ keep エ let

(4) 空所(4)に入れるのに最も適当な語はどれか。次のうちから1つ選び，その記号を記せ。

ア anything イ everything ウ nothing エ something

(5) 空所(5)に入れるのに最も適当な語はどれか。次のうちから1つ選び，その記号を記せ。

ア down イ in ウ out エ over

(6) 下線部(6)の意味に最も近いものはどれか。次のうちから1つ選び，その記号を記せ。

ア I didn't know why she spoke so softly.

イ I couldn't tell how she had changed her voice.

ウ The melody of her voice made it difficult to understand.

エ There was something unfamiliar about the way she spoke.

(7) 下線部(7)の意味に最も近いものはどれか。次のうちから1つ選び，その記号を記せ。

ア She wasn't holding out her hands.

イ Nothing was missing from the house.

ウ I couldn't tell anything from her face.

エ The situation was completely under her control.

— 286 —

2000 年　　入試問題

(8) 下線部(8)を和訳せよ。

(9) 空所(9)に入れるのに最も適当な語はどれか。次のうちから 1 つ選び，その記号を記せ。

　ア　direction　　イ　humour　　ウ　purpose　　エ　unease

(10) 下線部(10)の解釈として最もふさわしくないものはどれか。次のうちから 1 つ選び，その記号を記せ。

　ア　I was about to cry.

　イ　I was about to speak to her.

　ウ　I was about to open my eyes.

　エ　I was about to admit that I was awake.

(11) 空所(11)に入れるのに最も適当な語はどれか。次のうちから 1 つ選び，その記号を記せ。

　ア　at　　　　　イ　in　　　　　ウ　on　　　　　エ　over

— 287 —

入試問題

解答時間：120 分
配　　点：120 点

1 (A)　次の英文を読み，「オーラル・ヒストリー」の特徴と影響を 100 ～ 120 字の
日本語に要約せよ。句読点も字数に含める。

　　　In the second half of the twentieth century, oral history has had
a significant impact upon contemporary history as practised in many
countries.　While interviews with members of social and political elites have
expanded the range of existing documentary sources, the most distinctive
contribution of oral history is that it includes within the historical record
the experiences and perspectives of groups of people who might otherwise
have been 'hidden from history'.　Although such people may in the past
have been written about by social observers or in official documents,
their own voices have only rarely been preserved — usually in the form
of personal papers or pieces of autobiographical writing.　Through oral
history interviews, working-class men and women, and members of cultural
minorities, among others, have added their experiences to the historical
record, and offered their own interpretations of history.　Moreover,
interviews have documented particular aspects of historical experience
which tend to be missing from other sources, such as personal relations,
domestic work or family life, and they have resonated with the subjective or
personal meanings of lived experience.

　　　Oral history has challenged the historical enterprise in other ways.　Oral
historians have had to develop skills required for the creation of recorded
interviews, and to learn from different academic fields — including
sociology, anthropology, psychology and linguistics — to better understand
the narratives of memory.　Most significantly, oral history is based on an

－ 290 －

1999年　入試問題

active human relationship between historians and their sources, which can transform the practice of history in several ways. The narrator not only recalls the past but also asserts his or her interpretation of that past; and thus, in participatory oral history projects, the interviewee can be a historian as well as the source. Moreover, for some who practise it, oral history has gone beyond just making histories. In certain projects a primary aim has been the empowerment of individuals or social groups through the process of remembering and reinterpreting the past.

(B)　次の英文の下線部を和訳せよ。

He had crossed the main road one morning and was descending a short street when Kate Caldwell came out of a narrow side street in front of him and walked toward school, her schoolbag bumping at her hip. He followed excitedly, meaning to overtake but lacking the courage. What could he say to her? He imagined his stammering voice saying dull, awkward things about lessons and the weather and could only imagine her saying conventional things in response. Why didn't she turn and smile and call to him, saying, "Don't you like my company?" If she did, he would smile faintly and approach with eyebrows questioningly raised. But she did nothing. She made not even the merest gesture.

2 (A)　A大学では，カリキュラムの一環として，ボランティア活動への参加をとりいれている。あなたがA大学に入学して，何らかのボランティア活動を行うとすれば，どのような活動に参加したいか，それはなぜかを 40 ～ 50 語程度の英語で述べよ。文の数に制限はない。（内容よりも作文能力を問う問題であることに注意せよ。）

－ 291 －

<u>1999 年　　入試問題</u>

(B)　次の英文において，前後がつながるようにするには下線部(1)～(3)にどのような英文を入れればよいか。話の流れを考えて，適切な英文を，それぞれ5～10語程度で書け。

Maiko and Yuriko have just watched their friend Kazuko lose a tennis match. Maiko is surprised by the match results, whereas Yuriko isn't. On their way home they are discussing their different opinions.

Maiko : "Too bad Kazuko lost. Normally she's an excellent player, but today (1) _____."

Yuriko : "Oh, I don't think that's the real reason she lost. Just last month (2) _____.

So (3) _____.

And, of course, if a tennis player doesn't do that, she's in trouble."

4　次の各文には，それぞれ1つずつ，文法的な誤りがある。文法的な誤りを含んでいるのはどの部分か。その部分の番号を記せ。

(A)　One　way　to deal with　the　problems　were　to be　suggested by
　　(1)　(2)　(3)　　　　(4)　(5)　　　　(6)　(7)　(8)
　　the　committee.
　　(9)　(10)

(B)　I would　appreciate very much　if　you could　show me　how　to
　　(1)　(2)　　　　　　(3)　(4)　　　　(5)　　　(6)　(7)
　　put　the machine　back together.
　　(8)　(9)　　　　(10)

(C)　By　the time　the messenger　arrives,　the gate　will　have been
　　(1)　(2)　　　(3)　　　　(4)　　　(5)　　(6)　(7)
　　opened　to let　in him.
　　(8)　(9)　　(10)

— 292 —

<u>1999 年　　入試問題</u>

(D)　Everyone　who　saw them work　was amazed by　their ability　of
　　(1)　　　　(2)　　(3)　　　　　　(4)　　　　　　(5)　　　　　　(6)
using　so many　different kinds　of machines　at once.
(7)　　(8)　　　　　　　(9)　　　　　(10)

(E)　For　those of you　who don't　exercise regularly,　it will probably be
　　(1)　(2)　　　　(3)　　　(4)　　　　　　　(5)
extremely difficult　to　keep to run　for　more than 30 minutes.
(6)　　　　　　(7)　(8)　　　　(9)　(10)

(F)　I don't think　Mary could have been　the one　who somehow
　　(1)　　　　　(2)　　　　　　　　(3)　　　(4)
managed　to　put out the fire,　although　she is possible to　have called
(5)　　(6)　　　　　　　(7)　　　　　(8)　　　　　　(9)
the fire department.
(10)

5　次の英文は，有害物質の流出事故による環境被害を論じた新聞記事の一部である。
これを読んで，下の設問に答えよ。（便宜上，段落ごとに番号を付してある。）解答
は解答用紙の所定欄に記せ。

(1)　A spillage of poisonous waste in one of the most environmentally
sensitive areas on earth is threatening the wildlife of two continents. The
area affected is the Doñana National Park, which consists of marshlands
stretching for about 100 kilometers southwards to the sea from the
southern Spanish city of Seville.

(2)　The Doñana is an exceptionally important place for wildlife. Many
species of birds which spend the summer in the north of Europe, especially
in Scandinavia, come to these wetlands and stay from early autumn to early
spring to escape the bitter cold of the northern winter. The park is also one
of the last places where the rare Iberian imperial eagle can be found. In
addition to this, the park and its surroundings form the main resting place
for the many species of birds which pass through Spain as they migrate
each year between southern Africa and countries in northern Europe such
as Britain.

— 293 —

<u>1999 年　入試問題</u>

(3)　Disaster struck in the early hours of April 25 when the dam wall of a waste reservoir collapsed at a mining plant northwest of Seville. About 158,000 tons of waste, including heavy metals and other toxic material, were sent down the River Guadiamar towards the park.

(4)　But the event vanished from the front pages of newspapers within about a week, partly because the waste did not affect Seville itself (the Guadiamar flows some distance west of the city), and partly because the poisonous grey mud was, for the most part, blocked before reaching the heart of the Doñana. Only 3 per cent of the surface of the national park was covered. But the effects of the disaster are penetrating every aspect of life in southern Spain.

(5)　Some effects are relatively small. For example, pilgrims travelling in traditional covered wagons or on horseback from Seville for this month's annual midsummer festival at the town of El Rocio were warned not to take their usual route across the Guadiamar. Instead they had to take the main road to avoid the layer of toxic waste which still covers the banks of the river.

(6)　This waste is currently being removed, and the official agency in charge of the clean-up estimates that, at the present rate of slightly under 10,000 cubic meters per day, it can remove the last waste from the surface by October 27.

(7)　But Britain's Royal Society for the Protection of Birds estimates it could take as much as twenty-five years for the area to recover. A spokesman said: "We fear this will turn out to be the worst environmental disaster of its kind in Europe this century."

(8)

(9)　Despite the huge scale of the disaster, however, some experts remain

— 294 —

1999年　入試問題

unalarmed. The park's director believes that "the chances of wide-spread dangerous effects are small, if everything continues as it has done so far." But he is now in a minority. Spain's notoriously divided environmental pressure groups have joined in a declaration that the situation, because of its unusual nature, is much worse than is claimed by the regional and national authorities; the disaster, they say, is full of the potential for delayed effects.

(10)

(11) The animals and birds and fish that died as the poisonous tide poured down the Guadiamar are therefore likely to be no more than a small part of the eventual total number of deaths caused by the disaster. For the poisons have only just started to pass upwards through the food chain. The birds — such as terns, grebes and cormorants — that come to the area to feed on its fish and shellfish are particularly at risk.

(12)

(13) In the meantime, the metals in the mud — zinc, lead, copper and silver — will be seeping into the soil, creating a hidden danger for humans. According to Spain's Young Farmers' Association, several hundred acres of land growing crops for human consumption have been dangerously affected: although they were not covered by the waste, they use water from wells which may have been polluted.

(14) What would turn the disaster into a catastrophe would be if the heavy metals in the waste were to penetrate the aquifer under the park. Aquifer 27, as it is called, is up to 200 metres deep, and covers 5,200 square kilometres, and the well-being of the whole area depends on this huge

1999年　入試問題

underground lake.

(15) Initial tests suggest the poisons have not penetrated it. But nobody can be certain. As the head of Spain's Science Research Council remarked: "The fact that the first analyses indicate that the aquifer has not been polluted does not mean that one day it will not be."

(1) 上の英文には，第8段落，第10段落，第12段落が抜けている。それぞれ の空所を埋めるのに最もふさわしいと思われる文章を次のうちから1つ選び， その記号を記せ。

ア　At the moment, the number of birds in the park is rather small. Many birds had just left southern Spain to spend the spring and summer in northern Europe when the spillage took place. But, starting probably with the grey heron, they will begin returning in August. And not even the authorities are expecting the mud to be removed by then.

イ　"Heavy metals have a feature which is not noticeable at first," says a scientist who works with Spain's Association for the Defence of Nature. "They get into the body and slowly cause problems of many kinds. They affect growth, sexual development, the brain, and the immune system. They can also cause certain cancers."

ウ　He pointed out that the weight of the toxic material which poured out of the damaged reservoir at the mine was almost four times as great as that released in the Exxon Valdez oil tanker disaster of 1989, an accident that is widely regarded as having been the world's worst single incident of this type.

— 296 —

1999年　　入試問題

エ　The spokesman said that, in addition to its importance for wildlife, the area around Seville has a long history and rich cultural traditions; the religious festival at nearby El Rocio is just one example of this. The effect of the disaster on such traditions, he said, is very regrettable.

(2) 本文中, "poisonous"と同じ意味で何度か用いられている形容詞を1つ抜き出して記せ。

(3) 第2段落は, ドニャーナ国立公園が野鳥にとって大事な場所である理由をいくつか挙げている。次のうち, 理由として挙げられていないものはどれか。1つ選び, その記号を記せ。

　　ア　Birds come from Africa to pass the winter there.
　　イ　Birds which are making long journeys rest there.
　　ウ　Many Scandinavian birds spend the winter there.
　　エ　A rare kind of bird lives there.

(4) 次の地図のうち, 事故に関連する地域の位置関係を正しく記したものはどれか。1つ選び, その記号を記せ。（地図は, 上が北を指すものとする。）

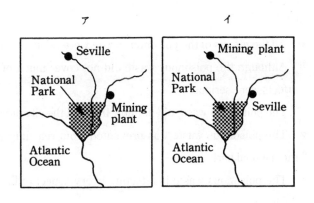

— 297 —

1999年　入試問題

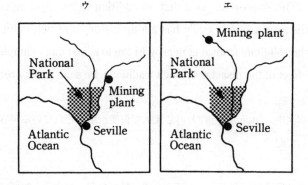

(5) この災害が重大ニュースとして扱われたのは、どのくらいの間であったか。また、それはどのような理由によるものか。次のア〜エの中から期間を1つ選び、その記号を記せ。さらに、オ〜ケの中から理由として正しいものを2つ選び、その記号を記せ。

〔期間〕

　ア　for only a day
　イ　for only a short time
　ウ　for about a month
　エ　for a long time

〔理由〕

　オ　All the effects of the poisonous waste were relatively small.
　カ　Although the poisonous waste did not cover much of the park, its effects were serious.
　キ　The poisonous waste did not flow through the city of Seville.
　ク　The poisonous waste was prevented from reaching the centre of the national park.
　ケ　The poisonous waste is affecting every aspect of life in southern Spain.

<u>1999 年　　入試問題</u>

(6) 第9段落によると，スペインの環境保護団体は互いにどのような関係にある
か。次のうちから1つ選び，その記号を記せ。

　ア　They usually agree with each other, and they agree about this
　　　disaster.
　イ　They usually agree with each other, but they don't agree about this
　　　disaster.
　ウ　They usually don't agree with each other, and they don't agree about
　　　this disaster.
　エ　They usually don't agree with each other, but they agree about this
　　　disaster.

(7) 第14，15段落の中で用いられている "aquifer" という単語は，そのいずれ
かの段落中において別の表現で言い換えられている。2語からなるその表現を
抜き出して記せ。

(8) 次の人たちの中で，事故の被害を最も楽観視していたのは誰か。1つ選び，
その記号を記せ。

　ア　the spokesman for the Royal Society for the Protections of Birds
　イ　the director of the Doñana National Park
　ウ　the members of Spain's environmental pressure groups
　エ　the members of the Spanish Young Farmers' Association

(9) 記事によると，次のうち，(a)最も軽い（あるいは，軽いと予測される）被
害，そして(b)最も深刻な（あるいは，深刻であると予測される）被害はどれか。
それぞれ1つ選び，その記号を記せ。

－ 299 －

<u>1999 年　　入試問題</u>

ア　People were unable to take their traditional route to a festival.

イ　Many creatures died when the poisonous waste came down the river.

ウ　Some water which is used by farmers has probably been polluted.

エ　The aquifer under the park may be polluted in the future.

入試問題

解答時間：120 分
配　　点：120 点

1 (A)　次の英文の内容を 80 〜 100 字の日本語に要約せよ。句読点も字数に含める。

What is the best way to protect the environment? Basically, there are two groups who give two different answers to this question. The answers they give depend on how they think the worth of nature can be determined. One group insist that the value of an untouched rain-forest, for example, or of an unpolluted river, simply cannot be calculated in terms of money. Such things, they therefore argue, must be protected from any industrial or economic use. Thus, they think the best way of saving the environment is to pass strong laws against pollution and the unwise use of nature.

The other group, however, say that it is better to rely upon market forces to achieve the same goal. They believe that it *is* possible to calculate how much the environment is worth; for example, according to their figures, pollution costs Europe five per cent of its GNP. They think that this cost should be paid by those who cause the pollution. In other words, companies should be taxed according to how much pollution they cause, so that they will be encouraged to use cleaner technologies and make cleaner products. If they don't do this, they will go out of business, because if polluting products cost more, people will buy fewer of them. Pollution taxes of this kind would send a signal to industrialists and consumers that pollution does not make economic sense, while the prevention of pollution does.

<u>1998 年　　入試問題</u>

(B)　次の英文の下線部を和訳せよ。

　　One of the biggest problems with modern computers is that they follow all commands mechanically. <u>Computers do what they are told to do, whether we meant it or not. Moreover, they cannot turn themselves on, nor can they ever begin something entirely new on their own.</u>

2 (A)　次の英語で示された見解に対して，賛成，反対，いずれかの意見を英語で述べよ。賛成の場合は I agree with this idea で，反対の場合は I disagree with this idea で書き出し，その語句を含めて 40 ～ 50 語程度にまとめること。文はいくつに分けてもよい。(内容よりも作文能力を問う問題であることに注意せよ。)

　　Young people in Japan should have the right to vote in elections from the age of eighteen.

(B)　次の英文(a)(b)において，それぞれ前後がつながるようにするには下線部にどのような英文を入れればよいか。それぞれ話の流れを考えて，適切な英文を，(a)については 10 ～ 15 語程度，(b)については 5 ～ 10 語程度で書け。

(a)

　　Why do John and I prefer to live close to the center of the city, in spite of the noise and the other difficulties of living there? There are two reasons. First, living in the middle of the city puts us close to things we want. For example, there are department stores and movie theaters within walking distance of our house. _____

_____ . If we lived in the suburbs, it could take hours to go to and from work. Thanks

－ 303 －

1998 年　入試問題

to the location of our home, however, both of us spend less than twenty minutes going to the office.

(b)

　　We know that many animals are capable of trying to deceive. Konrad Lorenz, a famous scientist, told a story about Bully, his old dog whose eyesight had become bad. Bully sometimes mistakenly barked in an unfriendly way at Lorenz when he returned home. After realizing his mistake, Bully would rush past Lorenz and bark angrily at a neighbor's gate, as if _____

_____. This episode made Lorenz realize that human beings are not the only creatures that try to deceive.

4　次の英文の下線部(1)〜(6)には，それぞれ文法上，あるいは文脈上必要な語が1語欠けている。どこにどのような語を入れればよいか。その語が入るべき位置の直前にある語と，入れるべき語を書け。

（例）I went school yesterday.　　（答）

直前にある語	went
入れるべき語	to

　　The total population of the world is more than 5 billion.　No one knows the exact number, as it rising constantly. 　The population of the world is growing faster now ever before. 　The recent calculations of experts suggest will double within the next forty years. 　Moreover, the population of the world is spread evenly around the globe, and this unevenness in population density has also been increasing since 1950. 　Many of the most densely populated countries are Europe and Asia. 　In the Netherlands, is

(1) (2) (3) (4) (5) (6)

－ 304 －

1998年　入試問題

one of the most crowded areas, an average of 360 people live in each square kilometer of land. In contrast, Australia has an average of only two people per square kilometer.

5　次の英文を読み，以下の設問に答えよ。解答は解答用紙の所定欄に記せ。

Simple Peter was walking to work in the fields one morning when he met an old woman sitting beside the road.

'Good morning, old woman,' he said, 'why do you look so sad?'

'I have lost my ring,' said the old woman, 'and it is the only one like it in the whole world.'

'I will help you find it,' said Simple Peter, and he got down on his hands and knees to look for the old woman's ring.

Well, he hunted for a long time, until at last he found the ring under a leaf.

'Thank you,' said the old woman, and slipped the ring on to her finger. Then she took a mirror out of her apron and gave it to Peter, saying, 'Take this as a reward.'

'What do I need a mirror for?' asked Peter.

'That is no ordinary mirror,' replied the old woman. 'It is a magic mirror. Anyone who looks into it will see themselves not as they are, but as other people see them.'

Simple Peter held the mirror up to his face and peered into it. First he turned one way, then he turned the other. Finally, he shook his head and said, 'Well, it may be a magic mirror, but it's no good to me. I can't see myself in it at all.'

The old woman smiled and said, 'The mirror will never lie to you. It will show you a true reflection of yourself as other people see you.' And with

— 305 —

1998年　入試問題

that she touched her ring, and disappeared.

Well, Simple Peter stood there in great surprise for a long while, and then he looked in the mirror again, and (　　　1　　　) himself, even when he put his nose right up against it.

Just then a farmer came riding past. 'Excuse me,' said Simple Peter, 'but have you seen my reflection? I can't find it in this mirror.'

'Oh,' said the farmer, 'I saw it half an hour ago, running down the road.'

'Thank you,' said Peter, 'I'll (2) if I can catch it,' and he ran off down the road.

The farmer laughed and said to himself, 'That Simple Peter is <u>a real goose!</u>'₍₃₎ and he went on his way.

Simple Peter ran on and on until he came to the blacksmith.

'Where are you running so fast, Peter?' called the blacksmith.

'I'm trying to catch my reflection,' replied Peter. 'John the farmer said it ran this way. Did you see it?'

The blacksmith, who was a kind man, shook his head and said, 'John the farmer has been telling you (4). Your reflection can't run away from you. Look in the mirror, and you'll see it there all right.'

So Peter looked in the magic mirror, and do you know what he saw? He saw a goose, with a yellow beak and black eyes, staring straight back at him.

'There, do you see your reflection?' asked the blacksmith.

'I only see a goose,' said Peter, 'but *I'm* not a goose. I'll show you all! I'll seek my fortune, and then you'll see me as I really am!'

So Peter (　　　5　　　).

Before long, he met a woodcutter and his family with all their belongings on their backs coming down the road towards him.

'Where are you going?' he asked them.

— 306 —

<u>1998 年　入試問題</u>

'We're leaving this country,' said the woodcutter, 'because there's a dragon here. It's fifty times as big as a man and could eat you up in one mouthful. Now it has carried off the King's daughter and is going to eat her for supper tonight. So, if you're going in that direction, you'd better be careful.' And with that they hurried on their way.

Peter went on, and suddenly he heard a terrible sound. He looked round a rock and there he saw the dragon. (　6　) the woodcutter had said, it was fifty times as big as himself and it was sharpening its teeth with a stone.

'Oh ho! Are you the dragon?' asked Peter. The dragon stopped sharpening its teeth and looked with great fierce eyes at Peter.

'I am!' said the dragon.

'Then I shall have to kill you,' said Peter.

'*Indeed*?' said the dragon, breathing fire. 'And how are *you* going to kill *me*?'

And Peter said, 'Oh, *I'm* not, but behind this rock I have the most terrible creature, that is fifty times as big as you, and could eat *you* up in one mouthful!'

'Impossible!' roared the dragon, and leapt behind the rock. Now Peter, who was after all not so (　7　) despite his nickname, had hidden the magic mirror there, and so when the dragon came leaping round the rock <u>it came face to face with it, and there, for the first time, it saw itself as</u>₍₈₎ <u>it appeared to others</u> — fifty times as big and able to eat itself up in one mouthful! And then and there the dragon turned on its tail and ran off over the mountains as fast as it could, and was never seen again.

Then Peter went into the dragon's cave, and found the King's daughter, and carried her back to the palace. And the King gave him jewels and fine clothes and all the people cheered him. And when Peter looked in the

— 307 —

1998年　入試問題

magic mirror now, do you know what he saw? He saw himself as a brave, fierce lion, (9). But he said to himself, 'I'm not a lion! I'm Peter.'

Just then the Princess came by and Peter showed her the mirror and asked what she saw there.

'I see the most beautiful girl in the world,' said the Princess. 'But *I'm* not the most beautiful girl in the world.'

'But that's how you appear to me,' said Peter, and he told the Princess the whole story about how he had (10) the mirror, and how he had (11) the dragon.

'So you see, I'm not really a goose, and I'm not really as brave as a lion. I'm just Simple Peter.'

When the Princess heard his story, she began to like him for his honesty. Pretty soon she grew to love him, and the King agreed that they should be married, even though Peter was just a poor farmer's son.

'But, my dear!' said the Queen. 'People will (12) because he is not a real prince.'

'Nonsense!' replied the King. 'We'll make him into the finest prince you ever did see!' But the old Queen was right....

On the day of the wedding, Peter was dressed up in the finest clothes, trimmed with gold and fur. But when he looked in the magic mirror, do you know what he saw? Instead of a rich and magnificent prince, he saw himself in his own rags —— Simple Peter. But it didn't worry him. He smiled and said to himself, 'At last! Everyone sees me as I (13)!'

(1)　空所（　1　）を埋めるのに最も適当な語句を次のうちから選び，その記号を記せ。

— 308 —

1998 年　　入試問題

ア　eventually he began to see

イ　now he could no longer see

ウ　now he could see

エ　still he could not see

(2)　空所（　2　）を埋めるのに最も適当な語を次のうちから選び，その記号を記せ。

ア　go　　　　イ　know　　　ウ　run　　　エ　see

(3)　文脈から判断して，下線部(3)の語句にはどのようなニュアンスが伴っていると考えられるか。最も適当なものを次のうちから選び，その記号を記せ。

ア　clever　　　イ　evil　　　ウ　fast　　　エ　stupid

(4)　空所（　4　）を埋めるのに最も適当な語を次のうちから選び，その記号を記せ。

ア　facts　　　イ　news　　　ウ　rumours　　エ　stories

(5)　空所（　5　）を埋めるのに最も適当な語句を次のうちから選び，その記号を記せ。

ア　began to see himself as he really was

イ　decided not to look like a goose

ウ　made up his mind to get rid of the mirror

エ　set off to seek his fortune

(6)　空所（　6　）を埋めるのに最も適当な語句を次のうちから選び，その記号を記せ。

ア　Just as　　　イ　Just that　　ウ　Such as　　　エ　Such that

(7)　空所（　7　）を埋めるのに最も適当な英語 1 語を記せ。

— 309 —

1998年　入試問題

(8)　下線部(8)に出てくる4つの it のうち，指すものが違うものが1つだけある。その it が何番目に出てくるかを数字で記し，さらに，それが指しているものを文中から選び，定冠詞（the）に続けて英語で記せ。

(9)　空所（　9　）に入れて意味が正しく通るよう，下の語を並べ替えよ。
　　　else　everyone　him　how　saw　was　which

(10)　空所（　10　）を埋めるのに最も適当な語を次のうちから選び，その記号を記せ。
　　ア　changed　　イ　found　　ウ　got　　　　エ　wanted

(11)　空所（　11　）を埋めるのに最も適当な語を次のうちから選び，その記号を記せ。
　　ア　attacked　　イ　burnt　　ウ　killed　　　エ　tricked

(12)　空所（　12　）を埋めるのに最も適当な語句を次のうちから選び，その記号を記せ。
　　ア　ignore us　　イ　laugh at us　ウ　look back at us　　エ　respect us

(13)　空所（　13　）を埋めるのに最も適当な英語2語を記せ。

(14)　この物語の登場人物のうち，次の描写にそれぞれ最も当てはまる人物は誰か。文中の語句を用いて，定冠詞（the）に続けて英語で記せ。
　a　The person who is worried about Peter's social position.
　b　The person who makes fun of Peter.
　c　The person who warns Peter about a danger.

— 310 —

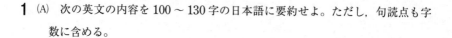

1 (A) 次の英文の内容を 100 ～ 130 字の日本語に要約せよ。ただし，句読点も字数に含める。

　　Until a few years ago, the common idea among archaeologists was that early human beings began to practice farming because they had no choice. Experts claimed that population growth led people to push some of their group members out of the most productive areas where it was easy to hunt and gather plenty of food from the wild.

　　Living on the poorer edges of the rich environments, according to the old thinking, these people noticed that seeds of gathered wild plants often began to grow where they had been thrown away or accidentally dropped. They then realized that planting crops intentionally in these poor areas provided a more plentiful and reliable source of food than hunting and collecting wild plants that could be eaten. As a result, according to the traditional idea, temporary camps in the poor areas developed into permanent settlements. Recent research, however, suggests it didn't happen quite that way.

　　Archaeologists now think that agriculture might not have begun just by accident. Instead, it might have begun because early humans did some scientific research. They say that because ancient peoples had experienced occasional bad years when wild foods were not easily available, people thought they should look for ways of making sure they always had enough food. So they experimented with particular wild plants, and eventually chose to grow the ones that seemed the best. Archaeologists say now that necessity was not necessarily the mother of the invention of agriculture.

1997 年　　入試問題

Instead, human creative ability was.

（注）　archaeologist：考古学者

(B)　次の英文を読んで，下線部(1)(2)の it の内容をそれぞれ 20 〜 30 字の日本語
で説明せよ。ただし，句読点も字数に含める。

　　When I came back to Malaysia after ten years in a foreign country,
I made a conscious attempt to regain my lost cultural self.　Being a
professional writer, my particular way of doing this was to try to involve
myself once again as deeply as possible with my mother tongue.　But, as
anyone who has gone through　it knows, such attempts, whether they
focus on language or not, can at best be only partly successful.　So was
mine —— and I don't regret　it.　To tell the truth, I didn't want to recover my
original cultural identity in its fullness and purity.

— 313 —

1997年　　入試問題

2 (A) 次の4コマ漫画がつじつまの合った話になるように2, 3, 4コマ目の展開を考え，次ページの1コマ目の説明文にならって2, 3, 4コマ目に対応する説明文をそれぞれ1文の英語で書け。

注意1　吹き出しの中に入れるべき台詞そのものを書くのではない。
注意2　1コマ目の説明文同様，直接話法を用いないこと。

1

2

3　　　　　　　　　　　4

1997年　入試問題

1 ： Susan's father was reading a newspaper when he noticed her happily getting ready to go out, so he asked her where she was going.

2 ： _____

_____

3 ： _____

_____

4 ： _____

_____

(B)　次の英文(a)(b)において，それぞれ前後がつながるようにするには下線部にどのような文を入れればよいか。それぞれ全体の内容を考えて，適切な英文1文を 8 ～ 15 語で書け。

(a)

In this country, traditionally people spent Saturday nights dining out and Sunday nights at home in front of the TV cheering on their favorite football team.　But a few years ago games began appearing on TV on Saturdays as well as on Sundays. _____

_____ . This is why restaurant owners have decided to boycott products advertised during televised matches.

(b)

Today, an average American home is full of labor-saving devices like washing machines and dishwashers. _____

_____ . Thus, average homemakers spend as much time doing housework now as fifty years ago — about fifty-two hours a

— 315 —

<u>1997 年　　入試問題</u>

week. Although they have the benefit of countless devices, they now have larger houses to clean, higher standards of cleanliness, and more wide-ranging life-styles, all of which keep them busy.

4 (A)　次の英文の下線部を和訳せよ。

Who ever reads a newspaper from cover to cover?　Clearly almost nobody. There isn't time in a busy day, and not all the articles are equally interesting. <u>All readers have their own personal tastes and purposes for reading, which cause them to turn immediately to whichever sections interest them, and to ignore the rest.</u>　Thus, most of the paper remains unread, yet you still have to buy all of it.

(B)　次の日本語の文章の下線部を英語に訳せ。

　人類には，おそらく，生活のなかに多少の閑の時間を見出した前史時代から，生まれながらの顔に対して化粧をほどこすという風習があった。<u>これは，他のいかなる動物にも見られないことである。二本足で立って歩くとか，言語を話すというのと同じような，基本的な人類の特徴だろう。</u>

(C)　次の英文の下線部(1)〜(5)には，取り除かなければならない語がそれぞれ1語ある。その語を記せ。

　（例）　<u>I saw him an yesterday.</u>　　（答）　an

　People have imagined ghosts since ancient times.　<u>They believe that when our bodies die, our spirits live on it.</u> Some spirits are happy in the
(1)
spirit world. But others are restless.　<u>They miss their former human</u>
(2)

— 316 —

1997 年　　入試問題

life, and keep coming back to the places where they were used to live.
Most ghosts are sad and quiet and make no trouble. <u>But among others,
especially the ghosts of murderers or criminals, are miserable.</u>₍₃₎ <u>They
terrify any more human being who sees them.</u>₍₄₎ In some parts of the world,
people go to church on a certain day and pray for dead people to lie quietly
in their graves. <u>Unless these prayers are said, people never believe, the
dead will rise up and try to revisit their former homes.</u>₍₅₎

5 次の英文を読み，以下の設問に答えよ。

As soon as he saw Benjie, Ezzie got up and said, 'Hey, what happened?
Where'd you go after school?'

Benjie said, 'Hammerman's after me.'

Ezzie's pink mouth formed a perfect O. He didn't say anything, but
his breath came out in a long sympathetic sigh. Finally he said, 'Marv
Hammerman?' even though he knew there was only one Hammerman in
the world, just as there had been only one Hitler.

'Yes.'

'Is after you?'

Benjie nodded, sunk in misery. He could see Marv Hammerman. He
came up in Benjie's mind ＿＿＿ monsters do in horror movies, big and
powerful, with the same cold, unreal eyes. It was the eyes Benjie really
feared. One look from those eyes, and you knew you were his next victim.

'What did you do?' Ezzie asked. 'Or did you do anything?'

At least, Benjie thought, Ezzie understood that. If you were Marv
Hammerman, you didn't need <u>a reason</u>.₍₂₎ He sat down on the steps and
looked down at his feet. 'I did something,' he said.

'What?' Ezzie asked. 'What'd you do? You bump into him or

— 317 —

1997 年　入試問題

something?'

Benjie shook his head.

'Well, what?'

Benjie said, 'You know that big chart in the upstairs hall at school?'

'What'd you say? _____, Benjie. You're muttering.' Ezzie bent
(3)
closer. 'Look at me. Now what did you say?'

Benjie looked up, and said, 'You know that big chart outside the history
room? In the hall?'

'Chart?' Ezzie said blankly. 'What chart, Benjie?'

'This chart takes up the whole wall, Ez, how could you _____ it?
(4)
It's a chart about early people, and it shows human progress up from the
apes, the side view of all those different kinds of prehistoric people, like
Cro-Magnon man and *Pithecanthropus*. That chart.'

'Oh, yeah, I saw it. So?'

Benjie could see that Ezzie _____ the good part, the violence.
(5)
His shoulders dropped. He wet his lips. He said, 'Well, when I was passing
this chart on my way out of history — and I don't know why I did this — I
really don't. When I was passing this chart, Ez, on my way to math —' He
swallowed several times. 'When I was passing this chart, I took my pencil
and I wrote Marv Hammerman's name on the bottom of the chart and then
I drew an arrow to the picture of Neanderthal man.'

'What?' Ezzie cried. 'What?' He could not seem to take it in. Benjie
(6a)
knew that Ezzie had been prepared to sympathize with an accident. He had
(6b)
almost been the victim of one of those himself. One day at school Ezzie
had reached for the handle on the water fountain a second ahead of Marv
Hammerman. If Ezzie hadn't glanced up just in time, seen Hammerman
and said quickly, '_____ ahead, I'm not thirsty,' then this unhappy figure
(7)
on the steps might be him. 'What did you do it for, Benjie?'
(6c)

'I don't know.'

— 318 —

1997年　入試問題

'You crazy or something?'

'I don't know.'

'Marv Hammerman!' Ezzie sighed. It was a sorrowful sound.
'<u>Anybody else in the school would have been better.</u> I would rather have
(8)
the principal after me than Marv Hammerman.'

'I _____.'
　(9)

'Maybe Hammerman doesn't know you did it though,' Ezzie said. 'Did
you ever think of that? I mean, who's going to go up to Hammerman and
say his name is on the prehistoric chart?' Ezzie leaned forward. *'Hey,
Hammerman,'* he said, imitating the imaginary fool, *'I saw a funny thing
about you on the prehistoric chart!* Now, <u>who in their right mind is going</u>
(10)
to —'

'He was <u>right</u> behind me when I did it,' Benjie said.
　　　　(11)
'What?'

'He was right behind me,' Benjie said stiffly. He could remember
turning around and looking into Hammerman's eyes. It was such a strange,
troubling moment that Benjie was unable to think about it.

(1)　下線部(1)に入れて意味が通る語句を次のうちから<u>すべて</u>選び，その記号を
　　記せ。

　　ア　as　　　　　イ　how　　　　ウ　just　　　　エ　the way

(2)　下線部(2)の a reason とは，誰が何をする理由か。日本語で述べよ。

(3)　下線部(3)を埋めるのに最も適当な文は，次のうちのどれか。その記号を記せ。

　　ア　I can't even see you

　　イ　I can't even hear you

　　ウ　I'm not even looking at you

　　エ　I'm not even listening to you

1997 年　入試問題

(4) 下線部(4)を埋めるのに最も適当な語は, 次のうちのどれか。その記号を記せ。

　ア lose　　　イ miss　　　ウ notice　　　エ view

(5) 下線部(5)の埋めるのに, 最もふさわしいように次の語を並べかえよ。与えられた単語はすべて, それぞれ一度ずつ使うこと。

　eager　for　get　him　on　to　to　was

(6) 下線部 (6a), (6b), (6c) は, Ezzie, Hammerman, Benjie のうちの誰を指すか。Ezzie を指すものは E, Hammerman を指すものは H, Benjie を指すものは B と記せ。

(7) 下線部(7)を埋めるのに, 次のうちのどれか。その記号を記せ。

　ア be　　　イ go　　　ウ look　　　エ make　　　オ see

(8) 下線部(8)の内容に最も近いものは, 次のうちどれか。その記号を記せ。

　ア　Somebody else should be chased by Hammerman.

　イ　Chasing Hammerman is as bad as chasing the principal.

　ウ　Hammerman is the worst person in school that can be after you.

　エ　You are the worst person in school for Hammerman to be after.

(9) 下線部(9)を埋めるのに最も適当な語は, 次のうちのどれか。その記号を記せ。

　ア do　　　イ know　　　ウ see　　　エ think

(10) 下線部(10)で, going to のあとを次のような形で補うとすれば, 空所にどのような語を入れればよいか。最も適当な英語1語を記せ。

　who in their right mind is going to (　　　) him that?

— 320 —

<u>1997 年　　入試問題</u>

⑾　下線部⑾の right に最も近い意味の right を含む文は，次のうちどれか。そ
の記号を記せ。

ア　Did I do it right this time?

イ　His turn came right after mine.

ウ　Turn right at the next traffic light.

エ　Now it's impossible to put things right.

1 (A) 次の英文の内容を 80 字～ 100 字の日本語に要約せよ。ただし，句読点も字数に含める。

From the outset, our civilisation has been structured in large part around the concept of work. But now, for the first time in history, human labour is being systematically eliminated from the economic process, and, in the coming century, employment as we have come to know it is likely to disappear. The introduction of a new generation of advanced information and communication technologies, together with new forms of business organisation and management, is forcing millions of workers into temporary jobs and unemployment lines. While unemployment is still relatively low, it can be expected to climb continuously over the coming decades as the global economy fully enters the Information Age. We are in the early stages of a long-term shift from mass labour to highly skilled "elite labour", accompanied by increasing automation in the production of goods and the delivery of services. Factories and companies without a workforce are beginning to appear. These developments, however, do not necessarily mean a dark future. The gains from this new technological revolution could be shared broadly among all the people, by greatly reducing the working week and creating new opportunities to work on socially useful projects outside the market economy.

— 324 —

<u>1996 年　　入試問題</u>

(B)　次の英文を読んで，空所（　1　）〜（　8　）に補うべき最も適当な語を
　　下の語群から選び，必要があれば語形を変化させて，解答用紙の所定欄に記せ。

　　Most children enjoy hearing a good story over and over again.　That's
the way it has always been.　The problem is that most grown-ups don't enjoy
telling the story as often as children like hearing it.　Sometimes, just to
（　1　）from being bored or to tease, a parent or grandparent will change
the words.

　　That became a little game between my children and myself when they
were little and constantly（　2　）for the same tale.　I would get into the
story and then pretend to be confused about various details.　The children,
in turn, would pretend to be angry that I could be so stupid.

　　Then, one day, I was reading a magazine and found a story about a
grandfather who did the same thing I did while telling the story of Little
Red Riding Hood to his grandchild.

GRANDFATHER：Once upon a time there was a little girl called Little
　　Green Riding Hood.

CHILD：No! *Red* Riding Hood!

GRANDFATHER：Oh, yes, of course, Red Riding Hood.　Well, one day her
　　mother called and said: "Little Green Riding Hood —"

CHILD：Red!

GRANDFATHER：Sorry! Red.　"Now, my child, go to Aunt May and take
　　her these potatoes."

CHILD：No! It doesn't（　3　）like that!　"Go to Grandma and take her
　　these cakes."

GRANDFATHER：All right!　So the little girl went off and in the wood she
　　met a giraffe.

CHILD：What a mess you are（　4　）of it!　It was a wolf!

－ 325 －

1996年　入試問題

GRANDFATHER : And the wolf said, "What's six times eight?"

CHILD : No! No! The wolf asked her where she was going.

GRANDFATHER : So he (　5　). And Little Black Riding Hood replied —

CHILD : Red! Red! Red!

GRANDFATHER : She replied: "I'm going to the market to buy some tomatoes."

CHILD : No, she didn't. She said: "I'm going to see my grandma, who is sick, but I've (　6　) my way."

GRANDFATHER : Of course! And this is what the wolf said: "Take the 75 bus, get out at the main square, turn right, and at the first doorway you'll find three steps. (　7　) up the coin you'll find lying on them, and buy yourself a packet of chewing gum."

CHILD : Grandpa, you're terribly bad at telling stories. You get them all wrong. But all the same, I wouldn't (　8　) some chewing gum.

GRANDFATHER : All right. Here's some money, then. Run along, now.

(注)　Little Red Riding Hood：赤ずきんちゃん

語群：　　ask　　be　　do　　get　　go　　have
　　　　　keep　know　lose　make　mind　pick

2 (A)　次の日本語の文章を読み，英文の手紙の空所(1)と(2)に，それぞれ与えられた条件をみたす英文を作成し，手紙を完成せよ。各空所はそれぞれ20 ～ 30語程度とするが，いくつの文で構成してもよい。

1996年　入試問題

純は今年の夏休みに，ロンドンから電車で1時間ほどのレスター
(Leicester) にあるレスター大学で，2週間の語学研修を受けることになっ
た。そこで純はスーザンに手紙を書こうとしている。スーザンは，以前純の
家にホームステイしたことがあり，現在ロンドンに住んでいる。純はロンド
ンのヒースロウ (Heathrow) 空港に8月2日（金）午後3時半に到着する。
レスターには8月4日（日）午後4時までに到着しなければならない。

---

(1) の条件　イギリスでの日程を知らせる。

(2) の条件　次の2点を丁寧な表現でたずねる。

　　㋐　空港に迎えに来てもらえるか。

　　㋑　レスターに行く前にスーザンの家に泊めてもらえるか。

July 3

Dear Susan,

　　Thank you for your last letter. I'm glad you're well, and it was good
to hear all your news. My big news is that the details of my two-week
language course in England have at last been fixed!

(1) _____

_____

(2) _____

_____

　　I hope to have the chance to meet you and your family, and I'm
very excited about the whole trip; it will be the first time I've travelled
outside Japan. Please give my best wishes to your parents and your
brother.

1996年　入試問題

> See you soon!
>
> Best wishes,
>
> 　　Jun

(B)　次の日本文(1)と(2)の下線部を英語に訳せ。

(1)　生きているうちは，特別に重んじもせず，大切にもしなかったのであるが，<u>彼女が死んでみてはじめて，やはりいい人だったと気がついた。もう少し親切にしてあげるのだった，と私は心から思った。</u>

(2)　あるアメリカ人の日本学者が言った。「日本人のふしぎなところは，いなかを一段下に見ることですね。<u>アメリカ人はニューヨークに住むよりも，いなかに住みたがります。日本人の場合，逆ではないでしょうか。</u>」

4　次の英文(A)(B)の下線部(1)(2)(3)を和訳せよ。

(A)　Fred and Ann were driving on the expressway to Minneapolis for Ann's health check-up. She was worried that she might have cancer, having read a lot about the disease in the newspaper, although the doctor in their hometown had told her she was all right. It was cold and raining, the traffic was terrible, huge trailers roared past them. Fred said, <u>"If it was up to me, I'd just as soon turn around and go home."</u>₍₁₎

It was the wrong thing to say, with Ann in the mood she was in. <u>But she had been expecting him to say it and had prepared a speech in her mind in case he did.</u>₍₂₎ "Well, of course. I'm sure you would rather turn around. You don't care. You don't care one tiny bit, and you never have, so I'm not surprised you don't now. You don't care if I live or die."

— 328 —

$$1996 \, 年 \quad 入試問題$$

(B) What are rights? If you ask ordinary people what exactly a right is, they'll probably be at a loss, and won't be able to give a clear answer. They may know what it is to violate someone's rights. They may also know what it is to have their own right to this or that denied or ignored by others. But what exactly is it that is being violated or wrongly denied? Is it something you acquire or something you inherit at birth?

5 次の英文を読み，以下の設問に答えよ。解答は解答用紙の所定欄に記せ。

Daguerreotypes are an early form of photographs. Paris street scenes, as they appear in those daguerreotypes, have an unreal quality about them. There are no people. Did the photographer wait until everybody was (1)? Did he or she snap the picture at dawn before anyone was up?

It took many minutes for these early cameras to take a picture, and during that time people would have come and gone, leaving not even a trace in the final print. What remained was only the solid, motionless part of the city. It probably did not strike these early photographers as strange that only permanent things appeared in the photograph; for them only the permanent was "real". Perhaps they would have found a modern photograph of a street scene unreal, with people caught in the middle of taking a step, or a child jumping rope miraculously suspended in the air, never to touch the ground again. On the other hand, it is equally possible that the modern photograph might have looked more real to them than their own, because even in their own time painters included people walking, and children playing, in their street scenes.

But whatever they might have felt, the "reality" of an image appears to be a matter of (3). The story is told about a man who approached Picasso after seeing *Les Demoiselles d'Avignon* and asked the artist, "Why

— 329 —

1996年　入試問題

don't you paint people the way they really look?" "Well," said Picasso, "how do they really look?" The man then took a photograph of his wife from his wallet. "Like this," he said Picasso looked at the picture; then, handing it back, he said, "She is small, isn't she? And flat."
(5)

Often we do not realize just how much information our brain has to add to a picture to make it a recognizable scene. The canvas by the American painter Mark Tansey, entitled *The Innocent Eye Test*, portrays a cow being shown a life-size painting of cows. A group of scientists is standing by, ready to record the cow's reaction. There doesn't seem to be any. The
(6)　　(7)
cow could be looking at a blank wall.

Neither the painting — the one that is hanging in the Metropolitan Museum of Art in New York — nor the painting within the painting is in full color. Instead, they are both the color of old photographs. This is to emphasize, no doubt, the fact that the "real" cow, the one being shown the image, is itself a painting, as flat and lifeless as the others. They are all painted, same size, same style, but we see one as a real cow, the others as a (　8　) of cows. The first cow is unimpressed. It has no concept of art, therefore it can't understand the painting.

(注)　*Les Demoiselles d'Avignon*：「アヴィニョンの娘たち」。ピカソの作品の題名。

(1)　空所（　1　）を埋めるのに最も適当な語句を次のうちから選び，その記号を記せ。

ア　empty

イ　in place

ウ　left

エ　out of the way

オ　turned off

— 330 —

<u>1996 年　　入試問題</u>

ア　きっと牛は塀ばかり眺めていたのだろう。

イ　牛の見ていた塀には何も描かれていなかった。

ウ　牛は絵の描かれた塀には興味を示さなかった。

エ　牛から見れば，絵も塀と変わりがなかった。

(8)　空所（　8　）を埋めるのに最も適当な英語 1 語を記せ。

1996年　入試問題

(2)　もし初期の写真家たちが現代の写真を見たとしたら，かれらが示すであろう反応について，この文章の筆者の考えに一致するものを次のうちから2つ選び，その記号を記せ。

ア　They might find a modern photograph real because it looks like some paintings from their own time.

イ　A modern photograph might impress them as real, because only the permanent appears in it.

ウ　A modern photograph might look strange because nothing permanent appears in it.

エ　They might be surprised to find people in a modern photograph.

オ　They might find modern people's behavior strange.

(3)　空所（　3　）を埋めるのに最も適当な語は，次のうちのどれか。その記号を記せ。

ア　convention　イ　course　　ウ　fact　　　　エ　minutes

(4)　下線部(4)を和訳せよ。

(5)　下線部(5)でピカソが言いたかったことに最も近いものは，次のうちのどれか。その記号を記せ。

ア　Photography does not interest me because it is too realistic.

イ　Since your wife is not interesting enough, I don't want to paint her.

ウ　This picture of your wife is only one way of representing reality.

エ　Small, flat photographs can't compete with life-size paintings.

(6)　下線部(6)のあとに補うのに最も適当な英語1語を記せ。

(7)　下線部(7)の解釈として最も適当なものは，次のうちのどれか。その記号を記せ。

— 331 —

入試問題

解答時間：120分
配　　点：120点

1 (A)　次の英文の内容を 60 字～ 70 字の日本語に要約せよ。ただし，句読点も字数に数える。

　　Traditional grammar was developed on the basis of Greek and Latin, and it was subsequently applied, with minimal modifications and often uncritically, to the description of a large number of other languages.　But there are many languages which, in certain respects at least, are strikingly different in structure from Latin, Greek and the more familiar languages of Europe such as French, English and German.　One of the principal aims of modern linguistics has therefore been to construct a theory of grammar which is more general than the traditional theory — one that is appropriate for the description of all human languages and is not biased in favor of those languages which are similar in their grammatical structure to Greek and Latin.

(B)　次の文章の空欄に入れるべき適当な一節を，それぞれ下から選んで記号で答えよ。

　　I think it was Conrad Hilton who first had the idea that travel would be greatly improved if as much of it as possible were spent in familiar surroundings.　Faraway places with strange-sounding names are all very well, (　1　).　What the weary traveler needs after being up to his neck in foreigners all day is a drink with plenty of ice, a straightforward dinner menu that doesn't require an interpreter, a decent bathroom and a king-sized bed.　Just like home.

— 334 —

<u>1995 年　入試問題</u>

The Hilton theory was, as everyone knows, a worldwide success. And this was for one very simple reason: even if you didn't always know where you were, you always knew what to expect. There were no surprises. A few touches of local color would creep in from time to time — mangoes instead of orange juice, waitresses in sarongs instead of skirts — (　2　). There was a certain standardization about the board and lodging that provided comfort and reassurance and familiarity even in the heart of the most exotic locations.

If the idea had stopped there — as one among many travel options — it would have been fine. Unfortunately, it proved to be so popular that it was adopted by one hotel chain after another, with varying degrees of local camouflage designed to add personality to a multi-national formula. With loud protestations that they were preserving the special character of each hotel they bought up, the new owners standardized everything that could be standardized, from bathroom fittings to color schemes, (　3　).

(a)　but for the most part it didn't really matter whether you fell asleep in Tokyo or Mexico City

(b)　while a traveler feels it difficult to walk around a new city, unless he has made beforehand a special study of its history and geography

(c)　until the only sure way of knowing which city you were waking up in was to consult the phone directory as soon as you got out of bed

(d)　provided there are scrambled eggs for breakfast, air-conditioning, toilets that work, and people who speak English, even if they speak it with a curious accent

1995年　入試問題

2 (A)　次の英文中の空所(1)(2)に入れるべき英文を自由に創作せよ。各空所は30語 (words) 程度とするが，いくつの文 (sentences) で構成してもよい。全体が一貫した話となるように，前後関係をよく考えること。

Jackie could never decide what to do when it was raining. Stuck indoors all day, she had explored every room in the house except one — the one door she had never dared to open. She remembered what the old man had told her: "＿＿＿＿＿＿＿＿＿＿＿＿＿＿＿＿＿＿＿＿＿＿＿

(1)

＿＿＿＿＿＿＿＿＿＿＿＿＿＿＿＿＿＿＿＿＿＿＿＿＿＿＿＿＿＿＿

＿＿＿＿＿＿＿＿＿＿＿＿＿＿＿＿＿＿"

But Jackie was tired of sitting reading, and decided to find out for herself. Creeping up the stairs, she approached the door. Carefully she turned the handle, and the door swung open. Then she saw it.＿＿＿＿＿

(2)

＿＿＿＿＿＿＿＿＿＿＿＿＿＿＿＿＿＿＿＿＿＿＿＿＿＿＿＿＿＿＿

＿＿＿＿＿＿＿＿＿＿＿＿＿＿

(B)　次の日本文(1)と(2)の下線部を英語に訳せ。

(1)　たとえば今の小学生あたりに，昔は電気を使わない，木でできた冷蔵庫があったのだと言っても，たぶん信じないであろう。<u>電気も使わないでどうして冷えるんだ，と反論されてしまうに違いない。</u>

　　今の冷蔵庫は氷を作る。だが昔の冷蔵庫は氷を別に買い，その氷の冷たさで他の食品を低温冷蔵したのだ。大人ならみんな知っていることである。

(2)　われわれのまわりでは現在でも，苦しいことに耐える苦行としての意味を読書にもたせていることが少なくない。<u>苦労のある読書の方がぼんやり見ていられるテレビなどより価値があるにきまっている，</u>と考えるのである。

－ 336 －

1995 年　　入試問題

4 次の英文(A)(B)(C)の下線部を和訳せよ。

(A) Creative thinking may well mean simply the realization that there's no particular virtue in doing things the way they have always been done.

(B) Most of us feel intuitively that time goes on forever of its own accord, completely unaffected by anything else, so that if all activity were suddenly to cease time would still continue without any interruption. For many people the way in which we measure time by the clock and the calendar is absolute, and by some it has even been thought that to tamper with either was to court disaster.

(C) Before the sun was full up I went out into the yard and I was shocked to see Ritchie still squatting there reading in the flowerbed; I walked over and spoke to him. But he didn't so much as take his eyes off the book to look at me; you'd have thought he didn't hear me.

5 次の英文を読み，以下の設問に答えよ。解答は解答用紙の所定欄に記せ。

Equivocation means using words ambiguously. Often done with intent to deceive, it can even deceive the person who is using the expression. Equivocation occurs when words are used with more than one meaning, even though the soundness of the reasoning requires that the same use be kept throughout.

'Happiness is the end of life.
The end of life is death;
So happiness is death.'

— 337 —

1995 年　　入試問題

'Half a loaf is better than nothing.

(　3　) is better than good health;

So half a loaf is better than good health.'

Equivocal use of words is misleading because it invites us to transfer what is true of one concept onto another concept which happens to have the same name. Logic, which deals with the relationship between concepts, is useless if the concepts themselves change.

> 'Elephants are not found in Britain, so if you have one, don't lose it or you will never find again.'
>
> (The word 'found' represents two different concepts here.)

Many of the equivocal uses are easy to spot. Many more of them are not. Fortunetellers specialize in equivocal expressions to protect themselves in case things turn out otherwise than they expect. Politics would be a totally different art if it had to avoid equivocation. So would business correspondence.

> 'You can rest assured that (4) your letter will receive the attention it fully deserves.'
>
> (As it makes a gentle curve in the air towards the waste paper basket.)

> 'Anyone who gets Mr. Smith to work for him will indeed be fortunate.'

Puns and music hall jokes often depend on equivocation.

— 338 —

1995 年　　入試問題

'My dog's got no nose.'

' How does he smell?'
(5)
'Terrible!'

The advice given to a political candidate facing a selection committee is
'When in doubt, equivocate.' The simple fact is that you cannot please
(6)
all of the people all of the time, but you can have a fairly good chance of
fooling most of them for much of it. The candidate assures those in favor
of the death penalty that he wants 'realistic' penalties for murder. To
(7)
those against, he wants 'humane consideration.' But he could be in favor of
realistic light sentences or humane killing.

　Equivocation is a particularly powerful paste for pouring into the cracks
of international discord. It joins irreconcilable differences with a smooth
and undetectable finish. Many 'full and frank' discussions are terminated
happily by the appearance of a joint treaty, whose wording is carefully
chosen to mean (　8　) things to each of the countries that have signed it.

　The vocabulary of equivocation may be learned from visitor's gallery
in the Houses of Parliament. If you have a seat in Parliament, there is
(9)
nothing you have to learn about it.

(1)　下線部(1)の解釈としてもっともふさわしいものは次のどれか。その記号を
　　記せ。

　　(ア)　だました人にだまされる

　　(イ)　自分が論理のわなにはまる

　　(ウ)　嘘をついたために損をする

　　(エ)　言葉のトリックを見破られる

— 339 —

1995 年　　入試問題

(2)　下線部 (2a)，(2b) はそれぞれどのような意味か。その記号を記せ。

(ア)　aim

(イ)　means

(ウ)　last day

(エ)　termination

(3)　空所(3)を埋めるのに適当な1語を記せ。

(4)　下線部(4)は2通りの意味に解することができる。それらにもっとも近いものを次の中から2つ選び，その記号を記せ。

(ア)　we will be honest in replying to your letter

(イ)　we will offer you good advice in response to your letter

(ウ)　your letter will be considered carefully because it is important

(エ)　your letter will be dealt with carefully because it may cause some trouble

(オ)　your letter will not be taken seriously because it is not worth bothering about

(5)　下線部(5)では，話し手と聞き手の間に smell という語についての誤解がある。それぞれの解釈にしたがって，下線部を2通りに訳し分けよ。

(6)　下線部(6)の言い換えとして，もっとも適当なものを以下から選び，その記号を記せ。

(ア)　if you are not sure what to say

(イ)　if you are suspected of dishonesty

(ウ)　if you are afraid of being deceived

(エ)　if you don't think you will be selected

(7)　下線部(7)を和訳せよ。

1995 年　　入試問題

(8) 空所(8)を埋めるのにもっとも適当な語句を以下から選び，その記号を記せ。

　(ア)　fairly indefinite

　(イ)　entirely different

　(ウ)　exactly the same

　(エ)　utterly unreasonable

(9) 下線部(9)の説明としてもっともふさわしいものを１つ選び，その記号を記せ。

　(ア)　If you are a politician, you must already be good at equivocation.

　(イ)　You don't have to know the art of equivocation in the world of politics.

　(ウ)　You should have studied the art of equivocation before entering Parliament.

　(エ)　If you are clever enough to be a politician, there is no need to resort to equivocation.

— MEMO —

— MEMO —

東大入試詳解
英語 第2版
2019〜1995

解答・解説編

駿台文庫

は じ め に

もはや 21 世紀初頭と呼べる時代は過ぎ去った。連日のように技術革新を告げる
ニュースが流れる一方で、国際情勢は緊張と緩和をダイナミックに繰り返している。
ブレイクスルーとグローバリゼーションが人類に希望をもたらす反面、未知への恐怖
と異文化・異文明間の軋轢が史上最大級の不安を生んでいる。

このような時代において、大学の役割とは何か。まず上記の二点に対応するのが、
人類の物心両面に豊かさをもたらす「研究」と、異文化・異文明に触れることで多様
性を実感させ、衝突の危険性を下げる「交流」である。そしてもう一つ重要なのが、
人材の「育成」である。どのような人材育成を目指すのかは、各大学によって異なっ
て良いし、実際各大学は個性を発揮して、結果として多様な人材育成が実現されてい
る。

では、東京大学はどのような人材育成を目指しているか。実は答えはきちんと示さ
れている。それが「東京大学憲章」(以下「憲章」)と「東京大学アドミッション・ポ
リシー」(以下「AP」)である。もし、ただ偏差値が高いから、ただ就職に有利だか
らなどという理由で東大を受験しようとしている人がいるなら、「憲章」と「AP」を
ぜひ読んでほしい。これらは東大の Web サイト上でも公開されている。

「憲章」において、「公正な社会の実現、科学・技術の進歩と文化の創造に貢献する、
世界的視野をもった市民的エリート」の育成を目指すとはっきりと述べられている。
そして、「AP」ではこれを強調したうえで、さらに期待する学生像として「入学試験
の得点だけを意識した、視野の狭い受験勉強のみに意を注ぐ人よりも、学校の授業の
内外で、自らの興味・関心を生かして幅広く学び、その過程で見出されるに違いない
諸問題を関連づける広い視野、あるいは自らの問題意識を掘り下げて追究するための
深い洞察力を真剣に獲得しようとする人」を歓迎するとある。つまり東大を目指す人
には、「広い視野」と「深い洞察力」が求められているのである。

当然、入試問題はこの「AP」に基づいて作成される。奇を衒った問題はない。よ
く誤解されるように超難問が並べられているわけでもない。しかし、物事を俯瞰的に
とらえ、自身の知識を総動員して総合的に理解する能力が不可欠となる。さまざまな
事象に興味を持ち、主体的に学問に取り組んできた者が高い評価を与えられる試験な
のである。

本書に収められているのは、その東大の過去の入試問題 25 年分と、解答・解説で
ある。問題に対する単なる解答に留まらず、問題の背景や関連事項にまで踏み込んだ
解説を掲載している。本書を繰り返し学習することによって、広く、深い学びを実践
してほしい。

「憲章」「AP」を引用するまでもなく、真摯に学問を追究し、培った専門性をいか
して、公共的な責任を負って活躍することが東大を目指すみなさんの使命と言えるで
あろう。本書が、「世界的視野をもった市民的エリート」への道を歩みだす一助とな
れば幸いである。

駿台文庫 編集部

《東大入試詳解 25 年　英語　執筆にあたられた先生方》

大	島	保	彦	勝	田	耕	史
駒	橋	輝	圭	斎	藤	資	晴
佐	山	竹	彦	武	富	直	人
廣	田	睦	美	増	田		悟

掲載内容について

　本書はリスニング問題をのぞく東京大学・英語入試問題を掲載しています。リスニング問題につきましては，同シリーズ『東大入試詳解 20 年　英語リスニング』(2019 ～ 2000 年度の問題を掲載) をご覧ください。

　下記の問題に使用されている英文や和文及び訳文は，著作権法第 67 条の 2 第 1 項の規定に基づく申請を行い，同項の適用を受けて掲載しているものです。

2017 年度：第 2 問(B)
2016 年度：第 4 問(B)
2015 年度：第 4 問(A)
2014 年度：第 1 問(A)
2013 年度：第 1 問(B)，第 4 問(A)
2012 年度：第 1 問(A)，第 4 問(A)
2011 年度：第 4 問(A)(1)，第 4 問(A)(2)，第 4 問(A)(3)，第 4 問(A)(4)，第 4 問(A)(5)
2010 年度：第 4 問(A)，第 5 問
2009 年度：第 1 問(B)
2008 年度：第 2 問(A)，第 4 問(B)
2007 年度：第 1 問(A)，第 5 問
2006 年度：第 1 問(B)，第 4 問(A)
2005 年度：第 1 問(A)，第 2 問(B)，第 4 問(A)(1)，第 4 問(A)(2)，第 4 問(A)(3)，第 4 問(A)(4)，第 4 問(A)(5)
2004 年度：第 1 問(B)，第 5 問（前半：斜体字部分）
2002 年度：第 1 問(B)，第 2 問(A)，第 4 問(A)
2001 年度：第 1 問(A)，第 2 問(B)，第 4 問(A)
2000 年度：第 2 問(A)，第 2 問(B)，第 4 問(B)，第 5 問
1999 年度：第 2 問(B)
1998 年度：第 1 問(A)，第 1 問(B)，第 2 問(B)(a)，第 2 問(B)(b)，第 4 問
1997 年度：第 2 問(A)，第 2 問(B)(a)，第 2 問(B)(b)，第 4 問(A)，第 4 問(C)
1995 年度：第 2 問(A)，第 4 問(A)，第 4 問(C)

目　次

出題分析と入試対策 ……………………………………………………………… 6

	問題	解答・解説
2019 年度 ……………………………………………………	4	20
2018 年度 ……………………………………………………	18	46
2017 年度 ……………………………………………………	32	72
2016 年度 ……………………………………………………	46	96
2015 年度 ……………………………………………………	62	120
2014 年度 ……………………………………………………	76	144
2013 年度 ……………………………………………………	90	166
2012 年度 ……………………………………………………	104	186
2011 年度 ……………………………………………………	118	206
2010 年度 ……………………………………………………	134	228
2009 年度 ……………………………………………………	150	250
2008 年度 ……………………………………………………	164	272
2007 年度 ……………………………………………………	180	294
2006 年度 ……………………………………………………	196	316
2005 年度 ……………………………………………………	210	336
2004 年度 ……………………………………………………	224	358
2003 年度 ……………………………………………………	238	378
2002 年度 ……………………………………………………	252	400
2001 年度 ……………………………………………………	266	420
2000 年度 ……………………………………………………	276	438
1999 年度 ……………………………………………………	290	456
1998 年度 ……………………………………………………	302	472
1997 年度 ……………………………………………………	312	488
1996 年度 ……………………………………………………	324	504
1995 年度 ……………………………………………………	334	518

出題分析と入試対策

年度	番号	項　目	分野・テーマ（表題）・問題レベル
2019	1	読　解	(A)　大意要約（記述）
			「ヨーロッパで生じた児童の人権に関する変化」
			(B)　文補充・単語補充（客観・記述）
			「音楽はある種の言語か？」
	2	英作文	(A)　自由英作文（記述）
			(B)　和文英訳（記述）
	4	文法・語法	(A)　文法正誤問題（客観）
			「ある偉大な女性数学者について」
		読　解	(B)　英文和訳（記述）
			「子育てとペットについての筆者の雑感」
	5	読　解	長文読解総合問題（記述・客観）「雲に魅了された男」
2018	1	読　解	(A)　全文要約問題（記述）
			「デマの拡散と人間の心理」
			(B)　文・英文要約（客観・記述）
			「Verbal Overshadowing について」
	2	英作文	(A)　自由英作文（記述）
			(B)　和文英訳（記述）
	4	文法・語法	(A)　整序英作文（客観）
		読　解	(B)　英文和訳（記述）「鳥の知力について」
	5	読　解	長文読解総合問題（記述・客観）
			「耳の不自由な女性とその母親」
2017	1	読　解	(A)　全文要約問題（記述）
			「国際ビジネスで大切なこと」
			(B)　文・単語補充（客観・記述）
			「経済的特権階級の利己的行動」
	2	英作文	(A)　自由英作文（記述）
			(B)　自由英作文（記述）

出題分析と入試対策

	4	文法・語法	(A)	文法正誤（客観）「ドキュメンタリー映画とは」
		読　解	(B)	英文和訳（記述）「一人でいること」
	5	読　解		長文読解総合問題（記述・客観）「ドリスと私の風変わりな関係」
2016	1	読　解	(A)	全文要約問題（記述）「社会の結束性を生み出す要因について」
			(B)	文補充（客観）「言論の自由はなぜ重要か」
	2	英作文	(A)	自由英作文（写真）（記述）
			(B)	自由英作文（空所補充）（記述）
	4	文法・語法	(A)	文法正誤（客観）「知識の重要性」
		読　解	(B)	英文和訳（記述）「アフガニスタンの戦争報道とその実態」
	5	読　解		長文読解総合問題（記述＋客観）「ホームレスの人々を排除しようとする社会環境」
2015	1	読　解	(A)	全文要約問題（記述）「危険察知における人間の非論理性」
			(B)	文・単語補充（客観・記述）「意思決定疲労で苦労していませんか？」
	2	英作文	(A)	自由英作文（イラスト）（記述）
			(B)	自由英作文（論説型）（記述）
	4	文法・語法	(A)	整序英作文（客観）
		読　解	(B)	英文和訳・内容説明問題（記述）「暗号として用いられたナバホ語」
	5	読　解		長文読解総合問題（記述＋客観）「母親と娘の間の複雑な愛情」

出題分析と入試対策

2014	1	読　　解	(A)	全文要約問題（記述）
				「人間の活動が地球環境に及ぼす影響」について
			(B)	文補充（客観）
				「機械化がさまざまな階層の労働に及ぼす影響」について
	2	英　作　文	(A)	自由英作文（会話文創作）（記述）
			(B)	自由英作文（論説型）（記述）
	4	文法・語法	(A)	取り除くべき一語の指摘（記述）
		読　　解	(B)	英文和訳・内容説明問題（記述）
				「福祉国家が与えるべき援助」について
	5	読　　解		長文読解総合問題（記述＋客観）
				「子育てに悩む父親のつぶやき」
2013	1	読　　解	(A)	全文要約問題（記述）
				「クモの巣の特徴とその応用可能性」について
			(B)	文補充（客観）
				「子供の時間認知能力の発達」について
	2	英　作　文	(A)	自由英作文（会話文創作）（記述）
			(B)	自由英作文（論説型）（記述）
	4	文法・語法	(A)	整序英作文（客観）
		読　　解	(B)	英文和訳・内容説明問題（記述）
				「人間の思考の落とし穴」について
	5	読　　解		長文読解総合問題（記述＋客観）
				「降霊術師にまつわる思い出」
2012	1	読　　解	(A)	全文要約問題（記述）
				「現代社会における移民」について
			(B)	段落整序など（客観）
				「マナーのあり方」について
	2	英　作　文	(A)	空所補充（記述）
			(B)	自由英作文（論説型）（記述）
	4	文法・語法	(A)	取り除くべき一語の指摘（記述）
		読　　解	(B)	英文和訳（記述）
				「Kazuo Ishiguro との対話」について

— 8 —

出題分析と入試対策

	5	読　　解	長文読解総合問題（記述＋客観）
			「NYでサリーを着用した1ヵ月」
2011	1	読　　解	(A)　全文要約問題（記述）
			「科学教育のあり方と展望」について
			(B)　段落整序問題（客観）
			"Don't worry, Dad"
			(C)　不要文選択，文補充，趣旨選択問題（客観）
			「コーヒーハウス」について
	2	英 作 文	(A)　自由英作文（空所補充）（記述）
			(B)　自由英作文（論説型）（記述）
	4	文法・語法	(A)　取り除くべき一語の指摘（記述）
		読　　解	(B)　英文和訳（記述）
			「クロスワードパズルの出現と影響」
	5	読　　解	長文読解総合問題（記述＋客観）
			「心の傷を負った少女と医師のやりとり」
2010	1	読　　解	(A)　全文要約問題（記述）
			「SFの存在意義」について
			(B)　読解（文補充・段落整序など）（客観）
			「小惑星帯から資源を獲得する可能性」について
	2	英 作 文	(A)　空所補充（記述）
			(B)　派生語補充問題（記述）
	4	文法・語法	(A)　取り除くべき一語の指摘（記述）
		読　　解	(B)　英文和訳（記述）
			「映画スターとは」
	5	読　　解	長文読解総合問題（記述＋客観）
			「William Porter（＝O. Henry）の伝記」
2009	1	読　　解	(A)　英文の趣旨をまとめる問題（記述）
			Annie Dillard: *Seeing*
			(B)　読解（文補充・段落整序など）（客観）
			「万年筆のコレクションについて」
	2	英 作 文	(A)　空所補充（記述）
			(B)　書き換え問題（記述）

— 9 —

出題分析と入試対策

	4	文法・語法	(A) 取り除くべき一語の指摘（記述）
		読　　解	(B) 英文和訳（記述）
			Mary Gordon: *Eleanor's Music*
	5	読　　解	長文読解総合問題（記述＋客観）
			New York Times, February 5, 2006: *Looking for the Lie*
2008	1	読　　解	(A) 全文要約（記述）
			「外見と内面の関係をどう考えるべきか」
			(B) 読解（文補充・段落整序など）（客観）
			「生命の起源について」
	2	英 作 文	(A) 空所補充（記述）
			(B) 1つのテーマに対する説明（記述）
	4	文法・語法	(A) 取り除くべき一語の指摘（記述）
		読　　解	(B) 英文和訳（記述）
			「通信革命における携帯とメールの違い」
	5	読　　解	長文読解総合問題（記述＋客観）
			「思春期の娘と母親の心情の交錯」
2007	1	読　　解	(A) 全文要約問題（記述）
			「詩の意味を誰が決めるか」
			(B) 文補充，段落整序，など（客観）
			「インドのゴミ処理について」
	2	英 作 文	(A) 英語による日本文要約（記述）
			(B) イラストを用いた自由英作文（記述）
	4	文法・語法	(A) 取り除くべき一語の指摘（記述）
		読　　解	(B) 英文和訳（記述）
			「医学の性質と役割の変化」
	5	読　　解	長文読解総合問題（記述＋客観）
			"Back Home"
2006	1	読　　解	(A) 要旨要約（記述）
			「民主主義の理想と現実」
			(B) 段落補充（客観）
			「Virginia州の小島で行われる子馬の競りについて」

— 10 —

出題分析と入試対策

	2	英　作　文	(A)	英語による日本文要約（記述）
			(B)	自由英作文（記述）
	4	文法・語法	(A)	整序作文（客観）
		読　　解	(B)	英文和訳（記述）
				「説得のコツ」
	5	読　　解		総合問題（客観＋記述）
				「有名人の悩み」
2005	1	読　　解	(A)	要旨要約（記述）
				「リズム感のある動きを維持する方法」
			(B)	段落補充（客観）
				「エスペラントについて」
	2	英　作　文	(A)	イラストを用いた自由英作文（記述）
			(B)	空所補充（記述）
	4	文法・語法	(A)	取り除くべき一語の指摘（記述）
		読　　解	(B)	英文和訳（記述）
				「科学革命について」
	5	読　　解		総合問題（客観＋記述）
				「灯台守と少年」
2004	1	読　　解	(A)	要旨要約（記述）
				「記憶の仕組み」
			(B)	段落補充（客観）
				「マダガスカルの環境保全」
	2	英　作　文	(A)	1つのテーマに対する説明（記述）
			(B)	英語による日本文要約（記述）
	4	文法・語法	(A)	整序＋適語補充（客観＋記述）
		読　　解	(B)	英文和訳（記述）
				「何が芸術作品を有名にするのか」
	5	読　　解		総合問題（客観＋記述）
				「分離独立に翻弄された祖母の人生」

— 11 —

出題分析と入試対策

2003	1	読　解	(A)	要旨要約（記述）
				「言語の消滅と新たな個別言語の出現」
			(B)	文補充（客観）
				「サーフィンとハワイ文化」
	2	英 作 文	(A)	グラフの読みとり（記述）
			(B)	英語による日本文要約（記述）
	4	文法・語法	(A)	整序（客観）
		読　解	(B)	英文和訳（記述）
				「神の存在」
	5	読　解	総合問題（客観＋記述）	
			「アメリカ人女性ジャーナリストのイランでの体験」	
2002	1	読　解	(A)	変形要旨要約（和文：30〜40字）（記述）
				「日本のテレビ番組の特徴」
			(B)	文補充（客観）
				「アメリカにおける雪」
	2	英 作 文	(A)	会話文空所補充（記述）
			(B)	英語による日本文要約（記述）
	4	文法・語法	(A)	取り除くべき一語の指摘（記述）
		読　解	(B)	英文和訳（記述）
				「祖母と母について」
	5	読　解	総合問題（客観＋記述）	
			「ギャンブラーの誤謬と経験に基づく予測の有効性」	
2001	1	読　解	(A)	要旨要約（和文：30〜40字）（記述）
				「物の価値について」
			(B)	段落整序（客観）
				「科学者の役割」
	2	英 作 文	(A)	英語による日本文要約（記述）
			(B)	会話文空所補充（記述）
	4	文法・語法	(A)	取り除くべき一語の指摘（記述）
		読　解	(B)	英文和訳（記述）
				「病気と闘うこと」
	5	読　解	総合問題（客観＋記述）	
			「家族の中で孤独な父親マクレディ」	

— 12 —

出題分析と入試対策

2000	1	読　　解	(A)	要旨要約（和文：40 〜 50字）（記述） 「人間の独自性とは何か」
			(B)	段落整序（客観） 「科学の発達と人類の幸福」
	2	英　作　文	(A)	グラフに基づく会話文空所補充（記述）
			(B)	空所補充（記述）
	4	文法・語法	(A)	整序（客観）
		読　　解	(B)	英文和訳（記述） 「偶然の裏切り」
	5	読　　解		総合問題（客観＋記述） 「新しい下宿人との生活と母の変化に対する少女の戸惑い」
1999	1	読　　解	(A)	要旨要約（和文：100 〜 120字）（記述） 「オーラル・ヒストリーについて」
			(B)	部分和訳（記述） 「登校中の出会い」
	2	英　作　文	(A)	１つのテーマに対する説明（記述）
			(B)	会話文空所補充（記述）
	4	文法・語法		誤り指摘（客観）
	5	読　　解		長文総合問題（客観＋記述） 「スペインでの有害物質の流出事故による環境被害」
1998	1	読　　解	(A)	要旨要約（和文：80 〜 100字）（記述） 「環境を保護する２つの方法」
			(B)	部分和訳（記述） 「コンピュータの問題点」
	2	英　作　文	(A)	１つのテーマに対する説明（記述）
			(B)	空所補充（記述）
	4	文法・語法		一語補充（記述）
	5	読　　解		長文総合問題（客観＋記述） 「マヌケなピーターと魔法の鏡」

出題分析と入試対策

1997	1	読　解	(A)	要旨要約（和文：100〜130字）（記述）
				「農業の誕生について」
			(B)	指示内容説明（記述）
				「自我を回復しようとする筆者の試み」
	2	英 作 文	(A)	4コマ漫画の説明（記述）
			(B)	空所補充（記述）
	4	読　解	(A)	下線部和訳（記述）
				「新聞の読み方」
		英 作 文	(B)	下線部［和文］英訳（記述）
		文法・語法	(C)	取り除くべき一語の指摘（記述）
	5	読　解		長文総合問題（客観＋記述）
				「学校の乱暴者に追いかけられる少年と友人のやりとり」
1996	1	読　解	(A)	要旨要約（和文：80〜100字）（記述）
				「労働の変化が及ぼす影響」
			(B)	空所補充（記述）
				「子どもに物語を話すこと」
	2	英 作 文	(A)	手紙文空所補充（記述）
			(B)	下線部［和文］英訳（記述）
	4	読　解	(A)	下線部和訳（記述）
				「フレッドとアンの会話」
			(B)	下線部和訳（記述）
				「権利とは何か」
	5	読　解		長文総合問題（客観＋記述）
				「写真や絵の画像がもつ現実性とは」
1995	1	読　解	(A)	要旨要約（和文：60〜70字）（記述）
				「現代言語学の文法理論」
			(B)	空所補充（記述）
				「ヒルトンホテルについて」
	2	英 作 文	(A)	空所補充（記述）
			(B)	下線部英訳（記述）
	4	読　解	(A)	下線部和訳（記述）
				「創造的な思考について」

出題分析と入試対策

			(B)　下線部和訳（記述） 　　「人々にとっての時間」 (C)　下線部和訳（記述） 　　「ある日の庭での出来事」
5	読　　解		長文総合問題（客観＋記述） 「遍在する曖昧語法」

出題分析と対策

◆分量◆

　例年大問5題が出題されている。最近は，1，2，4は(A)(B)の2題に，3（リスニング）は(A)(B)(C)の3題に分かれていることが多い。試験時間（120分で120点満点なので，単純計算すると1点につき平均所要時間1分ということになる）を考えると問題の分量はかなり多く，すばやく問題の狙いをつかみ，設問を処理する力が必要である。

◆出題分野◆

　「読む」「書く」「聴く」「話す」の4技能のうち，「話す」を除く3技能をカバーしている。

◆全体を通じての特徴◆

　東大の入試問題の最大の特徴は，「オールラウンドな学力」が求められていることである。出題分野に関して言えば，読解・作文はもちろんのこと，リスニング，さらには文法までが毎年出題されている。

　読解問題だけをとっても，4(B)のような英文和訳に限らず，1では「話の流れ」「論理の展開」を把握する能力が問われ，5では長文の読解力が求められている。また使用されている英文も論説文だけではなく，特に第5問では小説・エッセイ等が出題されることも少なくない。

　こうした出題を通じて，東大は受験生に「基礎を重視し，幅広くさまざまな分野をまんべんなく学ぶことで真の英語力は身につく」ということを訴えたいのであろう。受験生としてはこうしたメッセージを真摯に受け止め，特定分野に偏らないオールラウンドな学習を心がけることが重要である。

◆近年の特徴と対策◆

　1(A)　2000年～2002年は「制限字数」が30字～50字程度とそれ以前に比べかなり少なくなっていた要約問題だが，2003年～2005年は60字～70字程度に増加し，2006年以降は平均して70字～80字で解答をまとめることが要求されている。他大学の要約問題に比べると字数制限は依然として厳しく，英文の内容を「コンパクトに

— 15 —

出題分析と入試対策

表現する能力」が必要なことは間違いない。

　これまでの出題を見ると圧倒的に「要約」を求められる問題が多いが, 指示文が「一般的にどのようなことが言えるか」(2004 年), 「趣旨をまとめよ」(2009 年), 「要旨をまとめよ」(2016 年, 2017 年, 2018 年) となっている場合がある。2014 年のような例外はあるが, 「要約せよ」という指示文の場合は, 一般的に全体の話の流れを反映した解答が求められていると考えればよく, 「趣旨・要旨をまとめよ」という指示文の場合は, 英文全体の中で最も言いたいことを中心に答案をまとめればよい。

　1 (B)　1 (B)に継続的に段落補充・文補充の問題が出題されるようになったのは 2000 年以降だが, 2007 年～ 2012 年にかけては「段落補充・文補充問題」以外にも「不要文選択問題」や「タイトル選択問題」等も出題され, 分量的にかなり多く, 試験時間内に処理しきれない受験生もかなりいたと思われる。2013 年以降は負担が軽減され, その分かえって「点差がつく問題」になったであろう。2018 年には文補充に加えて, 15 ～ 20 語程度の英語で要約を求める設問があった。解答に際しては, 段落のテーマを押さえることが大前提となるが, その上で「指示語が表すもの」「冠詞 (a ＋名詞か the ＋名詞か)」「連結詞 (discourse markers) や but」「順序を示す表現 (年代, another, etc.)」「人名・名称」「時制・法」などがヒントになることが多いので, これらの表現に注意しながら文章を読み進める必要がある。また選択肢の英文を読む際に, 「内容的, もしくは文法的 (たとえば時制など) に選択肢をグループ分けできないか?」と考えてみることもヒントになる場合が多い。

　2　1998 年の入試以来, 東大は和文英訳問題は出題せず, いわゆる「自由作文」形式の問題しか出題していなかったが, 2018 年から和文英訳問題が再び出題されるようになった。「空所補充型」「日本文の要約」「イラスト・写真の説明 (会話作成)」「諺・格言などに関して自らの意見を述べる問題」の 4 種類が代表的だが, このうち「日本文の要約」は 2007 年を最後にそれ以降は出題されていない。一方, 空所補充型を拡充した「第 1, 2 段落の内容を踏まえ, 第 3 段落の内容を書かせる問題」(2016 年)や「手紙への返信」(2017 年) が新傾向の問題として出題されている。また 2017 年には「自分が今試験を受けているキャンパスについて書け」という「イラスト・写真の説明」を発展させた形の問題も出題された。設問を読んですぐに答案が書き出せるタイプの問題と, 英文をしっかり読み腰を据えてから書き出さなければならない問題が組み合わされて出題されるケースが多い。

　答案を書く上で重要なことは, 基本的な語彙を使った基本的な英文をあっさりと書くよう心がけることである。考えすぎるあまり複雑怪奇な内容を書こうとしたり, 自分が使える範囲内にない単語や熟語, 構文を用いてはならない。

出題分析と入試対策

4(A)　文法問題もしくは整序作文問題が出題されている。ただし2000年以降を見ても，整序作文が出題されたのは2000年，2003年，2004年，2006年，2013年，2015年，2018年だけであり，文法問題が出題されるケースの方が多い。文法問題とは言っても，むしろ読解問題に近く，「英文の構造・内容に気をつけながら読み進め，説明がつかない箇所を探す」というアプローチで対処すべき問題である。

4(B)　年によっては大問番号が違うものの，1997年から2000年にかけては英文和訳問題が1題のみ出題されていたが，「英文を読む力を測る手段として英文和訳問題はやはり有効」という判断が働いたのだろうか，2001年以降は増加に転じ，2001年，2002年は2題，そして2003年以降は3題出題されている。下線部のみではなく，より広い視野を要求される良問も多い。下線部だけで考えるのではなく，より広い文脈の中で単語の意味や英文の構造を考える姿勢を身につけてもらいたい。

英文和訳は，受験生の学力がストレートに反映される出題形式である。語彙力・熟語力を高める努力を日々重ねるのはもちろんのこと，文構造の正確な把握抜きでは英文の意味を正確につかむことは不可能だということを肝に銘じておいてほしい。

5　ここ数年，素材のジャンルは，体験に基づくエッセイ（2012年）→物語文（2013年）→体験に基づくエッセイ（2014年）→物語文（2015年）→体験に基づくエッセイ（2016年）→体験に基づく自伝的なエッセイ（2017年）→物語文（2018年）→伝記的要素を持つエッセイ（2019年）と変化してきたが，本文の長さは800語強（2012，2013年）→1,000語強（2014年）→1,000語弱（2015年）→800語強（2016年）→900語強（2017年）→900語弱（2018年）→1,000語弱（2019年）と推移し，平均して900語を超える英文が出題されている。登場人物の心情理解を求める設問も多いので，日ごろから物語文やエッセイを読む際には，登場人物の気持ちを追いかける練習をしておくとよいだろう。「一見平易に思われるが，文脈を考慮しないと読み誤ってしまう表現」もよく問われる。4(B)と同様，文章全体を視野に入れる必要があることは言うまでもない。

解答・解説

1 **(A)** **全訳** 産業化以前のヨーロッパにおいては，児童就労は広く受け入れられた現象で，経済制度の中で大きな意味をもつ要素であった。19世紀まで，そして19世紀中，6歳を過ぎた子どもは，その能力に応じて社会貢献することが求められていた。7歳頃から子どもは徐々に仕事の世界に入りはじめたが，それは大人と子どもが共に棲む世界であった。教育・学校教育・危険要因からの保護といった概念は，まれにしか見られないか，全く欠如しているかのどちらかであった。また，19世紀初頭には，子どもは一般に親の私的所有物だとみなされており，法的権利はほとんど，あるいは，全く与えられていなかった。親（主に父親だったが）は，子どもに対する力と支配権を無制限に与えられており，自分の望み通りに子どもを扱うことが許されていた。体罰も，ほぼ欧州全土で見られ，社会的に認められるものだった。

　このような状況は，19世紀が進むにつれ，変わり始めた。とりわけ1870年から1920年の50年間で，親や雇用主などに対する子どもの権利が法的保護という形で拡大していった。徐々にではあるが，子どもというものは別個の範疇に入るものであって，単に大人の所有物ではないという捉え方がされるようになっていった。子どもには経済的価値しかないという見方が変わり始め，子どもたちは独自の集団であり，社会にはこの集団を支援し，子どもたちが直面する様々な危険から守る責任があるという認識に変わっていったのである。

　この時代に生じたもう一つの変化は，親の虐待や育児放棄から子どもを守るようになったことであり，それらは政府の関係機関によって厳しく監視され，その妥当性がますます問題視されるようになった。1889年，フランスと英国は両国とも，親によるものも含め，子どもの虐待を禁止する法案を通過させた。国家が子どもの権利の擁護者となったわけである。そして，このように保護される権利を子どもが得たことによって様々な援助に対する権利が生まれ，中央政府が諸々の便益を提供する責任を負うことになった。医療，一定の水準を満たす住宅，遊び場が，労働からの解放や公教育を受ける機会と共に，子どもの権利を構成する要素として浮上した。

— 20 —

2019年　解答・解説

考え方

　本年度の出題は次の２つの特徴によって，例年の要約よりは処理しやすいという印象を受験者に与えたようである。

① 近年１(A)は，ほとんど「主張型の文章」（筆者の視点・考え方を中心とするもの）が素材となっていたのだが，本年度は「解説型の文章」（事の経緯や学説の紹介などを軸とするもの）になっている。

② 設問の指示書きに「ヨーロッパで生じたとされる変化の内容を」とあり，解答の核となる内容が予め提示されている。

　ただし，最初から素直に目を通していかないとポイントを見逃すことになる点は従来通りであって，怪しげな方法論だのストラテジーだの解法だのを信じて「全部読まずに済ませよう」などという安易な態度をとるべきではない。

◇　全体の概略

(1) 第１段落（産業化以前〜19世紀初頭）

　第１〜３文で，この時代は「児童就労」が当たり前だったこと，第４文で「ほとんど教育を受けることも保護されることもなかった」こと，第５〜６文では「子どもは親の所有物扱いされていた」ことが述べられている。

(2) 第２段落（19世紀後半以降）

　第１〜２文で「19世紀後半から子どもの権利を法的に守るようになっていった」とあり，第３〜４文で，子どもが「別個の範疇」だと捉えられ「社会が守らなければならない独自の集団」となったことが述べられている。

(3) 第３段落（19世紀後半以降）

　第１文で，もう一つの変化として「国の機関によって子どもを守るようになった」という点が挙げられており，第２文はその例で，第３文は，そのまとめ（言い換え）である。第４文では，国家レベルで子どもを守る法制度を作った結果，「様々な便益に対する権利が生まれ，政府が各種サービスを提供する責任を負った」という記述があり，最終文はその具体化となっている。

◇　着眼点

(1) 子どもには人権がなかった

　第１段落の，産業化（工業化）以前／19世紀前半までの部分については，大雑把に言えば「子どもには人権がなかった／人間扱いされていなかった」ということが表現できていればよいと思われるが，第５文に "also" があるので「労働力の一部だった／児童就労が当然だった」という点と，第２段落第３文の "not simply as the property of adults" との関連で「親の所有物だった」という点の両方に触れておく

― 21 ―

のが安全策と言える。

(2)　子どもを人間扱いするようになった

　第2段落第2文 (Particularly ...) で「1870年以降の50年間で子どもの権利が拡大していった」とあるが，これが第2段落の残りの部分と第3段落全体を支配する文になっていることに注意する。これを展開したのが第2段落第3〜4文と第3段落である。(つまり，形式段落は3つあるが，第2〜3段落は意味的には1つのブロックを成しているということ)。この構造が見えていないと，「何を2つの要素として抽出するか」がずれることになってしまう点に注意しなければならない。

　(以下の解説で，第2段落第3〜4文をAとし，第3段落をBとする)

A.　別個の人間集団とみなされるようになった。

　第3段落冒頭に "Another change" とあるのだから，第2段落から1つ目の変化を抽出することになる。第3文 (Gradually ...) に "a separate category"，第4文 (The view ...) に "a unique group that ..." という表現が出てくる。また，この部分で指摘されている変化は "perceive" や "perception" という語から分かるように「(子どもというものを) どう捉えるか」に関する変化であり，これは第1段落の内容と大きく対比を成す部分であるため，子どもは「別個の人間集団だという認識が生まれた」という点を解答に含めておくべきだと考える。あとは，"a unique category" の後の関係詞節を考慮して「社会が守るべき別個の集団 (存在) とみなされた；社会によって守られる独自の存在だと認識された」という程度にまとめておく。

B.　国家が法によって守る対象となった。

　第3段落第1文で「虐待と育児放棄から守る」とあるが，"which were ... by government authorities" の部分があり，第2文のフランス・イギリスの法制度化の例があり，そして第3文で "The nation became ..." という記述があるのだから「国家が (国家レベルで；国政レベルで；法によって) 子どもを保護するようになった」という点を2つ目の変化としてまとめる。

(3)　そして様々な権利が与えられた

　第3段落第4文 (The child's right ...) の "led to ..." という因果関係の表現に注意すること。国によって守られる権利を得た結果，「様々な provision に対する権利が生まれ，政府がサービスを提供する責任を負うことになった」とある。provision は provide の名詞形だが，この単語を知らなくても最終文の内容から「(政府が) 提供してくれるもの；援助」程度の意味がつかめていればよい。最終文は言うまでもなく "services" の具体例であり，個々の要素に触れる必要はないので「様々な (サービス／支援に対する) 権利が与えられた」という程度にしておくとよいだろう。

— 22 —

2019年 解答・解説

以上の点をまとめると，次のようになる。

---
① （産業化以前は）子どもには人権がなかった。
   (a) 労働力の一部だった　　(b) 親の所有物だった
② 19世紀後半から，社会が守るべき別個の集団とみなされるようになった。
③ 国家が法的に保護する対象となった。
④ その結果様々な権利が（国によって）与えられた。

時代の明記は不要かもしれないが，変化の起点となった「19世紀後半」は含めておくことにする。また，ポイント①は(a)と(b)に分けてあるが，第1段落は「子どもには人権がなかった／人間扱いされていなかった」という点が出ていれば可となるかもしれないため（解答例2）は，そのようにまとめてある。

解答例

［解答例1］　子どもは労働力の一部で親の所有物だったが，19世紀後半からは社会が守るべき別個の存在だと認識され，国家によって法的に保護され，様々な権利を与えられるようになった。(80字)

［解答例2］　産業化以前，子どもには全く人権がなかったが，19世紀後半以降は社会が守るべき独自の存在とみなされ，国家によって法的に保護され，様々な権利が保障された。(75字)
---

1 **(B)** 【全訳】　音楽は世界共通語である。少なくとも，そうであると音楽家たちは主張したがる。「音楽なら，英語やフランス語のような普通の言語では不可能なやり方で，文化的および言語的な境界を越えて意思を伝えることができる」と彼らは言うだろう。ある次元においては，この発言は明らかに真実である。フランス人作曲家のクロード・ドビュッシーによって書かれた楽曲を楽しむためにフランス語を話せる必要はない。　(1)　　それは「世界共通の」という語によって何を意味するか，および「言語」という語によって何を意味するかによる。

あらゆる人間の文化には音楽があるが，それは各文化に言語があるのと全く同じである。よって音楽が人間の経験の世界共通の特徴であるということは真実である。それと同時に，音楽体系と言語体系の両方が文化ごとに大きく異なっている。それにもかかわらず，外国の音楽体系がどれほど奇妙に思われたとしても，人々は自分に馴染みのない音楽形態において伝えられる感情，つまり，幸福と悲哀という少なくとも2つの基本的な感情を見抜くことにかなり長けているということが研究によって示され

— 23 —

ている。 (2) たとえば，音調がより高いこと，音調とリズムにより多くの変化
があること，およびテンポがより速いことは幸福を伝える一方，その逆は悲哀を伝える。

そうすると，もしかしたら，私たちは音楽的な感覚を持って生まれるということに
なるのかもしれない。しかし，言語にもまた旋律があり，それを言語学者は韻律体系
と呼んでいる。音調，リズム，そしてテンポといった音楽と全く同じ特徴が，諸言語
に共通であると思われるやり方で，話し言葉において感情を伝えるために用いられる。
フランス語や日本語，あるいはその他自分が話さない何かしらの言語で行われている
会話を盗み聞きしてみよう。話の内容は理解できないだろうが，話し手の揺れ動く感
情の状態は理解できるだろう。彼女は気分を害していて，彼は守りに入っている。す
ると今度は，彼女はとても怒っていて，彼は口を挟むのをやめている。彼は彼女に懇
願するが，彼女は納得していない…。私たちがこのやり取りを外国語で理解できるの
は，それが自分たち自身の言語でどのように響くかを知っているからである。同様に，
私たちが楽曲を聞く時，それが自分の文化のものであれ別の文化のものであれ，私た
ちは世界共通の韻律特性を反映する旋律の特徴を基にして感情を認識する。 (3)

しかし，音楽は一種の言語なのだろうか？　ここでも，私たちが用いる用語を定義
しなければならない。 (4) 生物学者は「ハチの言語」について語るが，それは
仲間のハチに新たな食料源の場所について教える手段である。人々は「花言葉」につ
いて語るが，それを通じて彼らは自分の意図を伝えることができるのである。「赤の
バラは…を意味する；ピンクのカーネーションは…を意味する；白のユリは…を意味
する」といった具合である。それから「ボディー・ランゲージ」がある。これは，感
情や社会的地位などを伝えるために私たちが用いるジェスチャー，動作，および表情
を意味する。私たちは話す時にボディー・ランゲージを用いることが多いのだが，言
語学者はそれを真の言語形態とは考えていない。そうではなく，いわゆるハチの言語
や花言葉と全く同様に，それは意思伝達の体系なのである。

定義上，言語とは意味を持つ一連の記号（単語）と，それらの記号を意味のあるさ
らに大きな単位（文）へと組み合わせる一連の規則（統語法）からなる意思伝達の体
系である。多くの生物種は意思疎通体系を持ってはいるが，これらのうちで言語に数
えられるものは１つもない。それらにはどちらか一方の構成要素が欠けているからで
ある。多くの生物種が警告を伝える音や食べ物のありかを知らせる呼び声を持ってい
て，それらは一連の有意味な記号から成ってはいるものの，そうした記号を規則に従っ
て生産的に組み合わせることはしない。同様に，鳥の歌声やクジラの歌声には，要素
を組み合わせる規則があるが，これらの要素は有意味な記号ではない。１つのまとま
りとしての歌にのみ（　ア　）があるのだ。

2019 年　　解答・解説

　言語と同様に，音楽にも統語法，すなわち，音，和音，休止などの要素を複雑な構造へとまとめ上げるための規則がある。　(5)　　むしろ，感情面での意味を伝えるのは，より大きな構造，つまり，旋律なのである。そして，話し言葉の韻律を反映することによってそのような意味を伝えているのである。

　音楽と言語は特徴を共有しているので，言語を処理する脳の部位の多くが音楽の処理も行うということは驚くべきことではない。　(6)　　私たちは，脳の特定の部位が専ら特定の機能のみに結びついていると考えがちである。しかし，言語であれ，音楽であれ，車の運転であれ，複雑な行動であればどんなものでも，多くの異なる脳の部位から寄与を受けるのである。

　音楽は確かに，地球上の任意の人に向けて任意の考えを表すためにそれを使うことができるという意味での世界共通の言語ではない。しかし音楽は，人類共通の経験の核心にある基本的な感情を呼び起こす力を実際持っている。それは文化を越えるものであるだけでなく，私たち人類が歩んできた過去へと深くつながってもいるのである。そしてその意味において音楽は，まさに共通言語なのである。

【考え方】

(ア)　正解は **meaning**。空所のある第5段落は，「言語は『単語』という有意味な記号と複数の単語を統語法という規則に則って組み合わせた『文』という有意味な単位からなるが，他の生物種が持つ意思疎通体系は，これら2つのどちらかが欠けているため言語とはみなされない」という内容である。空所を含む文は，1つ前の文と合わせて，言語における「単語」に相当するものが意味を持たないものの具体例を表している部分になる。このことから「同様に，鳥の歌声やクジラの歌声には，要素を組み合わせる規則があるが，これらの要素は意味を持つ記号ではない。歌全体にのみ意味があるのだ」という趣旨になるはずだと考える。これを設問の指示にある同じページの本文中（解説者注：第4段落の冒頭から第7段落第3文 (We tend to ...) の tied まで）から探すと，空所を含む段落の次の段落である，第6段落第3文 (Rather, it's the ...) の最後に meaning という語があるため，これが正解。

(イ)　【選択肢全訳】

a)　しかし，音楽は本当に共通言語なのだろうか？

b)　しかし，その逆は真実だろうか？つまり，言語は世界共通の音楽だろうか？

c)　しかし，このことは音楽が言語であるということを意味するのではない。

d)　この意味で，音楽は実際に感情を伝達する世界共通の体系である。

e)　音楽の具体的な特徴が，これらの感情を表現することに寄与する。

f)　科学者たちを含め，私たちは「言語」という言葉を「意思疎通体系」という意味

2019 年　　解答・解説

で用いることが多い。

g)　私たちは通例「言語」を「意思伝達」とは定義しない。

h)　しかし，これらの要素のどれも，それ自体だけでは特別な意味を持たないのである。

⑴　正解は **a)**。空所の直後の文に That「そのこと」とあるので，その指示対象となる内容が空所の文になければならない。直後の文は「それは "universal" という語によって何を意味するか，および "language" という語によって何を意味するかによる」という意味なので，universal と language が含まれる a) か b) に絞られる。b) は「しかし，その逆は真実だろうか？　つまり，言語は世界共通の音楽だろうか？」という意味で，これが入るためには続く第2段落の主題が「言語」になっていなければならないが，第2段落の主題は引き続き音楽であるため不可。以上より a) が適切。

⑵　正解は **e)**。空所の直前の文には「人々は…幸福と悲哀という2つの基本的な感情を見抜くことにかなり長けている」とあり，空所の直後の文には「たとえば，音調がより高いこと，音調とリズムにより多くの変化があること，およびテンポがより速いことは幸福を伝え，一方でその逆は悲哀を伝える」とある。e) を入れれば these emotions が手前の the two basic emotions of happiness and sadness を指し，Specific futures of music の具体例が pitch「音調」，rhythm「リズム」，tempo「テンポ」になるためこれが適切。

⑶　正解は **d)**。空所に入る文は第3段落の最終文であり，その直前の文は「同様に，私たちが楽曲を聞く時，それが自分の文化のものであれ別の文化のものであれ，私たちは世界共通の韻律特性を反映する旋律の特徴を基に感情を認識する」という意味。d)「この意味で，音楽は実際に感情を伝達する世界共通の体系である」を入れれば，直前の内容とうまくつながるし，「言語，音楽の両方に共通する感情の伝達および認識」が主題である同段落のまとめの文としても d) は適切である。

⑷　正解は **f)**。空所の直後の文に「生物学者たちは『ハチの言語』について語るが，それは仲間のハチに新たな食料源の場所について教える手段である」とある。f)「科学者たちを含め，私たちは『言語』という言葉を『意思疎通体系』という意味で用いることが多い」を入れれば，「科学者」の具体例が「生物学者」になり，「意思疎通体系」の具体例が「新たな食料源の場所について教える手段である」の部分になるため，これが適切。

⑸　正解は **h)**。空所の直前の文には「音楽にも統語法がある」という内容が述べられていて，空所の直後の文は「むしろ，感情面での意味を伝えるのは，より大きな構成，つまり，調べなのである」とある。このことから，1つ前の段落の「鳥

— 26 —

2019 年　　解答・解説

の歌声やクジラの歌声」と同様に，「個々の要素には意味がない」といった内容が空所に入ればよいのだと考える。よって h)「しかし，これらの要素のどれも，それ自体だけでは特別な意味を持たない」が内容上適切となり，these elements が notes, chords, intervals を指すことにもなる。

(6)　正解は **c)**。空所の直前の文には「言語を処理する脳の部位の多くが音楽の処理も行う」と述べられている。そして，空所の直後の文の後半である but 以降には「言語であれ，音楽であれ，車の運転であれ，複雑な行動であればどんなものでも，多くの異なる脳の部位から寄与を受ける」とある。これらから，空所には「処理を行う脳の部位の多くが共通していることは，言語と音楽が同じものであるという根拠にはならない」といった内容が入ると考えられる。c)「しかし，このことは音楽が言語であるということを意味するのではない」がこれを端的に表したものであるため，これが適切。

解答

(ア)	meaning				
(イ)	(1)－ a)	(2)－ e)	(3)－ d)	(4)－ f)	(5)－ h)	(6)－ c)

2 (A)

日本語でテーマを与え，それに従って英文を書くというのは 2017 年と同じ形式だが，盛り込まなければならない内容を細かく指定しているところは 2015 年のことわざの問題に似ている。

考え方

＜語数について＞

「60 〜 80 語」とあるから，この指定より多くても少なくてもいけない（語数超過はともかく，59 語以下の場合は減点あるいは 0 点にされる可能性が高い）。また，答案の最後に「○○ words」と書き添えよう。

＜内容のポイント＞

答案に盛り込まなければならない内容は以下の 3 つ。

(1)　「新たに祝日を設けるとしたら，どのような祝日を提案するか」

(2)　「その祝日の意義」

(3)　「そのような祝日が望ましいと考える理由」

問題文の最後に，提案する祝日が「国民のための祝日」「国内外の特定の地域の祝日」「全世界で祝うような祝日」のいずれでもかまわない，とコメントされているが，

— 27 —

2019 年　　解答・解説

通常「祝日」と聞いて我々が想像するのは「国民のための祝日」（日本を含めて，国が指定した，全国民にとって休日となる祝日）であろう。しかし，そのようなものでなくてもいいのですよ，とわざわざ教えてくれているだけなので，あまり気にしなくてよい。おそらく東大は，自由に想像力を発揮しなさい，と訴えているのだろう。

☆　(1)について

祝日と言えば「○○の日」という名前が通常ついているが，わざわざ英語で固有名詞的なものを創作する必要はない。説明的に「△△が ×× な日」とすればよい。むろん創作もＯＫだが，あまりに変な英語を作り，英語的に許容範囲を超えていて減点されるのが一番まずいパターンである。

英語の問題だが，個人が祝日を設ける権限を持つなど現実にはありえないことである。したがって「新たに祝日を設けるとしたら」の部分を英訳するなら（というか，英訳してもかまわない）仮定法を用いることになる（たとえば "If I were to create a holiday"）。英訳しないにしても，「提案する」は「新たに祝日を設けるとしたら」に続く部分だから，やはり仮定法になる（たとえば "I would (like to) propose ..."）。ただし，「提案」という意味の語を使わないのなら，たとえば "I think it should be ...." と直説法で処理することは可能。「…の日であるべきだ」という言い方をするのも 1 つの「提案」である。

ちなみに，この(1)は必ず答案の冒頭で明記すること。そして，(1)と同じような内容を答案の最後で繰り返さないこと。書くことが思い浮かばないと，語数稼ぎのために最後で "So I would propose ..." のごとき英文を書く受験生がいるが，同じことを二度も三度も繰り返せば減点対象になることは免れない。

☆　(2)(3)について

(2)だが，広辞苑によると，『意義』とは「① 意味，わけ」「② 物事が他との連関において持つ価値・重要さ」となっている。つまり，提案する祝日がどのような意味を持つのか，どうしてそのような祝日を設けることが重要なのかを説明せよ，ということだろう。(3)は「そのような祝日が望ましいと考える理由」なので，受験生諸君の個人的な思いを書けばよい。ちなみに，(2)(3)は順不同である。つまり，どちらを先に書いてもかまわない。

ただ，この(2)(3)はかなりの部分が重なっている。「その祝日が持つ価値・重要さ」＝「そのような祝日を望む理由」であると解釈してもおかしくないからである。したがって，この 2 つが厳密に分けられていなくても減点対象にはならないだろう。

また，「祝日が設定されたらどのような状況になるか」を記述する部分はすべて仮定法で書かなければならないことに注意。受験生諸君が一番間違えやすいのはここで

— 28 —

ある。(1)を仮定法で書くことは皆が比較的気をつけているが，第2文以降になると途端に仮定法を使い忘れやすくなるからだ。

＜答案作成＞

　ここで，答案の展開方法を具体例に沿って見てみることにする。

［解答例1］

　(1)　「ネットを使わない日」＝「一日ネットを使わないでいることを目的とした日」

　(2)(3)　「現代人はネットの仮想空間にとらわれすぎている」→「身の回りにある人や物が持つ価値を忘れてしまっている」→「科学技術から遠ざかり，家族や友人と話したり自然を楽しんだりすれば，現実世界がどれほど貴重なものかがわかるようになるだろう」

　(1)で "Offline Day" という固有名詞を創作したので，その具体的説明を付け足した。この解答例は(2)(3)ははっきりと分けていない。そのような祝日を設けるとネットに関連する現実の問題点をいかに解決するかを述べることで，その祝日の「意義」を表し，また，だからこそそのような祝日を求めるという「望ましいと考える理由」をも表している。

　ちなみに，"Today ... around them" は現実問題を表したものなので直説法である。また，先述したように，第2文 "The purpose of this day would be to stay ..." の "would be" が仮定法にするのを忘れやすい部分。

［解答例2］

　(1)　「地球の誕生日を祝う日」＋「地球が何月何日に誕生したかを知っている者はいないので，どの日付でもよい」

　(2)　「地球が現在直面している問題(地球温暖化など)について世界中の人が考える，よい機会になるから」

　(3)　「地球を顧みない数多くの人にもっと思慮を持ってほしい」

　「地球の誕生日」というのはかなり突飛な発想かもしれないが，思い切り想像力を駆使してみた。ただ，「地球環境について皆で真剣に考えよう」というのは，内容的にはありきたりなものである。また，「日付はいつでもよい」というのは蛇足のように思えるだろうが，語数稼ぎをするならこのようにしてほしい，というメッセージを込めてつけ加えてみた。

　ちなみに，"Of course ... existence" "Regrettably, ... the earth" は現実を表したものなので直説法である。また，unkind に quotation mark (" ") をつけたのは，通常 be (un)kind to の後に続くのは「人」で，ここでは故意に変則的な使い方をしているためだ。「たとえて言わば，地球に『不親切』」という感じである。

－ 29 －

<u>2019 年　　解答・解説</u>

解 答 例

[解答例 1]

　If I were to create a holiday, it would be "Offline Day". The purpose of this day would be to stay completely offline for one day. Today, people are too obsessed with the virtual world of the Internet. As a result, they've forgotten the value of the people and things around them. Spending this holiday away from technology, talking with family and friends or enjoying nature, would help people realize how precious the real world is. (76 words)

[解答例 2]

　I would recommend the new public holiday be to celebrate the Earth's birthday. Of course nobody knows the exact date it came into existence, so any date would be good. Such a holiday would be a good chance for everybody in the world to think about the problems our planet is now facing, such as global warming. Regrettably, there are a great many who are very "unkind" to the earth. Maybe they would start to be more thoughtful. (78 words)

2 (B)

考え方

(1)「もっとも重要なのは…である」**what is most important is ...**

☆ 「もっとも重要な（こと）」は what is most important / the most important thing / what matters most など。

☆ *it is the most important to − / what is the most important thing* は ×。

(2)「…と, 私たちひとりひとりが（中略）自覚すること」**for each of us to realize (that) ...**

☆ 「私たちひとりひとり」は each (one) of us / we each / every one of us / each and every one of us など。*every of us / everyone of us* は ×。*we all / all of us / everyone* などは「ひとりひとり」という感覚が乏しいので, 不適当だろう。

☆ for each of us が(1)に含まれていてもＯＫ（例：what is most important <u>for each of us</u> is to realize）。

☆ 「自覚する」は realize / recognize / understand / become [be] aware

— 30 —

[conscious] など。*find / notice* は「（知覚・感覚を通して）…に気づく」という意味合いで，「自覚」とは異なるので×。

☆ that each of us realize のように that 節を用いた場合，節中の述語動詞は「原形 [realize]」「should ＋原形 [should realize]」「単純現在形 [realizes]」のいずれもOK。

⑶ 「日々の暮らしのなかで」**in our daily lives**

☆ in our daily [everyday] lives が最も適切だが，単数形で life としてあっても，our が抜けていても減点対象とはならないだろう。

☆ realize that の that 節中に置かれていると，「自然環境を汚染している」に対する修飾語句であると確実に勘違いされるため，減点されるだろう。

⑷ 「…のは私たち自身である」**it is we ourselves who [that] …**

☆ it is us ourselves who [that] … / we are the ones who … もOK。単に we ourselves 〈are polluting〉としても減点されないだろうが，やはりひと工夫ほしいところ。

☆ 「自身」という感覚はほしいので，単に it is *we* [*us*] who [that] … は減点されるだろう。

☆ it is *ourselves* who [that] / *ourselves* are the ones who は ×。oneself を主語として使うことはできない。また，"people who … are *ourselves*" も ×。oneself が補語になる場合は "S be not oneself." のような表現に限られる（「S は普段と何か違う」という意味）。

☆ *by ourselves*（ひとりで；自力で）/ *for ourselves*（独力で；自分自身のために）は内容的に異なるため×。

⑸ 「かけがえのない自然環境を汚染している」**are polluting our precious natural environment**

☆ 「汚染している」は pollute / contaminate。時制は現在進行形が最適（「こうしている間にも汚染は続いている」という感じ）。

☆ 「かけがえのない」は irreplaceable または「貴重」という意味合いの形容詞（precious など）。*important / essential / indispensable* のような「重要」という意味合いの語は不適当である（具体的に何にとって重要か，という感じになる）。

☆ 「自然環境」は (natural) environment。our をつけるのが最適だが，the でもOK。

⑹ 「プラスチックごみによって」**with plastic garbage**

☆ 「ごみ」は garbage / trash / rubbish / waste / litter など。いずれも不可算

— 31 —

2019 年　　解答・解説

名詞であるため，不定冠詞の a や複数の s がついていると減点される。

☆　「によって」は with 以外に考えられない。*by − ing* を用いると，まるで意図的に汚染しているかのようになるため，減点されるだろう。

解答例

［解答例 1］

what is most important is for each of us to realize in our daily lives that it is we ourselves who are polluting our precious natural environment with plastic garbage.

［解答例 2］

the most important thing is that we each become aware in our everyday lives that we are the ones who are contaminating our irreplaceable environment with plastic waste.

4　(A)　**全訳**　(22)　女性は生まれつき数学の研究には向かないという古くさい固定概念は，2014 年に大打撃を被った。この年，マリアム・ミルザハニが数学において最も権威のある賞，フィールズ賞を受賞した最初の女性となったのである。同じくらい大きな打撃が，今から 300 年前に生まれたイタリアの数学者マリア・ガエターナ・アニェージによって与えられていた。アニェージは数学の教科書を著し，数学の大学教授の職を与えられた最初の女性だったが，彼女の人生は矛盾に満ちたものだった。聡明で，裕福で，著名であったにもかかわらず，彼女はつましく，貧者に献身する人生を送ることを最終的に選んだ。

考え方　正解は(a)［at → for］。「…に適している」は be suited <u>for</u> ... である。

全訳　(23)　1718 年 5 月 16 日にミラノで生まれたアニェージは，富豪であった父がもうけた 21 人の子どもの長子だった。成長過程で，彼女の特に語学における才能は異彩を放った。彼女にできる限り良い教育を与えることを 1 つの目的として，父親は当時の一流の知識人たちを家庭に招いた。アニェージが 9 歳のとき，彼女はラテン語のスピーチ（おそらくは彼女の家庭教師の一人が作成したものだろうが）を父の客たちの前で何度も暗唱した。そのスピーチは，芸術や科学における女性教育に対し当時一般的だった偏見，即ち家庭を治める人生にそのような学習は全く必要がないという考えに根ざしていた偏見を非難するものだった。男性が手に入れることのできるあらゆる知識を女性も自由に追求することができるようになるべきだという，明瞭で説得力のある論をアニェージは提示したのである。

— 32 —

2019年　解答・解説

(考え方) 正解は(d)［either → 削除］。either は①否定文で用いて「…もまた（〜でない）」②数量詞として用いて「（2つのものの）どちらか一方」という2つの意味を持つ。関係代名詞 which の節中は肯定文だから①ではない。②だが，この関係代名詞 which の先行詞は内容から考えて "prejudice" であるが，これでは「eitherは2つのものに対して用いる」という制約に反するため，②でもない。したがって，either が had と been の間に存在する理由がないため，これを削除して単に whichhad been grounded とするのが正しい。

　ちなみに，(a)の in part は副詞用法の to − を，(c)の likely は副詞で composedという過去分詞を修飾するもの。一見すると誤りのように見えるかもしれないが，いずれも正しいのである。

(全訳) (24)　アニェージは結局公の場で自らの知的能力を示すことに疲れてしまい，世間から引退して宗教的生活に身を奉じたいという願望を表明した。しかし，父親の二番目の妻が死去したとき，彼女は家や多くの弟妹の教育に対する責任を果たすことにした。この役割を通じて，イタリアの学生たちに近年の数学的発見をまとめた基本的な方法論を紹介するべく，包括的な数学の教科書を作成する必要性を感じたのである。

(考え方) 正解は(c)［her → herself］。dedicate の意味上の主語は "Agnesi" である。捧げる対象が他者ではなく自分自身であるから，再帰代名詞 herself を用いる必要がある。単に her とすると「第三者の女性」つまり「自分ではない他の女性」になってしまい，おかしい。

(全訳) (25)　アニェージは数学に特別な魅力を見出した。経験から得られた知識のほとんどは誤りが生じやすく，議論の余地が生まれるものであると彼女は考えていた。しかし，数学からは完全に間違いのない真理が生まれる。アニェージの著作は 1748年に2冊に分けて出版され，タイトルは『解析の基本原理』だった。それがラテン語ではなく（ニュートンやオイラーのような偉大な数学者の場合はラテン語で書くのが通例だった），イタリア語で書かれていたのは，学生により利用しやすいものにするためであった。1749年，アニェージの教科書はフランスの科学アカデミーから絶賛された。「互いに全く異なる数多くの数学者の研究の中で散逸していた発見を，ほぼ統一された体系にまとめあげるには，多大な技術と的確な判断が必要だった」。

(考え方) 正解は(e)［reduce almost uniform methods to discoveries scattered → reduce to almost uniform methods discoveries scattered］。この問題は難しい。reduce A to B という語法は確かに存在し，「A を B の状態にする；A を B に変える」と和訳する。ただ，そもそも reduce とは「減少させる；低下させる」という意味なので，この熟語は単なる「変化」ではなく，「複雑な［高度な］A を単純な［低

— 33 —

レベルの]Bに変える」という意味合いを持つ。ところが，この(e)ではAが "almost uniform methods"，Bが "discoveries scattered ..." となっている。内容から考えればわかると思うが，これではBの方がAより複雑になってしまう。したがって，"reduce <u>discoveries scattered ... to almost uniform methods</u>" という順番が正しい。しかし，本問の場合 discoveries に "scattered ... each other" という長い修飾語句（scattered は過去分詞で，discoveries という名詞にかかる形容詞用法）がくっついているため，AとtoBの部分を入れ替えて（つまり倒置にして）"reduce to <u>almost uniform methods</u> discoveries scattered ..." とするのが適切。

　ちなみに(a)だが，下線部(a)を含む文全体が倒置になっている。通常の順番で表現するなら "Truths that are wholly certain come from mathematics." なので，誤りはない。

【全訳】 ㉖　女性や貧しい者の教育の熱心な提唱者であったアニェージは，自然科学や数学は教育課程において重要な役割を果たすべきであると考えていた。しかし宗教への信仰心が厚い人間として，彼女はさらに，科学的数学的研究が，世界の創造に対する神の計画という，より大きな枠組みの中でとらえられるべきだとも考えていた。彼女の父が1752年に亡くなったとき，神のおぼし召しに答え，貧しい者への奉仕という彼女のもう一つの熱情に残りの人生を捧げることが自由にできるようになった。今日アニェージのことを記憶している人はほとんどいないが，数学史における彼女の先駆的役割は，性別に関する固定概念に対する勝利という，勇気づけられる話として役立っている。彼女は以後何世代にもわたり数学の世界で女性に明確な道筋をつけるのに貢献したのである。アニェージは数学に秀でていたが，数学を愛してもいて，数学を極めることには，彼女と同じ人間たち，そしてより高次の存在双方に奉仕する機会があることを認識していた。

【考え方】 正解は(e)[of→削除]。下線部の直前にある perceive は他動詞で目的語が必要だが，of があると in から order まででひと括りの前置詞句になり，目的語がなくなってしまう。of をとれば，an opportunity が perceive の目的語で，perceive と an opportunity の間に前置詞句 in its mastery が割り込んでいるという解釈になり，構文的に収まる。

　(a)だが，これは "<u>Being</u> a passionate advocate ..." という分詞構文から being を省略したものである。"being C" という形の分詞構文においては，being はしばしば省略される。

－ 34 －

2019 年　　解答・解説

解 答

| ⑵ー(a) | ⑵ー(d) | ⑵ー(c) | ⑵ー(e) | ⑵ー(e) |

4 **(B)** **(全訳)** 去年の７月，フレッドに会って両親と夏を過ごすためにホノルルに行った。両親と話をしたり親元を訪れることはそう頻繁ではないのに，というべきなのか，それだから，と言うべきなのかはわからないのだが，両親と私は良好な関係を維持している。一番最近親元を訪ねるまで，つまりこの前の７月までということだが，私は６年間親と会っていなかったのだ。私はニューヨークに住んでいて，両親はハワイに住んでいる。そしてハワイ諸島に行くにはある程度の時間がかかることは確かだが，自分が親元に立ち寄らない本当の理由は，訪れたい場所が他にあるからなのだ。両親が私に与えてくれたあらゆる贈り物や強みのうちで，最も素晴らしかったものの１つが，「親元を去り，やりたいことをやるのが子どもの義務であり，これを受け入れるだけではなくそれを促すことが親の義務だ」と彼らが確信していたことだ。私が 14 歳で初めて親元を離れて（親は当時テキサスの東部で暮らしていた），ホノルルの高校に通おうとしていたとき父に言われたのは，子どもに何であれ期待する親は皆必ずがっかりすることになる，なぜなら子どもを産み育てたことに対して子どもがいつの日か恩返しをするかもしれないと期待して子どもを育てるのは愚かで身勝手だからだ，ということであった。父はこれ以降ずっとこうした姿勢を貫いている。

こうした考え方が，なぜうちの親が，我々が一般にペットの理想と信じているものに多くの点で矛盾するペットが大好きなのかを説明してくれる。生活の中に動物が一緒にいる人は，自分たちが動物に対して何かを期待しているとは考えたがらないが，実際には期待をしているのだ。ペットに忠誠と愛情を示してほしいと思っているし，それらを我々に理解可能な形で表現してほしいと思っている。しかし，フレッドはこうしたものを一切示してくれない。彼は彼なりには友好的なのだが，こちらに対して特に何らかの愛情を持っていると感じさせる生き物ではないのだ。

(考え方)

(ア)　1．**while it is true that ...**「確かに…だが；…なのは本当だが」 while はここでは「譲歩」を表し，「…だが」の意。it は形式主語で that 以下を指している。It is true (that) S + V ... は「確かに（なるほど）…だ」の意を表す定型表現。（例）*It is true (that)* your idea is interesting, but I'm afraid it's difficult to put it into practice. （確かにあなたのアイディアは面白いが，残念ながら実行するのは難しいと思う）

2．**traveling to the islands requires a certain commitment of time**「ハワ

— 35 —

<u>2019 年　　解答・解説</u>

イ諸島へ行くことは一定の時間の投入を求める（ハワイ諸島に行くにはある程度時間を割くことが必要となる）」 traveling が主語として働く動名詞で，それに対する動詞が requires。the islands の訳語は「その島々」でもかまわないが，ここでの指示内容を明示して「ハワイ諸島」などと訳出してもよいだろう。the を無視して単に「島に行くことは」と訳したのでは「島一般」について論じたことになってしまうので，適切とは言えない。requires については「…に行くには－しなければならない」等を含め，様々な訳出が考えられる。a certain commitment of time は「時間の一定の投入」の意。commitment は「〈資金・時間・人などを〉利用すること，使うこと」，すなわち「〈資金・時間・人などの〉充当，投入」という意味で使われていることに注意。（例）They agreed to a *commitment* of funds to the project.（その計画に資金を投入することに彼らは同意した）「時間の一定の投入を必要とする」では日本語としてあまりに拙いので，まとめて「一定の時間を割かなければならない」などとすればよい。

3. **the real reason I stayed away is ...**「私の足が遠のいていた本当の理由は…」reason の直後には関係副詞の why が省略されている。stay away は「離れている；寄りつかない；足が遠のく」の意。

4. **that there were other places I wanted to visit**「私が他に行きたいところがあったということ」 places の直後には関係代名詞が省略されている。

⑴　1. **it was foolish and selfish to raise children**「子どもを育てることは愚かで身勝手だ」 it は to raise ... を指す形式主語。raise は「…を育てる」の意。この because 節の内部が it was foolish and selfish ... と過去形になっているのは「時制の一致」が適用されているためである。よって，訳出の際には「…は愚かであり身勝手である」と「現在」で訳しておけばよい。

2. **in the hope that ...**「…ということを期待して」 全体で raise を修飾する副詞句として働いている。that 節は直前の hope の内容を説明する同格節。

3. **they might someday pay back the debt of their existence**「子どもたちが自分たちが存在した恩をいつの日か返してくれるかもしれない〈と期待して〉」 debt はここでは「恩；恩義」を表し，pay back the debt で「恩を返す；恩返しをする」という意味になる。their existence は文字通り訳せば「子どもたちの生存（存在）」だが，要は「子どもが生まれ，ここまで育ってきたこと」を表しており，解答例や全訳のようにやや説明的に訳出した方が日本語としては自然であろう。子どもたちがここまで育つことが可能であったのは「親の世話のおかげ」であり，子どもはそれに対し「報いるべき恩義 (the debt)」があるという見方もあるだろうが，筆者の父親は「苦

－ 36 －

労をして育てたことに対して，いつか子どもが恩返しをしてくれることを期待して子育てをするのは馬鹿げていて，身勝手だ」と考えているのである。

（ウ）　1．**This philosophy explains their love for a pet**「こうした考え方がペットに対する両親の愛情を説明する；こうした考え方によって，ペットに対する両親の愛情が説明できる」 philosophy は「哲学；考え方」の意。their love for a pet は They love a pet. が名詞化したもの。

2．**that, in many ways, contradicts ...**「多くの点で…に反する〈ペット〉」 that は a pet を先行詞とする主格の関係代名詞。in many ways は「多くの点で」の意の副詞句。contradicts は「…を否定する；…と矛盾する」などといった訳語も可。

3．**what we generally believe a pet should be**「ペットはそうあるべきだと我々が一般に信じているもの；私たちが一般にペットの理想と思っているもの」 contradict の目的語として働く名詞節。この what 節は，We generally believe (that) a pet should be X.（我々は，ペットは X であるべきだと一般に信じている）から X を関係代名詞の what に変え，節の先頭に出すことででき上がったもの。内容的には「我々が一般に考えている理想のペット」を表すことになる。

解 答

> （ア）　ハワイ諸島へ行くには一定の時間を割かなければならないのは確かだが，足が遠のいていた本当の理由は，他に行きたいところがあったからである。
>
> （イ）　いつか子どもが，自分を生んで育ててくれたことに対して恩返しをしてくれるかもしれないと期待して，子育てをすることは愚かであるし，身勝手なことである。
>
> （ウ）　この考え方によって，私たちが一般にペットの理想と思っているものと多くの点で食い違っているペットに対する両親の愛情が説明できる。

5　**全訳**　ギャヴィン・プレイター＝ピニーは一息つこうと決めた。時は 2003 年の夏で，それまでの 10 年間，ロンドンでのグラフィックデザインの仕事に加えて，彼と友人の 1 人は *The Idler* という名の雑誌を発行していた。このタイトルが示唆するのは「怠け者のための文学」である。その雑誌は忙しさや仕事至上主義に異議を唱え，無目的に生きることの価値，想像力をひっそりと自由に働かせることの価値に賛同するものである。プレイター＝ピニーはあらゆる冗談を言われるのを予想していた。つまりそれは，あいつは何もしないことを主題とした雑誌の運営で燃え尽きてしまったのだ，などといった類の冗談だった。しかし，それは事実だった。その雑誌を発行

— 37 —

2019 年　　解答・解説

するのは骨が折れる作業であり，10 年もすると，しばらく雑誌の発行をやめて無計画に過ごす，つまり，良い意味で自分自身が怠け者になって新たなアイデアのための余裕を作るのが望ましいように思われてきた。だから彼は，ロンドンのアパートからローマのアパートへと移り住んだ。ローマでなら，すべてが新鮮で何が起きても不思議ではないと思われたのだ。

　プレイター＝ピニーは 47 歳で，長身で温厚な人物であり，白くなったあごひげを生やし，瞳は薄い青色である。彼は晴れやかな顔つきをしていることが多く，それはまるで，彼が物語を語り聞かせてもらっている真っ最中で，何らかの素晴らしい驚きが物語の中に出てくるのを感じ取ることができているかのようである。彼は 7 ヵ月間ローマに滞在し，その街を，特にその宗教芸術すべてをとても気に入っていた。彼が気づいたことが一つあった。それは，彼が目にする絵画に雲がたくさん描かれているという事実であった。雲は至る所にあった，「聖人たちのソファのように，この柔らかな雲がね」と彼は最近私に語った。しかし屋外に出て，プレイター＝ピニーが空を見上げてみても，現実のローマの空にはたいてい雲はなかった。彼はそのような無限に広がる青く何もない空間に慣れていなかった。彼はイングランド人で，雲に慣れ親しんでいたのだ。彼は，子どもの頃に自分が雲に魅了され，雲から綿を収穫するために人々は長いはしごを上っているに違いないと結論づけたことを思い出した。そして今ローマの地で，彼は雲について考えるのをやめられなかった。「私は雲がなくて寂しかったんです」と，彼は私に語った。

　雲。それは夢中になる対象としては奇妙なものであり，ことによると馬鹿げたものですらあったが，彼はそれに抗うことができなかった。当時の彼は（彼にはよくあることなのだが），具体的な目標もなければ全般的な方向性すら念頭においていなかったにも関わらず，雲に夢中になることを受け入れた。彼は物事の成り行きがどうなるかを確かめるのが好きなのだ。プレイター＝ピニーはロンドンに戻ると，いつも雲のことを口にしていた。雲に見とれながら歩き回り，「層積雲」のような雲の学術名やその雲を形作る気象条件を覚え，雲なんて陰気だとか退屈だとか不平をこぼす友人たちと言い争ったりした。後に彼が述べたところでは，「雲は不平不満の対象などではない。それは実際には，自然界の最も活動的で詩的な光景なのである」ということを彼は理解しつつあったのだ。

　のんびりと手を休めて雲を鑑賞することで，彼の生活は豊かになり，何でもないような光景の中に隠れている他のささやかな美を鑑賞する能力を研ぎ澄ますことができた。同時に，驚嘆の念を失いつつある時代に我々は突入しようとしているということに，プレイター＝ピニーは気づかずにはいられなかった。新しくて，驚くべきものと

— 38 —

2019 年　　解答・解説

思われる出来事がインターネット上であまりにも迅速に拡散してしまうので，彼の言葉を借りるならば，我々は皆，今では「あのさ，パンダが変わったことをしているのをネットで見たばかりなんだよ ―― 今度は何が僕を驚かせてくれるっていうんだい？」といった態度をとってしまう。雲に対する彼の情熱は，「我々は自分の周りにあるものに驚きや喜びを感じられるのだと実感する方が，我々の精神にとってははるかに望ましい」ということを彼に教えていたのだ。

　2004 年の終わりにプレイター＝ピニーは，友人に招かれて，サウス・ウエスト・イングランドで開かれた小規模な文芸フェスティバルで雲についての講演を行った。その前年は，聴衆よりも演説者の人数の方が多かったので，プレイター＝ピニーは大勢の人々を引きつけるために講演のタイトルを面白いものにしたいと思った。「雲が被っている悪評から雲を守る，つまり雲を擁護するような協会を作ったら面白くないだろうか？」と彼は考えた。だから彼は講演の名称を「雲鑑賞協会第一回年次講演」とした。そしてこれが功を奏した。場内は立見用スペースしか残らないほどだったのだ！　講演の後，人々は彼のもとへとやって来て，雲鑑賞協会についてもっと詳しい情報がほしいと告げた。彼らはその協会に加入したいと思ったのだ。「それで，まあ，実際には協会なんて作っていないと彼らに説明せざるをえなかったのです」とプレイター＝ピニーは言った。そういうわけで，彼は協会の設立に取りかかったのだ。

　彼は雲の投稿写真のギャラリーと会員申し込みフォームと大胆なマニフェストを載せた簡単なウェブサイトを立ち上げた。（そのマニフェストは，「我々は，雲は不当に侮辱されており，雲なしでは人生ははるかに貧しきものになるであろうと信じる」と始まっていた）　彼はまた，会費を請求して郵便で会員証を発行しようと決めた。彼がこうしたことを行ったのは，名目上でしか存在しないオンライン上の雲鑑賞協会に加入するというのは馬鹿げているように思われるかもしれないと認識していて，そのような協会への加入が無意味に思われることが絶対にないようにしたいと思っていたからであった。

　数か月のうちに，その協会の有料会員は 2,000 人になった。プレイター＝ピニーは驚き，そして喜んだ。そして，ヤフーは英国の "Wild and Wonderful Websites" の2005 年度リストの先頭に雲鑑賞協会を載せた。人々はそのリンクをひっきりなしにクリックした。それは必ずしも驚くべきことではなかったが，そのうちの何千もの人々がそれに続けてプレイター＝ピニー自身のサイトにもアクセスして，そして会費を支払ったのだ。他のニュースサイトも注目するようになり，雲鑑賞協会に関する独自の記事を掲載し，人々はその記事の中のリンクもクリックした。以前は，プレイター＝ピニーが雲に関する書籍を執筆したいと申し出ても，28 人の編集者に断られてきた。

― 39 ―

2019 年　　解答・解説

今では彼は，オンライン上の支持者が相当数いるインターネットで評判の人物となった。彼は，雲に関する書籍を執筆する契約を取り付けたのだ。

　執筆の工程は骨の折れるものであった。それまで本を書いたことが実は一度もなかったのに加え，彼は自らに完璧さを要求したので，作業の進捗は遅々としたものであった。しかし，2006 年に刊行された *The Cloudspotter's Guide* は，喜びと驚きに満ちあふれたものとなっている。プレイター＝ピニーは美術史や詩や現代写真における雲を概観しており，本の中盤あたりには雲に関するクイズもある。その第 5 問はある特定の写真を示して，「層積雲のこの層がこんなに魅力的であるのは一体なぜか？」と問いかけている。プレイター＝ピニーが挙げている解答は「あなたがそれを魅力的と感じる理由なら何でも正解です」である。

　この本はベストセラーになった。

［考え方］

　(A)　下線部の burn out は「燃え尽きる；疲れ果てる」という意味。ここでは直後に現在分詞 running が導く副詞句を従えて「〈彼は〉…するのに燃え尽きてしまった」という表現になっている。この run は「…を運営［経営］する」という意味の他動詞で，a magazine がその目的語となり，devoted to …「…を（専門的に）扱った；…を主題とした」という形容詞句が a magazine を修飾している。以上より，下線部全体の意味は，「彼は何もしないことを主題とした雑誌を運営するのに燃え尽きてしまった」となる。

　設問は「"all the jokes" の例であることがわかるように，その内容を日本語で説明せよ」となっているので，なぜこの下線部が joke「冗談」なのかを考える必要がある。「何もしない」ことの価値を重視しそれを主題とする雑誌であれば，その雑誌を運営しているプレイター＝ピニーも「何もしない」生活を本来は実践すべきであるはずなのに，その当の本人が雑誌の運営に忙しすぎて「燃え尽きてしまった」というところに面白みがあり，それを冗談交じりに皮肉っぽく表現したのが下線部ということになる。よって解答は，上記の内容がわかるように**「何もしないことを推奨する雑誌を作っていたはずなのに，本人がその運営に忙殺され燃え尽きてしまったという皮肉な状況」**などとまとめればよい。

　(B)　下線部の主節は we were entering an era で，an era「時代」が関係代名詞 which の先行詞となっている。さらに，a sense of wonder は「物事に対して驚きや不思議を感じる心；驚嘆の念」という定型表現なので，下線部全体の意味は「我々が驚嘆の念を失いつつある時代に我々は突入しようとしている」となる。ただし，設問が「内容を本文に即して日本語で説明せよ」となっているので，単に下線部を和訳し

— 40 —

ただけでは十分な解答とは言えない。「…時代に我々は突入しようとしている」という箇所の意味は，詳述されている部分が下線部の前後にないことから，これ以上の説明は不要と判断できるので，「我々が驚嘆の念を失いつつある」という部分の内容を「本文に即して」考える必要がある。

　下線部を含む第4段落の最終文 (His passion for ...) で「雲に対する彼の情熱は，『我々は自分の周りにあるものに驚きや喜びを感じられるのだと実感する方が，我々の精神にとってはるかに望ましい』ということを彼に教えていた」と述べられていることから，下線部(B)の a sense of wonder も「自分の身の周りにあるもの」に対する感情であると判断できる。さらに，現代人がそのような a sense of wonder を失いつつある理由を考えると，下線部直後の文 (New, supposedly amazing ...) に「新しくて，驚くべきものと思われる出来事がインターネット上であまりにも迅速に拡散してしまう」と記されているので，これが現代人が a sense of wonder を失いつつある理由であると判断できる。よって正解は，以上をまとめて「**驚くべき出来事があまりに速くインターネット上で拡散するので，実際に身の周りにあるものに対して人々が驚嘆の念を抱けない時代になってきているということ**」などとすればよいだろう。

　(C)　まず，下線部(C)で始まる文は疑問文になっているので，冒頭は疑問詞の what かあるいは is S ... かのいずれかである。もし what を先頭で使わない（＝ is が先頭）とすると，what は関係代名詞節か疑問詞節（いずれも名詞節）を構成することになるが，そうすると what 節内の述語動詞として使えるものが見当たらない。よって，先頭で what を使うことになる。

　ここで，is / it / that's から，強調構文によって疑問詞が強調される場合があることを思いつけたかがポイントである（例：*Where is it* that you want to go?「あなたが行きたいのはいったいどこなのですか」）。先頭の疑問代名詞 what が強調構文で強調されていると考えると，what is it that's ... という結びつきが得られ（what は that's の is の主語），is の補語になれるものを探すと形容詞 pleasing「楽しい；魅力的な」が見つかる。副詞の so が修飾できるのはこの pleasing しかないので，ここまでで what is it that's so pleasing「これほど魅力的なのは一体何なのか」となる。さらに，layer「層」は可算名詞の単数形なので単独では用いられず，this layer のように this をつけて使うことになるので，残っているのは about / this layer / of となり，下線部の直後に stratocumulus「層積雲」という名詞があることを考慮すると，about this layer of 〈stratocumulus〉とつなげれば文法的にも意味的にも適切なものになる。

　以上より，正解は **What is it that's so pleasing about this layer of** となる。

　(D)　(ア)　(27)　空所には動詞の -ing 形が入るので，その -ing は find myself C の C

－ 41 －

2019年　　解答・解説

として働く現在分詞となり，文の意味は「私は自分がそれ（＝雲）を（　　）のがわかった」となる。直前の記述から判断すると，この空所前後は，幼いころから雲に魅了されていたイングランド人のプレイター＝ピニーが，雲の少ないローマにやってきた際に感じた気持ちを表しているとわかる。そのような人間の心情として最も適切なのは **h)** の **missing**「〈雲〉がなくて寂しく思う」なので，これが正解となる。

⒇　空所に動詞の -ing 形が入ると，walk around -ing「－しながら歩き回る」という表現が完成するので，空所の前後は「彼はそれ（＝雲）を（　　）しながら歩き回った」という意味になる。これは，雲の少ないローマからロンドンに戻ってきたプレイター＝ピニーの行動を表しており，空所の前後の「いつも雲のことを口にしていた」「雲の学術名やその雲を形作る気象条件を覚えた」という記述も参考にして当時のプレイター＝ピニーの行動を想像すれば，正解は **a)** の **admiring**「〈雲〉に見とれる」となる。

⒈　空所に動詞の -ing 形が入ると，（　　）in plain sight が直前の other pockets of beauty「他のささやかな美」を修飾する現在分詞句となり，「何でもないような光景の中に（　　）他のささやかな美を鑑賞する（…）」となるので，この文意にふさわしい **e) hiding**「隠れている」が正解となる。

⒊　空所を含む文は，雲鑑賞協会についての講演をしたプレイター＝ピニーが，講演を聞いた人々に「実際にはその協会を作っていない」と説明した後の描写である。これ以降の文章では，彼が実際に雲鑑賞協会を設立してそれを運営していった様子が描かれているので，set about「…に取りかかる」の直後の空所に入れて適切な意味となるのは **g)** の **inventing**「…を創り出す」となる（one は a society を指す）。

⒊⒈　直前の段落の「会費を請求して」という内容を踏まえて空所に **i)** の **paying** を入れれば，paying members「有料会員（＝会費を支払っている会員）」となり，内容的にうまくつながる。よってこれが正解となる。

⒊⒉　空所の後ろを見ると，「それまで本を書いたことが実は一度もなかったのに加え，彼は自らに完璧さを要求したので，作業の進捗は遅々としたものであった」と記されているので，プレイター＝ピニーが著書を執筆する作業は困難を伴うものであったと推測される。空所に **c)** の **exhausting** が入れば，「骨の折れる；心身を疲労させるような」という意味の形容詞となって適切な文脈となるので，これが正解となる。

⒤　空所の前の and he ... 以降の意味は，「彼は絶対にそれが（　　）に思われることがないようにしたいと思っていた」となる（make sure that ... で「絶対に…ようにする」という意味）。下線部を含む文の前半には，「彼がこうしたことを行ったのは，名目上でしか存在しないオンライン上の雲鑑賞協会に加入するというのは馬鹿げているように思われるかもしれないと認識していたからだ」と書かれている。この部分の

— 42 —

2019 年　　解答・解説

... might appear ridiculous と空所を含む it did not seem（　）は，appear と seem が類語の関係にあり，文型も同じである。ここから，it は joining an online Cloud Appreciation Society「オンライン上の雲鑑賞協会に加入すること」を指し，空所部分は「その加入が"ridiculous（馬鹿げている）"と思われないようにしたい」というプレイター＝ピニーの心情を表していると考えれば，スムーズな文脈となる。選択肢のうちでこのような意味になるのは **d)** の **pointless**「無意味な；不毛な」なので，これが正解となる。a) の cloudy「雲の多い」，b) の expensive「高価な」，c) の lazy「怠惰な」，e) の serious「真剣な」は，いずれも上で説明した文意に合わない。

　㋒　正解は **a)**「ローマに行って初めて，プレイター＝ピニーは雲が魅力的であると気づいた」。第2段落第8文（He was an ...）および第9文（He remembered, as ...）で，ローマに移り住んだ際のプレイター＝ピニーの心情の説明として「彼はイングランド人で，雲に慣れ親しんでいたのだ。彼は，子どもの頃に自分が雲に魅了され（…）」と述べられているので，彼はローマに行く前の幼少期から雲の魅力に気づいていたことがわかる。よって，この a) が本文の内容と合致しない。

　他の選択肢については，以下の通り：

　b)　「ロンドンに戻った後にプレイター＝ピニーは雲について多くのことを学び，それが *The Cloudspotter's Guide* を執筆するのに役立った」：第3段落第4文（When Pretor-Pinney returned ...）および第5文（He walked around ...）で，「プレイター＝ピニーはロンドンに戻ると，いつも雲のことを口にしていた。雲に見とれながら歩き回り，『層積雲』のような雲の学術名やその雲を形作る気象条件を覚え（…）」と述べられている。第8段落（The writing process ...）に記されているように，この後でプレイター＝ピニーは雲に関する書物である *The Cloudspotter's Guide* を出版しているので，ロンドンに戻った後に学んだ知識が書物の執筆に役立ったと判断するのが妥当と考えられる。よって，この選択肢が本文の内容に合致しないとは言えない。

　c)　「プレイター＝ピニーの雲鑑賞協会はすぐに人々の注目を引いた」：第7段落第1文（Within a couple ...）に「数か月のうちに，その協会の有料会員は 2,000 人になった」と記されているので，雲鑑賞協会は「すぐに人々の注目を引いた」と判断できる。

　d)　「小規模な文芸フェスティバルでのプレイター＝ピニーの雲に関する講演は結果的に大成功を収めた」：文芸フェスティバルでのプレイター＝ピニーの講演に関しては第5段落で述べられており，その第5文（And it worked.）および第6文（Standing room only!）で，その様子が「そしてこれが功を奏した。場内は立見用スペースしか残らないほどだったのだ！」と描かれていることから，講演は大成功を収めたことがわかる。

— 43 —

2019年　　解答・解説

　e)　「プレイター＝ピニーは，*The Idler* の共同編集者の頃も雲鑑賞協会の創設者の頃も，いずれも忙しかった」：*The Idler* の共同編集者の頃のプレイター＝ピニーについては，第1段落第5文 (Pretor-Pinney anticipated all ...) に「彼は何もしないことを主題とした雑誌の運営で燃え尽きてしまったのだ」という冗談が記されており，同段落第7文 (Getting the magazine ...) にも「その雑誌を発行するのは骨が折れる作業だった」という記述がある。雲鑑賞協会の創設者としても，第8段落 (The writing process ...) で，インターネット上で評判の人物になったプレイター＝ピニーが書籍の執筆に苦労していたことが描かれている。以上から，どちらの時代もプレイター＝ピニーは忙しい日々を送っていたと推測するのが妥当なので，選択肢 e) が本文の内容と合致しないと見なすことはできない。

解答

(A)　何もしないことを推奨する雑誌を作っていたはずなのに，本人がその運営に忙殺され燃え尽きてしまったという皮肉な状況。

(B)　驚くべき出来事があまりに速くインターネット上で拡散するので，実際に身の周りにあるものに対して人々が驚嘆の念を抱けない時代になってきているということ。

(C)　What is it that's so pleasing about this layer of

(D)　(ア)　(27)－h)　　(28)－a)　　(29)－e)　　(30)－g)　　(31)－i)　　(32)－c)

　　　(イ)　d)

　　　(ウ)　a)

― 44 ―

解答・解説

1 **(A)** **全訳** 噂は，異なってはいるが共通点のある2つの過程によって広がる。すなわちポピュラー・コンファメーションとイングループ・モーメンタムである。最初の過程は私たち一人一人が他者の思考や行動に頼るために生じる。一定数の人がある噂を信じているように見えると，それが誤りだと考える十分な理由がない限り他者もそれを信じるのである。大部分の噂は，人が直接ないしは個人的に知り得たことではない話題を含んでいるゆえに，大部分の人は多数の人の言い分をあっさりと信じてしまうことがよくある。多数派の視点を受け入れる人が増えると，その集団が大きくなり，たとえ完全に間違いであっても大多数の人が噂を信じてしまうという危険性が現実に生まれるのだ。

イングループ・モーメンタムが示しているのは，考え方の似た人が集まると，以前の考えがより極端になったものを最終的に信じてしまうことが多いという事実である。たとえば特定国家の邪悪な意図に関する噂を，ある集団の成員が受け入れようとしていると考えてみよう。おそらく，話合いをした後の方がその噂を強く信じ込むことになるだろう。実際，新しい根拠がその集団の他の成員が信じていることのみであっても，最初はためらいがちにそう思っていたのが絶対的確信になっていくこともある。ここでインターネットの役割を考えてみるとよい。似たような考え方をしている人のツイートや書き込みを数多く見ると，噂が本当だと思いたくなる気持ちが強まっていくではないか。

私たちがこれら2つの過程によってデマを正しいと思ってしまうという危険を減らすために何ができるだろうか。最も明白な答え（標準的なものだが）は自由表現という仕組みに絡んでいる。つまり，人は公平な情報に触れ，真実を知る者が発する訂正に触れるべきなのだ。自由は通常の場合効力を持つものだが，状況によっては改善策として不完全なこともある。人は中立的に情報を処理しない。そしてしばしば感情が真実の邪魔をする。人は大変不公平な新情報の取り込み方をする。そして，特に強い感情移入が絡んでいる場合に言えることだが，デマを正しいと思った人が容易に自分の考えを捨てることはない。事実を提示してもなお人の考えを変えることは極めて難しいということがあるのだ。

考え方

設問の指示が「要旨をまとめよ」となっており，解答字数が最大80字しかない。

— 46 —

2018 年　　解答・解説

このような時は，通例，主張の中心をまとめ，残りは言葉を圧縮してまとめることになる。本問では第3段落の内容が筆者の結論を含む部分なので，この部分の大筋を外さないことが最も大きなポイントである。

◇第3段落の内容

(1) 換言／具体化に注目する

　第1，2段落で述べられた2つの過程を受けて「これら2つの過程によって誤った噂を正しいと思ってしまう危険を減らすにはどうすればよいのか」という問題提起が第1文にある。この答えに該当するのが第2文だが，"the system of free expression" といういう表現があることに注意。過去の出題でもよくあったことだが，「曖昧模糊とした，抽象度の高すぎる表現」がある場合には，意味不明な訳語を出すより，言いかえられた部分を使って言葉の意味を明確にする必要がある。ここでは，コロン（：）の後で「偏りのない情報と，真実を知る者が発した修正に触れるべきだ」という意味の文があるので，この部分を使ってまとめるとよい。"balanced information" は「偏りのない情報；公平な情報」でよいが，"corrections ... truth" の部分は「誤解の修正；正しい情報」という程度にまとめておく。ここまでをまとめると「誤った噂の拡散を防ぐには公平な情報と誤解の修正に触れるべき」となる。また，false rumours は「デマ」という言葉でもよいし，「真実を知るものが発する修正」というのは，つまり「正しい情報」ということなので「デマの拡散を防ぐには偏りのない正しい情報に触れるべき」とまとめることもできる。さらに，"balanced information" と "correction ... truth" の2つは，「公正な情報」と圧縮する手もある。

(2) 逆接に注意する

　第2文で1つの考え方を提示しているわけだが，そこで終わっていないことに注意。1つの視点（見方；考え方）を提示しておいて，それとは異なる視点を追記するというのは，東大の要約問題における頻出パターンになっている。本問では第3文の "but in some contexts ..." 以下で「（公平で正しい情報に触れても）うまくいかないことがある」という方向に進んでいることに注意。この文の an incomplete remedy「不完全な対策」という表現の意味を後続部分を基にしてふくらませる必要があるが，これは，第5文の "do not easily give up their beliefs" や第6文の "It can be extremely hard to change what people think" という表現を参考に「人の考えを変えるのは難しい；人の考えは容易には変わらない場合がある」という程度にまとめ，これを結論として使う。

　また，第4文に "emotions" そして第5文に "strong emotional commitments" という表現があるが，この「（強い）感情が邪魔をする；感情が影響する」という内容は，

－ 47 －

2018年　　解答・解説

上記の結論の原因と考えられるので追加しておくべきであろう。

　以上の内容を「誤った噂の拡散を防ぐには公平な情報と誤解の修正に触れるべきだが，感情が妨げとなり人の考えは容易には変わらないことがある」とまとめると59字，「デマの拡散を防ぐには偏りのない正しい情報に触れるべきだが，それでも感情が影響するため人間の考えを変えるのは難しい場合がある」とすると61字，「デマの拡散を防ぐには公正な情報にふれるべきだが，感情が影響するため人の考えを変えるのは難しい場合がある」とすると51字になる。(この「…ことがある」や「…場合がある」という表現は，第3文の "in some contexts" や，最終文の "can be" という表現を反映したものである)

◇第1，2段落の内容

　第3段落の these two processes は明らかに第1，2段落の内容を指しているので，これに触れておくべきだが，解答字数を考えると大変簡潔にまとめる必要がある。最初の popular confirmation を(A)，第2段落の in-group momentum を(B)とすると，「(A)と(B)による誤った噂の拡散を減らすには…」あるいは「(A)と(B)によって生まれるデマの拡散を防ぐには…」という形でつなぐのが字数を節約するまとめ方になるだろう。この2つの表現の意味を残りの部分から捉え，それを簡潔に表現できたかどうかも本問の大きなポイントとなっている。

　第1段落の "popular confirmation" は，要するに「多数の人が信じると(それを基に)ある噂が正しいと思ってしまうこと」ということなのだが，これを「周囲への同調；多数派との同調」という程度にまとめる。(もちろん「多数派の意見に影響されること」という意味になっていれば他の表現でもよいと思われる)

　第2段落の "in-group momentum" については，第1文の "like-minded people"，"extreme version" や，第4文の "move from being tentative believers to being absolutely certain" という表現から，「同じ考えを持つ集団内で意見が過激化していくこと」ということなので「同じ考え(似た考え)を持つ集団内の意見の激化(強化)」という程度にまとめる。

　以上の点を含めて，表現とつなぎ方を調整したのが以下の解答例だが，最終段落の内容を十分に，そして出来るだけ英語の記述に沿って，表現しようとしている点に注意してもらいたい。

— 48 —

2018年　　解答・解説

解 答 例

［解答例1］　多数派との同調や，同じ考えを持つ集団内の意見の激化によるデマの拡散を防ぐには公正な情報に触れるべきだが，感情が影響するため人の考えを変えるのは難しい場合がある。(80字)

［解答例2］　周囲との同調と，似た考えを持つ集団内の思考の激化によるデマの拡散を防ぐには公平で正しい情報に触れるべきだが，人の考えは感情が絡むと容易に変わらないこともある。(79字)

1　**(B)**　**［全訳］**　心に残るような過去の出来事を振り返って考えると，私たちの記憶は内面からの影響によって歪められる傾向がある。このことの起こり方として1つありえるのは，記憶を他者と共有することを通じてであり，これは人生における重要な出来事の後で，私たちのほとんどがやりそうなことである。それが，自分の家族に何かわくわくする知らせを伝えるために電話をかけることであれ，仕事での大きな問題について上司に報告することであれ，さらには警察に供述することであれ，他者との共有を行う。こういった類の状況において，元々は視覚的に（または他の感覚を通じてということも実際にある）受け取られた情報を，言語情報へと私たちは変換している。五感からの入力を言葉へと私たちは変えているのである。 ⎡ (1) ⎤ 。映像，音，あるいはにおいを受け取って，それを言語化するたびに，私たちは潜在的に情報を変更したり失ったりする。言語を通じて伝達できる細部の量には限界があるので，私たちは端折らざるをえない。つまり，単純化するのである。これは，心理学者ジョナサン・スクーラーによって考案された用語，「言語隠蔽」として知られている過程である。

　ピッツバーグ大学の研究者だったスクーラーは，同僚のトーニャ・イングストラースクーラーと共著で，1990年に言語隠蔽に関する最初の一連の研究を発表した。彼らの主な研究に関わった実験参加者たちは，最初に30秒間の銀行強盗のビデオを見た。それから20分間，無関係な作業をした後に，参加者の半分は，銀行強盗の顔の特徴を書き留めるのに5分費やし，一方，残りの半分の参加者は国とその首都の名前を言う課題に取りかかった。この後，参加者全員が面通しのために列になった8人の顔を提示されるが，彼らの顔は，研究者たちの言い方では，「言語的に似て」いるものだった。それが意味するのは，彼らの顔が，たとえば「髪がブロンドで，目が緑で，鼻はほどほどの大きさで，耳が小さく，唇が薄い」といったように，同じ種類の言語的描写に合致するということである。これは純粋に視覚的な類似を基に写真を合致させるのとは異なるのだが，それは，顔の造作の数学的な距離といった，言葉にしづら

― 49 ―

いものに焦点をあてることもあるからである。

　顔の見た目を言葉で描写して強化する回数が増えれば増えるほど，記憶の中にその映像をより保持できるはずだと私たちは思うだろう。　(2)　。研究者たちの発見によると，強盗の顔の特徴を言葉で書き留めた人たちの方が，そうしなかった人たちに比べて，面通しの人の列の中から正解の人物を特定する作業の出来が実は著しく悪かったのである。たとえば，ある実験では，犯罪者の人相を書き留めた参加者のうちで，列の中から正しい人を選んだのは27パーセントにすぎなかったが，一方で，人相を書き留めなかった人たちの61パーセントがそうすることに成功した。これは非常に大きな違いである。簡単に言葉にできる細部だけを述べることによって，参加者たちは，元の視覚的記憶の細部の一部を見落としてしまったのだ。

　　(3)　，それは，心理学における実験結果を再現するものとしては，おそらく史上最大の努力の結果によっても示されている。それは，33の研究室と100人近くの学者による巨大プロジェクトで，学者の中にはジョナサン・スクーラーとダニエル・シモンズも含まれており，2014年に発表されたものである。研究者全員が同じ方法に従い，実験がさまざまな研究者によって，さまざまな国々で，さまざまな参加者を相手に行われた場合でさえ，言語隠蔽効果は一定だった。映像を言葉にすると，かならずその映像に関する記憶が劣化するのである。

　スクーラーおよびその他の研究者たちによる，さらなる研究が示唆するところでは，この効果は他の状況や感覚にも転移するかもしれないとのことである。何かが言葉にしづらいときにはいつでも，それを言語化すると概して想起が劣化するようである。色，味，あるいはメロディを言葉で表そうとすると，それに関する記憶が劣化する。地図，決断，あるいは感情的判断を言語化してみると，元の状況の細部をすべて思い出すのが，より難しくなる。　(4)　。私たちが目にしたものを誰か他の人が言語化するのを耳にすると，その場合もまた，それに関する記憶が弱められる。友人が起きた事柄を言葉で説明してくれるときには，私たちを手助けしようとしているのかもしれないが，実はそうではなく，私たち自身の元の記憶を隠蔽しているのかもしれないのだ。

　スクーラーによれば，非言語的な物事を言語化することは，細部を失うことに加え，競合する記憶を生成することを私たちに行わせる。出来事を言葉で表したときの記憶と，実際にその出来事を経験したときの記憶の両方を手にする状況へと陥ることになるのである。この言語化による記憶は，元の記憶の断片を圧倒するようであり，その後は言語化したものを，起こったことの最も良い説明として思い出す可能性がある。写真による面通しのように，元の細部全てを取り戻す必要がある同定作業に直面すると，言語的描

写を越えたことを考えるのが難しくなる。要するに，私たちの記憶は，記憶を改善しようとする私たち自身の努力によって悪影響を受ける可能性があるようだ。

　　 (5) 　　。スクーラーの研究はまた，たとえば，単語リスト，発言内容，あるいは事実など，元々言葉の形になっている情報に関しては，記憶を言語化しても記憶能力を減じることはなく，改善させることさえありうる，ということも示している。

【選択肢全訳】

a)　このこと全ては驚くようなことではない

b)　しかし，この過程は不完全である

c)　この効果は，信じられないほど強大である

d)　しかしながら，その逆が真実のようである

e)　このことは間違いなく非常に注意を要する分野である

f)　これはまた，他者が私たちに物事を言語化してくれるときにも成り立つ

g)　この効果は，より複雑な記憶にも及ぶ

h)　このことは，言語化することが必ず悪い考えだということを意味するわけではない

【考え方】

(ア)

(1)　正解は **b)**。空所の直後の部分に「私たちは潜在的に情報を変更したり失ったりする」というマイナス面が述べられていることや，次の文で There is a limit to ...「言語を通じて伝達できる細部の量には限界がある」と述べられていることから，これを端的に「不完全な」と表している b) が適切。

(2)　正解は **d)**。空所の直前の文に「顔の見た目を言葉で描写して強化する回数が増えれば増えるほど，記憶の中にその映像をより保持できるはずだと私たちは思うだろう」とあるのに対し，空所の直後の文には「強盗の顔の特徴を言葉で書き留めた人たちの方が，そうしなかった人たちに比べて，面通しの人の列の中から正解の人物を特定する作業の出来が実は著しく悪かったのである」とあることから，空所手前にある記述の「逆のことが正しい」という内容である d) が適切。

(3)　正解は **c)**。空所を含む第4段落には，世界のさまざまな地域で同じ実験が行われたが，言語遮蔽効果は一定だったという内容が書かれている。これは，言語遮蔽効果が世界中で共通に見られる影響力の強い効果であることを示しているものなので，c) が適切。

(4)　正解は **f)**。空所の手前はあくまで自分が言葉にしづらいことを言語化するとそれに関する記憶が劣化するという内容が書かれているのに対して，空所の後ろには「私たちが目にしたものを誰か他の人が言語化するのを耳にすると，その場合もまた，そ

— 51 —

2018 年　　解答・解説

れに関する記憶が弱められる」と「他者が言語化すること」に話が転じている。よって，その転換を導入するものとなる f) が適切。

⑸　正解は **h)**。空所の後ろの文に「元々言葉の形になっている情報に関しては，記憶を言語化しても記憶能力を減じることはなく，改善させることさえありうる」と「言語化することの良い側面」が書かれていることから h) が適切。

㈠　問題の指示文は，"Jonathan Schooler らが発見したと言われていることの内容を，<u>15 〜 20 語程度の英語</u>で要約せよ。文章から答えを抜き出すのではなく，<u>できるだけ自分の英語で</u>答えよ"というものである。ここで，不明瞭な点がいくつかある。1 つ目は"Jonathan Schooler <u>ら</u>が発見した"という部分だが，これは Schooler 単独で発見したことは含まないという意味なのか，または Schooler 単独で発見したことと Schooler が他の人たちと共に発見したことの両方を含むという意味なのかが，やや不明瞭である。ここでは後者の意味で捉えることにする。2 つ目は"発見した<u>と言われていること</u>"という部分である。なぜこのような表現にしたかは不明だが，本文に Schooler らが発見したことと述べられていること，という解釈でよいだろう。3 つ目は"15 〜 20 語程度の英語"という部分である。どの程度まで許容範囲なのかが不明だが，15 〜 20 語の範囲に収まっているに越したことはない。4 つ目は"<u>できるだけ自分の英語で</u>"という部分である。本文の表現をどの程度借用すると減点対象になるかが不明だが，同じ語を全く用いずに書くことは不可能に近いので，可能な限り言い換えをすればよいだろう。

以上のことを前提として，要約に含めるべきポイントと考えると，以下のような内容になる。

「言葉によらない［言葉にしづらい］事柄を言語化すると，（後に）それを思い出すのがより難しくなる」

これを 3 つのポイントに分けて説明することにする。

1．「言葉によらない［言葉にしづらい］事柄」

第 1 段落から第 4 段落までは，五感（主に視覚）によって得た情報について書かれているが，第 5 段落第 1 文 (Further research by ...) で「この効果は他の状況や感覚にも転移するかもしれない」と述べられており，続く第 2 文 (It seems that ...) に「何かが言葉にしづらいときにはいつでも，それを言語化すると概して想起が劣化するようである」と書かれているので，元となる情報は五感によるものに限らず，言葉にしづらいもの全般である。さらにこれは，次の第 6 段落第 1 文 (According to Schooler, ...) に "verbalising non-verbal things"「非言語的な物事を言語化することは」と端的に言い換えられてもいる。以上より，experiences that are difficult

— 52 —

2018 年　　解答・解説

to put into words / a non-verbal experience[memory] / events (that) we have experienced non-verbally などの表現を用いればよい。

2．「を言語化すると」

　これに相当する表現は本文に幾度となく登場する。第 1 段落第 3 文 (In these kinds ...) の we are transferring ... into verbal information，第 1 段落第 4 文 (We are turning ...) の We are turning ... into words，空所 (1) の直後の we take ... and verbalise them，第 4 段落最終文 (Putting pictures into ...) の Putting ... into words，第 5 段落第 2 文 (It seems that ...) の verbalisation of it，同段落第 3 文 (Try to describe ...) の describe，第 4 文 (Try describing a ...) の describing，第 6 段落第 1 文 (According to Schooler, ...) の verbalising non-verbal things などがそうである。ここから put[translate] ... into words / describe ... / express ... in words といった表現を用いればよい。ちなみに，第 2，3 段落で述べられている実験の説明の中に「書き留める」(write down) という表現があるが，文章全体を読むと必ずしも書かなくても同じ効果が出てしまうことがわかるため，この表現を用いるのは不適切である。

3．「(後に) それを思い出すのがより難しくなる；それに関する記憶が低下する」

　本文のいくつかの箇所で，上記 2 つの述べ方をしているが，内容的には同じことなので，どちらかの表現を用いればよい。第 4 段落最終文 (Putting pictures into ...) の always makes our memories of those pictures worse，第 5 段落第 2 文 (It seems that ...) の generally diminishes recall，同段落第 3 文 (Try to describe ...) の you make your memory of it worse，第 4 文 (Try describing a ...) の it becomes harder to remember all the details of the original situation が主な例である。ここから，negatively affects our ability to remember those events / it will be more difficult to recall it later / makes our memory of them worse / can have a negative influence on our memory といった表現を用いればよい。

　ちなみに，第 1，3 段落に述べられている「情報の一部が削られる」という部分は「記憶が低下する」原因なのだが，第 6 段落第 1 文 (According to Schooler, ...) に「細部を失うことに加え，競合する記憶を生成することを私たちに行わせる」とあるので，「記憶が低下する」原因は 2 つあることになり，片方だけを含めるのは不適切である。Describing a nonverbal experience will make recalling it harder by creating another, edited, memory in addition to the original memory.（20 words）のようにすれば全て含めることはできるが，受験生には至難の業だろう。

　加えて，最終段落には「元の情報が言葉の形態になっている場合ならば言語化し

— 53 —

ても記憶は悪化しない」という主旨の内容があるが，これに関する記述は Schooler らが発見したことのうち，ごくわずかな部分しか占めないため，無視するのがよいだろう。Describing received information makes our memory of it worse except when the information was originally in word form. (18 words) のようにすれば問題ないだろうが，これも受験生には至難の業だろう。

　以上のことを踏まえ，下記の解答例のような英文を作成すればよい。

解答

> (ア)　(1)− b)　　　(2)− d)　　　(3)− c)　　　(4)− f)　　　(5)− h)
> (イ)　[解答例1]　Using words to describe events we have experienced non-verbally negatively affects our ability to remember those events. (17 words)
> 　　　[解答例2]　When we translate a non-verbal experience into words, it will be more difficult to recall it later. (17 words)

2 (A)

　文学作品からの抜粋を読んで思ったことを書かせるというのは新傾向の問題だが，モチーフになっているものが写真やイラスト，ことわざから変化しただけなので，本質的には同じ。

考え方

<語数について>

　「40～60語」とあるから，この指定より多くても少なくてもいけない（特に，少ない場合は減点あるいは0点にされる可能性が高い）。また，答案の最後に「○○ words」と書き添えよう。

<内容のポイント>

☆「二人の対話の内容について思うこと」とある。「思うこと」＝「感想」と考えれば，何を書いてもいいと考えるかもしれないが，それは間違いである。対話がテーマとしている内容を踏まえて，それについてのコメントをつけなければならない。したがって，「この二人が何を言いたいのかわからない」「シェイクスピアの作品は個人的に大好きである」「中世の英語が現代英語とあまりにも違うことに驚いた」など，テーマと無関係なことを書けば，大幅な減点対象となるだろう。

☆ 与えられた会話文のテーマだが，ブルータスのセリフ「目は，…他のものを通してしか自分自身を見ることができない」に対して，キャシアスが「きみ自身もまだ

— 54 —

2018年　解答・解説

知らないきみの姿を，あるがままにきみに見せてやろう」と返しているところがポイントである。要するに，人は自分のことは自分でわからず，自分の考えや行動の妥当性を判断するには他者の反応や意見などに注目しなければならない，ということ。まずこれを正確に理解した上で答案を展開することが重要。

＜答案作成＞

ここで，答案の展開方法を具体例に沿って見てみることにする。

［解答例1］

「この対話が語るところに同意する」→「自分では問題ないことをやっていると思いがち」→「他者が不快な顔をしているのを見て，初めて自分の行いが他者に迷惑をかけていることに気づく」

自分では全く問題がないと思っても，他者の反応を見て初めて自分の行いの不適切さがわかる，という趣旨。問題文の内容をもっともなことと肯定的にとらえている。

［解答例2］

「この対話は重要な教訓を教えてくれる」→「他者のためになると思っていることが，迷惑になることもある」→「常に他者の反応に注目をすることが大切」→「世間には他者の目を気にせず，勝手気ままに行動する者が多いのは残念だ」

前半は解答例1と同趣旨だが，後半では他者の反応を見ようとしない独断的な人間が多い現実を懸念する内容となっている。

［解答例3］

「我々は自分を直接見ることはできず，思っている自分と実際の自分はしばしば異なる」→「他者が自分の行動に対して忠告をしてくれたときは，謙虚に耳を傾けるべきだ」

どのような行動をとるかについては具体的に言及せず，日頃の行動すべてについて言及したもので，その点では解答例1や2よりも一般的な内容となっている。

解 答 例

［解答例1］

I agree with what this dialogue says. We tend to think we are doing the right thing and there is no problem with it. However, it is not until other people do something like making an annoyed face that we realize what we are doing is bothering them. (48 words)

2018年　解答・解説

［解答例2］

　This dialogue teaches us an important lesson. What we think will benefit others may turn out to be a terrible nuisance to them, so when we do something, we should always be careful to notice how they react. Unfortunately, there are many people who do things in any way they like, without caring what other people think.　(57 words)

［解答例3］

　We cannot see ourselves directly, and what we think we are is often different from what we actually are. Therefore, when other people try to give us some advice on how we should behave, we should never ignore it, but listen to it humbly. (44 words)

2 (B)

考え方

⑴ **「それは恐らく，…という意味であろう」** This probably means that ...

☆「それ」は This / That / It いずれもOK。ちなみにこの「それ」とは問題文冒頭にある小林秀雄の言葉のことであるから，「小林秀雄が言いたかったことは」と考えて，"He wanted to say that SV" "What he meant was that SV" などとまとめてもよい。

☆「恐らく…あろう」は probably が最適。

☆「…という意味で」は mean that SV。

⑵ **「自分が日常生活においてすべきだと思い込んでいること」** what you assume you should do in your daily life

☆「日常生活」は daily [everyday] life。所有格はつけてもつけなくてもよい。つける場合だが，本問は一般論であるから your か our（ただし our なら our daily lives と複数形にするのが通常）。

☆「すべき」は should [have to] do。

☆「思い込んでいる」は assume [think / believe] that SV。take it for granted that だが，これは自分に関する事柄に対しては用いないので誤り。

☆「こと」は関係代名詞 what または the things。「日常生活においてすべきだと思い込んでいること」は状況によってその都度決まる，つまり「特定」の事柄だから，関係代名詞 what が使える。thing を用いる場合，この「思い込んでいること」とは

－ 56 －

いろいろなものが考えられるので，複数形にする。

(3) 「…をやってそれでよしとしているようでは」**if you are happy with doing ...**

☆「…をやってそれでよしとする」だが，「…することに満足する」と解釈するなら be happy [satisfied / content] with – ing を使う。「…することで十分だと考える」と解釈して think [believe] it is enough [fine] to – などと表現することもできる。ちなみに，この部分は「すべきだと思い込んでいることをやって，それだけで満足する」というニュアンスなので，just や only などをつける方が望ましい。

(4) 「人生など終わってしまう」**your life will be over**

☆この部分は「人生があっという間に過ぎていってしまう」という時間経過の速さを表しているもので，「突然死を迎える」ということではない。したがって，your life will come to an end / your life will end / you will die などとするのは良くないのだが，減点対象とはならないだろう。別解としては you will be at the end of your life など。

☆時制だが，これはあくまでも予測であって事実ではないので，単純現在形は誤り。未来の表現 will を用いるべきである。

(5) 「いつの間にか」**before you know it**

☆「いつの間にか」という日本語の英訳としては before you know it / without realizing it などが定型表現のように見なされているが，後者の使用には注意が必要。without – ing はこの動名詞の意味上の主語が文の主語と一致していなければならない。したがって，your life will be over *without realizing it* は誤りとなる。

解 答 例

［解答例 1］
　This probably means that if you are happy with just doing what you assume you should do in your daily life, before you know it, your life will be over.
［解答例 2］
　It probably means that if you are satisfied with just doing what you believe you have to do in your everyday life, you will be at the end of your life without realizing it.
［解答例 3］
　He probably wanted to say that your life will be over before you know it if you think it is enough to do only the things you think you should do in your daily life.

— 57 —

2018年　解答・解説

4 （A）**【全訳】** 推理小説の起源はシェイクスピアまでさかのぼる。だが，エドガー・アラン・ポーが書いた，理性的な犯罪事件の解決を行う小説は，重要なジャンルを創出した。彼の物語は誰が犯人かという謎の解明を中心に展開し，(21-22)<u>その謎解きに読者も誘い込む</u>のである。

そのような物語に登場する重要人物は探偵である。ポーの小説に出てくる探偵オーギュスト・デュパンは，暇を持て余す紳士である。彼は働く必要がない。その代わり，「分析」を使って実際の警察が犯罪事件を解決する手助けをすることに没頭している。

シャーロック・ホームズの産みの親アーサー・コナン・ドイルでさえ，ポーの影響を認めざるを得なかった。シャーロックのように，デュパンはパイプを吸っている。さらに彼は異常なほど聡明かつ理性的で，(23-24)<u>思考力を用いて事件解決</u>という偉業を達成する，一種のスーパーヒーローである。そしてどちらの場合も，探偵に文字通りつきまとっている物語の語り手は，その同居人である。

ポーが用いた事件解決法は，19世紀の科学精神に訴えた。推理小説は，(25-26)<u>いかなる疑問でも推理によって答えを出せる</u>ことを約束するものだったからである。推理小説が流行ったのは，知性が勝利することを約束したからである。犯罪は理性的な探偵が解決してくれるだろう。科学が (27-28)<u>厄介者</u>を追跡してとらえ，<u>誠実な人々が夜安眠できる</u>ようにしてくれるだろう。

［考え方］

(21-22)　正解は **g)，b)**。並べ替えた英文：inviting readers **to** solve the **puzzle**

①　the をつけるなら readers か puzzle だが，直前に "solving the puzzle of ..." とあることから，solve the puzzle ではないかと考える。

②　invite には "invite ＋ 人 ＋ to ‒ "（〈人〉に‒するよう依頼する；誘惑する）という語法があるので，inviting readers to とし，さらに①と合わせて inviting readers to solve the puzzle とまとめる。構文的には inviting は分詞構文で，前半の情報に対する付加説明とすれば問題はない。内容的には，「ポーの小説は謎解きを中心に展開し，そこに読者も引き込んでくる」と考えればやはり問題はない。

(23-24)　正解は **d)，f)**。並べ替えた英文：who uses **powers** of thinking **to** accomplish

①　空所の直前が "He's also unnaturally smart and rational, a kind of superhero" となっていることから，空所は superhero を先行詞とする関係代名詞（who）節ではないかと考える。

②　uses は第3文型の動詞なので目的語が必要。したがって uses powers とまとめる。

— 58 —

2018年　解答・解説

③　空所直後の great feats of crime-solving は名詞句なので，目的語になっている可能性が高い。feats（偉業）という語の意味を考えると，組み合わせとしては accomplish（成し遂げる）が最適。accomplish は原形なので，その前に to をつけて to accomplish〈great feats of crime-solving〉としておく。

④　残った選択肢は is / of / thinking だが，①の続きを who is thinking of とすると of には目的語が必要だから who is thinking of powers とし，uses が「不要な語」となる。しかし，〈superhero〉who is thinking of powers to accomplish〈great feats of crime-solving〉は「〈事件解決という偉業〉を成し遂げる力を考慮中である〈スーパーヒーロー〉」が直訳で，全く要領を得ない。ここで発想を転換し，②の「力」とは「思考力」ということではないかと考え，is を不要な語とすると，who uses powers of thinking to accomplish となる。直訳は「〈事件解決という偉業〉を成し遂げるために思考力を用いる〈スーパーヒーロー〉」で，Dupin が理詰めで事件を解決しているタイプの探偵だったということがわかる。ちなみに，これは "think to − " ではなく，uses powers of thinking の後に「目的」（「結果」で解釈してもよい）の意味の副詞用法の to − が続いている。

(25-26)　正解は **d)**，**h)**。並べ替えた英文：reasoning could **hold** the answer **to** any

①　空所の直前は "because detective stories promised that" となっているから，空所は接続詞 that の節中の文であることがわかる。

②　could の後に続くのは answer か hold のみ。しかし，answer を動詞としてとらえると，その目的語に相当するものが見つからない（空所直後にある question に the をつけて answer the〈question〉とするのは無理がある）。したがって，ここは could hold とするのが妥当。

③　answer が名詞ならば，やはり空所直後の question とからめるのがよいだろう。answer も question も可算名詞であるから，原則として単数無冠詞では使えない。すると，考えられるのは the answer to any〈question〉か any answer to the〈question〉のいずれかになる。the〈question〉は「その疑問」という意味だが，指し示すものが見当たらない。したがって，前者つまり the answer to any〈question〉とまとめるのが適切。

④　残った選択肢は in / reasoning。①〜③において未決事項は could hold の主語だから，reasoning を主語として reasoning could hold the answer to any〈question〉とする。

(27-28)　正解は **c)**，**e)**。並べ替えた英文：troublemakers and **let** honest souls **sleep**

①　let が使役動詞なら "let ＋ O ＋原形" という形になるはずだから，とりあえず

— 59 —

2018 年　　解答・解説

let souls [または troublemakers] sleep" としておく。

　②　honest(誠実な)は内容的に troublemakers(厄介者)とはつながりにくいから，honest souls にしておく（この souls は「魂」ではなく「人」という意味）。

　③　空所の直前にある the に続く名詞は troublemakers か honest souls のいずれかだが，さらのその前にある track down が「…を追い詰めて捕まえる」という意味であることが大きなヒント。ただし，この表現を知らなくとも問題はない。①の段階で「厄介者を夜眠らせる」では意味がよくわからないので，こちらが let honest souls sleep であるなら，track down の目的語は必然的に〈the〉troublemakers となる。

　④　track down と let をつなぐ接続詞は and。nor は neither とセットで使う必要があるので，不適当。

解答

(21-22)　g)，b)	(23-24)　d)，f)
(25-26)　d)，h)	(27-28)　c)，e)

4 **(B)** **全訳**　一つの種として，鳥はこの地上に１億年以上にわたって存在している。鳥は自然界における偉大なサクセスストーリーの一つであり，生き延びるために新しい生存戦略を編み出したり，鳥ならではの独特な知力を用いたりしているのだが，そうした知力は少なくともいくつかの点で，我々の知力をはるかに超えているように思われる。

　霧に包まれたはるか遠い昔のある時期に，すべての鳥の共通の祖先が暮らしていた。今では約 10,400 種の異なった鳥がおり，これは哺乳類の種の２倍以上である。1990 年代の終わりに科学者は，地球上にいる野生の鳥の総数を推定した。そして２千億から４千億の個別の鳥がいるのではないかという話になった。(ア)これは人間一人当たりおおよそ 30 羽から 60 羽の生きた鳥がいるということである。人間の方がより成功を収めているとか進歩していると言えるかどうかは，本当のところそうした言葉をどのように定義するか次第なのだ。というのも，進化の本質は進歩ではなく，生存であるからだ。その本質は，自分の環境の諸問題を解決できるようになるということであり，それを鳥たちは極めて長い間にわたって，驚くほどうまくやってきたのだ。(イ)私が思うに，このために一層驚きなのは，これまで多くの人は，鳥は我々には想像ができない点で賢い可能性があるという考えを容易に受け入れることができなかったということである。

— 60 —

2018年　解答・解説

　鳥は学習する。新しい問題を解決し，古い問題に対して新たな解決策を編み出す。鳥は道具を作り，それを用いる。数を数える。他の鳥の行動を真似し合う。どこに物を置いたかを覚えている。(ウ)鳥の知力が我々の複雑な思考と完全に同じであったり似ていることはなくても，鳥の知力にそのもとになるものが含まれていることが多い。たとえばその一例に当たるのが洞察力で，それは試行錯誤を伴う学習がないまま完璧な解決策が突然現れることと定義されてきている。

【考え方】

(ア)　**That's roughly 30 to 60 live birds per person.**「それは，一人当たりおおよそ 30 羽から 60 羽の生きた鳥がいるということになる」

　That は前文の「2千億羽から4千億羽の鳥がいる」という内容を受けている。「thatの内容を明らかにせよ」という指示はないので，「それ；これ」と訳出しておけば充分である。roughly は「おおよそ；大雑把に言って」の意の副詞。live は「生きている」の意の形容詞で，直後の birds を修飾している。[laiv] と発音されることにも注意。per person は「一人当たり」の意。

(イ)　1．**This (S) ... makes (V) it (O) all the more surprising (C)**「このためにそれは一層驚くべきこととなる」　This は前の「鳥は長い間にわたって自分の置かれている環境にかかわる諸問題を驚くほどうまく解決してきたこと」を指している。「This の内容を明らかにせよ」という指示はないので，「これ」と訳出しておけばよい。all the more ... で「一層…」の意。(例) The movie is *all the more* interesting because of the special effects.（その映画は特殊効果のおかげでいっそう面白いものになっている）　it は後続する3．の that 節を指す形式目的語。

　2．**to my mind**「私の考えでは」　to ...'s mind で「…の考えでは」の意。(例) It was after two and, *to my mind*, time to go to bed.（午前2時をまわっていたし，私の考えではもう寝るべき時間だった）

　3．**that many (S) of us have found (V) it (O) hard (C) to swallow the idea**「我々の多くは…考えをなかなか受け入れることができなかった」　この that 節内の it は to swallow ... を指す形式目的語。swallow ... は「…を（簡単に）信ずる；鵜呑みにする」の意の動詞。

　4．**that birds may be bright**「鳥は頭がいいかもしれない〈という考え〉」　この that 節は3．の the idea と同格で働いている。bright はここでは「明るい」ではなく「頭がいい；利口な」の意の形容詞。

　5．**in ways we can't imagine**「我々には想像ができない点で」　be bright を修飾する副詞句。way は「方法」以外にも「面」や「点」といった意味で用いられる

— 61 —

ともあるので注意。(例) They are different in many *ways*.（彼らは多くの点で異なっている）　ways と we の間には目的格の関係代名詞が省略されている。

(ウ)　1．**Even when their mental powers don't quite match or mirror our own complex thinking**「鳥たちの知力が我々の複雑な思考と完全には同じではないか，似てはいない場合でさえ」　mental は「精神的な」以外にも「知能の；知的な」の意で用いることができる。ここはその後者の例。not quite は「完全に…ではない」の意の部分否定。(例) That movie was*n't quite* as good as we expected.（その映画の出来は完全に期待通りというわけではなかった）　match は「…に合う；一致する；匹敵する」，mirror は「…とよく似ている」の意。その二つの動詞の共通の目的語が our ... thinking である。

2．**they often contain the seeds of it**「それらはしばしばその種［もとになるもの］を含んでいる」　they は「鳥の知力」, it は「人間の複雑な思考」を受けている。この問題も「指示語の内容を明らかにして」とはなっていないので、they と it の内容を明らかにする必要はない。seed は「種；もと；原因」といった意味。(例) the *seeds* of doubt（疑念の種；疑いのもと）

3．**insight, for instance,**「たとえば洞察力」「人間の複雑な思考のもとになるものが鳥の知力には備わっている」と前で述べられているが、この「洞察力」はその一例として挙げられている。

4．**which has been defined as ...**「…と定義されている〈洞察力〉」　define A as B で「AをBと定義する」の意。それが受動態になると, A is defined as B となる。(例) Obesity *is defined as* a BMI of 30 or above.（肥満は BMI30 以上と定義されている）

5．**the sudden emergence of a complete solution without trial-and-error learning**「思考錯誤を伴った学習なしに，完全な解決策が突然現れること〈と定義されている〉」　emergence of a ... solution は A ... solution (S) emerges (V). という文が名詞化されたもの。「解決策の出現」という訳でも構わないし，名詞化される前の文を意識して「解決策が出現すること」などと処理してもよい。without ... learning は形容詞句で前の名詞句を修飾している。trial-and-error は, trial and error「試行錯誤」という名詞句をハイフンでつないで一語にまとめたもので，後続する learning を修飾する形容詞として働いている。

2018年　　解答・解説

解　答

(ア)　これは人間一人当たりおおよそ30羽から60羽の生きた鳥がいるということである。

(イ)　私が思うに，このために一層驚きなのは，これまで多くの人は，鳥は我々には想像ができない点で賢い可能性があるという考えを容易に受け入れることができなかったということである。

(ウ)　鳥の知力が我々の複雑な思考と完全に同じであったり似ていることはなくても，鳥の知力にそのもとになるものが含まれていることが多い。例えばその一例が当たるのが洞察力で，それは試行錯誤を伴う学習がないまま完璧な解決策が突然現れることと定義されてきている。

5　**全訳**　「ジェイニー，こちらはクラークさんよ。階段の下の部屋を見にいらしたの」　ジェイニーが単語一つ一つを口の動きから正しく読み取って理解できるようにと，彼女の母親は必要以上にゆっくりかつ慎重に話した。ジェイニーはそんなことはしなくてもよいと母親に何度も言ってきたが，母親がたとえ人前でもほとんどいつもそうしたので，ジェイニーは恥ずかしくなった。

　クラーク氏はジェイニーをじっと見つめ続けた。たぶん，母さんの話し方のせいで，あの人は私の耳が不自由だと思っているのね。それを言っていなかったのだとしたら，いかにも母さんらしいわ。ことによると彼は，少し間をおいて私が話すかどうかを確認して，自分が抱いている考えを裏付けようとしていたのかもしれない。ジェイニーはただ，自らの沈黙の意味を彼が勝手に解釈するがままにしておいた。

　「部屋をお見せしてあげて」と母親は言った。

　ジェイニーはもう一度うなずき，体の向きを変えてクラーク氏が自分の後ろをついてくるようにした。すぐ目の前の階段の一角の下に，一人用の寝室があった。彼女がドアを開けると，クラーク氏は彼女の横を通って部屋に入り，振り向いて彼女の方を見た。彼の視線を感じてジェイニーは不愉快な気持ちになったが，別に自分が彼から一人の女性として見られているという感じはしなかった（好みの男性にならそうしてほしいと昔だったら思ったかもしれない見られ方ではあったが）。もう恋愛をする年齢は過ぎ去ってしまったとジェイニーは感じていた。以前はその終焉を嘆き悲しんだものだったが，その後彼女はそれを克服していた。

　「いい部屋だね」と彼は手話で伝えた。「借りることにするよ」

　それだけだった。何の会話もなく，ジェイニーの耳が不自由だとどうして確信した

— 63 —

のかの説明もなく，どうやって自分が手話を使えるようになったかの説明もなかった。

　ジェイニーは母親のもとに戻り，ある疑問を手話で伝えた。

　「写真家さんよ」と母親は言ったが，今回も話し方は必要以上にゆっくりだった。「写真を撮りながら世界中を旅しているって言っているわ」

　「何の写真を？」

　「建物ですって」

＊　　　　　　　　　　　　　　　　＊

　音楽がジェイニーにとっての無音への入り口だった。まだほんの10歳だった頃，彼女は家の外の階段を上ったところにある縁側の端に座り，教会の聖歌隊の歌に耳を傾けていた。すると彼女はめまいを感じ始め，突如として音楽の中へと背中から倒れていった。

　数日後の夜に彼女が目を覚ますと，自分の部屋のベッドの中で無音に囲まれるようになった。子どもだったら誰もがそうするように，彼女は混乱して叫び声をあげ，母親がすぐにジェイニーのもとにやって来た。しかし，病と混乱がますます存在感を増していた彼女の内側を別とすると，音の聞こえ方がどこかおかしかった，いや，そもそも音が聞こえなくなっていた。彼女は自分の声も聞こえず，自分が発した「ママ」という呼び声も聞こえていなかった。そして，ジェイニーの母親が彼女の身体をすでにしっかりつかまえてはいたものの，ジェイニーはまた叫び声をあげた。しかし，その声は無音の世界へと投げかけられただけであり，そんな無音の世界に彼女は今生きているのだ。彼女はあまりにも長期間そこで生きてきたので，目に見えないその世界の中で不安に感じることはなかった。その世界が自分を救ってくれ，いつどんな時（実際にそういう時は存在した）にも彼女が必要とする分だけ閉じこもれる自分だけの居場所を与えてくれると，彼女は時折思ったのであった。

　ジェイニーの母親の怒りは，いつも床を通して伝わってきた。ジェイニーが最初にそれを知ったのは，まだ小さい子どものころに母親と父親が口論している時のことだった。両親の言葉は彼女にとっては音としては存在していなかったのかもしれないが，怒りがいつも自ずから振動を発していたのだ。

　ジェイニーは，当時両親がなぜ口論をしていたのか正確にはわかっていなかったが，子どもは子どもなりに，その口論がたいていの場合は自分に関するものだろうと感じとっていた。ある日，ジェイニーが家の裏にある森で遊んでいるのに母親が気づいて，ジェイニーがどうしても自分の後について家に帰ろうとしなかった時，彼女はジェイニーの腕をつかんで，ジェイニーを引きずりながら森の中を進んでいった。ジェイニーはしまいには腕を振りほどいて，言葉ではなく，彼女の感情すべてを1つの激しい振

2018年　　解答・解説

動で表現したような絶叫で，母親に向かって叫び声をあげた。母親はジェイニーの顔を強く平手打ちした。ジェイニーは母が震えている姿を目にして，母が自分のことを愛しているのだとわかった。しかし，愛情とは時に無音にも似て，美しくはあるが耐え難いものだった。ジェイニーの父親は，「母さんは自分の感情を抑えることができないんだよ」とジェイニーに言った。

＊　　　　　　　　　　　＊

数週間後，クラーク氏はジェイニーに「手伝ってもらえたりしないかな」と言った。「私にできるなら」と，ジェイニーは指を使って伝えた。

「建物に関してちょっと知っておく必要があるんだ，明日写真を撮ることになっている建物なんだけどね。もしよかったら，その建物の歴史を何かしら僕に教えてくれないかなあ」

彼女はうなずき，自分が必要とされ，ささいなことであっても役に立てることをうれしいと感じた。するとクラーク氏は，オークヒルの頂上にある古い家屋まで同行してくれるよう彼女に頼んだ。「楽しいんじゃないかな。少しの間ここから離れてみるのもね」

ジェイニーはキッチンのドアの方に目をやったが，なぜ自分がその方向を向いたか最初は自分でもわからなかった。ことによると彼女は，なんらかの無意識のレベルで，ほんの一瞬前には自分が理解していなかったことを理解したのかもしれない。そこには母親が立っていた。彼女はクラーク氏の話をずっと聞いていたのだった。

ジェイニーはもう一度彼の方を向くと，彼の唇の動きを読み取った。「明日一緒に行かないかい？」

ジェイニーは母親が近づいてくるすばやい振動を感じた。彼女は母親の方を向くと，母親の怒りと不安を目にした。それはいつも彼女が目にする様子と同じであった。ジェイニーは深く息を吸い込むと，耳障りなささやきのようにして，2つの単語を息だけを使って口から絞り出した。その音は，彼女が知る限りでは，病気の子どもや瀕死の人の口から発せられる音に似た響きのものだったのかもしれない。「行くわ」とジェイニーは言ったのだった。

ジェイニーの母親は驚いた様子でジェイニーを見つめた。母親の驚きが普段より大きかったのが，残されたわずかな声を自分が使ったことが原因なのか，それとも自分が言った内容が原因なのかは，ジェイニーにはよくわからなかった。

「だめ。絶対だめよ」と母親は言った。「明日は家事をいくらか手伝ってもらう必要があるの」

「いいえ」彼女は手話でそう伝えて，首を横に振った。「その必要はないわ」

— 65 —

2018年　　解答・解説

「ちゃんとわかってるでしょ，母さんには手伝いが必要だって。やらなきゃいけない掃除があるのよ」

「それは後回しよ」と告げると，ジェイニーは母親に返事をする隙を与えずに歩いて出ていった。

【考え方】

(A)　It is like ... to − で，通常は「−することはいかにも…らしい」という意味になる。(例) *It is like* him *to* behave so strangely. 「そんな奇妙な行動をするなんていかにも彼らしい」　また "to have 過去分詞" という完了不定詞は，主節に先行する時間（「…したこと」）を表す。よって，下線部の意味は「それを言っていなかったことは，いかにも彼女の母親らしいだろう」となる。

次に，直前の「彼女の母親の話し方のせいで，彼はジェイニーの耳が不自由だと思っているのだ」という内容より，it「それ」が指すのは「ジェイニーの耳が不自由であるということ」であると判断できる。

加えて，クラーク氏と初めて会ったこの場面でのジェイニーにとっては，このやりとりだけで「母親がクラーク氏に自分の耳が不自由だと言わなかった」とは確信できていないはずなので，ここでの not to − は，むしろ「−しなかったとしたら」という"仮定・憶測"を示すと解釈するのが妥当であり，そう考えれば，"推量・婉曲"の助動詞 would が使われているのも自然である。

さらに，下線部の直前の文の Maybe や直後の文の Perhaps より，下線部とその前後の合計3文は「ジェイニーの心理の描写」であると考えるのが妥当である（もし「語り手の考え」であれば，Maybe や Perhaps が使われているのは不自然であり，さらに，この状況で「−しなかったのは母親らしい」と感じる可能性があるのはジェイニー以外には考えられない）。このような心理の描写を受けて，段落最終文の「ジェイニーはただ，自らの沈黙の意味を彼が勝手に解釈するがままにしておいた」という客観描写につながっていくと考えれば，自然な文脈となる。

以上より，この下線部の意味を，「ジェイニーの心理の描写」であることも考慮に入れて自然な日本語に訳すと，**「私の耳が不自由だと言っていなかったとしたら，いかにも母らしいことだろう」**となる。ただし，「ジェイニーの耳が不自由だと言っていなかったとしたら［…言っていなかったことは］，いかにも彼女の母親らしいことだろう」といった解答もおそらく認められるであろう。

(B)　(B29)　ジェイニーの家の中の部屋を見に来たクラーク氏が，部屋を見て「いい部屋だね」と言った後に（手話で）ジェイニーに気持ちを伝える箇所である。この後の話の展開より，クラーク氏はその部屋を間借りして住んだことがわかるので，空

— 66 —

所には「この部屋を借りたい」といった意味の表現が入ることになり，これにふさわ
しいのは e) **I'll take it.**「この部屋を借りることにするよ」となる。

　(B30)　空所には，直前でジェイニーの母親が「写真家さんよ」，「写真を撮りなが
ら世界中を旅してるって言っているわ」と述べているのを受ける発言が入る。直後で
"Buildings"「建物ですって」と母親が答えており，そのような返答を引き出すのは「何
の写真を？」という疑問しかない。よって，正解は d) **Of what?**「何の？」となる。

　(B31)　この空所に入るジェイニーのセリフは，クラーク氏からの「明日一緒に
行かないかい？」という誘いに対する返事である。後ろに記された母親の反応から，
ジェイニーはこの誘いを受諾したと考えられるので，それにふさわしい表現は a) **I'll
go.**「行くわ」しかない。

　(B32)　翌日クラーク氏と外出すると告げた後に，それを聞いた母親から「だめ。
絶対だめよ」「明日は家事をいくらか手伝ってもらう必要があるの」と反論されたジェ
イニーが，「いいえ」と手話で自分の気持ちを伝え，首を横に振った後に伝える表現
が入る。ここで注目すべきは，空所直後の You know good and well I do.「ちゃん
とわかってるでしょ，母さんには手伝いが必要だって」という母親のセリフである
（good and well で「十分に」という意味の副詞句で，I do の前に接続詞 that が省
略されている）。この代動詞 do は空所の前の母親のセリフにある need you to help
me ... を指しているので，空所にも同じ意味の do を含んでいる f) **You don't.** (=
You don't need me to help you ...)「母さんにはその必要はない」を入れるのが正し
い。空所とその手前の部分だけを見ると，b) I can't. や c) I won't. でも良いように思
われるが，これらを空所に入れてしまうと後ろの I do につながらない。

　(C)　まず，1つ目の空所には動詞の過去形が入り，2つ目と3つ目の空所には動詞
の過去分詞形が入ることになる。よって，3つの空所に共通して入るのは，過去形と
過去分詞形が同じ形をしたものになるので，正解の候補は a) **ended** と c) **seemed** と
d) **sounded** に絞られる。さらに，1つ目と2つ目の空所付近は，ジェイニーが自分
の聴覚が正常ではないことに気づく場面なので，1つ目の空所に sounded が入れば，
sounded (V) wrong (C) という第2文型で「普通ではないように聞こえた：音の聞こ
え方がおかしかった」となり，2つ目の空所に sounded が入れば，第1文型で「（音
が）鳴っていなかった」となり，どちらも文脈上自然である。さらに，3つ目の空所
に sounded が入れば，sounded 〈...〉like 〜「（ジェイニーが発した音が）〜のように
聞こえた」となり，こちらも意味が通じるので，正解は d) **sounded** となる。

　seem には第1文型の用法はないので，c) seemed は不適。また，上で述べたよう
に，1つ目と2つ目の空所付近ではジェイニーの聴覚世界が話題にされているので，a)

2018年　　解答・解説

ended も明らかに不適である。

⒟　下線部の直前を見ると，at any given moment「いつどんな時にも」という表現があるので，下線部はこの moment を受けて「実際に（そういう）時は存在した」と述べていると考えられる。よって，この at any given moment の moment が「どういう時か」を考えればよい。下線部を含む文のダッシュの前までの意味は，「それ（＝無音の世界）が自分を救ってくれ，いつどんな時にも彼女が必要とする分だけ閉じこもれる自分だけの居場所を与えてくれると，彼女は時折思ったのであった」となっているので，その「時」とは，「彼女が必要とする分だけ閉じこもれる自分だけの居場所を無音の世界が与えてくれる」ような「時」であると判断できる。よって，これに最も近い意味を持つ **d)「彼女が無音の中へと引きこもる必要があった」**が正解となる。残りの３つの選択肢である a)「必要とされる際に彼女に与えられた」b)「彼女が不快な気分でなかった」c)「彼女の母親が彼女を行かせようとしなかった」では，上記の文脈にまったく合わない。

⒠　下線部のセリフは，ジェイニーの父親がジェイニーに言ったものである（下線部直前の Her father の Her と目的語の her は同一人物を指す）。よって，下線部の主語である She は，ジェイニーではなくジェイニーの母親を指しているとわかる（ジェイニーであれば You となるはずである）。次に，can't help oneself で「自分（の感情など）を抑えることができない」という意味になることを知っていたかがポイント（例：I was told not to go to the spot, but I *couldn't help myself.*「その場所には行くなと言われていたが，どうしても自分を抑えられなかった」）。よって下線部の意味は「母さんは自分の感情を抑えることができない」となる。次に，「ジェイニーの母親が自分の感情を抑えることができずにしてしまった行動」を直前の描写から探すと，家に帰ろうと母親に言われたジェイニーが叫び声をあげて反抗したことに対して，母親がジェイニーの顔を平手打ちしたという行動が見つかる。これが，ジェイニーの母親の「自分の感情を抑えられない行動」にあたるので，以上をまとめて，解答は**「ジェイニーが叫び声をあげたことに対して彼女の頬を平手打ちしたことからわかるように，ジェイニーの母親は自分の感情を抑えることができないということ」**などとすればよい。

⒡　写真家であるクラーク氏は，空所の後ろでジェイニーに「もしよかったら，その建物の歴史を何かしら僕に教えてくれないかなあ」と言い，ジェイニーにその建物まで翌日同行してくれるように頼んでいる。このような文脈を踏まえ，まずは I'll need to の後ろに（動詞の原形である）know を置いて，その後ろに know something about the buildings と続けて「建物に関してちょっと知っておく必要が

－ 68 －

2018 年　　解答・解説

ある」という意味にする。次に，設問文の「どこか 1 か所にコンマを入れること」という指示に着目し，the buildings と同格になる the ones を，コンマをはさんで the buildings の後ろに置き，I will photograph 〈tomorrow〉 をその後ろに続ければ，この部分が the ones を修飾する関係代名詞節（ただし関係代名詞自体は省略されている）になり，〈I'll need to〉**know something about the buildings, the ones I will photograph** 〈tomorrow〉．「建物に関してちょっと知っておく必要があるんだ，明日写真を撮ることになっている建物なんだけどね」となり，意味的にも通じる。

　ちなみに，know about the buildings としてしまうと something を使う場所がなくなってしまうので不可。また，先頭を（もう 1 つの動詞の原形である）photograph にしてしまうと，後ろが photograph the buildings, the ones I will know something about 〈tomorrow〉．となり，全体として要領を得ない内容になってしまう。

　(G)　翌日クラーク氏と一緒に外出すると主張するジェイニーに対して，母親が「掃除を手伝ってほしい」と訴える場面に続く箇所である。ここで，wait に「（物事や事態が）後回しにできる；急を要しない」という意味がある（この wait は can や cannot とともに使われることが多い）ことを知っていたかがポイントである（例：This is urgent, so it cannot *wait*.「これは至急なので，後回しにできない」）。空所に **d) wait** が入れば，「それ（cleaning）は後回しよ（＝私は絶対に外出する）」という意味になり，文脈に合う。a) do や b) not では，どの動詞の代用や省略と見なしても文脈がつながらない。c) postpone「…を延期する」であれば，be postponed とする必要があるので，これも不適である。

解答

(A)　私の耳が不自由だと言っていなかったとしたら，いかにも母らしいことだろう。

(B)　(29)－ e)　　(30)－ d)　　(31)－ a)　　(32)－ f)

(C)　d)

(D)　d)

(E)　ジェイニーが叫び声をあげたことに対して彼女の頬を平手打ちしたことからわかるように，ジェイニーの母親は自分の感情を抑えることができないということ。

(F)　know something about the buildings, the ones I will photograph

(G)　d)

— 69 —

解答・解説

1 (A) **[全訳]** 文化と国は大体交換可能だというのが，多くの人々が認める考え方となっている。たとえば，「日本式」のビジネスのやり方（婉曲的で礼儀正しい）があるはずで，これは「アメリカ式」（率直で押しが強い）とか「ドイツ式」（生真面目で能率的）とは異なるものであり，それゆえ成功を収めたければ，ビジネスの相手国のビジネス文化に適応しなければならない。

しかしながら，近年の研究は，このような仕事のやり方を疑問視する結果を出している。この新たな研究は，35年に渡る558の先行研究から得られたデータを使い，仕事に関する4つの姿勢を分析した。すなわち，個人対集団，階級と地位の重要性，リスクと不確実性の回避，そして競争対集団の和，の4つである。従来の考え方が正しければ，国の中での差異よりも，複数国の間の差異の方がはるかに大きいはずだ。しかし実際は，上記4つの姿勢における差異の80％以上が国の内部で見出されており，国と相関関係がある差異は20％未満であった。

したがって，少なくともビジネスの文脈においては，ブラジル文化やロシア文化について単純化して語ることは危険である。もちろん，歴史・言語の共有，食品とファッションの共有もあり，その他，その国特有の習慣と価値観の共有も多数ある。しかし，グローバル化（人間の移動と技術・思想の交換の両面におけるものだが）のもたらす数多くの影響のおかげで，この国ならこのビジネス文化だと一般化して考えることは，もはや妥当とは言えなくなっている。タイ在住のフランス人実業家が，祖国フランスの人よりもタイの実業家の方と共通点が多いということが十分あり得るのだ。

実際，出身国よりも職業と社会経済的地位の方が，仕事の価値観に関して，はるかに優れた予測をもたらしてくれる。たとえば，さまざまな職業のイギリス人100人よりも，さまざまな国から来た医者100人の方が同じ考え方をする可能性がずっと高いのである。言語を別とすれば，オーストラリアのトラックドライバーは，オーストラリアの弁護士よりも，インドネシアのトラックドライバーの方を馴染みのある仲間だと思う可能性が高いのだ。

交渉がうまくいくかどうかは，交渉相手の行動を予測できるかどうかで決まる。国際的な文脈においては，国民性に関する考え方をもとに判断するほど，誤った予測をし，不適切な対応をすることになるだろう。国をもとに文化的な固定観念を持つのは，全く見当違いなことなのである。

2017年　　解答・解説

【考え方】
　設問の指示が「要旨をまとめよ」となっており，解答字数が最大80字しかない。このような時は，通例，主張の中心をまとめ，残りは軽く触れる程度でよいと思われる。本問は，文章構成の点では典型的なパターンと言えるものなので，中心的な主張を外すことはなかったのではないだろうか。

◇段落ごとの内容
　第1段落に "one widely held view" とあり，多くの人が考えていることが紹介されている。interchangeable という語が使われているが，具体例から「日本なら日本式，アメリカならアメリカ式という風に，国固有のビジネスのやり方があるという考え方」であることが掴めていればよいだろう。そして最後に「成功したければ相手国の相手国のビジネス文化に適応しなければならない」とある。この段落の趣旨は「国ごとに固有の文化があるのだから外国相手のビジネスでは，相手国のビジネス文化に適応すべきだ」となる。

　第2段落で「最近の研究がこのやり方に疑問を投げかけている」とある。ここから第3段落までは，具体的な数値などを使いながら「1つの国に1つの考え方ということは実はあまりない」ゆえに「この国ならこのビジネス文化があると考えることは妥当ではない」と述べられている。

　第4段落では，「出身国よりも職業と社会経済的地位が，仕事の価値観についてはより良い predictor になる」とある。この段階では "predictor" という言葉の意味／意義は，ぼんやりしていてよくわからないが，具体例に「出身国より職種の方が共通点・共感がある」とあるので「国ではなく職業によって相手の考え方が予想できる」という点がわかっていればよい。

　第5段落では，第1文で「交渉が成功するどうかは相手の出方を予測できるかどうかで決まる」，第2文で「国民性を基に判断すると間違った予測になり対応を誤る」，第3文で「文化的に型にはまった考えをするのは間違いだ」とある。この第2文と第3文は，明らかに，第1段落の内容に対応するものになっている。

　このように「一般によくある考え方」に触れ，それを否定して「新たな視点」を紹介し，「結論」につなぐ，という文章構成は主張型の文章の典型の1つと言える。

<u>2017 年　　解答・解説</u>

◇ **全体のアウトライン**

> ＜第１段落＞
> 　各国固有のビジネス文化があるので，相手国のビジネス文化に適応すればうまくいく。
> ＜第２～３段落＞
> 　しかし，このやり方を疑問視する研究がある。
> ＜第４段落＞
> 　職業と社会経済的地位によって，仕事の価値観が，より予測可能になる。
> ＜第５段落＞
> 　１．交渉が成功するどうかは相手の出方を予測できるかどうかで決まる。
> 　２．国民性を基に判断すると間違った予測になり対応を誤る。
> 　３．文化的に型にはまった考えをするのは間違いだ。

◇ **解答のまとめ方**

　先に述べたように解答字数が 80 字しかないので，第５段落の内容を中心とし「相手国の文化に関する固定観念を基にして相手の動きを予想すると交渉は失敗する」（37 字）とまとめてみる。言うまでもなく，この文章は「外国相手のビジネス（国際ビジネス）」の分野に限定した話なので，この点も入れておく。これだけでは第４段落で紹介された新たな視点を無視することになるので「職業や社会的地位」を予測の判断基準として入れておくべきだろう。

　以上の点から「国際化時代のビジネスにおいては，〈Ａ〉ではなく〈Ｂ〉を基にして相手の動き（出方）を予想しようとすると交渉は失敗する」というフォーマットでまとめるのもよいが，それでは焦点にズレがあるように感じられるので「〈Ｂ〉ではなく〈Ａ〉を基にして相手の動き（出方）を予想しないと交渉は失敗する」というまとめ方にしたのが［解答例１］である。（〈Ａ〉には「職種や社会経済的地位」，〈Ｂ〉には「相手国の文化／国民性に関する固定観念」が入る）　これは，文章の書き方に沿ったまとめ方である。

　ただし，本年度は「要旨をまとめよ」という指示であり，要するに文章全体で言いたいことが反映されていればよい，という考え方もできるので「国際ビジネスにおいて成功したいなら，〈Ｂ〉ではなく〈Ａ〉をもとに相手の動きを予測して交渉すべきだ」というまとめ方でもよいと思われる。そのようにまとめたのが［解答例２］である。

2017年　解答・解説

解答例

[解答例1]　国際化時代のビジネスにおいては，相手国の文化に関する固定観念ではなく，職種や社会経済的地位を判断基準として相手の出方を予測しないと交渉は失敗する。(73字)

[解答例2]　外国相手のビジネスにおいて成功したければ，相手の国民性に関する固定観念を判断基準とせず，職種や社会経済的地位を基に相手の出方を予測して交渉すべきだ。(74字)

1 **(B)** **(全訳)** ダッハ・ケルトナー教授は，ある朝自転車に乗っていて命を落としそうな経験をした。「キャンパスに行こうと自転車をこいでいたんです」と彼は振り返る。「で，交差点の所まで来たんです。優先権は私にあったんですが，問題の大きな高級車がスピードダウンすらしなかったんです」 衝突まであと1メートルほどしかないというところで，そのドライバーはやっと止まった。「その人は驚いているようでもあり，同時に人を軽蔑しているようでもありました。彼の方に優先権があって私が邪魔してるみたいにね」 ケルトナーの最初の反応は怒りと安堵感の混ざり合ったものだった。勤務先の大学はその日心理学の教授を失わずに済んだというわけだ。次の反応は，より学問的だった。高級車の持ち主の行動と，その他のドライバーの行動の間に測定可能な差があるのだろうか，と彼は考えた。

　教授は心理学科の学生の集団に指示して，運転中のエチケットを監視し，車の型のメモをとらせた。どのドライバーが交差点で歩行者に優先権を与えたか，そしてどのドライバーが，歩行者が見えないふりをして高速で突っ切って行ったのかを記録した。結果は極めて明快であった。高級車のドライバーは，高級ではない車のドライバーと比べると，交差点で一時停止する見込みが4分の1，他の車の前に割り込む見込みが4倍となった。車が高級になるほど，自分は交通規則を破る権利があるのだと所有者は感じていたのである。

　（　1　）いくつかの実験で，ケルトナーと彼の共同研究者は，さまざまな所得層の参加者をテストした。また別の実験では，参加者に自分よりも力が強い人や弱い人のことを考えるよう頼んだり，自分自身が強い，あるいは弱いと感じた時のことを考えるよう頼んだりすることによって，参加者に自分は力がなくなったとか，力が強くなったと感じさせようとした。結果は全て同じ方向性を示していた。力があると感じた人は，そうでない人よりも比較的思いやりがなさそうであった。裕福な参加者は，ちょっとした金銭的報酬があるゲームで不正をしたり，やって来る子供が使うために

— 75 —

2017年　　解答・解説

印を付けてあるお菓子の瓶に手を突っ込んだりすることが多かった。小児ガンに関するビデオを見ている時，彼らの表情には同情の気持ちがあまり出ていなかった。

（　2　）ケルトナーと彼の同僚が2010年に，このテーマに関して影響力の高い論文を発表した時，マーティン・コルンデルファ，ステファン・シュムクレ，ボリス・エグロフという3人のヨーロッパの学者は，ドイツ政府によって行われた調査で得られた，はるかに大量のデータセットを使って，狭い実験室を拠点とする実験の結果を再現できるのではないかと考えた。この情報は，人々が日々の暮らしで何をしたと言ったかを記録したものだったが，それが人間の行動に関して，実験室で得られた結果と同じ全体像を与えてくれるかを確認するのが狙いであった。「我々は単に彼らの実験結果を再現したかったのです」とボリス・エグロフは言う。「それは，なるほどもっともだと私たちには思えるものでした」ところが，彼らが得た数値は想定したパターンに合わなかった。全体的に見れば，逆のことを示唆していたのである。このデータの示すところによると，特権階級の人々は収入に比例して，所得の低い同胞市民よりも，慈善事業にお金を出す気持ちが強く，ボランティアにも参加し，スーツケースを抱えて困っている旅行者の手助けをし，隣人のネコの面倒をみる可能性が高かった。

では，正しいのは誰か。力のある人の方が，ない人よりも良い人なのか，それとも悪い人なのか。これら2種類のデータセットから得られた相反する結果をどのように説明できるだろうか。（　3　）裕福な人は，人前で気前よくすることが利益をもたらすなら，老婦人が道路を渡るのを手伝う気持ちが強くなるかもしれないのだ。ドライバーは，車の中にいれば外から見えないので，乱暴な運転をして自分の評判を下げるのを心配しなくても済む。そしてこのデータは人々が自分の寛大さについて報告したことがもとになっていて，彼らの善行を現実に観察することがもとになっているわけではないとケルトナーは指摘する。「別の研究からもわかるのですが，富裕層の人は倫理的問題について嘘をついたり誇張したりすることが多いのです」と彼は言う。「経済学における自己申告のデータと心理学における対面調査のデータは異なるプロセスをとらえているわけです。自分が社会でしていると口で言っていることと，自分が実際の人間相手にどう振る舞うかは同じではないかもしれないのです」

（　4　）2015年8月，雑誌『サイエンス』の発表によると，バージニア大学の高名な心理学教授であるブライアン・ノゥゼックが率いる270人の学者集団が同類の100件の心理学的研究の結果を再現しようと試みていた。元の研究のうち97件が，検証対象となっている仮説に合致する結果を出していた。ノゥゼック教授グループの実験で同様に合致したのは，たった36件であった。このような数字は実験心理学の学説全体を覆すおそれがある。というのも，ある結果が再現できなければ，それは疑

— 76 —

2017 年　　解答・解説

わしいと考えざるを得ないからだ。（　5　）

選択肢全訳

a)　しかしながら，この結論を誰もが受け入れるわけではない。

b)　路上で起こったことは，実験室でも起こった。

c)　そうすると，（経済的）特権と利己性の関係は未だ証明されていないことになる。

d)　お金持ちの人は貧しい人よりも自分の利己性を隠すことに長けているのかもしれない。

e)　しかしながら，この考えは学界以外のところで一大センセーションを引き起こした。

f)　しかし，問題は調査データではなく心理学の実験にある，という可能性もある。

考え方

(1)　正解は **b)**。第2段落で路上の実地調査の概要が述べられている。そして，この第3段落ではケルトナー教授が主導して行った実験の概要が述べられているので，b) がふさわしい。

(2)　正解は **a)**。第3段落で「（経済的に）力のある人が，より利己的な行動をする」という趣旨の実験結果が示されている。そして，この第4段落では，コルンデルファたちの研究結果が示され，逆の結論，すなわち「裕福な人の方が利他的な行動をする」という結論が示されているので，a) がふさわしい。

(3)　正解は **d)**。第3段落と第4段落で，ケルトナーたちの研究と，コルンデルファたちの研究が逆の結果を示したことをふまえ，空所の直前で「どちらが正しいのか」「この結果をどう説明すべきか」と問い，直後に「人前で気前よくすることが利益をもたらすなら，老婦人が道路を渡るのを手伝う気持ちが強くなるかもしれない」という文があるので，It may be that ...「…ということかもしれない」という表現で裕福な人の心理を推測した d) がふさわしい。ただし disguise ...「…を隠す；偽る」という動詞の意味を知っていることが前提である。

(4)　正解は **f)**。この最終段落では，ノゥゼック教授による再検証で，仮説に合致する結果が少なかったことが紹介され，さらに，空所(5)の直前で「このような数字は実験心理学の学説全体を覆すおそれがある」と述べられているので，「しかし，問題は心理学の実験にあるかもしれない」という趣旨の f) がふさわしい。

(5)　正解は **c)**。ケルトナーとコルンデルファたちの研究が逆の結果を出し，ノゥゼックの研究でも同類の研究で再検証してみると異なる結果が出たということを考えると，富裕層の行動については決定的なことは言えないと考えられるので，最終文として c) がふさわしい。

（不要選択肢は e) で "outside the academic world" が本文の記述と無関係である）

— 77 —

空所(ア)　正解は **violate**。「高級車に乗っている人の方が乱暴な運転をする」ということが述べられた後なので，「交通規則を破る」という意味になり，かつ "v" で始まるものを考えると violate しかない。

なお，この文は The 比較級の構文だが，前半の部分は be 動詞 "was" の省略形であり，後半は its owner felt entitled to － (その所有者は－する権利があると感じていた) が基本となるものである。

解 答

(1)－ b)	(2)－ a)	(3)－ d)	(4)－ f)	(5)－ c)	空所(ア)－ violate

2 (A)

2013 年以来写真またはイラストを使った問題が続いていたが，本年は「与えられたテーマについて書く」というオーソドックスな形式になった。ただ，非常に意表を突くもので，問題文を見た受験生諸君はあわてて教室内や窓の外を眺めまわしたのではないだろうか。

(考え方)

＜語数について＞

「60 ～ 80 語」とあるから，この指定より多くても少なくてもいけない (特に，少ない場合は減点あるいは 0 点にされる可能性が高い)。また，答案の最後に「○○ words」と書き添えよう。

＜内容のポイント＞

☆「気づいたことを一つ選び」とあるのだから，二つ以上書けば減点は免れない。

☆「それについて (中略) 説明しなさい」とあるのだから，「気づいた」ことに関する具体的な説明をする必要がある。むろん諸君の感想を加えても構わないだろうが，まず説明を先に行うこと。

☆「感想」を加える場合，必ず自分の英語力で書きこなせる内容にすること。「教室の壁や廊下についたキズを見て，往時の学生に思いを馳せ…」のような文学的内容を書こうとしないこと。

＜答案作成＞

ここで，答案の展開方法を具体例に沿って見てみることにする (ちなみに，「あなたがいま試験を受けているキャンパス」とは「駒場キャンパス」か「本郷キャンパス」のいずれか。不公平にならないように，それぞれに当てはまる解答例を作成した)。

― 78 ―

2017 年　　解答・解説

［解答例１］

　［気づいたこと］＝「赤門」

　［説明］＝「日本史の教材に写真が載っていた」＋「意外ときれいだった」

　［感想］＝「ずっと見たいと思っていた」＋「江戸時代に作られたと思うと感動する」

　これは本郷キャンパスに関する例。「赤門」は大変有名なので，本郷で受けた受験生はこれをテーマに書いた者も多かったのではないか。実際に日本史の教科書でよく写真が掲載されているし，簡単な感想もつけやすい。

［解答例２］

　［気づいたこと］＝「キャンパスが広い」

　［説明］＝「多くの校舎，木々，そして池やバス停までもある」

　［感想］＝「東大生になったら校舎間移動が大変そうだ」

　「校舎」「樹木」「池」「バス停」と４つ記述されているが，これは「キャンパスが広い」という１つの事柄に対する具体例として扱っているので，問題文の指定には違反していない。

　「池」「バス停」とあるからには本郷キャンパスのことだが，駒場もキャンパスは非常に広い（特に奥行き）。したがって，「池」や「バス停」の部分を変えれば駒場にも応用できる。誰にでも書けそうな内容を簡単な英語でまとめることが重要。

［解答例３］

　［気づいたこと］＝「古い校舎と新しい校舎の混在」

　［説明］＝「おそらく明治時代に作られた洋風建築」＋「2000 年以降に作られた現代建築」

　［感想］＝「古い方の校舎で授業を受け，伝統的雰囲気を楽しみたい」

　これはどちらのキャンパスにも当てはまること。校舎を単に見た目だけで判断した内容だが，それで全く問題ない。むしろ，凝ったことを書こうとすると英語がついてこなくなる可能性が高い。

解答例

［解答例１］

　What caught my eye first was the red gate called Akamon.　Long ago I saw its photo in a textbook on Japanese history, and I have been wanting to see it with my own eyes since then.　I found it was much cleaner than I had expected.　When I think that the gate was made in the Edo period, I feel very impressed!　(63 words)

－ 79 －

2017年　解答・解説

［解答例2］

What strikes me most about this campus is that it is very large, so large that one could get lost while walking around. There are many buildings, trees, a pond, and surprisingly enough, a bus stop in the middle of the campus! I'm afraid that when I'm a student at this university, I will find it hard to move from building to building. (63 words)

［解答例3］

One thing I noticed is the unique mix of traditional and modern architecture. Some buildings are old and traditional. They were probably built in the Meiji period, and look similar to buildings found in many European cities. But there are also modern buildings, which must have been built in the twenty-first century. I would love to take classes in some of those traditional buildings and enjoy the traditional atmosphere.

(69 words)

2 (B)

新傾向の問題。答案に盛り込まなければならない要素が手紙に書かれているので，そこをしっかり把握することが必要。

【全訳】

ジュンへ

君は私のことは覚えていないだろうね。私は君の祖父で，君がまだ3つだったときに国を離れてしまったから。だが，私はもう余命いくばくもないが，人生で成功を収め，私の莫大な財産をすべて君に譲ることにした。君がそれを上手に使ってくれると私に納得させることができればの話だが。私のお金を「何」のために使うのか，また「なぜ」それに使うのかを教えておくれ。君の返事を楽しみにしているよ。

君の祖父より

マーリー

*　　　*　　　*　　　*　　　*

マーリーおじいちゃんへ

― 80 ―

あなたの孫より

ジュン

[考え方]

<語数について>

「60 ～ 80 語」とあるから，やはりこの指定より多くても少なくてもまずい。また，この問題も答案の最後に「○○ words」と書き添えること。

<内容のポイント>

答案に盛り込まなければならない要素は次の2つ。

① 祖父の金を何のために使うか

② なぜ①に使うのか

手紙で「教えておくれ」(Tell me ...) とあるのだから，この2つが答案に含まれている必要がある。順番も①②の順，つまり①を答案冒頭部で記述し，その後②に触れるという展開にする。さらに「お金の上手な使い方」でなければならない。どう好意的に判断しても「上手」とは思えない場合は減点対象となるだろう。

注意したいのは，この遺産相続は「決定事項」ではない。もし「君［＝ジュン］がそれを上手に使ってくれると私［＝祖父］に納得させることができれば」という条件付きである。当然のことながら，「納得させる」ことができなければ相続は白紙となる。要するに，「何に使うか」というのは，条件をクリアし，かつ相続した後に行うことなので，完全に「状況想定」である。したがって，「何に使うか」の部分は仮定法で書くべきだろう。むろん相続の可能性はあるのだから，直説法で書くこともあながち「誤り」とは言い切れない。しかし，手紙文に "*what* you would use my money for" とあることから，東大は仮定法を使って書くことを要求しているように思える。以上のことから，①については仮定法を用いなければ減点されるだろう。ちなみに②は自分の「想い」を書けば良いのだから，直説法でよい。

<答案作成>

以上の点を踏まえて，答案の展開方法を具体例に沿って見てみよう。

［解答例1］

[何に使うか] ＝「金のない老人が十分な介護を得られる施設を作る」

[その理由] ＝「日本は高齢化しつつあり，独居老人が増えている」→「老人が安
心して楽しく過ごせる施設にしたい」

「高齢化」という社会問題を念頭に置いて論を展開した答案。具体的な用途は「介護施設の建設」とし，実際に老人たちが抱える問題およびその解消策を理由とした。

－ 81 －

2017年　解答・解説

［解答例2］

　［何に使うか］＝「赤十字へ寄付」

　［その理由］＝「世界には食べるのに困っている人が多くいる」→「貧困層の救済
　　　　　　　　にお金を使うのが最善だと思う」

「恵まれない人の救済」を理由に考え，そこから「赤十字への寄付」という用途を
考えた。しかし，世界の困窮者の救済というからには，相当な額を寄付したい。とこ
ろがマーリーは金額には言及していないので，「いくら遺してくれるのかわからない
が，私が使えきれないくらいの金額だろう」という前振りをつけた。

［解答例3］

　［何に使うか］＝「2種類の学校を作る」（貧しい子供用と女子用）

　［その理由］＝「今人類が直面している最大の問題は『不平等』」→「貧富の格差，
　　　　　　　　性的不平等が日本では深刻」→「教育は格差是正のカギとなる」

「不平等」をテーマに，貧困と性という2つの項目を軸とし，「教育による解決」を
着地点として論を展開している。冒頭では「貧しい子供のための学校」「女子専用の
学校」という2つの学校の建設を用途として提起し，世界特に日本で深刻な状況にあ
ることを説明した後，だから教育が（つまり学校創設が）必要だと結んだ。

解答例

［解答例1］

　　With your money, I would build a nursing home where old people would
be provided with good care even if they didn't have much money. Japan is
aging rapidly, and there are an increasing number of poor old people who
live alone. I'd like to make the nursing home a place where old people can
relax and enjoy themselves. I hope you like my plan. (65 words)

［解答例2］

　　I don't know how much money you might leave me, but you said you made
a fortune, so it will probably be far more than I could use myself. Therefore,
I would donate most of it to the Red Cross. There are a lot of people in
the world who don't know where their next meal will come from. I think it
best to make use of your money for the poor and unfortunate. (74 words)

［解答例3］

　　If I inherited your fortune, I would use the money to start two schools —
one for poor children and the other exclusively for girls. I believe that the

biggest problem humanity is facing is inequality, and I want to devote my life to correcting it. I think the financial gap between the rich and the poor and gender inequality are especially serious in Japan, and education is the key to reducing such disparities. (73 words)

4 (A) 〖全訳〗 (21) 「ドキュメンタリー」という語は，(a) 以前から行われていた行為の中から紆余曲折を経て登場したものである。19世紀後半の起業家たちが初めて実生活における出来事の映像を記録し始めたとき，(b) 一部の者は自分たちが作っているものを「ドキュメンタリー」と呼んだ。しかしその語は何十年間も定着しなかった。自分たちの映画を "educationals" "actualities" "interest films" と呼んだり，たとえば「旅行映画」のように(c) おそらく主題に言及した人もいただろう。スコットランド人のジョン・グリアソンは英国政府の兵役についていた際この新しい形の映画を利用しようと決意し，「ドキュメンタリー」という語を偉大なアメリカの映画監督ロバート・フラハティの(d) 作品に当てはめることによって作ったのである。彼はドキュメンタリーを「現実の芸術的表現」と定義したが，その定義が今でも変わらない(e) 理由は，おそらく非常に順応性のあるものだからだろう。

(22) ドキュメンタリー映画は(a) 最初の映画が撮影された19世紀末に始まったが，さまざまな形をとりうる。それは「極北の怪異」（1922年）のように異国情緒あふれる土地や生活様式への旅の場合もある。それはヨリス・イヴェンスの「雨」（1929年）のように視覚化された詩の場合もある。この映画はある雨の日に関する物語だが，(b) クラシック音楽に合わせて作られ，そこでは嵐が音楽の構成と重なっている。それは(c) 巧妙なプロパガンダにもなりうる。ソ連の映画監督ジガ・ヴェルトフは，フィクション映画は有害で滅びつつある，(d) ドキュメンタリー映画にこそ未来がある，と宣言したが，「カメラを持った男」（1929年）を(e) 政治体制および映画形式双方のためのプロパガンダとして作成した。

(23) ドキュメンタリーとは何か？ 簡単に答えれば，「現実生活に関する映画」ということではないか。そしてそれこそが問題なのである。ドキュメンタリーは現実生活に「関する」ものであって，現実生活そのものではない。(a) 現実生活を眺める窓ですらない。それらは現実生活を描いたものであり，(b) 現実生活を原料として用い，(c) どのような話を誰に，どのような目的で伝えるべきかについていろいろと決定を下す芸術家や技術者によって作成されるものである。ならば，それは現実生活を描くことに最大限の努力をし，(d) それを操作することのない映画のことか，と言うかも

— 83 —

しれない。しかし，情報を操作しないで(e)映画を作成する方法はないのである。テーマの選定，フィルムの編集，音の編集などは皆操作である。放送ジャーナリストのエドワード .R. マローはかつて言った。「どの映画も『バランス』の取れた映像を撮らなければならないと信じている人は，バランスのことも映像のことも全くわかっていない」と。

⑭　どの程度操作するべきかという問題は(a)その映画形式と同じくらい古くから存在する。「極北の怪異」は最初の偉大なドキュメンタリーの１つであると考えられているが，その主題であるイヌイットは，(b)フィクション映画における俳優たちのように，監督のロバート・フラハティの指示で役割を演じた。フラハティは，たとえば槍でセイウチの狩りをするなど，(c)もはや彼らがやっていないことをやるよう彼らに依頼し，実際は理解している(d)事柄に対して彼らが無知であるかのように描いた。同時に，フラハティは(e)自らがイヌイットとともに何年も生活した実体験に基づいて話を作り上げたが，彼らは彼の制作に喜んで参加し，構想に対するさまざまなアイディアを彼に与えたのである。

⑮　ドキュメンタリーの重要性は社会現象としての(a)大衆という考えと結びついている。哲学者ジョン・デューイは，民主主義社会の繁栄にとって極めて重要な大衆というのは，(b)単に個人の集合体にとどまらない，と説得力を持って主張した。大衆とは公益のために共に行動でき，(c)だからこそ企業や政府が持つ強固な力に挑戦することができる人々の集まりである。それは(d)必要とあらば危機的状況に際しては団結できる非公式の集合体である。大衆は，彼らを奮い立たせてくれる出来事や問題と同じ数だけ存在する。直面する共通の問題について(e)互いにコミュニケーションを取る手段があれば，我々は皆いかなる大衆の一員にもなれる。したがって，コミュニケーションは大衆の生命なのである。

【考え方】　⑳　正解は(d)。apply to O（O に当てはまる）という慣用句は確かに存在する。しかし，by applying となっていることに注目。動名詞が動詞や前置詞の目的語になっている場合，その意味上の主語は主文の主語と一致しなければならないというルールがある。下線(d)を含む文の主語は John Grierson だから，「John Grierson が（フラハティの）作品に当てはまる」という解釈になり，要領を得ない。ここで，apply には apply A to B（A を B に当てはめる）という表現もあることを思い出そう。「Grierson がドキュメンタリーという語を（フラハティの）作品に当てはめた」という解釈ならおかしくないから，by applying it（= the term "documentary"）to a work" とすればよい。

⑫　正解は(b)。It ⟨S⟩ can be ⟨V⟩ a visual poem ⟨C⟩ という構文で，a visual

― 84 ―

2017 年　　解答・解説

poem の具体例が such as 以下の Joris Ivens's *Rain* (1929)，そしてこの *Rain* な
る映画についての言い換えがダッシュの後に続く a story about a rainy day である。
このような流れを見ると，is set の主語に相当するものが見当たらないし，is の前に
カンマが打たれているので a story を主語と見なすのもつらい。ここで set の語法だ
が，set A to B で「A を B に合わせる」という語法がある。set a story to a piece
of classical music → a story is set to a piece of classical music という変換を経て，
さらに a story を補足説明する分詞構文と考えれば，内容的にも文法的にも無理がな
くなる。したがって，is を削除するのが正しい。

　⒇　正解は⒟。下線の前に a movie that does its best とあるが，この that は
does の主語になっていることから関係代名詞で，先行詞が a movie である。そし
て下線部の所で and ⒟ that とあるから，この that も関係代名詞で，前の that と
の並列と考えるべき。ところが，それに続く it doesn't manipulate it の部分は，
manipulate が第 3 文型の動詞であるため完全な英文となり，英語として成り立たな
い。次の下線⒠で make a film without manipulating the information（情報を操作
せずに映画を作る）とあることから，ここも同じような意味合い，つまり「現実生
活を操作しない映画」ということではないかと考え，that doesn't manipulate it [＝
real life] とするのが正しい。

　⒇　正解は⒠。この段落ではフラハティという監督がイヌイットの生活を映画に
収めたことが述べられている。したがって内容的に「フラハティ自身がイヌイットと
生活を共にした経験」という意味になることは想像がつくだろう。into を削除して
years living with the Inuit とすればそのような意味合いになる。文法的には years
と live の間に〈S−V〉の関係が成り立たないので不可能なように思えるが，days /
years などの後に現在分詞を続けて「−した日々［年月］」という意味合いにするの
は英語ではよくあることである。

　⒇　正解は⒠。communicate は「コミュニケーションを取る」という意味の場合
は第 1 文型，「伝える」という意味の場合は第 3 文型をとる。本問は前者であるから，
communicate with each other とするのが正しい。

解答

⒇ − ⒟	⒇ − ⒝	⒇ − ⒟	⒇ − ⒠	⒇ − ⒠

2017 年　　解答・解説

4 (B) 〔**全訳**〕　一人でいられる能力は，どのように育まれうるのだろうか。それは，気を配ってあげることと，敬意をもって会話することによってである。

　子供たちは一人でいられる能力を，気を配ってくれる別の人物がいるところで身につける。母親が2歳の娘をお風呂に入れているところを想像してみよう。その娘がお風呂のおもちゃで楽しい空想にふけることができるようにしてやり，その中で娘は物語を作ったり，自分の考えとだけ向かい合うことができるようになるのだが，その間ずっと，母親は自分のそばにいて，相手をしてもらえるとわかっているのだ。しだいにお風呂は，一人で入ると，その子供が自分の想像の世界を心地よく感じる時間となる。愛情を持って接することが，一人でいることを可能にするのである。

　ある哲学者が，美しく明確に表現している。「言語は…他者なしでいることの痛みを表すために『孤独』ということばを作り出してきた。そして，他者なしでいることの素晴らしさを表すために『一人でいること』ということばを作り出してきたのだ」と。(ア)<u>孤独は，感情的に，そして肉体的にも痛みを伴うものであり，私たちがもっとも思いやりを必要とする幼児期にそれが欠けていることから生まれる。</u>一人でいること（満足して前向きに他者なしでいられる能力）は，ちょうどその時期に，人との好ましい繋がりによって形成される。ところが，私たちが一人でいることを経験しないと（そしてそれは今日よくあることなのだが），孤独と一人でいることを同じだと考え始めてしまう。このことは，私たちの経験の乏しさを映し出している。もし私たちが一人でいることの喜びを知らないとすれば，ただ孤独の恐怖しか知らないということになるのだ。

　先日，ボストンからニューヨークへ行く列車に乗りながらコンピュータで仕事をしている間，私たちは壮大な雪景色の中を通過したことがあった。(イ)<u>コーヒーを買いに行く途中に，たまたま外を見るということがなかったら，私は壮大な雪景色の中を通過したことは知らなかっただろう。</u>私はその時，列車に乗っている他のすべての大人が，コンピュータを見つめていることに気づいた。(ウ)<u>私たちは，一人でいることの恩恵を自分に与えないが，それは，一人でいるために必要となる時間というものを，もっと有益に使うための資源とみなしているからである。</u>近頃では私たちは，他者のいないところで，考える（あるいは考えない）ために時間を使うのではなく，何らかのサイバースペースでそれらを急いで埋めてしまうのだ。

〔**考え方**〕

　(ア)　1．**Loneliness is ... painful**「孤独は痛みを伴う（辛い）ものだ」　これが文の骨格。

　2．**emotionally and even physically**「感情的に，そして身体的にさえ〈痛みを

— 86 —

2017 年　　解答・解説

伴う〉」　emotionally と physically は painful を修飾する副詞。even は physically を修飾している。

　3．**born from a lack of warmth**「人の温かみがないことから生まれる」Loneliness を意味上の主語とする分詞構文 (Loneliness is born ... → [being] born ...)。and is born ... と同義ととらえて訳出すればよい。

　4．**in early childhood**「幼少期（幼児期）の」　a lack of warmth を修飾する形容詞句。

　5．**when we need it most**「我々がそれを最も必要とする〈幼少期〉」　it は warmth を受ける代名詞。問題の指示により，この it は「[人の] 温かさ，思いやり (= warmth)」と訳出しなければならない。when を関係副詞ととらえ後ろから訳し上げる場合は，「人の温かさを一番必要とする幼少期にそれがない」のように，a lack of warmth の warmth の方を「それ」と訳してもいいだろう。またこの when 節を in early childhood を言い換えたものととらえ，「〈幼少期，（すなわち）〉我々が人の温かさをもっとも必要とするときに」と処理してもよいだろう。

　(イ)　1．**I wouldn't have known this**「私は見事な雪景色の中を通過していることには気づかなかっただろう」　wouldn't have known は仮定法過去完了。this は前文の we passed through a magnificent snowy landscape を受ける代名詞。前の「単数名詞」を受けるときは it を用いることが多いのに対して，前の「内容」を受けるときは本問のように this を使うことが多い。

　2．**but for the fact that ...**「…ということがなかったら」　but for ... は if it had not been for ... と同義で「…がなかった（な）ら」の意の仮定条件を表わしている。(例) *But for* your help, I could not have done it.（あなたの援助がなかったら，私はそれをすることができなかったでしょう）　that ... は the fact と同格で働く名詞節。

　3．**I happened to look outside**「私はたまたま外を見た」　happen to − で「たまたま−する」の意。

　4．**on my way to get a coffee**「コーヒーを買いに行く途中に」　look outside を修飾する副詞句。

　(ウ)　1．**We deny ourselves the benefits of solitude**「我々は自分に一人でいることの恩恵を与えない」　deny O_1 + O_2 で「O_1 に O_2 を与えない」の意となる。(例) He *denies* his child nothing. (= He *denies* nothing to his child.)（彼は子供の言うことは何でも聞き入れる）　solitude は loneliness とは訳語を変えることが望ましい。第3段落より，「loneliness が苦痛なのに対して，solitude は素晴らしいこと」を指していることがわかるので，loneliness よりは肯定的な響きを持つ訳語を選択す

－ 87 －

<u>2017 年　　解答・解説</u>

ることが望ましい。

２．**because we see the time 〈...〉as ～**「我々は 〈…な〉時間を～とみなすからだ」　see A as B で「A を B とみなす」の意。as a resource を require(s) を修飾する副詞句と考えるのは誤り。

３．〈**the time**〉**[that] it requires**「それ（一人でいること）が求める〈時間〉；それ（一人でいること）に要する〈時間〉」　the time を修飾する関係詞節。

４．**a resource to use more profitably**「もっと有益に使うべき資源」　ここが，see A as B の B にあたる。to use ... は a resource を修飾する形容詞用法の不定詞。

解答

> ㈠　孤独とは，感情的に，さらには身体的にも辛いものであり，人の温かさを一番必要とする幼少期にそれがないことから生まれる。
>
> ㈡　コーヒーを買いに行く途中に，たまたま外を見なかったら，見事な雪景色の中を通過していることに私は気づかなかったであろう。
>
> ㈢　我々が一人でいることの恩恵を自らに与えないのは，それに要する時間を，もっと有益に使うべき資源と見なすからだ。

5　**全訳**　昨年ドリスが 94 歳で亡くなった時で，私が彼女と知り合って 50 年になっていた。その間ずっと，私が一度も決めることができなかったのは，私の人生における彼女の役割を的確かつ簡潔に記述する，彼女に対する呼び方だった（まして，彼女の人生における私の役割となってはなおさらだ）。通常は，母，父，娘，息子，おじ，おば，いとこといった，この上なく近い人間関係を記述する一連の便利な単語があるが，現代西洋社会では通常はその程度で限界なのだ。

　ドリスは私の母親ではなかった。一緒に暮らしてもらえるようにと私が彼女の家のドアをノックして，彼女がそのドアを開けるまでは，彼女とは面識がなかった。他の人に対しては，彼女のことを何と呼べばよいのだろう？　数ヵ月間私はドリスと一緒に生活し，彼女の友人の会社で働いて，タイピングを習った。その後，少しばかり努力をしてドリスは私の父を説得して，私が学校に戻ることを許すようにしてくれた。私が何年か前の 11 歳の時に，自分が入れられていた進歩主義的な男女共学の全寮制学校を（２階のトイレの窓から脱走して町でのパーティーに出かけたことを理由に）退学になった後，罰として父は，私をそれ以上学校に通わせることを拒否していたからだった。父は折れて，ドリスが私を新しい学校に入れてくれた。

　新しい学校では，十代の若者たちがいつも自分の親の話をしたり不平を言ったりし

— 88 —

ていたが，使っていたのは親を意味する普通の言葉だった。私はドリスを養母と呼ん
でよいのだろうか？　彼女は私を養子にしていなかったが，そうするよう提案はして
いた。私の母は，いつもの叫び声を上げるような発作を起こして，私を養子にしよう
とするのならドリスを訴えてやると脅した。だから，その話はひっそりと立ち消えに
なった。そうはいっても，私が「養母」と口にすることは時々あり，それは不正確だ
が手軽な解決法としてのことだった。問題なのは，彼女のことをどう呼ぶかであって，
私の保護者のことを呼ぶのに「ドリスっていう，私の…，まあ一種の養母というか…，
私の…ドリスが…」と口にする必要がある時はいつも，間違った印象を与えているの
ではないかという気がしていた。

　どういうわけか，正確であること，私の境遇をきちんと説明する単純な所有格表現
を見つけることは，とても重要だった。私は嘘をつきたくなかったし，自分の状況を
他人に正確かつ簡潔に示す方法を何か見つけたいと心底思っていた。しかし，私は養
子になっていたことはなかった。両親ともまだ存命で，（私からすれば残念なことに）
私とのつながりは切れていなかった。

　私は前の学校を退学になった後，バンベリーにいた父親のもとから逃げ出して，ホー
ヴにいた母親ととても小さなアパートで同居するようになった。同居がほんの数日間
続いた後ですでに，隅っこにうずくまり食べるのも口をきくのも拒否するのが最善の
措置だと思えた。「どうすればおまえは私にこんなことができるの？　なぜいい子に
できないの，他の子みたいに？」と，母は金切り声をあげた。

　私を両親から引き離しておくのは良い案だと思われたので，公的な援助で養っても
らった後で，私はホーヴにあるチチェスター婦人病院へ入れられた。大きな一戸建て
の建造物の中にある小さな精神科だった。私は，そこでみんなの子供のような存在と
なり，職員も患者たちも私の面倒をみてくれて，他の人たちのさまざまな問題の中で
も最悪のものから私を守ろうとしてくれた。私はやっとのことで，強く心を惹かれ，
かなり居心地良く自分が十分な世話を受けていると感じるようになった。

　不思議なことに自分は妊娠しており，医者は私がその現実を受け入れるのを待って
いるのだという人知れぬ恐怖を，私はつのらせていた。それ以外には，私は精神的に
おかしいところは何もなく，彼らは私を治療しようとすることもなかった。私は治療
を受けることもなく4ヵ月そこに滞在し，ホーヴの浜辺に腰を下ろして海を見つめな
がら（それは前例のないほどの氷と雪に覆われた冬だった）長い時間を過ごしたが，
かたや人々は，私をどう扱ったらよいかの答えを出そうとしていた。

　その時突然，私はドリスから手紙を受け取った。その手紙によると，私は彼女を知
らなかったが，彼女の方は，私の学校での同級生だった息子から聞いて私のことを知っ

— 89 —

ていた。想像に難くないことだが，そこでは，退学をくらって今は精神病院にいる非行少女ジェニファーについて，過剰興奮気味の噂話が広まっていた。

　（学校ではけっして仲が良くはなかったことからすると）まったく邪心のない心の広さで，ドリスの息子のピーターは母親への手紙で次のように書いていた。つまり，私が「けっこう頭が良い」ので，なんとかして彼ら母子が私に手をさしのべることができないものか，と。ドリスの私あての手紙には，初めて手に入れた家に引っ越したばかりで，（とりわけ彼女の自慢の）セントラルヒーティングもついていて，空いている部屋もあるので，そこで暮らすつもりはないだろうか，そして，私の父親は気乗りしないだろうが，学校に戻って試験を受けて，大学へ通うというのはどうだろうか，と書かれていた。滞在期間はどれくらいのものとして私が招かれているのかは，手紙では定かでなかったが，大学へ通うという考えからすると，それは長期にわたると思われた。

　私はその手紙を何度も読んだ。最初は肩をすくめるようにして：「ああ，そう。今度私の身に起きるのはそれってことね」。私の子ども時代には，思いがけない出来事がとても頻繁にどんどん起きたので，それが普通に思えたのだ。他人事のように受け身的な態度で，そういうものだと思うようになっていた。次に手紙を再読して，私には守護天使がいるのだと驚いた。次に恐くなった。次に，いくらかがっかりして，受け入れるべきかどうかについて，ちょっと現実的に考えた。そして最後には，こういったすべての反応が混ざり合って，自分自身の恐怖や期待にも，そして私を招いてくれたことに対してこの見ず知らずの人にも，どう反応したらよいかまったくわからなくなった。

　そんなわけで，ドリスは私の母ではなかった。そして，他人との間で生じるぎこちない瞬間を別にすれば，ドリスが私にとって何であるのかということは，考えないでおくのが一番良い他の疑問と一緒に棚上げにされたのであった。

（考え方）

　(A)　that は直前の mother, father, ... cousin という一連の語を指し，it は「家族関係の呼び方」を漠然と表している（as far as S go で「S の限界だ」という意味：例）That's *as far as* my knowledge goes.「それが私が知り得る限界です：私はそれしか知りません」）。よって，下線部を含む部分の意味は，「それが，現代西洋社会での通常の限界だ」となり，この箇所は，直前の mother, father, ... cousin の中には筆者とドリスの関係を適切に表す言葉が存在しないということを述べているとわかる。ここで次の例のような意味を持つ代名詞 all の用法を思いついたかがポイントである：例）This is *all* I can do for you.「僕が君のためにできるのはこれだけです」。空所

— 90 —

2017 年　　解答・解説

にこれと同種の all を入れれば，「我々が通常使うのはそれだけだ［その程度だ］」という意味になり，下線部の言い換えとして成立する。なお，構文的には空所に関係代名詞 what を入れることもできるが，「それが我々が通常使うものだ」では，下線部が持つ「限界；それしかない」のニュアンスが出せないので，what は正解とは言えない。

　(B)　下線部の意味は「肩をすくめるようにして」となる。shrug とは「肩をすくめる動作」という意味で，「絶望・当惑・無関心」を示す動作である。この時点での筆者の心理を探ると，直後に「『ああ，そう。今度私の身に起きるのはそれってことね』」「私の子ども時代には，思いがけない出来事がとても頻繁にどんどん起きたので，それが普通に思えたのだ。他人事のように受け身的な態度で，そういうものだと思うようになっていた」と記されている。よって，筆者が下線部のような反応をしたのは，【①自分の身に起こる思いがけない出来事を（淡々と）他人事のように受け止めるようになっていたから】【②その原因は幼少期からそのような出来事が頻繁に起こってきたから】となるので，解答はこの2点をまとめ，「**思いがけない出来事が幼少期から頻繁に起こってきたので，それを淡々と受け止める**ようになっていたから」とすればよい。

　(C)　下線部前後の文の意味は，「ぎこちない social な瞬間を別にすれば，ドリスが私にとって何であるのかということは，考えないでおくのが一番良い他の疑問と一緒に棚上げにされた」となるので，下線部の「瞬間」とは，「ドリスが私にとって何であるのか」という問いが棚上げにされない瞬間，つまり，「ドリスが私にとって何であるのか」という問いの答えを筆者が考えざるを得ない瞬間となる。

　ここで文章全体を見ると，第1段落 (When she died ...) に「その間ずっと，私が一度も決めることができなかったのは，私の人生における彼女の役割を的確かつ簡潔に記述する，彼女に対する呼び方だった」，第2段落 (Doris wasn't my ...) に「他の人には，彼女のことを何と呼べばよいのだろう？」，第3段落 (At the new ...) に「私はドリスを養母と呼んでよいのだろうか？；問題なのは，彼女のことをどう呼ぶかであって（…）」などと記されているので，これらが示しているのが下線部の「ぎこちない social な瞬間」であるとわかる。つまり，ここでの social は「人づきあいにおける；人と人との間の」という意味であり，下線部は「他人との間で生じるぎこちない瞬間」といった意味になる。よって解答は，上に記したような文脈を踏まえて，「**自分とドリスの関係を人に説明しなければならない，面倒な瞬間**」などとまとめればよい。

　(D)　(ア)　(26)　空所前後の意味は，「その間ずっと，一度も決めることができなかったのは，私の人生における彼女の役割を的確かつ簡潔に記述する，彼女に対する（　26　）だった」となる。つまり「彼女に対する(26)」は，「私の人生における彼女

－ 91 －

2017年　　解答・解説

の役割を的確かつ簡潔に記述する」という行為の主語になる名詞である。さらに，続く文の「通常は，母，父，娘，息子，おじ，おば，いとこといった，この上なく近い人間関係を記述する一連の便利な単語がある」も参考にすると，この「この上なく近い人間関係を記述する一連の便利な単語」と(26)が似たような意味になると考えられる。以上を満たすのは，**a) designation**「名称；呼称」となる。

(27)　空所前後の意味は，「（　27　）として父は，私をそれ以上学校に通わせることを拒否していたのだった」となる。つまり，「私をそれ以上学校に通わせることを拒否していた」という内容を一語で示した名詞が(27)に入ればよいことになり，これを満たすのは，**g) punishment**「罰」となる。空所に h) result を入れて as a result「結果として」としても，直前の内容とつながらない。

(28)　空所を含む文の意味は，「私は嘘をつきたくなかったし，自分の（　28　）を他人に正確かつ簡潔に示す方法を何か見つけたいと心底思っていた」となる。この前の文を見ると，「私の境遇をきちんと説明する単純な所有格表現を見つけることは，とても重要だった」と述べられている。よって，空所には circumstances「境遇」とほぼ同義の単語が入ることになるので，**j) situation**「状況」が正解となる。

(29)　空所前後の意味は，「最善の（　29　）は隅っこにうずくまり食べるのも口をきくのも拒否することだと思えた」という意味である。よって(29)には，「隅っこにうずくまり食べるのも口をきくのも拒否する」という行為を表す名詞が入る。これにふさわしいのは **e) move** しかない。この move は単なる「動き；運動」ではなく，「措置；行動」という意味である。場面を考えると，i) rush「突進；殺到」は意味的にふさわしくない。

(30)　空所には名詞が入り，空所直後の that 以下は同格節と考えられるので，空所前後の意味は「不思議なことに自分は妊娠しており，医者は私がその現実を受け入れるのを待っているのだという人知れぬ（　30　）を，私はつのらせていた」となる。この that 以下の意味から考えて，正解は **c) fear**「恐怖」となる。

(イ)　正解は **c)**「筆者の新たな学校で，筆者に関する悪いうわさが広まっていた」。第8段落 (Then, all of ...) にあるように，転入する前の学校では筆者に関する「悪いうわさ」が広まっていたが，転入した先の「新たな学校」でもそのような「悪いうわさ」が広まっていたという記述はない。よって，c) が本文に合致しないと判断できる。

a)　「筆者はドリスとの関係をはっきりさせようと努力した」：筆者は文章全体にわたって，「自分にとってドリスとはどのような存在か」という疑問に答えようとしているので，これは本文に合致する。

b)　「筆者の母親は，筆者がドリスの養子になるのを望まなかった」：第3段落 (At

— 92 —

2017年　解答・解説

the new ...) に「私の母は，いつもの叫び声を上げるような発作を起こして，私を養子にしようとするのならドリスを訴えてやると脅した」とあるので，これは本文に合致する。

d）「ドリスの息子は，筆者が非常に賢いので筆者を助けたいと思った」：第9段落 (In his letter ...) に「私が『けっこう頭が良い (quite intelligent)』ので，なんとかして彼ら母子が私に手をさしのべることができないものか」と書かれている。なお，quite intelligent のように「程度の差がある形容詞や副詞」の直前に置かれた quite は，アメリカ英語では「とても（＝very）」という意味だが，イギリス英語では「まあまあ；比較的」という意味になるので，後者の場合は quite intelligent は d) の very smart と意味が合わなくなってしまう。ただ，上記のように c) が明らかに本文に合致しない正解となっているので，この点については不問に付し，d) も本文に合致すると見なすしかない。

e）「ドリスからの手紙を受け取った時，筆者は病院に滞在していた」：第8段落 (Then, all of ...) に「その時突然，私はドリスから手紙を受け取った」とあり，その直前の第7段落 (I developed a ...) からは，「私は治療を受けることもなく4ヵ月そこに滞在し，ホーヴの浜辺に腰を下ろして長い時間を過ごした」，つまりこの時筆者は，第6段落 (It was considered ...) で登場した「病院」にいるとわかる。よって，e) も本文に合致する。

(ウ)　筆者は本文全体にわたって，ドリスと自分の関係を模索している（設問(C), (D) (26)(28)，(イ)a) などの解説を参照)。そのような「単純に言葉では説明できない」関係を表す語は，d) の unconventional「慣例にとらわれない；型にはまらない」しかない。a)「悲惨な；災害を招く」，b)「違法の；非合法の」，c)「情熱的な；熱烈な」，e)「不安定な；落ち着かない」は，いずれもこのような内容を表現するには不適切である。

解 答

(A)　all

(B)　思いがけない出来事が幼少期から頻繁に起こってきたので，それを淡々と受け止めるようになっていたから。

(C)　自分とドリスの関係を人に説明しなければならない，面倒な瞬間。

(D)　(ア) (26)－a)　　(27)－g)　　(28)－j)　　(29)－e)　　(30)－c)

　　　(イ)－c)

　　　(ウ)－d)

― 93 ―

解答・解説

1 (A) **[全訳]** 「想像上の家族」という概念は，集団意識が現実の家族を超えてどのように広がり得るかを理解する手助けになる。人類は，成員が緊密な関係を持つ小集団の中で進化してきたので，進化は，親密な家族の成員を手助けするよう形成された心理に有利に働いた。しかし人間社会の発達に伴い，異なる集団間の協調がさらに重要になってきた。家族内の言葉と感情を，家族ではない集団に拡大することによって，人類は「想像上の家族」を作り出すことができるようになったが，これは貿易，自治政治，防衛といった大規模な企てに着手する能力を持つ政治的・社会的共同体であった。

　しかし，このような捉え方は，これ自体では，なぜ我々がそのような共同体の全成員を平等とみなすのかを，やはり説明することができない。想像上の家族は現実の家族とは異なるものであり，その原因は遺伝的な繋がりが欠如していることだけではない。近縁と遠縁の区別が欠如していることによっても異なるのである。一般に，同胞あるいは祖国の全成員は，少なくともその集団の一員であるという点では，対等の立場にあるが，一方，現実の家族の成員は，その関係の度合いが異なっており，家族の一員であることやその範囲に関する一定不変の定義もない。人間を統合し，人間同士の強い絆を作り出す，もっと根本的な要因を探求する必要がある。

　より深いレベルで人間社会を統合しているのは，よく知られた心理的バイアスであり，これは普遍的なものだと考えられている。さまざまな文化圏で行われた児童発達に関する研究が示しているのは，どの文化圏の人でも，人種，民族性，服装といった人間の社会的範疇に何らかの本質的特性があると考えがちだということである。この心的態度が用いられて「内部集団」対「外部集団」の概念が生み出され，もともと結束性のなかった集団に結束性が与えられ，その集団の生存可能性が劇的に高まる。しかしまた，このことによって人間は「外部集団」を自分とは異なる生物種とみなすようになり，敵意と紛争の危険性が高まることにもなり得る。歴史を通して，さらに言えば，おそらく先史人類史を通して，人間は常に他者を異種に属するものとみなすことによって団結し，他者と闘い，他者を支配しようとしてきたのである。

[考え方]

1. 第2段落最終文をヒントにして，全体の方向性を決める。

　この文章の主題は「人間社会の結束性（まとまり；絆）」であり，それを「どの

― 96 ―

ように捉えるか」，それを「生み出す要因は何なのか」を論じるものとなっている。

第1段落に "imagined family" という表現が出てくる。これは人間の共同体を家族の拡大版と捉えるという見方であることが，特に最終文からわかる。第2段落に入って「しかし，この概念（＝imagined family という捉え方）では，なぜそのような共同体の全成員を平等だとみなすのか説明できない」と，その捉え方だけでは説明できない部分があることを指摘している。第2〜3文はその理由に該当する。すなわち，社会は家族のようなものだといっても，1）現実の家族と違って，想像上の家族は遺伝的繋がりも近縁遠縁の区別もないし，2）想像上の家族は集団の一員であるという点では対当の立場だが，現実の家族は関係の度合いが異なり家族の定義が決まっているわけでもない，という点である。ここまでは「人間の社会を家族にたとえて説明しようとしても，説明できない点がある（＋その理由)」という流れになっている。

そして，最終文で「人間同士を繋ぐ根本的な要因を探求する必要がある」という趣旨の文がある。

このように段落の最後に「次の展開を暗示する文」を入れるのは，論説・解説型の文章によくあるパターンである。

以上，1つの考え方を紹介し，その不備を指摘し，また別の視点に移行していくという流れがあり，"a more fundamental factor" という表現が使われているのだから，これを詳述した第3段落の内容を主軸に置いてまとめていくとよい。

2．「言い換え」，「指示語」，「因果関係」に注意しつつ，第3段落の内容をまとめる。

第2段落最終文の a more fundamental factor に該当するのが，第3段落第1文の a well-known psychological bias which is believed to be universal（普遍的だと考えられている，ある有名な心理的バイアス）だが，これだけでは何のことか不明である。このように General Statement（大雑把で概略的な表現）から Specific Statement（より具体的・個別的で明示的な表現）へ移行していくのも論説・解説型の文章のよくあるパターンで，これを明確にしてくれる部分が次にあるだろう，と思いながら読み進める。そうすると早速第2文に関連する「見方」が出てくる。（"universal → across cultures → everywhere" という関連語がこの点でヒントになっている）　この「人種・民族性・外見といった社会的範疇に本質的な意味があると考える」ことこそが，第2文の "bias" の意味するところなのである。

その見方を第3文の "This mental attitude" で受け，これが「内部集団 vs 外部集団」という概念を生み出し，集団に結束性 (coherence) を与えた，と述べているのだから，この心理こそが集団に結束性を与える元になるものだと考える。最後

— 97 —

の２文は「これによって外部集団を異なる種とみなすようになり，敵対関係を促すことにもなる。人間は有史以前から他者を異種とみなすことによって団結し，他者と闘い他者を支配しようとしてきた」という内容なので「外の集団を異なる種とみなす／敵対するものとみなす」ことも結束性を生み出す要因として加えておくとよいだろう。

◇ **解答のアウトライン**

以上の点から，次のような要素が含まれていればよいと思われるが，本年度は設問の文言が「要旨をまとめよ」となっているので，やはり第３段落の内容を中心に置き，第１～２段落は軽く触れる程度にしておく。

---

① 視点(1)

人間社会は家族のようなものだという捉え方がある

② その不備

これでは何故集団の全成員が平等だとみなされるのか説明できない

＋その理由（これは省くしかない）

③ 視点(2)

社会の結束性を生む元となるのは，人種などの分類に本質的な意味があると思うこと

その結果：１）内と外の区別をするようになる

　　　　　２）外部集団を異種として（敵対心をもって）見るようになる

解答例

［解答例１］　社会を擬似的家族として捉えても，その全成員を平等とみなす理由が説明できない。人間は人種などの分類に本質的な意味があると考えがちで，そこから内と外の概念が生まれ，外部集団を異種とみなすことによって集団の結束性が生まれるのである。（113字）

［解答例２］　社会を家族にたとえるだけでは，その全成員を平等に扱う理由が説明できない。人種などの社会範疇に本質的な意味を見出す姿勢が元になって内と外の概念が生まれ，同時に外部集団を敵対視することによって人間は団結する。（102字）

2016 年　　解答・解説

1 **(B)** **全訳** 言論の自由は，国旗やモットーのように単なる象徴にすぎないのだろうか？　私たちが比較検討する多くの価値観の一つにすぎないのだろうか？　それとも，言論の自由は基本的なもの（絶対的なとまでは言えなくても，厳密に規定された場合を除いては手放すことができない権利）なのだろうか？

その答えは，言論の自由は実に基本的なものだということである。その理由を想起し，その権利が問題になった時には，その理由を準備しておくことが重要である。

最初の理由は，言論の自由が基本的かどうかを問う際に私たちがしていること（意見を交換したり評価したりすること）そのものが，私たちには意見を交換し評価する権利があることを前提にしている，ということである。言論の自由（であれ何であれ）について語っている時，私たちは「語って」いる。力ずくで，あるいはコインを投げることによって意見の対立を解消したりはしていない。Nat Hentoff の言葉で言えば「言論の自由は私にはあるが，あなたにはない」とでも断言する気があるなら別だが，ディベートに参加して言論の自由に反対しようとすると，そのとたんに負けたことになる。言論の自由に反対するために言論の自由を使うなど意味を成さないのである。

（　1　）

もしかしたら近代史における最大の発見は（その後のあらゆる発見のために必要なものだったが）科学が登場する前に信念の元となったものは信頼できない，ということなのかもしれない。信仰，奇跡，権威，占い，第六感，社会通念，主観的確信は，過ちを誘発するものであり，排除すべきなのだ。

（　2　）

このような科学的手法が近代初期に支配力を持つようになると，古典的な世界観は一変することとなった。実験と議論が権威に取って代わり真理の根源となっていった。

（　3　）

言論の自由が人類の繁栄にとって基本的である三つ目の理由は，それが民主主義にとって不可欠なものであり，独裁政治に対する防御装置になっているということである。20 世紀のおぞましい体制は，どのように力を獲得し維持しただろうか。その答えは，凶暴な集団が批判者・反対者を沈黙させたということである。そして独裁政府はひとたび権力の座につくと，その体制に対するいかなる批判も罰した。これは大量殺戮などの残虐行為をしたことで知られる現代の政治体制にも言えることだ。

（　4　）

共通認識は公開情報によって作り出される。「裸の王様」という物語がこの論理の例証となっている。王様は裸だ，と叫んだ時，この少年は人々にまだ知らなかったことを伝えていたわけではないし，人々の目には見えないことを伝えていたわけではない。

— 99 —

2016年　　解答・解説

しかしそれでも，この子は人々の知識を変化させていた。他の者全員が王様は裸だという事実を知っていることを，これで全員が知ることになったからである。その共通認識によって，彼らは笑いをもって王様の権威に挑む勇気を持つことができたのだ。

（　5　）

たしかに言論の自由には限界がある。大衆が不正な個人攻撃をしたり，軍事機密を漏洩したり，他者が暴力をふるうよう仕向けるのを防ぐ法律を私たちは作るかもしれない。しかし，このような除外事項は厳密に定義し，個別に根拠付けをしなければならない。これらは言論の自由を数多くある交換可能な善の一つとして扱う言い訳にはならないのである。

そして読者諸氏が以上のような主張に反対するというのなら，私の論理の破綻やら私の考え方の間違いを明らかにしたいというなら，言論の自由という権利があるからこそ，そのようなことができるのである。

(選択肢全訳)

a)　また，私たちは言葉を武器として使って，権力者のみならず，要求の多い上司，自慢ばかりする教師，つまらないルールを強引に押しつける隣人といった，日常的に脅威を与える人物も挫けさせようとする。

b)　この純粋に論理的な推論に納得できない者は，人類史から得られる議論に目を向けてみるとよい。歴史を学べばわかるが，宗教的，政治的論拠によって排他的に真理を我が物にしようとした者は，しばしば誤っていることが示されてきた。しかも，往々にして滑稽なほど誤っていることが。

c)　では，私たちはどのようにして知識を獲得しているのだろうか。その答えは仮説と検証という手順である。現実の特性に関してアイデアが浮かぶ。それを現実に照らし合わせて検証し，それにより人々が誤った考えに反証することができる。この手順の仮説の部分は，言うまでもなく，言論の自由を行使できるかどうかに左右される。どの考えが検証の試みを超えて生き残るかを確認することによってのみ，誤った考えを回避できるのである。

d)　このような政府は，なぜ批判の声を一切認めないのか？　実際には，もし苦しんでいる人が数千万人共に行動すれば，どんな政府も彼らに抵抗できない。大衆が団結して独裁者に反旗を翻さないのは，共通認識，すなわち，皆がその知識を共有していて，それを共有していることを知っている，という意識がないからだ。人間が自らをリスクに晒すのは，そのリスクに他者が同時に身を晒すことを知っている場合のみなのである。

e)　この道程において，ひとつの重要なステップとなったのが，地球が太陽の周りを

— 100 —

2016年　　解答・解説

回っているというガリレオの論証であったが，この主張は激しい抵抗を乗り越えなければならなかった。しかし，このコペルニクス的大転回は，現在の世界観を祖先たちにとって認識不可能にするような一連の歴史的事件の中で最初のものだったにすぎない。私たちは今，あらゆる時代，あらゆる文化において多くの人が抱く確信（間違いなく私たちが現在抱いている確信もここに含まれる）が明確に誤りであることが証明される可能性があることを知っている。そして，そのために私たちは新しいアイデアの自由な交換を頼りにするのだ。

[考え方]

　本年度は，2012年度以前の段落補充問題に戻ったが，内容の関連度を考えて絞り込み，その上で指示語などの文法的手がかりを見落とすことがないように注意する，という点は文補充の場合と同じである。不要な選択肢がないので，従来よりも難易度は下がっている。さらに，本文空所(5)までの部分は，言論の自由の重要性を「論理」「歴史」「民主主義」の3つの面から支持しようとする文章となっており，内容のまとまりを把握しやすい文章なので，従来の設問よりも取り組みやすいと感じたはずである。

　(1)　正解は **b)**。第3段落の内容を this ... logical reasoning（論理的推論）で受けることになり，かつ後半にある「人類史に目を向ける」という内容が直後の段落の「歴史から得られる知見」とも関連するので，b) が最適である。

　(2)　正解は **c)**。空所直後で this scientific approach（科学的手法）とあるので，hypothesis（仮説）と testing（検証）について述べた c) が最適である。

　(3)　正解は **e)**。this path が，第7段落の「科学的手法が定着し，実験と議論が権威に取って代わった」という内容を受けることになり，ガリレオの話が例として成立するので e) が最適である。

　(4)　正解は **d)**。ここに d) を入れると，第9段落の the monstrous regimes of the 20th century（20世紀のおぞましい政治体制／政権）や the governments of today（現在の政府）を these regimes で受けることになる。また「国民が独裁者に反抗して団結しないのは，共通認識／共通知識 (common knowledge) がないからだ」という文があり，次の段落で"common knowledge"がどのように生まれるかを紹介している点も，ここに d) がふさわしい根拠となる。

　(5)　正解は **a)**。第9〜11段落で「民主主義を維持する手段，そして独裁政治に対する対抗手段として言論の自由は擁護すべきだ」という内容が述べられている。つまり「対権力者」の面が引き合いに出されていたので，この空所は「そしてまた，"those who are in power"（権力者）を抑えるだけでなく，"bullies in everyday life"（日常生活で強圧的な態度をとる人；いじめっ子）を抑えるためにも言論の自由を使う」と追加情報を出している a) が最適である。

— 101 —

<u>2016年　　解答・解説</u>

解 答

(1)－ b)　　(2)－ c)　　(3)－ e)　　(4)－ d)　　(5)－ a)

2 （A）

　写真問題はおととし以来だが，今回は会話文を作成するのではなく，「思うこと」を述べるという形式。そういう意味では昨年のイラストが写真に変わっただけとも言えるが，画像に写っている状況の説明は求められていない。ただ，少々の説明をつけるくらいなら大丈夫だろう（「少々」というのは，求められてもいないのに，指定語数の半分以上説明に費やせば減点対象になる可能性があるから）。

考え方

＜語数について＞

　「60 〜 80 語の英語で」とあるから，この指定より多くても少なくてもいけない（特に少ない場合は減点あるいは 0 点にされる可能性が高い）。また，答案の最後に「○○ words」と書き添えよう。

＜内容のポイント＞

① **画像に写っている状況を説明する場合**

　　むろんこれは書かなくてもよい。答案の書き出しから感想が始まっても一向に差し支えない。「説明するならば」という立場での解説である。

　☆　「猫」「指［または手］」の両方に関する記述が必要で，片方だけだと減点は免れない（これは次の「思うこと」に関しても同様）。

　☆　猫がどこに横たわっているかは自由。「じゅうたん」「ぼろきれ」「床」など何でもよい。むろん「横たわっている」という姿勢にはこだわりたい。

　☆　「猫」「指［または手］」が等身大，つまり「普通の大きさの人間の指［手］が普通の大きさの猫をつかもうとしている」という解釈は，いくら何でも無理があるため，減点対象になるだろう（これは次の「思うこと」でも同じ）。

② **「あなたが思うこと」について**

　　絵に対する反応として適切であれば，本当にどんな内容でもよいと思う。「心霊現象」「ミニチュア（おもちゃ）の猫」「遠近法」「インスタグラム等の SNS への投稿目的で撮られた」等々。ただし，自分の英語力で書ける内容にすることが重要。アイデアばかり先行して，英語として破綻するのが最悪のパターンである。特に，「猫はきれいに撮れているのに，指の方はピントがぼけている」「カメラの性能の悪さ」などを<u>答案全体のテーマにしているもの</u>はいかがなものだろうか。それも確かに「思

— 102 —

<u>2016 年　　解答・解説</u>

うこと」の 1 つではあるので，減点対象にはならないと思うが，やや想像力に欠ける答案になる。

＜答案作成＞

　ここで，答案の展開方法を具体例に沿って見てみることにする。

［解答例 1 ］

　　［絵に描かれた状況］＝「じゅうたんの上に横になっている猫」＋「おそらくはこの
　　　　　　　　　　　　　画像を撮った人間の手」（英語は 21 words）

　　［あなたが思うこと］＝「おもしろいけれどある意味こわい」＋「むろん画像を撮っ
　　　　　　　　　　　　た人間が左手にカメラを持ち，右手をカメラに近づけて
　　　　　　　　　　　　撮ったものだ」＋「邪悪な者の手が猫を捕らえようとしてい
　　　　　　　　　　　　るようにも見える」

　　画像の説明を入れた解答例。"This picture shows O" という定番の表現がある（「この写真［絵］には O が描かれている」が標準的な和訳）ので，使ってみた。この部分は先述したように「少々」がよい（20 語前後が適当）。その後はすぐに「思うこと」の部分に入るが，ここでは「心霊現象」的な内容にしてみた。「楽しいがある意味こわい」の「こわい」の部分に対しての説明を最後まで続けている。「このような巨大な手が現実には存在しない」という文言，さらにどうしてこのような画像が撮れたのかについての説明は諸君にとってくどく思えるかもしれないが，階段を一段一段上るように説明していくというのが自由英作文の常識（そうすることによって語数も稼げる）。日本語は「わかっていることは言わない」という言語なので，この［解答例 1 ］のような展開の仕方はしないだろうが，英語は逆に一段トバシで階段を上っていくことを嫌うのである。英語らしい展開法を身につけることが重要だ。

［解答例 2 ］

　　［あなたが思うこと］＝「この画像から遠近法がわかる」→「現実 2 本の指で猫はつ
　　　　　　　　　　　　まめない」＋「猫を指から離して撮ると，猫は実際よりも小
　　　　　　　　　　　　さく見える」＋「指でつまめるように見える」＋「物事は異な
　　　　　　　　　　　　る角度から見ると違って見えるものだ」

　　ここは「遠近法」をテーマにしている。遠近法とは何かをこの画像を使って 1 つ1 つ丁寧に説明した後，一般的な事物に当てはめて結論づけた。この遠近法についての説明部分には 44 語費やされているが，［解答例 1 ］でも述べたように，やはり階段を一段ずつ上っていくことが重要なのである。最後のように一般化しなくてもむろん構わないのだが，いきなり「物事は異なる角度から見ると違って見えるも

－ 103 －

2016年　　解答・解説

のだ」から始めて，どんどん哲学的な話を進めていくのはやめた方がいいだろう。内容があまりに抽象化して何を言いたいのかわからない，自分の英語力では書けない，破綻した答案ができあがるという最悪のパターンになりやすい。

［解答例3］

> ［あなたが思うこと］＝「一見ありえない状況」＝「巨人が指で寝ている猫をつまみ上げようとしているように見える」→「むろんこれはトリック写真」＝「手をカメラに近づけ，猫を遠くにおいている」→「凝った画像になると見て驚く者も多い」＋「人間の知覚はだまされやすいことの証明」

これは「トリック」をテーマにしたもの。書き出しは「状況説明」に近い。その後トリックの種明かしをし，最後には人間の知覚に触れて締め括っている。「種明かし」の部分が諸君にくどく思えるところかもしれないが，何度も言うようにこのような展開が重要なのである。ちなみに，「人間の知覚」から書き出し，この画像以外の状況で発生する「脳の錯覚」を全体テーマにするのも考えものである。やはり自分の英語力では書けない破綻した答案ができあがる可能性が高い（大脳の生理について語る場合はかなり専門用語が必要になる）。それに，［解答例2］で述べた「物事は異なる角度から見ると違って見えるものだ」から始める答案もそうなのだが，往々にしてこの画像から話がそれていってしまう危険性がある。自由英作文はあくまでも<u>与えられたものに関する内容を展開しなければならない</u>。「この画像の感想」に留まることが極めて重要で，答案を最後まで読んだら全く違う話になっていた，ではいけない。

解答例

［解答例1］

　This photo shows a cat lying on the carpet and a hand, apparently that of the person who took this photo. This is amusing, but also, in a sense, horrifying. Of course, such a huge hand doesn't really exist; this person simply took a photo of a cat, with his left hand holding a camera and his right hand very close to it. But it looks as if someone evil is trying to catch the animal. (76 words)

［解答例2］

　This picture tells us something important about perspective. In the real world, for example, you cannot pick up a cat with two fingers, but when the

— 104 —

2016 年　　解答・解説

cat is placed at a distance from your fingers, the cat looks smaller than it really is, and it looks like you can pick it up. So things look totally different from what they really are when you see them from a different perspective.

(70 words)

［解答例 3 ］

　At first glance, the picture seems to show something impossible. It looks as if a giant is about to grab a sleeping cat with his fingers. Of course, it is a trick photo: the hand is very close to the camera, whereas the cat is far away. This one is of low quality, but some very good ones surprise many of us, and they show how our perception can easily be tricked.　(72 words)

2 (B)

　新傾向の問題。作文の力はもちろん必要だが，読解の要素も大きい。さらに，与えられた英文がわかればよいというだけではなく，論理の展開を予測する思考力・想像力も必要。

【全訳】　動物の知性を研究するため，科学者たちは自分の手の届かない所にある食べ物を獲得させるために動物たちに長い棒を与えた。チンパンジーのような霊長類はその棒を使うが，象は使わないことがわかった。象は鼻を使って棒をつかむことはできるが，食べ物を獲得するのに使うことはない。かくして，象はチンパンジーほど頭がよくないという結論が下された。

　しかし，ワシントンにある国立動物公園にいる若い象のカンドゥーラが，最近その考え方に疑問を投げかけた。その象には棒だけでなく，大きな四角い箱やその他いくつかの物を与え，その一方で頭上の届かない所に果物を置いた。象は棒を無視したが，しばらくすると足で箱を蹴りはじめ，その箱を果物がある場所の真下に持って行った。それから前足でその箱の上に立つと，鼻を使って果物を取ることができたのである。

【考え方】

＜語数について＞

　「50 ～ 70 語」とあるから，やはりこの指定より多くても少なくてもまずい。また，この問題も答案の最後に「○○ words」と書き添えること。

— 105 —

<u>2016 年　　解答・解説</u>

＜各段落の要旨＞

① 第一段落

　棒を使って食べ物を獲得することができるかという実験の結果，象はチンパンジーほど知性がないという結論が出た。

② 第二段落

　別の実験の結果，ある象が棒以外のものを使って食べ物を獲得したため，第一段落で出された結論に疑念が生じている。

＜内容のポイント＞

　「導かれる結論を第三段落として書きなさい」という指示に注目してほしい。つまり，「考えられる展開」を書くのではなく，第一・第二段落の内容を踏まえた「結論」を書くのである。「考えられる展開」であればほぼどんなことを書いても大丈夫だろう。ところが，「導かれる結論」となれば，答案に盛り込まなければならない内容は限られてくる。つまり，この問題は「自由」英作文ではない。

　眼目は第二段落第1文にある **"has recently challenged that belief"** の部分。第一段落で出された「象はチンパンジーほど知性がない」という結論に疑義が生じるということは，要するに「象とチンパンジーの知性は同等である」ということ。これをテーマとし，なぜこのような結論が導かれるのか，その論証を続けるのが最も簡単だろう。ただ，「象とチンパンジーの知性は同等である」と明言しなくても，そのような内容を匂わせる書き方でも差し支えない。

　他の視点としては，「動物実験のあり方に対する提言」というのも考えられる。「棒」というたった1つの道具だけで結論を下してしまうことの早急さを批判し，今後の動物実験のあり方に対する意見を述べるという展開もよいと思う。

　以下にテーマとして<u>不適切</u>であると思われる例をあげておく。

★ 「<u>象の方が知性が高い</u>」

　箱を使うことが棒を使うことより「すぐれている」という結論を出すのは無理がある。

★ 「<u>一般的にどの動物が優秀か</u>を決めるにはもっと実験を重ねる必要がある」

　与えられた英文から導かれる結論としては，やはりチンパンジーと象に特化するべき。

★ 「人間」の知性を取り上げているもの

　この英文から「人間」の話をするのはおかしい。冒頭に書かれている「動物の知性の研究」の部分を読み飛ばしているとしか思えない。

★ 「<u>棒や箱だけで動物の知性を判断することはできない</u>」

－ 106 －

2016 年　　解答・解説

「棒だけで知性は測れない」ならば問題ない。しかし，「箱」まで入れてしまうと，結論を導くことができなくなってしまう。それに，象に関しては第二段落第2文に"not just sticks but a big square box and some other objects"とあるのだから，実際他にもいろいろな道具が与えられていることがわかる（具体的には示されていないが）。つまり，このような視点は「事実誤認」になる。

★　「これらの実験から動物の進化の様子がわかる」

evolution という視点で語るのはあまりにも無理がある。

★　「結局動物の知性は測れない」

要するに，英文で示されている実験は全く無意味だったということ。これを結論とするのは最も無理があるだろう。

★　「これらの実験を反面教師にして，我々も普段から幅広い視野を持つべきだ」

本文と全く無関係な内容で，あまりにも論理が飛躍しすぎている。

ちなみに，書くことが思い当たらないと同じ内容を繰り返す答案がよく見られる。たとえば，「チンパンジーと象の知性は同等」という趣旨の英文が繰り返されている，など。一カ所をグルグルと回っているだけで，話が前に進んでいない答案は大幅な減点対象となるだろう。

＜答案作成＞

以上の点を踏まえて，答案の展開方法を具体例に沿って見てみよう。

［解答例1］

　　［結論］＝「象はチンパンジーに劣らない知性を持っている」

　　［論証］＝「チンパンジーは棒を使ったが，象は箱を踏み台として使った」→「地面から果物までの距離を計算して，自分の鼻が届くかどうかを判断している」

　「象の知性はチンパンジーと同等」という内容を冒頭に明示したパターン。このような展開だと，読み手が答案の趣旨をつかみやすい。問題(A)でも述べたように，知性の存在に対する説明を階段を上るように積み重ねていくことが重要。

［解答例2］

　　［結論］＝「象には高い知性がある」

　　［論証］＝「象は道具が使えるだけでなく，いろいろな選択肢の中から目的達成に最適なものを選ぶことが出来る」→「実際に果物をとるのに役立つのは箱であって他の物ではないと判断した」

　内容的には［解答例1］と同じで，「象の知性はチンパンジーに劣らない」という内容を明示していないだけ。

— 107 —

<u>2016 年　　解答・解説</u>

［解答例 3 ］
　［結論］ ＝「動物の知性を研究する際は注意が必要」
　［論証］ ＝「一度望んでいた結果が出ると結論を下してしまう傾向にある」→「動物
　　　　　　の行動は単純ではないし，我々の期待通りに行動してくれるわけでもな
　　　　　　い」→「実験結果をさまざまな角度から再検証することが必要」
　　動物に対する実験を行う際の注意を喚起することがテーマ。緻密な検証の重要性
を説いている。

解 答 例

［解答例 1 ］
　This experiment shows that elephants have no less intelligence than chimpanzees. The chimpanzees used a stick to get food, but the young elephant used a box to stand on; clearly, he considered whether his trunk could reach the fruit or not, which means he calculated how high it was from the ground. (52 words)

［解答例 2 ］
　What Kandula did shows that an elephant can not only make use of a tool to get what he wants, but he can also choose from several options which one is the most suitable to help him achieve his goal. When he was given several tools, he considered the options given to him and understood the box would help him get the fruit, but not the other tools. (68 words)

［解答例 3 ］
　From these examples, we can see that we have to be careful when studying animal intelligence. We tend to think we have reached a conclusion once the desired results have been obtained. However, animal behaviors are not that simple, and animals do not always behave as we expect them to. So we need to always reexamine the results from different angles. (61 words)

－ 108 －

2016年　解答・解説

4 (A) 【全訳】 (21)　知識は我々の最も重要なビジネスである。(a)他のほとんどすべてのビジネスの成功はそれにかかっているが，その価値は経済的なものにとどまらない。知識の追求，生産，拡大，適用そして保持は(b)文明の中心的活動である。知識は社会の記憶であり，過去との結合である。そしてそれは社会の希望であり，未来への投資である。知識を生み出し，(c)それを行使する力は，人間の重要な特質である。そのようにして我々は(d)社会的存在として繁殖し，変化していく。つまり，(e)地に足をつけつつ，雲の中に頭を入れているのである。

(22)　知識は(a)常に不均等に分配されている一種の資本で，より多くの知識を持っている，あるいはより容易に知識を得ることのできる人は，(b)よりそうでない人に比べて有利な立場にいる。(c)これはつまり，知識は力と近い関係にあるということだ。(d)「知識のための知識」という言い方をするが，我々が知ることの中で，世の中との異なる関係性（たいていはよりよい関係性を我々は望むが）を(e)我々に持たせないものはないのである。

(23)　社会として，我々は知識の生産は無制限であるべきだ，(a)知識の獲得は普遍的であるべきだ，という原則に我々は傾倒している。これは民主主義の理想である。知識に関する限り，(b)常に多いに越したことはないと我々は考えている。(c)知らない方がよいこと，(d)一部の者のみ知るべきであることが存在するとは思っていない。それは，表現されるべきではない考え方，(e)選挙権を持つには無知でありすぎる市民が存在するとは思っていないのと全く同じである。

(24)　より多くの(a)情報や考えを生産すればするほど，そしてそれらをより多くの(b)人に利用できるものにすればするほど，よい決定を下す可能性が高くなると我々は信じている。それゆえ，我々は単に知識の生産と拡大，つまり研究と教育を(c)目的とする機関に大きな社会的投資をしているのである。我々は(d)これらの機関にあらゆる保護を与え，それらが(e)我々が望むような形で機能していないと思うとき，不安に思ったり，時として怒りを覚えたりするのである。

(25)　大学に対する期待の一部は非現実的なものである（(a)そして民主主義に対する期待の一部もそうである）。教えるということはやっかいな作業で，成功の度合いを測ったり，成功を(b)定義することさえ困難なものになりうる分野である。研究もまたやっかいである。あらゆるすぐれた考えや科学的主張に対する代償は，(c)数多くのあまりすぐれてない考えであり科学的主張なのである。すべての学生が十分な教育を受け，すべての学問または研究が価値あるものになるだろうと期待することは当然できない。だが，その制度は，(d)大きくまた多様ではあるが，我々にとって有利に働いていて不利に働くものではなく，我々が望む研究や教育を(e)可能にしてくれていると信じたい。

— 109 —

2016年　解答・解説

考え方　(21)　正解は(c)。put O to use で「O を利用する」という意味の慣用句で，*put use to* という英語はない。ちなみにこの use は名詞。

(22)　正解は(d)。for the sake of A / for A's sake（A は名詞）で「A のために」という意味の慣用句。この表現はしばしば A for A's sake / A for its own sake という形で用いられ，「A のための A」という意味になる（内容的には，本来「手段」であるべき A が「目的」になってしまっていることを示す）。本問はまさにこれで，「知識のための知識」，つまり何かを成し遂げる手段として知識を得るのではなく，知識を得ることが最終目的になってしまっているということ。したがって，for its own sake が正しい。

(23)　正解は(a)。段落(22)の第 1 文に "greater access to knowledge" とあるが，ここに正解が表示されているようなものである。access は名詞で，通常 access to O という形で用いる。したがって本問も access to it should be universal とするのが正しい。

(24)　正解は(b)。(b)が含まれている部分は "the 比較級，the 比較級" の構文になっている。the more people we make them(= information and ideas) available は we〈S〉make〈V〉them〈O〉available〈C〉という第 5 文型なので，the more people という名詞の役割がなくなってしまうため，英語として間違っている。the more people we make them available to とすれば正しくなる（available to more people ということ）。

(25)　正解は(a)。some are of our expectations では英語にならない。直前の英文にあるように some of our expectations とするべきだろう。さらに，"so + 疑問文の形の倒置" で「S もまた…である」という意味の構文があることを思い出し，and so are some of 〈our expectations about democracy〉(= and some of our expectations about democracy are also unrealistic) とすれば正しくなる。

ちなみに(c)の部分は正しいのだが，疑問を持った受験生も多いだろうから解説をつけておく。"The price ... is a lot of not-so-good ones" において主語は The price，補語は a lot of not-so-good ones で，主語が単数なのに補語が複数（しかも a lot of がついている）になっていることを変に思ったかもしれない。The price for every good idea or scientific claim は The price that has to be paid for good ideas or scientific claims（すぐれた考えや科学的主張に対して支払わなければならない代償）という意味合い，つまりすぐれた考えや科学的主張が確立されるには犠牲を払わなければならない，ということ。その「犠牲」とは「数多くのくだらない考えや科学的主張」（not-so-good は bad の婉曲表現，ones は ideas or scientific claims の代用）である。

— 110 —

2016年　　解答・解説

要するに，すぐれた考えや科学的主張は一朝一夕になしとげられるものではなく，それらに至るには数多くの取るに足らない考えや科学的主張が唱えられるという犠牲を払わなければならない，ということ。このように考えれば，(c)が正しいことがわかるだろう。

解答

⑵─(c)	⑵─(d)	⑵─(a)	⑵─(b)	⑵─(a)

4 (B) **全訳** 1990年代のアフガニスタン発のニュース報道には，過激派の軍事部隊によって破壊された廃墟と化した場所以外はほとんど何も描写しないという傾向があった。そうしたイメージがアフガニスタンの普通の暮らしの実態を見抜く洞察力によって釣り合いがとれたものとなることなどめったになかったのだ。戦争状態にある国々を描く報道陣は，とりわけ危険な場所においては，行動を共にし，個別の出来事だけを相互につながりのない形で報道しがちだ。(ア)カブールでは，訪れているテレビの取材班たちは，いつも決まって，その街の最もひどく攻撃を受けた地区へ連れていってくれるよう頼んだものだ。そしてある報道記者は，カブールを「90パーセント破壊されている」とすら報じたのである。

　戦争はものごとを複雑にしてしまう。戦争には人をひどく惹きつけてしまうところがあって，そのせいで戦争ほど目を引かない報道を影の薄いものにしてしまいがちだ。よく知られていることだが，紛争は正確に伝えるのが困難である。戦いは起こったり収まったりするし，しかも現代の紛争は，予測できない意志を自ら持って動く。重大な戦闘は夜の間に終わってしまい，そのあとは風景に溶け込んでいってしまう。(イ)いわゆる交戦地帯といえども，必ずしも危険な場所とは限らない。すなわち，大部分の報道が示唆するほど広い範囲に戦争が及んでいることはめったにないのだ。

　ところが，かの地について描写するのを妨げる，ひときわ根の深い障害が存在したのである。つまりアフガニスタンは，外部の者たちにとっては割れた鏡であり，観察者の見方によって幅広くもなり，あるいは狭小にもなる像を生み出していたということだ。(ウ)平和時であっても，アフガニスタンは外部の者たちに対して，あくまで短期間しか開かれてはいなかったのであり，それは1960年代から1970年代までの忘れ去られた時代のことだった。アフガニスタンは決して単一国家だったのではなく，歴史的に見ればありえないような人種と文化の坩堝であって，そのそれぞれが慣習や言語，そして世界観といった独自の宝を持っていたのである。

― 111 ―

2016 年　　解答・解説

考え方

(ア)　1.　**In Kabul, visiting television crews invariable asked**「カブールでは，訪れているテレビの取材班は例外なく求めた」　visiting は television crews を修飾する現在分詞。動名詞と解釈し，「テレビの取材班を訪れること」などとしたものは不可。television crews は「テレビの取材陣」などでもよいだろう。ただし，「テレビの記者」「テレビの解説員」「テレビのカメラマン」等，撮影に関わるすべての人ではなく一部の人間に限定してしまうものは不可。invariably は「例外なく」の意味が表わされていればよい。

2.　**to be taken to ...**「…に連れていかれること」　asked の目的語として働く名詞用法の不定詞（例　He asked to *see* the violin.「彼はそのバイオリンを見せてもらいたいと頼んだ」）。be taken to ... を「…へ［自分たちを］連れていくよう〈求めた〉」のように能動態に転換して訳出してももちろん構わない。take を「連れていく」の意に解釈していないことが明らかなもの（例：「撮影する」など）は不可。

3.　**the worst-hit parts of the city**「その都市（カブール）の被害が最も大きな地域（最も大きな被害を受けた地域）」　hit の訳語は「攻撃された，打撃を受けた」等広く認められるだろうが，最上級の意味が訳出されていないもの（例：「被害の大きかった」）は減点されても仕方がない。「最も被害の大きかった都市に〈連れていくよう求めた〉」のように parts を無視し，the worst-hit city と混同していることが明らかなものは不可。

(イ)　1.　**Even a so-called war zone is not necessarily a dangerous place**「いわゆる戦闘地域でさえ必ずしも危険な場所ではない」　so-called の訳出は「〈戦闘地域〉と呼ばれている（ような）〈ところ〉」などでもよいだろう。war zone は「戦争地帯」「戦いの場所」等の意味が通る表現なら広く認められるはず。not necessarily は部分否定。「絶対に〈危険な場所では〉ない」のような訳出は当然不可。

2.　**seldom is a war ... comprehensive**「戦争が広範囲にわたることは滅多にない」　seldom は「滅多に…ない」の意で，頻度が少ないことを示す否定の副詞。文頭に否定の副詞が置かれているため，文の中心の主語・動詞が「疑問文の語順」（倒置形）になっていることに注意。「ほとんど…ない」と訳したものも減点されることはなかったはず。comprehensive は「広い範囲で行われる」という意味に解釈できるものはすべて可だが，「理解可能」などのように comprehensible と混同しているものは当然不可である。「…ほど広範囲な戦争はめったにない」のように，comprehensible を補語ではなく，a war に対する修飾語と解釈しているように採点官に受け止められてしまう解答は英文和訳問題の答案としては避けた方がよい。

— 112 —

2016年　　解答・解説

3．**as ... as the majority of reports suggest**「報道の大部分が示唆しているほ
ど〈広い範囲で行われる〉」「報道の大多数が示唆している・よ・う・に，広範囲にわたる
ものではない」と処理したものは，比較構文であることを見落としたと見なされても
仕方ない。the majority of reports は「報道の大多数」でも「大多数の報道」でもよい。
majority に「…の多く」「多くの…」は避けておいた方が無難。reports を「記者」「報
道者」などと解釈した者もいたと思われるが当然不可である。suggest を「提案する」
の意に解していることが明らかなものは不可。

(ウ)　1．**Even in peacetime Afghanistan had been open to outsiders**「平時
でさえアフガニスタンは外部の人間に開かれていた」　形容詞 open の訳出は「開放
的な」などでもよい。outsiders は「よそ者，外国人」等を含め広く認められるだろう。
「アフガニスタンは開かれている」のように明らかに時制を無視したケアレスミスは
意外と多いので注意。

2．**for only a brief interval**「ほんの短い期間だけ〈開かれていた〉」「短い期間
しか〈開かれていなかった〉」　訳出の際には only を無視しないこと。interval はこ
こでは，閉鎖的な期間にはさまれた「合間」という意味で使われている（アフガニス
タンは平時においても外国人には基本的には閉ざされていたが，一時は開放政策が取
られた期間があった）。訳語は，「合間；時間」などを含めて広く認められるだろう。

3．**a forgotten period from the 1960s until the 1970s**「1960 年 代 か ら
1970 年代までの忘れられた期間」　a ... interval は直前の only a brief interval と同
格。「短い期間，つまり…の忘れられた時期」「…の忘れられた時期という短い期間」「短
い期間のみ外部の人間に開かれていたが，それは…の忘れられた時期だった」などい
ずれも問題ない。「1960 年代から 1970 年代までの忘れられた短い期間」のような訳
文はこの同格関係を訳出しているとは言えず，避けてもらいたいところ。

解答

(ア)　カブールでは，現地を訪れているテレビの取材班は，その街で最も被害を受
　　　けた地区に自分たちを連れて行くよう決まって頼んだ。

(イ)　いわゆる交戦地帯も必ずしも危険な場所ではなく，戦争が大多数の報道が示
　　　唆しているほど広範囲にわたるものであることはめったにない。

(ウ)　平時でさえ，アフガニスタンが外部の人間に開かれていたのは短期間のみ，
　　　すなわち，1960年代から1970年代にまでの忘れられた時期だけだった。

— 113 —

2016年　解答・解説

5　**[全訳]**　昨年，ロンドンの団地の建物の外で「ホームレス対策の」スパイクが使われていることに対する大規模な大衆抗議運動があった。私の住んでいる場所から遠くない所だ。スパイクは，コンクリートに打ち込まれた鋭い金属片で，その上に人々が座ったり寝そべったりできないようにするためのものだった。ソーシャルメディアは怒りにあふれ，請願署名が行われ，夜明かしの抗議行動が行われ，数日以内にスパイクは撤去された。しかし，「人を排除する」建築あるいは「優しくない」建築という呼び名でそれは知られているのだが，そういった建築を建てる現象は，依然としてありふれたものである。

　前方に傾いているバス待合所の座席から，散水スプリンクラー，固い管状の腰かけ，硬い仕切りのついた公園のベンチに至るまで，都会の空間は，柔らかい人間の身体をとげとげしく拒絶している。

　ロンドンであれ，東京であれ，都市環境の中で，こういった施策を私たちはいつも目にしているが，その本当の意図を把握していない。私も2009年にホームレスになる前は，ほとんどその存在に気づくこともなかった。経済危機があり，家族が一人亡くなり，突然の離婚があって，さらにそれにも増して突然の心の不調があれば，1年のうちに，けっこう余裕のある収入からホームレスにまで私が落ちぶれるのには十分だった。そんなとき，雨風をしのげる場所を見つけるという明確な目的をもって周囲を見回し始めてようやく，都市の残酷さが明らかとなった。

　その当時，私はロンドン地下鉄のサークル線が好きになった。他の人たちにとっては，それは地下鉄網の中でかなり非効率的な路線にすぎなかった。私にとっては，そして多くのホームレスの人たちにとっては，安全で，じめじめしていなくて，暖かい容器であり，ときには地上，ときには地下を，つねに移動して，まるでロンドンの中心部を正しい位置に縫い合わせている巨大な針のようだった。誰もこちらの存在を気にかけないし，あっち行けと言ったりしなかった。貧しさを共に連れて行くことを許されたのだ。しかし，土木工事がそれに待ったをかけたのだった。

　その次は，主要道路からちょっと入った所にある小さめの公園のベンチだった。古い木製のベンチで，歴代の何千人もの座り手によって滑らかにされていて，これ以上ないくらいにしつこい雨でなければ滴り落ちてくることのないほど葉が茂った木の下にあった。ぬくぬくとして守られていて，一等地だった。それが，ある朝，姿を消してしまった。その代わりに，三つの頑丈な肘かけのついた，居心地の悪い金属の座席が設置された。その日，私は相当な喪失感を味わった。伝わってくることは明白だった。私は一般市民の一員ではない。少なくとも，ここで歓迎される一般市民の一員ではない。私は他に行き場を見つけなければならなかった。

— 114 —

2016年　　解答・解説

　もっと大きな問題もある。こういった施策は，ホームレスの人たちと，もっと援助を受けるに値すると思われる人たちとを区別しないし，区別することもできない。貧しい人たちがバスの待合所で疲れた身体を休ませることができないようにすると，休むことが必要な高齢者や障害者や妊婦もまた憩うことができなくなる。都市が人の身体を受け入れないようにすることによって，すべての人間にとって都市が居心地の悪い場所になってしまう。

　優しくない建築がさまざまな段階で啓発的であるのは，それが偶然の産物でも無思慮の産物でもなく，考えた結果だからである。威嚇し，排除しようという明確な動機をもって，考えられ，計画され，承認され，資金提供を受け，実施されることになった種の意地悪なのである。

　この間，地元のパン屋に入ろうとした際に，（それまで何度か見かけたことのある）ホームレスの男から何か食べるものを恵んでくれないかと言われた。カウンターで働いている若い女性の一人であるルースに，ミートパイをいくつか別の袋に入れてくれと言って，事情を話すと，彼女の言葉は辛辣だった。「この人，物乞いであなた以上に稼いでるでしょうに」と冷たく言いあしらったのだ。

　おそらくそんなことはない。男の顔の半分は，ただれていた。黒ずんで，ひどい傷を負った足の指が，履き古した靴の穴から出ていた。最近あった何かしらの事故か喧嘩かが元で，左手は乾いた血でおおわれていた。このことを私は指摘した。ルースは私の抗議にびくともしなかった。「知らないわよ」と彼女は言った。「こういう人たちって，町の緑地を汚すのよね。危険よ。けだもの」

　優しくない建築が是認しているのは，まさしくこういう考え方なのである。ホームレスというのは，まったく別の種の生きもので，劣っていて，破滅しているのも自分のせいだ，と。追い払われるべきハトのように，あるいは，泣き声で私たちの睡眠を妨げる都会のキツネのように。パン屋で働いている，もっと年上の女性であるリビーが会話に割って入ってきて言った。「恥を知りなさい。その人だって，人の子なのよ」

　貧困は，隣に並んではいるが，隔離された現実として存在する。都市計画をする人たちは，貧困を私たちの目に見えないところに隔離しようと懸命に努力する。みじめすぎて，ため息が出るばかりで，痛々しすぎるので，戸口に眠っている人を見て，この人にも「親がいる」なんて考えられない。そんな人が目にうつっても，次のように問うだけの方が気楽だ。「この人がホームレスだってことが，私にとって何だというの？」だから，私たちは都市計画と結託して，見ないようにと必死に努める。見たくないのだもの。この隔離政策に，私たちは無言の同意をするのである。

　人を排除する建築は，貧困を見えないままにする。快適な生活をすることへの後ろ

— 115 —

2016年　解答・解説

めたさを隠ぺいする。広く言えば貧困，狭く言えばホームレスに対する私たちの態度を，無残なまでに顕わにする。心の寛大さを集団的に失っていることを，具体的に，スパイクのようにとげとげしく表出しているのである。

そして，言うまでもなく，私たちの安心感を高めるという基本的な目標の達成すらできていない。自分たちを鍵で閉じ込めることなく，他者を鍵で閉め出す方法などあるわけがない。都市環境を敵対的なものにすることで，ぎすぎすしてよそよそしくなる。誰にとっても生きることが前よりも少し醜悪になってしまうのだ。

考え方

(A)　正解は「ホームレスの人々がその場所に長時間居座れないようにするという意図」　下線部に含まれる代名詞 their が指しているのは，these measures「これらの施策」であり，具体的には直前の段落に列挙されている。ただし，そこには下線部の「それらの本当の意図」に相当する記述がない。それが書かれているのは，第1段落第2文 (The spikes were ...) の to keep people from sitting or lying on the ground「人々が座ったり寝そべったりできないようにするため」であるが，これはあくまで「ホームレス対策の」スパイクという例の意図なので，それを these measures すべてに当てはまるような表現に変えると正解が得られる。ちなみに，設問文には「具体的に」とあるので「ホームレスを社会から排除する」などと一般化しない方がよい。

(B)　正解は「ミートパイを別の袋に入れるのは，店の入り口にいたホームレスの男性にそれを分けてあげるためであった」　下線部に至る一連の状況は次のとおり。「語り手がパン屋に入るときに，顔見知りのホームレスに物乞いをされた」→「店員にミートパイをいくつか別の袋に入れてくれと頼んだ」→下線部→「店員が辛辣な言葉を言った」。以上のつながりに合致するように事態を整理すれば，解答が得られる。

(C)　正解は **human**。That is A you are talking about. という表現は主に，ある人やものが悪く言われている状況で，それを制止しようとして，「そんな悪い言い方をするな」という気持ちを込めて述べる表現。これは下線部(C)の前文の「『恥を知りなさい』とリビーが会話に割って入ってきた」という記述からも読みとれる。下線部(C)にある someone's son は「人の子」という意味合いで用いる表現なので，この文は「あなたが話しているのは人の子のことなのよ」という意味になる。これは，ルースがホームレスの人たちをあたかも他の動物であるかのような発言をしているのを受けて述べているものなので「ホームレスの人たちだって同じ人間なのよ」という意図の発言である。以上の内容を基に，本文中にある語から適切なものを探し，The man you're talking about is no less underline{human} than you are. 「あなたが話題している男の人は，あなたと全く同程度に人間なのよ」とするのが正しい。

— 116 —

2016 年　　解答・解説

(D)　(ア)　(26)　正解は，**h) rejecting**。空所の前後を直訳すれば「…は柔らかい人間の身体を攻撃的に(26)している」となる。人を寄せつけない設備が人間の身体に対して何をしているかを考えれば，rejecting が最適だとわかる。ちなみに，ここは現在進行形である。

(27)　正解は，**d) finding**。空所の前後を直訳すれば「雨風をしのげる場所を(27)することという明確な目的」となるので，finding「見つけること」を入れればよい。この finding は動名詞。ちなみに，2つ後の段落の末尾に，I had to find somewhere else to go「私は他に行き場所を見つけなければならなかった」とあるのも根拠になる。

(28)　正解は，**c) deserving**。空所を含む文の意味は「こういった施策は，ホームレスの人たちと，もっと(28)と思われる人たちとを区別しないし，区別することもできない」となる。後続の文には「高齢者や障害者や妊婦」が言及されており，この人たちは休息を必要とし，都市空間の中で優しく扱われるのがふさわしい人たちであることから，deserving「助けてもらうに値する」を選べばよい。

(29)　正解は，**a) accepting**。空所を含む文の直前の文にある「貧しい人たちがバスの待合所で疲れた身体を休ませることができないようにする」が手がかりになる。空所に accepting を入れれば「都市が人の身体を受け入れないようにすることによって」という意味になって，直前文と自然なつながりとなる。なお，accepting は動詞 accept の現在分詞が形容詞として使われるようになったもの。(例) Learning how to be more *accepting* of others is a very important skill.（他者をもっと受け入れるようになる術（すべ）を身につけるのは，とても大切な技能です）　ちなみに，この箇所の less accepting of the human body という言い回しは，(26)の rejecting soft, human bodies と類似した表現になっていることにも注意。

(30)　正解は，**i) revealing**。空所を含む段落が，そこまでの具体的な現象に対する評価を下していると気づけることがポイント。「優しくない建築がさまざまな段階で(30)である」という文に合うのは revealing である。この語は，reveal「顕（あら）わにする，明らかにする」という動詞の現在分詞が形容詞として使われているもので「物事の真相を明らかにするような」という意味。

(イ)　(31)　正解は，**e)**。「このホームレスの人が，私の人生にほんの少しでも関係があるというのだろうか？」　本文の下線部は，反語的疑問文で「この人がホームレスだってことが，私にとって何だというの？」という意味。最も適切な選択肢は，e) であり，どちらも「このホームレスは私と何の関係もない」という内容である。

ちなみに，他の選択肢の意味は，次のとおり。

a)　「このホームレスの人を見ると，私はうろたえる」

— 117 —

2016年　　解答・解説

b) 「彼がホームレスであるということは，皆にとって衝撃である」

c) 「このホームレスの人に私はどのようにして手助けをすることができるだろうか」

d) 「このホームレスの人は，戸口で眠る権利がない」

(ウ) (32)　正解は，**a)**。「人を排除する建築は私たち皆に有害だ」この選択肢は，二重否定の文である下線部を肯定文の形に変えたものである。本文の that は関係代名詞で，先行詞は way であるが，直訳すると「他の人たちを鍵で締め出す方法で，なおかつ，私たちを鍵で閉じ込めることのない方法なんて存在しない」となる。これはつまり「人を閉め出すと自分も閉じ込めてしまう」という意味であり，それがわかれば正解に至る。

ちなみに，他の選択肢の意味は，次のとおり。

b) 「ホームレスであることを無視しても，それがなくなるわけではない」

c) 「ホームレスの人たちを制限するのは，彼ら自身のためになる」

d) 「ホームレスの人たちは，私たちが何をしても，必ず目につくものだ」

e) 「安全のために，私たちはホームレスの人たちを目につくところから閉め出さなくてはならない」

解答

(A)　ホームレスの人々がその場所に長時間居座れないようにするという意図。

(B)　ミートパイを別の袋に入れるのは，店の入り口にいたホームレスの男性にそれを分けてあげるためであった。

(C)　human

(D)　(ア)　(26)－ h)　　(27)－ d)　　(28)－ c)　　(29)－ a)　　(30)－ i)

　　(イ)－ e)

　　(ウ)－ a)

解答・解説

1 (A) **[全訳]** 私たちは，人間がこの上なく論理的であり，衝動ではなく信頼に足るデータを元に意志決定をしていると考えたがる。しかし，このようなホモ・エコノミクス（正確な情報を与えられると，何よりもまず自己の利得のために行動する人）という人間観は，とりわけ危険認知という新しい分野における発見によって，その真偽が問われるようになってきた。人間は危険度を正確に測ることがなかなかできないということがわかってきたのである。論理と本能（理性と直感）という2つの強力な情報源から，相反する指示を出す仕組みを人間は持っている。

人間の本能的直感的反応は，飢えた野獣や敵対する部族に満ちあふれた世界で発達し，そこではこのような反応が重要な機能を果たしていた。胸に槍を突きつけられていることに新皮質（脳内の思考を司る部分）が気づくよりも，ほんのわずかだけ先に扁桃体（脳内で，感情のコアとなる部分）に危険の最初の兆候を引き受けさせることは，おそらく非常に有益な順応だったのだろう。現在でも，この直感的反応があるから，バスに轢かれたり，足にレンガを落としたりしなくてすむのだ。しかし，人間の扁桃核は，放射能検知器の音で危険を測定するような世界には不向きなのである。

野獣を避けるために作られた危険認知器官があるがゆえに，私たち現代人は脂肪分の多い食品から悲鳴を上げながら逃げることができなくなっている。ある研究者は「ある種の客観的に見れば危険な要因，たとえばハンバーガーとか自動車，そして喫煙などは，進化による備えができていないものであり，人間はこのような危険要因に対しては，たとえ意識レベルで脅威を認識していても恐怖心をほとんど持たずに反応するものなのです」と述べている。チャールズ・ダーウィンですら，危険認知に対する扁桃体の強い支配力を打ち破ることができなかった。1つの実験として，ロンドン動物園でガラガラヘビの檻に顔を寄せて，ヘビが板ガラスにぶつかってきた時に冷静さを保ち，動かないようにするという試みをしてみた。それは失敗に終わった。

空を飛ぶ恐怖を克服することを軸に1つの業界全体が発達してきた。しかし私たちは世界で毎年約500人いる航空機事故の犠牲者の1人にならないようにと祈る一方で，食料品店に車で行くことに関しては，ほとんど何も考えないのである。毎年自動車事故で亡くなる人が100万人を越えているというのに。

— 120 —

2015 年　　解答・解説

考え方

　本年度は「危険認知における人間の非論理性」に関する文章が使用された。第2段落以降は，細々した具体的な情報や引用が列挙されているように見えるが，これらは第1段落で述べた内容をより明確にするための要素だと考えることができる。次のような点に留意しつつまとめていけば，文章全体のトーンをすくい上げる要約文になるだろう。

1．第1段落第1～3文で大筋を作る。

　第1段落は，第1文「私たちは人間が論理的思考をすると思いたい」，第2文「しかし，この見方は危険認知の研究により揺らいでいる」，第3文「人間は危険度を正確に判定することができないことがわかった」という内容になっているので「人間は論理的な生き物だと私たちは考えたいが，危険認知の分野ではそう言い切れず，危険を正確に判断することができない」という方向性を捉えることが，まず最初のポイントになる。この「正確に危険［危険度］を判断［算定］することができない」というのはどういうことかを，第2段落以降の内容を参考に明確にしていく。

2．「論理（理性）＜本能（直感）」の関係を反映させる。

　第1段落第4文では「論理（理性）と本能（直感）両方が働きかける仕組みを持っている」と述べているだけだが，第3文までの流れから，危険認知は「論理のみに支配されるとは言えない」領域であることが暗示されている。

　第2段落は主に本能的・直感的な反応について述べられており，第2文では「危険に際し思考より感情の部分が優先して反応する，原始的な仕組み」について述べている。これがあるから怪我をしなくてすむというわけである。

　第3段落第3，4文のダーウィンのエピソードは「理屈で考えれば危険はないが，体が危険を察知して動いてしまう」ことの例として引き合いに出されている。

　このような記述から「人間は危険察知の際には，論理より本能が優先する［強く影響する］」という点を抽出しておくべきだと考える。

3．どのような危険要因を危険だと思えないかを明確にする。

　第2段落以降，危険要因と言えるものがいろいろと紹介されているが，これらは次のように2つに大別できる。

＜A群＞　spear, wild animal, flying

＜B群＞　radiation, fatty food, hamburgers, automobiles, smoking, driving

　このA群は「人間が本能的・直感的に恐怖を感じる（＝危険だと思う）もの」であり，B群は第3段落第1文の記述や第2文の引用から考えて「危険であることが意識的に認識はできても恐怖を感じないもの」となる。このような捉え方の差，すなわち

— 121 —

2015 年　　解答・解説

「A 群は危険だと思えるが B 群は危険だと直感できない」という差こそが，第 1 段落第 3 文の "have great difficulty in accurately gauging risk" という表現の意味であると考えられる。B 群のような危険要因は「（論理的には）危険だと認識可能なものだが，（直感的には）怖いと思えない」ものとして紹介されているわけである。

以上のような視点からポイントをまとめてみると次のようになり，これを元に解答例をまとめてみた。

Point 1

　　私たちは人間が論理的思考をするもの（理性的な存在）だと考えるが，人間は危険認識の際には危険度を正確に判断することができない。

Point 2（下線部の意味を明確に）

　　認識はできるが本能（直感）で感じられない危険要因は怖いと思わない。

Point 3（その背景／原因）

　　危険を察知する際は，論理的思考より本能的衝動に強く影響される面がある。

解 答 例

［解答例 1］　人間は論理的な生物とされるが，危険察知の際には論理より本能的衝動に強く影響される。たとえ認識可能でも本能的に恐怖を感じない危険は正確に把握できない。（74 字）

［解答例 2］　人間は合理的存在だと言われるが，危険察知の際には原始的本能が優先的に働くため，認識はできていても本能的に恐怖を感じない危険は正しく捉えることができない。（76 字）

1　**(B)**　**全訳**　なぜ普通の，分別をわきまえた人が，同僚や家族に腹を立て，お金を無駄にし，普段ならしないような決定をしてしまうのだろうか。「意思決定疲労」という捉え方がその説明に役立つ可能性がある。どれほど理性的であろうとしても，次から次へと意思決定をすれば，かならず生物学的な代償を支払うことになる。これは一般的な肉体的疲労とは異なる。メンタルな力は下がるが，疲労を自覚することがないのである。どうやら，1 日で行う選択が多くなるほど，それぞれの選択が脳にとって厳しいものになっていくように思われるのだ。

（　1　）その後参加者全員が自制心を試す典型的なテストの 1 つを受けた。氷水にできるだけ長く手を付けておくのである。衝動的に手を引き上げようとするものであるが，決定者の方がすぐにあきらめた。

— 122 —

<u>2015 年　　解答・解説</u>

（　2　）研究者は，買い物が終わった買い物客に面接をし，算数の問題を可能な限り解くように求めた。ただし，いつでもやめてよいと言った。案の定，店内で一番多くの決定をすでにしていた買い物客が，この算数の問題でも一番先にあきらめた。

どんな意思決定でも，イタリアとローマの属州ガリアとを隔てるルビコン川に敬意を表して，行動局面に関するルビコンモデルと呼ばれているものに分類可能である。カエサルが紀元前 49 年に，ガリア人を征服した後に帰郷する途中，この川にたどり着いたとき，ローマに戻る将軍は，ローマを侵略する行為とみなされないように，軍隊を率いてその川を横断することは禁じられているということを彼は知っていた。ルビコン川のガリア側で待っている時，すなわち「意思決定前の局面」にあった時，彼は内戦を始めることの危険と利益について熟慮した。やがて彼は計算をやめ，決定を下し，自軍とともにルビコン川を渡り「意思決定後の局面」に達したのである。

（　3　）研究者たちが示しているのは，どちらかの岸辺で生じること（ガリア側にとどまって自分の選択肢について考えるのであれ，ローマへ進軍することであれ）よりも，ルビコン川を渡ることが人を疲弊させるということである。

精神的に疲れ果ててしまうと，大変骨の折れる決定をする気がしなくなるものだ。この意思決定疲労のために，どういうタイミングでオファーを出すかを心得ているセールスマンのカモになってしまうのだ。ある実験がドイツの自動車販売代理店で行われた。客はそこで新車のオプションを注文するのである。たとえば，13 種のホイールリム，25 のエンジン配置，56 色の内装から選択をしなければならなかった。

客は，最初のうちは慎重に選択肢を比較検討していたが，意思決定疲労が始まると，勧められるものを何でも受け入れるようになった。（　4　）研究者たちは，自動車購入者の選択肢の順序を入れかえることで，客は結局さまざまなオプションで手を打つことを発見した。そして平均的な差額は車 1 台につき 1500 ユーロ（当時のレートで約 2000 ドル）以上にのぼった。客が追加料金を少し払ったか，たくさん払ったかは，その選択肢がいつ提示されるか，そしてどれほどの意思力が客に残っているかによって決まった。

買い物は，特に貧しい者にとって疲労感を与えることがある。意思決定疲労が貧しい人を罠に掛ける主要因になり得る（そして，見逃されていることが多い）と主張する研究者もいる。その経済的な状況ゆえに難しい決定を数多くしなければならないゆえに，学校，仕事，その他，中流階級への足がかりとなるかもしれない活動に注ぎ込む意思力が減ってしまうのである。（　5　）

また，貧しい人とお金持ちの人が買い物に行くと，貧しい人のほうが買い物の最中に間食をする可能性がずっと高いということもわかっている。これは彼らの性格の弱

－ 123 －

<u>2015年　　解答・解説</u>

さを裏付けていると思えるかもしれない（結局のところ，健康問題発生率を上げる原因となる調理済みスナックを食べるのではなく，自宅で料理をすれば栄養状態を良くすることもおそらくできるのだから）。しかし，スーパーマーケットに行くことが，お金持ちよりも貧しい人において，よけいに意思決定疲労をもたらすとすれば，貧しい人はレジに到達する前にチョコバーを我慢するために残された意志力が少なくなってしまう。こういう品物が衝動買いアイテムと呼ばれるのにはちゃんと理由があるのだ。

選択肢全訳

a)　しかし，なぜルビコン川を渡ることが，それほど危険なのか？

b)　この過程は全体的にどんな人の意志力も疲弊させ得るものであるが，この意思決定の過程の中で，最も人を疲弊させるのはどの局面だろうか。

c)　もう少し現実的な場面に入れて考え方を検証するために，この研究者たちは，巨大な現代的意思決定の場，すなわち郊外のショッピングセンターに入っていった。

d)　言いかえれば，経済的に貧しい者は意志力をほとんど持たないので，自分の生活を困難にしたと言って社会を非難しようとすることさえできない。

e)　そして，この過程の早い段階で出会う大きな選択肢が多いほど，すぐに疲れてしまい，提示されたオプションをほとんど抵抗もせず受け入れることに甘んじた。

f)　フロリダ大学の研究者によって行われた実験で，買い物客が自分の精神的疲労に気づいているということが，計算能力を測る単純なテストによって裏付けられた。

g)　これが重要な意味を持つのは，相次ぐ研究によって，自制心の低さが低所得のみならず，低学力，離婚，犯罪，アル中，不健康などその他数多くの問題と関連づけられることが示されているからである。

h)　フロリダ州立大学の研究者がこの考え方を検証する実験を行った。ある学生の集団が一連の選択をするよう求められた。「ペンがいいですか，ロウソクがいいですか？」「ロウソク，それともTシャツ？」　彼らは実際に選んだ品物をもらったわけではない。単にどちらを好むか決めるだけだった。一方，もう一つの集団（彼らを非決定者と呼ぶことにしよう）は，これら同一の製品すべてについて同じ長さだけ考えたが選択はしなくてもよかった。

考え方

(1)　正解は **h)**「フロリダ州立大学の研究者がこの考え方を検証する実験を行った。ある学生の集団が一連の選択をするよう求められた。『ペンがいいですか，ロウソクがいいですか？』『ロウソク，それともTシャツ？』　彼らは実際に選んだ品物をもらったわけではない。単にどちらを好むか決めるだけだった。一方，もう一つの集団（彼らを非決定者と呼ぶことにしよう）は，これら同一の製品すべてについて同じ長さだ

— 124 —

<u>2015 年　　解答・解説</u>

け考えたが選択はしなくてもよかった」。

　直後の文に定冠詞付きで "the participants"（参加者）が登場しているし，Afterward（その後）という副詞があるので，実験／調査の大筋を含むものになるはず。この時点で，f) か h) に絞られるが，同段落内に "the deciders gave up much sooner" という表現があることから，それと対比を成す "the nondeciders" を含む h) がふさわしい。

　(2)　正解は **c)** 「もう少し現実的な場面に入れて考え方を検証するために，この研究者たちは，巨大な現代的意思決定の場，すなわち郊外のショッピングセンターに入っていった」。

　直後の文で shoppers（買い物客）を実験対象にしたことが述べられている。この時点で c) か f) に絞られるが，f) は「買い物客が自分の精神的疲労を意識していたことが…を通して裏付けられた」という内容が空所直後の文とは無関係なので c) が適していると考える。

　(3)　正解は **b)** 「この過程は全体的にどんな人の意志力も疲弊させ得るものであるが，この意思決定の過程の中で，最も人を疲弊させるのはどの局面だろうか」。

　空所前の第4段落でルビコン川の話が引き合いに出されていて，"predecisional phase"（意思決定前の局面），"postdecisional phase"（意思決定後の局面）そして decision-making（決定を下すこと＝ルビコン川を渡る決定をすること）に触れているので，これを受ける文として b) がふさわしい。さらに直後の文で "Researchers have shown that ... is more tiring than ～" の文があるので，これが b) の問いに対する答えとしても成立すると考える。

　なお，ルビコン川の話なので a) を考えたかもしれないが，この選択肢には "so risky" という表現があることに注意。このような表現が出てくるとすれば，「ルビコン川を渡ることが危険だ」ということが前に書かれていなければならないが，そのような文がない。さらに，直後の "... more tiring than ～" の文も対応しないことになってしまうため不適当である。

　(4)　正解は **e)** 「そして，この過程の早い段階で出会う大きな選択肢が多いほど，すぐに疲れてしまい，提示されたオプションをほとんど抵抗もせず受け入れることに甘んじた」。

　第6，第7段落は自動車販売店の場面を例として述べている部分なので，この内容と関連性が最も高いと言える e) がふさわしい。

　(5)　正解は **g)** 「これが重要な意味を持つのは，相次ぐ研究によって，自制心の低さが低所得のみならず，低学力，離婚，犯罪，アル中，不健康などその他数多くの問

－ 125 －

題と関連づけられることが示されているからである」。

経済的に貧しい人と意思決定疲労の関係について「大きな意思決定を数多くしなければならないので，中流階級への手がかりとなるかもしれない活動に注ぎ込む意志力が減ってしまう」と直前にあるので，これと最も密接な内容を持つ g) がふさわしいと考える。言うまでもなく，This は直前の内容を指す。

なお，d) にも "the financially poor" が入っているが，「自分の生活を困難にしたといって社会を非難しようとすることさえできない」という内容が言い換えとして成立する文が直前にあるわけではないので不適である。

(ア)　正解は **eat**（あるいは **snack**）。

文法上は，likely to の後なので「動詞の原形」が入る。次に文脈上の視点だが，直後の 2 文が might seem ... But ～の構成になっており「これは貧しい人の性格の弱さを裏付けていると思えるかもしれないが，スーパーに行くことが貧しい人に対して意思決定疲労の大きな原因となるというのなら，レジにたどり着く前にチョコバーを我慢するために残されている意思力は（お金持ちより）少なくなってしまう」が大筋となる。

また，前半の after all 以下には「健康問題発生率を上げる原因となる調理済みスナックを食べるのではなく，自宅で料理をすれば栄養状態を良くすることもおそらくできるだろう」とある。

① 買い物の途中でしそうな行為
② 性格の弱さの裏付けとなり得るような行為
③ consume ...（…を摂取する；食べる）と同じ方向の意味になる行為
④ チョコバーを我慢できなくなってするような行為

以上 4 点に合う単語として eat がふさわしい。ただし，「間食をする；軽食をとる」という意味の snack という動詞も別解となる。

解答

(1)– h)　　(2)– c)　　(3)– b)　　(4)– e)　　(5)– g)
(ア)– eat（別解・snack）

2 (A)

イラスト問題は 2007 年以来の出題。この形式の復活は想定内のことだが，2007 年以前は「描かれている状況の説明」のみだったのに対し，本問ではそれに受験者の考えを加えるところが大きな変化である。

— 126 —

2015 年　　解答・解説

考え方

＜語数について＞

「60 〜 80 語の英語で」とあるから, この指定より多くても少なくてもいけない（特に少ない場合は減点あるいは 0 点にされる可能性が高い）。また, 答案の最後に「○○ words」と書き添えよう。

＜問題の指示＞

① 「絵に描かれた状況を簡単に説明する」

　「簡単に」とあるので, 20 〜 30 語くらいが適当ではないか。

② 「①についてあなたが思ったことを述べる」

　残り 30 〜 60 語をこの部分にあてる。

＜内容のポイント＞

① 「絵に描かれた状況」について

　☆　イラストにせよ写真にせよ, 過去の問題では男性か女性かをはっきりさせているのが特徴だったが, 本問の場合は性別は自由だろう。

　☆　「ある人物が（手）鏡を持っている」「鏡の中に違う顔があるのに驚いている」という 2 つの要素は必須。

　☆　鏡の中の表情は俗に言う「アカンベ」だが, これを英語で表現しようと思うと苦労する。「舌を出している」と考え, "be sticking one's tongue out" と処理すればよいのだが, この表現すら思い浮かばなかった場合は, 単に「違う顔がある」と考えて "there is a different face in the mirror" とすればよい。このような簡略化がはたして許されるのかどうか不安に思う者もいるだろうが, 逆にこのように逃げ道を見つけられることこそ東大が試したいポイントではないだろうか（stick one's tongue out という語彙を問うことが東大のねらいとは思えない）。

② 「あなたが思ったこと」について

　絵に対する反応として適切であれば, 本当にどんな内容でもよいと思う。「心霊現象だ」「目の錯覚だ」「疲れから幻覚を見ている」「動画に撮って売ればよい」等々。ただし, 自分の英語力で書ける内容にすることが重要。アイデアばかり先行して, 英語として破綻するのが最悪のパターンである。特に, この人物の深層心理について書こうとしないほうがよい。また, 「絵のような状況は非現実的だ［あり得ない］」という反応は, 想像力の欠如としか言いようがない。東大もこのような状況が現実に存在すると思って出題しているわけではないだろう。

— 127 —

<u>2015 年　　解答・解説</u>

＜答案作成＞

　ここで，答案の展開方法を具体例に沿って見てみることにする。

［解答例1］

　　［絵に描かれた状況］＝「鏡の中に違う顔があり，しかも舌を出しているのを見て，女性が驚いている」（英語は 28 words）

　　［あなたが思ったこと］＝「本当にあったら怖い」＋「こんな体験をしたら，幽霊か悪魔の仕業だと思い，悪霊を払うため霊能者を雇うだろう」

　イラストの客観的説明として "This picture shows O" という表現がある（「この絵には O が描かれている」が標準的な和訳）ので，使ってみた。「舌を出している」の部分はなくても大丈夫だろう。「思ったこと」だが，この解答例ではこのような状況は現実にはありえないという想定のもとで書いたので，全体的に仮定法を用いている。ちなみに，"A person who experienced this would think ..." の部分は，問題5・下線部(B)の部分をまねて書いてみた。

［解答例2］

　　［絵に描かれた状況］＝「ある女性が手鏡を見たら，自分が舌を出している顔が映っているので驚いている」（英語は 24 words）

　　［あなたが思ったこと］＝「動画に撮ってネットにアップするべき」＋「何百万の人が見て，そのうちテレビ局が買いに来る」＋「大金持ちになれる」

　イラストの説明は解答例1とほぼ同じ。「思ったこと」に関してはやや現実離れした（というか妄想が膨らんでいる）内容なので，「何百万の人が…」以降は仮定法を用いた。

［解答例3］

　　［絵に描かれた状況］＝「ある男子が手鏡をのぞくと，そこには自分の顔だが全く違う表情をしたものが映っているので，衝撃を受けている」＋「片目を閉じ，舌を出している」（英語は 48 words）

　　［あなたが思ったこと］＝「学校の課題のせいで疲れており，幻覚を見ている」＋「すぐに寝た方がいい」

　状況説明を少々多めにしている。問題文には「簡単に」と指示されていたが，さほど厳密に守らなくても大丈夫だろう。その分「思ったこと」はアッサリと済ませた。ちなみに "be seeing things" は「幻覚を見る」という意味の idiom（"be hearing things" なら「幻聴」になる）。

－ 128 －

2015年　解答・解説

解 答 例

[解答例1]

　This picture shows a woman who is astonished because there is a different face in the mirror she is holding, and moreover, it is sticking its tongue out.　If this kind of thing really happened, it would be quite horrifying.　A person who experienced this would think it was the work of a ghost or a demon, and would employ an exorcist to remove the evil spirit.

(67 words)

[解答例2]

　A woman is holding a hand mirror, and when she looks at it, she is quite astonished to see herself thrusting her tongue out.　I think she should make a video of this and upload it to a website like YouTube.　I'm sure millions of people would see it, and in no time many TV stations would offer her lots of money for permission to show it.　She would soon become a millionaire.

(73 words)

[解答例3]

　When the boy looks into the mirror he is holding, he sees someone that looks exactly like him, but with a different facial expression.　The boy in the mirror has one of his eyes closed and his tongue is sticking out.　Obviously, the boy is shocked at this.　I think he is so tired from working on his school project that he is seeing things.　He needs to get some sleep right away.

(73 words)

2 (B)

　昨年に引き続きことわざ・格言を問う問題。指示通りの順番で書けばよいので，答案の展開の仕方について悩む必要がない面では楽だが，そもそも与えられたことわざの意味する所がわからなければ書きようがなくなるところが難点。

考え方

<語数について>

　(A)と同じく「60～80語の英語で」とあるから，やはりこの指定より多くても少なくてもまずい。また，この問題も答案の最後に「○○ words」と書き添えること。

— 129 —

2015 年　　解答・解説

＜問題の指示＞

① 「２つのことわざの相反する部分についての説明」

　　最初に両方の定義を述べた後で，引き続き相反する部分を説明するのがよいだろう。この部分はどれだけ簡潔に書いても 30 語以上はかかる。

② 「あなたにとってどちらがよい助言と思われるか」

　　「こちらの方がよい」と明言するべきで，答案全体を読むことで察知させるという書き方はよくない。この部分は 10 語以下で書ける。

③ 「②の理由」

　　上記から考えると，この部分を 20 ～ 40 語で書くことになる。

＜内容のポイント＞

① 「２つのことわざの相反する部分についての説明」

　　Oxford Dictionary of English に掲載されている２つのことわざの定義は以下の通り。

　　"Look before you leap" ＝ you shouldn't act without first considering the possible consequences or dangers

　　"He who hesitates is lost" ＝ delay or vacillation may have unfortunate or disastrous consequences

　　むろん試験会場で辞書は引けないから，もしこれらのことわざを知らなければ，意味を推理するしかない。直訳はそれぞれ「跳ぶ前に見ろ」「ためらう者は道に迷う」だが，これらは「相反する」のだから，どちらか一方の意味がとれればよい。前者の方が見当がつけやすいだろう。「跳ぶ前に見ろ」とは「見てから跳べ」，つまり「まわりの状況をよく見てから跳べ」という意味合いで，行動に先んずる熟慮・観察の重要性を説くことわざである。後者はその逆，つまりとりあえず行動することの重要性を説くものである。したがって，対立点は「熟慮 vs 行動」ということになる。

② 「あなたにとってどちらがよい助言と思われるか」

　　"I think the first [second] proverb is better advice." と直訳するのが一番簡単。

③ 「②の理由」

　　注意しなければならないのは，この「理由」はややもすると①で述べたことわざの定義と同一の内容を繰り返してしまう可能性があるということだ。たとえば，「最初のことわざの方がよい助言だと思う。やはり行動する前にはいろいろなことを考えることが大切だ」という類のもの（下線部が定義の繰り返しとなっている）で，これは大きく減点される可能性がある。このような事態を避けるためには，選んだことわざの長所を力説するのではなく，選ばなかったことわざが持つ欠点を挙げる

― 130 ―

2015年　　解答・解説

のがよい。

＜答案作成＞

　以上の点を踏まえて，答案の展開方法を具体例に沿って見てみよう。なお，「①相反する部分」については別解が存在しない（英語の表現方法はいろいろあるだろうが）ので，「②どちらがよい助言か」「③その理由」の部分のみ記してある。

［解答例1］

　　［どちらがよい助言か］＝前者

　　［理由］＝「一度やったことは取り返しがつかない」→「自分が適切な行動を取っているのか慎重にならなければならない」

　相反する所の説明をかなり丁寧に行ったため，①の部分だけで英語が53語かかっている。したがって，②③は簡単に済ませた。

［解答例2］

　　［どちらがよい助言か］＝後者

　　［理由］＝「どれほど熟慮したところで，自分の行動がよい結果をもたらすかどうかは絶対にわからない」→「とりあえず行動してみて，うまく行けばそれでよし，うまく行かなければ違う行動に出てみればよい」

　相反する部分を33語で説明したので，こちらは②③をじっくり書いてある。先述したように，自分が選ばなかった前者のことわざの欠点を突くという展開。「とりあえず行動してみて」の部分は定義と同一内容になっているが，このように一部のみでとどまっているならば問題はない。

解 答 例

［解答例1］

　The first saying means you should think carefully about what you are about to do before you do it, and the second means someone who spends too much time thinking about what to do loses the chance to act; in short, the first lays emphasis on careful thinking, and the second on doing. I think the first is better. What is done cannot be undone. When you do something, you should be careful that you are doing the right thing.

(80 words)

［解答例2］

　The difference between these proverbs is that the first emphasizes the importance of thinking carefully before you do something, and the second

－ 131 －

says thinking carefully before you do something will get you nowhere. To me, the second proverb is better advice. However carefully you think, you'll never know whether what you do will bring about good results. So, you should just try something without thinking, and if you don't succeed, you should just try something different. (76 words)

4 (A) 【全訳】　生物学者クリスティーナ・リールは，「オオハシカッコウ」という熱帯地方の鳥が取る変わった協力的繁殖行動について研究している。オオハシカッコウの集団は一つの巣でヒナを一緒に育て，親鳥たちは皆で作業を分担する。ところが，意外なことに，これらの集団に属している鳥には必ずしも血縁関係がないのである。

　この半世紀の間，動物の協力行動については主として「血縁淘汰」という理論が支配的である。これは，動物は自らに利益がありそうな場合，もし自分にとって利益がなければ親族（家族や親戚）に利益がありそうな場合にのみ，互いを助け合うという理論である。このことが，彼らが遺伝物質の一部を常に次の世代に伝えることを確実にしているのである。だが，(ア)ヒナを育てるということになると，オオハシカッコウは血縁淘汰だけでは説明できない行動を取る。

　オオハシカッコウは互いに協力し合うが，他よりもずっと一生懸命に働く者がいることをリールは知った。どの集団にも，巣の中の卵の上に座るという(イ)骨の折れる作業を最終的に行うオスが一羽存在する。他の鳥が眠っている間，夜勤に就いている鳥は，自分のヒナの健康に関しても生存に関しても特別得になるとは思えないのに，余分な仕事を引き受けるのである。これは再び血縁淘汰のルールを破っている。

　オオハシカッコウはまったく利他的であるわけではない。メスは巣の手入れには協力するが，同時に他のメスの卵を巣から落とすことで自らのヒナの生存率を上げている。ここでも彼らの行動は変わっている。世界の1万種に及ぶ鳥の中で，このような卵を割るという無駄な行動を取るものはたった6種しかなく，「オオハシカッコウは動物の社会行動(ウ)に関し存在する種の中で最も興味深いものの1つである」というリールの主張を強固なものにしている。

【考え方】　(ア)　正解は(21) - **c)**，(22) - **d)**。when it comes to O で「O ということになると」という意味の慣用表現であることを知っていれば簡単。残った has / raising / their / young だが，これは本文2〜3行目に "raise their young" とあり，答えが書いてあるも同然。

　並べ替えた英文：when **it** comes to **raising** their young

— 132 —

2015 年　　解答・解説

　(イ)　正解は⑵ - **h)**，⑷ - **f)**。end up - ing で「最終的に - する」という意味の idiom。残った all / much / labor / the / tiring だが，perform の目的語となる名詞は labor しかない。tiring は形容詞なので labor を修飾させて tiring labor となるが，「形容詞」なのだから，強調する場合は much ではなく very を使うことになる。したがって，much tiring labor はあり得ず，all the tiring labor とまとめる。

　並べ替えた英文：ends **up** performing all **the** tiring labor

　(ウ)　正解は⑸ - **f)**，⑹ - **d)**。カッコの直前が "this is one of" となっているから，その後には複数形の名詞が続くはずである。さらに interesting / most / the から最上級を考え，the most interesting species とまとめる。問題はここからで，現段階で残っているのは except / existence / for / in。in existence で「現存の」という意味合いの idiom であることを知っていれば後は楽だが，知らなければ except for を考えてしまうだろう。"except for existence" としても "except for animal social behavior" としてもまったく要領を得ない。この問題は結局 in existence という idiom を知らないと破綻する仕組みになっているのである。

　並べ替えた英文：the **most** interesting species **in** existence for

解 答

(ア) (21) - c)	(22) - d)	(イ) (23) - h)	(24) - f)	(ウ) (25) - f)	(26) - d)

4 （B）　**【全訳】**　ユージーン・クロウフォードはナバホ族，すなわちアメリカの先住民族の一員である。彼は自分と友人がアメリカ軍に新兵として参加した日のことを忘れることができない。キャンプエリオットに到着するとすぐに，彼らは教室に案内されたが，その教室を見て，彼は子供の頃に寄宿学校で入った教室を思い出した。その記憶は決して楽しいものではなかった。先生にナバホ語をしゃべっているのを見つかったとき，口の中を洗うために先生が無理やり彼に使わせた茶色い石鹸の不快な味がほとんどしていた。彼のそうした思いは，教室のドアが突然開き，将校が入ってきたときに中断された。新兵たちは立ち上がって気をつけをした。「休め，諸君。座りたまえ」

　その建物で過ごした最初の1時間が彼らの人生を永遠に変えることになった。そしてその時点で生じたショックを彼らは今日に至るまで依然として感じている。彼らは，軍がどのようなプロジェクトのために彼らを新兵として採用したのかをまったく想像することはできなかった。中には，事前に知っていたなら，それほど熱心に参加することはなかったかもしれないと考えている者もいた。ナバホ語が秘密の通信内容を伝

— 133 —

2015 年　　解答・解説

えるための暗号に選ばれていたのだ。というのは，ナバホ族でない限り，ナバホ語は一言も理解できないのである。ナバホ語は複雑な言語で，発音のわずかな変化で伝達内容が完全に変わってしまう可能性がある。政府の決定は賢明なものだった。結果的にそれは敵が解読することができなかった唯一の暗号となったのだ。しかし，若いナバホ族の兵士にとってそれは悪夢だった。いついかなる状況下でも，許可なく，あるいは一人で建物を出ることは許されなかった。1968 年についに公表されるまで，家族さえ含め，彼らは誰に対してもこの計画について語ることは禁止されていたのだ。

　こうした兵士たちの多くは，この部屋に似た教室，同じ政府が管理している学校の教室で，ナバホ語を話すと，時には厳しく罰せられてきたのだ。過去においては自分自身の言葉を話したことに対して彼らを罰していたこの政府が，今では戦争に勝つ手助けをするためにナバホ語を使うように彼らに求めていたのだ。白人はナバホ族が想像していたよりも奇妙な連中だった。

[考え方]

（ア）　1．**He could almost taste the harsh brown soap**「彼には茶色い石鹸の不快な味がほとんどしていた」「can ＋知覚動詞」で「ある一定の期間知覚している状態」（「…が見えている」「…が聞こえている」「…を感じている」）を表すことができる。（例）I *can see* the stars.（星が見えている）／ I *can feel* something crawling up my leg.（何かが足を這いあがっている感じがしている）。「…な石けんをほとんど味わっていた」とは，ここでは「…な石けんの味をほとんど思い出していた」ということ。harsh は「〈音・光・色・味などが〉不快な，きつい，刺激が強い」の意。

　2．**the teachers had forced him to use to wash his mouth out**「口の中を洗うために教師が無理やり使わせていた〈石けん〉」 the ... soap を先行詞とする関係詞節で，関係代名詞は節内では use の目的語として働いている。to wash his mouth out は use を修飾する副詞用法の不定詞。wash ... out で「〈…の内側〉を洗う」の意。

　3．**when he was caught speaking Navajo**「ナバホ語をしゃべっているところを見つかると」 forced を修飾している副詞節。catch O － ing で「O が－しているところを目撃する」の意。（例）I *caught* the boy *stealing* fruit from our orchard.（その少年が我々の果樹園から果物を盗むところを目撃した） 問題文はこの表現を受動態にしたもの。

（イ）　1．**At no time under any circumstances were they to leave the building**「いついかなる状況下においても彼らはビルを出てはならなかった」 They were *not* to leave the building at *any* time. で「彼らはいかなるときもその建物を去ってはならなかった」の意。ここでは，be not to － で「禁止」を表していることに注意。

— 134 —

2015 年　　解答・解説

（例）You *are not to* tell anyone of this problem.（この問題については誰にも語ってはならぬ）　この文の not と any を合わせて no にすると，They were to leave the building at *no* time. という文が得られるが，ここから at no time を文頭に動かし，文の中心の主語・動詞を倒置してできあがるのが，At *no* time ... *were they to leave* the building. である。under any circumstances は「いかなる状況においても」の意の副詞句で，At no time と同様に were to leave を修飾している。

　2．**without permission or alone**「許可なく，あるいは一人で」　leave を修飾する副詞要素。without permission という副詞句と alone という副詞が or によってつながれている。

　(ウ)　1．**Now this government ... was asking them to use it**「今になってこの政府は彼らにそれを使うように求めていた」　them はナバホ族の新兵，it は彼らの使うナバホ語を指している。

　2．**that had punished them in the past for speaking their own language**「過去において，自分自身の言語を話したことに関し彼らを罰していた〈この政府〉」　this government を先行詞とする関係詞節。in the past, for speaking their own language はともに punished を修飾する副詞句。punish A for B「B に関して A を罰する」は punish の代表的な用法。（例）He *punished* a student *for* telling a lie.（嘘をついたため，彼は生徒を罰した）

　3．**to help win the war**「その戦争に勝つ手助けとなる（役立つ）ように」　use を修飾する副詞用法の不定詞。help の目的語は to 不定詞でも原形でも構わないことに注意。（例）I *helped (to) clear* up the mess.（私は後片付けするのを手伝った）

解答

　(ア)　彼は，先生たちにナバホ語を話しているのが見つかってしまったときに口を洗うのに用いるよう強いられた，きつい茶色の石けんの味を思い出しそうなほどだった。

　(イ)　いついかなる状況においても，彼らは許可なく，もしくは一人で建物を出てはならなかった。

　(ウ)　かつて自分自身の言語を話したことで彼らを罰したこの政府が，今度は彼らに戦争に勝つ手助けをするためにそれを使うよう求めていたのである。

－　135　－

2015年　　解答・解説

5　**【全訳】** レベッカは, 事業計画を立てたり, ローンを申し込んだりして, 書店を開業する準備を進めていた。「本屋さんですって？」と母親のハリエットが言った。「あなた程度の学歴で, お店を始めたがるの？　それも, お金になる見込みもないような店を。あなたの人生って結局, どうなるのよ？」

レベッカは傷つき, 怒り狂っていた。いつもながらの喧嘩をしたのだが, 相変わらずこういった喧嘩ができるということをレベッカがわかっていなかったので, いっそうひどい喧嘩となった。ハリエットの病気が始まって以来の, 最近の長い平和が, レベッカに間違った安心感を与えてしまっていたのだった。彼女は騙されたような気がした。

その後で, ハリエットはレベッカに小切手を送った。かなりの金額のものだった。「書店の助けになるように」とカードに書いてあった。

「こんな余裕はないはずでしょ」とレベッカは言った。

「私のしたいことなの」とハリエットが言った。

それから, 彼女はまた病気になった。

肺炎だった。命を危険にさらすものではなかったが, 回復するのに長い時間がかかった。レベッカは車で出かけていって, ハリエットにチキンスープとヴァニラカスタードを作り, ハリエットのベッドの足もとで横になった。

そのようにして, こんなことが, 何年も何年も続いた。ハリエットが病気になって回復し, レベッカが登場して引っ込む。何度も遮られながら, その合間に自分の人生を生きていく。

レベッカは疲れている。ハリエットは10年以上, 病気に罹ったり治ったりの繰返しである。レベッカは, ハリエットがいま暮らしているコネチカットの介護施設まで, ボストンから4時間かけて車でやってきたところだ。パートの店員に自分の代役の特別給を渡し, 経営している小さな書店を2日休んできている。ハリエットの好きなものを買い物袋にいっぱい詰めて持ってきた。部屋に入っていくと, ハリエットはテレビの方から視線をわずかにこちらに向けて挨拶をする。レベッカは椅子を引っ張ってきて, 母親と面と向かって腰かける。ハリエットは車椅子に座っているが, それはまたもや麻痺が起きたからで, 前にも経験済みだった。何かしら珍しい背中の病気にかかっているのだが, 今回は, 医者が言うには, ずっと消えることはない。

もっと頻繁に母親に会いに来なかったことで, レベッカは罪の意識を感じている。ハリエットは, 自分に必要なものをいつも話題にしてばかりいる。ラベンダーの入浴剤とか, 靴下とか, 車椅子で屋外に連れて行ってもらう時に脚にかける毛布とか。レベッカは, 多くの要望にときには感動し, だがしかしときには不愉快になりながら,

— 136 —

2015 年　　解答・解説

送れるものは郵送で送っている。

　前回レベッカが訪問したときは，ハリエットが介護施設へ移った日のことだったが，食事のトレーを持ってくる前に，看護師がハリエットに大きなビニールのナプキンをかけた。ハリエットはなされるままにしていたが，一種の，愕然としたような悲しそうな表情でレベッカを見た。その日には，いろいろ屈辱的なことがあったが，その中でも，このことに彼女は打ちのめされてしまった。「それ，彼女には必要ないです」とレベッカは看護師に言った。

　「どなたにもこうするのです」

　「そうかもしれませんが，母には必要ないです」

　そのようなわけで，ハリエットのナプキンをめぐる看護師とのやりとりは，レベッカがハリエットのためにそこにいて勝つべきささやかな戦いだった。レベッカがいなかったとしても，ハリエットは自分で見事に勝つことができたであろう。2 人とも，このことはわかっていた。それでも，この 2 人の間では，愛情はつねに示されねばならないものであり続けてきた。愛情はそこにある。そして証明される。何度も何度も。2 人の最悪の喧嘩のうちのいくつかは，なんとも紛らわしいことに，愛情を証明し，なおかつ反証するように思われる。もし 2 人の人間が互いに愛し合っていないのなら，そのように再三にわたって喧嘩することができないのは確かだ。

　15 年近く前，ハリエットは死にかけているように思われた。大腸癌のステージ 4 だったのだ。レベッカは母親が死にかけていると信じて，生まれて初めてのことだが，母親に親近感を抱き始めていた。ときおり夜になるとベッドに横になって泣いたが，1 人だけだったり，ハーバードで建築史を教えているピーター・ビゲロウと一緒だったりした。母親のことがわかりかけてきているのと同時に母親を失いつつあることがどれほどつらいことであるかについて彼女が語っている間，彼は彼女を抱きしめて耳を傾けた。

　信じられないことに，ハリエットは死ななかった。手術は成功し，さらに何度も手術を受け続けた。レベッカは車で出かけて母親と一緒に時間を過ごすということを続けた。しかし，ずっと続けることはできなかった。注意力，共感，友愛，母親の近くにいるだけの無目的な楽しさ，テレビのニュースを見ることなどなど。彼女は燃え尽きていた。

　ハリエットは，レベッカの訪問頻度が十分でないと感じ始めていた。たしかにそうで，前と比べると，やってくる回数が減っていた。それにしても，なんてことだろう。あの「十分」という言葉。傷つき不満を口にする，そんな 2 人の間に横たわっているのを 2 人とも見てとることができるので，母と娘の間に語られる必要さえな

— 137 —

<u>2015年　　解答・解説</u>

い，あのつかみどころがなく罪の響きのある言葉だ。大きくて，どぎつい色の傷口
のような言葉。

　結婚することについてどう思うかとピーターがレベッカに尋ねた。そういうのが彼
の流儀だった。申し出るというのではなくて，話し合う話題を導入するということだ。
彼女はよくわからないと言った。実は，彼がそのことを口にしたとき，彼女は胃の中
に冷たくて心地悪い気分がした。この，可愛げのある，親切で，思慮深い男を相手に，
彼女に一体どんな不都合があるというのだろうか。彼が一切のことにとても落ちつい
ているように見えること，彼女に首ったけでないこと，彼女が自分のものだというよ
うな否応なしの求めで彼女に迫って来ないことに彼女は神経をとがらせていて，そし
てまた，いらいらしていた。他方で，彼女もまた彼に迫っていなかった。

　そうこうするうちに，彼の本が完成して出版された。ある夜，彼は1冊持ってきて
くれ，彼女はシャンパンを1瓶用意していた。「ピーター，おめでとう。私もうれしいわ」
と言って彼にキスをした。彼女がページをめくると，自分の名前が飛び出すように向
かってきた。「…そしてレベッカ・ハントに。彼女は多くの楽しい時間を与えてくれた」。

　表現が控えめすぎるんじゃない？　互いを理解している2人の人間の間に存在しう
るような控えめさなの？　自分は何を望んでいるのだろう？　「レベッカのために。
彼女を私は心のすべてで愛しており，彼女のために死ぬとしてもかまわない」といっ
た献辞だろうか？

　こんなところに，彼女が自分の中に，ふいに見出して嫌悪したものがあったが，そ
れは彼女がハリエットから遺伝で受け継いだかもしれないものだった。それは，愛情
とは，熱烈に，声高に，はっきりと宣告され証明されなくてはならないものだという，
素朴な信念だった。

【考え方】

　(A)　正解は「そのようなわけで，**ハリエットのナプキンをめぐる看護師とのやりと
り**は，レベッカがハリエットのためにそこにいて勝つべきささやかな戦いだった。レ
ベッカがいなかったとしても，**ハリエットは自分で見事に勝つことができたであろ
う**」。

　1．**So that was one small battle ...**「そのようなわけで，ハリエットのナプキ
ンをめぐる看護師とのやりとりは…ささやかな戦いだった」　So は，これまでの文章
の流れを受けている。that は，設問にあるとおり指示代名詞で，看護師とレベッカ
のやりとりをさしていることは，後続する battle という単語からもわかる。

　2．**that Rebecca was there to win for Harriet.**「レベッカがハリエットのた
めにそこにいて勝つべき〈ささやかな戦い〉」　that は関係代名詞で，win の目的語。

— 138 —

be there to －で「－するためにそこにいる；そこにいて－する」という意味の定型
表現。

　　3．**Without Rebecca**「レベッカがいなかったとしても」　この箇所が仮定を表し
ていることは，後に仮定法の形 (could have won) が続くことからもわかる。

　　4．**Harriet could have won it**「ハリエットは…勝つことができたであろう」　仮
定法過去完了の典型的な形。

　　5．**just fine for herself.**「自分で見事に」　just は強意の副詞。fine は副詞で「見
事に」。

　⒝　正解は「もし２人の人間が互いに愛し合っていないのなら，そのように再三に
わたって喧嘩することができないのは確かだ」。

　　not が単独で否定文の代用をすることがある。（例）"I think the war will soon
end." "I'm afraid *not*. (= I'm afraid that the war will not soon end.)"「戦争は，も
うじき終わるだろうね」「いや，そうならないんじゃないか」

　　本文では not が直前の two people who didn't love each other couldn't fight
like that を指しているが，この文は，if two people didn't love each other, they
couldn't fight like that とほぼ同義。

　　certainly「たしかに…」「…なのはたしかだ」。repeatedly「何度も」。

　⒞

　⒄　正解は，**a)**。ハリエットが高額の小切手を送ってきたことに対するレベッカの
発言に使われている表現。afford「…の余裕がある」を使って「こんな余裕はありえ
ない」とすればよい。

　⒅　正解は，**e)** だが，本文に補充するとすれば，３人称単数現在の s をつけて，
owns とする必要がある。空所に入るのは the small bookstore を目的語とする動詞
と考える。本文冒頭にレベッカが書店を開業しようとしている旨の記述があることか
ら，owns を入れることになる。

　⒆　正解は，**i)** だが，本文に補充するとすれば，過去分詞の touched に変える必
要がある。空所を含む箇所が対句になっていることを考えれば，後方の annoyed と
対比的な表現を入れればよいとわかる。annoyed「不愉快にされて」と対比的になり
うる表現を選択肢から作り出すとすると，touched「感動させられて」とすればよい。

　⒇　正解は，**d)** だが，本文に補充するとすれば，現在分詞の finding に変える必
要がある。この箇所も⒆と同様に対比的に考えればよい。「⑶すると同時に losing
している」ということから finding「見出しつつ」とすればよい。

　㉛　正解は，**d) The word "enough"**。本文の該当箇所以前では，ハリエットが

－ 139 －

<u>2015 年　　解答・解説</u>

病気になるたびに，レベッカが世話をするために訪れるといったことが 10 年以上
も続き（空所㉗と㉘の間），それでいながら，レベッカは，もっと頻繁に (more
often) 会いに来るべきだった（＝十分でない）と罪の意識を感じているものの（空
所㉘と㉙の間），愛情を繰り返し確認する必要が逆に喧嘩を繰り返す原因となって（下
線部(A)から(B)にかけて）きたのだった。それを受けて，下線部を含む段落では，レベッ
カの訪問頻度が「十分で」(enough) あるかどうかを中心として語られているのだか
ら，下線部は enough という単語のことを指していると考えるのが最も自然である。
愛憎の混じり合った母娘の関係が，訪問回数が「十分」であったかどうかという形で
現れ，それが「傷口 (wound)」という比喩で表現されているのである。

　㉜　正解は，**b) She is more like Harriet than she thought.**　設問にあるとお
りに，本文の最後を参照すればよい。そこに「彼女が自分の中に見出して嫌悪したも
のがあったが，それは彼女がハリエットから遺伝で受け継いだかもしれないものだっ
た」とあることから考えれば，「彼女は自分が思っていた以上にハリエットに似ている」
という意味の b) が正解だとわかる。

　㉝　正解は，**c)「レベッカは，ピーターの本が出版されたことがとてもうれしかっ
たので，自分の名前を出してくれたことに感謝しつつ，彼にキスした」**　本文の末尾
から 2 つめの段落 (It was understatement ...) では，ピーターが控えめすぎるという
レベッカの思いが書かれていて，このことと c) は合致しない。

　ちなみに，他の選択肢に関しては，以下のとおり。

　a)「ハリエットはレベッカが書店を経営するのを望まなかったが，それは利益にな
らないだろうと思っていたからだ」は本文第 1 段落のハリエットの発言と一致する。

　b)「看護師が母親をまるで赤ちゃんのように扱ったのを知って，レベッカは怒って
いた」は，下線部 A の直前の箇所に書かれている内容と一致する。

　d)「レベッカと母親との関係は，後者がおよそ 15 年前に重病で入院した時に改善
した」は，空所㉚を含む段落に「母親に親近感を抱き始めていた」とあることと一
致する。

　e)「ピーターはレベッカが喜んで結婚すべきすてきな男性ではあるけれど，彼女は
彼が自分への愛を十分強く宣言しないときにはいらついた気分になった」は，正解の
c) の関連箇所の記述と一致する。

— 140 —

2015年　解答・解説

解　答

(A)　そのようなわけで，ハリエットのナプキンをめぐる看護師とのやりとりは，レベッカがハリエットのためにそこにいて勝つべきささやかな戦いだった。レベッカがいなかったとしても，ハリエットは自分で見事に勝つことができたであろう。

(B)　もし2人の人間が互いに愛し合っていないのなら，そのように再三にわたって喧嘩することができないのは確かだ。

(C)　(27)－a)　　(28)－e)　　(29)－i)　　(30)－d)　　(31)－d)　　(32)－b)　　(33)－c)

解答・解説

1 (A) **全訳** 私はエディンバラで，素敵な古い集合住宅に住んでいる。部屋が5，6階分あって，どの部屋も建物内部の砂岩でできた階段で行き来することができる。この建物は少なくとも100年前からあり，最近この砂岩の階段は，一段一段が少しすり減っているように見える。

この摩耗は100年分の人間が自分の部屋から上り下りした結果できたものだ。出勤したり帰宅したり，お店に行ったり，ディナーに出かけたりして，1日に何度も住人の足が一段一段を踏みしめてきたのだ。

地質学者なら誰でも知っているが，小さな力でも，かなり長期に渡って繰り返されると，実に大きな影響力になりうる。100年分の歩みはかなりのものだ。ここの住人35人が，それぞれ平均1日4回上り下りしたとすると，階段ができてから少なくとも1千万回は各段が踏まれたことになる。

私は，この階段を自分の部屋まで上る時に，人間はある種地質学的な力なのだということを日々思い起こしている。仮に1千万人が全員一人ずつこの階段を上らされると，その足で砂岩が1センチ摩耗するのに8ヵ月もかからないだろう。

では，1千万人の人間というのは現在世界にいる70億人の中では，ほんの一部にすぎないということを考えてみよう。何らかの方法で，この全人口の足を一度に使うことができたとすると，瞬く間に数メートル分の岩を摩耗させることができる。それを何度か繰り返すと，かなり大きな穴があく。数時間続けると，新しい谷を作ることもできるだろう。

こういう話は，かなり非現実的な思考実験のように思えるかもしれないが，これは実に文字通りに，カーボンフットプリントという概念（人間の活動が環境に与える影響をはかる基準）を浮き彫りにしている。人間のカーボンフットプリントに関して言えば，この惑星全体が階段なのである。消費しているエネルギーや出しているゴミなど，私たち一人一人の活動で原因となるものは，取るに足らないものだと思えるかもしれない。この惑星に影響を与えるものなどとは到底思えないかもしれない。しかし70億掛けると，誰であれ一人の人間が環境に及ぼす小さな影響も実に重大な一歩となる。地球が，私のアパートの古い階段同様，すり減っているのも不思議はない。

考え方

6つの段落から成る388語の文章。冒頭で，アパートの階段の話がはじまり，「いっ

— 144 —

2014 年　　解答・解説

たい何が言いたいのか？」と思わせる。そして最終段落に入ると「なるほど，それが
言いたかったのか！」と感じさせる。身近な事から導入して最後で一般化する，とい
う「仕組み」は 2014 年 1 (A)の "a penny" を象徴的に使った文章と大変よく似ている。
個々の現象描写や象徴的な表現などに振り回されず「言わんとしていること」を確実
に捉えることができたかどうかが，ポイントであろう。東大の採点基準の詳細は不明
だが，この文章なら，最終段落の内容を中心に据えてまとめておけば，全体のトーン
をすくい上げたことになり，評価の高い答案になると思われる。

　今回は設問の指示書きが「要約せよ」となっていたので，もしかすると，第5段落
までをやや具体的に含めつつ解答全体を「…と同様に〜である」というまとめ方をし
てもよいのかもしれないが，文章全体のトーンを考えて，より一般化してまとめる方
を取ってみた。

◇キーワードは the environmental impact of human actions

　最終段落第1文にある "the environmental impact of human actions"（人間の活
動が環境に与える影響）がテーマである。解答がこれに即した文章になっていること
がまず第1歩。

◇最終段落第3文，第4文で骨格を作る。

　第1，第2段落で，アパートの階段が毎日多数の人が上り下りしてすり減って
いると述べられているが，これが対応するのが最終段落第3文 (Our individual
contribution ...) だと考えてよい。この部分は「人間一人一人の活動は，取るに足ら
ないもので，地球に影響を与えるとは思えない」という内容が出ていればよい。字数
に余裕があるなら「エネルギーを消費／廃棄物を出す」という点を加えてもよいだろ
う。また，この文で may seem ... が使われているが，これは後の But と関連して「…
と思えるかもしれないが，しかし〜である」という典型的な「譲歩→逆接」の関係を
作っている。この But の後が「言いたいことの中心」である。

　第4文は，人間の数を増やしていってその影響を考えていった第3〜5段落の内容
を受けて書かれていると考えてよい。ここは「人類全体の規模になると，個々の人間
の活動が実に大きなものとなる」という内容が表現できていればよい（70億という
具体的な数字を出しても特に問題はないはず）。

　以上を暫定的にまとめると「一人の人間の活動が地球に及ぼす影響は，ほとんどな
いと思えるかもしれない。しかし全人類の規模になると，その影響は甚大なものにな
る。」（64字）となる。この大筋は答案の骨格として入れるべきであろう。

◇追加し，ふくらませる。

　第1〜5段落で，筆者があれこれ考えながら書いた部分に a century / four times

－ 145 －

<u>2014 年　　解答・解説</u>

a day / less than eight months / in a few moments / repetitions / for a few hours など「時間の流れと反復」に関する表現が散りばめられている。これを象徴するのが第3段落第1文の "repeated over a large enough stretch of time" である。これを「一定時間（大変長期にわたって）繰り返されると」とまとめて加える。それによって，第5段落までの内容をより正確に捉えることになる。

　最終段落最終文で，"not surprising" という書き手の評価を表す言葉が使われているので，これを加えてまとめたのが解答例である。字数に余裕があれば「ゆえに；だから；そう考えると」という表現でつなぐのもよいだろう。

　ここで使われている "wear down" という表現は「摩耗させる；すり減らす」という意味で，「地球が劣化している」ことを表す比喩である。ただし "is worn down" となっているので「現在すでに地球がすり減っている」というのが文字通りの意味であるから，「これからそうなる可能性がある」と読める言葉を出すと誤読になってしまうので要注意。

解 答 例

[解答例1]　一人の人間が地球環境に及ぼす影響は微々たるものに思えるかもしれないが，それが全人類によって長期に渡り繰り返されると甚大なものになる。人間の活動によって地球が劣化しているのも当然だ。(90字)

[解答例2]　個々の人間の活動はそれ自体取るに足らないものだと思えるかもしれないが，人類全体が同じ事を一定期間くり返すと多大な影響力を与えるものとなる。そう考えると地球が人類によって劣化しているのも不思議はない。(99字)

1 (B) 【全訳】 仕事の真の複雑さを判断する基準は複数あるが，その中で最もわかりやすいのは，どれほど容易に機械にやらせることができるかという基準である。自動化革命の初期の頃には，たいていの人が技術によって仕事が**ボトムアップで消滅する**だろうと考えていた。工場はこの削減が最初に生じる場所となるだろうと思われたのである。流れ作業で同じ数本のボルトを締めている作業員は，同じことをより速く，より効率よく，そして文句も言わずにかたづける機械に一掃されるだろう。中間管理職は，その他の労働力を管理する能力を持つロボットは存在しないので，それよりはましだろう。ただし，肉体労働をする人が減ると少なくとも部分的には管理職も減ることになるだろう。仕事が機械の影響をまったく受けないのは組織のトップのみ

－ 146 －

2014年　　解答・解説

になるだろう。

　それは，ある程度，その通りになった。ロボットがボルト締めの作業をする大勢の人間に取って代わったが，なくなったのはそこまでにすぎなかった。人間なら車のドアが枠にきっちりカチャッと閉まらないのを感じとったり，完成半ばの製品にある小さな欠陥に気づいたりしながらできる仕事に，複数の感覚を持ち込むことのできる機械など存在しない。ロボットは，純粋に機械的反復作業ができるかもしれないが，人間らしい複合的な技能や単独で考える能力を必要とする仕事は影響を受けなかった。

　一方，肉体労働者の一段上のレベル，すなわち中間管理職の仕事は，**従業員が必要とする直接指導が減って消滅し**始めた。しかし，階段の最上位，すなわち管理職や重役は，市場を細かく予測し，変動する需要と動向に巧みに対応することを求められる仕事をしており，大部分，その地位を失うことはなかった。

　コンピュータ革命は情報処理を自動化することで，さらに大きな影響を労働人口にもたらした。これが原因となって工場で始まった中間職の失業が，**ローンの申し込みを評価するような事務作業**にも広がっていった。このような展開は多数の勤勉な会社員を仰天させたが，実際それは予測可能な成り行きであった。

　非常に広範囲にわたる仕事や専門職は，その複雑さがU字曲線に沿ったものとなる。左端頂点には最もブルーカラーらしい仕事が来る。多くの場合まったく尊敬されず，たいていの場合最も薄給の仕事である。右端頂点には最もホワイトカラーらしい仕事が来る。大変尊敬されると同時に給料も高い。しかし，大部分の人は，その中間，U字の底辺のところ，仕事が一番単純なところで働いている。

　複雑さのU字曲線が実際はどう当てはまるかを具体的に示すには，航空会社のチケット発券担当者を考えてみるのが一番わかりやすい。かつては自動発券機に取って代わられるだろうと考えられていた地位の低い労働者である。今度空港に行ったら，以前とまったく変わらぬ数の係員を目にすることだろう。自動発券機はスーツケース1つの個人旅行者には何の問題もないかもしれないが，搭乗に手助けを必要とする障害者，一人で飛行機に乗る子供の面倒を見てもらう手配をしようとしている心配そうな親にとっては，まったく機能しない。特にちょっとした独創性を必要とする場合や，その人らしさを必要とする情緒的な面を含んでいる場合に言えることだが，人間の手助けが唯一の問題解決策であることが多いのである。

　U字のもう一方の端に来る仕事は，**それよりさらに知的かつ直観的技能に頼るところが大きい**。そのような職種にいるのが，さまざまな文書を読んで法的主張を組み立てる弁護士，試験結果をそろえて新たな治療法につながる直観的な飛躍を成し遂げる生化学者，言葉よりも雄弁な表情や声色や身振りに反応する心理学者たちである。

— 147 —

2014 年　　解答・解説

　少しばかり単純な状況になるのは，複雑さのＵ字曲線で下の方の部分だけなのである。その部分の仕事は**情報収集および情報伝達を含む**ことが大変多い。世界の産業化が進んだ地域において，コンピュータが以前に増してこの種の仕事をこなせるようになると，労働力の空洞化が生じ，事務系職員や簿記係が多数失業することとなった。

選択肢全訳

ア　ボトムアップで消滅する

イ　労働者に大きな個人的満足感を与える

ウ　情報を収集し伝達することを含む

エ　将来の繁栄に確固たる基盤を与える

オ　従業員が必要とする直接指導が減り，消滅する

カ　ローンの申し込みを評価するような事務系の作業に広がる

キ　経験から，価値のあるどんなものが取れるかを決定する

ク　知的かつ直観的な技能に頼るところが，さらに大きい

考え方

　今回は選択肢がすべて動詞の原形あるいは現在形から始まるので，選択肢オの as 節にある過去形以外は，まったく文法的な手がかりはない。全体の論旨をつかみ，各段落が「何に関して書いてあるか」をつかんだ上で，内容上ふさわしいものを考える。

(1)　正解は**ア**。

　直後の文で "this reduction" という表現があるので「仕事が削減される；なくなる」という内容になるはず。その内容を表しているのはアかオになるが，この後で「工場労働者の場合→中間管理職の場合→組織のトップの場合」と，下部から上層部へと話が進んでいくので "from the bottom up"（ボトムアップで）という表現が入っているアが正解となる。

　なお，この段落の第 3 文以降は，もちろん文法的には独立しているのだが，"it seemed" という挿入，would という助動詞によって，すべて「機械化が始まった頃の人々の考え」を表していることに注意。

(2)　正解は**オ**。

　中間管理職がどうなったかを考える。これは "started to" という過去形によって，過去の事実を描写していることがわかる。However で始まる次の文は，さらに上の管理職レベルの話になっていて "did keep their positions" とある。この内容と逆になるはずだから，オが正解。as 節内部の動詞が過去形になっている点も注意。

(3)　正解は**カ**。

　この文の主語 This は直前の文の内容を受けている。「コンピュータ革命が情報処

― 148 ―

2014 年　　解答・解説

理の自動化によって労働力に多大なる影響を与えた」ことの結果，「工場で始まった中間層の仕事の削減」がどうなるかを考えると，カが最も適切。

(4)　正解は**ク**。

　"the other end" は，前段落の内容から「右端」すなわちホワイトカラーの仕事だということになる。第 2 文以降で紹介されている「弁護士；生化学者；心理学者」の仕事がどのようなものかを考えると，クが最も適切。

(5)　正解は**ウ**。

　この段落の第 1 文にある "the lower parts of the complexity U-curve" とは，第 5 段落の内容から考えると，中間層・中間管理職的な仕事ということになる。この階層の仕事が「最も単純」であり，直後の文にあるように「コンピュータが得意とする作業」となるのでウが正解。

解答

(1)−ア	(2)−オ	(3)−カ	(4)−ク	(5)−ウ

2 (A) 考え方

<語数について>

　「50 ～ 70 語程度」とあるから，ゆるく解釈して 40 ～ 80 語くらい書けばよいと思う。また，答案の最後に「○○ words」と書き添えよう。

<問題の指示>

① 「左側の人物を **X**，右側の人物を **Y**」

　X と Y の取り違えに注意。単純なミスだが減点されるだろう。

② 「**X** と **Y** のどちらから始めてもよい」

　要するに「Y : --------- X : ---------」でも構わないということ。

③ 「それぞれ何度発言してもよい」

　問題用紙の書き方の例には「X : --------- Y : --------- X : --------- Y : --------- 」と書かれているが，それぞれ 2 回ずつの発言に留めなければならないという意味ではない。また，1 つの発言に一行使った方が見栄えがよい（解答欄が 10 行もあるのはそのためだろう）。

<内容のポイント>

① 答案に盛り込むべき必須情報を写真から読み取る

　写真を元にして会話文を作るわけだが，写真の中にあるどの情報を答案に盛り込むか，その取捨選択能力が問われる。最低限盛り込まれていなければならない情報は次

— 149 —

の４つ。

1）**Ｘは男性**

2）**Ｙは女性**

3）**２人は飲み物の自動販売機の前にいる**

4）**犬**

むろんこれら以外のことに言及しても構わないが，この４点を踏まえて会話文が作られていない場合は減点対象となるだろう。

② **見たままを素直に英語にする**

会話文全部を書くという設定だから，１つのきちんとしたストーリーを作らなければならないのではと思う受験生もいるだろう。むろんそれなりのまとまりは必要だろう（尻切れトンボの会話や，何を話し合っているのか要領を得ない会話はよくない）。しかし，そもそも「50 〜 70 語程度」という短い語数なのだから，起伏に富んだ内容にすることは無理で，またその必要もない。妙に凝った内容にしたために英語がついていけていないものが最低の答案と言えよう。

ちなみに，問題文には「自由に想像し」とあるが，写真の画像と明らかに異なることを書けば，減点は当然免れない。注意してほしいことは，犬が写り込んでいること。無視すれば当然減点対象だが，かといってこの犬にしゃべらせてはいけない（問題文の指示を無視して勝手に Ｚ：　　　　などとしないこと）。また，犬を中心とした過度の創作もやめたほうがよい（むろん理解可能な内容を正しい英語で書いてあるのなら問題はないが）。

＜答案作成＞

飲み物の自動販売機の前にいるのだから，どの製品を買うかをテーマにするのが常識的だろう。偶然自動販売機の前にいるだけ，という設定で，飲み物とは全然無関係な会話（たとえば単なる世間話に終始しているような会話）を展開すると，おそらく減点は免れないと思う。少しでもよいから飲み物と絡めた内容にすること。

ここで，答案の展開方法を具体例に沿って見てみることにする。

［解答例１］

［テーマ］＝何を買うか迷っている

［犬の処理］＝犬用の飲み物であるという設定

どのような答案を作るにせよ，まず最初に犬をどのように絡ませるかを考えてから会話全体の流れを決めたほうがよい。ここでは犬を中心にした「犬が冷たい飲料を欲しがっているのに，自販機には温かいものしかない」という内容に，「何を買えばいいか迷っている男性に女性が答える」くだりと，「冬場はどうしても温かい飲料が自

— 150 —

販機のメインになりやすい」という内容を付け加えて，全体を完成させた（男性→女性の順）。

[解答例2]

[テーマ] ＝欲しい飲み物が売り切れになっている

[犬の処理] ＝勝手について来たよその犬という設定

　この解答例では，犬を会話の流れの外に置き，最後に少々付け加える程度にとどめた（「その犬あなたの犬？」「ううん，勝手について来ただけ。僕のこと気に入ってるみたい」）。メインの流れは，女性が少々変わった飲料（桃ジュース）を求めていて，それがこの自販機でしか売っていないのだが，売り切れていてどうしよう，という話で展開した（女性→男性の順）。

[解答例3]

[テーマ] ＝優柔不断な男性

[犬の処理] ＝あきれた女性が最後に触れる

　男性が何を買うか悩んでいて，女性が助言をしてもまったく決められないので，あきれ果てた女性が最後に「そこの犬に聞いてみたら」と男性に言う，という，ややコントのような雰囲気で構成した。男性が悩んでいる部分を大きく膨らませることで語数を稼ぎ，犬への触れ方は最小限度である（女性→男性の順）。

解答例

[解答例1] 〈54 words〉

　X：I don't know what to choose.

　Y：You said you liked orange juice. Why don't you get that?

　X：It's not for me. It's for Maggie.

　Y：Maggie? Oh, you mean your dog.

　X：Yes. She likes cold tea, but this machine only sells hot tea.

　Y：In winter you sometimes have a lot of trouble finding cold drinks.

[解答例2] 〈59 words〉

　Y：Oh no!

　X：What's the matter?

　Y：I wanted a peach juice, but it's sold out!

　X：A peach juice? I didn't know you liked such strange stuff.

　Y：There are hardly any machines that sell peach juice. I only know this
　　　one. What should I do? Incidentally, is that your dog?

－ 151 －

X : No. For some reason, he's following me. Maybe he likes me.

［解答例 3］〈65 words〉

　Y : What do you want to get?

　X : Well, I wanted sugar free tea, but there isn't any here.

　Y : Then why don't you get a green tea? They don't contain sugar.

　X : I don't like green tea. I think I'll get either the grapefruit juice or the
　　　orange juice. Oh, the coke looks good too. I just can't decide.

　Y : Then why don't you ask the dog over there?

2 (B) 考え方

<語数について>

　「50 ～ 70 語」とあるからには，やはりこの指定より多くても少なくてもまずい。また，答案の最後に「○○ words」と書き添えよう。

<問題の指示>

「下の文（問題文の英語）をそのままの形で用いてはならない」

　要するに答案で "People only see what they are prepared to see." という英語をそのまま引用してはいけない，ということ。むろんアレンジは許されるであろう。

<内容のポイント>

　この問題は，"People only see what they are prepared to see." という英文が意味する内容を正しく理解していないと答案が書けないが，受験生諸君にとっては非常に難しかったのではないだろうか。まず，この英文が意味するところを説明しよう。

　be prepared to － は直訳すれば「－する準備が整っている」である。see は「見る」だが，ある物体の方へ意図的に目を向ける "look" と違い「視界に入っている状態」を意味する。したがって，全体を直訳すれば「人間は目に入る準備が整っているものしか目に入らない」だが，この「準備」は当然精神面のことで，肉体的なことではない。つまり，頭の中で「ああ，今これが目に映っているんだな」と考えているもの以外は一切目に映らない，ということ。これは要するに一種の「思い込み」で，人間は物事の表ばかりを見て裏を見ることができない，たとえ裏を見るにしても，「裏はこうなっているはず」と自分が決めつけるもの以外に考えが及ばない，と言いたいのである。

　たとえば，我々にいつも意地悪をする人間がいるとしよう。実はその人間は我々の為を思ってわざと意地悪な態度を取っていたのだが，我々はそんなことに一切思いが至らず，その人間のことをただ「意地悪な奴」としかとらえることができない。

— 152 —

2014 年　　解答・解説

　さらに一歩進めると，その人間の「善意」に気づくためにはきっかけが必要である。その「意地悪」な人間が陰で我々を応援してくれている姿を目撃してはじめて，その人間が実は「意地悪」ではなかったことに気づく。つまり，"People only see what they are prepared to see." という段階から抜け出るためには，さまざまなきっかけ（経験）が必要なのである。

　この "People only see what they are prepared to see." は 19 世紀のアメリカの思想家 Ralph Waldo Emerson の言葉で，「人は見たいものしか見ない」「人は見ようとするものしか見ない」など，いろいろに和訳されている。ただ，この英文が意図していることを忠実に解釈すれば，「人は目に見えるものしか見ない」と訳すのが適切ではなかろうか。

<構成上のポイント>

① **最初に結論を書く**

　答案の冒頭に，問題文で求められている答え，つまり諸君が与えられた英文について「どう考えるか」を具体的に述べる。答案全体を読まないと言いたいことがわからない，という展開はよくない。

　ただ，先述したように，この英文は人間の本質を突く言葉で，どんな人間にも英文が表すような部分は必ずある。したがって，「賛成」「反対」（agree / disagree）する性質のものではない。

② **その後の展開**

　通常の論説型の自由英作文はテーマが何らかの意見や提案であることが多いから，まず「賛成」か「反対」かを述べ，その理由を後に続ければよいのだが，この問題はそもそも意見でも提案でもないので，まったく異なるアプローチにしなければならない。"People only see what they are prepared to see." という英文の内容が理解できていることを大学側にアピールするためには，このような人間の本質を示す具体例を述べることが最も適当だろう。しかし，具体例だけで指定の語数を埋めるのはなかなか大変，ということなら，この英文の意味するところをまず説明し，それから具体例を展開するのも一つの策である。さらに，この本質的傾向を打破するにはどのような経験が必要かを書いてもよい。

③ **最後に①の結論を繰り返さない**

　本問は論の展開がかなり難しいので，語数稼ぎのために①の結論を繰り返す受験生も多いことだろう。しかし，50 語という短い英文の中で同じ内容を繰り返すのは，書くことが思い浮かばなかったと告白しているようなもの。意味のない行為で答案を埋め尽くすことは採点者に決してよい印象を与えないため，極力避けるべきである。

— 153 —

2014 年　　解答・解説

＜答案作成＞

　以上の点を踏まえて，答案の展開方法を具体例に沿って見てみよう。

［解答例1］

　　［どう考えるか］＝ある重要な真実を語っていると思う

　　［具体例］＝親の行為を子供がどう受け止めるか→子供自身が親となったとき，か
　　　　　　　つて自分の親がとった行為の真の意味を悟る

　親が欲しいものを買ってくれないと，子供はしばしば親のことを鬼のようなひどい
人間に感じることがある。「親の心子知らず」という状況こそがまさに "People only
see what they are prepared to see." を示す事例である。この解答例ではさらに「親
の心」に気がつくきっかけとなる経験を説明することで，人間の視野がどのように広
がっていくかに触れた。

［解答例2］

　　［どう考えるか］＝国際紛争の主原因になっている

　　［具体例］＝領土問題が発生するとき，関係国は自らの歴史観でしか物を見ない→
　　　　　　　解決のためには客観視できるようになる必要がある

　最初に「我々には自らの価値観で物を見る傾向がある」と英文の説明を軽く付けた
あとで，本題の「国際紛争」を提起し，相手の価値観を理解できないことからいかに
紛争が継続していくか，それを解決するには何をすればよいか，という順に展開した。

［解答例3］

　　［どう考えるか］＝当てはまらない例もある→「天才」

　　［具体例］＝「天才」は自分が見えない部分も見ようとする

　＜構成上のポイント＞のところで，「本問は賛成・反対する性質のものではない」
と述べたが，「人による」（つまり例外に触れる）というアプローチは可能。この［解
答例］では，「天才」をテーマにアインシュタインを具体例として，「目に見えない部
分を見ようとする」人間もいるという趣旨で展開した。

解 答 例

［解答例1］

　　I think this saying expresses an important truth. For example, children
often get mad when their parents don't buy the expensive toys they want.
They may even think their parents are wicked. But when they grow
up and have their own children, they realize it isn't good for children to
have excessively expensive things. They realize their parents were right.
Their experience has prepared them to see this. (68 words)

— 154 —

2014 年　　解答・解説

[解答例2]

　　We certainly have a strong tendency to see things according to our own belief system, and this is the main cause of international conflicts. For example, when two countries both insist that a certain piece of land belongs to them, each sees things from their own historical perspective and never compromises. In such cases, we must realize our own view may be wrong and seek for objectivity. (67 words)

[解答例3]

　　This quotation applies to almost everyone, except a few very rare exceptions: geniuses. Geniuses do not blindly accept what is widely believed as true at the time and can see things as they really are. For example, Einstein probably learned a lot from theories that existed at the time, but he was able to make his great discoveries only because he could truly see things objectively. (66 words)

---

4 (A) **[全訳]** 過去から受け継がれてきたあらゆる制度の中で，現代において家族制度ほど損なわれ，不安定になっているものはない。親の子に対する愛情，そして子の親に対する愛情は，幸福を生み出す最大の源になりうるが，実際今日では親子関係は双方にとって十中八九不幸を生み出す源となっている。このように，家族が原則として与えることのできる基本的な満足を与えていない状況こそ，現代に蔓延する不満感の原因として最も根の深いものの1つである。

　私としては，個人的に言わせてもらうと，親であることの幸せを，今まで経験してきた他のいかなるものよりも大きいと感じている。さまざまな事情で男性または女性がこの幸福感を味わえていないときには心の奥深くにある欲求が満たされないままであり，このことが原因がまったくわからない不満や不安を生み出していると思う。

　親としての愛情をまずほとんど感じない，あるいはまったく感じることのない親，あるいは自分の子供に感じる愛情とほぼ同じくらい強烈な愛情を他人の子供に感じる可能性のある親も確かに存在する。それでも，親の愛というのは特別な感情で，普通の人間なら自分自身の子供に感じることはあっても他人に感じることはないものだ，という一般的な事実は残っている。

[考え方] (1) **該当する語は has・直後の語は ×。**"none is ... so damaged and unstable as the family has" の部分は同等比較で，none という否定語があるため

— 155 —

2014年　解答・解説

so ... as が使われている。したがって，"none is damaged and unstable" と "the family is damaged and unstable" の比較なのだから，"none is ... so damaged and unstable as the family (is)" が正しい。

(2)　**該当する語は that・直後の語は in**。but 以下の構文だが，in fact / at the present day / in nine cases out of ten はすべて副詞句なので取り除くと，"<u>the relations of parents and children</u> ⟨S⟩ <u>are</u> ⟨V⟩ <u>a source of unhappiness to both parties</u>" ⟨C⟩" という第2文型。are that とするなら，that 以下には完全な英文が来る必要がある。

(3)　**該当する語は for・直後の語は which**。全体の構造は "<u>This failure ...</u> ⟨S⟩ <u>is</u> ⟨V⟩ <u>one of the most deeply rooted causes</u> ⟨C⟩" という第2文型。したがって "for which in principle it is capable of yielding" は "the fundamental satisfaction" を先行詞とする関係代名詞節ということになるが，yield は第3文型の動詞で「O を産出する；もたらす」という意味。第1文型の用法もあるが，"yield to O" という表現はあっても "yield for O" は存在しない。したがって，for which の for を取り除けばよい。

(4)　**該当する語は for・直後の語は remains**。全体の構造は "I believe that ..., and that ～ " で，believe の目的語である2つの that 節が and によって並列されている。さらに最初の that 節の中は，"when ... this happiness" までが接続詞 when による副詞節，"a very deep ... unfulfilled" がそれに対する主文である。したがって，"a very deep need ⟨S⟩ remains ⟨V⟩ unfulfilled ⟨C⟩ " でないと英文にならない。名詞の need には確かに "a need for 名詞 "（名詞に対する必要性）という語法があるが，本問でこのように解釈すると英文の構造が破綻する。

(5)　**該当する語は of・直後の語は other**。最後の "any of other human being" は英語として誤っている。"any of" ならばその後には特定の複数名詞または不可算名詞が続くことになるが，other human being は複数形でも不可算でもない。of を削除して any other human being（他のどの人間）とすれば正しくなる。

解答

	該当する語	その直後の一語
(1)	has	×
(2)	that	in
(3)	for	which
(4)	for	remains
(5)	of	other

— 156 —

2014年　解答・解説

4 **(B)** 【全訳】　ある福祉国家が，社会全体の利益になるように役割を果たしている場合，その国家は資源をその社会の個々人に同じ基準で配分してもよいし，あるいは選択的に働いて，援助を必要としている人々，また援助を受ける資格のある人々にのみ資源を提供してもよい。全体的，ないしは選択的な配分のどちらの方針についても，効率性の観点からその正当性を説明することができる。仮に十分な福祉手当とサービスが，誰に対しても同じ基準で充てられるとすれば，そのときはすべての人に，生活に必要な基本的なものを確保するための最低限の援助が保証される。誰もが同じものを手にするわけだから，そうした援助を受けるのを恥じることはないし，誰もそれを求めることに引け目を感じる必要はない。自分たちが受けるそのような援助を必要としない人々は，このシステムが累進課税を原資にしている場合，自分が受け取ってきたものを返還することができるだろうし，また社会の他の人々が受ける援助に貢献することもできるだろう。一方，仮に手当とサービスが，それを必要としている，あるいはそれを受ける資格のある人々にのみ充てられるとすれば，これらの資源は最も効果的な使途に投入されることになる。すなわち，援助を最も必要としている人々に対して，いっそう惜しみない水準の援助が与えられる可能性があるということだ。しかも，援助を必要としない人々は，高額な税金を課されることによって不当に扱われたと感じさせられることはないだろう。

【考え方】

(1)　**1. A case can be made ... for ～**「～を擁護する［支持する］ことができる」make a case for ～で「～を支持する立場を取る」の意の表現。(例) It is easy to *make a case for* retaining these regulations.（これらの規則を残すことに賛成の立場を主張するのは簡単である）　問題文はこれを受動態にしたもの。

　2. on grounds of efficiency「効率（性）を根拠に」　be made を修飾する副詞句。grounds は「根拠；基礎」の意。(例) She divorced her husband *on grounds of* irreconcilable differences.（彼女は性格の不一致を理由に夫と離婚した）

　3. either approach「いずれの取り組み方〈も支持することができる〉」　設問文より either approach の内容を明らかにしなければならない。either が用いられている以上，前に２つの取り組み方が紹介されているはず，と考える。第１の取り組み方が distribute resources on the same basis to every member of that community（資源をその社会の全ての成員に同じように分配する）であり，第２の取り組み方が operate selectively, providing resources only to those who need or deserve help（選択的に働き，助けを必要としているかそれに値する人たちだけに資源を提供する）である。resources は後で benefits and services「給付金［補助金，手当］とサービス」

— 157 —

2014年　　解答・解説

と言い換えられていることから,「お金・富」とするのは意味を限定しすぎである。「資源」なら「お金」のみならずより幅広い内容を指すことができるので,問題なかろう。ただし「天然資源」と混同されるおそれがあるので,解答例では内容を考慮して「援助」と表現した。

(2)　1．**all are guaranteed the minimum level of help**「すべての人が最低限の援助を保証される」　S guarantee(V) all(O) the minimum level of help(O) を受動態にしたもの。all は「すべての人」の意。

　2．**to secure their basic needs**「自分たちが基本的に必要としているものを確保するために［ための］」　the minimum level of help を修飾する形容詞用法と解釈しても,are guaranteed を修飾する副詞用法の不定詞と解釈してもよい。

(3)　1．**those people … will not be made to feel unfairly treated**「…の人々は不公平に扱われていると感じさせられることはないだろう」　S will not make(V) those people(O) … feel(C) unfairly treated. を受動態にしたもの。いわゆる「使役動詞＋目的語＋原形」の構文だが,受身にしたときには,be made *to* feel … と補語が「to 不定詞」の形になることに注意。those は後続する関係詞節の先行詞が people であることを明確にするために用いられており,あえて「それらの」などと訳出する必要はない。(例) *Those students who* came late to school were scolded by the teacher. (学校に遅刻した生徒たちは先生に叱られた)

　2．**who do not require help**「助けを必要としない人々」　those people を修飾する関係詞節。

　3．**by high levels of taxation**「高い税金で［税率で］」　be made to feel … を修飾する副詞句。「富裕層に支援を与えない」ということになると,その分だけ財源が少なくて済むので,富裕層が必要以上に課税されることはなくなり「不公平感を抱かなくなる」のである。

解 答

> (1)　社会の全員に同じ基準で公的援助を与える方針と,支援を必要とするかそれを受けるに値する人にのみ援助を与える方針は,いずれも効率性を根拠にして擁護することができる。
>
> (2)　すべての人は,自らが基本的に必要とするものを確保するために最低水準の援助を保証されている。
>
> (3)　援助を必要としない人が,重い課税によって不公平に扱われていると感じさせられることもないだろう。

— 158 —

2014 年　　解答・解説

5 【全訳】　7月上旬の今朝, セーヌ川沿いをさっと一走りしに出かけた。楽しかった。出ている人がとても少なくて, それでいっそう走りやすかった。パリという街は, ぶらぶら歩きをする人に向いていて, 走る人には向いていない。

　女性たちは, 自転車で町をこぎ抜けるが, ヘルメットを着けず, 丈の長い白い服を着ていたりする。あるいは, ピンクのカットオフショートパンツと, それに合ったローラースケートで, 駆け抜けていったりする。男性たちは, オレンジのズボンと, 白いリンネルシャツを着ている。彼らは, *un petit peu*（ちょっと）おしゃべりをしてから, 街角の向こうへ姿を消す。次に目にするときには, ポルシェを運転してサンジェルマン大通りをゆっくりと走り, 生活をエンジョイしている。パリのこの小さな一角では, 誰もが「どうでもよかったんだよ」という言葉の自分なりの形を体現しているように思われる。

　カップルたちがカフェで並んで座り, 通りを眺めている。何組ものカップルが列をなして集まっていて, まるで『ヴォーグ』のファッション写真に写っているみたい, あるいはお洒落なマネキンの展示みたいだ。みんなタバコを吸っている。彼らには行く手で待ち受けているものがわかっている。順不同で言えば, 恐ろしい死とか, 乱痴気パーティとか。

　戻ってシャワーを浴びて着替えた。通りの向こうまで歩いて, パンとミルクを買った。妻がコーヒーを淹れた。朝食をとった。それから, 猛烈な疲れが襲ってきて, 昼まで寝た。目覚めると息子が着替えを終えていた。妻はグレートギャッビーのTシャツ, サングラス, イヤリングそしてジーンズを身に着けていた。彼女の髪は後ろにまとめ, ブローをきかせて大きくきれいなアフロに仕立ててあった。外に出て, 郊外へ向かう電車をめざした。息子は大荷物を携えていた。これで息子とは6週間のお別れであった。

　自分がどうかしてしまったと気づいたのは, 電車の中だった。ボストンにいた頃に, 私は一冊のワークブックと古い語学テープをいくつか使ってフランス語の勉強を始めた。それから私はフランス語学校で授業をとることにした。そして家庭教師を雇った。うちの近くのカフェで会ったものだった。ときおり, 息子が立ち寄った。息子は残って一緒にいることを好むことに私は気づいた。ある日, 自分にもフランス語を習わせてくれないかと言ってきた。なんか変な気分だったが, 賛成した。5月, フランスへ来る前に, 息子は2週間, 1日8時間のコースをとった。授業に間に合うように午前6時に起床して, 12時間後までは戻ることがなかった。夕食を食べると建設労働者のように眠った。しかし, 彼はそれが気に入っていた。それで, 息子と妻と私が夏を過ごしにパリへ来るとすぐに, 私は息子を泊まりがけのフランス語づけ合宿へ送って

— 159 —

いくところだった。*Français tous les jours*（四六時中フランス語）という名称のものである。

　正気の沙汰ではない。私は，自分が幼少期に家庭で受けてきたしつけ，常に課される終わりなき難題という感覚を，暴力を用いずに示そうとしているのだ。私たちの世代で，厳しく育った多くの人は，かりにそれが体罰で与えられていたとしても，学んできた教えを尊重している。そういった教えを，私たちの子どもが，そうした力づくの目に合わないようにして伝えていくのには，どのようにすればよいのだろう。彼らに争いをもたらすような世界への準備ができるように，虐待にさらすことなく彼らを強くするには，どのようにすればよいのだろう。私の唯一の答えは，子どもたちを日常とかけ離れた別の場所に置くことであり，そこでは，それ以前に子どもたちがどこかで誰かに「賢いね」と言われたことを誰も気にかけてくれないのである。私の唯一の答えは，私が大人になってから経験した学習スタイルを踏襲し，それを子ども向けに調整しようとすることだ。

　そうは言っても，私には，褐色のわがうるわしき息子のことが気がかりだ。

　3週間前にアメリカで，私は父と同席し，私自身の息子の行いが悪いのをどうやって取り締まらなくてはならないかを父に語っていた。父親になるにあたって私に心の準備がなかったことが一つだけあって，それは，悪役になるのがどれほど辛いことであるか，どれほど息子を放免したいと思っているか，しつけをしているときはいつも，彼の痛みをどれほど感じているかということだったと，私は父に語った。私がそれを感じたのは，私自身が息子の年齢だった時のことを，そして自分が12歳であることがどれほど嫌だったかを覚えていたからだった。父が同意してうなずくのを見て私は衝撃を受けた。父は厳しい父親だった。厳しくすることを楽しんでいるとも思わなかったが，私たちのしつけのために，それなりの無理をしていたなんて思いもよらなかった。そんな面が見えないようにしていたのだ。父の原則は「母を愛せ，父を怖がれ」だった。それで父は仮面をつけていた。実のところは，私は父も母も恐かった。

　昨日，この話を息子にした。興味がないこと（たとえばピアノ）をやってみなさいと強制するつもりは決してないと彼に伝えた。しかし，いったん興味関心があると明言したら，道はただ一つ，何としても最後までやらせきるしかないのだ。パリの人々とは対極だ。でも彼に伝えた。この世の苦痛は不可避であり，選べるのは，自分で何かやって苦しむか，人から何かされて苦しむかのいずれかしかない，と。*C'est tout*（それでおしまい）。

　私たちは手続きをした。息子は試験を受けた。私たちは部屋を見て，ルームメイトに会った。息子に愛しているよと言った。それからその場をあとにした。

2014 年　　解答・解説

　息子が言った。「僕がメールしたら，必ずメールを返してね。そっちが無事だとわかるように」

　こっちが無事だとわかるように，だってさ。

　その場を離れる際に，妻が泣き始めた。電車の中で，このこと全て，つまり，取るに足りなく非常識な私たちが，今まさにこんなところにいるということが，狂気の沙汰であることについて，私たちは語りあった。まず隣近所を後にする。それから住んでいる地域を後にする。それから高校を後にする。自分の町，大学，そして最後に国を後にする。一歩ごとに，また一つの世界を後にして，一歩ごとに，暖かい重力，大きな愛が，自分を故郷へと引き戻しているのを感じる。そして，立ち去ることにいたたまれなくなる。そして，自分に対してこんなことをするなんて馬鹿げていると感じる。そして，子どもに対して誰がこんなことをするものかとも思うのである。

考え方

（1）　正解は**オ**。下線部そのものの意味「誰もが『どうでもよかったんだよ』という言葉の自分なりの形を体現しているように思われる」が，やや難しいが，本文中の他の箇所の「ヘルメットなし」，「ローラースケート」，「生活をエンジョイ」といったあたりをヒントと考え，さらに注に出てくる Porsches が「高級」スポーツカーであることを考え合わせれば，オ「努力を必要としない娯楽と気楽な生き方に身をまかせている」が選べるだろう。ちなみに第9段落で，興味を持ったことは最後までやりきるという生き方を「パリ的でない」と言っているが，これをこの問いへのヒントにするのは試験場心理ではかなり厳しいだろう。

　他の選択肢の大意は以下のとおり。ア「目的なく，自己破壊的な」。イ「健康志向で勤勉な」。ウ「自己規律的で悪徳のない」。エ「現実逃避的で過去憧憬的な」。

（2）　正解は**ウ**。下線部の意味は「**順**不同で」，「特定の**順番**ではなく」であるから，ウ「単語はアルファベット**順**に並んでいる」が正解となる。他の選択肢の意味は次のとおり。ア「彼女の部屋はいつもきちんとしている（order の意味は「**秩序**」）。イ「警察は公的**秩序**を回復することができなかった」。エ「彼は学生たちに整列するようにという厳しい**命令**を与えた」。オ「この本を 50 冊，急いで**注文**するつもりです」。

（3）　正解は「**これで息子とは6週間のお別れであった**」。東大の第5問では，ちょっとした表現を知っているかどうかを問う小問が出題されることがしばしばあるが，この問題は，その典型と言ってよい。（例）*This was the last* I ever saw of him. （彼を見たのはこれが最後だった。＜ I saw the last of him.）

（4）　正解は**オ**。空所を含む文の直前の文で，筆者の息子がフランス語を習いたいと言い出し，直後の文で，実際に習い始めていることから，筆者が息子の意見に同意し

— 161 —

たということがわかる。それゆえ，空所にオの with を入れれば，went with「同意した」
という表現ができるので，これが正解となる。go with という熟語を知らなかったと
しても，with の意味からだけでも正解に到達できるだろう。

(5) 正解は**エ**。東大の第5問では，ちょっとわかりにくい箇所に設問を設定し，文
脈把握力を見ようと，和訳文を選択させる小問が出題されることがある。この問題は，
そのタイプと言えよう。

　下線部だけを見ていても正解にたどりつくのは難しい。come up hard などという
つながりは，通常の勉強をしていても見かけない表現だからだ。直訳すれば「困難な
状況で生育する」だが，この文脈で「困難な状況」というのは「親から厳しいしつけ
を受けながら」と考えるのが自然である。さらに，下線部の前後や文章全体のテーマ
が「親が子をどのようにしつけていくか」だということを考えあわせれば，エ「親か
ら厳しいしつけを受けた人びと」が答えだということになる。イやウは文意にまった
く合わない。アは「一所懸命」と下線部の hard が，辞書的，局所的に対応している
ものの「努力を重ねてきた」の箇所は，本文と関係がない。オは，「現在の地位を築いた」
の類の記述が本文とまったく無関係である。ちなみに come up the hard way「コツ
コツとたたきあげて出世する」という熟語も存在するが，今回の出題とは無関係。文
脈的にも慣用的にも母語話者の語感からしてもオとする根拠はない。

(6) 正解は (6a) **オ**，(6b) **イ**，(6c) **ア**。

　空所を含む文は筆者が自分の父親に向かって「父親であることの大変さ」を語って
いる箇所であることを念頭において解き進める。

　(6a) は「父親であることについて私が（　　）唯一のことは…だった」というこ
とから，オ wasn't prepared「心の準備がなかった」を選べばよい。構文としては，
I wasn't prepared for N（名詞）の N の部分が関係詞となって省略された形。ちな
みにエ was looking を入れても構文的には成立するが「私が探していたのは how
much ...」となって意味的に成立しない。

　(6b)，(6c) は同時に考えればよい。「（ 6c ）のときはいつも（ 6b ）だった」
ということから，(6b) にはイ felt his pain「彼の痛みを感じた」を入れ，(6c) には
ア disciplined him「彼をしつけるとき」を入れればよい。前後関係が理解できれば，
易しい問題。

(7) 正解は**ア**。一つだけ異質な選択肢となっているア「筆者は息子の無礼さに驚く」
が本文とまったく無関係である。他の選択肢の意味は以下のとおり。イ「筆者は息子
の配慮に感動する」，ウ「筆者は息子が親の役割を演じることに驚く」，エ「筆者は息
子が先手をとったことに驚く」，オ「筆者は息子の成熟がどれほど急速であるかを知っ

— 162 —

て感心する」。

(8)　正解は「**愛着のある世界を離れてなじみのない世界に身を置き，寂しい体験をするという試練を与えること**」。

　該当箇所が直接意味しているのは，同じ段落で書かれているような，なじみのある場所を離れることである。それは何のためであるかが書かれているのは，第6段落 (It is insane ...) の後半部分であり，子育てについて，筆者が手にしている「唯一の答え」の部分である。具体的には子どもを「日常とかけ離れた別の場所に置くことであり」，「誰も気にかけてくれない経験を」させるということである。

　以上をまとめて該当箇所に代入しても成立するような言い方に整理すれば正解が得られる。

(9)　正解は2番目－ウ，6番目－キ。

　まず，小説やエッセイでは「出来事の順序」と「語りの順序」が同じとは限らないということに留意する。この問題では，パリから郊外のフランス語会話合宿の場所へ向かう話を枠組みとして，その中に，第5段落の最初 (It was on the train ...) から第9段落 (I told my son ...) の最後までが，回想シーンとして割り込んだ形になっている。

　具体的には以下のとおりである。

④第1段落　ア　筆者がセーヌ川沿いを走った。（7月と書かれていることにも注意）

⑤第4段落 (I came home ...)　カ　筆者と妻と息子が郊外へ行く電車に乗った。

①第5段落 (It was on the train ...)　回想シーンに入る。Back in Boston という表現や過去完了形に注意する。5月とあることに注意。エ　息子が2週間のフランス語の講座をとった。

②第8段落 (Three weeks ago, back in America, ...)　ウ　筆者が座って父と語った。

③第9段落 (I told my son this story yesterday ...)　ここで「昨日」とあることから，回想シーンが終わりに近づいたことに注意。オ　筆者はこの世の苦痛は不可避と息子に伝えた。

⑥第10段落 (We signed in ...)　ここが出来事としては第4段落につながる。キ　筆者と妻は没入式言語合宿の息子のルームメイトと会った。

⑦第13段落 (When we left ...)　イ　筆者の妻が泣きだした。

以上の流れから，エ→ウ→オ→ア→カ→キ→イとなり，正解が得られる。

－ 163 －

<u>2014年　解答・解説</u>

解答

---

(1)　オ

(2)　ウ

(3)　これで息子とは6週間のお別れであった。

(4)　オ

(5)　エ

(6)　(6a)　オ　　(6b)　イ　　(6c)　ア

(7)　ア

(8)　愛着のある世界を離れてなじみのない世界に身を置き，寂しい体験をするという試練を与えること。

(9)　2番目－ウ，6番目－キ

— 164 —

解答・解説

1 (A) **【全訳】** クモが巣を作り，獲物を捕らえ，天井からぶら下がるために使う糸は，我々が知る中で最も強い素材の一種である。しかし実際には，クモの巣にそのような耐久性をもたらしているのはこの素材の特別な強さだけではない。

土木・環境工学の准教授，マーカス・ビューラーは，段階によって変わるような分子の相互作用により強くなるクモの糸の複合構造を以前分析した。「巣を強くしてくれる素材の最も重要な特性は，引っ張られると最初は柔らかくなり，その力が強まるとまた固くなることだ」 彼は現在ではそう述べている。圧力がかかると柔らかくなる特性は，以前は弱点だと考えられていたのである。

ビューラーと彼の率いる研究チームは，異なる特性の素材が，同じ巣のパターンで配列された場合，局所化された圧力にどう反応するか分析した。そして，単純な反応を示す素材の方が，反応性がはるかに劣ることを発見した。

クモの巣は，加えられる損傷が局所化されるという性質があり，影響がほんの数本の糸（たとえば虫が捕まってもがき回った部分）にしか及ばない。このように局所化された損傷は，巣の適切な機能が維持できていればすぐに修繕できるし，そのままにしておいてもかまわない。「傷がたくさんあっても，相変わらずクモの巣は力学的にはほぼ同様に機能しているのです」とビューラーは述べている。

この発見を検証するために，ビューラーとそのチームは実際に野原に分け入ってクモの巣を押したり引いたりしてみた。どの場合でも，損傷は彼らが損傷を与えた場所のすぐ近くの範囲に限定されていた。

このことから言えそうなのは，反応が複合的な素材には重要な利点があり得るということである。ビューラーによると，構造全体が存続できるよう損傷の局所化を可能にする原理は，ゆくゆくは構造工学の専門家の指針となるかもしれない。たとえば耐震建築も，ある程度は歪むが，揺れが続くか強くなった場合には構造の特定の部分がまず壊れて損傷を吸収するということも可能性としてはあり得る。

また，この原理はもしかしたらネットワークシステムの設計にも使用できるかもしれない。ウイルスに攻撃されているコンピュータが，問題が拡散しないうちに即時シャットダウンするという風にできるかもしれないのだ。そして，その名を生むきっかけとなったクモの巣状の構造から得た教訓のおかげで，やがてはワールドワイド・ウェブの安全性も高まっていくかもしれない。

— 166 —

2013年　　解答・解説

［考え方］

　本年度は「クモの巣」について述べた７段落（345 語）の文章が素材になり，近年の出題と比較すると段落数が増え，やや長い文章になったように見える。しかし，これまでの出題と同様，要約問題にふさわしい構造を持った文章だと言える。本問の内容は「クモの巣の特性」と「人間界での応用可能性」の２点に大別できるが，これを大筋として含めること自体はほとんどの受験生ができていたと思われる。ただし，前半の第１～５段落の部分で読み違えや要素の欠落がないように注意しなければならない。

◇**ポイント１：クモの巣の特性①（第１～３段落）**

　第１～３段落は，クモの糸が強いのはなぜか，について述べている。第１段落第２文に "... it's not just the material's exceptional strength ..." 「〈巣に耐久性をもたらすのは〉単に素材そのものの強さだけではない〈ことがわかる〉」とある。この部分を解答に含めるのは誤りではないが，"not just" とあるし，第２段落で別の特性を研究結果として紹介しているので，解答字数も考えると含めなくてもよいだろう。

　では，クモの糸の強さの秘密は何なのか。第２段落第２文の Buehler という研究者の言葉に "a key property"（カギとなる特性）という表現があるので，この文の "the way it can soften ... as the force increases" が，糸を強くする決定的な特性になると考えてよい。これは訳すと「引っ張られると最初は柔らかくなり，その力が強まるとまた固くなる」となるが，このままでは字数をかなり費やすことになるので「外部からの力の強さに応じて反応する柔軟性がある［反応できる］」という程度にまとめるとよいだろう。なお，第６段落第１文の "whose responses are complex" という表現は，この内容をまとめたものであり，この complex は「複雑」ではなく「複合的」という意味である。

◇**ポイント２：クモの巣の特性②（第４～５段落）**

　この部分のキーワードは，やはり "localized" であろう。この表現だけでは，よくわからなくても "affecting just a few threads"（少数の糸にしか影響しない）という表現や，研究者が実際にクモの巣を押したり引いたりしてみたことを紹介する第５段落にある "damage was limited to the immediate area ..."（損傷はすぐ近くの部分に限定されていた）といった表現から「損傷が局所に限定される」という意味をとらえることはできたはずである。もちろん，この意味になっていればよいので「１ヵ所にしか及ばない；部分的にとどまる；広がらない；全体に及ばない」というまとめ方でもよい。

　以上，２つの特性については「①ゆえに②」という因果関係でまとめてもよいと思

— 167 —

2013年　　解答・解説

われる。

◇**ポイント3：応用可能性①（第6段落）**

ここでも Buehler という研究者の言葉として紹介されているが，"... guiding structural engineers"（構造工学の専門家を導いてくれることになるかもしれない）とあり，第3文に例もあるので，「建築（工学）；構造工学；耐震建築に応用可能かもしれない」という点が含まれていればよい。

◇**ポイント4：応用可能性②（第7段落）**

ここは also とあるので，2つ目の応用可能性として "the design of networked systems" を中心に「安全なインターネット［ネット；ウェブ；WWW；情報通信網］の構築に利用できるかもしれない」に触れていればよい。また「安全な」を「ウイルスに強い」とまとめてもよいだろう。

以上，2つの応用可能性の部分については，英文中で用いられた助動詞にも注意すること。第6〜7段落では，could / might / may を使っており，この文章中では「将来あり得る可能性」として述べているので，「…に応用できた；…に影響を与えた」などとまとめると英文の意味とは異なってしまうからである。

解答例

> クモの巣は外部からの力の強さに応じて反応する柔軟性を持ち，損傷を局所化できるという特性がある。これは建築工学や安全な情報通信網の構築に応用可能かもしれない。(78字)

1 **(B)** **全訳** 人は人生を二度生きる，と言われることがある。一度目は5歳まで，二度目はそれ以降。この発想の生まれる元となっているのは，おそらく，人生の最初の5年間が含む膨大な時間であろう。この5年間で，その後の70年あるいはそれ以上の時間で経験する時間に匹敵する時間を体感している可能性もあり得る。

人は生後数ヵ月間は全く時間を体感していないと思われる。心理学者ジャン・ピアジェの研究によれば，生後数ヵ月間，人は「空間のない」状態で生きていて，異なる物体間の差も，物体と自分自身の差もわかっていない。世界と混ざり合っていて，自分の終わりと始まりもわからない。また時間のない状態も経験する。物体間の区別ができないのと同様に，ある瞬間と次の瞬間の区別もできないからである。**ある出来事がいつ始まり，いつ終わるかわからない。**

分離の感覚が発達し始めると，ようやくこの時間のない状態から脱却し始める。ピアジェによると，これは生後7ヵ月前後に始まる。自分を周囲の世界とは切り離され

— 168 —

2013年　　解答・解説

た別個の実体として認識し始め，さらに異なる物体の区別を感知するようになる。同時に異なる出来事が別のものだということにも気づき始める。過去・現在・未来の時制を持つ言語の発達に後押しされて，**連続した時間の感覚，過去と未来の感覚を持ち始める**。この過程は4つの段階を経ると，ピアジェは言う。第1段階では，人が目の前にやってきて出来事が始まるのだということを認識する。第2段階では，人がどこかへ行ってしまい，出来事が終わるということを認識する。第3段階では，人や物が動くと，いろいろな距離を移動することを認識する。第4段階では，移動する異なる物と人の距離を測ることができるようになり，この段階で連続した時間の感覚ができたことになる。

　時間というものに「収まる」という，この段階を過ぎると，**ますます時間に支配されるようになる**。連続の感覚が，自分を別個の存在とみなす感覚の発達の結果であるとすれば，おそらく，自我が発達するほど連続の感覚も発達すると考えてよい。その結果，時間の流れは速くなるように思えてくる。時間の流れが速くなるというこの感覚は，大人になって初めて経験するものではなく，おそらく幼い頃からずっと生じているのだろう。2歳児にとっても時間は流れているのだろうが，途方もなくゆっくりとしか流れていないのではないか。しかし子供の自己感が発達すると，時間の速度も上がっていく。おそらく4歳児の時間は3歳児よりも速く流れ，6歳の子供より7歳の子供の方が時間の流れが速いのであろう。

　しかし，この年齢でも大人と比べると時間の流れは何倍も遅い。だからこそ，親なら誰でも知っているように，幼児は**実際よりも多くの時間が流れたと常に思い，物事に時間がかかりすぎだと，よくごねるのである**。小学校で，教員にとっては，たった40分の授業だろうと思える時間が生徒たちにとっては，その何倍にも長くなっている――これは生徒たちの気が散り始めた時に教員が留意すべき点である。

　さらに，それ以外の面でも幼児の時間感覚は，まだ完全にはできあがっていない。さまざまな出来事がどれくらい続くのか正確に推測できないのだ。意外かもしれないが，6，7歳の子でも数秒程度の長さでしか推測できない。また，**過去の出来事の連続性をきちんととらえる感覚もないのである**。2歳から4歳の子供が，自分のしたことを話したり，自分に起こったことをもう一度伝えたりする時には，通例，連続性ではなく関連性をもとに一つのまとまりを作ってしまい，必ずといっていいほど出来事の順序を間違えるものである。

〔選択肢全訳〕

ア　現在形でしか話すことができない

イ　さらに時間に影響されるようになる

— 169 —

2013年　　解答・解説

ウ　出来事の重要性を並べるようになる

エ　ある出来事がいつ始まって，いつ終わるかわかっていない

オ　過去の出来事の連続性に対する明確な感覚も持たない

カ　連続した時間に対する感覚，過去と未来の感覚を身につける

キ　常に多くの新しいことに遭遇するが，それでも一つ一つの出来事が他とは異なる
　　という感覚を保持している

ク　実際よりも多くの時間が過ぎていったといつも思っていて，物事に時間がかかり
　　すぎていると不満を言うことが多い

[考え方]

(1)　正解は**エ**。

　この段落では，生後数ヵ月は空間概念も時間概念も未発達であることが，ピアジェ
の研究を基に述べられている。さらに，直前の文で「ある瞬間と次の瞬間の区別もで
きないから，時間のない状態も経験する」と述べているので，このような内容と最も
密接に関係するのは，**エ**「ある出来事がいつ始まって，いつ終わるかわかっていない」
だと考える。

(2)　正解は**カ**。

　この段落では，生後7ヵ月頃になると，分離する感覚が発達し，自己を周囲と切り
離し，物体の区別もできるようになることが述べられている。また，直前の文で「異
なる出来事が別のものだととらえられるようになる」とあり，後ろから「過去・現在・
未来の時制を持つ言語の発達に促されて」という副詞句に修飾されているので，これ
らと最も自然に適合するのは，**カ**「連続した時間に対する感覚，過去と未来の感覚を
身につける」だと考える。さらに，後続の「このプロセスは4つの段階を経る」以下
で紹介された，第4段階の説明に "we have developed a sense of sequential time."
とあり，これも空所2にカが入る根拠となる。

(3)　正解は**イ**。

　第2文以降で「自我が発達するほど連続の感覚も発達する。その結果，時間の流れ
は速くなるように思えてくる」という趣旨の記述があるので，この内容と最も関連性
のあるのは，**イ**「さらにそれ（＝時間）に影響されるようになる」だと考える。なお，
空所直前の "'falling' into time" がわからなくても，this point とあるので，第3段落
の内容を受けているのだと考えればよい。

(4)　正解は**ク**。

　This is why ... という表現によって，直前の文が「原因」，why 以下の部分が「結果」
という関係が生じる。直前の「大人と比べると子供の時間の流れは何倍も遅い」とい

—　170　—

2013 年　　解答・解説

う内容の結果と言えるもので，かつ「親なら誰でも知っていること」と言えるのは，
ク「（幼児は）実際よりも多くの時間が過ぎていったといつも思っていて，物事に時
間がかかりすぎていると不満を言うことが多い」である。

(5)　正解は**オ**。

　この段落では，幼児の時間感覚は，（さまざまな段階を経て発達しつつあるが）や
はりまだ不完全である，ということが述べられている。直前の "They can't ..." の文
と同様に，この空所にも「否定的な内容／幼児たちにできないこと」が入るはずである。
否定的な意味合いを持つのはア，エ，オの3つだが，ここは "don't have ... , either"
と "the sequence of past events" という表現を含むという点から，**オ**「過去の出来
事の連続性に対する明確な感覚も持たない」が最も適切である。この文がここにある
と，空所直後の「幼児が過去のことを話す時には，連続性ではなく関連性をもとにま
とまりを作ってしまい，出来事の順序を間違える」という文が補強の文として成立す
る。

解 答

(1)－エ	(2)－カ	(3)－イ	(4)－ク	(5)－オ

2　(A)　考え方

＜語数について＞

　「60 ～ 70 語程度」とあるから，ゆるく解釈して 50 ～ 80 語くらい書けばよいと思う。
また，答案の最後に「○○ words」と書き添えよう。

＜問題の指示＞

① 「左側の人物を **X**，右側の人物を **Y**」

　後でも述べるが，話を組み立てる際，何かを指さしている Y から話を始める方がス
ムーズな展開になりやすい。ところが，X・Y と並んでいればどうしても X から書き
始めたくなるし，また問題用紙に与えられている書き方の例が「X:　　　 Y:　　　」
となっている。くれぐれも X と Y を逆にしないよう注意すること。

② 「**X と Y のどちらから始めてもよい**」

　要するに「Y:　　　 X:　　　」でも構わないということ。

③ 「**それぞれ何度発言してもよい**」

　問題用紙の書き方の例には「X:　　 Y:　　 X:　　 Y:　　　」と書
かれているが，それぞれ 2 回ずつの発言に留めなければならないという意味ではない。

— 171 —

2013年　　解答・解説

＜内容のポイント＞

① **答案に盛り込むべき必須情報を写真から読み取る**

　写真を元にして会話文を作るわけだが，写真の中にあるどの情報を答案に盛り込むか，その取捨選択能力が問われる。最低限盛り込まれていなければならない情報は次の4つ。

　1）**Xは男性**

　2）**Yは女性**

　3）**Xは手を耳に当てている**

　4）**Yは上の方を指さしている**

　むろんこれら以外のことに言及しても構わないが，この4点を踏まえて会話文が作られていない場合は減点対象となるだろう。

② **見たままを素直に英語にする**

　会話文全部を書くという設定だから，1つのきちんとしたストーリーを作らなければならないのではと思う受験生もいるだろう。むろんそれなりのまとまりは必要だろう（尻切れトンボの会話や，何を話し合っているのか要領を得ない会話は×）。しかし，そもそも「60〜70語程度」という短い語数なのだから，起伏に富んだ内容にすることは無理で，またその必要もない。妙に凝った内容にしたために英語がついていけてないものが最低の答案と言えよう。

　ちなみに，問題文には「自由に想像し」とあるが，写真の画像と明らかに異なることを書けば，減点は当然免れない。

＜答案作成＞

　上記＜内容のポイント＞で述べたが，「Xは手を耳に当てている」というのは「何かが聞こえない」「何かを聞こうとしている」と解釈するのが妥当で，たとえば「Xの耳が遠い」「Yの声が小さい」「何か大きな音がしているためよく聞こえない」などという設定がよいだろう。また，「Yは上の方を指さしている」だが，Yが上の方にある○○にXを注目させようとしていると考えるべきである。この○○だが，上の方を指さしているのだから，「木の上」「空」にあるもの，たとえば鳥・花・雲・飛行機などが考えられる。問題は，<u>聴覚</u>に訴えるXと<u>視覚</u>に訴えるYとの間にどう折り合いを付けるかで，それが会話文作成のポイントとなるだろう。

　ここで，答案の展開方法を具体例に沿って見てみよう。

— 172 —

2013 年　　解答・解説

［解答例１］

　　［X が手を耳に当てている理由］＝ Y の声が小さい

　　［Y が何を指さしているか］＝木の上にいる鳥

　Y は木の上にいる鳥を指さし，鳥を驚かせないように小声で話しかけているという設定で会話を進めた。鳥の正体を探っている過程で「ニワトリ」の話を盛り込んでいるが，これは「おかしみ」を出すのと同時に語数稼ぎも兼ねている。

［解答例２］

　　［X が手を耳に当てている理由］＝高齢で耳が遠い

　　［Y が何を指さしているか］＝木の間に咲く花

　X を老人，Y をその孫という設定にしたため，Y には "Grandpa" と呼ばせている。このような情報の明確化は必要である。しばらく「耳が遠い」ことに関連する内容で語数を稼ぎ，最後は「花の写真を撮っておばあちゃんに見せてあげたい」で話を収めた。

［解答例３］

　　［X が手を耳に当てている理由］＝単に Y の言葉が聞こえなかった

　　［Y が何を指さしているか］＝木の枝にうごめくヘビ

　X が手を耳に当てている理由は特別なものを考えず，単に聞き落としたという設定にしてある。木にヘビがうごめいているのを目撃したことから，なぜそこにヘビがいるのかを２人で考え，結論を出すという展開。

解 答 例

［解答例１］〈70 words〉

Y : Can you see the bird on top of that tree?

X : Yes ... but why are you speaking in such a low voice? I can't hear you.

Y : So I won't frighten the bird.

X : Then I have to speak quietly, too.

Y : What do you think it is?

X : I don't know. Maybe a chicken?

Y : Be serious. Chickens can't fly. Isn't it an eagle?

X : I don't think an eagle would come to a city park.

［解答例２］〈60 words〉

Y : Look, Grandpa. How beautiful!

X : What did you say? Speak louder, will you? You know I'm hard of hearing.

－ 173 －

2013年　解答・解説

　Y : Oh, sorry. I said "how beautiful." I mean, the flowers over there. Can
　　　you see them?

　X : Yes, and you're right. What are they? Do you know what they're
　　　called?

　Y : No. Anyway, I'll take a picture. I want Grandma to see them, too.

［解答例3］〈62 words〉

　Y : What's that in that tree?

　X : What did you say?

　Y : There's something in that tree. See it moving?

　X : Oh! Is it a snake?

　Y : I think so! I didn't know snakes could climb trees.

　X : Neither did I. I wonder if someone put it there.

　Y : What? Climbed the tree and left the snake? I doubt it.

　X : Yes, I guess the snake climbed up there itself.

2 (B) 考え方

＜語数について＞

　「50 ～ 60 語」とあるからには，やはりこの指定より多くても少なくてもまずい。
また，答案の最後に「○○ words」と書き添えよう。

＜問題の指示＞

① 「あなたが最も大切だと思うことは何か」

　「学校や学校以外の場で」となっているが，これはつまりどこでもよいということ
だから，全く意味のない文言である。「これまで学んできたことのなかで」だが，「学
び」は学問的なものとは限らない。「人生勉強」という言葉があるように，結局はど
のような事柄でも構わないのである。注意してほしいのは，「最も大切だと思うこと」
であるから，はっきりとポジティブな意味合いのものを選ぶこと。たとえば「コミュ
ニケーションの取り方」「友人とのつき合い方」などにすると大幅な減点となる。な
ぜなら，これらは良いやり方も悪いやり方もあるからだ。「コミュニケーションを取
ること」「友人」なら問題ない。

② 「それはなぜか」

　要するに「なぜそれが最も大切だと思うのか，理由を書け」ということ。論説型の
自由英作文を書く上で「理由」を述べるのは当然のことである。

— 174 —

2013年　　解答・解説

③　「英語に関すること以外について述べること」

　なぜこのような条件をつけたのか，よくわからない。おそらく「英語」に関しては受験生があまりにも訓練を受けていて，パターン的な答案（「英語は世界語だから，英語を知っていれば世界中どこへ行っても人とコミュニケーションがとれる」のような）しか出てこないことを嫌ったのだろう。

＜内容のポイント＞

① 　最初に結論を書く

　答案の冒頭に，問題文で求められている答え，つまり諸君が「最も大切だと思うこと」を具体的に述べる。答案全体を読まないと言いたいことがわからない，という展開はよくない。

② 　「理由＋α」を書く

　結論と理由だけで50語は埋まらない。「＋α」にどれだけ語数を割けるかが答案を完成させる決め手となる。たとえば，「ある経験からそれが最も大切であると悟った」という設定にし，その「経験」つまり「大切だと思う」に至った過程を述べると簡単に50語に達する。あるいは，諸君の中には「最も大切だと思うもの」として「愛」「友情」「誠実さ」などの抽象概念を選ぶ者も多いだろう。抽象概念を抽象的に論じると，結局何が言いたいのか今ひとつ不明瞭になりやすい。こういう時は，極力具体化することで語数を稼げばよい。

＜答案作成＞

　以上の点を踏まえて，答案の展開方法を具体例に沿って見てみよう。

［解答例1］

　[最も大切だと思うこと] ＝友情

　(理由) 友人がいなければ生きていけないから

　友人が自分にとっていかに重要な存在かを自らの日常を紹介することで説明した。

［解答例2］

　[最も大切だと思うこと] ＝誠実さ

　(理由) 他者と強固な人間関係を構築する鍵となるから

　誠実であることがなぜ強固な人間関係を作る鍵になるのかを説明する「ブリッジ」の部分がもちろん書かれていなければならない。この解答例では「誠実ならば相手が自分の誠実さに敬意を表し，自分の意見を重視してくれる」という内容を盛り込んである。

［解答例3］

　[最も大切だと思うこと] ＝他人にやさしく話すこと

— 175 —

2013年　　解答・解説

（理由）言葉は人を傷つけうるから

「話し方によっては相手を傷つける」という事実にたどり着いた経緯を，かつての自分や姉妹に発生した出来事などを通して説明してある。

解答例

［解答例1］

　　Friendship is more important than anything else. I have a lot of friends at my school. When I feel sad, they try to comfort me; when I have a problem, they listen to me and try to think of a solution. I've learned that without friends, I wouldn't be able to do anything. (53 words)

［解答例2］

　　The most important thing I've learned in school is that honesty is the best policy. Telling the truth and being honest all the time has a positive influence on your life. If you are always honest, people will begin to respect your honesty and value your opinion. Honesty is the key to building strong relationships with others. (57 words)

［解答例3］

　　I've learned that it is important to always speak kindly to others. I used to often say unkind things to people. I never thought about how it affected them. But one day my sister came home crying. Someone had told her she was stupid. Since then I've paid attention to what I say. I know words can hurt people greatly. (60 words)

---

4 (A) 【全訳】 個人情報はインターネット上のソーシャルネットワークを動かす燃料のようなもので，ユーザーの関心も広告業者の関心も引いているが，そのようなネットワークの運営者は個人情報の扱いに関してほぼ自由な裁量権を持ってきた。だが，それほどの情報がどのように集められ，使用され，また保護されているかに対して現在注目が集まっているが，運営者が幾度となく個人データの保護を怠ってきた結果，ユーザーはあらゆるリスクにさらされていることが判明した。運営者の多くは，自分たちは現行の法律に従っており，これ以上の規制は不要であり，また逆効果でさえあると主張しているが，これは不思議なことではない。たとえば，彼らの主張によれば，ネットワークサービスを利用し始めてもいない段階から，自分の個人情報へのアクセスをどのように規制してもらいたいと思っているかに関して多くの細かい質問

— 176 —

2013年　　解答・解説

を受けると，ユーザーは頭が混乱して，プライバシーについて下手な選択をしてしまうこともある。それでも，業界の個人データの管理法は近いうちに変わらなければならなくなる可能性が高いように思われる。

【考え方】(1)　正解は**ウ・ア**。まず，本文全体のテーマが「個人情報」であるから，"〈Personal〉information"という並びは明白。これに対する述語動詞は is か powers だが，空所の直後にある online social networks という名詞句の処理を考えると，"〈Personal〉information is" "powers〈online social networks〉"という組み合わせが最適。残りは fuel / the / that なので，fuel を先行詞とする関係代名詞節を考えて，"〈Personal〉information is the fuel that powers〈online social networks〉"とまとめる。

　　並べ替えた英文：information **is** the **fuel** that powers

(2)　正解は**イ・カ**。この設問は，本文を一目見た段階で take a close look at ... の受動態であることが見抜けないと，解くのはほぼ不可能だろう。空所の後は information is collected という完全な英文が続いていることから，"the way S V"（S が V するやり方）の形を考える。この段階で"〈a close look is now being〉taken at the way〈information is collected〉"となる。残った選択肢は all / that だが，all は information につけるしかない。that を関係副詞と解釈して the way that all〈information is collected〉とすると構文的には収まるが，「あらゆる情報の集められ方」というのは内容的におかしい。別にすべての情報を集めるわけではなく，ソーシャルネットワーク上に集められる個人情報の話をしているのだから，all that〈information〉とするべきである。

　　並べ替えた英文：taken **at** the **way** all that

(3)　正解は**エ・ア**。空所の直前に about という前置詞があるが，これの目的語になるのだから，全体が how による疑問副詞節でまとめられているのではと考える。次に空所の直後に information controlled とあるが，control は第3文型の動詞なので，この controlled は確実に過去分詞である。過去分詞がこの位置にある理由としては"want + O + 過去分詞"以外には考えづらい。この段階で"how they want〈information controlled〉"となるが，残っている選択肢は access / their / to の3つ。前後の内容を見ると，個人情報保護の話であるから，「規制」(control) されるのは「情報」というよりも「個人情報へのアクセス」と考えるべきである。「…へのアクセス」は access to ...。残りは their だが，実はこれをどこに置くかが正解・不正解の決め手となるため，極めて重要である。*their* access to information とすると，「自分たちが情報にアクセスする」ことに対する規制を求めることになり，要領を得ない。

— 177 —

2013 年　　解答・解説

ここで問題になっているのは，あくまで「他者が自分の個人情報にアクセスしてくる」ことに対する規制であるから，access to their information としなければならない。最終的に，"how they want access to their ⟨information controlled⟩" とまとめる。

　　並べ替えた英文：how **they** want **access** to their

解答

(1)　ウ・ア　　(2)　イ・カ　　(3)　エ・ア

4 **(B)** **全訳**　すでに変わってしまった知識や考えの過去の状態を完全には元の状態に戻せないということが人間の精神の一般的な限界だ。いったん世界に関して（あるいは世界のどの一部に関してであれ）新しい見方を取り入れてしまうと，考えが変わる前に信じていたことを思い出す能力の多くを即座に失ってしまうのだ。

　多くの心理学者たちは，人々が考えを変えると何が起こるかを研究してきている。人々の考えが完全には固まっていない話題（例えば，死刑制度）を選び，実験者は注意深く被験者の持つ考え方を測定する。次に，参加者たちはそれに賛成または反対する説得力のある意見を目にするか，それを耳にする。それから実験者は被験者の考え方を再度測定する。すると被験者の持つ考え方は，彼らがさらされた説得力のある意見により近づいていることが多い。そして最後には，参加者は自分が以前に持っていた意見を発表するのだ。この作業は驚くほど難しいものとなる。以前に抱いていた考えを再度言うように求められると，人々はそれをせず，今自分が持っている考えを繰り返す（これが「置き換え」と呼ばれる行為の一例である）のであり，多くの人は自分が（さっきまでは）違う感じ方をしていたなどと考えることもできない。過去に抱いていた考えを再び抱くことができないために，必然的に，過去の出来事に自分がどれほど驚きを感じたかを過小評価することになってしまうのだ。

　こうした「最初からわかっていた」と人に思い込ませる効果が存在しているがために，我々は残念な結果に終わった良い決定に関し意志決定者たちを非難する傾向にあり，事後になって初めて明白であるように思えるようなうまい策を講じた場合も，彼らの功績をあまりに不当に評価してしまう傾向にある。結果が悪いと，人々は意志決定者たちがその兆候を見逃したと非難するが，その兆候は見えないインクで書かれていたのであり，そのインクは後になってようやく目に見えるものなのだということを，彼らは忘れているのだ。

－ 178 －

2013年　解答・解説

考え方

(1)　**1. Asked to reconstruct their former beliefs**「前の考えを再現する（再び述べる）よう求められると」　When people are asked to reconstruct ... と同義の分詞構文。

　2. people repeat their current ones instead「人々は代わりに現在の考えを繰り返す」　ones は beliefs を指す。設問の指示は「their current ones の内容がわかるように訳せ」となっており，どこまで説明すればいいのかやや不明瞭だが，単に「代名詞の指すものを明らかにして訳せ」という指示ではないので，もう一段詳しく説明しておいた方が無難と思われる。下線部の前の箇所に実験についての記述があり，その中で「まずは人の考えがはっきりと定まっていない話題を選び，それからそれについて説得力のある意見を見せる，あるいは聞かせる」とある。「現在の意見」とはまさにこの「説得力のある意見に触れた後に持つようになっている意見」なので，「その代わりに人々は説得力のある意見に影響された今の考えを繰り返す」などとまとめておけば十分であろう。

(2)　**1. Your inability(S) to － ... will inevitably cause(V) you(O) to underestimate(C) ...** とつながる第5文型。Your inability to － は You are unable to － という文が名詞化されたもの（「人が－できないこと」）。cause O to － で「O に－させる」の意。（例）The injury *caused* him *to* lose his job.（そのけがが彼に仕事を失わせた→そのけがのせいで彼は仕事を失った）　問題文もこの例文同様無生物主語なので，全体を「－できないために，人は…を過小評価してしまう」などとまとめるのがよい。

　2. reconstruct past beliefs「過去の考えを再現する（思い出す）〈ことができないこと〉」

　3. the extent to which you were surprised by past events「過去の出来事によって驚かされた程度」　to which ... は the extent を修飾する関係詞節（You were surprised by past events *to the extent.* → *the extent to which* you were surprised by past events）。「どの程度過去の出来事に驚かされたか」などと処理してもよい。

(3)　**1. they**　the signs を受ける代名詞であるが，単に「その兆候」などとしたのでは不十分。「その」の内容を明示し，「失敗に終わる兆候」「結果を暗示する兆候」などとしてもらいたいところ。下線部の「説明」が求められているときは，代名詞の内容は必ず明示すること。

　2. were written in invisible ink「目には見えないインクで書かれていた」とは「（当初は）認識不可能であった」ということのたとえ。

— 179 —

<u>2013 年　　解答・解説</u>

3．**that became visible only afterward**　「後になって初めて目に見えるように
なった〈インク〉」とは「結果が出た後で初めて兆候が認識可能になること」を示し
ている。

解答

(1)　以前の考えを再度述べるよう求められると，その代わりに人々は説得力のあ
　　　る意見に影響された今の考えを繰り返す。
(2)　過去の考えを思い出せないために，必然的に，過去の出来事にどの程度驚か
　　　されたかを過小評価してしまう。
(3)　[解答例1]　失敗に終わるという兆候は当初から感知できるものではない
　　　　　　　　　ということ。(33字)
　　　[解答例2]　結果を暗示する兆候は，その結果が出た後になって初めて認識
　　　　　　　　　可能だということ。(37字)

5　全訳　11歳のとき，私はケイティ・マッキンタイアという名の女性から，週
に一度，バイオリンのレッスンを受けていた。彼女は町の建物に，大きくて日当たり
のよい4階にある練習室を持っていて，建物の下の階には，歯医者と紙問屋と安っぽ
い写真屋が入っていた。練習室へは，古風なエレベーターに乗って行くのだが，それ
は4階へ上る際には，危険なくらいに揺れた。その4階を使っていたのは，もう1人
だけ，E・サンプソンという女性で，死者と交信できる降霊術師だった。

　母の友人たちの間で交わされたのを聞きつけた噂話から，私はサンプソンさんにつ
いて知っていた。有名な医者の娘で，クレイフィールド大学へ通い，頭がよく，人気
があった。しかしその後，彼女の才能が表に現れた。そのような言い回しを母の友人
たちは用いていた。その才能は，彼女の賢さやよい性格を全く変えることなく，だし
ぬけに正体を現したのである。

　彼女は死者の声を借りて話すようになったのだ。それは，郊外の公園で殺害された
小さな女の子たち，戦死した兵士たち，行方不明になった息子たちや兄弟たちといっ
た人々だった。ときおり，レッスンに早めに着いたときに，彼女と一緒のエレベーター
に乗り合わせることがあった。バイオリンのケースをギュッと抱きしめ，エレベーター
の壁に身をグイと押しつけたのだが，それは，彼女がひょっとしてエレベーターの中
に連れてきたかもしれない霊の存在に居場所を作るためだった。

　建物の入り口のエレベーターの脇に，歯医者や写真屋や私の通ったマッキンタイア
先生と並んで「E・サンプソン　降霊術師」と，とても大胆に表札が掲げられている

－　180　－

2013年　　解答・解説

のを見るのは違和感があった。当時は，階下で営まれているような日常的な出来事（歯医者のドリルがキューンという音を出したり，海外渡航する人々にパスポート用の写真を撮ったりすること）と，音楽は別物であるべきだというのは適切なことだと思われた。しかし，私はサンプソンさんのことを，実務的な靴と仕事向きのスーツにもかかわらず，にせ医者みたいに思っていて，サンプソンさんや，はるばる彼女の部屋までやってきて，エレベーターの最後の階を私たちとともにした，悲しい目をした大勢の女性たち（たいていが女性だったのだ）と，マッキンタイア先生やクラシック音楽が，一緒くたにされるのを心苦しく思っていた。女性たちは，ひょっとすると銀行の支店長をしている夫を持っていたかもしれず，とうとうこんなところまでやってきているのにもかかわらず，粋な帽子と手袋をして，あごを少し上に傾けていた。あるいは，病院の調理場とかオフィスで働いていた女性とかが，このときは皆，上品に手袋や帽子でめかしこんでいたものの，居合わせている人々や，エレベーターで連れてこられた高みが怖い様子だった。女性たちは，上品な女性らしい身のこなしで肘を使うのだが，使いはして，エレベーターが混んで距離が近づきすぎると，「失礼」とか「すみません」とか礼儀正しく言いながら，距離をとろうとしていた。

そんなときは，積載量の限界で，エレベーターは，どうにかこうにか仕事をした。そしてその古い機械をシャフトのところで軋ませていたのは，単に身体の重さだけでなく（掲示では定員8人と警告されていた），あらゆるそういった悲しみ，あらゆるそういった絶望と一縷の望み，うちに秘められた悲嘆の中のあらゆるそういった尊厳の重さなのだと私は思った。ゆっくりと，私たちを乗せたエレベーターは上っていった。

ときには，サンプソンさんは（そういうものを持ちえたとしての話だが）気まぐれな好奇心からといった様子で，少しの間私に目をとめることがあったのだが，そんなときには，小さな11歳の向こう側に何が見えているのだろうと，私は激しく疑問に思った。その年頃のたいていの男の子と同様に，私には隠しておくべきことが山ほどあった。しかし，彼女は私のことを見ていたようであり，透視していたのではなかったようだった。彼女は微笑み，私はそれに応え，なんとか声を出そうと咳払いをして，彼女をだまくらかして，私の秘密をそっとしておいてくれるように私が願っていた育ちのよいやり方で，「こんにちは，サンプソンさん」と言ったものだった。彼女自身の声は，親戚のおばさんと同じくらいにどうということのないもので，「まあ，こんにちは」と言った。

だからなおのことびっくりだったのは，マッキンタイア先生の自慢の生徒のベン・スタインバーグがマックス・ブルッフの曲を演奏している間，練習室のすぐ外で，イスの1つに座って待っていたとき，挨拶のときと同じものであるサンプソンさんの声

－ 181 －

が奇妙に変わって，オフィスの半分開いたドアを通して聞こえてくることだった。そこにいた女性たちの息づかいよりも大きな声だったものの，普段よりも一段階，いや数段階低い声で，まるで別の大陸から聞こえているかのようだった。それは彼女を通してインド人が語っている声だった。

それは，エレベーターの中にいた女性とはもはや思えない存在で，私が思い出したのは，かつて，私の乗った列車が蒸気を立てながら線路上に停車していたときに，客車の窓から見えたものだった。待合室のガラス越しの3人の老いた男と，ホタルがいっぱい入った瓶のように，彼らが吐く息で輝いた閉じた空間だった。それはまぎれもない現実だったのだが，見え方のせいで，その現実が様変わりし，そのことにより，その距離では，あるいは肉眼では，とうてい見えなかったであろう細部を思い起こすことができたと，印象深く気づいたのだった。それは，1人の老人の目の緑がかった灰色と，シャツの襟の近くのしみだった。サンプソンさんの部屋をのぞき込むのは，そんな感じだった。見えすぎてしまった。くらくらして，汗が出始めた。

物語性はなく，どこかへ通じていたり，何かを証明したりする一連の出来事もない。中間も，終わりもない。ただ単に，半分開いたドアを通して見えた一抹の光景である。

考え方

(1) 正解は**ウ**。「君の外出中に，ジョンソンとかいう人が会いにきたよ」と訳せることからわかるように，この不定冠詞は「…とかいう人」の意味。ちなみに，この用法は，本文の a Miss Katie McIntyre のように，Mr や Ms などをつけるのが通例なので，選択肢も，A <u>Mr</u> Johnson の方がよかったかもしれない。ア「玄関先に停めてある車は，フォードみたいに見える」は「…の製品」という意味。イ「彼を知っている人は皆，彼がエジソンみたいな人だと考えた」は「…みたいな人」。エ「その美術館で私は初めてピカソの作品を見た」は「…の作品」。オ「彼女は，ジョン・スミスと結婚する前はアダムズという苗字だった」は「…家の一員」という意味。

(2) 正解は (2a) **ク**，(2b) **ウ**，(2c) **ア**。

(2a) は，「4階を唯一の（ 2a ）入居者と共同利用していた」という文意から考えれば，クの other「他の」であることは自明だろう。the other ... に「2つ［2人］のうちの残った方」という意味があるのは必修事項。

(2b) は，文脈から「頭のよさや，気持ちのよさを，何も変えることなく」という意味になるだろうと考えて，ウの any を入れればよい。in no way「少しも…ない」という言いまわしがあるが，without に否定の意味が含まれているので，without in any way となったと考えればよい。

(2c) は，「私はサンプソンさんのことを，実務的な靴と仕事向きのスーツ（ 2c ），

— 182 —

2013年　　解答・解説

にせ医者みたいに思っていて」という前後関係から「…にもかかわらず」という意味になるのではないかと考え，for all という熟語を思い出せればよい。ちなみに，表現のまとまりを分断して設問にするのは東大英語の定番である。

(3)　正解は **the dead**。サンプソンさんが降霊術師であること，そして，下線部の後に「エレベーターに連れてきそうな」とあることから，ここでの the presences は死者の霊が現れることだと考えればよい。したがって，第1段落末尾と，下線部を含む段落の冒頭にある the dead が正解となる。

(4)　正解は**エ**。「マッキンタイア先生とクラシック音楽が…されるなんて」の部分は，本文とすべての選択肢に共通。本文の be associated with「…と結びつけられる」に最も近いのは，エの be coupled with である。さらに，下線部直前の表現から，当該個所の内容は「心苦しく思うようなこと」でなければならないが，それには，エ「マッキンタイア先生とクラシック音楽が，サンプソンさんのような品位に欠ける人と結びつけられるなんて」という内容がふさわしい。ア「…が，サンプソンさんの仕事に関わりをもつなんて」は「関わり」も「仕事」も不適。イ「…が，サンプソンさんのような人に影響されるなんて」は「影響」が不適。ウ「…が，サンプソンさんよりもいっそう軽蔑されるなんて」は比較の部分が不適。オ「…が，サンプソンさんと同じくらい素人だと思われるなんて」の「素人 (unprofessional)」が不適。

(5)　正解は**ア**。下線部の「居合わせている人々や，エレベーターで連れてこられた高みが怖い様子だった」という意味に最も近いのは，ア「エレベーターの中の他の女性たちや，エレベーターがどれほど高く上りつつあるかということを怖がっている様子だった」が最も近い。ちなみに本文の the heights には，単なる物理的な「高さ」という表面上の意味に加えて，「高次元の世界」「上流社会」といった比喩的な意味合いも含まれている。本文の looking scared が第2文型であるのに対して，イ「4階まで上るエレベーターの中の他の女性たちを怖そうに見ながら」や，エ「エレベーターが永遠に上昇し続けるように見えたので恐ろしくなり，エレベーターの中の他の客たちを不安そうに見ながら」は，第1文型なので不適。ウ「高い階まで連れて行くエレベーターの中の見慣れぬ女性たちへの恐怖を示しながら」は，根本的に間違えている。オ「彼女たちを雇っている会社や，不安定なエレベーターが上って行く高みのことを，どうやら怖いと感じながら」は，company の語義を間違えている。

(6)　正解は**エ**。本文は「私の秘密をそっとしておく」という意味。それゆえ，エ「彼女に私の心を読ませない」が正解となる。それ以外の選択肢，ア「私の罪悪感を隠す」，イ「私に一人でいることを楽しませる」，ウ「私の行儀のよさを彼女に確信させる」，オ「彼女が私の秘密を他の人に話さないようにする」は，いずれも文意に合わない。

— 183 —

<u>2013 年　　解答・解説</u>

(7)　正解は**ア**。下線部の all the more「なおさらいっそう」という表現は，その前後に「…だから」があるのが通常の用法。(例) I love him *all the more because he is my youngest child.* (彼は末っ子なので，なおさらいっそうあの子のことがかわいい)　この表現が，段落の冒頭近くにあることから，その直前の段落との関係を考えればよい。すると unremarkable「これといった特徴のない」声から，oddly changed「奇妙に変化した」声へと，変わったことがわかる。よって，ア「サンプソンさんは，ふだんは穏やかな声で話したから」が最も適切だとわかる。イ「ベン・スタインバーグは同じ声が奇妙に変わったのを聞いたから」は主語がおかしい。ウ「ますます多くの人々がサンプソンさんの声を怖がったから」，エ「マッキンタイア先生の練習室にあるピアノは，まるで遠くにあるように聞こえたから」，オ「サンプソンさんの声は，他のすべての女性よりもよく聞こえたから」は，まったく文意に合わない。

(8)　正解は「**その距離では，あるいは肉眼では，とうてい見えなかったであろう細部を思い起こすことができた**」。

　1．**I could recall details**「私は細部を思い起こすことができた」　この could は神経質にならずに「できた」と訳せばよい。

　2．**I could not possibly have seen**「とうてい見えなかったであろう」　直前に関係詞を補って考えるのは容易。possibly は，2011 年度 5 番 6 に出題されたばかりであり，「おそらく」などと訳すと減点されるだろう。could not ... have seen は「どうやったとしても」という仮定の含みがあるが，そこまで訳出する必要はない。

　3．**at that distance or with the naked eye**「その距離では，あるいは肉眼では」

解答

---

(1)　ウ

(2)　(2a) ク　(2b) ウ　(2c) ア

(3)　the dead

(4)　エ　　　(5)　ア　　　(6)　エ　　　(7)　ア

(8)　その距離では，あるいは肉眼では，とうてい見えなかったであろう細部を思い出すことができた。

— 184 —

解答・解説

1 (A) **全訳** 多くの先進国が移民（より良い機会を求めて他国からやってくる人々）の目的地となり，民族の混合比率が変化しつつあるが，これとともに，国内共通語と共通の価値観に象徴される国家的アイデンティティーの喪失に対する懸念が生まれている。一部の民族集団の分離とも言えるような現象が顕著になっており，これを憂慮する傾向が強まっている。たとえば合衆国で行われた調査によると，英語力がほとんど，あるいは全くないために家庭でも仕事面でも主にスペイン語に頼っている移民は，離婚・同性愛など論争の元になる社会問題について英語話者とは全く意見が異なっているのである。

ところが，このような異民族同時共存には，もう一つの面もある。現在私たちが暮らす世界では，移民が数世代にわたって新たなアイデンティティーを獲得していく過程の第一歩を踏み出すために友人や家族との繋がりを断ち切る必要がないのである。電子メールや電話で「本国の」社会と緊密な連絡を毎日維持することができるし，それだけではなく，出身国の社会で読まれているものと同じ新聞を読んだり，衛星放送で同じテレビ番組を視聴したり，同じ映画を DVD で借りたりすることもできる。

過去の世代では断ち切られていたソーシャルネットワークの繋がりが，あらゆるところで再結合されつつある。数世代前には引き離されていた家族や共同体が再び繋がりつつある。社会的な繋がりが再結合されることにより，これまでとは異なる社会が生まれつつある。それは，従来よりも広範囲に広がる，地理的近接性に依存しない社会なのである。

考え方

本年度は「現代社会における移民の状況」がテーマの文章。全体のアウトラインは以下のようになる。

［文章のアウトライン］

〈第1段落〉
(1) 移民の流入により国家のアイデンティティーが失われるという不安が生まれている。
(2) 一部の民族集団の隔絶［孤立］に対する懸念が大きくなっている。
(3) 合衆国の例。

— 186 —

2012年　解答・解説

〈第2段落〉
(1)　異民族同時共存には別の面もある。
(2)　現在は，移民が本国との関係を断ち切る必要はない。
(3)　様々な手段によって本国との社会関係を維持できている。

〈第3段落〉
(1)　かつては断ち切られていた繋がりが復活しつつある。
(2)　以前は引き離されていた集団が再び繋がりつつある。
(3)　社会的な繋がりの復活により，地理的に広範囲に渡る新たな社会が生まれつつある。

　第1段落は，第1文が主題，第2文が補強，第3文が例示と考えてよいので，第1文後半のand以下（ここはwith this (M) has come (V) the fear of ... (S)の倒置形で，as represented以下はidentityを修飾）を中心にまとめるとよいだろう。この文のnational identityは「一国家としてのアイデンティティー」の意味だが，英文和訳ではないので「国の統一感：国家としてのまとまり」のような表現でもよいだろう。また，the fearとあるので「移民の流入により国の統一感がなくなるという不安[懸念]」という程度に触れておけばよい。第2文は，内容面では第1文の補強と思われるので，こちらを使って「移民の民族的な孤立が懸念されている」とまとめても可であろう。いずれにせよ，この部分で字数を使いすぎないように言葉の圧縮を工夫しなければならない。

　第2段落は，第1文の "another side" の意味を第2文を使って明確にし「移民は本国[出身国]との関係を断ち切る必要がない→関係を維持できる」という点に触れておけばよいだろう。第3文は，字数に余裕があれば「様々な手段で」という程度に触れてもよい。

　第3段落は，第2文が第1文の補強[換言]なので「以前は切れていた本国との繋がり[社会関係]が復活している」という内容に触れておきたいが，過去と現在の対比が分かる言葉にするのがポイント。さらに，最終文のhelping ... 以下の部分で新たなとらえ方が紹介されているので，「地理的には拡散した新たな社会／地理的に広範囲に渡る社会の形成に繋がっている」という内容を解答に盛り込むとよい。

　「移民」と言えば，本国から遠く離れているし，受け入れ国の中でも言語や価値観の相違により孤立し，社会が 'a melting pot' というよりは 'a salad bowl' の様相を呈する可能性がある，というのはよくある視点。この文章は「そういう面だけではなく，移民が昔とは違って本国の方ときちんと繋がっている面もあるのだ」と言いたいよう

— 187 —

<u>2012 年　　解答・解説</u>

である。したがって全体的には「移民流入には，〈A〉の面もあるが，〈B〉の面もある」
という方向でまとめ，〈A〉（＝第１段落）は可能な限り短めに触れ，〈B〉（＝第２〜
３段落）の方をふくらませる書き方にしておけば英文全体のトーンを反映した解答に
なるであろう。

解答例

［解答例１］　移民流入による国家の統一感の喪失も懸念されるが，現在は移民
　　が本国との関係を維持でき，途切れていた社会的繋がりも復活して地理的に
　　拡散した社会が形成されつつある。(79字)
［解答例２］　移民の民族的孤立が懸念される一方で，今は移民が本国との社会
　　的な関係を維持できるため，以前の隔絶も解消されて地理的に広範囲に渡る
　　新たな社会が出現している。(76字)

1　**(B)**　**全訳**　その朝，いつもの停留所で，なんとか乗り込んだときに，バスに
は席がなかった。数ブロック進むと，息子のニックは車内の半分ほど後方の片側に空
いた席を見つけ，彼の妹のリジーと私は反対側の列に座った。

リジーが何かについてしゃべっているのを聞いていると，ニックが席を立ったの
で私は驚いた。　ア　年かさの，でもおばあちゃんというほどではない，見覚えの
なさそうな女性に，ニックが礼儀正しく話しかけているのを私は見ていた。　イ
ささやかなことだけれど，それでも私は，なんともすばらしいと胸が一杯になった。
　ウ　我が家では，バスの車内で何をすべきであり，何をすべきでないか（「すみま
せん」と言う，咳をするときには口をおおう，人を指でささない，見かけが普通でな
い人をじっと見ない）について常々話してきたものだが，今回のことは，息子に躾(しつけ)て
きたことではなかった。　エ　ささやかな親切行為だが，彼が自分から思いついた
ことだった。　オ

私たちは，人はどう振る舞うべきだと思っているか，どう振る舞うのを期待してい
るかを，自分の子どもに実際に見せたり，口で教えたりしようとするものだが，子ど
もが分かっているということを思わせる行動をしてくれると，衝撃であり，喜びであ
り，正直ほっとする。ニックが育っている世界では，私たちが彼の年齢だった頃と比
べて，社会的やりとりを支配しているルールがはるかに曖昧になっているから，なお
のことそう言えるのである。容認できることについて，ましてや，賞賛されることに
関する合図が競合した形で存在し，複雑な混乱状態であることに子どもたちは曝(さら)され
ている。きちんとしたマナーとは何なのか，もう分かりにくくなっている。

－　188　－

2012 年　　解答・解説

※空所×4

　そういった状況の下では，きちんとしたマナーは，これまでとは比べものにならないほど想像力を必要とする。向かいに座っている人が（見知らぬ人であれ，友人であれ）あなたから期待していること，必要としていること，望んでいることを知るのがはるかに難しくなっているという理由だけであるにしてもそうなのである。公式のルールブックを持っていないときには，さらにきちんと耳を傾け，さらに敏感になり，臨機応変に対応する用意がなくてはならないのである。

【考え方】

　(1)　正解はイ。この文は「ふと，私は事情が飲み込めた。ニックは彼女に席を譲ろうとしていたのだ」という意味。空所　イ　の直後に "A little thing, but ..."（ちょっとしたことだが，なんともすばらしいと胸が一杯になった）とあるので，この空所でNick の行動の意図が筆者に判明していなければならない。また，この文の 'her' の指示対象が前になければならない。

　(2)　正解はア。〈A〉, let alone 〈B〉のパターンでは，通例〈B〉の部分で「はるかに可能性の低いこと；ありそうもないこと」を引き合いに出し，「〈B〉は言うまでもなく…；〈B〉はもちろんのこと…；〈B〉どころか…」という訳が充てられることが多い。（例）I hardly have time to *think* these days, let alone *relax*.（最近は，くつろぐどころか，ほとんど考える暇もない）　つまり，〈A〉と〈B〉の内容は意味的に同じライン上にあって比較しうるものでなければならない。この文では，admirable「賞賛に値する」と同じ方向の形容詞で，かつ，意味的に一歩手前のものとして acceptable「容認可能な」がふさわしい。

　(3)　【選択肢全訳】

　ア　言うまでもなく，こういった類の混乱は，公共交通機関でのエチケットの話にとどまらず，はるかに多くのことに関わっている。お互いに何をすべきか，お互いに何を期待してよいかということにも関わっている。なにしろ，男性女性のいずれであるか，若いのか年取っているのかということによって，自分の役割がすぐに決まってくることはなくなってしまっている御時世だから。

　イ　先日も電車の車内で，あの出来事を思い出していた。その朝も車内は混んでいて，高価なスーツを着た若者が，読みかけのニューヨークタイムズのページもそのままに空いた席に滑り込み，白髪の紳士も，流行の服装をした若い女性たちも，まんまと出し抜いた場面を見ていたときのことだった。

　ウ　男性に権力と機会の大半が与えられ，女性にバスの席の大半が与えられる社会

— 189 —

<u>2012 年　　解答・解説</u>

契約が消失したことを，一瞬たりとて私は悔やんでいない。しかし，契約なしでやっていくのは，落ち着かないという面もある。行動の仕方を，もはや誰もよく分かっていないかのようになっていて，あらゆる場面で予測が不可能なので，私たちの末梢神経が外の世界にさらされている。そして，こういった混乱は，誰が最初にドアを通るかを決めるということから，誰がデートの費用を払うのかということに至るまで，あらゆることに及んでいる。

エ　子どもたちを学校へ連れて行く途中で，またもや親に特有の，こういった経験をしたのだった。子どもが初めて一人で外遊びをしたときや，帰宅してから学校で起きたことについて熱く語っているときや，前はいやがっていた食べ物をうれしそうに食べるときとちょうど同じように，そういう時は他の誰にも見えないが，頭の中で何度も思い返すものである。なぜなら，そういうことで，自分の子どもの何か新しい面に気づかされるからである。ただし，今回についていえば，あの経験は人前で演じられたことであり，それでなおのこと，私にとって意味深いのだった。

オ　私がまず最初に思ったのは，この若者のお母さんが見たら恥ずかしいと思うだろうなということだった。それから，ちょっとおもしろいなと思ったのは，私がどうしようもなく時代遅れだということだった。案外，老紳士からすれば，自分より二，三十歳年下の人から席を譲られたら侮辱だと思ったかもしれないのだ。私の想像だが，女性たちの方も，自分たちに対する礼儀正しい振る舞いを差別と考える可能性もある。さらにまた，その若いエリートサラリーマンだか投資銀行の行員だかは，たぶん女性たちと職を争わなければならなかったのだろう。競争相手になりそうな人に，どうして席を譲りたいと思うだろう。

正解は，不要となる段落＝エ，(a)＝イ，(c)＝ア。

◇イ → オ

　　これは，本文第 1，2 段落の内容に対する，もう 1 つのエピソードとしてまとめればよい。イの 'a young man' がオの第 1 文の 'his' と 'him' に対応するし，この 2 つの段落が共に「過去形」で書かれているのも，このセットを作る 1 つの手がかりとなっている。また，イの 'this incident' が第 1，2 段落の自分の子どもの出来事を指すので，このセットが最初の部分にふさわしい。

◇ア → ウ

　　これは，具体的なエピソードを受けて，一般化していく部分としてまとめる。アの 'much more than etiquette on public transportation' に対して，ウの 'the confusion extends to everything ...' という表現，さらに，アの 'our roles are

－　190　－

no longer closely dictated by whether ...' に対して，ウの 'the passing of the social contract' の対応が手がかりとなるだろう。また，この2つの段落が「現在形」で書かれているのも1つの手がかりだし，最終段落の内容につなぐものとして，このセットは後半がふさわしい。

◇以上の点から，「現代社会におけるマナーのあり方」について具体的なエピソードから一般化した内容を述べようとする文章になっているので，段落の並び順はイ→オ→ア→ウとなり，不要な段落はエとなる。

(4) ア　筆者は，時代が変わっても行儀作法は同じままだと考えている。

　イ　筆者は，現代社会では行儀作法がなくなってしまったと不満を述べている。

　ウ　筆者は，次世代の人が社会的な行動の新たなルールを見出すだろうと論じている。

　エ　筆者は，今日の社会における行儀作法は多くの思慮や努力を必要とすると信じている。

　オ　筆者は，既定の社会的ルールに沿って私たちがこれからも行動することを推奨している。

正解は**エ**。最終段落の内容と照らし合わせて決定すればよい。'require a good deal more imagination' や 'have to listen harder' 'be more sensitive' などの表現が，エの 'demand much thought and effort' に対応していると考える。なお，本文最終文の 'play it by ear' は，設問を解く際に知っている必要はないが「臨機応変に対応する」という意味のイディオムである。

解答

(1)　イ　　(2)　ア　　(3)　不要となる段落＝エ，(a)＝イ，(c)＝ア　　(4)　エ

2 (A) 考え方

(1) 訳文：「その地域は土壌が肥沃なため，農業利益が非常に高い」

語義：[地表部分で植物が育つところ]

正解は **soil**。地域全体で1つの土壌と考えるため，単数形に限る。

(2) 訳文：「そのような急激な物価上昇は誰も予測できなかっただろう」

語義：[何かが発生するだろうと予測した]

正解は **anticipated**。could have に続くものなので過去分詞形にすること（語義も "expected" となっている）。

(3) 訳文：「その3人の姉妹は，母親が亡くなった後，家を相続した」

語義：[死んだ人から遺産として受け取った]

－ 191 －

2012 年　　解答・解説

正解は **inherited**。「母親が死んだ後」の話であるし，語義が "recei<u>v</u>ed" となっていることからも，過去形で提示すること。

⑷　訳文：「警察は車を止め，不審な行動をとっていた数人の若者に職務質問した」

語義：[行動していた]

正解は **behaving**。語義にある "conduct oneself" という表現を知らないかもしれないが，英文の内容がわかりやすいので，behave にたどり着くことはできるだろう。were に続くもので，語義が <u>conducting</u> となっていることから，現在分詞形にすること。

⑸　訳文：「健康上特別な配慮を必要とする人の多くは，購入する食品の包装すべてに記載されている原材料表をチェックしなければならない」

語義：[料理を作るのに使用される食材]

正解は **ingredients**。この語は可算名詞であり，かつ本問では内容的に複数の原材料でないとおかしいので，複数形にする必要がある。

解 答

⑴　soil	⑵　anticipated	⑶　inherited
⑷　behaving	⑸　ingredients	

2 ⑻ 考え方

＜語数について＞

「50 ～ 60 語で」とあるからには，やはりこの指定より多くても少なくてもまずい。また，答案の最後に「○○ words」と書き添えよう。

＜答案を書く上での注意＞

人間は超能力者でもない限り他人の心を読むことはできないのであるから，「他人の心が読める世界」について記述する場合には当然仮定法を使って表現する必要がある。特に if 節を省略した英文の場合，would / could / might のいずれかが使われていないと減点対象になる。だからと言って答案全体をすべて仮定法にすればよいということではない。現実世界にも当てはまることなら直説法で書くのである。その使い分けが本問の場合重要になる。

＜内容面でのポイント＞

①　「考えられる結果」は1つでも2つ以上でも構わない。また，どうしてそのような結果が考えられるのか説得力を持たせるために，理由や説明を付記する必要がある。

②　「他人の心が読める」のが自分だけに発生することなのか，人類全体に発生する

－ 192 －

2012年　　解答・解説

事態なのかを考えておかなければならない。前者の場合，自分だけが他人の心を読むことができ，まわりの人間は相変わらず嘘と欺瞞の世界で暮らしていることになる。後者の場合は誰もが他人の心を読めるのだから，この世に嘘や欺瞞は存在せず，常に本音で接し合うことになる。つまり，どちらの世界を選ぶかで，答案に書く内容が全く変わってくるのである。

＜答案作成＞

答案の展開方法を具体例に沿って見てみよう。

［解答例1］

　［考えられる結果］＝いい友人を作るのがはるかに楽になる

　（理由）相手が嘘をついているかいないかがすぐにわかるから

　（＋α）常に本音しか語らない人と時間を過ごして，友人関係を結べばよい

　自分だけが人の心を読める存在になったと仮定し，それがもたらすメリットを［結果］として挙げ，続けてその理由を述べた。最後に，具体的な友人の作り方を示し，それが［結果］で書いたようにいかに簡単かを補足してある。

［解答例2］

　［考えられる結果］＝この世は退屈なところになる

　（具体例）友人にプレゼントを買う→相手が欲しがっているものがわかるから手間
　**　　　　　は省ける→相手にとって何が一番いいものかを考える楽しみがなくなる**

　これは「人の心が読める」のが個人的なこととも，人類全体に発生することとも解釈できる。また，この解答例は具体例を1つ挙げ，それを中心に心が読めることのデメリットを述べている。

［解答例3］

　［考えられる結果］＝人間社会に悲惨な結果をもたらす

　（＋α）良好な友人関係を築くには，時として本当の気持ちを隠す必要がある

　（［結果］の具体化1）人の心が読めたら，人間は互いに敵意を抱くであろう

　（具体化2）これは個人的にも国際的にも問題を起こす

　これは人類全体の場合。冒頭の「悲惨な結果」だけでは何のことだかわからないので，それを後で解き明かす形式にしてある。そして，なぜ人間関係が悪化するのかを説明するために，そもそも人間関係はどのようにして成り立っているのか，第2文で現状に触れている（したがって，ここだけ直説法になっている）。

— 193 —

2012年　　解答・解説

解 答 例

［解答例1］

If you could read other people's minds, you would be able to make good friends far more easily, because you would have no difficulty knowing whether people were lying or not. All you would have to do is to spend time with people who always said what they really meant and then make friends with them. (56 words)

［解答例2］

The world would be a boring place for you if you could read other people's minds. For instance, suppose you were going to buy a present for a friend. It would certainly save you trouble if you knew what she wanted, but you wouldn't be able to enjoy choosing something that you thought was best for her. (57 words)

［解答例3］

This would bring about disastrous consequences for human society. Sometimes we have to hide our true feelings in order to create good friendships. If mind reading were possible, people would often feel hostile towards each other. This would cause trouble not only at the personal level but also at the international level. (52 words)

4 **(A)** **全訳**　荒野で道に迷ったときはどうやって生き残ればよいか，ということについて書かれた記事を時折読むが，笑いを禁じえない。これらの記事を書く専門家は生存法については何でも知っているが，道に迷うことについてはほとんど何もわかっていない。私は道に迷うことの専門家だ。今までに9カ国，43の都市，7つの国有林，4つの国立公園，無数の駐車場，そして1つの旅客列車で私は迷ったことがある。妻が言うには，一度高いビルのエレベーターに乗ったときにも迷ったことがあるそうだ。ただそれは，13階が存在しないことに私が混乱した経験を元にした誇張である。（もし君が高所恐怖症なら，建物の階がしかるべき場所にちゃんとあることを確認したいと思うだろう。そして12階と14階の間に空間があることに対していろいろな言い訳など聞くつもりはないだろう。）　このような道に迷った経験すべてを生き延びてきたのだから，私も生存に関する相当な専門家ということになる。

— 194 —

2012年　解答・解説

考え方 (1) 「荒野で道に迷ったときはどうやって生き残ればよいか，ということについて書かれた記事を時折読むが，笑いを禁じえない」　正解は **is**。"when is lost" では主語がなくなってしまう。is を削除すれば接続詞 when の節中から we are が省略された形となり，正しい英文になる。ちなみに，副詞節中の主語が主文の主語と一致し，述語動詞が be 動詞の場合，この〈S be〉はしばしば省略される。本問は "how to survive" となっているのでわかりにくいが，これは意味的に "how we should survive when we are lost" ということなので，we are を省略したのである。

(2) 「これらの記事を書く専門家は生存法については何でも知っているが，道に迷うことについてはほとんど何もわかっていない」　正解は **it**。next to nothing で「ほとんど何もない」（= almost nothing）という意味の慣用句。ここでは "know everything about survival" と "know next to nothing about getting lost" が対比されている。

(3) 「今までに9カ国，43の都市，7つの国有林，4つの国立公園，無数の駐車場，そして1つの旅客列車で私は迷ったことがある。妻が言うには，一度高いビルのエレベーターに乗ったときにも迷ったことがあるそうだ」　正解は **of**。countless は「数え切れないほど多くの」という意味の形容詞なので，直接 parking lots を修飾すればよい。この設問はおそらく，regardless of（「…に関係なく」という意味の慣用句）の連想で，*countless of* という表現もあるのでは，と受験生に勘違いさせることをねらったものだろう。

(4) 「そして12階と14階の間に空間があることに対していろいろな言い訳など聞くつもりはないだろう」　正解は **all**。be about to - で「まさに-しようとしている」という意味の慣用句であることは有名だが，be not about to - で「-する気は一切ない」という意味がある。内容的には，ここは筆者がある建物に13階がなくて混乱した経験を語っている部分。下から数えて13番目には13階があるのが当然なのに，たとえば「13は縁起が悪いから12の次を14にしました」などと言い訳されても腹立たしくて聞く耳を持てない，という筆者の怒り，および筆者が現場で混乱したことを正当化しようとしているのである。単に語法だけでなく，これらの内容も踏まえないと正解を導き出すことは不可能だろう。

(5) 「このような道に迷った経験すべてを生き延びてきたのだから，私も生存に関する相当な専門家ということになる」　正解は **Ever**。ever since という表現は確かに存在するが，これは since が「…以来」という意味の場合に限る。また，この意味で接続詞 since が使われているのなら，主文は当然完了形になっているべきだが，本問では it follows（that の節中も I am）と現在形になっている。さらに，「…以来」

— 195 —

2012年　　解答・解説

で直訳しても内容的に合わない。以上３点から，この since は「理由」を表している
のではと考える。「理由」の since ならば，ever をつけることはできない。注意とし
ては，答案では必ず Ever と大文字にすること。

解 答

(1) is	(2) it	(3) of	(4) all	(5) Ever

4 **(B)** **全訳** イシグロには音楽的な側面があるということは恐らくあまり知ら
れていないだろう。彼にインタビューしたのは彼と知り合って数年経った後であった
が，その時点では彼の持つ音楽的な側面については，たとえ気づいていたとしてもぼ
んやりとだけであった。これは彼が自分のことをあまり外には表さないことを示すよ
い例である。イシグロはピアノとギターを弾く。しかも両方ともうまい。いったい何
本のさまざまなギターを今彼が実際に持っているかははっきりとしないが，本数が２
桁に達していても驚きはしない。彼の妻のロルナは歌を歌い楽器の演奏もする。そし
て彼の娘もそうだ。イシグロの家で夜になると音楽の演奏会が開かれることも全然珍
しいことではないにちがいない。

　私が自分の人生で悔やんでいる数少ないことの１つは，音楽のきちんとした基礎知
識を習得したことがないということだ。音楽教育を受けたこともないし，音楽を身に
つけることを可能に，あるいはほぼ確実にしてくれるような「音楽好きな家庭」で育っ
たわけでもなかった。そして音楽というのは自分とは違う「音楽の才能のある」人た
ちがやることだと，常にかなりたやすく決めつけていた。一方，本を読んで育つこと
がなかった大多数の人々は，物を書くということは自分とは違う「作家に向いた」人
たちがやることだと恐らく感じていたのであろうが，私はそうした気持ちになったこ
とは一度もない。

　しかし，物を書くことと音楽をこのように対比するのはおかしい。というのは，物
を書くことに関わる私の本能の多くは実際のところ音楽的なものだと私にはますます
感じられてきており，執筆と音楽は根本的にはそう離れてはいないと私は思うからだ。
物語の基本要素（間の取り方，テンポ，流れ，緊張と解放，テーマの反復）は音楽の
基本要素でもある。そしてリズム（話を構成する大きなリズム，ないしは，段落を構
成する小さなリズム）がなければ文章などあり得ないのである。

考え方 (1) 「**彼が自分について多くを語らないことの好例**」

　１．**a good example of ...**「…の好例」「…を示すよい例」のように言葉を加え，
わかりやすくしてもよい。

— 196 —

2012 年　　解答・解説

2．**how he doesn't give much away**「彼が自分について多く語らないということ」　ポイントは give away と how の 2 つである。give away は「〈正体・秘密など〉を表す，漏らす」の意の熟語。よって，he doesn't give much away で「彼は自分の正体をあまり明かさない」→「彼は自分について多くを語らない」の意となる。次に，how はその直後に how が修飾する形容詞や副詞が置かれている場合は「程度」を表すが〔(例) He told me *how honest* he was.（彼は私に自分がいかに正直であるかを語った）〕，下線部の how の直後にはそうした形容詞や副詞はない。よってこの how を「程度」に解釈することはできない。一般に how の直後に「主語＋動詞」が現れるときは，how は「方法」を示すが〔(例) I don't know *how he did* it.（私は彼がそれをどのようにやったのか知らない）〕，下線部を「どのように彼が多くを語らなかったかということの好例」と訳すのは明らかに不自然である。そのような場合には，how を意味的にほとんど that と変わらぬ接続詞「…ということ」として解釈すると適切な意味になる場合がある〔(例) He told me *how* he was honest.（彼は自分は正直だと私に語った）／ It is good *how* he always remembers my birthday.（彼がいつも私の誕生日を覚えていてくれるのがうれしい）〕。よって，この下線部も「彼が自分について多くを語らないことの好例」などと訳出すればよい。

⑵　「一方で，**読書に親しまずに育った非常に多くの人**は，**物を書くことなど自分以外の『作家になりそうな』人がするものだ**と恐らく感じているが，**私はそのように感じたことは一度もない**」

1．**I've never felt, on the other hand, ...**「一方，私は…を感じたことはない」

2．**though a great many people ... have perhaps felt it**「きわめて多くの人たちはそれを恐らく感じたが」　a great (= a good) は全体で「かなり，とても」の意の副詞。it は後続する 4．の that 節の内容を指している。

3．**who didn't grow up reading books**「本を読んで育っていない〔成長期に本を読んでいない〕〈きわめて多くの人たち〉」　reading ... は「補語」として働き「どのような状況で成長していったか」を説明している（「付帯状況を表す分詞構文」と考えてもよい）。(例) Mary stood there *watching* him.（メアリーはそこに立って彼を見つめていた）

4．**that writing is what those other, ... people do**「物を書くということは自分とは違う…な人たちがやることだということ」　この that 節は 1．の felt の目的語として働いている。節内は writing (S) is (V) what ... (C) とつながる第 2 文型。those は「あの例の」といったニュアンスで用いられているが，特に訳出しなくてもよい。other は「自分以外の」の意。なお，設問の指示より訳出の際には 2．の it の

— 197 —

<u>2012 年　　解答・解説</u>

内容を明示する必要があるが，だからと言ってこの 4. の that 節を 2 回訳す必要はないであろう。2. を「とても多くの人々は，書くことは…と感じたが」と訳し，その部分を訳文上で先行させたなら，I've never felt ... that writing is ... は「私はそう感じたことはない」でよい。

5．**writerly**「作家らしい」　なじみのない単語であろうが，前出の musical と対比して意味を類推してもらいたい。musical home と言えば「音楽が頻繁に流され，それに親しんでいる家庭／音楽的才能のある人たちが暮らしている家庭」を想像することはそれほど難しくはないはずである。同様に musical people といえば「音楽に対して興味や才能を持っている人／音楽に慣れ親しんでいる人」であろう。そこから類推して「物を書くということに対して興味や才能を持っている」などと処理してもよいだろう。

(3)「リズムがなければ，物を書くということはどうなってしまうのだろうか？」

where という疑問副詞が，ここでは「どんな状態（状況，立場）に」の意を表していることに注意。(例) *Where* would we be without technology?（科学技術がないと私たちはどうなるだろうか）／ *Where* will we be if an earthquake occurs?（地震が起こったら私たちはどんなことになるだろう）

解答

> (1)　彼が自分について多くを語らないことの好例
>
> (2)　一方で，読書に親しまずに育った非常に多くの人は，物を書くことなど自分以外の「作家になりそうな」人がするものだと恐らく感じているが，私はそのように感じたことは一度もない。
>
> (3)　リズムがなければ物を書くということはどうなるのであろうか？

5　**全訳**　1 ヵ月間，サリーを着る。大したことではないはずだったのだが，実際には大したこととなった。なにしろ，私はインドでサリーを着ている女性たちに囲まれて育ったし，私の母はサリーを着たまま寝ていたほどだった。

インドでは，サリーは大人が着るものだ。私も 18 歳になってから，美しいサリーをときおり着たが，それは，結婚式や祝祭日の折に，そして寺院に出かけるときにであった。しかし，絹のサリーをインド式パーティーへ着ていくのとは，勝手がちがう。ニューヨーク暮らしをしながら，それも洋服を 10 年間着た後で，毎日サリーを着ることを決行するのは，とんでもないことに思われた。この私にさえも。

サリーというのは，6 ヤードの布地をたたんで，優美ではあるが実用的でない服に

— 198 —

したものだ。着くずれしやすくて，いつなんどき，ほどけてしまってもおかしくない。着こなし方がよいと，この上なく優美で女性らしさのあるものである。

　そうはいっても，犠牲にしなくてはならないこともある。赤信号に変わる寸前に，通りを走って横断するわけにはもういかなかった。サリーを着ていると，歩幅を前より短くするしかなかった。胸を張って，姿勢に気を遣わなければならなかった。混雑している地下鉄の車内へと押し入って乗るわけにもいかなかった。誰かがうっかり私のサリーを引っ張ってしまうといけないから。片手にはスーパー帰りの袋を4つ，バランスよく持ちながら，もう一方の手で，使い勝手のよいポケットから家のカギを取り出すなんていうこともできなかった。最初の1週間が終わるまでには，ストレスがたまり，自分に腹が立っていた。私は一体何を示そうとしているのだろうか。

　サリーを毎日着るという考えは，私には比較的新しいことだった。大学生時代は，インドのたいていの女の子がきまってサリーを着始める年代だが，私は芸術専攻の学生としてアメリカで勉強していて，他の学生たちとまったく同じように，カジュアルな服装をしていた。結婚してからは，もっとファッショナブルな服装を試すような主婦になった。要するに，長年にわたって，私はアメリカ人のような話し方，歩き方，ふるまい方をしようとしていた。

　その後，私はニューヨークに引っ越して，母親になった。3歳になった娘に，インド的な価値観や伝統を教えたかった。宗教の点でも（我が家はヒンドゥー教の家庭だ），食習慣の点でも（うちはベジタリアンだ），年中行事のお祭りごとの点でも，娘は遊び友だちとは根本的にちがうことになるとわかっていたのだから。サリーを毎日着ることは，自分らしさ［独自の味わい］を保ちながら，人種のるつぼに溶け込むことができるということを娘に見せてあげる私なりの方法だった。

　サリーを着ようと決めたのは，娘のためを思ってというだけではなかった。自分を周囲に合わせようとすることがいやになっていたのだった。アメリカ人の歌手で，私のお気に入りのインド人の歌手ほどに，深く私に語りかけた人は1人もいなかった。アメリカの人気の歌を，私のお気に入りのインドの歌ほどに，私がすんなりと歌えたことは一度もなかった。アメリカの食べ物を美味しく食べてはいたものの，インド食なしでは4日ともたなかった。サリーと，それから真っ赤なビンディーで，私の民族性を示す頃合いだった。私は移民になろうとしていたのだが，あくまでも私なりのやり方で，と思っていた。今度は，アメリカが私に合わせる番だった。

　徐々に，サリーを着るのがしっくりしてきた。サリーは私の掌中に，私はサリーの掌中にあった。混雑した書店をさっそうと歩いていると，見ず知らずの人たちが私を凝視した。目を合わせて微笑みかけてくる人もいた。最初のうちは，見世物扱いに腹

— 199 —

<u>2012 年　　解答・解説</u>

が立った。それから私はふと思った。ひょっとすると，あの人たちは，私を見て，インドでのすばらしい休日や，お気に入りのインド料理の本を思い出したのかもしれない。店員たちは，私に話しかけるときに，はっきりと単語を発音してくれた。どこへ行っても，サリーを着ているおかげで私が権威でもあるかのように，インドについての質問に私は立ち止まることになった。タイムズスクウェアの近くにいた日本人の女性なんて，一緒に写真を撮ってもいいですかと尋ねてきた。ある観光客は，私のことも観光客だと思っていた。それも家から出てすぐのところで。

　しかし，思いがけない長所があった。通りに出てタクシーを止めようとした瞬間に，インド人のタクシー運転手が，さっと車線変更をして，私の目の前で止まった。セントラルパークで娘がジャングルジムの高い所に上ったとき，私はサリーの裾をまとめて娘についていこうとした。マリリン・モンローのドレスみたいに裾がふくらんでしまうことがないように願いながら。近くに立っていたパパさんたちのうちの１人が，私が困っていることを見てとって，娘の後について登ってくれると申し出てくれた。ニューヨークの騎士？　私だから？　それともサリーだから？

　なにより良かったのは，家族が賛同してくれたことだった。夫がほめてくれた。両親は自慢に思ってくれた。色鮮やかなサリーを私が出してきたとき，娘は感服の溜め息をもらした。娘を腕の中でやさしく抱きしめていると，サリーを清新にするために夜の間に私が使っていた甘い香りのハーブの小さな香袋からの匂いが，布地の襞（ひだ）からただよって，娘はすやすやと眠りこんでしまった。こうやって赤ちゃんを抱きゆすったインドの母親たちの脈々と続く伝統に，私もその一員として連なっている気持ちになった。

　やがて，決めていた１ヵ月が終わった。自ら課した義務は終わりを迎えようとしていた。解放感ではなく，不安という鋭い痛みを私は感じた。自分のサリーが楽しいと思い始めていたのだった。

　アメリカで生きていくにはサリーは実用的じゃないのよ，と私は自分に言い聞かせた。これからも着ることは着るけど，毎日っていうことじゃなしに。実用的でカジュアルな服装に戻る潮時だった。

【考え方】

　(1)　正解は，アの extreme「極端な；普通では考えられない」。単語の知識の問題。本文の outrageous は「とっぴな；とんでもない」という意味であり，類義の語は１つしかない。かりに outrageous を知らなかったとしても，空所補充問題だと考えて，ア extreme を選ぶことはできただろう。

　(2)　正解は，(2a) コ，(2b) ア，(2c) ク。

－　200　－

<u>2012 年　　解答・解説</u>

(2a) は，後続の文に，今まで出来たことなのにサリーを着たことで出来なくなったことが書かれていることから，コの sacrifices「犠牲（になったこと）」を選べばよい。

(2b) は，後続の文に，サリーを着たことで良かったことが書かれているので，アの advantages「長所；利点」を選べばよい。対応する動詞が were になっているので，イの assistance は不可。(2a) と (2b) は離れた箇所にあるが，内容的な対比になっていることにも注意しておきたい。

(2c) は，空所を含む文を訳すと「自ら課した（　　）は終わりを迎えようとしていた」となり，本文全体から考えれば，クの obligation「義務」を選べばよい。対応する動詞が was になっているので，ウの attempts は不可。

(3)　正解は，(3a) ウ，(3b) キ，(3c) ケ。

(3a) では，サリーを着たことで筆者が「肩を（　　）しなければならなかった」とあり，具体的動作を思い描いてみれば，throw my shoulders back「肩を後ろにそらす→背筋をきちんと伸ばす」と考えられ，ウ back を選ぶことになる。

(3b) は，「混雑している地下鉄の車内へと乗り込む」ということなので，キ into を選ぶ。直前の squeeze を知らなくても正解は得られる。

(3c) は，pull out ... keys ... (　　) the other (hand) というつながりに注目して，ケ with を入れることになる。

(4)　正解は，(4a) オ，(4b) ウ，(4c) イ。

(4a) は，空所を含む文の意味「私は何を（　　）しようとしているのか」から考えて，オ prove「証明する」を入れればよい。ここでの prove の使い方は慣用的である。(例) What are you trying to *prove*?「何が言いたいのですか？；どういうおつもりですか？」 ただし，文章全体が筆者の実験的試みであることから考えても，正解にたどりつけただろう。

(4b) では，空所を含む文が「私は（　　）しようとすることに飽きていた」という意味であることから，空所以前を参考にすることが求められる。直前の段落末尾にある melt into the pot「人種のるつぼに溶け込む」という表現を参考にして，ウ fit in「溶け込む」を選ぶ。なお，ここでの in は副詞扱いなので目的語は不要。

(4c) では，サリーを毎日着用する試みを終了しようとする筆者が，サリーのことが気に入り始めている局面だということを理解して，イ enjoy「楽しむ」を選ぶ。

(4)の３問とも，文法・語法的な空所補充ではなく，内容理解が求められていることにも注意しておきたい。

(5)　正解はカ。(5a)を含む段落では，アメリカに溶け込もうとしているインド人としての筆者の思いが書かれていることから，immigrant「移民」が入ることになる。

<u>2012 年　　解答・解説</u>

(5b) よりも (5c) の方が考えやすい。サリーを着たことで自分が（　5c　）になったかのように，インドについて尋ねられる，とあることから，(5c) には authority「権威」を入れればよい。(5b) に入る exhibit「見世物；さらしもの」の名詞としての用法は，受験生にはなじみがないであろう。

(6)　正解は「**ある観光客は，私のことも観光客だと思っていた。それも家から出てすぐのところで**」。

1．A tourist had thought that ...　a tourist は「ある観光客［旅行者］」と訳す。不定冠詞がついているので，直前の one Japanese lady とは別人であることに注意。過去完了形になっているのは「ある時点まで」ということであるが，訳出に神経質になる必要はないであろう。

2．I was one, too　ここでは one = a tourist であるのは明らか。

3．just steps from my home　直訳すれば「私の家からほんの数歩のところで」となるが「家からすぐ近くなのに」と訳してもよい。「自宅のすぐ近くだっていうのに観光客だと思われてしまった」というユーモラスな雰囲気。

(7)　正解は**ア**。下線部そのものは「ニューヨークの騎士？」ということであるが，文脈を考えればよい。困っている筆者に手を差し伸べてくれる男性がいたということから，ア「ニューヨークで見知らぬ人を助けてくれるほどやさしい男性がいることに筆者は驚いている」を選べばよい。イ「高貴な生まれの男性が，そんなに大胆にニューヨークで行動するということに筆者は驚いている」，ウ「ニューヨークでは美しい女性を助ける機会が男性にはたくさんあるのだろうかと筆者は思っている」，エ「ニューヨークで，ある父親が自分自身の子どもたちより筆者の娘を優先してくれたことに，筆者は困惑している」，オ「ニューヨークで，ある男性が自分とは外見が異なる人と知り合いになろうとしていることの熱心さに，筆者はショックを受けている」は，いずれも下線部の説明として成り立たない。

(8)　正解は**ア**の but not every day「しかし毎日ではない」。空所直後に，筆者が洋服に戻ると書かれているので，サリーを着るのは毎日ではなくなると考える。ちなみに，オの only to show I am an Indian mother「インド系の母親であるということを示すためだけに」を選んでしまうと，サリーを着ることは着るのだが，それはもう，ただひたすらインド系の母親であることを示すことだけが目的だという意味になり，西洋式の服に戻ることにはつながらないので誤り。イ「解放されたと感じるために」，ウ「どれほど不便であっても」，エ「そして甘いハーブの香りを楽しむ」は，いずれも前後関係にまったく合わない。

(9)　正解は**ア**。「インド人としてのアイデンティティーを示したくて筆者はサリー

－ 202 －

を着ることにした」は，第6段落の「サリーを毎日着ることは，自分らしさを保ちな
がら，人種のるつぼに溶け込むことができるということを娘に見せてあげる私なりの
方法だった」という記述に一致する。イ「サリーがとても優美で女性らしさがあるの
で，筆者は当然のごとく，優雅にふるまった」は，下線部(7)を含む段落（＝第9段落）
で，筆者がサリーの裾をまとめてジャングルジムに登ろうとしたという記述と一致し
ない。ウ「最初はサリーを着るのがいやだったが，徐々に筆者はインドの専門家になっ
た」は，空所(5c)を含む文で，as if を使った仮定法で「まるで権威であるかのように」
とあることと一致しない。エ「店員が筆者に非常に丁寧に話しかけたのは，サリーを
着ているのを見て，敬意を持って応対しなくてはならないと思ったからだった」は，「敬
意を持って応対」以下の箇所が本文にないので不可。

解 答

(1) ア
(2) (2a) コ　　(2b) ア　　(2c) ク
(3) (3a) ウ　　(3b) キ　　(3c) ケ
(4) (4a) オ　　(4b) ウ　　(4c) イ
(5) カ
(6) ある観光客は，私のことも観光客だと思っていた。それも家から出てすぐの
　　ところで。
(7) ア
(8) ア
(9) ア

－ 203 －

解答・解説

1 **(A)** **全訳** 基礎科学に慣れ親しむことは、これまで以上に重要になっているのだが、伝統的な科学の基礎課程では必要な理解が得られているとは必ずしも言えない。知識そのものは、ますます分野間の境を越えつつあるにもかかわらず、大学教授は世の中で話題になっていることよりも、自分の専門科目の方法論と歴史を中心に授業を組み立てるきらいがある。むしろ科学の課程は、学問分野よりも実質的な内容を中心に組み立てるべきなのだ。つまり、物理学、天文学、化学よりも物質的宇宙を、生物学よりも生物を中心にすべきなのである。

　心理学の示すところによると、人間の頭は、事実が物語やメンタルマップや理論といった概念構造の中に織り込まれている時に一番よく理解できるようである。頭の中で相互に繋がっていない事実はウェブ上でリンクされていないページのようなもので、それは存在しないと言ってもよい。常々望まれていることだが、科学というものは、知識が学生たちの頭の中で有機的に繋がるよう教えるべきなのである。

　授業を組み立てる枠組みとして時間を利用してみるというのも、1つの手である。宇宙の始まりとなったビッグバンは、物理学の中心的テーマの始まりとなっている。太陽系と地球の形成は、地質学のような地球科学の始まりであった。生物学は生命の出現とともに生まれた。そして、このように教えるようにすれば、時間という視点で構成された科学の教育課程が世界史そして文明や思想の歴史を教えることにも自然につながり、そうすることによって、ことによると一般教養課程全般の統合をもたらすかもしれないのだ。

考え方

　従来東京大学の要約問題では「主張型」の文章が素材として用いられていて、誰かの視点・考え方が含まれている。それを抽出し、解答の中心に据えるのが最も大きなポイントである。

　本年度は「科学教育のあり方と展望」がテーマの文章（245 words）で、全体のアウトラインはこのようになる。

— 206 —

<u>2011 年　　解答・解説</u>

［アウトライン1］

〈第1段落〉
(1)　従来の科学教育では必要な理解が得られているとは言えない。
(2)　知識は分野の境界線を越えているのに，分野中心の授業になっている。
(3)　科学教育は分野よりも内容を軸にすべきだ。

〈第2段落〉
(1)　事実は概念構造に有機的に組み込まれると，よく理解できる。
(2)　頭の中で相互に関係していない知識は，存在しないに等しい。
(3)　科学は知識が有機的に繋がるように教えるべきだ。

〈第3段落〉
(1)　時間を科学教育の枠組みに取り入れるべきだ。
(2)　ビッグバンは物理の中心的テーマの起源となっている。etc.
(3)　一般教養課程全体の統合にもつながり得る。

　これを，もう少し抽象化して単純化すると，この文章は次のような構造になっていることがわかる（第1，第2段落のそれぞれ第2文は前文の補強だと考えてよいし，第3段落の第2文は例だと考えてよい）。

［アウトライン2］

〈第1段落〉
A.　科学教育の現実（第1〜2文）
B.　科学教育のあるべき姿（第3文）
　　＝分野ではなく内容を中心に授業を構成すべき

〈第2段落〉
A.　事実の理解について（1〜2）
B.　科学教育のあるべき姿（3）
　　＝知識が有機的に繋がるよう教えるべき

〈第3段落〉
A.　1つの提案（1〜2）
　　＝時間を（科学）教育の枠組みとして使う
B.　展望（3）
　　＝教養課程全般の統合になり得る

　このラインに沿って各段落のA，Bの要素をすべて含めると，次のような文章にな

— 207 —

<u>2011 年　　解答・解説</u>

る。当然ながら，これでは指定された字数には収まらず，答案にはならない。

［草案 1］

> 　従来の科学教育では十分な理解をさせているとは言えない。知識は境界を越えるものなのに，科学の授業は専門分野を中心として行われている。それよりも科学教育は学問分野より内容を中心とするべきだ。事実の理解が最もよくできるのは，事実が概念構造の中に関連性を持って組み込まれる時であるから，科学は知識が有機的に繋がるように教えるべきだ。そのためには時間を科学教育の枠組みとするのも手で，そのようにすれば，他の分野も含めて一般教養課程全般の統合になるかもしれない。(223 字)

　ここから，さらに切りつめてみよう（もちろん，試験時間中にこんな作業をやっている余裕はないので，アウトラインのメモを書きながら頭の中で処理しなければならない）。要約問題で複数の段落がある場合は，全ての段落の内容に触れるのが原則であるが，この文章で筆者が言いたいことの方向性は，第 3 段落にあると考えてよい。これを「時間を教育の枠組みとして使えば教養課程全体の統合につながり得る。」とまとめると 32 文字になる。残りの字数を考えると，第 1，第 2 段落については，それぞれ［アウトライン 2］のポイント B を中心にまとめるしかない。

［草案 2］

> 　科学教育は，学問分野よりも内容を中心に構成すべきだ。理解を促すため知識が有機的にまとまるよう教えるべきであり，そのために時間を教育の枠組みとして使えば，一般教養課程全体の統合につながり得る。(95 字)

　これでもまだ制限字数を大幅に超えているので，第 1，第 2 段落の内容は思い切って圧縮してまとめざるをえない。テーマが「科学教育のあり方」であるから，【科学教育は，[A] であり [B] であるべきだ。そのために [C] すると，[D] になり得る。】というフォーマットでまとめておけば，全体を網羅し，かつ，文章のトーンをすくい上げる答案になるであろう（なお，第 1，第 2 段落にある understanding (understands) を含めたのが解答例 2，3 である）。

解答例

> ［解答例 1］　科学教育は分野よりも内容を中心にし，知識が有機的につながるよう教えるべきだ。そのために時間を枠組みとして使うのも手で，それは教養課程全体の統合にもつながり得る。(80 字)

－ 208 －

2011年　　解答・解説

[解答例2]　科学教育は学生の理解を促すよう，特定分野を超えた知識の整理を目指すことが望ましい。そのために時間を枠組みとして使えば教養課程全体の統合につながり得る。(75字)

[解答例3]　科学教育では，実質内容を中心にし，理解のために知識が有機的に繋がるよう教えるべきだ。そのために時間を教育に組み込めば，教養課程全体の統合にもつながり得る。(77字)

1 **(B)** **全訳**　僕は16歳です。先日の夜，週末に何をしようかとか，それを誰としようかとか，大切な人間関係上の問題について，思いめぐらしていたときに，両親が未来についてキッチンで話をしているのがたまたま耳に入りました。父は動揺していました。父や母が，そして想像するに多くの親が心配しそうな，僕がどの大学へ行くかとか，それが家からどれくらいの距離にあるかとか，いくらくらいかかりそうなのかといった，普通の話題ではありません。そうではなくて，父の世代が僕の世代へバトンタッチしつつある世界，暗く困難な未来（まあ，そもそも未来があるとしてですが）を持つと父が懸念する世界について父は動揺していたのです。

※空所×5

　その夜，僕と僕の世代に対して未来が何をもたらすのかについて父が不安を述べているのを聞きながら，僕は父を抱きしめたくなりました。そして父がいつも僕に言ってくれたことを言いたくなりました。「心配しなくていいよ，パパ。明日の方がもっと良い日になるよ」

選択肢全訳

ア　父は言った。「これから来るのは，何百万人もの命を奪う伝染性の病気，ひどいエネルギー危機，恐ろしい世界的規模の不況，そして，怒りのあまり引き金を引かれる核爆発だ」

イ　僕が小さな子どもだったときからずっと，僕がうまくいかなかった日にいつも，父は僕を抱きしめて断言してくれました。「明日はもっと良い日になるさ」って。あるとき父に確認してみました。「どうしてわかるの？」　父は言いました。「わかるものはわかるのさ」　僕は父の言うことを信じました。僕の曾祖父母がそれを信じ，祖父母がそれを信じ，そして僕もそれを信じるのです。そして今，突如として僕にははっきりとわかりました。父に気分を良くしてもらうようにするのは，僕の

— 209 —

番だっていうことを。

ウ　僕は，祖父母と曽祖父母が生涯で経験した恐ろしい物事のいくつかを考えました。
2つの世界大戦，疫病，人種差別，核爆弾などです。でも，彼らは他の，もっと良
いことも経験しました。2つの世界大戦の終結，新薬，市民権法の成立などです。
ボストン・レッドソックスがワールドシリーズを勝ちとるのも経験しました。二度
です。

エ　同様にして，僕の世代も良いことを経験するだろうと思います。僕たちは，次の
ような時を経験するでしょう。エイズが治り，ガンが撲滅される時，中東に平和が
訪れる時，シカゴ・カブスがワールドシリーズを勝ちとる時（たぶん一度だけです）
を。今の僕には信じられないようなことを経験するでしょうが，それは，祖父が
16歳だったときに月ロケットがそうであり，父が16歳だったときにインターネッ
トがそうであったのと同じです。

オ　そういった物事のうちで最も恐ろしいものの1つは，第一次世界大戦でした。私
の曽祖父母は元々はスウェーデン出身ですが，その国は第一次世界大戦に参戦して
いませんでした。アメリカにやってきて数年以内に，曽祖父は軍務局に呼び出され，
フランス戦線に送り出されました。後になって幾分回復しましたが，そしてそれは，
彼が野球に見出した大きな喜びのおかげでもありましたが，フランス戦線で彼がし
た経験は，彼の生涯にわたって暗い影を死ぬまで投げかけたのでした。

カ　リビングのソファに寝そべって，父の言葉を聞き，父が描写する未来について気
にし始めていると，ふと，我が家系の何枚かの昔の写真を僕は見ていました。士官
学校の制服を着た祖父の写真がありました。祖父は1942年の学生，戦時クラスで
した。その写真の横には，ヨーロッパから移民してきた曽祖父母の何枚かの写真。
それらの写真を見ていると，僕は気分がずっと楽になりました。明日は今日よりも
良いだろうというのが僕の考えです。僕の世代が成長して入っていく世界は，悪く
なるのではなく，良くなるだろうということです。あの写真は，僕の理解を助けて
くれました。

[考え方]

　まず，整序ゾーンの前後，つまり本文の第1段落と最終段落が，語り手と父との関
係であることに留意しておこう。最初に語り手は父の言葉を偶然に耳にする。そして，
最後には，父を抱きしめて言葉を投げかけたくなっている。

　整序ゾーンには，父が登場する段落もあれば，祖父母や曽祖父母が登場する段落も
あるので，登場人物の移り変わりに注意してみる。すると，段落カの冒頭で，父の言
葉から，祖父や曽祖父母の写真へと移っており，段落エの最後に父が再登場する。

2011 年　　解答・解説

　残りの段落のうちで，ウとエが対比的な記述になっており，しかもエの冒頭の In the same way を考え合わせると，ウ → エのつながりがわかる。この 2 つの段落の趣旨は，世の中には悪いことばかりでなく，良いこともたくさんあるということである。

　父親の言葉の具体的内容が述べられている段落アが，本文冒頭の直後につながること，つまり整序ゾーンの冒頭に来ることに気づくのは比較的容易であろう。

　以上の点を考え合わせれば，ア → カ → ウ → エ → イとなって，正解が得られる。

　なお，段落オは，冒頭の those things の指示内容が不明であること，「悪いこと」しか書かれていないこと，曽祖父母の記述の仕方が他の段落（とくにカ）と円滑につながらないことなどから考えて不要な段落だとわかる。

　参考までに表にすると，以下のとおり。

本文冒頭段落 ア	父の言葉を偶然耳にする 具体的な父の言葉
カ ウ エ	祖父と曽祖父母の写真を見て思いをはせ，認識が改まる 祖父母と曽祖父母の世代…悪かったことも良かったことも 私の世代…これからも良いことがあるだろう
イ 本文最終段落	父からの言葉「もっと良くなるよ」を今度は僕から父へ 父を抱きしめて言ってあげたい

解答

不要となる段落：オ　　(b)に来る段落：カ　　(d)に来る段落：エ

1 (C) **【全訳】**　カフェインは世界で最も広く使用されている薬品で，国際商品市場で取引されるコーヒーの価値を凌いでいるのは石油のみである。しかし人類史の大半を通じ，コーヒーはエチオピア高原の狭い地域を除いては知られていなかった。16 世紀後半にオスマン帝国を旅していた数名の旅行者が最初に認識してから，コーヒーはヨーロッパにおいて，好奇心旺盛な科学者や商人の中で定着していった。キリスト教世界における最初のコーヒーハウスは，1650 年代初頭になってようやくロンドンで開店した。

　コーヒーハウスはコーヒーを売るために存在するのではあるが，このような基本的商業活動をする場所だと単純化して考えることはできない。サミュエル・ジョンソン

－ 211 －

2011 年　　解答・解説

は，その有名な辞書で，コーヒーハウスを「コーヒーを売り，客に新聞を提供する娯楽の場」と定義した。ジョンソンの言によれば，コーヒーハウスはコーヒーを売るだけではなく，思想であり，生活様式であり，社交様式であり，哲学なのである。しかしコーヒーハウスは，コーヒーとは切っても切れない縁にある。依然としてコーヒーは支配的な記号なのである。コーヒーハウスが繁盛してコーヒーは大衆向けの商品となった。ここに行けば緊張感を持つものだ，そしてそれゆえ真面目に振る舞い，活発な議論をするものだという感覚ゆえに，コーヒーハウスは現代の都市生活と風習における独特の位置づけを得ているわけだが，これは酒場とは極めて大きな対照を成すものである。

　コーヒーハウスの歴史は，ビジネス史ではない。初期のコーヒーハウスには，商業面の記録がほとんど残っていない。しかし歴史家は，その他現存する史料をずいぶんと利用してきた。公文書には，政府機関のスパイがコーヒーハウスで聞いた会話の報告が多々含まれている。初期の新聞でも，その広告や報道記事の中で，さらに史料が得られる。17，18 世紀に書かれた有名な日記でも，当時コーヒーハウスが社交の中心であったことが示されている。

　しかしコーヒーハウスの生活世界を語る場合に，最も説得力のある証拠の多くは文学に絡むものである。　ア　コーヒーハウスでの経験が持つ多様性，そしてその特質によって，コーヒーハウスは相当な量の風刺的ジョークとユーモアの主題となった。　イ　文学として考えれば，この分野の一連の文章は面白く刺激的であり，熱狂と怒りの潮流によって活発になり，特定かつ地域限定の論争に対する言及に満ちている。　ウ　コーヒーハウスの描写において，現代の都市生活におけるコーヒーの位置づけを確立させ，定着させたのは，何よりもこのような文学的資料であった。　エ　描写対象を誇張し，愚行・悪行を際だたせ，題材を極めて華麗な文体で描くのが風刺文学の本質である。　オ　それでもやはり，コーヒーハウスの風刺は文学作品のみならず，史料とみなすこともできる。あの野卑な風刺は単にコーヒーハウス人生を批評したものではない。それは，そこに集う人々の会話の一部であり，都市の社会生活について今も続いている議論における発言の 1 つなのである。

考え方

　(1)　正解は(d)。設問に「取り除いても段落の展開に最も影響の小さいもの」とあるので，この段落全体の趣旨に沿って考える。第 1 文に「コーヒーハウスはコーヒーを売る場所だが，それだけに単純化して考えることはできない」とあり，これがトピックセンテンスに相当するものなので，「コーヒーハウスがどのようなものか，どのような位置づけになるものか」に触れていないものを選ぶ。そうすると，(c)と(d)が候補

― 212 ―

2011 年　　解答・解説

になるが，(c)には Yet があり，これを削除すると(d)の文が唐突に現れることになるので，(d)の方を削除可能と考える。

(2)　正解は**エ**。この文は「しかしながら，この証拠（史料）を使うことは簡単ではなく，歴史家を長年困らせてきた」という意味。この段落は「コーヒーハウスの位置づけを知る史料として風刺文学が有効である」ということを第 1 文から空所エの手前までで述べている。挿入すべき文の however と troubled historians に注目し，　エ　に入れると，その直後の文 (It is ...) が理由付けとしても成立する。

(3)　正解は**ア**。

ア「17 世紀半ばを過ぎると，コーヒーハウスは近代ヨーロッパの都市生活の社会的中心となった」

イ「コーヒーハウス文化は，17，18 世紀の公文書やその他の出版物に見られる」

ウ「16 世紀後半にコーヒーがヨーロッパに持ち込まれ，コーヒーハウスは文学，とりわけ風刺文学において中心的な話題となった」

エ「コーヒーがヨーロッパに持ち込まれたのは 16 世紀後半になってからであったが，コーヒーハウスによって，コーヒーはまもなく国際的に取引される商品として定着した」

設問に「文章全体の」とあるので，表題選択問題と同様，部分的な情報にしか触れていないものを消去して答えればよい。イは第 3 段落のみ，ウは第 4 段落のみに関係する内容になっている。エは，第 1 段落で「16 世紀にヨーロッパに持ち込まれた」ことは述べられているが，「コーヒーハウスによって国際的に取引される商品となった」とは述べられていないので不適。したがって，アが正解となる。

解答

(1) － (d)　　　(2) － エ　　　(3) － ア

2 (A)【全訳】

キヨシ：今日の新聞読んだ？　イギリスではペットを 16 歳未満の子供に売るのは違法らしいんだ。金魚もだめなんだって！　子供はきちんと面倒を見られないだろうからってことが理由なんだけど，違反者は懲役 1 年になる可能性もあるらしい。

ヘレン：へぇー！　（　1　）

キヨシ：うん，確かにそうだね。でも（　2　）。

ヘレン：その通りだと思うわ。

— 213 —

2011 年　　解答・解説

【考え方】

＜語数について＞

「15 〜 20 語で」とあるからには，この指定より多くても少なくてもまずいだろう。答案を書いたら，最後に「○○ words」と書き添えるのが望ましい。

＜答案を書く上での注意＞

⑴の書き出しは大文字，⑵の書き出しは文の途中を埋めるので小文字であるべきだろう。

＜内容面でのポイント＞

⑴は **Kiyoshi** が説明したイギリスの事情に対する **Helen** の反応を書く。どのような反応にするかはかなり自由で，賛成でも反対でも，驚き・怒りなどでも構わない。ただし，<u>Kiyoshi が後で「うん，確かにそうだね」と受けられるような内容にする必要がある。</u>たとえば，この⑴で「あなたはどう思うの？」のごとき内容にしてしまうと，Kiyoshi がその後で「うん，確かにそうだね」とは答えられなくなる。したがってこのような答案は不適切。

⑵だが，But の後に続けるのだから，⑴の内容に対する反論，⑴が抱える問題点の指摘，⑴が見落としている事柄の補填などを書く。つまり<u>⑴と⑵は逆接の But をはさんでいることから，対立点が含まれていなければならない。</u>このことは⑴を書く段階から意識しておくことが重要。

＜答案作成＞

答案の展開方法を具体例に沿って見てみよう。

［解答例 1 ］

⑴　「イギリスのペットショップは商売上がったりね。ペットをほしがるのは大体子供なのだから」

⑵　「大した問題じゃないと思う。子供はお金を持っていないのだから，ペットを買うのは普通親だよね」

　「イギリスではペットを 16 歳未満の子供に売るのは違法」に対して「ペットショップは儲けが出しづらくなる」と考えるのはごく自然な流れで，Kiyoshi が「うん，確かにそうだね」と答えるのもおかしくない。続く⑵では Helen が問題視していることは「大した問題ではない」と反論し，Helen が⑴で述べた「ペットをほしがるのは子供」の部分と対立する形で「ペットを買うのは親」と指摘している。

［解答例 2 ］

⑴　「つまり子供がペットを欲しければ，誰かからのプレゼントという形をとるしかないということね」

— 214 —

2011 年　　解答・解説

⑵ 「親は子供の誕生日にハムスターや籠の鳥など喜んで買ってあげるんじゃない」

　「イギリスではペットを 16 歳未満の子供に売るのは違法」ということは「子供が自分で買えない」ということで，ならば「プレゼントとしてもらうしかない」となるのは当然の帰結。ただ「親は喜んで買ってくれる」のだから，子供は全く困らないという流れにすることで，⑵は⑴が見落としている点の補填となっている。

［解答例 3］

⑴ 「子供にたかが金魚を売ったくらいで懲役 1 年というのは厳しすぎるんじゃないかしら」

⑵ 「こういう法律は必要だよ。飼い主がちゃんと面倒を見ないから被害を被っているペットが多すぎる」

　⑴は Kiyoshi のセリフの最後にある「違反者は懲役 1 年になる可能性も」の部分に対する反応。「厳しすぎる」とは言い換えれば「法律を修正（または廃止）せよ」という意味合いなのだから，⑵はそれに対する反論としてまず「このような法律は必要」と発言した。引き続き Helen が見落としていると思われるペットの現状を説明することで，論に説得力を持たせている。

解 答 例

　［解答例 1］

⑴ Pet shops in England must have great trouble making money, because it's mainly children who want to buy pets. (19 words)

⑵ I don't think it's a big problem. Normally it's their parents who buy pets because children don't have the money. (20 words)

　［解答例 2］

⑴ That means, if children want pets, they can only get one as a present from somebody. (16 words)

⑵ most parents are very happy to give their kid a hamster or a caged bird for their birthday. (18 words)

　［解答例 3］

⑴ Sending someone to prison for a year just for selling a goldfish to a child seems a little harsh. (19 words)

⑵ I do think such laws are necessary. Too many pets suffer because their owners don't take care of them. (19 words)

2011年　　解答・解説

2 (B) 考え方

<語数について>

「50 ～ 60 語で」とあるからには，やはりこの指定より多くても少なくてもまずい。またＡと同様，答案の最後に「○○ words」と書き添えよう。

<答案を書く上での注意>

「understand と pain はそれぞれ１回しか用いてはならない」と指示されている。２回以上使用した場合だが，さすがにそれだけで答案全体が０点にされるとは思えない。使用のたびに１点なり２点なり減点，ということであろう。

<内容面でのポイント>

「他人の痛みは理解できない」について思うところを書け，とあるのだから，「賛成」「反対」ばかりでなく，個人的な感想や体験談でもよいのだろう。ただ，英語で書きやすい内容を，文法上・語法上の誤りが含まれない英文で書くことが至上課題であることを忘れずに。

　１つ注意だが，与えられた英文の内容は「他人の痛みは理解できない」であって「他人の気持ちは理解できない」ではない。あくまでも「痛み」にこだわる必要がある。

<答案作成>

　答案の展開方法を具体例に沿って見てみよう。

［解答例１］

・「賛成」→「人によって感じ方が違う」（理由）→「ある人にはつらいことが他の人には快適なこともある」（具体化）→「他人の痛みを理解したいのなら，その本人になるしかないが，それは不可能」

　ぐるっと一周して，最終的に「他人の痛みを理解するのは無理」という出発点にたどりついている。

［解答例２］

・「賛成」→「似た経験をしたことがあっても，他の人がどう感じているかを正確に判断することはできない」（理由）→「相手の方が自分よりもっと悪い気分でいるかもしれない」（具体化１）→「相手の痛みは自分より小さいのに，相手の方がより大騒ぎしているかもしれない」（具体化２）→「結局自分の経験しか理解できない」

　これもいろいろと具体化することで，最終的に「他人の痛みを理解するのは無理」という出発点まで一周して戻っている。

［解答例３］

　・「不賛成」→「他人の痛みを完全に理解することは無理かもしれないが，理解しようと努力することはできる」（譲歩・逆接）→「ある人の母親が亡くなったとする」（具

－ 216 －

体化）→「それと似た状況（親・祖父母・友人・ペットなどの死）で自分が感じたことを思い出すことで，相手の気持ちをおしはかることはできる」

　「痛みを推測する」ことと「痛みを理解する」ことを等号では結べないかもしれないが，少なくとも「理解できない」と断言することには反論している。

解答例

[解答例1]

I agree with this opinion. Different people feel differently about the same thing. For example, what is painful to one person may be pleasant to another. So it can be said that if we really want to understand another person's pain , the only way is to be that person, but that's absolutely impossible. (53 words)

[解答例2]

I agree. Even if you have had a similar experience, there is no way of knowing exactly what another person is feeling. Their circumstances may make them feel much worse than you did. Your pain may actually have been much worse than theirs, but they may complain more loudly. Ultimately, we can only understand our own experiences. (57 words)

[解答例3]

I don't agree with this view. Certainly it may be impossible to fully understand another person's pain , but we can at least try. Suppose a person's mother died. We can imagine his feelings by remembering how we felt in a similar situation; the death of our parents, grandparents, friends, pets, etc. (51 words)

4 (A) 考え方

(1) 「それらの政治上の展開がもたらす多くの結果の1つとして，あまりにも複雑で政府が対処できないことが最終的に判明するようなものがあった」

　取り除く語は for，その直後の語は one。was は過去形であるから述語動詞となる。その主語だが，"Among the many consequences" "of those political developments" はいずれも前置詞句なので主語にはなれない。was の後に続く "for one" も前置詞句なので主語としては機能できない。このままでは英文が成り立たなくなってしまうので，among / of / for の中で削除可能なものを考える。the many

— 217 —

<u>2011 年　　解答・解説</u>

consequences と those political developments は複数形で was だとおかしくなる
ため，削除可能なのは for のみである。

(2)　「その二国が世界経済を再び安定化させるために払わなければならないと言わ
れた犠牲は，完全にとは言わないまでもほぼ互いに相反するものである」

取り除く語は are，その直後の語は to。The sacrifices は文頭の名詞なので，英
文全体の主語になっている可能性が高い。直後の that 以下の構造だが，make の目
的語がないことから that を関係代名詞と考え，もともとは "the two countries have
been told they must make *sacrifices*" だったと考えれば構文的にも内容的にも収
まる。ならば，"The sacrifices (S) ... are (V) to restore (C) という構文になる
が，ここで問題になるのが 2 番目の are の出現である。restore までで収まってい
る構文が，この 2 度目の are のせいで再びおかしくなるので，いずれかの are を削
除する必要がある。2 番目を削除すると "... restore (V) stability (O) to the world
economy almost if not completely the opposite ..." となるが，これでは to the
world economy 以下の構造が全く要領を得ない。したがって，1 番目の are を削除
することが正解。

(3)　「その国は経済的に繁栄したばかりでなく，その市民たちはいくつかの別々の
民族集団から構成されているにもかかわらず，1 つの国民としてある程度の心理的統
一感を抱くにいたった」

取り除く語は became，その直後の語は consisted。consist は第 1 文型の動詞で
あるから受動態にはなれないため，become consisted という表現は文法的に誤り。
ちなみに，consist of O で「O から構成されている」という慣用句。

(4)　「科学は時として，以前は無関係だと思われていた現象を同じ法則にまとめあ
げる理論を作り出すことによって物事を単純化し，そのようにして一見複雑に見える
宇宙に対する我々の理解を高めてくれる」

取り除く語は were，その直後の語は unrelated。previously considered は直前
の名詞 phenomena を修飾する過去分詞であるから，phenomena と consider の間
には〈O － V〉の関係が成り立つ。したがって，本来は consider (V) phenomena (O)
unrelated (C) という第 5 文型の関係として考えなければおかしいので，were は余
計である。ちなみに that 以下だが，本来 "... that reduce phenomena to the same
law" だったものが，phenomena の後に修飾語句が続いている都合上 phenomena
と to the same law の位置が入れ替えられている，つまり倒置されているという構造
になっている。

(5)　「それらの集団に対する首相の支持を正当化することがいかに難しいことだっ

－ 218 －

たのかもしれないにせよ，その後十年間大きな反対があったにもかかわらずこの立場を貫くことで彼女は自分が信念の人間であることを証明した」

取り除く語は had，その直後の語は been。"may have been ＋過去分詞"ならあり得るが，"may have had ＋過去分詞"という英語は不可能である。ちなみに，本文は "It may have been hard to justify ..."（it ～ to - の構文）の hard に however が付いて文頭に移動した形。

解答

> (1)　for / one　　(2)　are / to　　(3)　became / consisted
> (4)　were / unrelated　　(5)　had / been

4 (B) **全訳** 20 世紀初頭の生活の変化の過程は，自動車輸送，航空，無線といった分野における科学技術上の発明の点から，ないしは時に相対論や精神分析のような新しい理論のモデルに言及することによって示されるのが最も普通である。しかし言語の領域にも革新があった。今では文化的重要性を持つ出来事としてはほとんど記憶されていないが，1924 年のクロスワードパズルの出現は，教養のある大衆と英語の語彙の間に新たな種類の関係が生まれたことを示すものと見ることもできるかもしれない。クロスワードパズルは新聞（紙上）での流行から始まり，現金の賞を出すことで普及が図られたが，まもなく国の1つの伝統として確立することとなった。このことは，1930 年から英国の新聞 *The Times* にクロスワードパズルが毎日掲載され始めたということから確認できる。この時点までには，クロスワードパズルのファンは小説にも現れ始めていた。クロスワードパズルに熱心に取り組んだことと，明らかに謎解きの魅力を持っていた推理小説が1930 年代に大流行したことの間に関連があるのかどうかは推測の域を出ない。より確かなことは，クロスワードパズルが言葉に対する広範な興味を高めたということである。かくして新聞の読者は自分たちが読んでいる新聞から急いで辞書に向かうはめになり，図書館は何度も辞書を補充しなければならないと苦情を言った。というのは，クロスワードパズルの愛好家たちの辞書の扱いが荒かったり，彼らが辞書を盗みさえしたからだ。結局のところ，クロスワードパズルは，綴りの標準化を含めそれ以前から行われていた言語統制や，広く評価されている辞書が利用可能になったことに強く依存しているのだ。

考え方

(1)　1. **The processes of change in early twentieth-century life are ... presented**「20 世紀初期［初頭］の生活における変化の過程は…提示されてい

<u>2011 年　　解答・解説</u>

る」　The processes (S) are presented (V) が文の骨格。

　2．**most commonly**「最も普通に」 are と presented に挟み込まれた副詞。「…
は最も普通に提示されている」ではややぎこちないので，訳出上は「…提示されるの
が最も普通［一般的］である」などと処理する方が良いだろう。commonly を補語
と解釈し，「…の過程は最も普通である」などとしたものは不可。

　3．**in terms of technological inventions**「科学技術上の（様々な）発明と
いう観点で」 in terms of ... は「…の観点で」の意の熟語。（例）She thinks of
everything *in terms of* money.（彼女は何でもお金に換算して考える）　この部分は
are ... presented を修飾する副詞句として働いている。

　(2)　1．**Whether ... can only be guessed at.**「…かどうかということは推測す
ることしかできない［推測の域を出ない］」 S can only <u>guess at</u> whether ... という
文を，guess at を 1 つの動詞句と見なして受動態にしたもの。whether 節「…かど
うかということ」が文の主語，can ... be guessed at がそれに対する動詞である。

　2．**there is a connection between ...**「…の間に関係がある」　この部分が
whether 節内の中心。

　3．**enthusiasm for the crossword and the 1930s boom in detective
fiction**「クロスワードパズルに対する熱狂と 1930 年代の推理小説［探偵小説］の大
流行」　ここが between A and B の A and B にあたる箇所。for the crossword と
in detective fiction はいずれも直前の名詞を修飾する形容詞句。

　4．**with its obvious puzzle-solving appeal**「明らかに謎解きの魅力を持った」
detective fiction を修飾する形容詞句。with は「…を持った」の意で「所持・所有」
を表す。its は detective fiction を受ける代名詞。puzzle-solving は solve puzzles（謎
を解く）を出発点にした形容詞として働いている。全訳のように後ろから訳し上げて
もよいし，下記の解答のようにカッコを使って処理するのもよい。

　(3)　1．**From their newspapers**「彼らが読んでいる新聞から」 were sent を修
飾する副詞句。their は後続する readers を先取りしたもの。

　2．**readers were thus sent hurrying to dictionaries**「かくして［それゆえ］
読者は急いで辞書に向かうはめになった」 send O － ing で「O に－させる」の意。
（例）Oil producers *sent* the price of oil *skyrocketing.*（石油の生産者は石油の価格
を急騰させた）／Tokyo's summer temperatures have *been sent soaring.*（東京の
夏の気温は急上昇している）　ここではNにあたる readers が主語になった受動態で，
「読者は辞書に急いで向かった」の意となる。

　3．**which libraries complained they had repeatedly to replace**「図書館は，

－ 220 －

2011 年　　解答・解説

辞書を繰り返し取り替えなければ［買い替えなければ：補充しなければ］ならないと苦情を言った」　which は dictionaries を先行詞とする関係代名詞で，関係詞節内では replace の目的語として働いている。Libraries complained (that) they had ... to replace *the dictionaries*. → *which* libraries complained they had ... to replace φ と考える。

解答

> (1)　20世紀初期の生活における変化の過程は，科学技術上の発明という観点から提示されるのが最も普通である。
>
> (2)　クロスワードパズルに対する熱狂と1930年代における推理小説（これにも明らかに謎解きの楽しさがある）の大流行との間に関係があるのかどうかは推測の域を出ない。
>
> (3)　かくして読者は新聞を開くと辞書に急いで向かうことになり，図書館は何度も辞書を買い替えなければならないとこぼすこととなった。

5　【全訳】　ある朝，玄関でノックの音がした。ノックの音は続き，誰かの大きい声がした。「誰かいるの？」　ブローディ夫人だったのだが，彼女は数軒先に住んでいる近隣住人だった。彼女はまず，自分がどうしても覚えることのできない名前を持つ不幸な子どもの姿を目にした。それから，その子の母親の姿を目にして，口に手をあてて言った。「まあ，たいへん！」　母親を病院に連れていくための救急車を彼女は手配した。その一方で，パーディタは，ラムゼー夫妻，フローラとテッドの所へ引き取られたのだが，この夫妻は，2人とも60代で，成人した子どもたちがどこかにいた。気配りがよく，思いやりのある人たちだった。

　パーディタは，母親がどこにいるのか，そして，ちゃんと食べて体力を回復させているのかと思うことが多々あったが，実のところは，ほとんど解放されたといってもよかった。ラムゼー夫妻の物分かりのよさと，やんわりとした気づかいのおかげで，パーディタは自由に息ができる状態に戻れたのだった。フローラとテッドはパーディタがくつろげるよう骨を折った。パーディタが夫妻と一緒に暮らし始めて1ヵ月もしないころ，医者に診てもらうことになるわよとフローラ・ラムゼーがパーディタに告げた。パーディタは同意したものの，自分の言葉づかいを見知らぬ人間に診断されるのが怖かった。「ただ検査するだけよ！」とフローラは言って，細かいことは伝えなかった。そして，パーディタは小児科病院に付随した診療所の建物に到着した。

　勇敢でいなくちゃ，とパーディタは心に決めた。しかし，受付の看護師が名前を綴

－ 221 －

2011年　解答・解説

るよう求めてきたときに微笑んでくれたのに，やっぱり勇気を手に入れるのは容易ではなかった。今回もまた，自分の名前を綴ろうとすることで，彼女の状態が明らかになった。そこでフローラは，思慮深い女性だったので，パーディタの代わりに全ての話をした。

　ここ，パーディタがとても怖い思いをした診療所の裏手にある小さなオフィスで，担当医のヴィクター・オブロフ医師に面会した。彼は，ロシアのノボシビルスク生まれで，第一次世界大戦末期に商船に乗ってオーストラリアにやってきた。戦時中は，軍医として働き，心理的問題を抱えた兵士たちの治療をしていた。彼はフローラに向かって自己紹介をしていたが，パーディタもじっと聞いていた。話の内容からすると，刺激的で，興味深い人物のようだった。髪は薄く灰色で，かっこいいとは言えない長髪。金縁の眼鏡をかけていた。シャツを腕まくりしていて，まるで今から肉体労働をするぞといわんばかりだった。パーディタはすぐに惹きつけられた。彼の話し声は穏やかで低く，これは，医者という職業にはすばらしい資質だった。

　「お目にかかれてうれしく存じます」と彼は言った。まるで，本気でそう思っているかのようだった。診察室は乱雑で，医療の場にふさわしいものでなく，物腰は，よい意味でびっくりするほどのものだった。

　オブロフ医師は，ガラス製の物体，つまりは文鎮，をいくつか机の上に置いてあったが，それをときおり手にして，繊細な手の中でまわしてから，元の位置に置いた。そのうちの1つは，固く完全な円形のガラスで，中には鮮やかな青い色の不思議な花，自然界にはとうてい存在しえないような花が入っていた。2つめは，嵐の波を航海する小さな船が入っており，3つめは，明るい黄色の蝶が入っていた。贈り物をめったにもらったことがなく，宝物と考えてもよさそうなものといったら1枚の真珠貝以外はほとんど何も持っていなかった子どもだったので，パーディタは，このガラスの置物を喜ばしく魅力的なものだと思った。

　この初診のときに，いくつかの問診があったが，他にはほとんど何もなく，パーディタはオブロフ医師がそもそも医者だとはほとんど思わなかった。3つのガラス製の置物を手でもてあそんでいたときにパーディタが見ているのがわかったので，医師は，どれか1つを選んで問診中に手に持っていたいかと尋ねた。その方が話すのが楽になるだろうからね，と言った。そんなのはバカバカしい提言だとパーディタは思ったが，そうすることに同意した。彼を喜ばせるためでもあったし，文鎮の1つを手にしたらという誘いは，彼女も願っていたことだったからだ。彼女は不思議な花の入ったのを選んだ。

　「私に話をするときは」とオブロフ医師は言った。「こんな風に想像してごらん。つ

2011 年　　解答・解説

まりね，自分の声が，君を超えて文鎮の中へ投影されて，魔法のように青い花の中心から出てくるっていう風にね」

今度もまた，パーディタは，バカバカしい提言だと思った。彼が自分のことを子ども扱いしていると感じたのだ。しかし，その文鎮がとてもきれいだったので，そのおかげで，その気持ちを，どういうわけか乗り越えることができた。文鎮を手にすると，それは冷たく完璧で，彼女がそれまでに見た中で最もきれいな物の１つだということを認めざるをえなかった。そのように文鎮を持ちながら医師の簡単な問いに答えていったのだが，問いかけの声はとても小さかったので，彼女にはほとんど聞き取れなかった。

そうです，症状は２年くらい前に始まりました。父の死を目にしてからです。そうです，悪化しています。ますます話さないようになりました。そうです，苦労しないで話せるときもあります。シェークスピアの文章をいくつかまるごと暗誦できるんです。母から習いました。

この答えに，オブロフ医師は椅子にのけぞり，指をからみ合わせた。

「シェークスピア？」

「そう言ったんですよ，この子は！」とフローラが大声でさえぎった。

パーディタは，目を上げて彼女を見て微笑んでから，視線を戻してガラスの文鎮の複雑な美しさを覗き込んだ。

「ちょっといいですか」と医師は尋ねた。「１行か２行だけでも？」

何の造作もなかった。パーディタはハムレットの有名なセリフを暗誦してみせたのだが，彼女にとっては最も簡単な部分だった。言葉が自分の舌からスラスラと流れ出るのを一種の誇らしい気持ちを持って聞いていた。

オブロフ医師は感心した様子だった。フローラの顔に幸せな笑みが広がり，まるで有名な俳優に出会ってゾクゾクしている少女のようにハンドバッグを握りしめた。

「なるほど」と医師は言った。

彼は広げた掌を差し出した。パーディタは医師の手の中に文鎮を注意深く置いた。それは光を捉えて，宝石のように輝いた。

「いつか，言葉がまたスッと出てくるようになったときには，家へ持って帰っていいよ」と彼は言った。

パーディタは，一瞬，わくわくしたが，それから彼の言葉を疑い始めた。医師に守る義務のある約束ではとうていなかったからだ。しかし，オブロフ医師は彼女に微笑み，握手をしようと手を差し出したのだが，やっぱり子どもではなく，もう一人の大人だと彼女のことを見なしているかのようだった。彼女は医師の手を真摯に受け止め，大人のように握手をすると，やってきてよかったと思った。

<u>2011 年　　解答・解説</u>

考え方　(1)　正解は，(1a) ウ，(1b) イ，(1c) カ，(1d) オ。

　(1a) では，ドアをノックする人が言いそうなセリフを選べばよいので，ウ Anyone there?「誰かいるの？」が正解となる。ちなみに，ア Who was it? は不可。ドアをノックされて「どなた？」という意味で，'Who is it?' と言うことがあるが，これは文意に合わず，しかもアでは過去形なので，さらにおかしい。

　(1b) が，少女を病院に連れて行こうとしているフローラのセリフであることから，イ Just to check!「ただ検査するだけよ！」が最適。この問題を正解するには，check に「検査する；(健康) 診断をする」という意味もあるという知識が必要。

　(1c) は，少女の言葉に対して意外な驚きを感じた医師に対するフローラのセリフである。ここでは，カ That's what she said!「それがこの子の言ったことです！→そう言ったんですよ，この子は！」を入れればよい。設問(10)の解説も参照のこと。

　(1d) は，(1c) に続く場面の医師のセリフなので，オの Would you mind? を入れることになる。この表現は，Would you mind - ing?「－していただけませんか」という高頻度の表現があるが，その省略形と考えればよい（たとえば，Would you mind reciting something from Shakespeare? と補ってみればわかりやすい）。

　(2)　正解は，(2a) ア，(2b) イ，(2c) オ。この文章の冒頭段落の人物関係は，かなり錯綜しているので，本番でも戸惑った受験生が多かっただろうと思われる。

　(2a) の the unfortunate child は，文章全体から考えれば，容易にア Perdita だとわかる。

　(2b) の her は「それから，その子の母親の姿を目にして，口に手をあてて言った」という文意から考えて，文の主語の she と同一人物だとわかる。そして she が，その前文，そしてさらにその前文の主語のイ Mrs. Brodie だとつきとめるのは難しくない。

　(2c) の her は，病院に送られている人物である。直後の文で，Meanwhile（その一方で）とあり，これは，娘の Perdita を対比させていることのマーカーと考えられるので，下線部が指しているのはオの Perdita's mother ということになる。

　(3)　正解はエ「彼女は心の安らぎを取り戻すことができた」。下線部そのものの直訳は「彼女が自由に呼吸できるようにした」ということになるが，ここは比喩表現となっており，直前の almost a liberation「解放といってもよいもの」を手がかりとするのがよい。ここは，少女が，問題のある母親の元を離れ，ラムゼー夫妻という里親のおかげで心の安らぎを回復する場面なのである。その他の選択肢の意味は以下の通り。ア「彼女は風邪を治すことができた」，イ「彼女は自分の意見を表明することができた」，ウ「彼女は自分の興奮を共有することができた」

— 224 —

2011 年　　解答・解説

⑷　正解はイの obtain「手に入れる」。これは熟語の知識の問題。come by には自動詞として「通り過ぎる」という意味もあるが，ここでは他動詞として「手に入れる」という意味で使われている。下線部⑷を含む文の骨格が，courage was not easy to come by であり，これは概ね it was not easy to come by courage と同義であることにも注意。

⑸　正解は **about to engage in physical labour**。空所を含む文の意味が「シャツを腕まくりしていて，まるで（　5　）」であることから，engage in physical labour「肉体労働に従事する」というつながりを使うことになると推測できる。残りの選択肢から about to と組み合わせれば，空所直前の were とつながって，be about to 不定詞（今にも…する）という熟語ができあがり，文脈に最も適合し，正解が得られる。ちなみに，interested to としてしまうと「肉体労働に従事することに興味がわいた」あるいは「肉体労働をして興味がわいた」という意味になってしまって，文脈に合わなくなる。

⑹　正解はウの possibly「〈否定文で can とともに〉とても」。空所直前の could not が手がかり。副詞 possibly は，否定文で can や could とともに用いられると，「とても〈…できない〉」「どうしても〈…できない〉」という意味での強調表現となる。(例) I *could not possibly* afford such a sum.（とてもそんな金額は出せなかった）

⑺　正解はウの hoped。空所を含む箇所の意味は「文鎮の１つを手にしたらという誘いは，彼女が（　7　）していた」となる。空所直後の for を考え合わせると，hoped for「…を願った」が最も適切である。それ以外の選択肢は文意に合わない。それぞれ，ア lived for「…のために生きた」，イ asked for「…をねだった」，エ prepared for「…への準備をした」という意味になる。

⑻　正解は「そのガラスの文鎮のおかげで，彼女は自分が医師から子ども扱いされているという気持ちを，どういうわけか乗り越えることができた」。

１．**it**　下線部を含む箇所は，いわゆる so that 構文であり，主節の部分の倒置を元に戻せば，the object was so beautiful that ... となる。この object は空所⑹を含む段落の冒頭にあるように paperweight のことである。本設問⑻の主語 it も，素直に「文鎮」とすればよい。

２．**somehow**「どういうわけか」という意味の副詞。

３．**allowed her to ...**　第５文型で「彼女が…することを可能にする」の意。ここを「許す」と訳すのは拙劣。

４．**overcome**「克服する；乗り越える」

５．**that feeling**　同一文内に，he was treating her as a little girl, she felt とあ

— 225 —

ることから「医師が自分を子ども扱いしているという気持ち」とすればよい。

(9)　正解は**ウ**。下線部の次の段落にある 3 箇所の Yes が，医師の質問に対する少女の答えであることに気づけたかどうかがポイント。1 つめの Yes が本設問の選択肢イに対応し，2 つめがア，3 つめがエに対応している。そこで「質問内容と合致しないもの」はウとなる。

(10)　正解は**ア**。前後の行と考え合わせて流れを考えればよい。具体的には以下のとおり。

　　…シェークスピアの文章をいくつかまるごと暗誦できるんです。母から習いました。

　　At this オブロフ医師は椅子にのけぞり，指をからみ合わせた。

　　「シェークスピア？」

　この流れから，医師が少女の言葉に驚いて反応しているのだということが読み取れれば，容易に正解が得られる（ちなみに，Perdita という名前は，シェークスピアの『冬物語』に出てくる王女の名前でもある。王女は父王の命により捨て子にされる）。

解答

(1)　(1a)　ウ	(1b)　イ	(1c)　カ	(1d)　オ
(2)　(2a)　ア	(2b)　イ	(2c)　オ	
(3)　エ	(4)　イ		

(5)　about to engage in physical labour

(6)　ウ　(7)　ウ

(8)　そのガラスの文鎮のおかげで，彼女は自分が医師から子ども扱いされているという気持ちを，どういうわけか乗り越えることができた。

(9)　ウ　(10)　ア

解答・解説

1 (A) **【全訳】** SF は大変おもしろいものだが，それだけではなく人間の想像力を広げるという大切な目的にもかなっている。我々は人間の心が科学の未来の発達にどう反応するかを探ることができる。そして，その発展がどのようなものか想像することができるのだ。

SF と科学の間には双方向のやりとりがある。SF は，科学者が自らの理論に含める概念を提唱するが，時に科学がどんな SF よりも奇抜な概念を提示することがある。ブラックホールがその一例で，物理学者ジョン・アーチボールド・ホイーラーが付けた見事な名前が大いに後押しすることになった。仮に「凍結した星」とか「重力によって完全に押しつぶされた天体」など元々の名前のままだったら，ブラックホール関連の書物は半分も出ていなかったであろう。

SF が注目した概念の 1 つが，超光速移動である。仮に宇宙船を亜光速で飛ぶように制限したとすると，銀河の中心までの往復が乗組員には数年しかかからないように見えるが，地球上ではこの宇宙船の帰還までに 8 万年がたっていることになる。これでは帰還して家族の顔を見るなど不可能だ。

幸いなことに，この問題を回避する可能性はアインシュタインの一般相対性理論によって示されている。時空を曲げる，あるいは，たわませることによって，行きたい場所に近道をすることができるかもしれない。このように時間と空間をたわませることが将来は人間の能力の範囲内に入るかもしれないのだ。しかし，このような方向で科学的な研究がそれほど本格的になされてきたわけではない。それは 1 つには，そのような考え方があまりにも SF 的に思えるからだと私は思う。高速宇宙移動の帰結の 1 つとして，過去に遡ることが可能になるというのもあるだろう。政府が時間旅行研究の資金援助をしていることが公になった場合，納税者の税金を無駄にしているという不満が出ることを想像してみよう。このため，この分野で研究している科学者は，「時間的閉曲線」などという，実際には時間旅行を意味する専門用語を使って本当の関心を隠さねばならないのだ。しかしそれでも，今日の SF が明日の科学的事実になることはよくある。SF の背後にある科学は間違いなく研究に値するものである。

考え方

従来の要約問題と違って「挙げられた例にも触れながら」という指示があるが，文章の大筋・骨格を抽出するのが最優先であることには変わりない。「例をすべて完全

— 228 —

2010 年　　解答・解説

に列挙せよ」などと書いてあるわけではないし,「たとえば…」に相当する部分は軽く触れる程度でなければ到底この解答字数には収まらない。この指示書きに過剰反応してあれこれ盛り込もうとしないよう注意すること。このような設問の解答の手順としては大筋をまずまとめ,残りの字数で例を加えていくのが最も無難である。

①アウトライン

　各段落の大筋は以下の通りである。第 1 段落と第 2 段落は,それぞれ第 1 文がTopic Sentence（主題文）である。第 3 ～ 4 段落目は最後の部分に至る流れに注意。

＜第 1 段落＞

　SF は人間の想像力を広げる

＜第 2 段落＞

　SF と科学は双方向のやりとりがある

　　（例）ブラックホールという科学の概念が SF に取り上げられた

＜第 3 段落＞

　　（例）SF が注目する「超光速移動」について

＜第 4 段落＞

　光速移動の問題は一般相対性理論で回避はできる

　→ しかし,あまりに SF 的で科学研究の対象となっていない

　→ 時間旅行の研究に国が援助をしたら納税者から苦情が出るだろう

　→ だから,科学者はこの分野に興味があっても表立っては言えない

　→ それでも,今日の SF が明日の科学的事実になることが多い

　→ （ゆえに）SF 的な科学も研究に値する

②全体的に「SF の意義」を主軸に置いてまとめる

　この文章は,SF と科学の関係について述べられているが,第 1 段落冒頭の表現と第 4 段落最後の 2 文の書き方から考えると,「SF の科学に対する意義」を中心的主題としてまとめるべきである。第 2 段落で「双方向のやりとり」があるという文があるが,「科学 → SF」の方向は,やはり第 3 ～ 4 段落の流れから考えると軽く触れる程度でよいだろう。

③例を加える

　「SF は人間の想像力を広げ,科学と影響し合う。SF 的発想も将来は科学の事実になる可能性はあるので研究に値する」（53 字）　これで大筋がまとまった。あとは第 2 段落～第 4 段落前半の「ブラックホール」「光速移動」「時間旅行」の例を加えればよい。

・第 2 段落の "There is a two-way trade ..." の文を使ってまとめたのが解答例 1 だ

<u>2010 年　　解答・解説</u>

が，この文は「ブラックホール」の話に触れ，かつ，「時間旅行」以下の話に触れて
いれば，すなわち，〈科学 → SF〉〈SF → 科学〉の両面に触れていれば，内容的に
は同等なので省いてもよいだろう（→ 解答例 2 を参照）。

・第 4 段落の最後の部分を中心に据えることを主眼に置き，第 2 段落は「ブラックホー
ル」という言葉を使わずに軽く触れたのが解答例 3 である。

・第 2 段落は主題文のみに触れ，第 4 段落最後の部分を中心にまとめたのが解答例 4
である。制限字数の下限に近い字数でまとめるとすると，「ブラックホール」の方は
触れずにまとめるしかない。

解 答 例

> ［解答例 1 ］　SF は想像力を広げ，科学と影響し合う。ブラックホールのような
> 　　科学の概念が SF でよく取り上げられる。逆に光速移動や時間旅行も今は SF
> 　　的だが将来は科学的事実になり得るため，科学研究に値する。(93 字)
>
> ［解答例 2 ］　SF は人間の想像力を広げる。ブラックホールのような科学の概念が
> 　　SF で取り上げられることもあり，時間旅行など現在は SF 的で真面目な研究対
> 　　象にできない考えも将来は科学的事実になり得るため研究に値する。(98 字)
>
> ［解答例 3 ］　SF は想像力を広げるもので，科学と相互作用がある。科学の概念
> 　　が SF によって広がることもあるし，逆に SF 的で真剣な研究対象とはなって
> 　　いない光速移動や時間旅行も将来は科学的事実になり得るため研究に値する。
> 　　(100 字)
>
> ［解答例 4 ］　SF は人間の想像力を広げ，科学と相互に作用しあう。SF 的であ
> 　　るがゆえに科学研究の対象になっていない超光速移動や時間旅行も将来は科
> 　　学的事実になる可能性があるため，SF の着想も研究に値する。(93 字)

1 (B) 【全訳】　初めて提案されたのは 20 世紀初頭だったが，小惑星から資源を
得ようという考えは相変わらず注目を集めている。地球近傍の小惑星，すなわち地球
に近づく軌道を持っている小惑星から物質を得るというのが基本的な考え方となって
いる。この惑星群は，火星と木星の間で軌道を描くメインベルト小惑星とは明確に異
なるものである。小惑星から得た物質は宇宙空間で，宇宙飛行や宇宙ステーション，
さらには月面基地のために利用可能であろう。また，この資源を持ち帰り，ここ地球
上で利用することもできるであろう。

　　ア 　まず第一に興味を引く資源は，地球近傍の小惑星から得られる水というこ
とになろう。この小惑星は（炭素が豊富な）C 型小惑星あるいは枯渇彗星核のどちら

— 230 —

かである。 イ おそらく，これらの惑星を全部合わせると，地球近傍の小惑星の
半分あるいはそれ以上を占めるであろう。 ウ その水はロケット燃料用の水素と
酸素を作るために使用されることになる。 エ もちろん，その水と酸素は宇宙で
人間の生命維持にも利用可能であろう。 オ これらの物質は地球上のみならず小
惑星でもごく普通に見られるものなので，それを宇宙で構造物として利用することも
できるだろう。

※空所×4

　宇宙空間で得ようとする資源が物質であれエネルギーであれ，やはり，それらを得
る技術を開発する必要がある。地球近傍の小惑星まで行くために必要な技術は現在で
きてはいるが（実際，これらの天体の中には到達に必要なロケットの推力と燃料は月
に行くのより少なくてすむものもある），小惑星を採掘し小惑星の資源を処理したり
持ち帰ったりするために必要な技術はまだ開発されていない。また，これがどれほど
困難でどれほど費用がかかるか明らかになっていないし，この作業がロボットででき
るのか，あるいは人間の監督が必要なのかということも分かっていない。一部の宇宙
開発機関はロボットで小惑星を探索しているし，有人探査計画の可能性も議論されて
はいるが，小惑星を採掘する具体的な計画はまだできていない。

[選択肢全訳]

ア　初期の小惑星採掘の考え方の大半は，人間が小惑星に行って採掘するというもの
　　だったが，最近の考え方の中には完全にロボットのみの探査も含まれている。1つ
　　の手は単に小惑星の断片を地球に持ち帰り，処理工場を建てるどこか遠くの場所で
　　つぶすことであろう。また，もう1つの手は物質を他ならぬ小惑星で処理すること
　　であろう。

イ　さらにもう1つの潜在的資源になりそうなのが，地球に持ち帰ることのできる貴
　　金属類である。小惑星から得られる金属の中で最も有望なものとして，地球上では
　　希少かつ高価で多くの工業利用が可能なプラチナ類の金属がある。惑星を研究する
　　天文学者は，平均的な小惑星には，地球の（場合によっては月でもそうだが）典型
　　的な岩石よりもこれらの金属がはるかに多く存在すると考えている。

ウ　しかし，宇宙から物質を持ち帰ることはコストが高すぎるかもしれないが，経済
　　学者は，地球で使用する電力を宇宙で発生させることに関わる大変興味深いチャン
　　スがあることも指摘している。たとえば，地球の高軌道上に太陽発電衛星を配置し，
　　マイクロ波エネルギーの形で地上へ太陽エネルギーを伝送することもできよう。月

－ 231 －

面で得られるヘリウム３も，月面で核融合を起こしそのエネルギーを地球に伝送するということを考えると，経済的には魅力的かもしれない。

エ　これと同様，太陽熱収集器を月面に月にある素材で作り，地球に太陽エネルギーを送り返すこともできるかもしれない。発電所のローテク大型コンポーネントを小惑星で，場合によっては月で，作った素材を利用して宇宙で生産すれば，原理的には宇宙での太陽発電所建設は地上よりはるかに低コストでできるようになる。さらに地球から遠く離れると，巨大惑星（とりわけ天王星と海王星）ではヘリウム３貯蔵量が莫大であり，その大気から核融合の燃料を得る計画ができれば，太陽が燃え尽きるまで地球に電力供給が可能である。

オ　しかし，一部の経済学者は，小惑星の物質を地球に持ち帰って利益になるのか疑問を呈している。たとえば，宇宙から得たプラチナ類の金属の供給が地球で急増すると，需要が同程度に伸びない限り，これらの金属の価格が急落し，結果的に利益がなくなり，さらに投資する気もなくなることになる。これ以外に宇宙から得る可能性がある物質（たとえば実験室での分析に用いられる希少物質）は市場が限定されているだけではなく，そのような物質は将来的には分析技術が上がると需要も下がると考えられている。

[考え方]　本年度も，2007年度以降の設問構成を維持している。

(1)　正解は(c)。これ以外の文は「(a) 小惑星から資源を得る」「(b) 小惑星から物質を得る」「(d) その物質の利用法」「(e) その資源の利用」という内容を含んでおり，小惑星から資源や物質を得て利用することに関係しているが，この文のみ，そのような内容とは直接関係のない内容になっていることから考える。

(2)　正解はオ。この文は「宇宙で利用できるもう１つの資源は，ほぼ間違いなく鉄やコバルトのような金属である」という意味。Another resource とあり，metals とあるので，「水」の話の後に追加するべき文だと考える。また，空所オに入れると，次の文で **These substances** が metals を指すことにもなり，うまくつながる。

(3)　【不要な段落】ア

全体的に小惑星から資源や物質を地球上での利用のために持ち帰ることに関する文章であり，ア以外の選択肢はすべてこれに関わる内容となっていることから考える。

【一番目と三番目の段落】イ，ウ　（ イ → オ → ウ → エ）

以下のようなポイントに注目して並べ替えればよい。

◇第２段落 → イ

選択肢イの冒頭 Yet another ... という表現に注意。これは still another ... と同様，「さらにもう１つの…」という意味で項目を追加していく時に使うものである。これ

－ 232 －

2010 年　　解答・解説

を最初に置くと，第２段落で言及した「水」と「金属」に加えて precious metals「貴金属」を小惑星から得られる資源・物質として列挙するという流れができる。

◇イ → オ → ウ

この部分の流れについては，いわゆる「逆接関係」を作る言葉が２つあるので，何と何が逆接（対立）の関係になっているかに注意すること。

第２段落と選択肢イで，小惑星から得られる資源・物質とその利用［恩恵］に触れた直後に選択肢オを置くと「経済学者が指摘する問題点」が逆接の however でつながることになる。また，ウは economists also point to ... の also に注目する。選択肢オで経済学者の指摘する「問題点」に触れ，ウで But を使って経済学者の指摘する「新たな可能性」に触れているのだから，オ → ウとつなぐ。

◇ウ → エ

選択肢エに Similarly（これと同様に）とあることに注目する。ウの「宇宙での発電」の可能性の後に，「太陽発電衛星 (solar-power satellites)」を地球の軌道上に配置するという記述がある。この後に選択肢エを置けば「太陽熱収集器 (solar collectors)」を月面に設置するという記述が Similarly でつながることになる。また，ウとエはどちらも「エネルギー」の話になっていることに注意。これを空所後半に置けば，第７段落第１文の "Whether the resources ... are <u>materials</u> or <u>energy</u>" という表現にも自然につながることになる。

(4)　正解は**イ**。

設問に「文章全体との関係を考えて」「最後の段落の要点として」とあることに注意。パッセージ全体の表題を選ぶのではなく，あくまで最終段落の内容に近いものを選ぶ，ということである。本年度の設問については消去法で対応するしかないだろう。

ア　「宇宙旅行の課題」

これは space travel が無関係と考える。

ウ　「小惑星採掘の費用と便益」

costs and benefits については整序部分では経済学者の視点で触れているが，最終段落では明確に触れていない。これが正解になるためには，もっと具体的に費用と便益の検討が文章中でなされていなければならない。

エ　「地球近傍の小惑星が地球にもたらす危険性」

地球に及ぶ危険性については触れていない。

オ　「小惑星資源の獲得：人間によるかロボットによるか」

似たような内容が第３文に登場するが「ロボットでできるのか人間の監督が必要なのかは分からない」という書き方であり，最終文にも登場するが Although 節の内容

— 233 —

<u>2010 年　　解答・解説</u>

として触れているにすぎない。

イ　「実現されるべき夢」

この段落の「宇宙に資源やエネルギーを求める技術をこれから開発しなければならない」（第1, 2文），「困難度やコストが不明；人間が必要かどうかも分からない」（第3文），「小惑星採掘の具体案はまだできていない」（最終文）といった内容から，宇宙から資源・エネルギーを得る可能性は，現段階ではまだ具体性を持つ計画とはなっていないということになる。また，第1段落冒頭で「小惑星から資源を得ようという考えは相変わらず注目を集めている」とあることから，「資源を得る新たな可能性として宇宙に目を向けたいが，まだまだ実現には遠い段階にある」というトーンで書かれていると考え，これを正解とみなす。

解 答

---

(1) – (c)　　(2) – オ

(3)　不要な段落：ア　一番目の段落：イ　三番目の段落：ウ　　(4) – イ

2　(A)　**考え方**

＜語数について＞

「50〜60語で」とあるからには，この指定より多くても少なくてもまずいだろう。答案を書いたら，最後に「○○ words」と書き添えるのが望ましい。なお，書き出しとして与えられている "If there were only one language in the world," の部分は，この指定語数には含めない。

＜答案を書く上での注意＞

文の途中を埋めるので，書き出しは当然小文字となるだろうが，大文字にしても減点はないだろう。

＜問題文について＞

☆ 書き出しである「現在，全世界で約3,000から8,000の言語が話されていると言われている」の部分は，解答を求められている内容と無関係であるから，言及する必要はない。まして，この部分を英訳したものを答案に盛り込むのはよくない。

☆「全世界の人々がみな同じ1つの言語を使用しているとしたら」の部分は，問題文にも解答用紙にも英訳が印刷されている (If there were only one language in the world,) ので問題はないだろうが，言うまでもなくこれは「世界の言語が1つしかなかったら」という想像である。誤って<u>「世界の言語を統合して1つにする」という積極的な行為として解釈しないように</u>注意すること。

— 234 —

2010 年　　解答・解説

☆「我々の社会や生活」とあるが,「社会」と「生活」のそれぞれについて別個に言及する必要はない。「社会」について書くことは結局「生活」について書くことであり,逆もまたそうである。

☆「〈我々の社会や生活は〉どのようになっていたと思うか」だが,この日本語はたとえば「江戸時代はどのようになっていたか」という意味,つまり「過去」を表すものではない。「我々の社会や生活は現在どのようなものになっているか」ということなので,内容的には「現在」である。

＜内容面でのポイント＞

☆「言語が１つしかない世界」は想像の産物で,非現実である。したがって,このような世界について言及する場合は**仮定法**を用いる必要がある（印刷されている英語も仮定法が使われている）。時制は,先述したように現在のことを表現するのであるから,**仮定法過去**となる。ただし,これは答案すべてを仮定法で書くという意味ではない。答案で現実世界についても当てはまる事柄に言及する場合は直説法の使用が必要になってくる。

☆「言語が１つしかない世界」を肯定的にとらえるか否定的にとらえるかは自由だが,「言語」に関するテーマなので,コミュニケーションに話をつなげるのが最も楽な展開だろう。むろん「言語と文化」「言語と民族性」のような話題にしてはいけないわけではない。しかし,自由英作文を処理する際の重要ポイントは**「書きたいことを書くのではない」「英語で書けることを書く」**ということ。文化論や人類学的な内容を英語で表現するには相当な英語力が必要なので,一般の受験生はこのような内容を書こうとするのは避けるべきだろう。

＜答案作成＞

答案の展開方法を具体例に沿って見てみよう。

［解答例１］

・「他者とのコミュニケーションが楽になる」＋「誤解が減る」

→「世界に平和がもたらされる」

（理由）「紛争の多くはコミュニケーション不足と相互の誤解から生じるため」

・「人種上宗教上の違いは残る」（譲歩）→「人々が話す言語が１つなら,この差異も乗り越えられる」（逆接）

「コミュニケーション」から「誤解の減少」に続け,さらには「世界平和」を着地点とした。ただ,なぜ「平和」につながるのか今ひとつ不鮮明なので,はっきりとした理由を追加した。しかし紛争の原因は「コミュニケーション不足」「誤解」だけではなく,人種や宗教の問題もある。「言語が１つになれば平和が訪れるというのはあ

— 235 —

2010 年　　解答・解説

まりに楽観的」と反論する人々もおそらく存在するだろうと考え，それらの問題は認めつつ，自分の主張の妥当性を強調するという〈譲歩―逆接〉で語数を稼いだ。

　ちなみに，「紛争の原因」を説明する部分（第2文 because 以下）は事実であるから直説法，その他は「言語が1つしかない世界」における状況だから，すべて仮定法を使っている。

［解答例2］

・「生活がずっと楽になり，良くなる」

・（具体化）「国際コミュニケーションが容易になる」→「商業・科学・政治などの，国際的協力が必要な分野で大きな進歩につながる」→「世界が住みよい場所になる」

　問題文にある「我々の社会や生活はどのようになっていたと思うか」の部分を意識し，まず「生活は…になる」から始めた。しかしそれでは具体性に欠けるので，「コミュニケーションが容易」→「国際協力の分野での飛躍」→「よりよい世界」という展開で話を進めた。

　ちなみに，「商業・科学・政治などの分野で国際的協力が必要」というのは事実なので，ここだけは直説法にしてある。

［解答例3］

・「世界は退屈な場所になる」

・「コミュニケーションや国家間の問題を解決するのは楽になる」（譲歩）→「多様性に欠ける世界になる」（逆接）

→「世界は多様であるからこそ興味深く刺激的」（第1文の理由）

　「言語が1つしかない世界」を否定的にとらえている例。「多様性の欠如」という視点からとらえたが，最終文 (Our world, I ...) がないと，なぜ「多様性がないと退屈なのか」が曖昧になるだろう。

解答例

［解答例1］

　　[If there were only one language in the world,] it would be far easier to communicate with others, and there would be far fewer misunderstandings. This would certainly bring about peace, because many conflicts arise mainly from lack of communication and mutual　misunderstandings. Of course, there would still be racial and religious differences, but if all people spoke the same language, they could overcome them more easily. (58 words)

2010 年　解答・解説

［解答例２］

　　[If there were only one language in the world,] life would be a lot easier and better than it is now. International communication would be very easy, and this would lead to dramatic breakthroughs in the fields of commerce, science, politics and anything else that requires international cooperation. This would surely make the whole world a better place to live in. (52 words)

［解答例３］

　　[If there were only one language in the world,] the world would be a boring place to live. It would probably be possible for us to communicate with each other and solve problems between countries more easily, but we would be living in a world without much diversity. Our world, I believe, is all the more interesting and exciting because of its diversity.

(54 words)

2 (B) 考え方

(1)　「その橋は地震によって弱くなり，修理のため閉鎖しなければならなかった」

　　正解は **weakened**。be 動詞と前置詞 by にはさまれているので，受動態であることは容易に察することができただろう。

(2)　「その目撃者たちが事故の発生の仕方について昨日異議を唱えたので，警察がまだ調査中である」

　　正解は **disagreed**。The witnesses に続く部分なので，述語動詞になっていることはすぐにわかるし，yesterday とあるから過去形であることもわかる。しかし，後半の「だから警察がまだ調査中である」という部分を考慮に入れないと，うっかり agreed にしてしまう可能性があるので，注意が必要。

(3)　「彼女はケガをした後，ジムの会員を辞めざるをえなかった」

　　正解は **membership**。her という所有格に続くので，空所には名詞が入るが，そもそも member 自体が名詞である。直後に in the gym とあることから，「ジムの会員であること」という意味を考え，membership とする。

(4)　「その作曲家の新しい交響曲は，明るいメロディーと悲しいハーモニーを独特に組み合わせたものである」

　　正解は **combination**。a unique に続くので，空所に入るのは名詞だから，単に

— 237 —

2010年　解答・解説

combine の名詞形を考えればよい。

⑸ 「その界隈の住民は大変効果的に協力し合ったので，地域の犯罪を減らすことができた」

正解は **effectively**。work together に続くので，空所に入るのは副詞だから，effect → effective → effectively と考えていけばよい。

⑹ 「この1ヶ月間，野党の党首は首相が政府の金を無駄遣いしていることを批判している」

正解は **criticizing** [または **criticising**]。空所の後に the prime minister for wasting と続いていることから，動詞の criticize [criticise] を考え，それがさらに be 動詞に続いていることから進行形と考えて現在分詞に変えればよい。

⑺ 「火曜日，その国はイギリスからの独立50周年の記念日を祝った」

正解は **independent**。内容的に「独立」という意味合いはすぐに見当がついただろうが，空所の直後に from Britain となっていることに少し躊躇したかもしれない。通常は be independent of で，be independent *from* は誤りだが，「…から独立する」という意味合いに限り become independent from と表現する。

⑻ 「そのデータをどうやって正しく解釈すればよいのかを教えてくれる専門家に相談することが必要かもしれない」

正解は **specialist**。a に続くのだから，空所に入るのは名詞。さらにその直後に関係代名詞 who が続いていることから，〈人〉を表すものである必要がある。したがって，specialist 以外考えられない。

解答

⑴ weakened	⑵ disagreed	⑶ membership
⑷ combination	⑸ effectively	⑹ criticizing [または criticising]
⑺ independent	⑻ specialist	

4 (A) 考え方

⑴ 「発見とは，そのことについて『発見者は誰か』という問いを問うことが妥当であるような類の過程ではない」

正解は **finding**。which の後に続く英文は動詞 ask を中心とした受動態で，能動態は S appropriately ask the question "Who discovered it?" となる。これでわかるように，この部分は完全な英文になっており，足りない要素は1つもない。すると困るのは which である。which は疑問代名詞か関係代名詞だが，いずれにせよそ

— 238 —

2010 年　　解答・解説

の節中で S・O・C のいずれかになっていなければならない。したがってこのままでは which の働きがなくなってしまう。which を削除すれば finding that から that が省略されたものと考えて文法的にはおかしくなくなるが,「発見とは『誰がそれを発見したのか』という問いが適切に問われていることに気づくことに関する過程ではない」という意味になり, 全く要領を得ない。そこで, finding を削除すると, "The question "Who discovered it?" is appropriately asked about the process" の the process が関係代名詞 which に変化したことになり,「(発見という)過程について,『誰がそれを発見したのか』という問いを発することは妥当だ」という意味になり, 内容的に明瞭なものとなる。ちなみに appropriately は本問では文修飾で使われており,「問いを発すること」=「妥当なこと」という意味合い。

(2)「新しい現象を発見するということは, 必然的に複雑な事象となり, あるものが存在するということ, そしてそれが何であるのかの両方を認識することを伴う事象なのである」

　正解は **of**。which を非制限用法の関係代名詞ととらえると, 先行詞は当然 a complex event であろう。one of which となっているが, この one of ... は「…の１つ」という意味だから, 当然「…」の部分には複数形の名詞が続く。したがって, one of the complex events となる必要が出てくるが, これでは先行詞と異なる形になってしまうので, 文法的に誤っている。of を削除すれば, one は event の繰り返しを避けるための代名詞, which は one を先行詞とする関係代名詞, "a complex event, one which ..." の部分は「複雑な事象, すなわち…のような事象」という同格となり, すべて矛盾はなくなる。

(3)「科学とは, 理論と事実をより緊密に一致させることを実際目指しているし, また絶えず目指さなければならないもので, その営みは, 検証すること, すなわち, 真であるか偽であるかを探求することと見なすことができる」

　正解は **in**。"try to bring theory and in fact into closer agreement" の部分だが, これでは and が何と何をつないでいるのかが全くわからない。in を削除すれば "bring theory and fact into ..." つまり theory と fact が共に bring の目的語になっていることがはっきりする。

(4)「発見によって科学者は, 自然現象をより広範囲に, またそれまでは未知であった現象のいくつかをより正確に説明することができるようになる」

　正解は **were**。与えられた英文全体の構造だが, "Discovery makes it possible for scientists to −" は make の第５文型でその目的語が it ... for 〜 to − の型になっている。to 以下だが, "to account for a wider range ..." と "to account ... for some

− 239 −

2010 年　　解答・解説

of those" という 2 つの account for が接続詞 or でつながれている。したがって，those were previously unknown という完全な英文が最後に登場するのはおかしい。were を削除すれば，previously unknown は those を修飾する形容詞句となり，some of those で前置詞 for の目的語となって，構文的に収まる。ちなみに，those は phenomena の繰り返しを避ける代名詞。

(5)「ニュートンの運動の第二法則は，作り上げるには何世紀にもわたる困難な事実的理論的研究を必要としたが，ニュートン理論にくみする人々にとっては，どれほどの観察をおこなっても偽であることを証明できない純粋に論理的な命題のように扱われている」

正解は **seem**。与えられた英文全体の構造だが，"Newton's second law of motion ... behaves" が〈S―V〉で，この 2 つの間に though 節が挿入されている。問題は behaves の後。behave は第 1 文型の動詞なので，その後には目的語も補語も来ず，続くとすれば副詞や前置詞句などの修飾語句以外にない。そのように考えると，"behaves for those committed to Newton's theory seem" の seem がひっかかる。これを削除すれば，committed ... theory は those（＝ people）を修飾する過去分詞，そのような人々にとって「運動の第二法則」はどのような扱われ方がされているのかを説明しているのが very much like 以下，ということになり，内容的に要領を得る。

解答

(1) finding　　(2) of　　(3) in　　(4) were　　(5) seem

---

4 (B)　**全訳**　スターは利益をあげるために作られる。市場という観点からすると，スターは映画を売る方法の 1 つなのだ。映画にある特定のスターが出ていることで，その映画を見に行けば目にすることになるものが保証される。同じように，スターは新聞や雑誌も売るし，食品，ファッション，車，そして他のほとんどすべてものを売るのに使われる。

スターのこうした市場的役割は，スターの持つ経済面での重要性の 1 つの側面に過ぎない。スターはまた財産であって，その名前の威光で映画を作るためにお金を集めることができるのだ。スターはスター本人，そしてスターを管理するスタジオやエージェントにとっても資産なのだ。また映画を製作する費用の大半を占めるのもスターだ。スターはなによりも（まず），利益を求めて市場で売り出すことができる商品として映画を製作する労働者の一部なのである。

スターは自分自身を商品にすることにも関わる。スターは労働者であると同時に労

― 240 ―

働者が生み出すものでもあるのだ。彼らは1人で自分を作り出すのではない。その人間の肉体，心理状態，一連の技能全体に手を加え，スターのイメージを作り上げなければならないのだ。人という素材からスターを作り出すというこの作業がうまくいくかどうかは，その素材の基本的な性質がどれほど尊重されるかにかかっている。化粧，髪型，服装，減量，ボディビルは元々の体の特徴を様々な形で活かすことができるし，技能を習得することができるし，個性さえ変えることができるのだ。こうした仕事を行う人には，スター自身のみならず，メークアップアーティスト，ヘアドレッサー，衣装デザイナー，栄養士，パーソナルトレーナー，演技や踊りなどの指導者，写真家，ゴシップコラムニストなどが含まれる。

（考え方） (1) 1．**The star's presence in a film is a promise of ...**「ある特定のスターが映画に出ていることは…の約束である」 主部である The star's presence in a film は，The star is present in a film.（ある特定のスターが映画に出ている）という文が名詞化されたもの。a promise はここでは「約束，保証」といった意味。「ある特定のスターが映画に出ていることは…の約束である」とそのまま訳しても構わないだろうし，主部が「無生物」であることから，「ある特定のスターが映画に出ていると…の約束［保証］になる」と副詞的に処理してもよい。

2．**what you will see if you go to see the film**「映画を見に行けば何を見るかということ［見るもの］」 what は名詞節をまとめるとともに，節内では最初の see の目的語として働いている。この what は疑問代名詞と関係代名詞のどちらに解釈してもよい。if ... は最初の see を修飾する副詞節。

(2) 1．**They are also property**「スターは同時に財産でもある」 They は「スター」を受ける代名詞。「They が何を指すか明らかにして訳すこと」という指示があるので，「彼ら」はもちろん不可。property の訳語は「資産」でも構わないが「所有物，特性」等は不可。

2．**on the strength of whose name money can be raised to make a film**「その名前に基づいて映画を作るためにお金を集めることができる」 関係詞節が whose name から始まっていると考えると，They are also property on the strength of. という文と Its name money can be raised .... などといった文が関係詞を使って1文にまとめられたことになるが，いずれの文も文法的に成り立たないので，関係詞節の始まりはここではない。of whose name から関係詞節が始まっていると考えた場合は They are also property on the strength. と Money can be raised to make a film of its name. という2つの文が合体したことになるが，この両文もともに意味不明なので，この切り方も正しくない。関係詞節の切れ目がさらに前にあると考え，on the

— 241 —

strength of whose name ... から関係詞節が始まると考えられたかどうかがポイント。
つまり，この文は They are also property.（スターはまた財産である）と Money
can be raised to make a film on the strength of its name.（その名前に基づいて，
映画を作るためにお金を集めることができる）が関係詞を使って１つにまとめられ
たものである。on the strength of ... は，そのまま「…の力に基づいて」と訳しても
よいだろうが，全体で「…に基づいて，…を当てにして」の意の熟語。（例）He was
convicted *on the strength of* the evidence.（その証拠に基づいて彼には有罪判決が
下された）　関係詞節が長く，また節内の構造もこみ入っているため，ここは解答例
にもあるように，関係詞節を前から訳し下した方が訳しやすい。

　(3)　1．**This work ... depends on ～**「この…作業は～にかかっている」の意
だが，「この…作業がうまくいくかどうかは～にかかっている」のように言葉を補っ
た方が訳文としてはわかりやすい。

　2．**of making the star out of the raw material of the person**「人という素
材からスターを作り出すという〈この作業〉」 of making ... の of は「同格」の of。
make A out of B は「B から A を作る」の意。raw は「生の」という意味の形容詞。よっ
て raw material 全体で「原材料，素材」という意味になる。of the person の of も同格。
「人という素材」などと処理すればよい。

　3．**how much the essential qualities of that material are respected**「そう
した素材の本質的な性質がどれだけ尊重されているかということ」 The essential
qualities of that material are respected *very much.* → *how much* the essential
qualities of that material are respected と考える。how は「程度」を表す疑問副詞で，
much を修飾しながら名詞節をまとめている。respected に「尊敬される」は不可。

解 答

(1)　映画にある特定のスターが出ていることで，その映画を見に行けば目にする
　　ことになるものが保証される。
(2)　スターは同時に財産でもあって，その名前に基づいて映画を作るためにお金
　　を集めることができる。
(3)　人という素材からスターを作り出すというこの作業がうまくいくかどうか
　　は，そうした素材の本質的な性質がどれだけ尊重されているかということにか
　　かっている。

－ 242 －

<u>2010 年　　解答・解説</u>

5　**全訳**　ウィリアム・ポーターは，ヒューストンを離れ，二度と戻ることがなかったが，彼が立ち去った理由は，オースティンにただちに来て，First National Bank of Austin に勤務していたときに銀行の金に手を出したことで裁判を受けなければならないという命令を受けていたことだった。

　出頭していたら，まちがいなく無罪の宣告を受けていただろう。「境遇の犠牲者」というのが，公判の推移を最も近くで見守っていたオースティンの人たちの判断である。数多くのインタビューをした後で私が知りえたかぎりでは，彼らの誰ひとりとして，ポーターが何か悪事を働いたことで有罪であるとは思っていなかった。その銀行は，閉鎖してから長いこと経過していたが，管理がずさんだったことがよく知られていた。顧客は，昔ながらのしきたりで，銀行に入ってきて，カウンターの背後に行き，100 ドルか 200 ドルを手にして，1 週間後に言うのだった。「ポーター，先週 200 ドル取ったから。メモを残しておいたかどうか確認しといてくれ。そのつもりだったけど」銀行の金の流れを把握するのは不可能だった。銀行業務の管理があまりにもずさんだったので，ポーターの前任者は辞職し，後任者は自殺未遂に追い込まれた。

　オースティンへ行くつもりでポーターがヒューストンで列車に乗ったのはまちがいない。私の想像では，彼の首のまわりに重くひっかかっていた裁判がようやく行われることとなり，彼の無実が公式に宣言されることに一種の安堵感さえ彼は感じていた。友人たちは彼の無実を確信していた。彼らのうちの 1 人でもポーターに同行していたら，事態はすっかり別物になっていただろう。しかし，オースティンへの道のりの 3 分の 1 ほどにあるヘムプステッドに列車が到着したときに，ポーターには，裁判の場面を想像し，自分が囚人になっている姿を思い浮かべ，未来をのぞき込むと自分に疑惑の烙印を押される姿が目に浮かぶ，といったことをする時間があった。想像力が理性を凌駕し，ニューオーリンズ行きの夜行列車がヘムプステッドを通ると，ポーターはそれに乗車したのだった。

　彼の心はすっかり決まっていたようだ。自分と家族を世間の恥さらしにすることから救うだけでなく，新天地で人生の再出発をするつもりでいた。スペイン語ができて，ホンジュラスのことを知らないということで，小さな中米の共和国が逃亡先には打ってつけだと思われた。ホンジュラスから妻に宛てて出された何度かの手紙によれば，彼は中米を自分たちの故郷にすることを決めたのであり，娘の教育のための学校もすでに選んであった。

　ホンジュラスへ行く前に，ポーターがニューオーリンズにどれくらいの間滞在したのかはわかっていない。おそらく，ホンジュラスに向かう途中ニューオーリンズは通過しただけで，ホンジュラスの海岸へ向かう最初の船便に乗って，プエルトコルテス

－ 243 －

2010年　　解答・解説

かトルヒーヨに着いたのだろう。ともあれ，彼がトルヒーヨにいて波止場に立っていると，よれよれの礼服を身につけた男が到着したばかりの船から降りてくるのが見えた。「なぜそんなにあたふた出てきたんだい？」とポーターは聞いた。「ひょっとするとおまえさんと同じ理由かもな」と初対面の男は答えた。「行先は？」とポーターが尋ねた。「行先に行くのを避けるためにアメリカを去ったのさ」というのが返事だった。

　男の名前はアル・ジェニングズ。アメリカ南西部に存在した史上最悪の列車強盗一味の一つの首領だった。彼と兄弟のフランクはガルベストンで船をチャーターしたが，出発がとても慌ただしかったので，礼服と山高帽子を，もっと普通の服に着替える時間がなかったのだった。ジェニングズとフランクはラテンアメリカで犯罪歴を重ねていくつもりはなかった。ただ単に，自分たちと，すでに自分たちを追跡していた捜査官との間に距離を保っていただけだった。ポーターは彼らと連れ立って，南米の海岸一帯を回った。これは，ポーターにとって最も長い航海であり，まちがいなく最も奇妙な航海だった。

　この放浪をともにしながら，たぶんジェニングズは，ポーターの人生の一面を，他の誰がそれまでに見たよりも深く見たのだろう。友人宛ての手紙に彼は書いている。「ポーターは，たいていの人には気難しい人柄にうつるのだろうが，男というものが空腹をともにし，食事をともにし，死に直面して笑うという経験をしたならば，お互いのことがわかると言ってかまわないだろう。そしてまた，人生の中で，おそろしい空腹のときほど，その人間独特の個性を示す時期はないだろう。そのことを我々の友人と共に身をもって知り，彼について私は何の欠点も見い出せなかった。私が彼のことを知っているように世の中が彼のことを知ることができさえしたならば，捜査のサーチライトは彼の美しい魂に光をあて，それは嵐の雲が過ぎ去った後の太陽の光と同じくらいに染みひとつなく清らかだとわかるだろう」

　最初の3週間が過ぎると，ポーターから妻宛ての手紙が定期的にやってきた。手紙はオースティン在住のルイス・クライスル宛ての封筒に入っていて，彼がポーターの妻に手渡していた。「奥さんは夫からの手紙を，いくつか選んで私に読んで聞かせてくれましたよ」とクライスルは語った。「手紙に書かれていたのは，彼が落ち着いたらすぐに奥さんとマーガレットを呼び寄せる計画でした。大変なときだったのに，手紙は元気と希望にあふれ，奥さんへの愛情にあふれていました。奥さんのご両親は，奥さんとマーガレットを援助するつもりがもちろんあったのですが，奥さんの方が依存したくなかったのです。離れ離れになっているのがどれくらいの期間になるのかわからないので，お金を稼げるようなことをするつもりだと奥さんは言っていました。奥さんは実業系の大学で受講をし始めたのですが，病気で頓挫しました。クリスマス

— 244 —

<u>2010 年　　解答・解説</u>

がやってくると，レースのハンカチを作り，それを 25 ドルで売り，旦那さんに贈り物の箱を送りました。中にはオーバーと，上等な香水と，ほかにおいしいものをたくさん入れて。そのような意志力を見たことは私には一度もなかったです。ベッドから起きなかったのは，亡くなった日の当日だけでした」

　この箱は，体温が華氏 104 度（摂氏 40 度）のときに妻が荷造りをしてくれたものだとポーターが知ったのは 1 ヶ月たってからのことだった。それを知るとすぐに，彼はラテンアメリカで我が家を構えるという望みをすべて捨て，オースティンへ向けて出発した。自首し，運命または法廷が用意していた処罰がいかなるものであってもそれを受ける決意をかためながら。

[考え方]　(1)　正解は**ア**の **victim**「犠牲者」。直前文の「まちがいなく無罪の宣告を受けていただろう」がわかれば容易に正解が選べるはず。イ nature「性質，自然」，ウ creature「生物」，エ punishment「罰」は，いずれも文脈にまったく合わない。

　(2)　正解は**ウ**の **which had been closed for a long time**「それは長い間閉鎖されていたが」。下線部は直前の the bank を修飾する挿入句であり，long since は for a long time の意味の副詞句。したがって，下線部を含む文は「その銀行は，閉鎖されて長い間経っていたが，ひどい経営をしていたことはよく知られていた」という意味になるので，ウが正解となる。ア「それが閉鎖していた間」とイ「それはとうとう閉鎖されたが」は明らかに意味的に不適。エは「それは大昔に閉鎖されていたので」という意味になり，理由を表す because が言い換えとして不適切である。

　(3)　正解は**ウ**の「そのつもりだったが，忘れたかもしれない」。「mean to −」は「−するつもりだ」という意味の表現。下線部の省略を補うと，I meant to leave a note about it となるはずだとわかれば正解に至る。それ以外の選択肢は，いずれも意味が異なり，文脈にも合わないので不適。

　(4)　正解は「**ポーターの友人の 1 人でも彼と一緒にいたならば，状況はすべて違っていただろう**」。下線部の them が直前の his friends をさしているのは明らかであり，with は「一緒に」の意味。(例) I enjoy being *with* her.（彼女と一緒にいるのが私は好きだ）　all には「万事」の意味もあることを知らないと後半を間違う可能性がある。(例) See that *all* is well.（万事よろしく頼む）

　(5)　正解は**ア**「**自分が無罪の宣告を受けそうだと思っていたものの，彼は裁判が恐かった**」。下線部は「想像が理性を凌駕した」「想像が理性の上をいくものだった」という意味。すべての選択肢に共通の「彼は裁判が恐かった」が「想像」の内容であることはすぐにわかる。outran「凌駕した」「上をいった」ということから，想像と理性の間に葛藤があったはずなので，even though で接続したアとウは可，because

— 245 —

2010 年　　解答・解説

で接続したイとエは不可。アの「自分が無罪の宣告を受けそうだと思っていた」は文脈に合致するが，ウの「自分がなぜ銀行から金を盗んだのか思い出せない」はまったく文脈に合わない。

(6)　正解は**ア**の **prison**「刑務所」。下線部そのものは「私の行先」の意味。その少し前から訳せば「私の行先に近づかないように」であるが，犯罪者が行きたくない場所とは刑務所のこと。ウ「銀行」やエ「彼の家」では文脈に合わない。イ「強盗」は場所ではないので不可。

(7)　正解は **sudden they had not had time to exchange**。例年どおり，東大の語整序問題にありがちな「該当部分の前後を考慮しなければならない」タイプの問題。構文的には，the departure(S) had been(V) so（　7　）their dress suits and high hats(A) for plainer clothing(B) ということから，so の直後に had been の補語になる形容詞 sudden を置く。並べかえる要素の中に S＋V があることから，so ～ that S V ...「とても～なので S V…」という構文を思いつくことができたかがポイント（この構文の接続詞 that は省略されることがある）。後続部分を exchange A for B の形にすることは比較的容易。時制を考慮して，they had not had time to exchange という形に仕上げることができるかどうかが最終関門である。不要な語は with となる。

(8)　正解は**ア** crime「犯罪」。本文には「（　8　）の経歴を続ける」とあるので，彼らがそれまでにやっていたことを考えれば容易に正解が得られる。

(9)　正解は**イ** knowledge of ...「…を知ること」。空所を含む段落は「人が人の人格を知ること」をトピックにしていると理解することが解答への前提条件。ア「…にとって利用価値がない」，ウ「…に絶望する」，エ「…を心配する」は，いずれもトピックに合わない。

(10)　正解は，(10a) **イ**，(10b) **ウ**，(10c) **エ**，(10d) **ア**。まず，cheerful and hopeful and full of (10a) for his wife とあることから，(10a) には cheer や hope と並列しうる意味の語で，妻に対して抱くようなものが入ると考えると, affection「愛情」となる。(10b) は就学することの妨げとなるものだと考えて，ill health「病気」となる。such (10c)「そんな (10c)」とあることから，ポーターの妻の行動をまとめる語として，willpower「意志の力」が最適。(10d) は gave up の目的語であるから，断念するような意味内容のものは何かと考えて hope「望み」を選ぶ。ちなみに，この話に登場した人物の William Porter という名は，『最後の一葉』『賢者の贈り物』などの短編小説で知られる作家，O. Henry の本名である。

－ 246 －

2010 年　　解答・解説

解 答

---

(1) - ア　　　(2) - ウ　　　(3) - ウ

(4) - ポーターの友人の 1 人でも彼と一緒にいたならば，状況はすべて違っていた
　　だろう。

(5) - ア　　　(6) - ア

(7) - sudden they had not had time to exchange

(8) - ア　　　(9) - イ

(10) - (10a)　イ　　(10b)　ウ　　(10c)　エ　　(10d)　ア

－ 247 －

解答・解説

1 (A) **【全訳】** 私は6，7歳の頃，よく自分の小さなコイン（たいてい1ペニー硬貨だったが）を持って行って，誰かが見つけてくれるよう隠していた。なんとなくだが，私は決まってそのペニーを同じ歩道沿いに「隠して」いた。たとえば大きな木の根元のところとか，歩道に開いた穴に置いていた。そしてチョークを持って，その区画のどちらか一方の端から描き始めたのだが，両方向からそのペニーにつながる大きな矢印を描いた。字が書けるようになると，その矢印に「前方に意外なプレゼント」とか「お金はこちら」などという文字を添えた。そうやって矢印を描いている間，価値はともかくとして，宇宙からの無償の贈り物をこんな風に運良く最初に受け取る通行人のことを考えて，かなり興奮していた。

さて，私が大人になってこんな記憶を呼び起こしたりするのは，最近，見るということについて考えているからである。見るべきもの，無償の驚きがたくさんあるではないか。世界は恵みの手があちらこちらに投げたペニーに満ちているではないか。しかし，ここが大事なところだが，どんな大人が単なるペニーに興奮するというのか。1本の矢印に従って進み，揺れる枝を見ようと道ばたにじっとしゃがみこむと，1頭の鹿がびくびくしながら用心している姿に報われる。あなたは，その光景を取るに足らぬと考え，歩き続けるだろうか。疲労や多忙のあまり立ち止まってペニーを拾うことができなければ，それはまさに極貧である。しかし，ペニーの発見が自分にとって真の意味を持つように清廉潔白で純真な心を育むならば，世界にはまさにペニーが潜んでいるのだから，あなたはその清貧で生涯続く発見を得たことになるのだ。

【考え方】

本年度は，文章のスタイルが全く変わり，筆者の個人的体験を持ち出しておいて，その後に言わんとすることを記すという構成になっている。また，設問も「要約せよ」ではなく「趣旨をまとめよ」になった。

設問の指示文には，「突然変異」的な言葉が時折登場する。2004年度の「事例から一般的にどのようなことが言えるか記せ」がその一例である。今回の「趣旨をまとめよ」という指示も，これまでの1(A)の伝統の中では，ある種の突然変異なのかもしれない。出題者の真意がどこにあるのか，出題意図がこれまでと異なるのか否かに関しては，どう考えようと推測の域を出ないのであるが，従来の「要約せよ」に近いスタンスで考えてみることにする。

— 250 —

2009 年　　解答・解説

◇第1パラグラフは，具体例に相当

　筆者は第1パラグラフで，自分が子供の頃にした，ちょっとした悪戯を描写している。これは，従来の論説文の「具体例」に相当すると考えてよいだろう。ただし，このパラグラフにも第2パラグラフにも登場する penny（1ペニー硬貨）が何を象徴するのかには注意しておいた方がよい。

◇ penny の意味

　ペニーは元々英国の通貨で，日本円の感覚だと「1円硬貨」程度のもの。これが象徴する意味については，第1パラグラフおよび第2パラグラフ第2文の内容から，「一見無価値に思えるもの；小さな驚き；些細な発見；普段は見過ごしがちなもの」というとらえ方ができていればよい。これを含めて，冒頭から第2パラグラフ第2文までは「世の中［人生］は小さな驚き［発見］に満ちている」という程度にまとめることができる。

◇ seeing について

　第2パラグラフ第1文で，筆者は「（ものを）見ることについて最近考えている〈から，昔のことを思い出す〉」とあるので，これを解答の要素として一言入れておきたい。

◇趣旨の中心は最終文

　第2パラグラフ第3文で「どんな大人がただのペニーに興奮するのか」という文がある。これまでの出題でもそうだったが，「疑問・問いかけ・問題提起」には，それに答えようとする部分が伴ってくる。この文章では「それは…な大人である」という表現はしていないのだが，この文章で第4文から第6文の流れを考えると，やはり「言いたいこと」の大筋は最終文にまとめられていると思われる。この文の If 節の内容，so that 節の内容，そして主節の内容に沿っていけば「趣旨」に相当する内容になるであろう（since 節の内容は，反復・旧情報なので不要である）。

◇ a healthy poverty and simplicity of mind という表現

　この poverty は，キリスト教的「清貧」の意味が裏にあるようだが，これは直訳しなくても「純粋な心；清らかな心；素直な心」の意味になる表現ができていれば十分だと思われる。第1パラグラフの内容を考慮して，「子供のような」と加えてもよいだろう。

　以上のような点を考えた上で，最終文を中心にまとめたのが以下の解答例であり，これらは，if 節，so that 節，主節，それぞれの部分の記述に即したまとめ方である。

— 251 —

<u>2009年　　解答・解説</u>

　　最初に述べたように出題意図が不明なので，もう少し英文の記述から離れて，「人生は様々な驚きに満ちているもので，一見無価値に思えても，小さな発見を見逃さないよう，子供のような清廉で純粋な心を持ってものを見るべきである。」とか，「世の中は思いがけない発見に満ちているものだ。些細なものでも，子供のように純粋で欲のない見方をするとよい。そうすればいくつもの発見ができるものである。」という方向でまとめてもよいかもしれない。そのような言葉でも「筆者の言いたいこと」をまとめたものとしては許容範囲に入るのではないだろうか。

解 答 例

［解答例１］　世の中は小さな驚きに満ちており，些細なものであっても，それが自分にとって意味を持つように純粋な心で見れば，発見に満ちた人生を手にしたことになる。(72字)

［解答例２］　人生は一見無価値に思えるものに満ちているが，ささやかなものであれ，その発見が有意義なものになるよう清廉潔白な心で見るならば，発見に満ちた人生を得たことになる。(79字)

［解答例３］　人は，子供のような，すこやかな慎ましさとあどけない心でものを見るようにすれば，一生の間，世の中のささやかなものに潜んでいる驚きを発見し続けることができる。(77字)

［解答例４］　人生は小さな発見に満ちており，大人はそれを見逃してしまうが，それが意味を持つよう子供のように清らかで純粋な心で見るならば，一生発見は続くものだ。(72字)

1 **(B)** **全訳** コレクションという趣味は，普通の切手やコイン，バッジ，最近ではポケモン・トレーディングカードなど，何であれ，昔から人気があります。しかしコレクションの中にはアマチュアの知識では対応できないものもあります。万年筆はそういう範疇に入るものです。安くて便利なボールペン，ローラーボールペンが幅をきかせてきたために，日々の筆記用具としての万年筆は今ではめったに見かけなくなってしまいました。まさにそれが理由で，万年筆はコレクターの目を捕らえてきたのです。

　　ア　コレクターにとって，品物の価値を高めるのは，その希少性だけではありません。その品物についてきらびやかな物語がどれだけあるかということも価値を

2009 年　　解答・解説

高めるのです。そして万年筆の長い歴史にはそのような物語がたくさんあります。
　イ　たとえば，万年筆の素敵な起源は書記法そのものの発達と切っても切れない
縁にあります。　ウ　中国が紀元 104 年頃，「墨汁」を使う毛筆用に，紙という極め
て重大な発明をしたことは皆さんご存じの通りです。　エ　しかし，それ以前にエ
ジプト人が約 4000 年前からパピルスに文字を書くために中空の葦のペンを使ってい
たことを考えてみて下さい。　オ　「泉」が乾くことのない理想のペンである現代の
万年筆の基本原理ではないとしたら，これは一体何になるのでしょうか。

　中世時代から，ヨーロッパでも他の地域でも文筆家はガチョウの羽軸など鳥の羽を
使っていました。その中には苺類の果汁，あるいはインクが入っていました。鵞ペ
ンは映画などで見かけるとロマンチックな雰囲気が漂うし，シェークスピアがそうい
うペンで傑作を創作している姿など想像することもあるでしょう。しかし現実には鵞
ペンは見た目も悪く，汚いことが多かったのです。しょっちゅうインクをつけたりナ
イフで削ったりしなければなりませんでした。文字を書いたり手で触ったりしている
だけで，すぐに磨り減ってしまいました。

※　空所×4

　しかし今やこの黄金時代も，ローラーボールペンからコンピューターへと，文書作
成術の新しい時代へと移りつつあるため，万年筆とその物語を絶やさないようにでき
るかどうかは，私のような凡庸なコレクター次第なのです。実を言うと，私は最近に
なって初めて蒐集価値のある万年筆を購入しました。英国のデ・ラ・ルー社は 1821 年，
製紙・印刷会社として設立されました。現在でもイングランド銀行の紙幣が印刷され
ているのは，デ・ラ・ルー社の偽造防止用紙なのです。ところが 20 世紀初頭，しば
らくの間この会社は，私が現在所有しているようなペンも製造していたのですが，実
はそのペンでこの会社はかなり有名になったのです。他ならぬこのデ・ラ・ルー社の
ペンをなぜ私が欲しくなったかを説明する前に，そのきっかけとなった作家のことに
まず触れておかなければなりません。

　オノト・ワタナという 19 世紀の作家が，かつて西洋と日本に関する大変好評を博
した小説を英語で書きました。彼女は英国の読者に日本の言語，文化，風俗習慣を伝
えたかったのです。本名を明かすことはありませんでしたが，ある時「オノト・ワタ
ナ」はただのペンネームだと認めました。まさしく文字通りに，「オノト」とは，デ・
ラ・ルー社の万年筆の名前でもあったのです！

　オノト・ワタナが何者であるかは，すでに知っていました。ウィニフレッド・イー
トンは，中国人と英国人の混血で，カナダと米国で育ちました。日本語は全く話さな

－ 253 －

<u>2009 年　　解答・解説</u>

かったし，日本に行ったこともありませんでした。私は後になってたまたま「万年筆はオノト」という 1920 年代の日本の広告を見て，そのペンに注目したのです。見た瞬間，そのペンが日本製であり，オノトのペンネームはここから巧く取ったんだと思ってしまいました。ところが，オノトの万年筆は 1905 年「オノト・ワタナ」にちなんで英国で生まれたものでした。つまり，ウィニフレッド・イートンが先にそうしたように，デ・ラ・ルー社も世界の日本趣味に追従し，そしてイートンのでっち上げ和名を借用してしまったわけです。ペンと作家の真実を調べるきっかけとなったこの勘違いが出発点となって，意外な物語を持つ珍しい万年筆の蒐集熱が新たに生まれてきました。

[選択肢全訳]

ア　彼の場合には，まさに「必要は発明の母」だったのです。同じことを繰り返さないよう，彼は研究にとりかかりました。彼が考案した新しいインク送り方式のおかげで，インクはペンの筐体内部にあるタンクから特別に設計されたペン先，「ニブ」に問題なく流れるようになりました。

イ　19 世紀に科学が発達し多くの発明が可能になりました。その 1 つがチャールズ・グッドイヤーの柔らかいゴムを硬くする化学処理の発見で，これによりゴムが万年筆の筐体を強くしたり，ブーツやコートを防水にするのに最適な素材になりました。

ウ　技術と設計のおかげで万年筆の信頼性が上がると，単に使いやすさだけではなく，美しさにも注意が向くようになりました。世界中のペンメーカーがクオリティとステイタスを目指して競い合い，世界の有力指導者，有名人，戦場の兵士，そして普通の消費者それぞれに向けて販売するペンを作ったのです。

エ　皮肉なことに，こうした問題をすべて解決し，万年筆の技術革新をもたらしたのは，ある事故だったのです。1883 年，実業家ルイス・ウォーターマンは，ある契約書に署名をしてもらう必要が生じました。彼は自分の万年筆を顧客に渡して，ただ単に署名してもらおうと思っただけなのですが，何の前触れもなくインクがこぼれ，文書一面インクだらけになってしまったのです！　ウォーターマンは取引に失敗し，そして激怒しました。

オ　長きにわたる発達を通じ，万年筆は常に似たような問題に直面しました。インクを内部にどう保つか，いつも切れ込みを入れたりインク瓶につけたりしなくても，そして，乾くことも漏れることもなくインクを一定して紙に送るにはどうしたらいいのか，という問題でした。今でも粗悪なペンのインク漏れで突然手がインクだらけになるという不愉快な経験をした人は多いのですが，万年筆の黎明期にはそのような事態は当たり前のことだったのです。

— 254 —

2009 年　　解答・解説

考え方　(1)　正解は**オ**。2006 年度以降の設問と同様の文補充問題。この文は「歴史家によると，このような大変初期の筆記具も，インクを一定して先端に供給する，ある種の内蔵タンクを持っていると見なすことができるようです」という意味である。最大のポイントは "these very early writing instruments" が，空所オの直前にある，エジプト人が使っていた "hollow reed pens" を指すということ。さらに，これをオの位置に入れると，この文の "a sort of internal tank" を直後の文の this で受けるという対応も成立する。従来同様，指示語・代名詞に注目することがポイントである。

(2)　設問の書き方は変わったが，パラグラフ整序設問の趣旨は同じである。

【不要なパラグラフ】イ

　これは万年筆の発達とは無関係な情報が含まれていることから不要と判断する。たしかに "a stronger body for the fountain pen" という表現は入っているが，「科学の発展で多くの発明ができた」，「グッドイヤーの発見によって，ブーツやコートの防水処理が可能になった」などは，万年筆の発達とは無関係な内容である。

【1番目と3番目】オ，ア　（ オ → エ → ア → ウ）

　以下のようなポイントに注目して並べ替えればよい。

◇オの第1文に "similar problems" とあるので，これが第3パラグラフ最後の2つの文 (It had to be .... It quickly became ....) の内容に対応すると考える。

◇エの第1文に "all these problems" とあるので，これが，第3パラグラフおよび選択肢オの内容，すなわち，昔の万年筆の問題点を受けて使われたものと考える。

◇アの he, his は，エの実例に登場する Lewis Waterman を受ける代名詞である。

◇ウの「万年筆の信頼性が上がると，美しさやクオリティなどの付加価値を求めるようになった」という内容は，オ・エ・アの後に来るべきであり，かつ，「ペンメーカーが様々な階級・業種の人向けに販売するペンを作った」という内容が，第8パラグラフの "this Golden Age" につながる。

(3)　正解は(c)。

◇(a)の文は，筆者がこのパラグラフ以降で，ある万年筆をなぜおもしろいと思うかについて述べているので，その導入の文として残すべきだろう。

◇(b)の文を抜いてしまうと，次の "Even today" と "De La Rue's" が唐突に現れることになってしまうし，(d)の But や also が無意味になるので，取り除くべきではない。

◇(d)の文を抜いてしまうと，De La Rue Company が「製紙・印刷業をやっていた」という内容のみになってしまい，「ペンを作って有名になった」話が出てこなくなるので，取り除くべきではない。

— 255 —

2009年　　解答・解説

◇(e)は，第9パラグラフ以降の展開を予告する内容なので，取り除くべきではない。

　以上の点から(c)を「取り除いても展開に最も影響の小さいもの」だと考える。「英国の紙幣がこの会社の紙に印刷されている」というのは，万年筆の歴史とは関係が薄い，と考えてもよい。

(4)　正解は**イ**。

　ア「オノト・ワタナの正体を暴露する」

　イ「なぜ私が万年筆を集め始めたか説明する」

　ウ「万年筆の一番最近の歴史を述べる」

　エ「デ・ラ・ルー社の製品を紹介する」

　オ「デ・ラ・ルー社が自社のペンを『オノト』と名付けた理由を明らかにする」

　設問に「文章全体との関係において」とあることに注意。最終パラグラフ最終文(Sparking my search ...)や，第8パラグラフの(a)の文の内容，さらに第2パラグラフ第1文の内容を考えると，この中ではイが最適である。ア・エ・オは第8～最終パラグラフの内容に触れてはいるものの，「文章全体」に関わる要素が欠落している。

解 答

---

(1)－オ　　　(2)－不要となるパラグラフ：イ ／ 1番目：オ ／ 3番目：ア
(3)－(c)　　　(4)－イ

---

2 (A) 【全訳】

質問：読書は今日の世界を生きていくのに必要な知識を得る上で役に立つと思いますか？

回答：私の答えは YES と NO です。

「はい。なぜなら(1)（　　　　　　　　）」

「いいえ。なぜなら(2)（　　　　　　　　）」

【考え方】

＜語数について＞

　「それぞれ20～30語で」とあるからには，この指定より多くても少なくてもまずいだろう。答案を書いたら，最後に「○○ words」と書き添えるのが望ましい。

＜答案を書く上での注意＞

☆　空所(1)(2)ともに文の途中を埋めるので，書き出しは当然小文字となるだろうが，大文字にしても減点はないだろう。

☆　「それぞれが複数の文になってもかまわない」とあるが，「20～30語」で書くの

— 256 —

だから，多くても2文程度が適当だと思われる。

＜内容面のポイント＞

　YES / NOの両面から書かなければならないところが大変だろう。問題にされているのは，「読書が知識を得る上で役に立つ（立たない）理由」ということなので，どのように「役に立つ（立たない）」のかを具体的に明示しなければならない。単にメディアとしての「本」を問題にして，インターネットなどと利便性に関する比較論を展開してしまうと，内容的に不適切なものになる。

　ちなみに「現代世界を生きていくのに必要な知識」という要素も何らかの形で反映されていればベストだが，反映されていなくても減点はないだろう。

＜答案作成＞

　答案の展開方法を具体例に沿って見てみよう。

空所(1)

［解答例1］

「読書をすることで多くの知恵が得られる」

＋「この複雑な世界を生きていこうとする際に大いに役立つ知恵が」

　読書が具体的にどう役に立つかを説明し，さらに「読書から得られる知恵」と「現代」を結びつけた。

［解答例2］

「本から得られる知恵を利用しないと問題解決ができない」

＋「現代は複雑で理解しがたい世界だから」

　［解答例1］よりも「現代世界」という要素と緊密に関わらせている。

［解答例3］

「古典などの様々な本を読むことによって，知恵や重要な教訓が得られる」

＋「今日の世界で使うことのできる知恵や教訓」

　基本的に［解答例1］と同様の視点からまとめている。

空所(2)

［解答例1］

「読書によって得られる知識には限界がある」

＋「現代は急速に変化している」

　英文上にはっきりとは書かれていないが，「世の急速な変化に読書の知識では追いつかない」→「だから役に立たない」という流れである。

［解答例2］

「本だけではすべての問題を解決できるだけの知識は得られない」

－ 257 －

2009年　　解答・解説

＋「現代はとても複雑だから」

provide me となっていることからもわかると思うが，これは個人的な事柄ととらえている。これは設問文の［質問］にある you を「個人」と解釈したのである。

［解答例3］

「本は程度の差はあっても所詮はフィクションである」

＋「フィクションでは現実世界の助けにはならない」

"fiction" と "real world" を対比しているところがポイントなのだが，学生諸君にはなかなか思いつかない発想かもしれない。

解答例

(1)

［解答例1］

　　[Yes, because] by reading books we can definitely gain a lot of wisdom that will be of great use to us as we try to live in this complicated world.

(28 words)

［解答例2］

　　[Yes, because] today's world is so complex and hard to understand that we cannot solve our problems without making use of the wisdom to be found in books.　(26 words)

［解答例3］

　　[Yes, because] by reading various books, such as classic literature, we can gain wisdom and learn important lessons that can be used in the world today.　(24 words)

(2)

［解答例1］

　　[No, because] things are rapidly changing in today's world and there is a limit to how much you can acquire by reading books.　　(21 words)

［解答例2］

　　[No, because] today's world is so complicated that it would be impossible for books alone to provide me with enough knowledge to completely solve all my problems.　(25 words)

［解答例3］

　　[No, because] all books are, in one way or another, nothing more than

— 258 —

2009 年　　解答・解説

fiction. I don't think reading fiction can help us survive in the real world.

(25 words)

2 (B) 【考え方】

(1) 「彼女が授業を欠席することはまずめったにない」

「授業を欠席しない」という内容をそのまま変えずにいくなら，miss〈class〉/ be absent from〈class〉と［否定語］を組み合わせればよい。この［否定語］は「まずめったに」なので almost never とする。別のやり方としては，「授業をめったに欠席しない」→「ほとんどいつも出席している」と解釈して，be in〈class〉/ attend〈class〉と almost always の組み合わせにする。

注意事項としては，主語が she なので，述語動詞には三単現の s をつけ忘れない（be 動詞ならば is にする）こと。class を単数無冠詞として扱うことは，設問文に "miss class" と書かれているのだから，間違えることはないだろう。また，almost never / almost always の置き場所は，「一般動詞の前，be 動詞の後」が原則。

(2) 「彼は目がとても悪いので，ほとんど字が読めない」

主語が His eyesight から He に変わっているところがポイント。〈人〉を主語にして「目が悪い」と表現するなら，have poor eyesight を用いるのが最も簡単で，かつ一般的（suffer from poor eyesight とすることもできるが）。あとは「…ので〜」という「因果関係」を表現するのに，"so ... that" を such ... that に変更すればよい（ちなみにこの that は省略可能）。

注意事項としては，eyesight は不可算名詞なので，such a poor eyesight とすると誤りになることである。

(3) 「天気が悪かったので，電車が遅れた」

"the trains were late" の部分は(a)(b)共通なので，"Because the weather was bad" をいかに to を使いつつ "... weather" という形に変えるかを考える。「天気が悪かったので」とはすなわち「悪天候のために」ということで，「…のために」という原因を表現する語句の中で to を用いるものは due to / owing to 以外考えにくい。「悪天候」は電車が遅れたときの天候だから the bad〈weather〉が普通だが，the が抜けても減点はないだろう。ただし weather は不可算名詞なので，a bad〈weather〉は誤り。

(4) 「それは今まで私が受けた賛辞の中で最高のものだ」

書き換え文の冒頭は "No one has ever" だから，"ever" の後に過去分詞を続けて「今まで誰も私にそのようなすばらしい賛辞を送ってくれたことがない」という内容

— 259 —

の英文を作ればよい。「賛辞を送る」において，compliment と組み合わせる動詞はいろいろとあるが，設問文に pay が使われているのだから，わざわざ別の動詞を考える必要はない。

注意事項としては，「そのような」という要素を無視して単に *paid me a* ⟨nice compliment⟩ としないこと。これは誤答として扱われるだろう。また，such は不定冠詞の前につけるのがルールだから，*a such* compliment は誤り。ちなみに，当然のことだが，不定冠詞 a の使用が必要条件であるため，such を使わず paid me *that* [*the*] ⟨nice compliment⟩ とすれば誤りになる。

⑸ 「その車を買う余裕は我々にない」

can't afford は通例金銭面での余裕に使われる。つまり設問文は「金がなくて買えない」ということだから，書き換えは「(その車は) 高くて買えない」という内容にする。us を使うことが必要条件だから，too ... for 〜 to − を用いて書く。「高い」は「値段が高い」のだから expensive。したがって too expensive for us to ⟨buy⟩ となる。逆の発想，つまり「我々が買えるほど安くない」という解釈だが，これだと ⟨That car is⟩ *not cheap enough for us to* ⟨buy.⟩ となって 1 語オーバーしてしまい，不正解。

解 答 例

⑴ [She] is almost always in [class.]
[She] almost always attends [class.]
[She] is almost never absent from [class.]
[She] almost never misses [class.]

⑵ [He] has such poor eyesight that [he can hardly read.]
[He] suffers from such poor eyesight [he can hardly read.]

⑶ [The trains were late] due to the bad [weather.]
[The trains were late] owing to the bad [weather.]

⑷ [No one has ever] paid me such a [nice compliment.]

⑸ [That car is] too expensive for us to [buy.]

4 (A) 〔全訳〕 もし見知らぬ人の腕の中に倒れ込めと言われたら，君はその人が自分を受け止めてくれるだろうと信頼するだろうか？ この例は，心理学ではよく用いられるもので，やや極端ではあるが，毎日ほとんどの人は見ず知らずの人をある程度信頼している。他の動物とは異なり，我々人間は見知らぬ他者のまわりでかなりの時間を過ごす傾向にある。たとえば都会に住む人々は，いつも多くの見知らぬ者の間

— 260 —

2009 年　　解答・解説

を歩き，危険だと感じられる人のことはよけて行こうとする。彼らは，たとえば目的地までの正確な道案内をしてくれそうな人や，どうみても実際自分に危害は加えないであろう人を識別するのも同じように上手である。

考え方 (1) 「もし見知らぬ人の腕の中に倒れ込めと言われたら，君はその人が自分を受け止めてくれるだろうと信頼するだろうか？」　正解は **have**。trust には名詞と動詞の両方があるが，その後に the other person と続いているのだから，ここでは動詞として使われている。ならば，"have trust" は「have ＋原形」ということになって，英語としておかしい。have を削除すれば "would you trust ... " となり，全く問題がなくなる。

(2) 「この例は，心理学ではよく用いられるもので，やや極端ではあるが，毎日ほとんどの人は見ず知らずの人をある程度信頼している」　正解は **on**。put trust in ... で「…を信頼する」という意味の慣用句。some degree of などが挟まっているので少々わかりづらいかもしれないが，この慣用句を知っていれば簡単。

(3) 「他の動物とは異なり，我々人間は見知らぬ他者のまわりでかなりの時間を過ごす傾向にある」　正解は **all**。"others who ... " となっていることから，others は「他人」（＝ other people）という意味の代名詞で用いられている。この場合 others には通常数量詞は一切つけない。

(4) 「たとえば都会に住む人々は，いつも多くの見知らぬ者の間を歩き，危険だと感じられる人のことはよけて行こうとする」　正解は **familiar**。この(4)は，都会に住む人々がどのように見知らぬ人の中で日々暮らしているかを述べた部分。どの語も削らず直訳すると，「常に多くの見知らぬ者の間を歩き，危険だと感じられるよく見知った人のことはよけて行こうとする」となるが，「見知らぬ者の間を歩」いているのだから，そこに危険人物であろうがなかろうが「よく見知った人」が登場するのはおかしい。これは唯一文脈から判断して解かなければならない設問。

(5) 「彼らは，たとえば目的地までの正確な道案内をしてくれそうな人や，どうみても実際自分に危害は加えないであろう人を識別するのも同じように上手である」正解は **other**。接続詞 "or" が何と何をつないでいるのかを理解することがポイント。確かに "some ＋単数名詞＋ or other" で「何らかの（名詞）」という慣用表現は存在するが，問題は other の後に続く who。この who はどう見ても関係代名詞であるから，先行詞は当然〈人〉である。ところが，直前の other も destination も，さらに directions も先行詞にはなり得ない。"others" については上記(3)で解説したように「他人」という意味があるので，これなら先行詞になれるが，"other" は別。したがって，other を削除してしまえば，"identifying others who will, ... or who will, ～ " となり，

— 261 —

<u>2009 年　　解答・解説</u>

関係代名詞 who の並列（先行詞は共通で others）と解釈できる。

ボックス解 ボックス答

(1) have　　(2) on　　(3) all　　(4) familiar　　(5) other

4 (B)　【全訳】　彼女は何と自分の母親を愛していたことか！　彼女の母は 86 歳にしてまだ完璧な美しさを保っていた。(1)母親が自分の年齢に唯一譲歩したのは，補聴器をつけるという点だけだった。「私の耳よ」と母親はその補聴器を呼んでいた。彼女の母親は，触れるものすべてに慎重に触れ，それは母親が触れたがゆえに前より少しなめらかなものになり，幾分かより上品なものになっていた。母親にまつわるすべてのものは彼女に季節とともに変化する木々を思い出させ，母親が身にまとっていた一着一着の衣装を見るたび，彼女は何らかの種類の葉の色を，すなわち，かすかに黄色が混じった春の薄緑，夏の盛りの濃い緑，ときにはまた（オレンジのスカーフや髪を飾る赤いリボンを通じて）明るい秋の細部を思い起こしていた。冬はウール，夏は綿というように，母親が人工繊維を肌身につけることは決してなかった。母親がしばしば口にしたことだが，(2)便利という名の下に，しまいにはより手間がかかることになり，小さいが本当の喜びを人から奪うような無精が，彼女にはどうしても理解できなかった。湿った布に対する温かいアイロンの香り，かつて生きていたものが体に触れる安らぎ。母親は自分では自然だと考えるような労苦から自分を解放しないことが正しいと信じきっていた。彼女は電子フードプロセッサーを持とうとは決してしなかったし，クレジットカードも持とうとはしなかった。野菜を刻むのが好きで，(3)何かの代金を払うときは，その代価を指先で，そして手のひらで感じたい，と彼女は述べた。

【考え方】　(1)　1.　**The only concession she'd made to her age …**「彼女が年齢に対してした唯一の譲歩は…」　only は冠詞と名詞の間に挟まれているので，「唯一の」の意の形容詞。she'd (＝she had) made to her age は関係代名詞が省略された関係詞節で，直前の The only concession を修飾している。この関係詞節を元の文に戻すと she'd made *the concession* to her age（彼女は自分の年齢に対してそうした譲歩をした）となるので，この部分をそのまま訳せば「彼女 (＝her mother) が自らの年齢に対してした唯一の譲歩／彼女が自分の年齢に譲った唯一の点」などとなる。また譲歩とは「仕方なく認める」という意味なので，「彼女が年を取ったことを仕方なく認めてした唯一のこと」などと噛み砕いた訳をしてもかまわない（[解答例 2]参照のこと）。

— 262 —

2009 年　　解答・解説

2. **was a pair of hearing aids**「1 組 の 補 聴 器 だ っ た」 was が The ... concession に対する動詞で, a pair of hearing aids がそれに対する補語。補聴器は両耳にはめるものと考えて a pair of ... が用いられているが,「1組の」は必ずしも訳出しなくてもよいだろう。

(2) 1. **the kind of laziness which, ...**「…の種類の［のような］無精［手抜き］」 which の先行詞は the kind of laziness 全体。「the kind [sort, type] of 名詞＋関係詞節」は英語ではよく見られる言い回しの1つで,「…な種類の［…のような］名詞」などと処理することが多い。

2. **in the name of convenience, in the end**「便利さという名の下に, 結局は」 in the name of convenience と in the end はいずれも関係詞節の中に置かれている副詞句で, 後続する動詞を修飾している。in the name of ... は「…という名の下に」の意の熟語表現。（例）I detest killing animals *in the name of sport.*（スポーツの名の下に動物を殺すのは嫌いだ）

3. **made more work**「より多くの仕事を作り出す；手間を増す」 made は, 関係詞節内で which に対する動詞として働いている。

4. **and deprived one of the small but real joys**「そして, 小さいが本物の喜びを人から奪う」 deprive は, which に対する関係詞節内の2つ目の動詞。deprive A of B で「A から B を奪う」の意。（例）His anger *deprived* him *of* all reason.（彼の怒りは彼からすべての理性を奪い取った→怒りのあまり彼はすっかり理性を失った） 下線部において deprive の目的語として働いている one は「人」を表し, small と real はともに joys を修飾する形容詞として働いている。よって, 全体では「人から, 小さいが本物の喜びを奪う」という意味になる。

(3) 下線部(3)を含む文の文頭近くにある ", she said," は「S ＋ V の挿入」。よって, この文は She *said* that she *liked* ... and when she *paid* ..., she *wanted* to feel, ... と書かれているのと同じということになるので, 下線部が過去形になっているのは「時制の一致」の結果と考えることができる。時制の一致で過去形になっているものは, 日本語訳では「現在」に訳すことになるため, 下線部も現在時制で訳しておけばよい。（例）He *said* that she *was* ill.（彼は彼女は病気であると言った）

1. **when she paid for something**「彼女が何かの代金を払うときには」 後続する主節を修飾する副詞節。pay for ... で「…の代金を払う」の意。

2. **she wanted to feel, ..., the cost**「彼女はその代価を…感じたい」 feel の目的語が the cost であることがつかめたかどうかがこの下線部のポイント。

3. **on the tips of her fingers**「彼女の指先で」 feel を修飾する副詞句。on は「…

— 263 —

2009 年　解答・解説

の上［表面］で」，…に接触して」といった意味を表している。

4. **on the palms of her hands**「彼女の（両）手のひらで」　これも feel を修飾する副詞句。

解 答

---

(1)

［解答例１］　彼女が自分の年齢に対してした唯一の譲歩は補聴器をつけるということであった。

［解答例２］　彼女が高齢になったことを認めてしたことといえば，補聴器をつけることくらいだった。

(2)

［解答例１］　便利さという名の下に，結局は仕事を増やし，ささやかではあるが本当の喜びを人から奪うような無精

［解答例２］　便利さを標榜して，結局はより手間がかかることになり，小さいが本当の喜びを人から奪うような手抜き

(3)　彼女が何かの代金を払うときは，その代価を指先で，そして手のひらで感じたいのだ。

5　**【全訳】**　人間がお互いを欺く方法についての論説を書いているのだと人々が聞くと，すぐさま嘘つきの発見法について語ってくれる。嘘つきはいつも左の方を見るのだと何人かの友人は言う。嘘つきはいつも口を隠すものだと，飛行機で隣の席に乗り合わせた男が言う。嘘をつくとどんな外見になるのかということについての信念は多数あって，矛盾することも多い。嘘つきだとわかるのは，身体の動きが多いからだとか，まったく身動きしないからだとか，足を組むからとか，腕を組むからとか，上を見るからとか，下を見るからとか，目線を合わせるからとか，目線を合わせないからとかである。指の動かし方に十分な注意を払えば嘘つきの人間を察知できるものだとフロイトは考えた。ニーチェは「口は嘘をつくかもしれないが，それでもやはり，嘘をつくせいで生じる表情は本当のことを語る」と書いた。

　たいていの人々が，自分は嘘つきを察知するのが上手だと思っているが，研究が示すところは逆である。専門的訓練を受けた人々が嘘つきを正確に察知する能力を持つことを期待するのは間違っている。概して，裁判官や税関の係員のような，嘘つきをつきとめることを専門にしている人々でさえ，調べてみると，偶然と比べても大して出来は良くない。言い換えると，専門家でさえ，コインを投げて決めたとしても，正

― 264 ―

<u>2009 年　　解答・解説</u>

解率はあまり変わらないだろうということになる。

　誰が嘘をついていて，誰がついていないのかを判断するのが難しいのとちょうど同じように，何が嘘で，何が嘘でないのかを見分けることもまた，私たちが考えがちであるよりもずっと困難である。「誰もが嘘をついている。毎日，毎時間，起きていても，寝ていても，夢を見ながら，喜びながら，悲しみながら」と，マーク・トウェインは書いた。

　第一に，何かを言わないことで成り立つ嘘がある。妹と，そのハンサムなボーイフレンドと一緒に夕食に出かけて，その男がまったく気に入らないと思ったとしよう。その後，その晩のことについて妹と話をするときに，レストランについては語っても，ボーイフレンドについて口にしなければ，嘘をついていることにならないか？　見た目の良さについて語っても，不快な人柄について語らなかったらどうなのだろう？

　次に，事実とちがうとわかっていることを言うことで成り立つ嘘がある。こういう嘘の多くは，お互いうまくやっていくことを可能にしてくれる無害な嘘である。使えない贈り物を受け取ったときや，気にくわない同僚とのランチに招待されたときには，「どうもありがとう，最高の贈り物だよ」とか「行きたいけど，歯医者の予約があってね」とか言う可能性が高く，それよりも不快な真実を語りはしないだろう。これらは，私たちが自分の子どもにも用いるよう教える嘘であり，それを私たちは礼儀作法と称する。近所の人が「お元気ですか？」と機械的に尋ねるのに対して，「元気です」と私たちが同じくらい自動的に応答することでさえ，多くの場合，突き詰めて考えれば，嘘である。

　もっと重大な嘘には，広範囲にわたる動機や含みがある。たとえば，ライバルを首にするために，その行動について嘘をつくことである。しかし，その他の場合には，すべての嘘が暴露される必要のあるものでは必ずしもない。私たち人間は，自発的で創造的な動物であり，存在するものをまるで存在しないかのように，そしてまた，存在しないものをまるで存在するかのように表現することができる動物なのである。隠しごと，ほのめかし，沈黙，あからさまな嘘 —— すべては人間社会の平和維持に役立つのである。

　嘘をつけるようになることは，大人になることの重要な一部である。子どもたちが嘘をつき始めるのは，通常は３歳か４歳頃のことだが，それを可能にしているのは，心の理論，つまり，自分の頭の中で起きていることは，他人の頭の中で起きていることとは異なるという発想を育み始めているということなのである。親に初めてついた嘘でもって，力の均衡が少しずれる。つまり，この時点で彼らは親が知らないことを知っているのである。嘘を新たに１つつくたびに，自分の言うことを信じる人々に対

－ 265 －

<u>2009 年　　解答・解説</u>

する支配力を少しだけ増すのである。しばらくすると，嘘をつく能力は，感情に関して子どもたちが持つ特性の，ただの一要素となる。

　嘘をつくことは，あまりにありふれたもので，私たちの日常生活や日々の会話の一部になりきっているので，私たちはそれにほとんど気づかない。実は，多くの場合，人々は嘘をつくよりも本当のことを言う方が，難しく，能力を試され大変で，ストレスの多いものだ。なにしろ，欺くということは，高度な知性が進化したことと結びつく1つの特性と言えないだろうか？

　現在，「信頼性評価」のための効率的な機械，つまり，完璧な嘘発見器を，「テロリズムとの戦争」における国家の安全保障レベルを上げるための手段として開発しようとする試みが合衆国連邦政府によってなされている。しかしながら，国をより安全にしようとする，このような探求は，まったく思いがけない形で，私たちの日常生活に影響を与えるかもしれない。どのようにして，新たに開発された装置は，どれが本当に危険な嘘であり，どれが無害で，心の優しさから出てきた嘘，ないしは，利己的だが危険でない嘘だと識別できるのだろう？　テロリズムに対する戦いにおいてだけではなくて，国家の安全とほとんど何の関係もない状況，たとえば，就職面接，税務調査，教室，寝室といった状況においても，真実でないことを探知することのできる道具をある日気づくと手にしていたということになったら，どんなことが起こるのだろうか？

　完全な嘘発見器ができたら，私たちの暮らしをひっくり返すことになろう。まもなくして，私たちは語り合うのをやめ，テレビは廃止され，政治家は逮捕され，文明は停止することになるだろう。機械がきちんと作動しないかもしれないということは，私たちが考え慣れている類の危険性であるが，その場合に何が起きる可能性があるかということだけでなく，機械がきちんと作動したらどんなことになる可能性があるかということも考慮しないうちに，そんな装置を性急に市場に出すとしたら間違いだろう。不確実性に満たされた世界，誰が誰に嘘をついているのかを確実には決して知りえない世界に暮らすことよりももっとひどいのは，どこに嘘があるかについての確実性に満たされていて，それゆえ，私たちがお互いに真実しか語らざるをえない世界に暮らすことなのかもしれない。

[考え方]　(1)　正解は**ウ**の **what lying looks like**「嘘をつくことがどのように見えるか」。空所を含む文を訳せば「（　1　）についての意見は多数あって，矛盾することも多い」となり，この文の前後には，嘘をつく人たちの外見・様子について書かれていることを考えれば，容易に正解が得られるだろう。ア why people lie「人々が嘘をつく理由」，イ the timing of lying「嘘をつくタイミング」，エ the kinds of lies

－ 266 －

2009 年　　解答・解説

people tell「人々がつく嘘の種類」は，いずれも文脈にまったく合わない。

　(2)　正解は**イ**の **not much better than chance**「偶然と比べてあまり良いわけではない」。空所を含む文の前後が，いずれも「専門家の嘘発見率でさえあまり高くない」という趣旨の文になっていることから選べばよい。ア as accurately as expected「予想されているのと同じくらい正確に」では専門家の嘘発見率が高いものになってしまうので不可。ウ somewhat worse than average「平均よりもやや悪い」では嘘発見率が低いことになり，エ far better than non-professionals「専門家でない人たちよりもずっと良い」では差が大きすぎてしまう。「比較対象」や「差の程度」は東大の頻出事項である（次の設問も参照のこと）。

　(3)　正解は **than we tend to think to**。東大の語整序問題にありがちな「該当部分の前後を考慮に入れなければならない」タイプの問題。構文的には

Just as it is 　　　　　 hard 　　to decide 　　who is lying and who is not,
it is also much more difficult （　3　）　　tell what is a lie and what is not.

という対比の鮮明な文章であり，it が to 以下をさす形式主語であることも一目瞭然であるから，tell の直前に to を置くことになる。そこで必要なのは，much more という比較級の比較対象であり，それを than we tend to think という形で表せばよい。「現実」と「考えていること」との比較である。ダミーの選択肢 look を使うとしたら，「現実」と「見かけ」の比較ということになるが，今回の文脈，構文では使えない。

　(4)　正解は**ア**の **how you really feel**「本当はどう感じているか」。下線部を含む文が，you're likely to say A rather than speak B という形で，A がウソ，B がホントであることから考えれば正解に至る。この問題も比較対象である。イ the lies children tell「子どもがつく嘘」では対比にならず，下線部そのものとも矛盾する。ウ a visit to the dentist「歯医者へ行くこと」，エ why you don't like lunch「あなたがランチを好きではない理由」は，いずれも具体例に関わりを持たせたダミーの選択肢。

　(5)　正解は「**存在するものをあたかも存在しないかのように，そして存在しないものをあたかも存在するかのように表現することができる**」。この represent は express「表現する」という意味。what exists だけで名詞節を構成し，as if it did not は represent を修飾する。and 以下も同様の構文。as if S + V ... は「あたかも…であるかのように」という意味の表現で，節内の動詞が仮定法になっている。

　(6)　正解は**ア**の **They become less dependent on others.**「他人に前ほど依存しなくなる」。下線部の主語 they は，嘘をつけるようになり始めた子どもを指しており，当該パラグラフの最初に「嘘をつけるようになることは，大人になることの

－ 267 －

2009 年　　解答・解説

重要な一部である」とあることから，ここでは嘘をつくことが，親をはじめとする
他者からの自立であるということについて述べていることを踏まえれば，正解に至
る。イ They learn more clearly to tell right from wrong. 「正しいことと間違った
ことをもっと明確に区別できるようになる」，ウ They realize that their parents are
just like other people. 「自分の親が他の人たちと似たようなものだと理解する」，エ
They understand that they are being encouraged to learn how to lie. 「嘘のつき
かたを学ぶように奨励されているのだと理解する」は，いずれもパラグラフの趣旨に
まったく合わない。

(7)　正解は**イ**の **after all**「なにしろ」。空所を含む文は「欺くということは，(　7　)，
高度な知性が進化したことと結びつく１つの特性と言えないだろうか？」という意味
の修辞的疑問文（反語）であるが，これは直前の文「実は，多くの場合，人々は嘘を
つくよりも本当のことを言う方が，難しく，障害があり，緊張するものだ」への理
由づけになっている。after all には「理由づけ」の意味があることに注意。（例）He
shouldn't be working so hard. He is 78, *after all*. （彼はそんなに一所懸命働くべ
きでない。なにしろ78歳なのだから）　それ以外の選択肢，ア in vain「むだに」，ウ
in no way「少しも…ない」，エ by contrast「対照的に」は，いずれも文意に合わない。

(8)　正解は**ウ**の **in other words**「言い換えると」。空所の前後が，an efficient
machine ... = a perfect lie detector という２つの名詞句の言い換えになっている。
ア all the same「それにもかかわらず」，イ by all means「ぜひとも」，エ on the
other hand「他方」は，文意に合わない。

(9)　正解は**エ**「**利己的だが，国家にとって安全な嘘**」。下線部を直訳すれば「危険
であることなく利己的な」となるが，ここでの「危険」とは，下線部以前の記述から「国
家に対して危険」であるという意味なので，エを選ぶことになる。ちなみに元々の
New York Times の記事では，この直後に in situations that have little to do with
national security「国家的安全にほとんど関係がない状況」という記述が続いている。

(10)　正解は「**嘘発見器が嘘を見抜けないという危険性**」。下線部そのものの意味は「そ
してそれは，私たちが考え慣れている類の危険性である」ということであり，直前の
if it didn't work「嘘発見器が作動しない場合」ということの内容説明になっている。
これだけでは「具体的」な「説明」になっていないので，後方の記述も参照すると，「不
確実性に満たされた世界，誰が誰に嘘をついているのかを確実にはけっして知りえな
い世界」とあることから，「嘘発見器が作動しない」→「嘘発見器が嘘を見抜けない」
と展開すればよい。答案の末尾には risk の訳語も明示するようにして「…という危
険性」とまとめる。

— 268 —

2009 年　　解答・解説

⑾　正解は，(a) **avoid**　(b) **protects**　(c) **maintained**　(d) **revealed**。この「まとめ文」に関連するのは，第5パラグラフ第2文「こういう嘘の多くは，お互いとうまくやっていくことを可能にしてくれる無害な嘘である」や第6パラグラフ最終文「人間社会の平和維持に役立つ」などであり，比較的容易に空所を補充することができるが，以下のような手がかりもある。まず(a)は，前後が cannot（　a　）－ing という形なので，cannot avoid －ing「－することは避けられない」を想定しうる。(b)は，（　b　）A from B なので，protect A from B「A を B から守る」が思い浮かぶ。(c)は前掲の第6パラグラフ最終文に peace-keeping とあり，keep ≒ maintain と考える。(d)に関しては，下線部⑸の1文前の not every lie is one that needs to be uncovered「すべての嘘が必ずしも暴露される必要のない嘘である」も参考になる。

　この文章の大意は以下のとおり。「人間として，私たちはときおり嘘をつくことが避けられない。実際，ときには，嘘をつくことが人を不必要な対立から守ってくれる。多くの場合，人間社会の平和は，必ずしもすべての真実が明らかにされないから維持される」

解答

⑴－ウ

⑵－イ

⑶－ than we tend to think to

⑷－ア

⑸－存在するものをあたかも存在しないかのように，そして存在しないものをあたかも存在するかのように表現することができる。

⑹－ア

⑺－イ

⑻－ウ

⑼－エ

⑽－嘘発見器が嘘を見抜けないという危険性。(19字)

⑾－(a) avoid　　(b) protects　　(c) maintained　　(d) revealed

— 269 —

解答・解説

1 (A) **〔全訳〕** 自分が好意的に見ることのできない人物を魅力的だとか，せめて感じの良い人だと思えるかどうかが，顔に関する大きな問題となっている。私たちは概して顔つきの評価よりも道徳的評価の方に重きを置くものだが，これはもう，たいていの人がほとんどいつもそうしていると言ってよいだろう。それで，道徳的に低い評価をしている人を前にすると，せいぜい「あの人は見かけは良さそうな人だ」という言葉が出るぐらいなのだが，これに「これは表面的な印象にすぎませんが」などと付け加えることもある。しかし，どうやら私たちが実際しているのは，ある人物の過去の品行を知り，そこから，顔に残るその品行の形跡を探るという，いわば逆読みなのである。

　外見と内面が直接相互関係を持つと考えるのには慎重になる必要がある。ある人物の外見だけを見て下した評価から信頼に足る結論を出すのは実際きわめて難しいものだ。また，その人をよく知るようになると，最初の評価がまったく誤りだったことが分かることも多い。ヒトラーが現れ，権力の座についた最初の数年間は，今は彼の顔に極めてはっきりと見える非人道性に気付いた人はほとんどいなかった。口髭をたくわえ，仰々しいジェスチャーをする小男の外見に必ずしも邪悪なところがあるわけではないのだ。身振りと口髭が笑いと共感を誘った，あの有名な喜劇役者チャーリー・チャップリンにもまったく同じ描写が当てはまるだろう。そればかりか，ある有名な映画で，チャップリンは普通の人と悪徳政治指導者の一人二役を演じたが，その演じ方は両者の区別ができないほど似ていた。

〔考え方〕

① 文章のテーマと結論／主張をしっかり捉える。

　要約問題で最も重要なのは，文章全体のテーマを捉え，全体の流れを網羅する答案を目指すことである。断片をつまみ食いしたような印象を与える答案や，勝手な解釈を加えてテーマから乖離していると思われる答案は大失点の原因となりかねないので絶対避けなければならない。また，東大の要約問題では，最近「論説型・主張型」の文章がよく用いられている。筆者の考え方がどこかに述べられているはずで，それを見逃さないように注意すること。

— 272 —

<u>2008 年　　解答・解説</u>

② 文章のアウトライン

＜第 1 パラグラフ＞

1) 顔の問題：自分が好きではない人の顔を魅力的だと思えるかどうか。

2) 概して道徳的な判断をしがち。

3) 道徳的評価が低い人のことは，「見かけは良いが」などと言うことが多い。

4) 人の過去の行動に関する知識から，その証拠が顔に出ていると考える。

＜第 2 パラグラフ＞

1) 外見と内面が直接関係していると考えるのは慎重になるべき。

2) 外見だけの判断から信頼できる結論を出すのは極めて困難であり，その人を
よく知ると最初の判断が間違いだったと分かることが多い。

3) 第 3 文以下→ヒトラー，チャップリンの例

　本年度は，2 段落 264 語から成る文章で「外見と内面の関係をどう考えるべきか」
をテーマとするものである。この文章なら，やはり第 2 段落第 1 文を結語として使う
べきであろう。そこで解答全体は「〈第 1 段落〉だが，外見と内面が直接関係してい
ると考える際に慎重になるべきだ」という部分を中心としたまとめ方にする。もちろ
ん，この文の意味（＝筆者の考え方）をすくい上げていればよいので，「外面と内面
に直接関係があると考えるべきではない［…と考えるのは危険だ］」といったまとめ
方でもよいだろう。大筋としては，よく用いられる文章の構造になっていることに注
意。すなわち，第 1 段落で「一般によくある考え方」を出しておいて，第 2 段落で「筆
者自身の視点」に持ち込むというスタイルである。

③ 第 1 パラグラフ

　ここは「人の顔をどう思うか」について述べたものだが，2 行目の "someone of
whom we cannot approve"「好意的に見ることのできない人」，5 行目の "a person
one has a low moral opinion of"「道徳的に低い評価をしている人」という表現から，
「好意を持てない人／嫌いな人／自分にとって嫌な人」の顔について述べているのだ
と考える。これは，要約問題では過剰な一般化は危険だからである。次に，第 2 文の
"give more weight to moral judgments"「道徳的判断［評価］に重きを置く」から，
この段落の趣旨は「嫌いな人の顔は，一般に道徳的判断によって評価している」といっ
た方向でまとめておくとよいだろう。

　ここで "moral judgments" の内容をもう少しふくらませるなら，最終文の "reading
backward, from knowledge of a person's past behavior to evidence of that

－ 273 －

2008年　解答・解説

behavior in his or her face" を使うしかない。ここで述べられているのは，要するに，「人の顔を見て，いかにも悪そうな人だと考える」のではなく，逆に「ある人物の過去の行動［悪事］を知っていて，それが顔に出ていると考えてしまう」ということなのだが，すべて書くわけにはいかないので，「その人物の過去の行動を道徳的基準に照らして見ている」という程度にまとめるしかない。以上の点から，第1段落は「嫌いな人の顔はその人の過去の行動を道徳的基準に照らして評価しがちだ（33字）」とする。

④　第2パラグラフ

第3文以下は，ヒトラーやチャップリンの例を使って補強した部分なので，ここは先に述べたように，第1文を中心としてまとめるとよいだろう。この文章は全体的に論旨展開の交通標識的な役割を持つ言葉が用いられていない。この部分もそうで，第2文は第1文に対する「言いかえ」とも「補強」とも「理由付け」とも解釈できる。これは人によって意見の分かれるところであろう。そこで，採点官が「理由付け」と解釈したと想定して，まとめることにする。第1文の内容だけでも全体の大筋は表現できるのだが，複数の可能性がある場合は「より厳しい方」を基準にする，という考え方によるものである。

解 答 例

> ［解答例1］　嫌いな人の顔はその人の過去の行動を道徳的基準に照らして評価しがちだが，外見だけで決めるのは困難だし判断が変わることも多く，外見と内面の関係は慎重に考えるべきだ。（80字）
>
> ［解答例2］　嫌な人の顔は，その過去の行動をもとに評価しがちだが，外見のみで結論は出せず最初の判断も変わることが多いので，外見と内面に直接関係があると考えるのは危険だ。（77字）

1 **(B)** **全訳**　人間は頭脳が進化し，ある時，地球外生命の可能性を考えるようになった。もしかしたら，それは数千年前の星降る夜で，原始人が洞窟から歩み出て空を見つめ，初めてあの「私たちしかいないのか」という意味深い問いを発した時かも知れない。以来我々はこれを問い続けてきた。ほんの数年前まで，地球外生命をどこに求めるべきかに関わる重要な鍵が，まさにこの地球上に，それも地中にあるなどとは，誰も想定できなかった。

地球上の生命の起源を探る最近の調査で，地下数千メートル，超高温高圧の環境で繁殖する微生物の興味深い発見がいくつもあった。 ア 岩石や粘土の中で，これ

— 274 —

らの微生物は水を得ることはできるのだが，たいてい，それ以外に我々なら必要だと考えるものがほとんど得られない。　イ　たとえば，多くの微生物は数億年も太陽光線から隔絶されている。　ウ　この微生物は，地表の植物と同様，地下の食物連鎖の基盤をなしている。そして，このような地下の微生物群の存在が証明されたことにより，地球上および地球外の生命に関する我々の考え方は全く変わってしまった。　エ　これは多くの人が高校の生物学で学んだ内容，すなわち，あらゆる生命体は結局太陽エネルギーに依存しているという内容と矛盾することになる。　オ　現在一部の科学者は，これらの地下微生物は地球で最初の生命体の直系子孫なのかも知れないと考えている。

　天文学者などの科学者は，宇宙の惑星の多くは地球によく似た地表下の環境を持つ可能性があるという共通見解を持っている。これらの惑星の中には，内部の気温と気圧の状態が水を保持できるものすらある。さらにこれら惑星の内部深い所には，近い将来，そして遠い将来，人間社会にとって大変有益になると思われる貴重な天然資源が存在するかも知れないのだ。地下深くの極限状況の中で存続する生命体もいるのだから，火星の地下深くに存在してもよい，というわけである。また，一部の科学者が考えているように，もし生命の起源が地下にあるというのなら，太陽系の，いや，宇宙のもっと広い範囲で，多くの似たような環境の一つで生命体が生まれた可能性はないと言えるだろうか。太陽からエネルギーをもらう生命以外には考えられないという我々の偏狭な考え方の中では，もし生命体を維持できる惑星がどこかにあるなら，それは，表面の状態が地球に似ている範囲に収まるという想定をしてきた。しかし現在では，一般に広く認められたこの前提が間違いであり，生命維持が可能な範囲については，地球内部でも宇宙全体でも，想定範囲が狭すぎていたように思われる。

　地球内部の調査をする者にとって，最も興味深い部分は，ある意味，遠くの惑星と全く同様遠く離れている。自分ではその部分に行くことができないので，地下深くから掘り出した土や岩石を実験室で研究することに甘んじてきた。

　しかし最近になって，少数の科学者が，世界で最も深い南アフリカの東ドリエフォンテン金鉱山に入り，夢を実現させる道を見つけた。ここではいくつかのトンネルが地下3kmを超える深さまで掘り下げられている。この金山は建設に数十年かかっており，いかなる基準で考えても工学上の驚異である。典型的な金産出の勤務シフトだと，5千人を超える労働者が地下にいて，新しいトンネルを作り，補強構造物を組み立て，金を含む岩石を掘り出している。

　1998年秋，プリンストン大学の科学者チュリス・オンストットは，慎重な人選を経た科学者の集団とともに，数週間にわたって地下金鉱の労働者の仲間入りをした。最

<u>2008 年　　解答・解説</u>

初の日に研究者チームは，さっそく一番最近掘られた最深部に向かうことにしたが，そこは地表の微生物から生じる汚染が最も少ないと思われる部分であった。地底深くに向かう途中，研究者たちは気圧が上がり，気温が上がるのを感じた。最深部に到達する頃にはひどく発汗しており，水筒に手を伸ばさなければならなかった。地上から 3 km の深さだと，岩石の表面温度は 60℃に達していた。

※　空所×4

選択肢全訳

ア　数ヶ月たってやっと，彼らは持ち帰ったサンプルの分析を実験室で終えることができた。サンプルの一部は，1 グラム当たり 10 万から 100 万という，予想をはるかに上回る数の微生物を含んでいることが分かった。この微生物の多くは実際，極めて独特な生命維持の仕方をしていた。

イ　この南アの金鉱山から珍しい微生物が発見されたことにより，科学者たちは，地球の生命体がどう進化したかを知りたいなら地中のさらなる研究が絶対必要であるという確信を持つに至った。彼らは地球外生命の問題を研究する際，現在では宇宙同様地球の奥深くにも注目しているのである。

ウ　そこは全体的に活気のある場所だった。研究者たちは，ドリルなど掘削用の器具の騒音に負けないよう大声を出してお互いの声を確認しなければならなかった。労働者のヘルメットに取り付けられたランプが，埃の充満した暗闇のあちこちに見受けられ，火薬の臭いが漂っていた。騒音も，身体の不快感も，そして何よりも事故の危険が現実にあることも忘れて，研究者たちは仕事にとりかかった。

エ　サンプルを入れる袋がすべて一杯になると，彼らは暫くの間あたりを見渡してみた。その翌日には戻る予定だったが，彼らは興奮のためその場を去る気にはなれなかった。やがて，体力がなくなり始め，彼らは地表まで乗るエレベーターに戻った。

考え方　(1)　正解はウ。2006 年と同様の文補充問題。この文は「こうしたすべてのことにも関わらず，これらの微生物はその大きさに全く不釣り合いな重要性を持っている」という意味だが，"all this" の内容が前にあり，かつ，微生物の持つ "an importance" の内容が後で詳述されることになる位置を考える。空所ウに入れると，this が第 1 文の「超高温高圧で生きている」や「水以外には，生存に必要だと思われるものがほとんど得られない（たとえば太陽光線）」など，微生物にとって「不利な点」を指すことになるし，空所ウ以下で述べられた「食物連鎖の基盤を成す」や「その存在が科学者の考え方を変えてしまった」という内容が an importance の展開部分と

— 276 —

2008 年　　解答・解説

して対応することになる。

(2)　正解は(a)。この段落は，「生命体の存在条件・誕生の条件」に関する科学者の見解をまとめたものである。したがって，(a)「さらに，これら惑星の内部には，人間社会にとって大変有益になると思われる天然資源があるかも知れない」という文は，生命体がどこにどんな条件で誕生しうるか，また存続しうるか」という論旨とは「最も関係のうすい」文だと考える。決定的な根拠ではないが，"life"という言葉が(b)〜(e)にはあるが，(a)にはないこともヒントになるかも知れない。

(3)　正解はウ−エ−ア−イ。東大の1(B)では，「解説型」の文章で，事の進展・経緯を時系列に沿って記述するものが多い。この設問もその特徴を反映しており，ポイントは「論理関係」ではなく「経過」である。「地下に降りる」→「サンプルを集める」→「地上に戻る」→「実験室で分析する」→「さらに研究の必要性を確信」という流れで考えればよい。

また，この設問では指示語・代名詞・冠詞・言いかえなどの手がかりは「解答の裏付け」程度に利用すればよいだろう（ウの "The whole area" が南アの金鉱山内部を指し，アの "Many of these microbes did indeed have unusual ways of ..." がイの "the strange microbes" に対応する）。

(4)　正解はウ。

ア「他の惑星に生命を探す」

イ「微生物が地下でどのように生きているか」

ウ「生命の基盤に関する新たな理解」

エ「科学者が工学上の驚異を調査」

オ「東ドリエフォンテン金鉱山の重要性」

一般にタイトル選択問題は，「過剰一般化の表現」を含むもの，「過剰限定の表現」を含むもの，「無関係な内容」を含むものを排除し，消去法で絞り込んでいけばよい。このパッセージ全体が「生命の起源」について述べたもので，これまで思いもよらなかった「地下に潜む微生物にその起源があるかも知れない」という内容なので，正解はウとなる。

解答

(1)−ウ　　(2)−(a)　　(3) ウ−エ−ア−イ　　(4)−ウ

— 277 —

2008年　解答・解説

2 (A) 【全訳】（メッセージ文のみ）

> ヨシコとジョンへ
>
> 　来週タルボット先生の授業でやるグループ発表のことなんだけど，どんなふうに準備を進めたらいいかお知恵拝借，ということでお二人にメールしました。僕の案なんだけど，まず一人が温暖化とか，高齢化社会とか，環境問題など今問題になっている事柄について下調べをして，一人がそれについて短いまとめを書き，残り一人がそのまとめを基にグループ代表で発表をする，というのはどうかなと思ってます。どう思いますか？
> では。
> ケン

> ケンへ
>
> 　メッセージありがとう。あなたの提案はとてもいいと思うんだけど，(1)(　　　　)。だから，私は(2)(　　　　)と提案したいです。
> よろしく。
> ヨシコ

> ケンへ
>
> 　僕もヨシコの案がいいと思うな。明日もっと話しあおうよ。
> 　よろしく。
> ジョン

【考え方】

＜語数について＞

　「それぞれ 15 ～ 20 語で」とあるからには，この指定より多くても少なくてもまずいだろう。答案を書いたら，最後に「〇〇 words」と書き添えるのが望ましい。

＜答案を書く上での注意＞

☆ 空所(1)(2)ともに文の途中を埋めるので，書き出しは当然小文字となるだろうが，大文字にしても減点はないだろう。

☆ 15 ～ 20 語という語数，および空所の最後にピリオドが打たれていることから，1つの空所には一文を書くことが望ましいとは思うが，二文以上になってしまっても減点はないだろう。

— 278 —

2008 年　　解答・解説

☆ 空所(1)と(2)の内容は連動していなければならない。内容的につながりのないことを書けば当然減点。

☆ 空所(2)は直前に "suggest that" とあるので，述語動詞は仮定法現在（つまり動詞の原形）または「should ＋原形」にしなければならない。

＜内容面のポイント＞

空所(1)

空所の直前に "Your suggestion sounds very interesting, but ..." とあるが，逆接の接続詞 but が使われていることから，実際には "interesting" ではない，つまりヨシコなりの不満があることがわかる。したがってここには，**ケンの提案に対する反論・注文・不満点などが具体的に書かれている必要がある**。さらに，単に不平不満をいうだけでなく，その理由も含まれているべきであろう。ただ，何分にも語数が少ないので，簡潔に書くこと。

空所(2)

空所の直前は "So, I would rather suggest that ..." となっていることから，ケンの提案に対する**ヨシコの代替案・改善策が書かれている必要がある**（繰り返して言うが，空所(1)で述べた内容に対応していること）。この代替案をヨシコがすすめる理由だが，空所(1)で書いた内容から明らかな場合は割愛してよいだろう。

＜答案作成＞

空所(1)(2)は内容が連動しているため，解答例を素材にこの２つをまとめて考えてみる。

［解答例１］

(1) 「下調べ・まとめ・発表という作業の担当を一人ずつに振り分けるべきでない」（反論）＋「不公平だ」（理由）

(2) 「全員が３つの作業に携わるべし」（代替案）

「一人が一作業」に反対するのだからこのような結論にするか，または「発表は一人でもいいが，他の作業は…」のごとき内容にするべき。

［解答例２］

(1) 「下調べはとても一人で出来る作業ではない」（注文）＋「下調べには時間と労力がかかる」（理由）

(2) 「下調べは全員で行うべし」（代替案）

「理由」は空所(1)に書かれているのでカット。補足説明として「この方が能率がよい」とつけくわえた。

— 279 —

<u>2008 年　　解答・解説</u>

［解答例３］

⑴ 「誰が発表を行うか決めるのは難しい」（注文）＋「発表をするのは大変な作業だから」（理由）

⑵ 「発表を３つのパートに分けて，一人がひとつずつ担当するべし」

「理由」は空所⑴に書かれているのでカット。

解 答 例

［解答例１］

⑴ I don't think it is fair to divide the entire work among the three of us

(16 words)

⑵ each of us do research, write a paper, and do his or her own share of the presentation (18 words)

［解答例２］

⑴ I think doing the research will take time and effort, and that is more than just one person can do (20 words)

⑵ all of us should work together on doing the research; I believe this would be far more efficient (18 words)

［解答例３］

⑴ we'll have trouble deciding who should give the presentation, because giving the presentation is a very tough job (18 words)

⑵ we divide the presentation into three parts, then each of us will be in charge of one part (18 words)

2 ⒝ 考え方

＜語数について＞ → ⒜ の解説を参照のこと。

＜内容面のポイント＞

　盛り込まれていなければならない内容は次の２点。この２つにそれぞれ何語くらい割くかを気にする必要は全くない。両方が書かれてさえいれば，そのバランスは問題ではないからだ。

① 「今から 50 年の間に起こる交通手段の変化」

　空想的世界でも現実的な事柄でも構わない。なぜそのような変化が訪れるのか，原因・理由を書く必要はない（むろん書いても構わないが，長く書きすぎて次の②が落ちてしまうようなら減点になる）。

— 280 —

2008 年　　解答・解説

② 「①が人々の生活に与える影響」

　人々の日常生活に与える影響を書く。プラスに働くことでもマイナスに働くことでもよいが，必ず具体的に書くこと（設問で指示されている）。抽象的・概念的なことを書けば減点されるであろう。

＜答案作成＞

　解答例を素材に，どのような流れで書くかを検討してみよう。

［解答例 1 ］

☆「個人用の『空飛ぶ絨毯』のようなものが発明されるだろう」

　「交通手段の変化」をまず具体的に述べる。

☆「個人用の『空飛ぶ絨毯』＝ 遠くの場所へすみやかに運んでくれる乗り物」

　単に「個人用の空飛ぶ絨毯」ではどのようなものかわからないので，読み手がわかりやすいよう定義した。

☆「この発明により，バス・電車・飛行機などは消滅」

　ここまでが①の「交通手段の変化」に相当する。

☆「いつでもどこでも好きな所に旅行できるようになる」

　非常に少ないが，これが②の「人々の生活に与える影響」である。

［解答例 2 ］

☆「温室効果ガスを放出する乗り物はすべて禁止される」

　「禁止される」理由として，「温暖化の問題のために」と一言触れてある。ちなみに，この「乗り物」の具体例は次の項目で書き表している。

☆「車・バイク・タクシー・バスなどはすべて電気か水素で動くものになる」

　「すべて禁止される」だけでは具体性がないので，「禁止された」後どうなるのかを述べている。ここまでが①の「交通手段の変化」に相当。

☆「どこへ行くにも今より時間がかかるようになるから，大変不便」＋「空気がきれいになる・人々がより健康になる」

　これが②の「人々の生活に与える影響」。交通手段の変化がもたらすマイナス面を最初に挙げ，「譲歩－逆接」でプラス面を強調した。

［解答例 3 ］

☆「どこへ行くにも自分の足で移動するしかなくなる」

　理由として，「化石燃料の枯渇」を挙げてある。さらに「徒歩・自転車など」と書き足すことで具体性を持たせている。これが①。

☆「職場や学校の近くに住まざるをえなくなる」

　導入として「これは人々の生活を大きく変える」という趣旨の英文をつけている。

－ 281 －

2008 年　　解答・解説

これと次が②。

☆「コミュニティを中心とした生活が復活する」

　とりあえずポイントを箇条書きしたが，実際の答案では箇条書きするわけにはいかない。これらをどうまとめるかも採点上のポイントとなる。つまり，英語が正しければ何をどう書いてもいい，ということではないのである。1つのまとまった passage にするためには，有効な discourse marker を使うことが重要だ。

解答例

［解答例1］

　Something will be invented like a personal flying carpet, that is, a personal vehicle that can take a person to a distant place very quickly. People who have one will no longer have to take a bus, a train or an airplane, so these means of transportation will disappear. People will be able to travel whenever and wherever they like. (60 words)

［解答例2］

　Because of the problem of global warming, all vehicles that emit greenhouse gases will be banned. Cars, motorcycles, taxis, and buses will run on electricity or hydrogen. Certainly people may feel a little inconvenienced because it'll take far longer to get anywhere, but the air will be much cleaner and people will become more and more healthy. (57 words)

［解答例3］

　Within fifty years, we'll run out of fossil fuels, and we'll have no choice but to depend on ourselves to move around, like walking and using bicycles. This will drastically change the way we live. We will have to live close to work, school, or anything necessary to our lives, so a community-based lifestyle is sure to revive. (58 words)

4 (A) **【全訳】**　3カ国語を話すことが私にとって何を意味するのか，説明するのに苦労してきた。私はそれを3カ国語を「話す」ことだとは考えていない。むしろそれらの言語の中に生き，それらを呼吸しているような気分なのである。自分は実際多言語使用者ではなく，むしろ3つの言語の1つを使っているのであると説明しようと

― 282 ―

2008 年　　解答・解説

していた時期がかつてあった。その頃私の生活は実際３つの世界に分割されていたため，そのように感じたのである。今日では，より統合された生活様式，つまり３つの言語およびそれらが属しているさまざまな世界を行ったり来たりする生活様式に落ち着いたように思われる。それらの世界と私との関係，決して安定せず，常に強力で，時としてこわかったり厄介だったり，また時として刺激的だが，決してあいまいなものになることのない複雑な関係を，私は見失うことはない。

　私の人生は，私の周りにあった言語，絶対に学ぼうとしなかった言語，学びたくてしかたがなかった言語，専門的に研究した言語，そして私が物を考えたり，書いたり，人をおもしろがらせたり，仕事をしたりするときに使う，親しみを感じる言語など，さまざまな言語との関わり合いだと見なすことができる。時折私は，１つの言語の中で生まれ，育ち，大人としての人生を過ごしてきた人たちのことをとてもうらやましいと思う。安心感，安定感，自己制御感というものを私は持たないが，この人たちは持っていることだろう。いつものように，これらの感情が他の感情にもなりうるなどと全く意識することなく。

考え方　(1)「自分は実際多言語使用者ではなく，むしろ３つの言語の１つを使っているのであると説明しようとしていた時期がかつてあった」正解は **than**。"I was not really multilingual, but rather than monolingual" の部分だが，これは not A but B の構文。したがって，multilingual と monolingual の並列と考えるべきなので，than は不要である。rather とくれば than，という条件反射的な考え方をいましめる設問。

　(2)「今日では，より統合された生活様式，つまり３つの言語およびそれらが属しているさまざまな世界を行ったり来たりする生活様式に落ち着いたように思われる」正解は **hardly**。下線部の直前に "my life was really split between three worlds" とあり，下線部冒頭には "have settled into a more integrated lifestyle" とある。つまり，「筆者の生活が３つに分かれていた」時期と，「１つにまとまっている」今日という対比がつかめれば，hardly seem to と否定文になっているのはおかしい。

　(3)「私の人生は，私の周りにあった言語，絶対に学ぼうとしなかった言語，学びたくてしかたがなかった言語，専門的に研究した言語，そして私が物を考えたり，書いたり，人をおもしろがらせたり，仕事をしたりするときに使う，親しみを感じる言語など，さまざまな言語との関わり合いだと見なすことができる」正解は **them**。"I think in, write in, am funny in, work in them" は完全な英文の形をとっているが，そうすると those とのつながりが問題になる。ここは「目的格の関係代名詞の省略」と考えないと整合性がなくなってしまうので，them を削除する。

— 283 —

2008 年　　解答・解説

(4)「時折私は，１つの言語の中で生まれ，育ち，大人としての人生を過ごしてきた人たちのことをとてもうらやましいと思う」　正解は **at**。envy は第３文型をとる動詞であるから，at が存在すると envy の目的語がなくなってしまう。

(5)「安心感，安定感，自己制御感というものを私は持てないが，この人たちは持っていることだろう。いつものように，これらの感情が他の感情にもなりうるなどと全く意識することなく」　正解は **not**。下線部最後にある "it could not be otherwise" だが，この it は the feeling of comfort, of certainty, of control を指す。この下線部が言わんとしていることは，「筆者は３つの言語の中で生まれ育ったので，常にアイデンティティのゆらぎがあったが，１つの言語の中で生まれ育った人間にはそれがないから常に精神的に安定しており，よもや言語の問題で自分の心がゆれる可能性があるなどと考えてもいないだろう」ということ。したがって，not が不要となる。これは文脈を的確に把握していないと解けない設問なので，むずかしい。

解答

(1) than　　(2) hardly　　(3) them　　(4) at　　(5) not

4 (B) 【全訳】　われわれが現在，コミュニケーションに対する取り組み方に関して大きな変化を経ていることは議論の余地がない。そうした変化の２つの最も明白な象徴は，携帯電話と電子メールである。こうしたコミュニケーションツールの出現が世の中の景観に対して与える影響を見ると，電話によるコミュニケーションにおいて生じている変化の方が２つのうちで大きいように思えるかもしれない。というのは，それが路上でも，エレベーターの中でも，そしてレストランでもあまりに目につくからだ。しかしこれは単なる技術上の変化に過ぎない。コードがない電話は，とても小さいのでポケットに収まり，非常に奇跡的な技術を内蔵しているので，ロンドンのタクシーの後部座席からよく考えずに家に電話をすることができるが，それでもそれは電話に過ぎないのである。

対照的に，郵便の本質の変化の方がはるかに重大であり，そこに含まれる意味合いは革命的以外の何ものでもない。電子メールは，異なった手段を使って手紙を書くことに過ぎないように一見思えるかもしれない。しかし，もっとよく見ると，この新しいコミュニケーションの手段は，我々の情報処理能力だけでなく，人間の接触の本質にも重大な変化をもたらしている。その使用は見た目には簡単であるように思えるため，我々はそれについて知らなくてはいけないことはすべて分かっていると考えてしまうかもしれないが，実際には電子メールは，それが何であるかを我々が本当に理解

— 284 —

しないままに，我々の生活に浸透してしまっているのだ。

考え方 (1) 1. **A phone without wires**「コードのない電話」 要は携帯電話のこと。文全体の主語になっている。

2. **so small that it fits in a pocket**「あまりに小さいのでポケットに収まる」 it は a phone without wires を受けている。a phone を修飾するように訳し上げても（「あまりに小さくポケットに収まる電話」）解答例のように副詞的に処理して訳し下してもかまわない。

3. **containing such miracles of technology that ...**「…のような技術の奇跡（奇跡的な技術）を内蔵していて」 この箇所の処理も 2．と同様，訳し上げても訳し下してもよい。

4. **one can call home from the back seat of a London taxi without thinking twice**「ロンドンのタクシーの後部座席から家に，よくよく考えなくても電話ができる」 one は「人」を表す用法であり，特に訳出しなくてもかまわない。think twice は「よく考える」の意の熟語。without thinking twice（よく考えないまま）全体は call を修飾する副詞句として働いている。

5. **is still just a phone**「〈電話は〉それでも電話に過ぎないのだ」 1．の主語に対応する動詞が is で，just a phone が is の補語。still は「それでもなお」の意。just は only と同義。

(2) 1. **the shift in the nature of mail**「郵便の本質の変化」 the shift が文の主語。nature は「自然」ではなく，「本質，性質」の意。また，mail を「メール」と訳すと日本語では一般に「電子メール」を指してしまうが，この箇所は「電子メール」の性質が変わったということを論じているわけではないので，「メール」という訳語はここでは不可。

2. **is by far the more profound**「…は，はるかに深い（重大である）」 by far は直後の比較級を強調しており，訳出上は「はるかに，ずっと」などと処理するのがよい。the more profound と比較級に the がついているのは，the more profound のあとに of the two が省略されているため。(例) Bill is *the taller* of the two. (二人のうちではビルの方が背が高い)

3. **and its implications are nothing less than revolutionary**「そして，それに含まれている意味合いは革命的以外の何物でもない」 its は the shift を受ける代名詞。implication は「含意，意味合い」の意。nothing less than ... は「まさに…にほかならない；…以外の何物でもない」の意の熟語的な表現。(例) It is *nothing less than murder*. (それはまさに殺人も同然だ)

— 285 —

2008 年 　 解答・解説

⑶　1.　**e-mail has overtaken us**「電子メールは我々の生活にすっかりと入り込んでいる」　ここで overtake を「…を追い越す」と訳しても文意が不明確である。文脈上，ここでは overtake を affect suddenly and powerfully（突然，そして強く影響を与える）といった意味に解釈するのが妥当。「突然として我々に大きな影響を与えるようになっている」という意味合いに解釈できる訳語は広く認められるであろう。

　2.　**without our really understanding what it is**「それが何であるか我々が本当に理解しないまま」　understanding が without の目的語として働く動名詞で，our がその動名詞の意味上の主語。what it is という名詞節が understanding の目的語になっている。

解答

> ⑴　コードがない電話は，とても小さくポケットに収まり，きわめて奇跡的な技術を内蔵しており，ロンドンのタクシーの後部座席からよく考えずに家に電話をすることができるが，それでもそれはなお電話に過ぎないのである。
> ⑵　郵便の本質の変化の方がはるかに重大であり，そこに含まれる意味合いは革命的以外の何ものでもない。
> ⑶　電子メールは，それが何であるか我々が本当に理解しないまま，我々の生活に浸透してしまっているのだ。

5　全訳　ジャッキーは，窓枠にぼんやりともたれかかって，家の前の浜辺をじっと見ていた。浜辺の遠くの方に，青い服を着た見慣れた人影がゆっくりと家に向かって来るのが見えた。ジャッキーは，こういう時間が好きだった。娘をこっそりと観察できる時間だ。トニーは急速に成長していた。ジャッキーが，戸惑い気味の7歳の娘を連れてここへやってきてから，まだ間もないような気がした。トニーがどんなに父親のことを敬愛していたことか！　娘がまだほんの5歳か6歳のころ，家族みんなで都会から浜辺へと毎週末に長旅をしたものだ。そんなときに，娘は父親とこの上なく大きな荒波へと出ていって，勇敢にも父の背中にしっかりしがみついて，一緒に波遊びをしながら喜びの叫びをあげたものだった。娘は父親を心底信頼していた。それから，父親は母娘を捨てた。何の書き置きも，他の何もなかった。何の前兆もなく。

　今やトニーの姿がずいぶんくっきりと判別できた。トニーが波打ち際の岩の上に靴を置き，濡れた砂の中へと足を踏み入れてから，手を腰にあて，首をかしげて下の方を見つめながら，突っ立っているのをジャッキーは目にした。あの子は何を考えてい

— 286 —

2008 年　　解答・解説

るのだろう？　　ジャッキーは愛情が込み上げてくるのを感じたが，それはほとんど衝
撃的といってもよいほど強いものだった。「あの子のためだったら何でもするわ」と
彼女はふと声に出して言った。「何でも」

　8年前に都会からこの家へ引っ越してきたのもトニーのためだった。過去に別れを
告げ再出発をしたかったのである。きっと，こちらの方が，子育てをするのが簡単で
安全で楽しいだろう，と。そして確かに，そのとおりだった。トニーは，自転車で学
校へ行き，友人たちの家に走って出入りして，安全に，浜辺を散策することができて
いた。放課後，ジャッキーが仕事をしている間，トニーが出かける場所に事欠いたこ
とは一度もなかった。親子関係も順調で，トニーは何一つ面倒をかけさせなかった。
そんなわけで，残るところあとわずか3年もすれば，ジャッキーの心づもりとしては，
都会に戻って，ティムと一緒に入居して，ことによっては，結婚するかもしれない。

　彼女は時計を見上げた。4時だった。7時には彼がここへ来るだろう。いつもの金
曜日とちょうど同じように。トニーを別にすれば，彼女が世界でいちばん愛している
のは彼だった。毎週末に，彼がやってきて，家族のように一緒に過ごした。ティムは，
一緒に都会へ行って暮らしたい気持ちをジャッキーに押しつけたことは一度もなかっ
た。トニーが卒業するのをまず見届けたいとジャッキーが考えているのがわかってい
たのだ。彼女に心の準備ができるまで喜んで待つつもりだと言っていた。ジャッキー
は，そんなとりはからいが気に入っていた。平日の間，顔をあわせないことで，かえっ
てずっと新鮮な関係でいられた。毎週金曜日になると，話したいことがたくさんでき
ていた。準備をすること，たとえば，髪を洗って乾かしたり，お気に入りの服を着て，
かわいらしく見えるようにしたりといったことが，とても楽しかった。ジャッキーは，
トニーとティムのことを神に感謝した。

＊　＊　＊

　トニーは濡れた砂の中に足をさらにいっそう押しつけた。まだ家に帰りたくなかっ
た。考えないといけないことがあまりにも多すぎた。家ではママがあわただしく動き
まわって，歌ったり，掃除したり，ティムのための準備をしたりしているだろう。すっ
かり興奮して。ママの年頃の人があんな風にふるまうなんて！　あれはちょっとやり
すぎだわ，まったく，とトニーは考えた。ちょっとかわいそうと言ってもいいくらい。
ティムはすばらしいけれど…トニーは認めざるをえなかった。パートナーがいるとい
うことで，ママには本当に良かったと思う部分もあったが，その反面，とまどう部分
もあった。いや，今はまだ家には帰らないぞ，と。

　彼女は顔を上げて浜辺を見渡した。誰もいなくてほっとした。この服を着ていると
ころを人に見られるのがいやだった。派手で，女の子っぽすぎるんだもの。土曜日に

— 287 —

<u>2008年　　解答・解説</u>

することになるバイトに応募してきたところで，ママが着せたものだった。「ねえ，すてきじゃない。それを着ているとかわいく見えるわよ。いい印象を与えるっていうのは大切よ」と彼女は言っていた。そう，それでバイトは合格。ママは今頃，私のことを待っていて，その知らせを聞きたがっている。そして，まるで賞か何かを受けたみたいに大興奮してしまうでしょうよ。彼女はときおり，ママが物事にそんなに興奮しなければいいのにと願った。ただし，一つ良いことがあった。今回は自分自身のお金を手にすることになり，気分転換に欲しいと思う服をいくらかは買えることになる。

　一つ，確かなことがあった。今夜は，この服を着ていかないということだ！　ママに外出許可をぜったいもらえるように，家を出るときには着ているけれど，クリシーのところで着替えるつもり。全てがやや複雑な状況になっていた。それまでは，こんなことをする必要は一度もなかった。ダンスに出かける許可をママからもらうだけでも，十分大変だった。

　「監督の役割をする人はいるの？」「お酒は出るの？」「終わりは何時？」といった質問が次々と。まるで警察の尋問だ。他の子の親たちは，ママみたいにくどくない。でもともかく，出かける許可はもらえた。今回は初めてのビーチ・クラブなのだ！

　外出許可をもらおうとすることすらしなくたっていいわよとクリシーは言っていた。「ママとボーイフレンドが寝床に入ったら窓から出ればいいだけのこと」というのが彼女のアドバイスだった。「どうせ盛り上がるのは遅くなってからだからね」　でも，トニーにはそんなことはできなかった。今回は最初の一回であり，そんなことは決して無理だった。トニーがかなり早口にまくしたてた後で，ともあれママは出かけてもいいと言ってくれていた。いくつか嘘をつく必要があったけれど，結局，ママはのんでくれた。「クリシーの両親が連れてってくれるの。監督役の親が5組，来るわ。お酒はなしよ。11時半までには戻るわ」

　最後の嘘に，彼女はとりわけ気まずい思いになっていた。11時半なんて，無理にきまってる！　でも，いったん家を出てしまえば，ママにはわからないわ。トニーは砂の中へ足をさらに深くねじこんだ。あれこれの嘘のことで，ほんのちょっとだけ不安だった。でも，なぜ心配する必要があるの？　誰だって嘘をつく必要があるのよ。そうしなかったら，どこにも行けないじゃないの。クリシーをごらんよ。もう1年もの間，彼女がまんまとすり抜けてやってきたことを見てごらん。

[考え方] (1)　正解はイの **It seemed like only yesterday that**「…はほんの昨日のことのようだった」。本文の It seemed no time since を直訳すれば「…以来，ゼロの時間のようだった」となることから「…以来，ほとんど時間が経過していないようだった」という意味だと考えれば，正解に至る。ア It appeared to be so

－ 288 －

2008 年　　解答・解説

long ago that「…はずいぶん昔のことのように思われた」では意味が逆。ウ It had always been such a rush since「…以来ずっとこのように慌ただしかった」や，エ It allowed her little time to think since「…以来，彼女にはそのせいで考える時間がほとんどなかった」も意味が通らない。

(2)　正解は **out**。make out は，受験生なら当然知っているはずの「わかる」という意味の熟語。ここでは「見えたり聞こえたりしたものが判別できる」という意味で使われている。(例) I could just *make out* a figure in the darkness.（暗闇の中に，かろうじて人影が見えた）

(3)　正解は，2番目 **behind**，5番目 **start**（与えられた語をすべて並べ替えると past behind them and start again となる）。まず，空所の手前が wanting to put the となっていることを確認する。定冠詞があることから，基本的には名詞表現が続くことになるが，child を入れても後が続かない。そこで past を続け，put the past という表現を得ることになるが，これだけでは「過去をどう put」するかが不明なことと，本文の文脈を考え合わせて，put the past behind them「過去を忘れる，過去を考えないようにする」という表現にすればよい。その後に続く and start again が原形なのは，空所の手前の to と結びついた不定詞だからである。空所の部分だけを見ているとうっかりしやすいポイントなので注意が必要。ちなみに，put the past behind and start them としてしまうと，them の指示内容が不明になってしまうので誤りとなる。

(4)　正解はウの **no trouble**。まず空所直後に否定を強める whatsoever があることから，弱い否定語の little ではなく強い否定語の no を含んだ選択肢のア no joy かウ no trouble に絞られる。空所の手前の部分に，母と娘の二人の人間関係が順調だったという趣旨の記述があることから，ウを選び，「トニーは彼女をまったく心配させなかった」とすればよい。

(5)　正解はウの **wait until Toni finished school**。下線部のうちで see Toni through school は「トニーが学校を卒業するのを見届ける」という意味。空所4の直後に，ジャッキーが3年後には都会へ戻りたいと思っているとの記述があり，ティムが都会へ戻ることをジャッキーに押しつけたことはないと述べられた後に，この下線部が続いているという流れからも文意は自然に把握できるはず。ア「トニーが学校へ出かけるのを見送る」，イ「トニーが学校で一番になるのを助ける」，エ「トニーが学校へ行く姿を見るのを楽しむ」は，いずれも文意に合わない。

(6)　正解は「年甲斐もなく，恋人の来訪を待ち焦がれ興奮している態度。」　まず，下線部そのものは「ちょっとやりすぎ」という意味。設問文に「母親のどのような態

— 289 —

2008 年　　解答・解説

度」とあることから，母親を主語として，母親を描写している文を検討することになる。該当箇所は，下線部の直前の２つの文（家ではママがあわただしく動きまわって，歌ったり，掃除したり，ティムのための準備をしたりしているだろう。すっかり興奮して。ママの年頃の人があんな風にふるまうなんて！）となる。ここを制限字数にまとめれば，①恋人を迎え入れるために，②興奮する姿が，③年齢不相応，ということになり，これを字数以内の自然な日本語にすれば正解が得られる。

(7)　正解はイの **She is looking forward to spending her wages on new clothes.**「新しい服に給料を使うのを楽しみにしている」。トニーが新しいバイトで新しい服を買えると考えているということは，段落末尾に書かれている。この選択肢は，設問の「段落に描かれている Toni の心理」から考えると，枝葉末節の記述にも見えるが，他の選択肢が以下のように，まったく見当はずれなので，イを正解にするしかない。ア「獲得した賞を受けとるのを楽しみにしている」，ウ「仕事についての母親のニュースを聞くのを楽しみにしている」，エ「雇い主に良い印象を与えるのを楽しみにしている」。

(8)　正解はウの「母親に対して不誠実である」。直前の文のトニーの行動が何を意味するかを考えればよい。トニーは，母親に言われた服を「家を出るときには着ているけれど，クリシーのところで着替える」ことにしているのであり，これは母親に隠れた行動をすることになる。ア「服を買う」は前の段落のことであり，この下線部と直接関係がない。イ「友だちの家に泊まる」は本文にない。エ「窓から家を出る」という２つ後の段落の内容は，指示語として遠すぎるし，トニーの行動についての部分的な記述にすぎないので不可。

(9)　1. **Look at ...**「…を見てごらん」　通常の命令文と異なり，トニーの心中表現であることに注意する。

2. **what she had been getting away with ...**「クリシーがまんまとすり抜けてやってきたことを」　get away with ... は「…をうまくやってのける，まんまと成功する，とがめられずにすむ，罰せられないでやりとおす」という意味の熟語。(例) I can't let you *get away with* such statements. (君にそんなことをぬけぬけと言わせておくわけにはいかない)

3. **for a year now**「もう一年もの間」　for＋期間＋now で「もう…の間」という意味になる。(例) I have lived here *for nearly two years now*. (私がここに住みついてもう２年近くになる)

(10)　正解はウの **Toni and her mother moved to a house by the beach when Toni was seven.**「トニーと母親は，トニーが７歳のときに海辺の家へ越してきた」。

－　290　－

2008 年 解答・解説

下線(1)の直後に she and the confused little seven-year-old had arrived here「彼女と戸惑い気味の7歳の子がここへやってきた」とあるのが，ジャッキーとトニーのことだと理解するのは容易であろう。ア「トニーの父親はトニーが7歳のときに一人で暮らすために都会へ引っ越した」は，同段落末尾にトニーの父親の行方がわからないと書かれていることに矛盾する。イ「トニーと両親は，トニーが7歳になるまで海辺の家で暮らしていた」，エ「トニーの父親は，トニーが7歳になるまで週末に会うために海辺にやってきた」も本文と矛盾する。

(11) 正解は，(a)－オ，(b)－イ，(c)－エ，(d)－ア（空所に適合した形で言えば，**realize, fails, loves, become**）。まず，動詞の文型（後にどのような形が続くか）を考えるだけでも選択肢がかなり絞り込めることにも注意しておきたい。(a)は that 節が続くので，realize か wish ということになるが，節の中が現在進行形であることから，realize を選ぶのが自然である。(b)には fail を入れて，fail to 不定詞「…しない，…できない」の意とする。(c)は「トニーは依然として彼女を…している」という意味から考えて，love を入れる。(d)は直後に形容詞相当語句が続いているので，become を入れるのがよい。

この文章の大意は以下のとおり。「ジャッキーは，娘が急に，それもひょっとすると自分が望んでいるよりも急速に大人になっているということを理解していない。トニーにはトニーなりの考えや思いがあるということを理解できていないのである。トニーは依然として母親を愛しているものの，親子関係にはちょっと居心地の悪い思いをしていて，もっと自立したいと願っている」

解答

(1)－イ　　　(2)－ out

(3)　2番目－ behind　　　5番目－ start

(4)－ウ　　　(5)－ウ

(6)　年甲斐もなく，恋人の来訪を待ち焦がれ興奮している態度。(27字)

(7)－イ　　　(8)－ウ

(9)　もう一年もの間，クリシーがまんまとすり抜けてやってきたことを見てごらん。

(10)－ウ

(11)　(a)－オ　　　(b)－イ　　　(c)－エ　　　(d)－ア

解答・解説

1 (A) **[全訳]** 私たちは一般に，詩の意味（その他どんな文学作品の意味もそうなのだが）を創造し固定したのは作家だと考えている。読者側は，著者の言いたいことを知るだけでよい，というわけである。とはいえ，思考や洞察に言語形式を与えるのはたしかに詩人なのだが，この言語形式を意味と私的反応に変換するのは読者なのである。読書とは実際には，個々の読者の感じ方，記憶，そして過去の読書経験が作用する創造的過程なのである。まさに読書にこのような特性があるゆえに，どんな詩にも複数の解釈が生まれ得るのである。

しかしながら，このように読者側が意味を生み出すことに力点を置いた考え方も絶対に正しいというわけではない。妥当だと万人が同意できる解釈と，乱暴で受け入れがたい解釈の間に境界線を引くのが困難なことがあるからである。読者はしばしば自身の詩との出会いを基に自分だけの意味を創作したがるようだが，その意味は，読者自身にとってどれほど筋が通っていて納得のいくものであれ，詩人の意図したものではなかったかもしれないし，他の読者の共感も得られないかもしれないのである。

そうすると，意味を決定する権威を持っているのは実際のところ誰なのか。意味を創造するものとしての作家と読者を厳密に区別したところで，それは役に立たない。もちろん，読者の貢献と作家の貢献の差を考えたり議論することは，いくつかの点では有効であるが，そうしたからといって読書がある種の相互作用であるという根本的な事実は変わらないのである。詩の意味や価値が，いずれかによって一方的に支配されているなどと考えるのは誤りであろう。

[考え方] 本年度の要約問題に使用されたのは 3 段落 281 語から成る文章で，読解量は過去数年の問題よりやや多いが，英文そのものは平易である。解答字数が 80 字以上となったのは 1999 年以降初のことだが，この文章の全体像を網羅するならこの字数が必要という判断であろう。字数が増加したために戸惑った受験生がいたかもしれないが，要約問題の取り組み方そのものは変わらない。

① 全体を網羅し，テーマに沿った解答を心がける。

要約問題でもっとも重要なのは，文章全体のテーマに密着し，全体の流れを網羅する答案を目指すことである。断片をつまみ食いしたような印象を与える答案や，勝手な解釈を加えてテーマから乖離していると思われる答案は大失点の原因となりかねないので絶対避けなければならない。

— 294 —

<u>2007 年　　解答・解説</u>

　本問では，第 1 パラグラフに 'the meaning of a poem' とあり，全体的に 'poem' や 'poet' という語が登場すること，また，第 3 パラグラフで「そうすると，誰が意味を決定する力を持つのか」という問いがあることから，「詩の意味を創造する［決定する］のは誰か？」をテーマとする文章だと考える。

② 　第 1 パラグラフ

　ここでは，第 1 文と第 2 文の書き方に注意。'We *usually* think ....　*However,* ...'「一般には［たいていは；通例］A と考える。しかし，B である。」という流れができている。これは，一般論［常識］をまず出しておいて，逆接で新たな視点（時に筆者の視点）に持ち込む書き方であるから，「詩の意味を誰が創造するか」というテーマについて，「普通は作家が作ると考える」と「詩人の言葉を意味や私的反応に変換するのは読者だ（＝意味を作るのは読者だ）」という二つの視点を，この順序で，逆接表現を使ってまとめておくとよいだろう。ここで「作家 vs 読者」の対立を出しておくと，最後の部分で自然に内容がつながる，という利点もある。第 3 文，第 4 文は第 2 文の補強であり，また，第 2 段落第 1 文でその内容が吸収されているという点もあるので，大きく取り上げる必要はない。

③ 　第 2 パラグラフ

　第 1 文の 'This' と 'however' に注意。第 1 パラグラフ後半で述べられた「読者側［読者の解釈］が意味を決定する」という内容を 'This emphasis on the reader as the source of meaning' という表現で受けている。そして，それが 'problematic'「問題がある；正しいとは言えない」だと述べ，since 以下でその理由を「皆が妥当だと賛同する解釈と，乱暴で容認できない解釈の区別が時に困難なことがあるから」だと述べている。この理由の部分は，すべてを訳すと字数を使いすぎることになるので，「妥当な解釈の判断［判定］が困難」という程度に圧縮するとよい。第 2 文はその補強である。

④ 　第 3 パラグラフ

　過去の出題でもそうだったが，問題提起の部分があると，それに答えようとする部分が登場するはずである。第 1 文の「では，意味を決定する権威［権限；支配力］を誰が持っているのか？」に対する答えは，結局，最終文の「詩の意味は（読者か作家の）どちらか一方のみの支配下にあると考えるのは誤りだろう」という文になる。ここを「作家あるいは読者のどちらか一方だけが決めるとは言えない［…決めると考えるのは誤り］」という程度にまとめる。字数に余裕があれば，第 3 文を使って「読書は相互作用なので」を加えてもよいだろう。

— 295 —

2007 年　　解答・解説

＜全体のアウトライン＞

〈第1パラグラフ〉

詩の意味を創造する［決定する］のは作家だと普通は考える。

　↓しかし

読者の（多様な）解釈によって意味は生まれる。

〈第2パラグラフ〉

しかし，読者が意味を生むという考え方にも問題がある。

その理由：妥当な解釈の判定が困難だから。

〈第3パラグラフ〉

Q：では，誰が意味を決定するのか？

　↓

A：作家あるいは読者のどちらか一方が詩の意味を決定するとは言えない。

解答例

［解答例1］　詩の意味は作家が決めると考えがちだが，読者の解釈が決めるという見方もある。しかし妥当な解釈の判定が困難であるゆえ，この見方にも問題がある。実際は作家あるいは読者が一方的に意味を決めるとは言えない。(98字)

［解答例2］　詩の意味は作家が創造するのではなく読者の解釈で決まるという考え方は，妥当な解釈の判定が困難なため正しいとは言えない。読書は作家と読者の相互作用だから，どちらか一方が意味を決めるとは言えない。(95字)

1　**(B)**　**全訳**　ニューデリーの美しい芝地から遠く離れたところに，西デリーのスワラジパーク工業地帯がある。いたるところプラスチックがある。地面を覆い，風に舞い，分類され，溶解され，破砕されている。大型トラックが出入りして，屈強な男たちが積み下ろしする巨大な袋を運び，また別の男たちは外部の者には理解できない特殊な言語で，ややこしい取引をしている。

スワラジパークはアジア最大のプラスチック再処理市場である。4 km^{2}ある敷地には，露天の小さな保管所が何百とあり，プラスチックがうずたかく積み上げられている。ビジネスは昼夜を問わず動いていて，プラスチックを小商人が購入し多くの再生工場へと転送している。

インドでは，ゴミの回収と再生と処分は政府機関，非公式団体，そして民間企業が

— 296 —

2007 年　　解答・解説

行っている。最近までは，固形ゴミはすべて政府機関が回収し再生し処分するものとされていたが，うまくいかないことが多かった。結果的に，たとえばデリーでは，スワラジパークにおいてそうであるように，ほぼすべてのリサイクル処理は公式に承認されていない団体によって，非公式に行われるようになった。しかし現在ではゴミの処理が正規の民間企業に委託されつつあり，もぐりの業者の仕事が危機に瀕している。

　　ア　　ゴミ管理の作業に含まれるのは，まず街路，家庭，会社，工場からの回収，次に様々な素材を分離する分別，最後にリサイクルそのものである。　イ　　デリーではゴミの回収は伝統的に *pheriwallahs*, *binnewallahs*, *khattewallas*, そして *thaiwallahs* という非公式の組織によって行われてきた。　ウ　　*pheriwallahs* は街中で大きなビニール袋を持ち歩いているのをよく見かける。彼らの仕事はまだ使える *maal* がないかどうか，通りを調べることである。*maal* とは，紙，プラスチック，ガラス，金属を問わず，なにか価値のあるものを指す。*binnewallahs* は特定区域に市が設置したゴミ箱からのみ *maal* を拾い，*khattewallahs* は会社のゴミだけを回収する。*Thiawallahs* は会社や家庭から *maal* を買うが，彼らの物はずっと質が良いので高い値段を請求することができるのが普通である。　エ　　ゴミが回収されると，40 以上の種類に分別される。　オ　　事実上，この分別作業によってゴミには高い価値が生まれ，リサイクルが容易になる。

　このような非公式経済活動は，リサイクルを基盤としたビジネスモデルと共に，デリーにとって大変役に立っていると思われる。しかし，もぐりのゴミ回収はおそらく非合法でもあり，このサービスには政府の承認がほとんど得られていない。もぐりの業者の中には，政府がもっときちんとこの業界を認めてくれたら安い日給も上がるのではないか，と感じている者もいる。現時点で，平均的な *pheriwallah* の日給は約70 ルピー（日本円にして 180 円程度）である。また，政府による承認を支持する者は，それによって汚く危険な労働条件が良くなるのではないかという期待も持っている。

　しかしながら，政府公認にも課題が残るであろう。この非公式業界がうまく機能している最大の理由は，生産費用の安さと基準の緩さなのである。政府の規制が発効すれば，融通は利かなくなるであろう。さらに政府承認は，最も保護を必要としている者に恩恵をもたらさないかもしれない。認可制度によって，ただ免許があるだけで大もうけをする特権集団が生まれることにしかならない可能性があるからだ。

＜設問(3)の選択肢＞

（i）　もう一つの対立の原因は，都市部のゴミはすべて複雑な規則に従って分別せよという新しい規制である。これらの規則は，もぐりの処理業者が従いにくいため，多くの地域はゴミの回収と分別を民間のゴミ処理会社に委譲しつつある。

— 297 —

<u>2007 年　　解答・解説</u>

(ii)　ゴミ回収の場合，デリーの民間ゴミ処理会社は重量によって料金を受け取っている。これによって，民間会社は既存の非公式ゴミ処理と直接対立することになる。もぐりの回収業者がゴミを 1 kg 集めると，その分，民間会社の収入源となるゴミが 1kg 減るからである。

(iii)　大企業がこれまで以上にゴミ管理にたずさわることになれば，現在のような非公式の経済活動は危機を迎えることになる。民間の会社がすぐに分別所，倉庫，最後にリサイクル工場を作ることになるだろう。最終的に，このような会社によって非公式の回収業者，輸送業者，取引業者の仕事がなくなり，スラワジパークの巨大な再生システム（これが，デリーの生活独特の色彩豊かな部分となっているのだが）が消滅してしまうだろう。

(iv)　最高裁判所が 2000 年にデリーの汚染企業をすべて閉鎖するよう判決を出した結果，そのような事態が発生した。この決定によって隣接するハリヤナ州に多くの工場が移転することになった。しかし取引業の免許がなければ，どんな物も州の境界線を越えて移動させることはできない。この免許を持つ会社はごく少数だったので，結果的に，ただ州境を超えて素材を運ぶだけで巨額の利益を得る業者が台頭することとなった。

[考え方]　2000 年度以降，1(B)は「パラグラフ補充／整序」のみの単純な形式であったが，本年度は設問のヴァリエーションが増え，(1)文補充，(2)文削除，(3)パラグラフ整序，(4)表題選択，の四種融合問題となった。形式の変化に戸惑った受験生も多かったに違いないが，設問の趣旨はこれまでと同じで，要するに設問(1)～(3)は「文と文の関係」に注目すればよいのである。

(1)　正解はウ。補うのは「それぞれのカテゴリー（範疇；種類）は，明確な［一定の］仕事を持っている」という意味の文である。まず，'Each category' とあるので，複数のカテゴリーがこの文の前ですでに登場しているはずだと考える。また，'has a specific task' とあるので，この文の category は「事柄」ではなく，「人間の集団」であると考えるのもポイントである。さらに，この各集団がしている 'a specific task' が，この文の後で具体的に説明されるはずである。

　以上の点から，デリーにおける *pheriwallahs, binnewallahs, khattewallas, thaiwallahs* という非公式の組織の紹介をした後であり，かつ，それぞれの作業内容が具体的に述べられる前の位置，すなわち，空所ウが正解となる。

　なお，空所オの直前の文に '40 categories' とあるが，これは「ゴミの種類」のことであり，category の指示内容がまったく異なることに注意。

(2)　正解は(d)。第 5 段落の各文の大意は次の通りである。

— 298 —

2007年　解答・解説

- (a) このような非公式経済活動はデリーに役に立っていると思われる。
- (b) しかし，もぐりのゴミ回収は非合法的で，政府の承認を得ていない。
- (c) もぐりの業者の中には，政府が認めてくれれば安い日給も上がるのではないか，と感じている者もいる。
- (d) 平均的な *Pheriwallah* の日給は約 70 ルピー（日本円にして約 180 円）である。
- (e) さらに，政府による承認を支持する者は，それによって労働条件が良くなるという期待も持っている。

大意要約問題のアプローチと同じで，「取り除いても大意に影響を与えない」文といえば，まず「具体例」や「言いかえ」となる文である。この段落では，(d)の 'an average *pheriwallah*' と 'about 70 rupees ... a day' が，それぞれ(c)の 'Some informal workers' と 'their low daily wages' の「具体例」となっているので，この文を削除可能と考える。

(3)　正解は**エ**。4つの段落の順列組合せの可能性がすべて列挙されているわけではないので，以下のような点に注目し，選択肢を絞り込んでいけば容易に解答できる設問である。

①「指示語」に注目する。

空所直前の段落（= Government recognition で始まる第6段落）で，「もぐりの業者を公認することの問題点」が述べられている。第3文の also によって，2番目の問題点が追加されているが，その内容は「免許制にすることによって一部の業者に特権を与える事になってしまう」ということ。この部分を(iv)の 'Something like that' という指示表現が指すと考える。この段落では「免許制度にすることで実際に一部の業者にのみ利益が集中した事例があった」ことが述べられており，内容的にも第6段落に続くものとしてふさわしい。

②「追加の表現」に注目する。

選択肢(i)の冒頭に 'Another source of conflict'（対立のもう一つの原因）とある。another を使っている以上，この段落の前に「対立の原因」について述べたものが来るはずである。選択肢(ii)の最初の2文で「従量制によって民間会社ともぐりの業者の間で対立が生まれている」と述べられているので，この内容を受けて 'another source of conflict' を使っていると考え，(ii)→(i)の順序にする。この順列が逆になっているアとウは，この時点で消える。

以上2点から，(ii)→(i)の順列を含み，かつ，(iv)が最初にあるエが正解となる。

(4)　正解は**エ**。

ア　「もぐりの業者が新たな仕事を見つける」

— 299 —

2007年　解答・解説

イ　「インドにおけるリサイクル活動の重要性」

ウ　「スワラジパークの汚染悪化」

エ　「ゴミ処理で競合する制度」

オ　「西デリーが政府の規制に抵抗」

　タイトル選択問題は，過剰一般化の表現を含むもの，過剰限定の表現を含むもの，無関係な内容を含むものを排除し，消去法で絞り込んでいけばよい。本文については，第1，第2段落は全体の趣旨とは無関係なので，第3段落以降の内容に合致するものを選ぶことになる。

　第3段落では，インドのゴミ処理は'government agencies'（政府機関）と，'informal groups'（非公式団体：もぐりの業者）と，'private companies'（民間会社）が行っていることが紹介され，「政府機関による処理は非効率的→非公式の処理に頼ることになった→今では民間会社に委託され，非公式業者の仕事が危機に直面している」と述べられている。第4段落は非公式業者のゴミ処理の詳細を述べたもの。第5段落は非公式のゴミ処理にまつわる問題について，第6段落では政府による認定のもたらしうる問題について述べており，(iv)でその種の事例，(ii)と(i)では民間会社と非公式業者の対立関係，(iii)では非公式業者がさらに直面しうる危機について述べられている。このような展開から考えると，エが最もふさわしいと言える。

解答

(1)－ウ　　(2)－(d)　　(3)－エ　　(4)－エ

2　(A)　考え方

<語数について>

　「50〜60語で」とあるからには，この指定より多くても少なくてもまずいだろう。答案を書いたら，最後に「○○ words」と書き添えるのが望ましい。

<必要条件>

　設問文で与えられている指示に従って，解答には次の3点が必ず盛り込まれていなければならない。

　①　生徒がどのような悩みを持っているか

　②　生徒の英語学習のどこが間違っていたか

　③　教師はどのようなアドバイスをしたか

<答案作成>

①　生徒がどのような悩みを持っているか

— 300 —

2007年　　解答・解説

　生徒の最初のセリフ「(いくら練習しても)英語の聴き取りがうまくできるようにならないんです」こそ，まさに生徒が抱えている悩みである。「いくら練習しても」の部分はなくてもよい。

② **生徒の英語学習のどこが間違っていたか**

　生徒の4番目のセリフ「とにかくたくさん英語を聴けばいいんだと思っていました」が，この生徒の英語学習の誤りを最も端的に表現している。生徒の2番目のセリフ「ケーブル・テレビやインターネットで英語のニュースを見たり聞いたりしてはいるんですけど」は「とにかくたくさん英語を聴けばいい」の具体例に相当する部分。したがって，4番目のセリフの方が解答として適しているが，こちらを採用しても大丈夫だろう(別解2を参照)。ただ，2番目の方を採用するにせよ，「ケーブル・テレビ」「インターネット」はカットして，単に「英語のニュースを聴く」と処理したいところだ。

③ **教師はどのようなアドバイスをしたか**

　先生の最後のセリフにある「毎日やさしめの英文の聴き取りをやって，それと同時に，内容的に関連する読み物を，(辞書を引きながら)丁寧に読んでごらん」という部分を英訳するのが解答として最適である。先生の最初のセリフにある「やっぱり地道に勉強するしかないよね」は一見アドバイスのように見えるが，実は全く中身のないコメントで，とてもアドバイスとは呼べない。先生の3番目のセリフ「聴いて，ある程度中身が理解できるくらいの教材を選ばないと」だが，これをもっと具体的に表現しているのが先生の最後のセリフなのだから，やはりここも解答としては不適切。

＜英訳のポイント＞

①について

☆「英語の聴き取り」

　実はこれが一番難しい。外国語を学習する際には「読む」「書く」「聴く」「話す」という4つのスキルが必ず問題にされる。「読む」「書く」「話す」は read / write / speak でよい。問題は「聴く」で，これをうかつに listen とすると危ない。たとえば，reading ability は「読解力」という意味だが，listening ability とすると耳の機能の問題になってしまう。俗に言う「リスニング」は「聴力」ではなく「聴解力」なので，英語では「聴き取る」は understand spoken English，「リスニング力(を上げる)」は (improve) one's listening comprehension / (improve) one's ability to understand spoken English と表現する。

☆「…がうまくできるようにならない」

　単純に「can't ＋原形」を用いるのが一番楽。have trouble [difficulty] －ing などを用いるのもよい。

— 301 —

<u>2007 年　　解答・解説</u>

②について
☆「とにかくたくさん英語を聴く」 listen to as much English as possible
☆「(テレビやネットで) 英語のニュースを聴く」 listen to English news (on TV and the Internet)
③について
☆「(毎日) やさしめの英文の聴き取りをやる」 listen to easy [easier] English (every day)
☆「内容的に関連する読み物」 materials related to the English he is listening to / materials related to it / related materials

解 答 例

> This student has trouble understanding spoken English. He mistakenly thinks that the best way to improve his listening comprehension is to listen to as much English as possible. His teacher advises him to listen to easy English for practice every day and at the same time to carefully read materials related to the English he is listening to. (58 words)

別解 1　This student is trying to improve his listening comprehension, but so far he hasn't been successful. He believes he should listen to as much English as possible. His teacher tells him it is no use listening to English he can't understand, and that he should listen to easy English and take his time to carefully read materials related to it. (60 words)

別解 2　This student says he cannot understand spoken English no matter how much he studies. He is trying to improve his ability by listening to English news on TV and the Internet. His teacher tells him that is his problem, and that he should listen to easier English and also read materials with similar content. (54 words)

2 (B) 考え方

<語数について> →(A)の解説を参照のこと。
<必要条件>
　次の4ポイントを含んだ答案が望ましいと思われる。
①　「男の子が UFO に関する本を読んでいる」
②　「窓の外に UFO が飛んでいる (のを女の子が見た)」

— 302 —

2007 年　　解答・解説

③　「女の子が男の子に向かって叫んでいる」

④　「男の子は本に夢中で聞いていない」

　2005 年の問題の解説でも述べたが，「絵に描かれた状況を自由に解釈し」という指定がクセモノである。上記の 4 点を踏まえた上でのストーリー展開は，あまりにも見たままで，東大がそのような単純な解答を求めているはずがない，などと考えてしまうと大変難しい問題になり，書けなくなるのである。わざわざ突飛な発想でとらえたり，受けをねらった答案など書こうとせず，見たままを素直に英語で表現すれば，この上なく簡単。2005 年に続いて 2 回目の出題なので，構えずに書けた受験生も多かったとは思うが。

＜英訳のポイント＞

①　「**男の子が UFO に関する本を読んでいる**」

　a boy is reading a book with the title 'All About UFOs'（解答例）

　the boy is reading his book about UFOs（別解 1）

②　「**窓の外に UFO が飛んでいる（のを女の子が見た）**」

　この「女の子」を誰にするかだが，「男の子」の姉妹・友人・ガールフレンドなど，誰でも構わないだろう。

　his sister has just seen a UFO in the sky（解答例）

　his sister happens to see one in the sky（別解 1）

③　「**女の子が男の子に向かって叫んでいる**」

　(she) is shouting at him to look［解答例 1］

　she tries to get him to look out of the window（別解 1）

　she is trying to tell him about it（別解 2）

④　「**男の子は本に夢中で聞いていない**」

　he is so absorbed in his reading that he doesn't listen to [notice / hear] her

＜英文のまとめ方＞

　①～④の英訳例を箇条書きしたが，実際の答案では箇条書きするわけにはいかない。これらをどうまとめるかも採点上のポイントとなる。つまり，英語が正しければ何をどう書いてもいい，ということではないのである。ストーリーとして 1 つの流れを作り出すためには，有効な discourse marker を使うことが重要だ。ただ，ストーリー仕立てでなくとも，別解 2 のようにイラストの説明に徹底した解答でもよい。

— 303 —

<u>2007 年　　解答・解説</u>

解 答 例

A boy is reading a book with the title 'All About UFOs'. His sister has just seen a UFO in the sky and is very excited, and is shouting at him to look, but he is so absorbed in his reading that he doesn't listen to her. (47 words)

別解 1　While the boy is reading his book about UFOs, his sister happens to see one in the sky. Excited, she tries to get him to look out of the window, but he is so absorbed in his reading that he doesn't notice her. (43 words)

別解 2　This picture shows a boy reading a book about UFOs and a girl, apparently the boy's sister, shouting to him. The girl has seen a UFO in the sky. She is trying to tell him about it, but he is so absorbed in his reading he doesn't hear her. (49 words)

4 (A) **全訳** カリフォルニアとワイオミングの地中深くに，2 つの巨大な休火山がある。これらの超大型火山が噴火したら，すさまじい地震を引き起こし，合衆国西部は火山灰で埋め尽くされるだろうと科学者たちは考えている。昔の噴火によってできた，地表に露出している火山灰の堆積層にある証拠が示すところによると，それらは過去二百万年間において最低でも三回は噴火していることがわかる。これらの巨大火山を噴火させる原因は何か，いつ再び噴火しうるのか，噴火すればどれほどの被害が発生しうるのか，ということについて，研究者たちは熱心に情報を探し求めている。火山灰の堆積物の中で発見された極めて小さな水晶を最近分析することで，いくつかの答えが指摘されている。これらの発見により，次の大噴火が発生するかなり前の段階で，警告となる予兆をとらえることが可能になるだろうと，科学者たちは自信を深めている。

考え方 (1)「これらの超大型火山が噴火したら，すさまじい地震を引き起こし，合衆国西部を火山灰で埋め尽くすことだろうと科学者たちは考えている」 正解は **have**。「カリフォルニアとワイオミングの地下に眠る火山がもし爆発したら」という日常の事柄に関する仮想であるから，全体を仮定法過去にする必要がある。would *have* set off は仮定法過去完了なので，誤り。

(2)「昔の噴火によってできた，地表に露出している火山灰の堆積層にある証拠が示すところによると，それらは過去二百万年間において最低でも三回は噴火していることがわかる」 正解は **for**。for は「期間」を表す語句の前につけるもので，本問のように「回数」を表す語句にはつけられない。

— 304 —

2007 年　　解答・解説

⑶　「これらの巨大火山を噴火させる原因は何か，いつ再び噴火しうるのか，噴火すればどれほどの被害が発生しうるのか，ということについて，研究者たちは熱心に情報を探している」　正解は **an**。information は不可算名詞なので，不定冠詞をつけることはできない。

⑷　「火山灰の堆積物の中で発見された極めて小さな水晶を最近分析することで，いくつかの答えが指摘されている」　正解は **of**。「数量詞＋of」はその後に特定の名詞が続く場合。本問では単に answers となっているから，of は不要。

⑸　「これらの発見により，次の大噴火が発生するかなり前の段階で，警告となる予兆をとらえることが可能になるだろうと，科学者たちは自信を深めている」　正解は **ever**。ever は使える場合が限られている。通常は疑問文または否定的文脈で用い，強調のため最上級と共に使うこともある。だが，本問のようにごく普通の平叙文で使われることはない。

解答

⑴　have	⑵　for	⑶　an	⑷　of	⑸　ever

4　**(B)**　**全訳**　医療の性質と役割は過去1世紀の間に徐々に変わってきた。かつては病人の世話をすることを目指したコミュニケーション主体の活動であったものが，技術主体の作業となっており，それによってますます成功裏に病人を治療することができるようになっている。こうした技術面での前進を放棄して過去に戻りたいと思う人はほとんどいないだろうが，医療が伝統的に持っていた世話をするという役割は，治療行為がより確立されるにつれて，置き去りにされてしまった。患者の治療法が医学的に分からないうちにさえ，医療を患者にとって非常に役立つものとした人間的な触れあいを失ったと医療は今では批判されている。

　問題は簡単であるように思える。「人間的なコミュニケーション」対「技術」なのだ。しかしながら，医療においては，その2つを区別することは決して簡単ではないということを我々は誰でも知っている。医療行為の研究が示しているのは，患者の体の状態は医師と患者の間のコミュニケーションの質によってしばしば影響を受けるということである。治療が引き起こす可能性のある影響を説明するといったような，患者に対する初歩的な形態の配慮でさえ，治療の結果に影響を与える可能性があるのである。我々はまた，医療がまだ効果的な治療を施すことができない症例においては，昔ながらの看護が特に強く求められるということも知っている。それゆえ，現代の医療が持つコミュニケーションに関連した側面を忘れずにおくことは重要なのである。

— 305 —

2007 年　　解答・解説

考え方 (1)　1．**What was once a largely communicative activity ... has become a technical enterprise**「…主として言葉による活動であったものが…技術的な作業になった」 what 節 (What ... the sick) が文の主語で，has become がそれに対する動詞。largely は communicative を修飾する副詞で，communicative は activity を修飾する形容詞。「解答例」にもあるように，「コミュニケーション主体の活動」などと処理してもよい。これと対比されているのが technical enterprise で，こちらは「技術的な営み→技術主体の作業」などと処理すればよい。

2．**aimed at looking after the sick**「病人の世話を狙った（目的とした）」 aimed at ... は直前の activity を修飾する過去分詞で，「…を狙った」の意。(例) a TV show *aimed at* children（子供を狙ったテレビ番組→子供向けのテレビ番組） the ＋形容詞で「…な人」という意味を表すことができるので，ここも the sick は「病人」の意。

3．**able to treat them with increasing success**「ますますうまく［成功裏に］病人を治療できる〈技術的な作業〉」 a ... enterprise を修飾する形容詞句。もちろん後ろから訳し上げてもかまわないが，「解答例」にもある通り「〈…技術的作業になっていて〉それによってますますうまく患者を治療することができるようになっている」「それによって可能となった治療はますます成功を収めている」などと処理してもよい。

(2)　1．**it is criticized now for losing the human touch**「医学は人間的な触れ合いを失ったと今では批判されている」 it は medicine を受ける代名詞。blame, praise 等の「非難・賞賛」を表す動詞は一般に V A for B の形を取るが，ここも criticize A for B（B に関して A を非難する）が受け身になっている。human touch は「人間的な触れ合い」でよい。もちろん「人情味，人間味」といった訳出も可。

2．**that made it so helpful to patients**「医学を患者にとって非常に役立つものとした〈人間的な触れ合い〉」 the human touch を先行詞とする関係詞節で，節内は made(V) it(O) so helpful(C) とつながる第 5 文型。it はここでも medicine を指す。

3．**even before it knew how to cure them**「医学が彼らの治療の仕方を知らないうちにさえ」 before が導く副詞節で，made を修飾している。even は before ... を修飾する副詞。it はここも medicine を受ける代名詞。文末の them は patients を受ける代名詞。「医学が知る前に」＝「医学が知らないうちに」であることに注意。

(3)　1．**Even ... an elementary form of consideration for the patient**「患者に対する基本的な［形の］配慮でさえ」 Even は「…さえ」の意の副詞。form は「形」の意だが，あえて訳には出さなくてもよい。

2．**such ... as explaining the likely effects of a treatment**「治療のもたらし

— 306 —

得る影響を説明するというような…」 such A as B で「Bのような A」の意。この下線部では，such と as がかなり離れているので，両者の関係を見落とさずに読めたかどうかがポイント。the likely effects は「〈治療の〉もたらしうる影響」の意。

3. **can have an impact on the outcome**「(治療の)結果に影響を与え得る」 can have が such an elementary form に対する述語動詞。can は「可能性」を表す。

解 答

---

(1) かつては，病人の世話をすることを目的とした，コミュニケーション主体の行為であったものが，今では，技術を重視した作業となっており，それによって可能となった治療はますます成功を収めている。

(2) 患者の治療法が医学に分からないうちにも，医学を患者たちに非常に役立つものにしていた人間的な触れ合いを医学は失ってしまったと今では批判されている。

(3) 治療のもたらし得る影響を説明するといった患者に対する初歩的な配慮でさえ，治療の結果に対して影響を与え得るのである。

---

5 【全訳】 レベッカの母親がバス停の建物の外に立っていると，バスが到着した。日曜日の朝7時35分。彼女は疲れた様子だった。「道中はどうだった？」と彼女は尋ねた。

「オハイオに着くまでは寝つけなかったの」とレベッカは答えた。ニューヨークからの夜行バスでやってきたのだ。ミシガンの初夏の懐かしい匂いがあたりを満たすなか，母親の車の所へと歩いていった。「でも大丈夫よ」とレベッカは言った。

母親が家までの10ブロックほどの道のりを運転しているとき，レベッカは窓の外を見ていた。町には人影がほとんどなかった。メイン・ストリート沿いでは，かつてデパートがあった場所に靴の安売り店が立っていて，薬屋だった所はクリーニング屋になっていた。しかし，リンカーン・アベニューでは，ボーナス・バーガー，ピザ・デライト，タコ・タイムといったファーストフードの店は，彼女の記憶しているとおりだった。彼女が育った通りである，ウィロウ・ストリートの家並みもそうだった。母親の家から2軒先の家だけが様子が変わっていた。

「ウィルソンさんの家，どうしたの？」とレベッカは聞いた。「壁を塗ったか何かしたの？」

「ケンタッキーへ引っ越したのよ」と母は答えた。

無言の時が続いた。母はまだ以前持っていた陽気さを取り戻していないということ

— 307 —

2007 年　　解答・解説

をレベッカは悟った。

「誰か他の人が引っ越してきたわよ」　母親は自宅の私設車道に駐車し，二人は車を降りた。

家に入るとガランとしていた。レベッカの義父のヘンリーは，化学工場の早番の勤務に出ていた。昼下がりまでは帰ってこないだろう。スーツケースを運んでダイニングを通る際に，レベッカは，双子の兄弟であるトレイシーの，壁にかかっている写真を見ないようにした。

「教会へ行かなくちゃ」と母親は言った。「車を後で使いたいのなら，私は正午までには戻るから」

子どものときに使っていた寝室は模様替えされていた。ベッドが新しくなり，カーペットは緑だったのがグレーになっていて，天井からたれ下がっているのはヘンリーの模型飛行機コレクションだった。廊下を行った先には，トレイシーが昔使っていた部屋のドアが依然として閉ざされていたが，それはもう長いことそうなっていた。

ベッドの脇にスーツケースを置くと，レベッカはキッチンへ行った。コーヒーをいれ，テレビのスイッチを入れて，座ってクイズ番組を見た。

＊　＊　＊

その日の午後，レベッカは母親の車を運転して，町はずれのショッピングモールへ出かけた。レベッカが生まれる前からあったものだ。高校生のときには，そこが町で最もわくわくする場所だったので，晩には店が閉まるまで，友人たちとたむろしていたものだった。でも，何年もの間ブルックリンに暮らし，マンハッタンで勤務することで，レベッカの見る目が変わってしまったので，ショッピングモールは地味でおもしろくないように見えた。日曜日の午後だというのに，店には客がほとんどいなかった。

彼女はシャンプーとコンディショナーを買った。母親はレベッカが使っている種類のものを持っていなかったからだ。それから，飲食コーナーのテーブル席に座って炭酸飲料を飲んだ。子どもたちがテーブルの間を走り回り，母親たちは近くでおしゃべりをしていた。レベッカは仕事の後にほぼ毎晩通っていた，ニューヨークのコーヒーショップのことを思った。35 番街にあって，ブロードウェイのすぐ東，両脇にはスウェーデンパンの店とサーカス用品店があった。給仕の一人は 18 歳か 19 歳の男の子で，彼女が注文するものをいつも覚えており，彼女が店に入るとニッコリと微笑んでくれた。すみのテーブルに陣取っては，客たちが出入りするのを眺めていた。あらゆる年齢の，あらゆる国籍の，あらゆる種類の服装やヘアスタイルの客たちを。自分がそのような豊かな文化的織物の 1 本の糸となっていると感じることで，彼女はゾク

— 308 —

2007年　　解答・解説

ゾクするのだった。

　レベッカがその場を去ろうと立ち上がると，母親たちのうちの一人がやってきた。「レベッカじゃない？」と言った。

　レベッカは一瞬ためらった。それから，大声をあげた。「ジュリアじゃない！」彼女が立ち上がると，二人は抱き合った。「最初はあなただってわからなかったわよ！」

　「久しぶりね」

　トレイシーを偲ぶ会以来だとレベッカは思った。

　ジュリアは腰かけて言った。「今でもニューヨークで暮らしているの？」

　「そうよ」とレベッカは答えた。「今回は，2・3日の予定で戻ってきてるの。でも，ミシガンに戻ってこようかと思っているのよ」

　「どうして？　あなたはニューヨークが気に入っていると思ってたけど」

　「それがね，ルームメイトが結婚して出て行くことになったから，新しいルームメイトを見つけるか，引っ越すかしなきゃいけないの。あっちでは家賃が本当に高いのよ」

　「そうらしいわね」

　「義父が言うには，化学工場で事務系の仕事を見つけてあげられるって。明日，面接を受けるの」

　「それはよかったわね」と言ってからジュリアは一呼吸おいた。「つきあっている人，いるの？」

　「いないわ」と言ってからレベッカは尋ねた。「ジェリーはどうしてる？」

　「元気よ。あいかわらず，父親の所で働いているわ。今日は釣りに行ってるから，私が子どもたちをショッピングモールに連れてきて走り回らせてあげてるのよ」

　レベッカとジュリアは高校時代の友達だった。ジュリアはトレイシーとかなり本気でつきあっていたが，高校を出ると別れた。トレイシーがアフガニスタンで戦死したときには，ジュリアは既にジェリーと結婚していた。

＊　＊　＊

　その晩の夕食のときに，ヘンリーは工場で起きた事故について語った。「…それから，熱分解装置が過熱状態になって，その処置もしなくてはならなくなって，その一方では還流のラインの方も流し出していたんだが…」10代だったときよりもいっそうのこと，ヘンリーが何を言っているのかわからなくて，レベッカはばつが悪い思いがした。彼女も母親も，あまり口をきかなかった。それから，レベッカはヘンリーを手伝って食器を洗って片づけた。ヘンリーが母親と結婚して引っ越してきたのは，レベッカとトレイシーが11歳のときだった。実の父親は，その3年前に家を出ていた。レベッ

— 309 —

カは 20 年間，実父と会っていなかった。

「明日の 11 時に君が会社に来ると上司には言ってある」とヘンリーが言った。「ママは私が仕事に連れて行くから，君は彼女の車を使っていいからね」

「ありがとう」

「上司は，雇う前に君に会っておきたいだけなんだ。給料については聞かなかったけど，大丈夫なはずだ。前任の女の子は不平を言ってなかったからね」

バス旅行の疲れが，その晩早くにレベッカを襲ったので，母親とヘンリーにおやすみを言ってから，ベッドに入った。すぐに眠りに落ちて，ぐっすり眠った。朝の 4 時ごろ，外がまだ薄暗く静かなうちに，彼女は目をさました。ベッドの中にとどまって，天井から下がっている模型飛行機をじっと見ていた。ジュリアがショッピングモールで子どもたちと日曜の午後を過ごしていることや，そんなことを自分がしている場面なんて想像できっこないということに，彼女は思いをめぐらせた。ヘンリーが働いている化学工場や，母親がクレジットカードのトラブルについての遠距離からの問い合わせに受け答えをして日々を過ごしている町外れの電話受付センターについて，思いをめぐらせた。ニューヨークのこと，騒がしい通り，混雑した歩道，アパート近くの小さな韓国レストラン，35 番街のコーヒーショップの若者について，思いをめぐらせた。

それから，けっして 23 歳よりも上の年齢になることのないトレイシーについて，思いをめぐらせた。小さかったときに二人で喧嘩したが，そんな時には母親が穏やかな仲裁役であったこと，父親が去ってから二人が喧嘩をしなくなった状況を，彼女は思い出した。なぜ喧嘩をやめたのだろう。そしてなぜ，トレイシーが死んでからは母親が自分に対して何も言わなくなったのだろう。レベッカは無力感が大きく自分に襲いかかるのを感じた。

彼女がベッドから出て，音を立てずに荷造りをしたときには，まだ 5 時前のことで，家は依然としてひっそりとしていた。彼女に決心させたのは何だったのか？　彼女には確信がなかった。しかし，母親とヘンリー宛てにメモを書いた。「私，戻ることにしました。ごめんなさい」

メモをキッチンのテーブルの上に置くと，彼女は玄関のドアからひっそりと外へ出た。12 ブロックほど町の中心部の方へと歩いてデトロイト行きの始発バスに乗った。そしてそこから，別のバスに乗って，ニューヨークへ戻るのだ。

【考え方】 (1) 正解は**エ**の **as she remembered**「彼女が記憶しているとおり」。前の文では「街並みが以前とは変わってしまった」ということが述べられている。それと But によって逆接的に結ばれているのだから，空所を含む文は故郷の街並みで「以前と変わっていない」ところの説明になっているはずと考える。ア as she left「彼

— 310 —

2007年　解答・解説

女が去ったように；彼女が去った際」やウ as she was a child「彼女が子供だったように；彼女が子供だったので」を入れても意味不明。イ as her childhood「彼女の子供時代として」も意味が通らない（「子供の時代に」なら *in* her childhood のはず）。意味が通るのは as she remembered だけである。（例）Everything was *as I remembered.*（すべてが私の記憶のとおりだった）

(2)　正解はア。空所の直後の表現「以前持っていた陽気さ」と意味的につながるのはア **recovered**「〈…を〉取り戻す；回復する」だけである（選択肢は過去形であるが，ここでは原形としての意味を掲げる）。それ以外の選択肢の意味は次の通り。イ reformed「〈…を〉作り直す；変形させる」，ウ replaced「〈…を〉置き換える；〈…に〉取って代わる」，エ revised「〈…を〉見直す」。

(3)　正解は **「廊下の少し先のところでは」**。まず，部屋は廊下沿いにあると考えるのが普通。よって hall は「ホール」や「玄関」ではなく「廊下」の意と考えるのがよい。また，ここの down は必ずしも「下へ」ではなく「…の先に；…を行った所に」を意味することもできることに注意すること。（例）She stopped halfway *down* the passage.（彼女は通路を半分行った所で立ち止まった）　なお，空所(1)の直後の文にある two doors down from ...「…の２軒先」も参照のこと。

(4)　正解はアの **perspective**。空所を含む箇所の文意が「ブルックリンに暮らし，マンハッタンで勤務する年月が，彼女に新しい（　4　）を与えた」ということ，そしてまた，空所直後に「ショッピングモールは地味でおもしろくないように見えた」とあることから，レベッカの「見方」が変化したことを表現しているのではないかと考え，ア perspective「見方」を選ぶ。イは sight は「視野；眺め」の意味で不可。ウ transformation「変形」，エ way「方法」では全く文意に合わない。

(5)　正解はア。空所（　4　）の直後で故郷のショッピングモールが「地味でおもしろくないように見えた」とあり，それと対比されるような文脈で，下線部(5)を含むパラグラフのニューヨークの街の描写が続いていることに注目する。よって「豊かな文化的織物」は「ニューヨークの文化の多様性」を指し，「１本の糸となっている」とは「そこに参加している」ことを示し，また「ぞくぞくした」と述べられていることから，その多彩な文化に参加していることを「肯定的」に捉えていることがわかる。以上の内容を満たしているのはアだけである。

(6)　正解はエ。「最初はあなたを（　6　）しなかったの」が空所を含む箇所の文意。声を掛けられたレベッカは「一瞬ためらった」と述べられている。それはすなわち相手のことがすぐには分からなかったことを意味しているので，エの **recognize**「…を認識する；…だとわかる」が最適。それ以外の選択肢，ア appreciate「正しく評価する；

— 311 —

2007年　　解答・解説

高く評価する」，イ confirm「確かめる」，ウ foresee「予見する」は文意に合わない
ので不可。

(7)　正解は (7a) －エ，(7b) －カ，(7c) －オ，(7d) －イ。

(7a) は，レベッカがミシガンに戻ろうと思っていると言ったことに対して，「ニュー
ヨークが気に入ってたのでしょ？」とジュリアが反応する場面。こうした応答からジュ
リアにはレベッカが戻ってきた理由が分からなかったはずと考え，エ How come?
「なぜ？」を入れる。ちなみに，ア Why not?「なぜそうしないの？；いいじゃない」
では文脈に合わないことに注意。

(7b) は家賃が高いというレベッカの言葉に対する「相槌」として働くことができ
るカ That's what I hear.「そうらしいわね←それは私が聞いていることだ」がよい。

(7c) は明日面接があるというレベッカの言葉に対する相槌となる，オ That's
great.「それはよかったわ；すごいじゃない」がよい。

(7d) は「ジェリーはどう？」という質問に対する答えなので，イ He's okay.「元
気よ；問題ないわ」が最適。ウの Here he is. は「ここにいるわよ；ほら彼が来たわよ」
の意。直後にジェリーは「釣りに行ってる」とあり，その場にジェリーはいなかった
ので不可。

(8)　正解は**2番目 than ／5番目 been**。まず不要な語が would であることは，動
詞の形（原形の語がないこと）から分かる。与えられた語の中に she があることか
ら，SV の組み合わせを作れば，she had been と続くことがわかる。この段階で可
能性がある語順として① Even as she had been more than a teenager　② Even
more than as she had been a teenager　③ Even more than she had been as a
teenager などが考えられるが①では意味が通らないし，②は as の用法・意味が不明。
よって③が正解。「10 代のときに彼女がそうであった（＝当惑した）よりもなおさ
らいっそう」の意。even が比較表現の前に置かれると「さらに」という強めの言葉
となることにも注意。

(9)　正解はイの **complain**「不平を言う」。空所を含むヘンリーの発言「給料につ
いては聞かなかったけど，大丈夫なはずだ」が最大のヒント。「大丈夫」と言い切れ
るのは「前任の女の子が『不平を言って』いなかったから」と考えると筋が通る。ア
の claim はあくまで「主張する」の意。これを日本語の「クレーム（＝文句）をつける」
と解釈してはならない。ウ demand「要求する」，エ insist「主張する」はいずれも
文意に合わない。

(10)　正解は**再び暮らそうと戻ったものの, もはやこの街になじめず, むしろニュー
ヨークが故郷に思えたこと。**（45字）「心境の変化」が問われている以上「元々ど

－ 312 －

2007 年　　解答・解説

ういう気持ちであったのか」「それがどのように変わっていったのか」を解答に入れようとするのが大切である。英文の前半から，レベッカの故郷はミシガンであり，この先もニューヨークに残るという選択肢はあったものの故郷に戻る決断をしたことが読み取れる。ところが，実家に滞在し，故郷の街や自分の家族の様子，さらにはニューヨークの記憶を頭の中で反芻し，引き比べた結果，自分にとってミシガンはもはや居心地が悪く，今やニューヨークが故郷になっていると悟るのである（レベッカが残したメモが，単に "I've decided to go (back)." あるいは "I've decided to leave." ではなく，"I've decided to go back home." となっていることに注意）。つまり，タイトルとなっている BACK HOME の意味が，実家へ戻る前と実家滞在中で大きく変わったという文章全体の理解が大前提となる。字数制限があるので，細部の具体例にこだわらず，「故郷であるミシガンに戻る決意をした」→「戻ってみると居心地が悪かった」→「自分の故郷はもはやニューヨークであると感じられた」という流れを答案にまとめることが大切である。

⑾　正解は**エ**の**28歳**。空所⑻の後続の記述「ヘンリーが母親と結婚したのは，レベッカとトレイシーが11歳のときだった。実の父親は，その3年前に家を出ていた。レベッカは20年間，実父と会っていなかった」から考えればよい。11 − 3 + 20 = 28 となる。

解答

> (1)－エ　　　(2)－ア
>
> (3)　廊下の少し先のところでは
>
> (4)－ア　　　(5)－ア　　　(6)－エ
>
> (7)　(7a)－エ　(7b)－カ　(7c)－オ　(7d)－イ
>
> (8)　than ／ been
>
> (9)－イ
>
> ⑽　再び暮らそうと戻ったものの，もはやこの街になじめず，むしろニューヨークが故郷に思えたこと。(45字)
>
> ⑾－エ

— 313 —

解答・解説

1 **(A)** **全訳** 民主主義の成立には国民の自由な政治参加が不可欠である。民主国家の国民は，その活動を通じて，政治家になる人物を決定し政府の活動に影響を与えようとする。政治に参加することによって，国民が自らの関心や目標や必要に関する情報を伝え，かつ対応を要求できるような仕組みが生まれるのである。

民主的政治参加の中核をなすのは，国民の声と平等である。有意味な民主主義国家では，政策立案者が国民の関心を理解できるよう，また国民の声に注目せざるをえなくなるよう，その声が明瞭で，かつ大きく響くものでなくてはならない。民主主義では必然的に，国民の関心に対応して政府が動くのみならず，国民一人一人の関心を平等に考慮することにもなるため，民主的な政治参加が平等であることも必須である。

参加の平等という理想を実践している民主国家は（もちろん合衆国も含めてのことだが）存在しない。選挙で投票する，あるいはもっと積極的な参加の仕方をする国民もいるし，そうしない人もいる。事実，アメリカ人の大半は投票する以外には全く政治的な活動を行っていない。さらに，参加している者も，いくつかの重要な点で一般市民全体の代表とは言えない。彼らは社会的特徴も異なるし，要求や目標も異なっているのである。市民活動家は，恵まれた層から集められる傾向にある。すなわち，教育があり，裕福で白人の男性になりがちなのである。したがって，参加によって表明される国民の声は，国民の代表とは言えない，一部の限られた市民集団から届いているのである。

考え方 244 語から成る「民主主義の理想と現実」に関する文章で，過去数年の出題と比較すると，いたって素直な要約問題であり，解答語数もここ数年の傾向通りである。（解答に際しての基本的な注意は 2005 年度の解説を参照のこと）

1．"One Topic in One Paragraph" の原則

本年度の文章は，3つのパラグラフの内部構造が英語の文章構成の基本通りになっており，パラグラフの基本構成要素として Topic Sentence（主題文）と Supporting Details（支持文）があること，そして，論説文では「1つのパラグラフに主題は1つ（One Topic in One Paragraph）」が原則であることを既習の人には，いたって素直で御しやすい問題だったと言える。字数（65 〜 75 字）を考慮すると，各パラグラフの内容を言わば「総括」する役割を持つ主題文の内容をまとめて繋げば，全体の内容を網羅する要約文になる。それぞれ第1文が主題文となっているので，以下の3

— 316 —

2006 年　　解答・解説

点を全体のアウトラインとして解答に含めるとよいだろう。

〈第1パラグラフ〉
　民主主義は国民が自由に政治参加できなければあり得ない。
　→民主主義には国民の政治参加が不可欠
〈第2パラグラフ〉
　（参加にとっては）声と平等性が重要。
〈第3パラグラフ〉
　（平等性については）その理想を実践できている民主国家はない。

2．言葉の意味を明確に

　第2パラグラフでは，"voice"と"equality"が重要だと述べられているのが，この"voice"については，解答では単に「声（が重要）としただけでは言葉足らずの印象を免れ得ないであろう。ここはやはり，その内容を分かりやすく説明した第2文に注目して，「国民の声［意見］が為政者に確実に伝わること」という程度にまとめるとよい。

解 答 例

［解答例1］
民主主義には国民の参加が不可欠で，その声が明確かつ確実に為政者に伝わり，参加が平等であることが肝要だが，平等の理想を実践できている民主国家はない。（73字）
［解答例2］
民主主義の要諦は国民の自由な政治参加であり，その意見の確実な伝達と参加の平等が最も重要だが，平等の理想を実現できている民主国家はない。（67字）

1 (B) 【全訳】

1

　両島では18世紀初頭から，野生生物の定期的管理の一環として羊やポニー（小形種の馬）の祭りが行われていたのだが，現在のような形のポニー祭が始まったのは1924年であった。当時，シンコティーグの自警消防団は消防装置の資金を調達するために年に一度の祝祭でポニーの販売を始めたのである。毎年ポニーを売ることによって，この消防団は活動資金を得ることが可能となり，かつ，この島の自然の平衡に適したポニーの個体数を維持することができるようになった。意外なことに，自警消防

－ 317 －

団によるポニー祭は2つの小島を世界地図に載せる動きの第一歩にすぎなかった。

2

　ポニー祭が海外からも観光客を引き寄せるようになる以前は，両島の名を知る人は，合衆国にすら，ほとんどいなかった。なんといっても，シンコティーグとアサティーグは，かつては人間よりも野鳥とポニーの方が多かった小島なのである。数世紀にわたってポニーはほとんどの場合人間と接触することなく過ごしてきた。しかし次第に人間がシンコティーグに定住するようになり，その結果，ポニーは現在でも無人のアサティーグ島だけに生息するようになった。自警消防団やカーニバルや観光などが島に出現するよりもずっと以前からポニーは両島に生息していたのであり，ポニーにまつわる話は大変多くの観光客を引きつけてやまないものになっている。

3

　まさに，生息環境が厳しく，何世紀にもわたって孤立していたことによって「シンコーティーグ・ポニー」は生まれたのである。このポニーは元をたどれば馬であり，実際，仔馬の時にこの島から連れ出して普通の馬と同じように餌をやり馬小屋で育てると，時には馬の大きさになり，体高が58インチを超えるということが知られている。しかし，両島では天候が厳しく，虫なども多く，さらに，餌がほとんどの場合海岸に生える堅い草であり，この馬は環境によってまさに文字通り小形化したのである。

4

　世界中から観光客が何千人もこの祭りにやって来る。特に子供のいる家庭に対してはそうなのだが，ポニーを売るのはたやすい。子供たちはミスティに似たポニーを見つけようとこの祭りにやってくるし，大人は島の質素な生活や，シンコティーグ，アサティーグ両島の歴史について学ぼうとやってくる。観光の国際化が特定地域の習慣を保存する最善の策であることは現代の常識となっている。毎年夏に大挙してやって来る観光客に人気がなければ，おそらく野生のポニーは生きていけなくなるだろう。ポニー祭は地元経済にとってなくてはならないものとなっているわけだが，ポニー同様，シンコティーグの漁師や住民もポニー祭が終わると平穏な生活に戻ってホッとしているに違いない。一方，観光客は野生のポニーが自由に向かって泳ぐ光景を見て，なんとか気持ちを新たにしつつ，短い夏休みから慌ただしい現代生活に戻っていくのである。

ア　しかし，生活が困難であるにもかかわらず，ポニーはアメリカ西部に数多く生息する野生馬のようには痩せてもいないし，醜いわけでもない。逆にポニーは，主として塩分の多い海草，湿地に生える植物，海藻を餌にしているために，普通の馬よりもはるかに多くの水を飲むことになり，結果的「太って」健康に見えるのである。

2006年　　解答・解説

ひとたび人間に飼い慣らされると，おとなしい動物になることも知られている。実際は，サイズが小さく，頭がよく，見かけが美しいからこそ，これらのポニーは子供たちにとって格好のペットになったのである。

イ　しかし，本当の意味で有名になったのは，1947年に『シンコティーグのミスティ』という本が出版された時である。この本はベストセラーになった児童書で，世界中の言語に翻訳された。この物語で，著者のマーガレット・ヘンリーはビービ一家が，ミスティという名の頭の良い小さなシンコティーグ・ポニーを家族の一員として受け入れる様子を描いたのだが，それだけではなく，都市部の現代的な生活の猛烈な慌ただしさとは無縁に見える島民の習慣や生活様式も描いている。平和で，昔と変わらず，不便きわまりない――こういう島暮らしの特性はシンコティーグに来た現在の観光客に大変魅力的なのだが，まさにこれらの特性を持つがゆえに両島はかくも長きにわたって大勢の人にとって未知の島であり続けたのである。

ウ　この両島のような多くの場所では，かつて強力な存在であった先住アメリカ人の言語と歴史が豊かであるにもかかわらず，現在ではその原住民の名前しか残っていない。これはアメリカ史における悲惨な史実となっている。実際，シンコティーグとアサティーグという名前を最初に付けたのは，ジンゴ・ティーグと呼ばれる先住アメリカ人であった。たとえば「シンコティーグ」は「海の向こうの美しい国」という意味だと言われている。英国人入植者がこの両島に来始めたその時その名前を残したが，それは先住アメリカ人がこの地域から完全に追放され，先住民のみが居住を許された，「特別保留地」と呼ばれる土地に追いやられてからずいぶん後のことであった。

エ　ジョージ・ブリーデンは，シンコティーグで町の土産物店を経営している。彼はこう述べている。「ここに住み始めてもう80年近くなりますが，うちの一族は私が生まれる何百年も前にこの島にやってきました。植民地からここに送り込まれた最初の入植者は罪人だったと言う人もいますが，私の一族はそうではなかったと思いますよ。どこにそんな証拠があるんですか」　フリーデンとその仲間の島民たちはシンコティーグに最初に住み着いた家族のリストを正式にまとめた。これらの家の人々は，自分の家がこの島で長い歴史を持つことを誇りに思っている。しかし，彼らは過去の歴史的事実について知るよりも，今では観光で儲けることに興味があるのだと批判する人もいる。

オ　毎年7月になると，合衆国中部大西洋岸の沖に浮かぶ島に世界中から観光客が集まる。「ポニー祭」という行事に参加するためで，これはロッキー山脈の東部にのみ残る野生のポニーが1日だけ自由でなくなるお祭りである。ポニーが泳いで水

－　319　－

2006年　　解答・解説

しぶきを上げる。人々は歓声を上げ、「ウォーター・カウボーイ」たちが、シンコティーグ、アサティーグという名前の2つの小島を隔てる狭い水路を渡らせる。ものの5分もするとポニーは上陸。シンコティーグに上陸するとポニーは健康状態を検査され、その一部が販売される。翌日、ポニーはアサティーグの自由な生活へと泳いで帰り、これをもって世界中で知られた、町のお祭りは終わりとなる。

カ　その魅力の一つが、謎に満ちたその起源である。ポニーは何百年も前からシンコティーグとアサティーグにいるが、どのようにこの島にやってきたかは分かっていない。ある物語によると、近海で16世紀にスペインの船が暴風雨で沈み馬だけが泳いで避難し生き残ったということである。またある伝説ではスペインの海賊が貴重な馬をこの孤島に隠したということになっている。しかし、大部分の歴史家が主張するところでは、植民時代のヴァージニア、メリーランドの入植者が英国から馬を持ち込み、その後、動物税を逃れるために馬を離島に隔離したということである。しかし、どの話を信じるかは別にして、野生のポニーの起源には虚実織りまざった言い伝えがいろいろとある。これに劣らず興味を引くのが、その生態である。

[考え方]　段落補充（あるいは、文補充）問題は、2000年度以降連続して出題されており、文章の内容は様々であっても取り組み方自体は基本的に同じである。指示語、冠詞の使い方、代名詞、論理展開を示すDiscourse Marker、時間の流れ、内容のつながりなどに着目していけばよい。本年度は選択肢イの判断がやや難しかったかもしれない。

[不要な選択肢]　ウ・エ

　本年度の設問は、不要な選択肢が比較的明らかである。選択肢ウは「アメリカ先住民（アメリカンインディアン）の歴史」について、選択肢エは「島の一族の家系」について述べたもので、本論とは無関係なものである。残るア、イ、オ、カについて、手がかりが明確なものから述べることにする。

[空所1]　正解はオ。

　第1パラグラフが空所になったのはこれが初めてだが、この行事を紹介する文章の導入としてふさわしいものを探すとよい。この行事の「名前(Pony Day)」、それが行われる「時期（7月）」、「場所（中部大西洋岸の島）」、その行事の「概略（馬が1日だけ海峡を渡って島を移動しオークションにかけられること）」に触れた「オ」が最もふさわしい。

[空所3]　正解はカ。

　直前の第4パラグラフ最後に "their story is the one that continues to draw the most visitors" とあり、これとの関連で選択肢「カ」を入れると "that appeal"（そ

— 320 —

2006 年　　解答・解説

の魅力）がうまく対応することになる。また，「カ」では「シンコティーグ・ポニーの起源に関する諸説」が紹介されているが，最終文で "No less interesting is their biology." とあることに要注意。この biology は「生物学」ではなく，「（動植物の）生態」の意味がある。この表現がこの空所にあることによって，続く第6パラグラフの「厳しい環境ゆえに，この馬の特性が生まれた」という内容への導入となる。

［空所2と4］正解はイとア。

　空所2については，直前の第2パラグラフで，島の消防団が資金調達のために馬を売り始めたことが紹介されているが，最終文で「この活動は2つの小島を世界地図に載せる（＝世界中に知らしめる）最初のステップにすぎなかった」とある。ここに選択肢「イ」を入れると，1942 → 1947 という時間軸に沿った流れができるし，「本当に有名になったのは，ポニーを題材にした児童書の出版がきっかけだった」という内容が however でうまくつながることにもなる。さらに「イ」の最後には，島暮らしの特性ゆえに「長年無名であった」ことが述べられており，これと第4パラグラフ第1文の「この島の名を知る人はごく少数だった」という内容との連結もうまく成立する。

　この選択肢で紹介された "Misty of Chincoteague" という本で，Misty という名前のポニーが登場する。最終パラグラフに「子供たちは Misty に似たポニーを探しに来る」とあるために，空所4に入れることを考えたかもしれない。しかし，そうすると選択肢のアが空所2に入ることになってしまい，第1文にある "Despite their hard lives, however," という表現が説明無しで唐突に出ることになってしまう。やはり「ア」はこの表現を手がかりに，空所4に入れるべきであろう。そうすると直前の第6パラグラフで述べられた「厳しい環境」を受けて "their hard lives" という表現が生きることになる。

解 答

```
［1］－オ　　［2］－イ　　［3］－カ　　［4］－ア
```

2 (A) 考え方

　1．まず語数だが，「60～70語で」とあるからには，この指定より多くても少なくてもまずいだろう。ただ，解答スペースがかなり大きく（167 mm × 9 行），すべてを埋めてしまうと，小さめの字で書いた場合は確実に100語くらいになってしまう。多忙な採点官がいちいち答案の語数を数えているとも思えないので，おそらく7行書いてあれば十分であろう。できれば答案の最後に「○○ words」と書くのが望ましい。

— 321 —

<u>2006 年　　解答・解説</u>

2．設問文を読むと，「A先生とB先生の主張とその根拠を明確に伝えるような形で，議論の要点を英語で述べよ」とある。したがって，盛り込まれていなければならないポイントは次の4つということになる。

① 「A先生の主張」
② 「A先生がそのように主張する根拠」
③ 「B先生の主張」
④ 「B先生がそのように主張する根拠」

3．① 「A先生の主張」

A先生の最初のセリフ「今回の運動会では，競争心をあおるような種目をやめてはどうでしょうか」こそ，まさにA先生が一番訴えたいことである。

② 「A先生がそのように主張する根拠」

A先生の2番目のセリフにある「みんなで協力することの大切さを教えるべきです」というのが，A先生の主張の根拠である。「敗北感を味わったりするのは（子供に）よくないと思うんですよ」の部分を含めてもよい。

ちなみに，A先生の3番目・4番目のセリフでは具体的な種目名が羅列されているだけなので，ここには設問で求められている「議論の要点」と呼べるのは含まれていない。

③ 「B先生の主張」

B先生のセリフ全体を通して，B先生は基本的にA先生の意見に反対しているということがわかる。特に4番目のセリフにある「子供にはもっと競争させるべきだと思いますよ」の部分に注目すべきであろう。

④ 「B先生がそのように主張する根拠」

B先生の2番目のセリフ「勉強においてもある程度の競争心が刺激になる」，および4番目のセリフ「いい意味でのライバル意識を育てるために（競争が必要）」が，B先生の主張の根拠である。単純に言えば，「競争することが子供たちにとっては重要である（必要である・よいことである）」ということになろう。

「競争心をあおる種目をやめてしまうと運動会がつまらなくなる」を根拠としてもOKだとは思うが，「競争することが子供たちにとっては重要である」の方がA先生の「みんなで協力することの大切さを教えるべき」という根拠と好対照になるので，より適当であろう。

4．以上の4点を，極力平易な英語を使ってまとめあげること。日本語に合わせて直訳しようとすると減点される危険性が高くなる。

① 「今回の運動会」the next [coming] sports day　前置詞をつけるなら on。

— 322 —

2006 年　　解答・解説

「競争心をあおるような種目」直訳すると events that will stir up a sense of rivalry（解答例）だが，このようにはなかなか書けないだろう。別解1・2のように competitive events と簡単に処理するのがよい。

「やめる」not have [hold] events

②　「みんなで協力することの大切さを教えるべき」children should learn the importance of cooperation（解答例）／ it is important to teach children the value of cooperation（別解1）／ children should be taught the importance of cooperating with each other（別解2）　注意してほしいのは，cooperate は自動詞で目的語をとれないため，必ず cooperate **with** O としなければならない。

「敗北感を味わったりするのは（子供に）よくない」experiencing a feeling of defeat is not good for children（解答例）／ defeat will have a bad effect on the children（別解1）／ experiencing defeat will do the children more harm than good（別解2）

③　「B先生はA先生の意見に反対」Ms. B disagrees (with Mr. A)（解答例・別解1）／ Ms. B does not think so（別解2）

④　「競争することが子供たちにとっては重要である」it is very important for children to compete with each other（解答例）／ competition has a positive effect on children（別解1）／ children should compete more（別解2）

「勉強においてもある程度の競争心が刺激になる」別解1のように，encourage ＋ O ＋ to − などを用いて書くのが簡単。

解 答 例

> Mr. A suggests that on the next sports day they not have any events that will stir up a sense of rivalry. He believes that experiencing a feeling of defeat is not good for children, and that they should learn the importance of cooperation. Ms. B disagrees with Mr. A, saying that it is very important for children to compete with each other to improve their overall abilities.
>
> (68 words)

別解 1　Mr. A says that no competitive events should be held on the coming sports day. He believes that defeat will have a bad effect on the children and that it is important to teach them the value of cooperation. However, Ms. B disagrees. She thinks that competition has a positive effect on children because it encourages them to study harder. (60 words)

— 323 —

2006 年　　解答・解説

別解 2　Mr. A disagrees with the ideas of holding competitive events on sports days.　In his opinion, experiencing defeat will do the children more harm than good.　He says they should be taught the importance of cooperating with each other.　However, Ms. B does not think so.　She believes children should compete more because, by engaging in friendly rivalry with each other, they will be able to develop their overall abilities.　(70 words)

2 (B)　考え方

1．語数に関しては(A)の解説を参照のこと。

2．答案を書く上でおさえるべきポイントは，設問文に与えられている次の３つ。これからを採点官が読んでわかるような形で明確に述べなければならない。

① 「その時点でどのような選択肢があったか」

② 「そこで実際にどのような選択をしたか」

③ 「そこで違う選択をしていたら，その後の人生がどのように変わっていたと思われるか」

③は実際には行わなかった事柄であるから，英語にするときは仮定法を用いる必要がある。

上記３点をおさえることはさほど大変なことではない。難しいのは，「あなたが今まで下した大きな決断」としてどのような事柄を選定するかである。「人生を左右するような大きな決断」と言っても普通思い浮かべるのは，「就職」「転職」「結婚」「出産」などだが，受験生の中にこれらを経験したことのある者はまずいない。受験生の年齢は平均すると 20 才前後であろうから，そのような短い人生の中で，人生を大きく変えた決断などしたことがあるかどうかも疑問。ただ，設問文に「適宜創作をほどこしてかまわない」という文言がわざわざついているところを見ると，ひょっとしたら，この(B)は最初から受験生の「創造力」をためすことを目的にしている問題なのかもしれない。

3．具体的な答案作成法を，解答例に沿って見てみよう。

〈解答例〉

☆テーマ→「留学」（受験生が実際に経験することが可能）

① 存在した選択肢→「渡米」か「日本の学校への進学」か

② 実際の選択→「渡米」

③ 違う選択をした場合→「今頃は日本人的な物の見方しかできていないだろう」

（この③につなげるため，「視野を広げるためには日本の外に出る必要があると考え

— 324 —

2006 年　　解答・解説

た」という伏線をあらかじめ張ってある）

〈別解1〉

☆テーマ→「結婚」（創作）

① 存在した選択肢→「結婚」か「大学進学」か

② 実際の選択→「結婚」

③ 違う選択をした場合→「今頃は退屈な学生生活を送っているのだろう」

〈別解2〉

☆テーマ→「親元離れての一人暮らし」（創作）

① 存在した選択肢→「自宅から大学へ通学」か「一人暮らしをしてアパートから通学」か

② 実際の選択→「一人暮らしをしてアパートから通学」

③ 違う選択をした場合→「今のように楽しく学生生活を過ごしていないだろう」

（この解答例は 2004 年度に出題された問題 2 (A)を意識して作ったもの）

解 答 例

> When I was the third year of junior high, I decided to study at a high school in the U.S. Of course, I could have gone on to high school in Japan. However, I believed it was necessary to go to school outside of Japan to broaden my horizons. If I had stayed in Japan, I'd now be able to only see things from a Japanese point of view. (70 words)

別解 1　When I was eighteen, I decided not to go on to college but to get married and start a family. Naturally, my parents objected, saying that I was too young and should go to college, but I didn't follow their advice. If I hadn't made the choice I did, I would now be leading a boring life as a student.

(60 words)

別解 2　When I was admitted to college, I decided to rent an apartment and move away from my parents. My college was only two hours by train from my parents' house, so I could have stayed with them and commuted to school, but I chose not to. If I had stayed at home, I wouldn't be enjoying college life as much as I do now. (64 words)

2006年　　解答・解説

4 (A) 【全訳】　コウモリには問題がある。それは暗闇でどのようにして動き回るかということである。夜間に狩りをするので，食料を見つけたり障害物を避けたりするのに役立つ光を使うことはできない。もしそれが問題だとしたら，それは自業自得なのではないか，単に生活習慣を変え，昼間狩りに出かければ問題は解決するのではないか，と皆さんは言うかもしれない。しかし，鳥などの他の生物はすでに日中に活動するようになっている。コウモリは夜間に生活を営むことができ，代わりに日中の活動は他の動物によって占められていることを考えると，コウモリは自然淘汰によって夜間に狩猟活動することで成功を収めるようになっているのである。

　ところで，我々哺乳類はすべて，大昔は夜間に狩猟活動を行っていた可能性がある。日中の活動は恐竜たちによって独占されていた時代，我々の祖先は夜間に生活するすべを見つけたからこそ，かろうじて生き延びることがおそらくできたのだろう。約6千5百万年前になぜか恐竜が消滅してしまったが，その後になってようやく我々の祖先たちは大挙して昼間の世界に入っていくことができたのである。

　コウモリ以外に，物を見づらい，あるいはまったく見えないような状況で暮らしているものが現代の動物の中で多く存在する。暗闇の中でそのように動き回ればよいかという問題に対し，技師ならどのような解決法を考えるだろうか。まず考えつくのは，サーチライトのようなものを使うことだろう。魚の中には自ら光を発する能力を持つものがいるが，その行為は大量のエネルギーを使うと思われる。照射された場所の1つ1つからはねかえってくる小さな光の粒を目でとらえなければならないからである。したがって，光源を道を照らすヘッドライトとして用いるためには，他者への合図として用いる場合よりもずっと明るくなければならない。ともかく，その理由がエネルギー消費量であろうとなかろうと，おそらく一部の深海魚を除き，道を見つけるのに人工の光を使っている動物は人間以外いないのが実情であるように思われる。

【考え方】　(1)　正解は**キ・エ** (cannot **use light** to help them find)。find / help / use という3つの動詞をどう処理するかがポイント。直前に「コウモリは暗闇の中でどうやって道を見つけるかが問題」とあり，直後には「食料を…し，障害物を避ける」とあることから，暗闇の中で食料をどうやって「見つける」かが問題であると考え，food の直前に find を置く。次にアの cannot だが，暗闇の中だから「光が使えない」のではと考え，cannot use light とまとめる。残った help には「help ＋ O ＋ (to) 原形」という語法があることから，help ＋ O ＋ (to) find とつながっていく可能性を考える。ここで to の使い道だが，help them to find としてしまうと，cannot use light と help 以下をつなげる手段がなくなってしまう。したがって，「光は暗闇の中で食料を見つける手助けとなる」のではないかと考え，この to を light を修飾する

— 326 —

2006年　解答・解説

形容詞用法の不定詞と解釈し，cannot use light to help them find とまとめあげる。

(2)　正解は**キ・ア** (goes **way back** in the history of)。直後に，恐竜時代哺乳類の先祖たちがどのように闇の中で生きてきたかについての記述があることに注目。つまり，哺乳類は大昔には夜活動していたということ。選択肢に back / goes / history があることから，「歴史をずっと昔にさかのぼる」という内容を考え，goes back in the history of (all us mammals) とまとめる。ここで問題になるのはwayの置き場所。way には副詞としての用法があり，副詞や前置詞句を強調して「ずっと」という意味を持つ。本問では「ずっとさかのぼる」ということだから，back の前につける。(例) Her IQ is *way* above average. (彼女の知的指数は平均をずっと上回る)

(3)　正解は**エ・イ** (were **our ancestors** able to come out)。were able to come というつながりを見つけるのは容易だろう。主語は当然 our ancestors で，残った out の置き場所は come の直後以外考えられない。ところが，焦って our ancestors were able to come out としてしまうと誤りになることに注意。空所(3)を含む英文は "Only after ..." で始まっているが，これは「…以後しか～でない」という意味で，否定の副詞句という扱いになる。否定の副詞が文頭にある場合はその後に「疑問文の形の倒置」を続けなければならないというルールがあることを思い出し，were our ancestors able to come out とすれば正解になる。(例) **Never** *have I been* abroad. (私は外国へ行ったことがない)

(4)　正解は**オ・エ** (the **question of** how to move around)。the は定冠詞で名詞につけるものであるから，the question しかない。また，how / move / to より「疑問詞 + to –」の形を考えて how to move とする。残った選択肢は around / of だが，the question と how to move の関係は意味的に同格関係なので the question of how to move とし，around は move の直後につけて「動き回る」という意味にすればよい。

(5)　正解は**ウ・イ** (whether **or not** the reason is)。not / or / whether より whether (...) or not という並びは容易に発見できる。また the は定冠詞なので名詞 reason につくことも明白。問題は or not の位置だが，ここは the reason is ⟨the energy expense⟩ と続いていくため，whether the reason is *or not* と並べるわけにいかなくなる。したがって，or not は whether の直後に置いて，whether or not the reason is ⟨the energy expense⟩ とまとめる。

解 答

(1)－キ・エ	(2)－キ・ア	(3)－エ・イ	(4)－オ・エ	(5)－ウ・イ

－ 327 －

2006年 解答・解説

4 (B) 【全訳】 単に提案をするだけでは，聞き手がそれを受け入れなければならないということには決してならない。かりに「我々は幹線道路の建設にお金を使うべきだ」と述べても，そうした措置を講ずるべきだと主張したにすぎない。聞き手の視点からすれば，「なぜ我々はそうすべきなのだ？」という疑問をこちらが喚起したにすぎないのだ。単にこちらが提案を口に出したからという理由だけで，その提案がよいと信じなければならない理由は，その聞き手たちのうちの誰にもないのである。しかし，もしこちらが「なぜならば…」と言い，聞き手全員がなぜこちらと同じことをまさに言うべきなのかを示す理由をいくつか挙げることができれば，自分の主張の正しさを証明することができるだろう。こちらの話を聞いている人が，もし聞かれたら，幹線道路への資金投入の重要性に合意する方に傾けば，こちらの目的は達成したことになるのだ。

【考え方】 (1) 1. **If you say, "We should spend money on highway construction,"**「もしあなたが『我々は幹線道路建設にお金を使うべきだ』と述べても」 if は even if「(たとえ) …しても」という意味で用いられている。highwayは「幹線道路」の意であり，「高速道路 (freeway, expressway)」ではないことに注意。

2. **all you have done is to assert ...**「あなたがしたすべては…と主張することだ→あなたは…と主張しただけにすぎない」 all と you の間に関係代名詞が省略されている。you have done が関係詞節で all を修飾し，is が all に対する動詞で，to - が名詞用法の不定詞で is の補語。

3. **that such a step should be taken**「そうした措置が講じられるべきだということ」 take a step で「措置 [手段] を講ずる」の意。

(2) 1. **No person in that audience has any reason to believe ...**「その聞き手の中の誰も，…と信じる理由を持っていない [その聞き手の中の誰にも，…と信じる理由はない]」 to believe は reason を修飾する形容詞用法の不定詞。「信じる理由がない」の部分は「信じる必要はない」「信じることはできない」などと処理してもよいだろう。

2. **that the proposal is good**「その提案はよい [妥当だ] ということ」

3. **simply because you have voiced it**「単にあなたがそれ [その提案] を口に出して言ったからという理由で」 simply は because ... を修飾する副詞。because節は believe を修飾している副詞節。voice はここでは動詞で「…を口に出す」の意。

(3) 1. **You have achieved your purpose**「あなたは自分の目的を達成したことになる」

2. **when your audience would ... lean towards agreement on the**

— 328 —

2006年　解答・解説

importance of highway spending「あなたの聞き手が幹線道路への支出の重要性に合意する方に傾くとき」　would lean は仮定法過去。lean towards ... は「…に（向かって）傾く」の意。agreement on ... は「…についての意見の一致，合意」の意。highway は spending を修飾する名詞で，両者で「幹線道路に対する［関する］支出」の意。

　3．**if asked**「もし聞かれたら」　if they（＝ your audience を受ける）were asked から they were が省略された形。「聞き手が幹線道路への支出について意見を求められたら」の意。

解答

> (1)　「幹線道路の建設に資金を使うべきだ」と言っても，そのような措置を取るべきだと主張したことにしかならない。
>
> (2)　こちらが発言したというだけの理由で，その提案が良いものだと信ずべき理由は，その聞き手の中の誰にもないのである。
>
> (3)　聞き手が，自らの意見を聞かれた場合に幹線道路に対する出費の重要性に合意する方向に傾けば，こちらは自分の目的を達成したことになる。

5 **全訳**　数か月前に，ニューヨークの通りを歩いていたときに，ちょっと離れた所で，私のよく知っている男の人が私の行こうとしている方向へ向かっているのが見えた。困ったことに，彼の名前や，どこで会ったのかを思い出せなかった。こういうことは，とくに母国で会ったことのある人に外国の都市で出会ったり，その逆だったりするときに，経験する感情の一つである。思いがけなく遭遇する顔は混乱をもたらす。しかし，その時私は考えた。あの顔にはなじみがあるから，立ち止まり，挨拶をして，話しかけなくてはならないのは間違いない。ひょっとすると，あの人はすぐに反応するかもしれない。「ウンベルトさん，お元気ですか？」あるいは「私に言っていた件はなんとかなりましたか？」とまで言うかもしれない。そして，私はまったく途方にくれることになるのだろう。その人物を避けるには遅すぎた。彼は依然として通りの反対側を見ているが，今度は私の方へ視線を向け始めた。私の方から手を打った方がよいのかも。手を振っておいてから，彼の声，彼の最初の言葉を手がかりにして，彼が誰であるかを推測することにしようか。

　もう，互いの距離はわずか数フィートになり，私が満面の笑みをたたえようとしたときに，突然，誰だかわかった。有名な映画俳優のアンソニー・クインだ。当然，今まで私が彼に，そして彼が私に出会ったことは一度もなかった。電光石火の早業で，

— 329 —

2006年　　解答・解説

私は思いとどまることができ，彼の脇を通り抜ける際は，宙を見つめていた。

　後になって，この出来事を考え直し，そういうことが，まったくもってごく普通のことであるのがわかった。かつてあるとき，レストランで，チャールトン・ヘストンを見かけて，挨拶をしたい思いに駆られた。この種の顔は，記憶に刻まれている。スクリーンを眺めて，こういう顔と多くの時間を共有しているので，身内の人たちの顔と同じくらい，さらにはそれ以上というくらいに，私たちにとってなじみのものとなっている。マスコミを研究し，現在の効果や，現実との想像の間の混同を論じ，ある種の人々がこの種の混同に永続的に陥る様子を説明することもできる。しかし，それでもやはり，自分自身が，この種の混同を免れることができないのである。

　映画俳優にまつわる私の問題は，言うまでもなく，すべて頭の中の出来事だった。しかし，もっとひどいこともある。

　かなり頻繁にテレビに出ていて，ある程度の期間にわたり，マスメディアに関わってきた人から，話を聞かされたことがある。この上なく有名なメディアスターの話をしているのではなくて，公の場面に登場する人，誰だかわかるくらいにトーク番組によく登場してきた専門家の話である。そういう人たちは皆，同じ不快な経験について不満を述べる。さて，一般的に，個人的に知らない人を見かけると，私たちは，顔をしげしげと覗き込んだり，その人を指さして脇にいる友人に知らせたり，当人に聞こえるような場面で声高に話題にしたりすることはない。そういうふるまいをしたら，無礼だし，度を越すと侮辱したことになるだろう。しかし，客とカウンターで応対するときにけっして指さしたりせず，客がすてきなネクタイを締めていることを友人に指摘したりしない人が，有名な顔を相手にするとまったく別の行動をとる。

　私自身の比較的有名な友人たちが強く主張することだが，キオスクや書店で，あるいは電車に乗ろうとしているときや，レストランのトイレに入ろうとするとき，たまたま出くわした人たちが，内輪で次のように声に出して言っていることがある。

「見てよ。Xがいるよ」

「ほんと？」

「もちろん，ほんとだよ。Xさ。まちがいない」

　そして彼らは，Xさんに聞こえているのに，内輪の会話をおもしろそうに続け，当人に聞こえているかどうか気にかけていない。まるで当人が存在していないかのようだ。

　そういう人たちは，マスメディアの想像上の世界の登場人物が思いがけず実在の世界に入り込んできているという事実に混乱するものの，それと同時に，実在の人物が存在しているというのに，依然としてその人がイメージの世界に属しているかのように，まるで当人がスクリーンに映っていたり，週刊写真雑誌の中にいるかのようにふ

— 330 —

2006年　　解答・解説

るまうのである。本人のいないところで話しているかのように。

　ひょっとすると，私はアンソニー・クインの腕を取り，電話ボックスまで引っぱっていって，友人に電話をかけて次のように言った方がよかったのかもしれない。

　「わかるかい？　今，アンソニー・クインと一緒にいるんだ。聞いてくれよ。本当にいるみたいだぜ！」　そしてその後，私はクインをほったらかしにして，自分の用件をあれこれしゃべるだろう。

　マスメディアは想像の世界のものが実在の世界のものであるということを私たちにまず説得しておいてから，今度は実在のものが想像の世界のものであるということを私たちに説得しようとしている。そしてテレビの画面が現実を示せば示すほど，私たちの日常生活が映画のようになる。そしてついには，ある哲学者たちが主張するように，私たちは自分が世界の中で孤独であると考え，他のすべてのものは，神か何かの悪霊が私たちの眼前に映し出している映画であると考える。

【考え方】　(1)　正解は (1a) ア context，(1b) オ space，(1c) イ fact。(1a) と (1b) は選択肢を代入して前後に合いそうなものを選ぶのが近道だろう。out of context は「文脈なしに；文脈から切り離して」ということから「脈絡なしに；出しぬけに」と考える。Staring into space は「虚空を見つめる」ということから「宙を見つめる；視線を合わせないでいる」と考える。(1c) は，同格の that 節が続くことから fact を選ぶ。

　(2)　正解はイの get away from ...「…を避ける；…から逃れる」。空所の手前に「立ち止まり，挨拶をして，話しかけなくてはならない」が，そうなると「まったく途方にくれることになる」とあることから，筆者が当該の人物から距離をおいておきたいということがわかる。よって正解はイとなる。それ以外のア「追いつく」，ウ「利用する」，エ「友人となる」は，いずれも文意に合わない。

　(3)　正解はアの nor he me。時制と省略がポイント。まず，私が彼に会ったことがなく彼も私に会ったことがない，という文意から，アかイが残るが，イは時制が異なってしまうので不可。なお，文章を完全な文に復元すると，... and he had never met me in his life, either. となる。

　(4)　正解はウの normal「通常の；ありふれた」。ここは文の流れから考える。Anthony Quinn と出会った経験を語った後で，さらに Charlton Heston と出会った例，友人たちの例へと話題を続けていることから，正解を選ぶ。ア foreign「異質な」イ lucky「幸運な」エ useless「無益な」では流れに合わない。

　(5)　正解は **familiar to us than our relatives' faces**。もしかりに 1 語で答えるとしたら familiar となるところ。7 語にするためには，後続の語句を補って，

— 331 —

familiar to us than our relatives' となるが，これでもまだ1語不足なので，さらに
faces を補うことになる。実際の答案では，as を than に変更することを忘れたり，
綴りのミスが発生したりしやすいので注意が必要。なお，設問文はやや誤解を招きや
すい。「"so" を7語の英語で置き換えよ」とすべきだったかもしれない。

(6) 正解は「メディアでの露出度が高いと，面前で失礼な態度を取られること (29
字)」。下線部を含む短いパラグラフが「もちろん～だが…」という構造で，ここま
での記述と，後続の記述をつぐ役割をはたしていることに注意する。ここまでが筆者
の頭の中での出来事であったのに対して，後続の記述では，有名人が実際に目の前
で自分のことを話題にされる経験について語っているので，それをまとめればよい。
appearing fairly frequently on TV や public figures や become recognizable など
を「メディアでの露出度が高い」とまとめ，when he or she can hear us や while
X hears them などから「面前で失礼な態度を取られていること」とまとめればよい。

(7) 正解はアの as a rule「概して；一般的に言って」。ここは後続の文との意味的
なつながりから判断する。空所8の直後で「しかし，一般人には反応しない人が，有
名な顔を相手にするとまったく別の行動をとる」と逆接関係の「例」をあげているこ
とから，空所(7)から一般論が始まっていると考える。ウは as is often the case の形
で「よくあることだが」といった意味を表すが,as is the case では不適切。イは「そ
れにもかかわらず」，エは「善かれ悪しかれ」という意味である。

(8) 正解はアの if carried too far「度を越すと」。carry ... too far は「…をや
りすぎる」という意味の熟語。本文における省略を補えば if such behavior were
carried too far となる。ここは文の流れから程度を問題にしているのだと考える。エ
の if made too frequently「あまりにも頻繁になされると」は頻繁なので文脈に合
わない。イ if noticed too soon「あまりにもすぐに気づかれると」やウ if taken too
seriously「あまりにもまじめに受け取られると」は，いずれも受け止め方を考えて
いるので不可。

(9) 正解はイの I can't believe they're talking like that in front of me!「私の目の
前でそんなことを言うなんて信じられない」。この箇所の文脈については，(6)の解説
の後半部分を参照せよ。ア「私を誰か別の人と間違えているのだろうか」，ウ「私に
関して何を言うつもりなのかを私は知りたい」，エ「彼らの名もどこで彼らに会った
のかも私には思い出せない。どうしたらよいだろう？」は,いずれも文脈に合わない。

(10) 正解は **absence**。in ～'s absence で「～のいないところで」という意味の
熟語。直前の文の in the presence と対比関係にあることを参考にする。(例) The

— 332 —

decision was made *in my absence*. （決定は私のいないところで行われた）

(11) 正解は「そしてその後，私はクインをほったらかしにして，**自分の用件をあれ
これしゃべるだろう**」。前の文の内容を指す関係詞節 which ... が，このように主節か
ら独立した文として用いられることがある。throw aside は「放棄する，捨てる」と
いう意味の熟語。go on about ... は「…のことをぺちゃくちゃしゃべる」という意味
の熟語。ここでは business は「仕事」ではなく「用事，用件」の意味であることに
も注意。

(12) 正解はウ (a) imaginary，(b) real。該当箇所の前半が過去形，後半が現在形で
あることにまず注意する。そして直後に，現在のこととして「テレビが reality を示
せば示すほど，日常世界が movie-like（つまり imaginary）となる」と書かれてい
ることから，現在の状況は real から imaginary へという方向だとわかる。

解答

---

(1) (1a) － ア (1b) － オ (1c) － イ

(2) － イ   (3) － ア   (4) － ウ

(5) familiar to us than our relatives' faces

(6) メディアでの露出度が高いと，面前で失礼な態度を取られること（29字）

(7) － ア   (8) － ア   (9) － イ   (10) absence

(11) そしてその後，私はクインをほったらかしにして，自分の用件をあれこれ
しゃべるだろう。

(12) － ウ

解答・解説

1 (A) **[全訳]** 私たちは，かくも多くの自然なリズムとハーモニーを，単に持って生まれるにすぎない。したがって，その両者を維持する術を探求し開発しなければならない。私が50年にわたり一流のスポーツ選手を教え励ましてきた経験から分かったのは，完全に調和のとれた運動は水中の魚に似ているということである。魚は尻尾をひと振りすれば，速度と方向を難なく変えながら進んで行く。最小の労力を使い，最大の結果を得ているのである。

ペレ，モハメド・アリ，ビヨン・ボルグといった，スポーツ史に残る偉大な英雄たちは皆，リズム感のある，なめらかな始動をした。完全停止の状態から突然動きに入るなどということはしなかった。いきなり動き出すのではなく，ゆらゆらと流れるように動きながら考えていたのである。彼らが身につけていたのは，いわば高度な意識とでも言えるものであったが，これこそ，その世界で頂点を目指すスポーツ選手に絶対不可欠なものなのだ。

誰もが知るように，不安と緊張が原因になって動きが悪くなったりミスをしたりするものだが，この高度な意識を常に念頭においた生活をすれば，それらを最小限に抑えることができる。何かを拾い上げようとする指にそうするように，身体を集中させ，意識させなければならない。身体全体が，指のように，空間の中で占める位置に敏感でなければならない。徐々に自分独自のリズム感が生まれ，それが結果的に，よりすぐれた，より一貫性のある動きに現れるようになる。

[考え方] おそらく運動心理学 (Sport Psychology) の専門家が書いた文章を出典としているのだろうが，書き出しがやや唐突なところもあって，戸惑った受験生が多かったかもしれない。たった217語の文章であり，英文そのものの読解に苦労はしなかったはずだが，いざ「要約する」となると，どこを骨格とするかの判断が難しい。英文そのものは「易」だが，要約問題としては「やや難」とでも言える問題である。

1. 基本方針

全文の内容を要約するのであるから，可能なかぎり「全体の流れ」をすくい上げる解答を心がけるべきである。中には1文をピンポイントする問題もあるが，一般的には具体例や言い換え部分を理解の道具としつつ，文章全体の骨子をまとめるのが基本となる。複数の段落から成る文章の場合は（具体例のみの段落は別だが）全段落の内容に触れるように心がけること。

— 336 —

2005年　　解答・解説

　また，文章の内容から乖離することのないよう注意すること。要約問題では「そこに書いてあること」をまとめるのであり，自分の主観や感想を含めてはならない。

2．本文のアウトライン

〈第1パラグラフ〉

第1文　生得的な「リズムとハーモニー」を維持する術を探究開発すべき。

第2文　一流運動選手は魚の動きに似た調和の取れた動きをすることがわかった。

第3文　（すなわち）最小の努力で最大の効果を生む（ということ）。

〈第2パラグラフ〉

第1文　一流運動選手はリズム感のある流麗な動きをする。

第2文　完全停止から突然動きだすのではなく，ゆらゆら揺れながら考えていた。

第3文　彼らは一流選手に不可欠な，高度な意識を身につけていた。

〈第3パラグラフ〉

第1文　不安と緊張が動きの悪さやミスの原因となるが，この高度な意識がそれを最
　　　　小限に抑える。

第2文　身体を集中させ意識を持たせなければならない。

第3文　身体全体が空間の中に占める位置に敏感でなければならない。

第4文　徐々に自分独自のリズムが生まれ，より良い動きに現れる。

3．要約のポイント

　① 「目標」と「手段」

　　a. 第1パラグラフ第1文で「自然に持って生まれた "rhythm and harmony" を
　　　維持する方法を探求し，開発しなければならない」と述べられている。これが，
　　　いわば「目標」となる部分。

　　b. 次に，第1パラグラフ第2文から第2パラグラフにかけて「一流の運動選
　　　手」が引き合いに出されているが，彼らはまさに "rhythm and harmony" を
　　　持つ動きができているから参考にしているのである。では，なぜそのような
　　　動きができるかというと，第2パラグラフ最終文にあるように "high-level
　　　awareness"（高度な意識）を身につけているからである。そうすると「一流
　　　運動選手のように高度な意識を持つようにすること」が，先の目標に対する「手
　　　段」となる。ここまで，次のような流れをまとめることができる。

— 337 —

2005 年　　解答・解説

持って生まれた "rhythm and harmony" を維持する必要がある。《目標》

→（そのためには）一流運動選手のように "high-level awareness" を身につけ
るべきである。《手段》

---

c. なお，第3パラグラフ第1文は，第2パラグラフの内容を逆から述べている
だけで，新しい情報とは言えない。このパラグラフの重要性は，第2文，第3
文から "awareness" の意味を掴むことにある。

② 文脈中での「意味」の把握

d. 全体の流れがまとまると，あとはそこに含まれる表現の意味を明確にしてい
くことになる。「目標」の部分に含まれる "rhythm" は「（運動における）リズ
ム感」でよいが，"harmony" については，第1パラグラフ第2文，第3文か
ら「（運動における）無駄のなさ；効率の良さ」のことを言っているのだと考
える。

e. 次に「手段」の部分に含まれる "awareness" については，第3パラグラフ第
2文，第3文から「自分の身体の動きや位置について意識を集中させ，敏感に
なること」だと分かる。high-level awareness をただ訳すのではなく，「それ
がこの文脈ではどのような意味で用いられるか」を掴み，それを解答に表現す
るのがポイント。

以上，①，②の点を考慮してまとめたのが，以下の解答例である。なお，制限字
数の下限（本問では60字）を下回ると明らかな内容不足となり，採点対象外になる
可能性もあるので注意すること。

解 答 例

［解答例1］　リズム感のある効率の良い動きは生得的なものだが，これを維持す
るには一流運動選手の動きを参考にして自分の身体の動きについて敏感にな
るべきだ。(69字)

［解答例2］　先天的に備わった，無駄がなくリズム感のある動きを維持するため
には，一流運動選手のように自分の身体について敏感な感覚を持つことが重
要だ。(67字)

［解答例3］　無駄がなくリズム感のある自然な動きを維持していくためには，一
流運動選手を手本にし自分の身体について常に敏感であらねばならない。(63
字)

2005年　解答・解説

1 **(B)** **【全訳】** 1860年代のビヤウィトクは不寛容と恐怖によって分裂していた。この都市は，現在のポーランド北東部に位置し，当時はロシア支配下にあったが，主に四つの民族集団，すなわち，ポーランド人，ロシア人，ドイツ人，そしてユダヤ人の住むところであった。この民族集団は，離れて暮らし，共通言語を持たず，互いに強い不信感を抱いていた。暴力沙汰は日常茶飯事であった。

（　　1　　）

ザメンホフは，両親のしつけでポーランド語，ドイツ語，ロシア語，イディッシュ語，ヘブライ語を話すようになっていたが，英語とフランス語にもかなり通じていた。だから既存の言語でうまくいくものはないということが分かっていた。それは一つには，こうした言語がすべて特定の国家，民族，文化を連想させるために，国際語が受け入れられるために必要となる中立性が欠如するということになるからであった。

（　　2　　）

しかし，言語を発明しても勘定が支払えるわけではないので，ザメンホフには職業が必要だった。彼は医学を学び，眼科医になった。昼間は眼科医として働き，夜には自ら考案した言語，エスペラントに取り組んだ。エスペラントはすばらしく単純な言語で，基本ルールは16しかなく，しかも例外が1つもない。おそらく不規則変化の動詞を1つも持たない言語はこれ以外にはないし，（フランス語には2千以上，スペイン語とドイツ語には各々700ほどの不規則動詞がある），動詞の語尾はたった6つ習得すればよいだけなので，たいていの初学者は1時間もすれば話せるようになるのではないだろうか。

（　　3　　）

ザメンホフの見事な言語は，単一国家，単一文化を連想させるものではなかったが，その語根の4分の3はラテン語，ギリシャ語，現代西欧語から取ったものである。これには，世界人口の約半分がその語彙の大半をすでに知っているという利点がある。英語話者にとって，エスペラント習得はスペイン語やフランス語の5倍，ロシア語の10倍，アラビア語や中国語の20倍は楽だと思われる。

（　　4　　）

ア　同時期に，ドイツの聖職者ヨハン・シュライヤーは，彼の新言語，ボラピューク（「世界語」の意）に取り組んでいた。シュライヤーの言語は，1878年にドイツで初登場し，1890年までに設立されたボラピューク協会は283団体に上回った。しかし一般の評価では，シュライヤーの言語は奇妙で醜悪，ラテン語同様習得は容易ではないとされていた。

— 339 —

2005年　解答・解説

イ　さらに，これらの既存の言語は複雑な文法規則を持ち，個々の規則にその例外があったために，普遍的第二言語に欠かせないもう一つの特徴が欠落していた。すなわち，一般人にとって学びやすくなかったのである。そして習得困難という要因は，ラテン語も古典ギリシャ語も普遍語としての力をさほど持たないということも意味した。ザメンホフの取るべき道は一つしかなかった。自分の言語を考案せざるをえなかったのである。

ウ　1859年，相互理解の欠如によって民族間の憎悪が生まれ，街中で日々その憎悪が噴出していたこの地にルドビック・ザメンホフは生まれた。母親は語学教師で，父親も複数の言語を学んでいた。ルドヴィク少年は，15歳になるまでに，自分の町で目にする暴力にうんざりし，様々な民族集団の相互理解を可能にする共通言語が必要だと確信するに至ったのである。

エ　当然ながら，欠点となるが，非西欧語の話者がエスペラントを始めるには，多少余計な努力が必要になるという点である。しかしエスペラント使用者は，ザメンホフの言語体系は単純であるがゆえに，その語根を知らなくても全く問題ないと主張している。彼らは，エスペラントがハンガリー，フィンランド，日本，中国，ベトナムで普及していることを誇らしげに指摘し，これは相互伝達と相互理解を目指して世界語を造ったザメンホフの功績を証明していると言う。

オ　エスペラントは語彙もきわめて単純である。ザメンホフは必修語の膨大なリストを作らず，大変基礎的な語根の体系と，その意味を変える単純な仕組みを考案した。たとえば，"mal-"をエスペラントの語頭に付けるとその語は反対語になる。エスペラント使用者は既存の語を2，3語組み合わせると簡単に新しい単語を作ることができる。このような語形成法はエスペラント使用者から見れば，この言語の魅力を高める一種の創作過程なのである。

カ　エスペラントが，かくも習得しやすいという点は，それが成功を収める鍵となっている。言うまでもなく英語はルドビック・ザメンホフの時代と比べると，世界語として今日さらに重要性を増している。しかし英語は，実用性がさらに増しているとはいえ，まったく簡単にはなっておらず，そうだからこそエスペラントは今でも大変人気がある。母国語が何であれ，最初にエスペラントをやってみる。西欧語の使用者でも優位に立てるわけではない。エスペラントは，正真正銘，現代の世界を意思表示をし聞き入れてもらう機会を万人に，平等に与える言語なのである。

考え方　段落補充（あるいは，文補充）問題は，2000年度以降連続して出題されており，文章の内容は様々であっても取り組み方自体は基本的に同じである。指示語，冠詞の使い方，代名詞，論理展開を示す Discourse Maker，時間の流れなどに着目

— 340 —

2005 年　　解答・解説

していけば比較的容易に解答できたであろう。ただし本問では，最後の空所に要注意。

　(1)　正解はウ。選択肢ウの第 1 文に It was here, where ... とあるが，この here が第 1 パラグラフで述べられた Bialystok の町を示す指示副詞となる（なお，この文は It ... that 〜副詞を強調した強調構文）。また，エスペラント開発者ザメンホフの生い立ちを述べるものとしても，ウはこの空所にふさわしい内容を持っている。

　(2)　正解はイ。選択肢イの第 1 文に These existing languages とあり，これが第 3 パラグラフの all of these languages を指す指示形容詞となる。また，also had ... の also にも注意。ザメンホフは世界共通語の必要性を感じていたのだが，既存の言語ではうまくいかない理由が第 3 パラグラフ最終文で述べられている。選択肢イの「文法規則が複雑」という点も欠点であり，既存の言語が共通語としては不備がある理由を続けるものとして，ここにイがあるのがふさわしい。さらに，この選択肢の最終文では「（既存の言語ではうまくいかないから）自分で考案しなければならなかった」と述べられており，これが第 5 パラグラフ冒頭の But 以下の内容にうまくつながる。

　(3)　正解はオ。選択肢オ第 1 文の ... is also very simple. に注目する。第 5 パラグラフ第 4 文 (Esperanto is a beautifully simple language ...) 以下でエスペラントの特徴が述べられており，選択肢オも also によってその特徴を追加記述していると考える。

　(4)　正解はエ。第 7 パラグラフでは，特に第 2 文 (The advantage to this ...) 以下で，エスペラントの利点が述べられている。選択肢エは，第 1 文で "The disadvantage ..." とあるが，第 2 文の But 以下の内容に注意。「非西欧語話者にとっては習得が難しい → しかし，その単純さゆえどの言語の話者でも問題ないし，実際多数の国で普及している」という内容を考えると，ここはエがふさわしい。

　不要な選択肢のうち，アは無関係なものとしてすぐに排除できたであろう。カは第 1 文に「エスペラントは習得が簡単」という内容が入っているので，空所(4)にふさわしいように見える。しかし，この選択肢の第 5 文 (Not even ...) には「西欧語話者でも利点をもっているわけではない」とあり，これは第 7 パラグラフで述べられた西欧語話者にとってのエスペラントの利点と矛盾する記述になってしまうため，不要と判断する。

解答

(1)−ウ　　(2)−イ　　(3)−オ　　(4)−エ

－ 341 －

2005 年　　解答・解説

2 (A)　[考え方]

1．まず語数だが，「30 ～ 40 語で」とあるからには，この指定より多くても少なくてもまずいだろう。ただ，解答スペースがかなり大きく（167 mm×6 行），すべてを埋めてしまうと，小さめの字で書いた場合は確実に 5，60 語行ってしまう。多忙な採点官がいちいち答案の語数を数えているとも思えないので，おそらく 4 行書いてあれば十分であろう。できれば答案の最後に「○○ words」と書くのが望ましい。

2．「絵に描かれた状況を<u>自由に解釈し</u>」という指定がかなりクセモノである。ここで言う「自由な解釈」とは，下記の 3．で指摘する 3 つの要素を押さえつつ，**自由な発想でストーリーを仕立て上げよ**，という意味に解釈するのがよい。「女性は顔に笑みをたたえている」とか「男性は家から逃げた」とか「ウィスキーの瓶が割れている」などという突飛なことを書いてはいけない。**「自由な解釈」と「勝手な解釈」は違うことを心得ておいてほしい。**

3．答案を書く上でおさえておかなければならないポイントは 3 つ。この 3 つのすべてが盛り込まれていないと減点対象となるだろう。

①　**花瓶をめぐる話になっていること**
②　**女性についての記述があること**
③　**男性についての記述があること**

まず①だが，「花瓶が割れている」という記述が必要。someone has broken a vase / a vase is broken でもいいし，単に a broken vase でもよい（「花瓶」が英語で書けないのは論外）。

②だが，この女性はどう見ても「怒っている」ので，angry という語はほしい。

③だが，この男性は明らかに「女性の後ろいて，ドアのところで覗いている」ので，a man is looking through the door behind her / there is a man behind her / the man standing behind her などという書き方がよいだろう。a man is hiding behind the door は「扉のかげに隠れている」つまり「開いている扉の後ろに身を潜めている」ことになるため，厳密に言うとおかしいのだが，許容範囲であろう。

4．以上の 3 点を膨らませてどのようなストーリーに仕立てるかが，設問文に書かれた「自由な解釈」である。むろん 3 点すべてをクローズアップする必要はない。どれを膨らませるかは語数と相談である。具体例をあげてみよう。

★「花瓶」についての詳細
「女性が一番気に入っている花瓶」the woman's favorite vase [4 words]
「女性が長年大事にしてきた花瓶」the vase the woman had long cherished [7 words]（別解 3）

— 342 —

2005 年　　解答・解説

「有名な陶芸家に作ってもらった高い花瓶」an expensive vase the woman had a famous potter made [10 words]（別解 4 ）

★「男性」と「女性」を誰にするか

　この二人を夫婦（別解 2 ・ 4 ）あるいは親子（別解 3 ）ととらえても構わないし，親戚にしてしまってもよい。また John や Mary などと名前をつけるのも自由（別解 3 ・ 4 ）。どちらかを「自分」ととらえて，一人称の "I" と記述することも可能だろう。

★「女性」についての記述

「怒って割れた花瓶を見つめている」the woman is staring angrily at the broken vase [9 words]（別解 1 ）

「怒って割れた花瓶の前に立っている」the woman is standing angrily in front of a broken vase [11words]（別解 2 ）

★「男性」についての記述

「男性は不安げである」the man looks worried [4 words]（解答例）

「とまどっている」the man doesn't know what to do [7 words]（別解 4 ）

「女性にあやまる勇気がない」the man doesn't have the courage to apologize to the woman [11 words]（別解 3 ）

「花瓶を割ったのはおそらく男性である」it seems very likely that he is the person who broken the vase [13 words]（解答例）

5．まとめ方だが，このような状況説明をする場合，英語ではすべて現在形で表現するのが普通である（花瓶が割れたことは現在完了で表現する）が，時制はあまり厳密に守られていなくても構わないだろう。さらに大事なのが物語の構成で，1 つの流れを持ったストーリーを展開する必要がある。**このような「構成力」も東大の試験では重要な得点ポイントとなる**ことを忘れないように。

　具体的にどのように展開させればよいのかを，解答をサンプルに説明してみよう。

★「解答例」について

　状景描写に徹した書き方で，ストーリーはない。絵から見てとれない内容は一切書かず，客観的な説明に終始している。

★「別解 1 」について

　「解答例」のようにほぼ客観的な記述だが，男性の心情を書き加えている。

★「別解 2 」について

　二人を「夫婦」と解釈し，男性をメインにして，かなり自由に物語を創作している。

★「別解 3 」について

— 343 —

<u>2005 年　　解答・解説</u>

二人を「親子」と解釈し，子供（男性）には名前をつけている。花瓶の背景，さらにはこぼれた水についての記述を書き加え，男性の心情にも踏み込んでいる。

★「別解4」について

二人を「夫婦」ととらえて，「別解3」と同様名前をつけている。花瓶の背景をかなり膨らませている。

以上を見ればわかると思うが，書き方にはいろいろある。30 〜 40 語でまとまりのある話をいかに英語で書き上げるかが勝負となるだろう。

解 答 例

> The picture shows a woman who is very angry because someone has broken a vase. The man standing behind her looks very worried. It seems very likely that he is the person who broke the vase. (36 words)

別解1　A woman is staring angrily at her vase, which has been broken. A man is looking through the door behind her, and he seems to be frightened of her. He must have broken the vase. (35 words)

別解2　A husband comes home and see his wife standing angrily in front of a broken vase. He hesitates to come in, because he feels he might be yelled at even though it wasn't this fault. (35 words)

別解3　John broke the vase his mother had long cherished, and the water in it has made the carpet wet. She looks so angry that he doesn't have the courage to apologize. He is just standing behind her. (37 words)

別解4　Mr. Smith is looking at his wife through the door. Apparently, he broke the vase. She looks very angry. The vase was one she had a famous potter make, and it cost a fortune! He doesn't know what to do. (40 words)

2 **(B)** **考え方**　1．語数だが，「空所すべてを合わせて 40 〜 50 語」という指定が大変面倒である。解答用紙は空所(1)〜(3)すべてが 167 mm× 3 行だが「合計 40 〜 50 語」なので，極端な話(1)で 5 語・(2)で 5 語・(3)で 30 語でもよいということだ。この問題こそ採点官がいちいち答案の語数を数えるなどありえないだろう（むろん(A)と同様，各空所の最後に「○○ words」と書くのが望ましい）。

2．答案を書く上で注意したいのは，本文中にある "For example" "while" "Therefore" の 3 語。この 3 つの語より，おさえるべきポイントが見えてくる。

① (1)(2)に **communication style** の具体例が書かれていること **(For example)**

－ 344 －

2005 年　　解答・解説

②　⑴と⑵は対立する内容になっていること **(while)**

③　⑶にはコミュニケーションにおける大切な事柄を⑴と⑵の内容を踏まえて書くこと **(Therefore)**

この３つが守られていなければ当然減点対象となるはずである。

この問題の難しさは "communication style" が何を意味しているのか理解できていないと全く的外れな答案となり，下手すると０点にされる可能性があるということだ。communication style とは，相手とのやりとりにおいて，どのような物言いで発言するか，また相手の意見をどのような態度で聞くかということ。したがって，「携帯で話すか直接話すか」「手紙を書くか電話をするか」「ジェスチャーを交えるか交えないか」などはすべて解答として不適当である。これらのような，**コミュニケーションの手段を答えるのではない。**

３．communication style の具体例

これは⑴⑵共通である。上記①で書いたように，互いに対立するものの組み合わせでなければならない。

★「ひたすら yes-man で，自分の意見を言わない」⇔「自分の意見を押しつけて，相手の言うことを聞かない」（解答例）

★「直截的な物言い」⇔「遠回しな言い方」（別解１）

★「大げさな物言い」⇔「控えめな物言い」（別解２・３）

★「言葉を選んで話す」⇔「思いつきで話す」（別解４）

４．結論に何を書くか

要するに空所⑶の埋め方であるが，ここに書くことはほとんど決まってしまう。本文の流れを確認すると，まず冒頭で「コミュニケーションスタイルには個人差がある」と述べられ，その具体例が⑴と⑵である。最後に結論として「したがって人間のコミュニケーションで最も大事なことは」とあるのだから，空所⑶にはその「個人差」をどうすればいいのかを書くしかない。具体的に言うと，「どこが違うのか理解し，相手の真意を汲み取ろうと努める」（解答例，別解１・２）か「違いにとらわれることなく，相手の真意を汲み取ろうと努める」（解答例，別解３・４）のいずれかしかないだろう。したがって，たとえ⑴⑵で不適切な例をあげられているとしても，空所⑶で正しい内容が書かれている可能性は十分ある。注意してほしいのは，上記後半部の「相手の真意を汲み取ろうと努める」という内容が書かれていることが重要で，単に「コミュニケーションスタイルには個人差がある」だけでは単に本文冒頭文を繰り返しているにすぎなくなり，解答としては０点である。

<u>2005 年　　解答・解説</u>

解 答 例

---

(1)　do nothing but agree with others, being too hesitant to express themselves

(2)　try to force their opinions on others, not bothering to listen to them at all

(3)　to understand what style of communication another person has, and to adapt to it（合計 41 words）

別解 1

(1)　are very direct in the way they express themselves

(2)　typically express themselves in ways that seem intended to hide their meaning rather than express it

(3)　to try to understand what others are really saying, rather than simply assuming that it is obvious（合計 42 words）

別解 2

(1)　prefer to exaggerate things, and try to make them seem exciting than they are

(2)　prefer to understate things, and just let the facts speak for themselves

(3)　to understand the other person's communication style so that you won't be misled by it（合計 41 words）

別解 3

(1)　use a lot of big words when they speak because they want to sound intelligent

(2)　use very plain language

(3)　not to pay too much attention to differences in style, but attempt to understand what other people are really trying to say（合計 41 words）

別解 4

(1)　try to use very precise expressions when they are speaking

(2)　don't really concentrate very much on what they are saying and just say whatever comes to mind

(3)　not to let such differences interfere with our attempts to understand each other（合計 40 words）

2005年　解答・解説

4 (A) **[考え方]** (1)「太陽熱暖房に対する初期段階の試みにおいては，太陽からのエネルギーは二重のガラス板におおわれた大きな金属シートによって吸収されていた」　正解は **and**。energy from the sun was absorbed by で「太陽からのエネルギーは…によって吸収されていた」となるが，by の目的語がないままに and が出てきている。続く large metal sheets covered by を large metal sheets *was* covered by から was が省略されたものととらえ，double plates of glass が absorbed by と covered by の共通の目的語であると解釈した者もいるかもしれないが，これには無理がある。もしこのような共通関係が存在するなら，カンマを使って energy from the sun was absorbed by, and large metal sheets covered by, double plates of glass とするのが通常であるからだ。さらに，ここでは太陽熱暖房の仕組みが説明されているから，energy from the sun を主語に据えた記述と考えるべきである。and を削除すれば，absorbed by に続く目的語が large metal sheets で，さらに covered 以下が large metal sheets を修飾する過去分詞句となり，構文的にも明確になる。

(2)「道端の植物が枯れたことで，環境保護主義者たちはさらに調査を進め，道路の氷結防止に塩を使用することから生じる問題が，実際いかに広範囲に及んでいるかを知るに至ったのである」　正解は **from**。prevent という動詞の語法は prevent A (from B) で，単に prevent from B という使い方はない。to 不定詞の形容詞用法，または関係代名詞の省略など，A が欠落する理由も見当たらないので，from を削除し prevent とするのが正しい。

(3)「すでにわかっているものと，その他のまだよくわかっていないものとの間に存在する関係にある賢い人間が気づいたから，科学的大進歩がもたらされた，という場合もある」　正解は **noticed**。a connection between A and B で「AとBの間の関係」という意味。ここではAが a subject で，that was already understood はこの subject を修飾する関係代名詞節となっている。Bだが，noticed 以下を another にかかる過去分詞句と解釈するのは無理。notice は第4文型をとらず，第5文型になっても補語に分詞以外は来ない。したがって，過去分詞句として機能する場合，「notice＋名詞」という形にはならないのである。第3文型の notice が過去分詞として subject を修飾しているという考え方は可能だが，noticed still mysterious という並び，つまり「過去分詞＋副詞＋形容詞」はおかしいし，内容的にも「気づかれた不思議なもの」では要領を得ない。noticed を削除すれば，構文的にも内容的にも明確なものとなる。

(4)「21世紀の初頭，ユニセックスな服装の傾向が非常に進んだ状態に到達して

— 347 —

2005 年　　解答・解説

いたので，服をすべて剥ぎ取って裸にしないと男性なのか女性なのかほとんど区別ができないくらいになった」　正解は **from**。「到達する」という意味の reach は第3文型の動詞なので，その後には目的語が続かなければならない。advanced は「高度な」という意味の形容詞であるため，構文的におかしい。from を削除すれば，so advanced a state が reached の目的語となって正しくなる。ちなみにこれは「so ＋形容詞＋ a ＋名詞」の形で，such an advanced state と同意。

⑸　「司書たちはいかにして本を分類するかという問題をめぐって意味のある口論をしているが，言い争いに勝つか負けるかを判断する基準には，ある分類法が他と比べて「正しい」あるいは「間違っていない」ということは含まれないだろう」正解は **themselves**。まず第一に，but 以下が the criteria (S) ... will not include (V) the "truth" or "correctness"(O) という第3文型の構文になっており，relative to ... は「…と比べて」という意味の副詞句であることがわからないと，正解を見つけるのは難しいだろう。次に，by themselves を放置すると，その後に続く which arguments are won or lost において which 自身の節中での役割がなくなってしまう。一方 which を疑問形容詞とし（「どの主張が勝つのか負けるのか」），criteria と同格関係にあると考えたとしたら，それはあまりに内容を無視した無理な解釈である。「基準」は勝ち負けを決めるものであって，「どちらが勝ち負けか」とイコールではないからだ。themselves を削除すれば，the criteria *by which* arguments are won or lost となり，by which 以下の先行詞 criteria を修飾する関係代名詞節と解釈することができるようになる。これは本来 arguments are won or lost *by the criteria*（「その基準により口論の勝ち負けが決まる」）で，the criteria を which に変え，「前置詞＋関係代名詞」の形へと変化したもの。

解　答

(1) and　　(2) from　　(3) noticed　　(4) from　　(5) themselves

4 **(B)** **〔全訳〕**「科学革命」は，16，17 世紀のヨーロッパの天文学と物理学が成し遂げた偉大な知的勝利を説明するのに伝統的に使われる用語である。1700 年頃までには，教養ある人間たちは宇宙を時計のような機械的な仕組みを持つものと捉え，地球は太陽の周りを回る惑星とみなされていた。科学革命と結びついた知的革命の結果として，自然を探求しそれを支配することには価値があるという新たな確信が生まれたが，こうした発展は現代社会における科学の重要性を理解する土台となるものである。

— 348 —

2005 年　　解答・解説

　技術の革新と自然界の理解を通じ人間が進歩するという潜在的な可能性をめぐる新たな楽観主義もまた，17 世紀の特徴だった。自然を理解し支配することで工業技術や農業技術が向上するだろうという見込みが表明された。しかしながら，科学知識の応用に関する意図と実績の間には大きな溝があった。自然についての知識が実際に有用だとか，自然についての知識は技術の進歩にとって将来的に重要だという主張はよく見られたが，科学の進歩は人間とその周囲の環境の関係にはほとんど何の影響も与えなかった。それでもやはり，自然についての知識の追求と結びついた文化的な価値観は 17 世紀の社会の重要な特徴であった。科学は，技術の進歩，知的理解，そしてこの世界を創造する際に神が示した英知を祝うことといった様々な価値観を表明した。自然界の敵対的で神秘的な環境は，人間が調べればその秘密を明かすことになるのだろうと人々は信じていた。人間には自然を支配する能力があるという考え方を正当化したのは，自然という神の書を研究することと，神の言葉を集めた書物である聖書の研究には密接な関係があるという主張であった。

　文化的な物の見方の点におけるこうした重要な変化は，宇宙についての考え方および自然界における人間の立場についての考え方を劇的に変えた。宇宙は機械であって，宇宙には地球のような世界が他にもあるかもしれないという信念は，人間の独自性にまつわる様々な従来からの前提を脅かし，宇宙は人間のために創られたという教義の否定へとつながった。

考え方　(1)　「**自然界を理解し支配することで，農工業における技術が革新されるだろうという見込みが表明された**」

　1．**Hopes were expressed**「期待［見込み］が表明された」　これが文の中心の主語と動詞。

　2．**that** は節内が完全な文になっていることから接続詞。that 節全体は hopes に対する同格として働く名詞節であることに注意。

　3．**the understanding and control of nature would improve techniques**「自然を理解し支配することが技術を向上させるだろう」　understand and control nature（自然を理解し支配する）→ the understanding and control of nature と考える。of nature が control のみを修飾していると考えるのは誤り。would は will が時制の一致で過去形になったもの。「自然界を理解し支配することで，技術が革新されるだろう」のように主部を副詞的に処理してももちろん構わない。

　4．**in industry and agriculture**「工業［産業］と農業における〈技術〉」　in は「分野」を示す用法。句全体は直前の techniques を修飾する形容詞句。

　(2)　「自然界の敵対的で不思議な環境は，人間の探求によってその秘密が明かされ

— 349 —

ると人々は信じていた」

1. **The hostile and mysterious environment of the natural world**「自然界の敵対的で神秘的な環境」が下線部全体の主部。hostile は「敵対的な」の意の形容詞。

2. **would ... yield its secrets to human investigation**「人間の調査に対してその秘密を明らかにするだろう」 yield ... は「…を譲り渡す」の意の動詞。「自らの秘密を譲り渡す」とは「秘密を明かす」ということ。

3. **people believed** は主語と動詞が挿入された形。このような挿入は，文頭に置いて People believed (that) the ... environment ... would yield ... としたのと意味的には同じ。（例）She has, *I believe*, a villa.（彼女は確か別荘を持っていると私は思う）

(3)「宇宙は一つの機械であって，宇宙には地球のような世界が他にもあるかもしれないという考えは，人間は唯一無二の存在であるというそれまでの前提を脅かし，宇宙は人間のために創造されたという教義を否定することにつながった」

1. **The belief** (S) **... threatened** (V) **traditional assumptions** (O)「考えが伝統的な前提を脅かした」 これが文の骨格の SVO。

2. **that the universe is a machine**「宇宙は機械だという〈考え〉」 節内が完全な文であることから that は接続詞。節全体は主語の the belief と同格。

3. **and that it might contain other worlds like the earth**「地球のような他の世界は宇宙を含むかも知れないという〈考え〉」 and は前後の that 節をつなぐ接続詞。よって，この that 節も the belief と同格。it might contain other worlds は「宇宙 (＝it) が他の世界を含むかもしれない」の意。これは「他の世界が宇宙にある［宇宙には世界が他にもある］かもしれない」などと工夫してもよい。like the earth は直前の other worlds を修飾しており，「地球のような〈他の世界〉」となる。なお，「宇宙は機械だという考えや，地球のような他の世界を宇宙が含むかもしれないという考え」と訳すと複数の belief が存在することになってしまい，意味が変わってしまうことに注意。

4. **leading to a denial of the doctrine**「教義の否定につながる」 leading ... は「分詞構文」。文末の分詞構文はしばしば and (S＋)V と同義になるので，ここも and led と読み替えてやればよい(その場合 and は threatened と led を結ぶことになる)。a denial of the doctrine（教義の否定）は deny the doctrine（教義を否定する）が名詞化した形。

5. **that the universe had been created for the benefit of man**「宇宙は人間のために作られたという〈教義〉」 この that 節も直前の the doctrine と同格。for the benefit of ... は「…の（利益の）ために」の意。

― 350 ―

2005年　　解答・解説

解答

(1) 自然界を理解し支配することで，農工業における技術が革新されるであろうという希望が表明された。

(2) 自然界の敵対的で不思議な環境は，人間の探究によってその秘密が明かされると人々は信じていた。

(3) 宇宙は一つの機械であって，宇宙には地球のような世界が他にもあるかもしれないという考えは，人間は唯一無二の存在であるというそれまでの前提を脅かし，宇宙は人間のために創造されたという教義を否定することにつながっていった。

5 **（全訳）**　その古い灯台は白く丸い形をしていて，小さなドアと，てっぺんには丸窓と，そして巨大なランプがあった。ドアはふだんは半開きになっていて，螺旋階段が見えた。人を誘うようなところがあったので，ある日，僕は中に入る気持ちを抑えきれずに，ちょっと中へ入って，上がっていった。僕は13歳で，元気のよい黒髪の少年だった。今では入れない場所に，当時は入ることができ，軽い気持ちで，歓迎されないことを心配する気持ちもなく，中へと身を滑り込ませた。

螺旋階段を登って，てっぺんのドアをノックした。男の人がやってきてドアを開けたが，彼はいかにも灯台守のイメージにぴったりのように見えた。パイプをくゆらし，ごま塩のあごひげを蓄えていた。

「どうぞ，どうぞ」と彼は言って，すぐに，一部の人に備わっている，人を落ち着かせる不思議な力で，彼は私をくつろがせてくれた。男の子がやってきて灯台を訪れるのはごく当然のことだと彼は考えているようだった。もちろん，僕の年代の男の子は灯台を見たいだろうし，もっと多くの人が灯台に興味を持ち，訪れてもいいものだと，彼の物腰全体が語っているようだった。その場所を訪問者に見せるために彼がそこにいて，灯台がまるで博物館とか歴史的に重要な塔か何かであるのも同然という，そんな気持ちを実際に僕に抱かせかけていた。

もちろん，灯台はそんなものではなかった。船がいて，船は灯台が頼りだった。目をやると，船のマストのてっぺんが見えた。港の外にはブリストル海峡があって，反対側の，かろうじて見えるくらいの約30マイル離れた所には，サマセットの海岸があった。「で，これが気圧計だ」と彼は言った。「針が下にいくと，嵐が近い。小さな船は気をつけなくちゃいかん。今は「変わりやすい」をさしている。つまり何が起きるか本当のところはわからないということだ。ちょうど我々のようにね。そしてそれ

－ 351 －

2005年　　解答・解説

が」と彼は誇らしげに，いちばんいい所を最後に残しておく人のように付け加えた。「ランプだな」

強力な電球の中に入っている巨大レンズを僕は見上げた。

「そしてこんなふうにスイッチを入れる。日没のときに」　彼は壁の近くの制御盤に近づいてレバーに手を置いた。

僕のためにスイッチを入れることはないだろうと思っていたが，本当にスイッチを入れた。するとライトがゆっくりと力強く点った。頭上にランプの熱を感じることができた。太陽みたいな熱。僕がうれしくてニッコリすると，彼は満足そうな様子だった。「きれいだなあ。すばらしいなあ」と僕は叫んだ。

「3秒光って，それから2秒消える。1，2，3。1，2」と時計を測りながら彼は言ったが，まるでピアノを教えている先生みたいだった。そして光はそのとおりに従っているようだった。点っている時間の長さを彼は正確に知っていた。「1，2，3」と言って，片手を下ろすと，光は消えた。それから両手で，神様のようにして，光あれとでも言うかのようにすると，光がついた。

僕は見ていてゾクゾクした。

「どこから来たの？」と彼は僕に聞いた。

「イタリア」

「よろしい，世界中にあるすべての光は，場所によってリズムがちがう。船の船長は，光を見てリズムを知れば，それがどこの光かわかることになる」

僕はうなづいた。

「さて，お茶はいかがかな」と彼は言った。青と白のカップと受け皿を出して，お茶を注いだ。それからビスケットを一枚くれた。「いつか，暗くなってから光を見に来るといい」と彼は言った。

ある晩遅く，僕はもう一度出かけた。灯台の放つ光が，海や船や海岸に細長く投げかかり，それに続く暗闇は，一層暗いように見えた。その暗さといったら，灯台の光は，強力ではあったけれども，マッチの光とさほど強さが変わらないように，また，マッチの光とほとんど同じくらいすぐに消えてしまいそうに見えた。

その夏の終わりに，僕はイタリアへ戻った。クリスマスプレゼントに，パンフォルテを買って，灯台守に送った。パンフォルテというのは，フルーツケーキの一種で，僕の住んでいた町の名物だった。僕はもう灯台守に会うことはないだろうと思っていたが，なんと翌年，僕は再びウェールズへ戻ることになった。今度は休暇ではなく，戦争から疎開するためだった。到着した翌朝に，灯台へ行ってみると，あの灯台守は

— 352 —

2005 年　　解答・解説

引退しているとのことだった。

「でもまだここに来るよ」と，ずっと年下の後任の男が言った。「毎日午後になると，そのあたりに座っているのを見かけるよ。天気がよければね」

昼食後に僕が再び行ってみると，そこで，灯台のドアの脇のベンチに座って，パイプをふかしていたのは，あの灯台守だった。小犬を連れていた。前の年よりもドッシリとしているように見えたが，それは体重が増えたからではなくて，ベンチにずしりと身を置いて，助けがなかったら，ベンチから離れるのも容易ではないように見えたからだった。

「こんにちは」と僕は言った。「僕のことを覚えていますか。去年，お目にかかったのです」

「どこから来たの？」

「イタリアからです」

「そうか，イタリアから来た子と知り合いになったことがあったなあ。とってもすてきな男の子だった。クリスマスプレゼントにフルーツケーキを送ってくれてね」

「それは，僕です」

「ああ，彼はすてきな子だった」

「僕が送ったんです」

「そう，あの子はイタリアから来たんだった。とってもすてきな男の子だったなあ」

「僕ですよ。その子は僕です」と僕は引き下がらなかった。

灯台守は，一瞬，僕の目をのぞきこんでから，目をそらした。僕は泥棒になった気分だった。つまり，その権利もないくせに他人の立場を横取りしようとしている人の気分だったのだ。「なんとまあ，とってもすてきな男の子だった」と彼は繰り返した。まるで，今，目にしている客が去年の客とけっしてそぐわないかのように。

それから，僕について彼がそれほどすてきな思い出を抱いているのがわかったので，僕はそれ以上にこだわらなかった。イメージを壊したくなかったのだ。男の子が突如としてぎこちなくなり，二度と取り戻せないもの，つまり何か子どもの初々しさを失い，たくさんのことが結びついて少年の行動の愛らしさをだめにしてしまうような新たな段階へと入るような時期に，当時の僕はあったのだった。もちろん，この変化，僕自身の中のぎこちない時期が，僕には見えなかったが，彼の前に立つと，前の年の僕のようにすてきでいられるようになることはけっしてない，たぶんけっしてないだろうと，僕は感じた。

「なんとまあ，とってもすてきな男の子だったよ」と灯台守は再び言って，考えに沈みこんでいるように見えた。

— 353 —

<u>2005 年　　解答・解説</u>

「そうだったのですか？」と僕は言った。まるで僕の知らない誰かについて話しているかのように。

考え方　(1)　正解は，**エオアイウ**。つまり ... and (without) (worrying) (about) my not (being) (welcome) という語順にすればよい。まず my not を見て，この後には動名詞が続いて「私が…しないこと」という意味になるだろうと考える。(例) She was furious at *my not* believing her. （私が彼女の言うことを信じないことに彼女は激怒していた）　動名詞として being welcome と worrying about の二つが考えられるが，残された前置詞 without も用いながら文意に相当する語順を考えれば正解がえられる。

(2)　正解は「**すぐに，一部の人に備わっている，人を落ち着かせる不思議な力で，彼は私をくつろがせてくれた**」。immediately ... he made me feel at home が骨格部分で，途中は挿入部分。that は strange power が先行詞であることを予告しているだけなので，訳出には及ばない。その後は have の目的語が関係詞になって省略された形で，to put 以下は power を修飾している。ここを <u>have to 不定詞</u> と続けて読むと関係詞の元の位置がなくなってしまうので誤り。

(3)　正解は**イ**。下線部の the sort「その種のもの」は，直前の「博物館とか歴史的に重要な塔」をさす。さらに下線部直後には，船が灯台を頼りにしていたとあることから，イ「灯台の重要性は歴史的というよりは実用的なものだった」を選ぶ。正解以外の選択肢，ア「船のおかげで灯台は訪問者に非常に人気があった」，ウ「博物館や歴史的な塔に比べると灯台は価値がなかった」，エ「船は依然として灯台を頼りにしていたが，灯台は博物館としても機能していた」は文意にまったく合わない。

(4)　正解は順に**アイ**。「(4a) なものを (4b) に残す」という枠組と，灯台守が説明の最後に灯台のランプを紹介したこと，そしてランプがその後の重要な話題となっていることから，「もっとも良いものを最後に残す」と考える。

(5)　正解は**エ**の I didn't think he'd switch it on just for me「僕のためだけにスイッチを入れることはないだろうと思っていた」。下線部の直後に but he did, and the light came on ... とあるので，この did は正解の選択肢中の switch it on だと考えればよい。正解以外の選択肢のうちでイ「間違いなく彼は日没まで待つだろうと思った」を選んでしまうと，直後の he did で矛盾してしまうので誤り。それ以外の，ア「レバーを見て僕は驚いた」，ウ「ランプがどんな仕組みになっているのか見せて欲しいと僕は頼んだ」は文意と無関係。

(6)　正解は **different**。空所の次の文に「船の船長は，光を見てリズムを知れば，それがどこの光かわかることになる」とあるのを手がかりにして，空所を含む文は

— 354 —

2005 年　　解答・解説

「灯台によってリズムがちがう」という意味なのではないかと考え，different を重ね
て使うことを思いついたかどうかがポイントとなる。(例) *Different* people reacted
in *different* ways.（反応の仕方は人によって異なっていた）

　(7)　正解は「灯台の光は，強力ではあったけれども，マッチの光とさほど強さが変
わらないように，また，マッチの光とほとんど同じくらいすぐに消えてしまいそう
に見えた」。The lamp's light(S) ... seemed(V) が骨格部分。powerful as it was は
though it was powerful と同義。was と seemed は「実際」と「見かけ」の対比と
なっている。比較級の強め much を not が否定しているので「はるかに…というこ
とはない」の意味となる。match's (light) と補って考える。and は not much 以下
と almost as 以下を並列している。最終部は as short-lived (as match's light) と補っ
て考える。

　(8)　正解はウ。空所の前に灯台守が引退したとあり，空所を含む後任者の発言には
「まだここに来る」とあるので，空所には逆接の副詞 though が入る。ア「ことによ
ると」，イ「だから」は文意に合わない。エの yet には逆接の意味もあるが，その際
には文頭になければならないので，この問題の場合には不可。

　(9)　正解はア。下線部の最終部に「助けがなかったら，ベンチから離れるのも容易
ではないように見えた」とあるのをヒントにして，ア「彼は年老いて疲れているよう
に見えた」を選ぶ。正解以外の選択肢，イ「彼はその場を去りたいように見えた」，ウ「彼
は以前と変わりなく丈夫そうに見えた」，エ「彼は以前よりも関心がないように見えた」
は，いずれも文脈に合わない。

　(10)　正解は「老人の記憶にある素敵な少年は自分だと思い出させようという態度か
ら，それを諦めて思い出を大切にする接し方へと変化した」。(10a) の発言の時点で，
灯台守の記憶にある少年が自分であるという点で「引き下がらなかった (insisted)」
が，(10b) の時点になると，自分の「知らない誰かについて話している」かのよう
な接し方へと変化している。自分の主張へのこだわりを捨てたのは (10a) の 2 つ後
のパラグラフ冒頭に，And seeing that he had such a nice memory of me, I didn't
insist further とあるように，灯台守が自分に対してすてきな思い出を抱いているの
がわかったからである。以上の点を踏まえてまとめればよい。ちなみに，設問には「接
し方」とあるので，少年期における心のあり方の変化の類の内面的描写を書く必要は
ない。

— 355 —

2005 年　　解答・解説

解 答

(1)　エオアイウ

(2)　すぐに，一部の人に備わっている，人を落ち着かせる不思議な力で，彼は私をくつろがせてくれた。

(3)−イ　　(4)−ア・イ　　(5)−エ　　(6)− different

(7)　灯台の光は，強力ではあったけれども，マッチの光とさほど強さが変わらないように，また，マッチの光とほとんど同じくらいすぐに消えてしまいそうに見えた。

(8)−ウ　　(9)−ア

(10)　老人の記憶にある素敵な少年は自分だと思い出させようという態度から，それを諦めて思い出を大切にする接し方へと変化した。(58字)

— 356 —

解答・解説

1 (A) **全訳** チェスの名人は盤面の駒の位置について素晴らしい記憶力を発揮することがある。ある研究では，国際試合で活躍する名人は実際の試合の盤面にたった一度，5秒間向かうだけで25ある駒の位置をほぼすべて記憶したが，初心者の方は4つくらいしか駒の位置を記憶できなかった。さらに，盤面の記憶が後になってテストされることを名人が知っているかどうかは問題ではなかった。記憶しようと意図しないで盤面を見た時の成績もまったく同じだったのである。ところが，駒がでたらめに配列されていて，意味のある試合状況を示さない盤面を見せられると，名人の記憶力は初心者と変わらなかった。

　経験豊かな俳優も自分の専門知識の分野においては卓越した記憶力を持っている。彼らは比較的容易に長い台本を記録することができるわけだが，なぜそうできるのかはチェスの名人の場合とほぼ同じなのである。最近の研究の示すところによると，俳優は一語一句記憶しようとするのではなく，登場人物の動機や目的を知るための手がかりを求めて台本を分析し，無意識のうちに長年の経験の上に構築された知識全体に台本の言葉を関連付けている。記憶とは，意味を探るこのような過程で自然に生じる副産物なのである。ある俳優がこう述べている。「べつに暗記しているんじゃありません。そこには何も苦労もありません…ただそうなるんです。早い段階で，ある日セリフを覚えてしまっているんですよ」。俳優が台本を理解しようとする時は，しばしば登場人物が使う言葉そのものをかなり専門的に分析するのだが，それがまた，発せられた言葉の一般的な言葉のみならず，その言葉を正確に思い出すことの手助けにもなっているのである。

考え方 04年度は，英文中で与えられた「事例」から「一般的に言えること」をまとめる，という設問になったが，具体例は道具として扱いつつ議論の骨子を探るという従来の全文要約の方針を踏襲すればよいのであって，今回の設問独特の発想法・対処法があるわけではない。ただし，「一般的に言えること」という指示を無視し，慌てて本文中の記述のみをまとめたりすると到底満足な得点にはならないので，その点には十分配慮する必要がある。

— 358 —

2004年　　解答・解説

1．アウトライン

〈第1パラグラフ〉チェスの名人について

第1文　チェスの名人はずば抜けた記憶力を見せることがある。

第2文　実際の試合の盤面を5秒間見ただけで駒の配列を記憶した例がある。

第3文　記憶するつもりがあろうとなかろうと結果は同じであった。

第4文　しかし，駒の配列がでたらめで意味のある盤面になっていないと，名人であっても覚えることができなかった。

〈第2パラグラフ〉経験豊かな俳優について

第1文　経験を積んだ俳優も（長い台本を覚えるのだから）非凡な記憶力を持つと言える。

第2文　俳優は台本を分析し，登場人物や動機や目的を探り，無意識のうちに台本の言葉を自分の知識全体に関連付けている。記憶は意味を追求した結果自然に得られるものである。

第3文　ある俳優の言葉を引用。

第4文　台本の理解は，登場人物の言葉を専門的に分析することを含み，これがセリフを正確に思い出す手だてとなっている。

2．一般化

①　「記憶力が優れているとされる人でも，意味や必然性のあることしか記憶できない」

　　a．チェスの名人と経験豊かな俳優は，一般に「すぐれた記憶力を持つとされる人物」の代表として引き合いに出されている。ただし，どんなことでも等しく記憶するのではなく，「意味のあること」なら覚えられる（＝無意味なことは覚えられない）ことが第1パラグラフ最終文から分かる。

　　b．第2パラグラフ第1文の後半に「なぜそうなのかは，チェスの名人の場合と同じだ」とあるので，俳優も同様だと考えてよい。また第2パラグラフ第2文〜最終文で，俳優は一字一句暗記するのではなく，台本を分析し登場人物の気持ちを俳優自身の経験に裏付けられた知識に関連付けることで特に苦労もなくセリフを覚えられることが述べられている。

　　c．このような記述から「どんなに記憶力が優れているといっても（どんな人でも），意味のあることや必然性のあることしか記憶できない」という点をまとめる。もちろん「チェスの名人」とか「俳優」などという具体的な情報は含めるべきではない。

②　「記憶力は意味を探る過程で自然に得られるものである」

— 359 —

2004 年　　解答・解説

a. 本文が「人間の記憶」について何かを述べようとしているのは明らかである。そのような文章全体のトーンは漠然としたものであるが，なんとかすくい上げておきたい。そうすると，やはり「人間の記憶（記憶力）とは…なものである」という言葉でまとめておくのが理想であろう。

b. 人間の記憶について一般化して述べているのは，第2パラグラフ第2文の最後にある "memorization is a natural by-product ..." である。ここをヒントとし「記憶は，意味を探る過程で自然に得られたものである」という内容をまとめる。

以上①, ②のポイントを指定字数内でまとめる。制限字数の下限（本問では60字）を下回ると明らかな内容不足となり，採点対象外になる恐れもあるので注意すること。

解答例

> どんなに記憶力のある人でも意味のあることや必然性のあることしか記憶できないことから，記憶は意味を探る過程で自然に生じる副産物だと言える。(68字)

別解1　記憶力の優れた人でも容易に記憶できるのは与えられた状況において有意味なものだけであり，記憶とは意味追求の結果自然に得られるものである。(67字)

別解2　人間は個々の場面や状況において意味や必然性があるのなら容易に記憶することができる。記憶とは意味を求める過程で自然に生じるものである。(65字)

---

1 (B) 【全訳】

フランスとほぼ同じ大きさで，カリフォルニアよりやや大きい熱帯の島マダガスカルには，今日世界で最も興味深く重要な意味を持つ植物群や動物たちが生息している。しかし，マダガスカルの生態系は独特ではあるが，直面している危険はマダガスカルに限ったことではない。その他世界に数多くある貴重な野生の地と同様，今日マダガスカルは人間が大きな問題となっている。

（　1　）

しかし人間は，マダガスカルで暮らしている比較的短い期間に，その生態系に深刻な被害を与えてしまっている。伝統的なマダガスカルの農業では，農夫が森の一部を伐採し，焼き払い，更地になった所に稲を植える。米を収穫した後，森を蘇生する時間を十分に与えるべく，その土地を20年間放置しておく。しかしもし農夫たちが同じ区域に戻ってくるのが早すぎると，土壌は痩せてしまう。結局このせいで広大な森林地帯が何も生えない荒れ地となるのである。

（　2　）

このバランスをとるのが難しい。荒廃の多くは個々の農民によるものではあるが，

— 360 —

2004 年　　解答・解説

マダガスカルの環境問題の原因はその島の社会的状況及び歴史に深く根ざしている。マダガスカルは世界の最貧国の１つで，平均個人所得は年 250 ドルを下回っている。国民の約 80％が農家で，ほぼ全面的に土地に頼ってその生活を支えている。多くの農民は伝統的な伐採と焼き払いによる農業を行い続けているが，それは他の方法を知らず，他に生計を立てる術を持たないからである。

（　　3　　）

　肝心な点は，野生生物の保護と地域の発展の両立を強調することである。新しい公園の近くに住む住民が公園から恩恵を受け，その計画に積極的に参加するようにすることがその目的となる。たとえば，もし公園が外国人旅行者を呼び寄せ，ある地域に経済効果をもたらせば，地元住民は，公園がなければ農業に利用できたであろう土地であっても，そこに公園を設立することを支持してくれるだろう。また，公園設立計画は今や地元住民が雨林独特の蝶を育て，それらを世界中の蝶の博物館に売る手助けとなっており，公園における観光業が地元社会に多くの利益をもたらすことにもなっている。

（　　4　　）

ア　歴史的に見ると，人間の不在がその島の独特な生態系が発達した主な理由の１つであった。つまり，マダガスカルの生態系が確立できた理由は，その島が比較的大きく，地理的に孤立しており，熱帯に存在しているということばかりでなく，人間がその自然環境を荒らし始めたのがほんの約２千年前だったということでもある。

イ　かつてマダガスカルでのみ成長していた植物が，今では米国南部も含めて世界中のさまざまな地域で販売用に栽培されている。例えば Madagascar Rosy Periwinkle（マダガスカル産ツルニチニチソウ）のピンクと白の花は，一部の大変有効な治療薬で使用するために栽培されている。花から作られた薬品は，小児ガン，高血圧，高血糖値など多くの病気を治療するために使用されている。

ウ　野生生物の保護計画を立てる場合には地元の農民の需要や伝統的生活様式にも注意を払わなければならないと考えて，マダガスカル政府は全国環境保護行動計画と呼ばれる事業を立ち上げた。この計画は環境破壊の連鎖を断ちきり，貧困を減らし，天然資源の管理計画を作成し，生物の多様性を保護することを趣旨としている。この計画の中心となっているのが国立公園の創設である。

エ　マダガスカルの土地の多くは，小規模な農家による，この活動が徐々に進行することですでに荒れ果ててしまっている。人口の増加は，恒久的な荒廃を与えずにこれらの活動を行うことができる段階を越えてしまっている。森林が破壊されるのと

－ 361 －

<u>2004 年　　解答・解説</u>

同様，マダガスカル独自の動植物の生息地も破壊される。今日，マダガスカルに元から存在する森林はたった 10％しか残っていない。マダガスカルが直面している最大の問題は，いかにして環境を保全しつつその住民の需要を満たすかということである。

オ　マダガスカルの全国環境保護行動計画が 1980 年代に開始されて以来，政府は 8 つの保護区を新たに創設し，その全面積は 6,809 平方メートルに及ぶ。今日マダガスカルは，「野生生物と人間双方のための公園」への現実的な取り組みをしようと努力してきたことを誇りにしている。公園が子々孫々に至るまで保護され続け，マダガスカルのすばらしく多種にわたる植物・鳥類・動物には生息地を与え，マダガスカル国民には資源を与えることを確実にしたという点で，希望の持てる第一歩をすでに歩み出しているのである。

(考え方)　段落補充（あるいは，文補充）問題は，2000 年度以降連続して出題されており，文章の内容は様々であっても取り組み方自体は基本的に同じである。**指示語，冠詞の使い方，代名詞，論理展開を示す Discourse Marker，時間の流れなどに着目していけば比較的容易に解答できたであろう。**

本問で用いられた文章は Ecotourism や Sustainable Development に関係するものであり，環境保護と経済発展の両立を目指す取り組みをマダガスカルを例に解説したもの。近年全国の大学入試でもよく見られる内容であり，内容面で馴染みのある人も多かったのではないだろうか。

(1)　正解は**ア**。選択肢アには「マダガスカルの生態系が保全されているのは，人間の存在期間が短いためでもある」という内容の記述がある。この空所にアを入れると，後続の第 3 パラグラフ冒頭の「しかしながら，人間は比較的短い期間に，その生態系に深刻な被害を与えてしまっている」が自然な展開としてつながることになる。逆説の however によって生まれる展開，および，**the** relatively short time がアの最後の because 節の内容に対応することに注意。

(2)　正解は**エ**。後続の第 5 パラグラフの冒頭，**This** is a difficult balance to achieve に注目する。「達成困難なバランス」に該当するものが直前になければならない。選択肢エの最後に「最大の問題は，いかにして環境を保全しつつその住民の需要を満たすかということ」という記述があるので，これが This の指示内容に該当すると考える。

(3)　正解は**ウ**。選択肢ウでは「野生生物の保護と地元農民の需要や生活様式に対する配慮」を両立しようとするマダガスカル政府の取り組みとして「国立公園設立」の案ができたことが述べられている。これを(3)に入れると後続の第 7 パラグラフに

－ 362 －

2004 年　解答・解説

自然につながることが，The Key point has been ..., The idea is ..., the new parks, Park projects といった表現からも分かる。

⑷　正解は**オ**。この文章のまとめとしては，1980 年以来行われてきたマダガスカル政府の取り組みが「現在」どのような段階にあり，どのように評価されているかを述べたオがふさわしい。

不要な選択肢は**イ**である。

解答

(1)　ア　　(2)　エ　　(3)　ウ　　(4)　オ

2 **(A)** 考え方　1．語数だが，「50 語程度の英語」と指定されているので，±10 語つまり 40 ～ 60 語を目安に書く（下記の解答例のように答案の最後に「○○ words」と書けばとても親切である）。ただ，採点官が受験生の解答の語数をいちいち数えているとはとても思えない。実際の解答用紙は 7 行ドリになっているので，**4 行以上書いてあれば十分であろう。**

　2．「いくつかの理由を挙げ」となっているので，少なくとも 2 つは理由を書くこと。**1 つしか挙げられていない場合は減点対象となるはず。**ただ，「50 語程度」の英文であるから，4 つ以上理由を挙げるのは非常に厳しい。

　3．書き方として，まず「自分は自宅から通学する」「アパートを借りる」という主張を Topic Sentence とし，その後「理由」に移るのが読み手にとってわかりやすくてよい。注意したいのは，"I'd prefer to live at home. *Because* ..." という文を絶対に書かないこと。**because の節を独立させてしまうのは，自由英作文で最もよく見られる誤りである。**むしろ because を使わないで「理由」を書く訓練をしてほしい。

　4．「電車で片道 2 時間の距離にある大学に通う」という設定があるが，この「電車で片道 2 時間の距離」を答案に盛り込まれなければ減点，ということはないであろう。これは「アパートを借りる」ことのメリットとしては利用しやすいが，「自宅から通学」を選んだ場合は特に必要ないからである。しかし，いちおう設問文に書かれていることなので，盛り込むに越したことはない。

　5．「理由」は何を書いてもよいだろうが，必ず「自宅から通うことのメリット（デメリット）」「アパートを借りることのメリット（デメリット）」に関わる内容でなければならない。「新聞が読める」「長電話ができる」など，**自宅通学ならでは，あるいはアパート住まいならでは，とは言えないことを理由にすると，説得力がなくなって減点される。**

— 363 —

2004年　解答・解説

6.「自宅から通うメリット」として考え得る理由としては,「家事を自分でやらなくて済む」(解答例1,別解1,2,3),「家賃がかからない」(解答例1,別解2,3)などがあるが,さらに「朝起こしてもらえる」(別解1)などでもかまわないだろうし,「通学時間の有効利用」(別解3)に触れてもよい。

7.「アパート暮らしのメリット」としては,「親からの独立,自立の機会」(解答例2,別解5),「通学に疲れない」[解答例2],「時間の無駄が省ける(より多くの勉強時間が確保できる)」(解答例2,別解5),「より自由な生活がおくれる」(別解4),「友達と遊びやすい」(別解4,6)などが考えられる。また別解6のように「終電の心配がない」などでもよいだろう。

8.箇条書き的な考え方(たとえば "There are three reasons." と前置きして,First, ... Second, ... Third ... と続ける)は,あまり面白みある答案とは言えないが,本問の場合はこのような書き方でも十分である。

9.「大学に通うとしたらどうするか」という,あくまでも想像の世界を語るのだから,本来仮定法で書くのがベスト。ただ,仮定法を用いていなくても減点はないだろう。

解答例

解答例1.自宅から通う

　I'd prefer to live at home, even though traveling four hours a day would be hard. If I lived in an apartment, I'd have to do the housework all by myself. Furthermore, I'd have to pay the rent, and since my family is not very rich, I'd have to work part-time. I would surely have little time to study. (59 words)

解答例2.アパートを借りる

　I'd move to an apartment without hesitation. There are three reasons. First, I've been wanting to live away from my parents for a long time. Second, being on the train for two hours each way would be too tiring. Third, living near my college would give me more time to study. (51 words)

〈自宅から通う〉

別解1　I'd definitely not choose to live alone in an apartment. When I come back home tired from the day's activities, my mother will give me supper immediately and the bath will already be hot enough. In the mornings, if I oversleep, she will wake me up. Home is paradise to me. (52 words)

別解2　I would stay with my parents. Renting an apartment would cost more

— 364 —

2004 年　　解答・解説

than I could afford, and living alone would mean I would have to do everything myself, like cooking, cleaning, washing, shopping and so on, every day. Living with my parents would save both money and time. (48 words)

別解 3　I would choose to commute. Spending four hours on the train every day would be good because I would have plenty of time to read. Living at home would be much cheaper, too. Perhaps the most important reason is that I cannot cook, and would probably die if my mother did not cook for me. (55 words)

〈アパートを借りる〉

別解 4　I'd prefer to live alone in an apartment. Living alone would give me the freedom to do everything in my own way. I could invite as many friends over as I wanted to; I could play video games all night; I could stay in bed all day if I didn't feel like doing anything. (54 words)

別解 5　I would rent an apartment and live alone. Commuting four hours everyday would be a waste of time. I would like to spend that time studying. Also, living alone would be a big challenge for me. I believe looking after myself every day would be part of my education. (49 words)

別解 6　For several reasons, I would get an apartment. I could stay out as late as I wanted without worrying about catching the last train; I could invite friends over anytime; I would have much more time to relax and do whatever I wanted; and I would have more time to study, if I wanted to. (55words)

2　**(B)**　**考え方**　1．語数だが，「60 語程度の英語」と指定されているので，±10 語つまり 50 〜 70 語を目安に書く。実際の解答用紙は(A)と同様 7 行ドリになっているので，**5 行以上書いてあれば十分である。**

　2．「要点を英語で述べよ」という設問なので，(A)のような自由英作文とは違い受験者の個人的見解を書くわけではない。しかし，「要点」とあるからには，全文を和文英訳してはいけない。あくまでも「要点」をピックアップして英語で表現することが大切である。

　3．盛り込まなければならない「要点」は次の 5 つである。

①　出発の時間になった

②　雲行きが怪しい

③　雷雨に見舞われる危険性がある

— 365 —

2004年　解答・解説

④　しばらく様子を見る

⑤　天気が回復すれば出発，ぐずつけば明朝に延期

　4．スタイルだが，［英語圏から来た留学生の隊員に質問されたと仮定し］と設問文にあるので，隊長 (the team leader) を主語として書くのもよいし（解答例，別解1，3），あるいは通訳になったつもりで，隊長の言葉をそのまま書いてもよいのだろう（別解2）。

解答例

> The team leader said that the time has come to leave, but that the sky is beginning to look threatening. He has decided to wait a while because if we left now, we would be in danger of getting caught in a thunderstorm. He has decided that if the weather improves, we'll go, but if it doesn't change within two hours, we'll postpone our departure until tomorrow. (67 words)

別解1　The leader said that the weather looks threatening, and if we start right now, we might have heavy rain on the way. So he suggested we stay here for a while, and if the weather clears up, we'll start. But if the weather is still bad two hours from now, we'll out off our departure until tomorrow morning. (58 words)

別解2　The time has come for us to leave, but the sky is beginning to look threatening. If we leave now, we may be caught in a thunderstorm, so we've decided to wait for a while. If the weather improves within two hours, we'll go, but if nothing has changed, we'll postpone the departure until tomorrow. (55 words)

別解3　The team leader is saying that even thought we're supposed to be starting off now, the weather doesn't look good and we might get caught in a thunderstorm. He says he thinks we should wait a couple of hours to see if the weather gets better. If it does, we can go. Otherwise, he thinks we should wait until tomorrow morning. (61 words)

4　(A)　考え方

(1)　前半部に「部屋に入れない」とあり，選択肢に stupid があることから，何か愚かなことをして部屋に入れなくなったことを想像する。さらに lock out は「締め出す」という意味なので，自分で自分を締め出してしまったのではないかと考え，

— 366 —

2004年　解答・解説

myself を思いつく。注意しなければならないのは，「(c)と(e)にはア～エに与えられている語句が入る」という設問の指示。lock out myself ではこの条件に反するので，必ず lock myself out とすること。ちなみに lock me out は誤りである。

完成した英文　[I was] stupid enough [to] *lock* **myself** *out*.
　　　　　　　　（部屋に入れない）。愚かにも自分で自分を締め出してしまった。

(2)　「これらの写真のポスターとしてどれも使えない」という前半部の内容，および選択肢に look / older があることから，写真では彼が老けて見えることを想像する。さらに後半部の主語が They（＝写真）であることから，無生物主語構文となっていると判断する。したがって，使役動詞 make を用いて「写真が彼を老けて見えさせる」という内容の英文を完成させる。

完成した英文　[They] **make** him *look* [a lot] older *than* [he really is.].
　　　　　　　　（ポスター用にこれらの写真はどれも使わないことにしよう。）彼が
　　　　　　　　実際よりもかなり老けて見えるから。

(3)　この設問は内容から解答を割り出すのは極めて難しい。take には "It takes (＋O) 時間 to do" で所要時間を表現し，「(O が) …するのに（時間）がかかる」という意味になることを知っている者は多いだろうが，実は所要時間だけでなく「必要条件」をも表現することができる。

（例）　It will *take* this paint *three hours* to dry.（このペンキが乾くのに3時間かかるだろう）［所有時間］
　　　　It *takes talent* to become a leading dancer.（トップダンサーになるには才能が必要だ）［必要条件］

本問の take も必要条件を示すもので，この表現を知らないと問題は解けないだろう。ちなみに本問は，"It takes X to be a good journalist"（優秀なジャーナリストになるには X が必要だ）の X を関係代名詞の what に換えて "*what* it takes to be a good journalist"（優秀なジャーナリストになるのに必要なもの）となっている。

完成した英文　[she just doesn't have] what **it** *takes* to be [a good journalist.].
　　　　　　　　（彼女は頭はいいが，）優秀なジャーナリストになるのに必要な資質
　　　　　　　　を全く持っていない。

(4)　設問を解く鍵となるものは2つ。1つは "S（感情など）get the better of 人" で「感情が人を支配する」という意味の慣用句であることを知っていること。もう1つは使役動詞 let には「許可」の意味ばかりでなく「O が…するのを黙って見過ごす」という意味もあることを知っていることである。

（例）　I *let* my daughter travel abroad.（私は娘を海外旅行へ行かせてあげた）［許可］

— 367 —

2004 年　　解答・解説

I *let* one week pass by before answering his letter.（彼の手紙への返事を書かないうちに 1 週間が過ぎてしまった）［見過ごす］

この第 2 例の直訳は「1 週間が過ぎていくのを黙って見過ごした」で，この「見過ごす」という意味合いになるとき，目的語には通常〈物〉が来る。本問の場合も「私の感情が支配するのを黙って見過ごすべきではなかった」が直訳となる。

完成した英文　[I shouldn't have] **let** my emotions [get] *the* better *of* [me.]
　　　　　　　　（昨日あのようなことを言って本当にごめんなさい。）もっと感情を抑えるべきでした。

(5)　you will need は容易に結び付けることができると思うが，will you need と疑問文の型にしないよう注意する。疑問の対象となっているのは，「君がどう思うか」であって，「どのくらい必要か」ではない。したがって，「どう思うか」に相当する部分は do you think と疑問文の型にし，「必要か」の部分は you will meed と通常の主語・動詞の語順でよい。

how が「程度」の意味（「どのくらい」）となるときは，"how ＋形容詞または副詞"という型をとるが，この「形容詞または副詞」は必ず原級でなければならない。比較級が続くときは必ず "how much ＋比較級" にする。

（例）　How *old* are you?（何歳ですか）
　　　　How **much** old*er* are you than your brother?（弟さんよりいくつ年上ですか）

完成した英文　[How] **much** longer [do you think] *you* will *need* [to spend on your homework?]
　　　　　　　　（もう 1 時間以上も君を待っているんだよ。）宿題にあとどれくらい時間がかかると思う？

解答

(1)	補う単語：myself	(c)	イ	(e)	ウ
(2)	補う単語：make	(c)	イ	(e)	エ
(3)	補う単語：it	(c)	イ	(e)	ア
(4)	補う単語：let	(c)	エ	(e)	ウ
(5)	補う単語：much	(c)	エ	(e)	イ

— 368 —

2004年　　解答・解説

4 **(B)** **【全訳】**なぜモナリザは全世界で最もよく知られた絵画となっているのであろうか。モナリザの特徴の一部を見るだけで（それは彼女の輪郭でも，目でも，ことによると手だけでもいいかもしれない），絵に興味も情熱も持たない人でさえ，それがモナリザだとすぐに分かるのである。モナリザはどの他の芸術作品よりもはるかに広告で商業利用されているのだ。

　芸術作品の中には，作られて何世紀も経っているのにいまだに愛され楽しまれているという意味で，普遍的であるように思われるものもある。そうした作品は世界中で何百万人もの人が見てすぐにそれだとわかるのだ。そうした作品は，自らが生まれた時代（つまりそうした作品がそもそも対象としていた比較的少数の鑑賞者）だけに対して語りかけているのではなく，それを越えた世界，将来の世代，そして，その作品を作った人たちも生まれるとは思いもしなかった国際的な通信網によって結び付けられた大衆社会に語りかけているのだ。

　このように人々が普遍的に魅力を感じているということとそうした作品を有名にする仕組みとを切り離して考えることはできないという，まさにその理由のために，芸術作品の成功はその作品自体の中にあるという考えは疑ってみる必要がある。これほど多くの傑作が西洋で生まれたということは，作品が世界的なものになっていくためには，政治，イデオロギー，そして技術の適切な支援が必要だということを示唆している。

　モーツァルトがその生涯の間にも大いに評価されたことは我々も知っているが，それはヨーロッパだけの話である。録音機器の発明，映画音楽，そして彼の生涯を描いた演劇や映画がなければ，モーツァルトは今日のように世界中で広く知られていることはないだろう。モーツァルトは，適切な技術的支援やマーケティングの支援なしには，偉大な普遍的芸術家としての「モーツァルト」ではなくなるであろう。

【考え方】　(1)　1．**A simple glimpse at even some of her features**「彼女の特徴の一部でさえちらりと見ること」　A simple glimpse が文の主語。at ... は glimpse を修飾する形容語句。features は「特徴」の意。訳出の工夫については 3 を参照のこと。

　2．**her silhouette, her eyes, perhaps just her hands**「彼女（モナリザ）の輪郭，彼女の目，ことのよると単に彼女の手だけでも」　前の some of her features の具体的な内容を説明している同格要素。「手」も含まれているため，features は「容貌」ではなく「特徴」と解釈した方がよい。

　3．**brings instant recognition**「即座の認識をもたらす」　さすがに「一瞥が…に即座の認識をもたらす」では訳文の意味がはっきりしないので，訳出には何かしら

— 369 —

2004 年　　解答・解説

の工夫をした方がいいだろう。recognition の動詞形 recognize は「…が誰［何］だか分かる」の意を表すことができる。(例) I *recognized* her by the perfume.（香水の匂いで彼女だと分かった）　よってこの英文の recognition を「それがモナリザだと分かること」と解し，全体を「それがモナリザだとすぐに分かる」などと訳せばよい。

　4．**to those who have no taste or passion for painting**「絵画に対してなんの興味も情熱も持っていない人たちに」　to those ... は bring を修飾する副詞句。taste は「好み，嗜好」，passion は「情熱」の意。for ... は taste と passion の両方を修飾していることに注意。

　(2)　1．**a mass society**「大衆社会」　これはいわば決まり文句であり，「巨大社会」等の訳語は不可。

　2．**connected by international communications**「国際的な通信によって結びつけられた〈大衆社会〉」　connected は形容詞句を導く過去分詞で，a mass society を修飾している。テレビ，電話，インターネット等の発達によって大衆社会が結びつけられていることを思い浮かべればよい。

　3．**that their creators could not suspect would ever come into being**「芸術作品を作った人たちが，生まれるなどとは思いもしなかった〈…大衆社会〉」　a mass society を先行詞とするこの関係詞節は，Their creators could not suspect (that) the society would ever come into being. という文から，the society を関係代名詞に変えることでできている。これが把握できていれば，「芸術作品を作った人たちはそうした社会が生ずるだろうと考えることはできなかった」→「芸術作品を作った人たちが，生ずるだろうと考えることができなかった社会」などとまとめられたはず。なお，関係詞節の中の ever は，否定の気持ちを強めるために用いられている。

　(3)　1．**He would not be as widely known as he is today throughout the world without ...**「…がなければ，モーツァルトは世界中で今日ほど広く知られてないだろう」　主節の動詞である would not be ... known は仮定法過去になっており，後続する without ... が仮定条件として働いている。

　2．**the invention of recording equipment, film music, and plays and films about his life**「録音機器の発明，映画音楽，彼の生涯にまつわる演劇や音楽」「録音機器，映画音楽，演劇，映画の『発明』」というように the invention of の後が and で結ばれていると考えたのでは，意味的に不自然である。よって，the invention of recording equipment でひとまとまりで，それが film music と plays and films と並列されていると考える。about his life は plays and films を修飾する形容詞句。

— 370 —

2004年　解答・解説

解 答

(1) 輪郭であれ，目であれ，ことによると手だけであれ，モナリザの容貌の一部でさえちょっと見るだけで，絵画に対して何の興味も情熱も持っていない人でも，すぐにそれがモナリザだと分かるのである。

(2) 芸術作品を作った人たちも，生まれるとは思いもしなかった国際通信によって結びつけられた大衆社会。

(3) 録音機器の発明，映画音楽，彼の人生を描いた演劇や映画がなければ，彼は今日ほど世界中で知られてはいないだろう。

5 **【全訳】** ダッカを首都とする現在のバングラデシュという国は，伝統的にはベンガルと呼ばれている地域の東半分である。カルカッタを州都とする西半分はインドに属している。ベンガルの両地域の人々は同じ言語を話しているけれども，宗教が異なっており，東の地域の人々の大多数はイスラム教徒であり，西半分の大多数はヒンズー教徒である。この地域の全体が大英帝国に属していた時には，ベンガルは単一の属州だった。1947年にイギリスが手を引くと，大英帝国のインド地域は2つの独立国に分割された。大部分がヒンズー教徒であるインドと，大部分がイスラム教徒であるパキスタンである。後者は西パキスタン（現在のパキスタン）と，東パキスタン（かつてのベンガルの東半分，現在のバングラデシュ）から成っていた。この分割（「分離独立」と称される）の結果として，多くのイスラム教徒がインドからパキスタンのどちらかの地域へ避難し，多くのヒンズー教徒がパキスタンの両地域からインドへ避難した。人々の，このような入れ替わりは，非常に暴力的なもので，およそ五十万人が命を落としたと見積もられている。百万人以上が東パキスタンからインドの西ベンガルへと移動したが，以下の物語文に登場する祖母は，そのうちの1人だった。1971年に，東パキスタンはパキスタンから独立を獲得し，バングラデシュとなった。

　数週間後，夕食の時に，父は満面の笑みをたたえて，テーブルごしに祖母の方へ封筒をぐいと渡した。「はい，これ」と父は言った。

　「なあに，これ」と祖母はいぶかしそうに言った。

　「ほら，ちょっと見て」と父は言った。

　祖母は封筒を手にして，開封し，中身をちょっと見た。「わからないねえ。何なの」と言った。

　父は噴き出すように笑い始めた。「飛行機の切符ですよ。ダッカ行きの。1月3日

— 371 —

2004年　　解答・解説

です」

　その夜，数カ月ぶりに，祖母は本当に興奮しているように見えた。寝る前に，祖母に会いに上の階へ行くと，顔をほてらせて，目をキラキラさせて部屋をゆっくりと歩き回っていた。私はうれしかった。私が生まれてから11年間で初めて，私にも完全に理解できる反応を祖母が示してくれた。私自身も飛行機に乗ったことがなかったので，祖母が初めて飛行機に乗ることになるということですっかり興奮するのも，私には当然極まりないことに思えたのだった。しかし，祖母のことが気がかりな気持ちも抑えがたかった。というのも，私と違って，祖母が飛行機にかけてまったく無知であるということも私には分かっていたからであり，私はその夜，眠りに落ちるまでには，祖母が出発するまでにきちんと心積もりができているように，私がしっかりやっておこうと心に決めたのだった。しかし，ほどなく，祖母に分かってもらうのは容易なことではないということが私にもはっきりと分かった。祖母が父に尋ねる問いの傾向からして，一人にしておいたら［放っておいたら］，飛行機について何も分からないでいるだろうということが私には分かった。

　例えば，ある晩，私たちが庭に出て座っていたとき，飛行機からインドと東パキスタンの国境が見えるのかどうかを，祖母は知りたがった。父が笑って，おやまあ，国境っていうのは，教室の地図みたいに長い黒い線になっていて，その線の片側が，緑，反対側が赤にでもなっていると本当に思っているんですかと言ったとき，祖母はいらだつというよりも困惑していた。

　「いや，そういう意味じゃなかったのだよ」と祖母は言った。「当たり前でしょ。でもね，まさか何もないってことはないでしょ。ひょっとすると柵とか，兵隊さんたちとか，お互いに狙いをつけている銃だとか，なんなら，何もない帯状の地面っていうのだけでも。無人地帯とかいうのじゃなかったかね」

　父はすでに旅慣れていた。噴き出すように笑って言った。「いいえ，雲以外には何も見えませんよ。ひょっとして，運が良ければ，緑の平原が見えるかな」

　父が笑ったので祖母はむっとした。「冗談はやめなさい」と祖母は言った。「私がまるであなたの会社の秘書であるみたいな口のきき方はやめてほしいね」

　今度は父が気分を害する番だった。私にも聞こえる場所で祖母が父にきつい口調で話したものだから，父はうろたえた。

　「それくらいのことしか言えませんよ。それだけ」と父は言った。

　祖母はこのことについてしばらく考え込んでから言った。「でもね，柵かなんかがなかったら，どうやってわかるのかね。つまりさ，それだったら，どこに違いがあるというの？　それに，違いがなかったら，どちらの側も同じっていうことになるよ。

— 372 —

<u>2004 年　　解答・解説</u>

前と何も変わってないっていうことに。私たちがダッカで列車に乗ると，誰にも制止されることなく次の日にはカルカッタで列車から降りていた当時と比べて，のことだけど。だったら，あれは，つまり分離独立とか，殺戮とかの一切合財は，なんのためだったのだい？　もし途中に何もないのだったら」

「母さんが何を期待しているのか分からないのですけど」と父が言った。「ヒマラヤ上空を飛んで中国に行くのとはわけがちがう。現代世界の話ですよ。国と国の境目は境界線にあるのではなくて，まさに空港の中になるんです。分かりますよ。いろんな公式の書類やなんかを記入しなければならない時に，国境を越えるんです」

祖母は椅子の所で落ち着きなく身体を動かした。「どんな書類？　そういう書類でどんなことを知りたがっているの？」と祖母は言った。

父は額をこすった。「あのですね…国籍とか，生年月日とか，出身地とか，そういうことですね」と父は言った。

祖母は目を大きく開けて，椅子に深々と身体を沈めた。

「どうしたんですか？」と父は驚いて言った。

少しふんばって，また背筋を伸ばし，髪を後ろへなでつけた。「別に…なんでもないんだよ」と祖母は言って頭を振った。

その時，祖母が絶望的な混乱状態になりかかっていることが私にはわかったので，飛行機の旅や飛行機そのものについて，祖母が自家薬籠中のものにしておかなくてはと私が思った不可欠の情報をすべて父に尋ねる役回りを私が引き受けた。例えば，私が言っておかなければ，飛行中に祖母が窓を開けようとするだろうと確信した。

長い年月が経った後でようやく，祖母の頭のその時突然浮かんだことが私にははっきりと分かった。祖母は，その書類の出生地の欄に「ダッカ」と記入しなければならないだろうし，そう考えると，物事がきちんとして筋が通っているのが好きな祖母にしてみれば，落ち着かないということなのだった。そしてその瞬間に，自分の出生地と自分の国籍がしっくりとはいかなくなってしまったのはどういうことなのか，理解がつきかねたのだった。

考え方　(1)　正解 は **イ** の **natural**。it seemed the most (1) thing ... that the prospect of her first flight should fill her with excitement.「初めて飛行機に乗ることになるという見込みが祖母をすっかり興奮させることは，この上なく(1)なことに思えたのだった」　文脈から natural「当然の」を選択することは容易。空所の前だけを見て「私自身も飛行機に乗ったことがなかったので，(1)に思えたのだった」と考えると，うっかりエにしてしまうので注意。

(2)　正解 は (2a) は **オ** の **I would make sure**，(2b) は **カ** の **she was properly**

— 373 —

2004 年　　解答・解説

prepared, (2c) はアの **she left**。I made up my mind that (2a) that (2b) before (2c).「(2c) の前に (2b) することを (2a) するように私は決めた」　直後の文で「祖母に分かってもらうのは容易なことではない」と言っていることから，ここでは語り手が祖母が旅立つ前に，飛行機の旅について教え，確実に準備をしてもらおうとしたのだと考える。正解以外の選択肢のうち，ウ「彼女は行く準備ができている」は現在形なので不可。イ「私は成長した」，エ「彼女は旅行すべきだ」は無関係。

(3)　正解は「**彼女を放っておいたら**」「**彼女のするままにしておいたら**」。leave her to herself で「彼女を彼女の好きにさせる」の意。下線部はこれを受け身にし（→ she *was left* to herself），さらには分詞構文にしたもの（→ *[being] left* to herself）。直後の主文が she would となっていることから，この分詞構文は仮定条件を表していると考える。

(4)　正解は**ア**。not so much A as B は必修の熟語。「A というよりもむしろ B」という意味に合致しているのは選択肢のアだけである。

(5)　正解は**エ**の **turn**。it is ～ 's turn to － で「～が－する番だ」の意。

(6)　正解は**ア**の **where the border is**。if there isn't a fence or anything, how are people to know「柵かなんかがなかったら，どうやってわかるのかね」　直後に続く祖母の言葉から考えれば，選択肢ア「国境がどこになるのか」であることは明らか。

(7)　正解は「**だったら，あれは，つまり分離独立とか，殺戮とかの一切合財は，なんのためだったのだい？**」　it の指示内容は，直後の partition and all killing and everything の箇所。what ... for は「なんのために」の意味。all は it と同格。then「それなら，だったら」を訳し落とさないように注意したい。

(8)　正解は**エ**の **troubled**。4 行前の nervously「落ち着きなく」と，4 行後の a hopeless mess「絶望的な混乱」を考え合わせれば，troubled「混乱した，不安な」だとわかる。

(9)　正解は**イ**の **end**。end up in ... で「結局…な状態になる」という意味の熟語。(例) If you do not sleep well, you may *end up in* a bad mood.（十分睡眠をとらないと，機嫌が悪くなってしまいますよ）

(10)　正解は**ア**の **command**。have ... at ～ 's command で「…を～の思い通りにする」という意味の熟語。本文では…に相当する部分が関係代名詞 that になって前方に移動していることに注意する。

(11)　正解は (11a) **Dhaka**, (11b) **Hindu**, (11c) **Indian**。本文の最終パラグラフから，出身都市が Dhaka であることは明らか（ただし見慣れない地名なのでスペルミスをしないように注意）。説明文の末尾近くに，祖母は東パキスタンからインドへ

— 374 —

<u>2004 年　　解答・解説</u>

逃れた人であると書かれており，さらにその前に，パキスタンからインドへと逃れたのはヒンズー教徒だと書かれているので，祖母の宗教はヒンズー教だとわかる。国籍に関しては物語文末尾から推測が必要である。「自分の出生地と自分の国籍」が合致していないとあることから，祖母は出身地 Dhaka と矛盾する国の国籍だと考えられる。よって Indian となる。

⑿　正解は**イの 1963 年**。物語文は「分離独立」以後の話であるから，説明文の記述より，1947 年以降のことでなければならない。さらに，物語文の下線部⑷を含むパラグラフに「東パキスタン」とあることから，時代設定はバングラデシュの独立以前ということになり，説明文から 1971 年以前ということになる。よって正解は，イの 1963 年である。

解答

⑴　イ

⑵　(2a)　オ　　　(2b)　カ　　　(2c)　ア

⑶　一人にしておいたら

⑷　ア　　　　⑸　エ　　　　⑹　ア

⑺　だったら，分断とか殺戮などはいったい何のためだったの？

⑻　エ　　　　⑼　イ　　　⑽　ア

⑾　(11a)　Dhaka　　　(11b)　Hindu　　　(11c)　Indian

⑿　イ

－　375　－

解答・解説

1 (A) **[全訳]** 現在世界で話されている言語の数は，どれを方言と見なし，どれを個別言語と見なすかにもよるが，およそ5千と推定されている。これらには，今でも学校で教えられている（古代ギリシャ語とラテン語），あるいは宗教的儀式で用いられている（サンスクリット語とゲーズ語）一握りの「死語」を加えることもできよう。言語学者の予測によれば，こうした様々な言語のうち確実に半数以上は今後半世紀も経たないうちに，母語話者がいなくなるという意味で，消滅するということである。その大部分は，現時点での母語話者が千人に満たず，しかも，その話者の大半がすでに高齢者になっている言語である。すでにささやかれているように，たった2つの言語が世界を支配する時が来るかもしれない。そして，現在の使用状況を考えれば，それが英語と中国語になることはほぼ間違いない。この多様な言語の喪失は，もちろん，遺憾なことである。それらを失うと共に，人類は過去の断片も失うことになるのだ。というのも，言語とは民族の歴史，その経験の蓄積，その移住，そして彼らが受けた侵略を象徴するものだからである。

　しかしこのような見解は，人間の行動が持つある不思議な特徴を見逃している。すなわち，人間は新たな方言を，その喪失と同じ速さで作り出す傾向があるという特徴である。英語は世界中に広がり，どの大陸にもこれを国語とする国家があるばかりでなく，貿易，政治，科学の共通言語にもなっている。とはいえ，これと同時に，話者同士の相互理解がほとんど成立しない地域方言も多数発達しているのである。現在では大半の言語学者が，ピジン（ニューギニアの「ピジン英語」），黒人英語（米国の主要都市で主に黒人が話すような英語），カリブ・クレオール語（カリブ諸島の英語），クリオ語（西アフリカのシェラレオネのクレオール語），さらにはスコットランド語（スコットランド低地地方の英語）でさえ，個別言語とみなしている。

[考え方]

◇「言語の消失」に関する文章だが，第2段落で「新たな視点」を持ち出していることに注意。このように，ある現象をとりあげ，それに対して複数の視点を紹介するのは典型的な文章構成の1つである。

<第1段落>

・第1文 (There are estimated ...) 〜2文で「世界に現存する言語についての事実」が述べられている。

— 378 —

2003 年　　解答・解説

- 第 3 文 (Linguists expect that ...) ～ 5 文で「多数の言語が消滅するだろう」という言語学者の予測が紹介されている。
- 第 6 文 (The loss of ...) ～最終文で「言語の喪失は遺憾なことだ」という考え方とその理由が紹介されている。

＜第 2 段落＞
- 第 1 文 (But this observation ...) で「しかしこの見解（考え）は，人間の 1 つの特徴を見逃している」とあり，コロンの後で，それはすなわち「新たな方言を生み出す傾向」である点が明記されている。
- 第 2 文 (English has spread ...) で「英語が共通語として拡大しているが，同時に相互に理解不可能な方言が生まれている事実」が紹介されている。
- 第 3 文 (Most linguists now ...) で「大部分の言語学者がピジンなど英語の亜種を個別言語だと認めている」ことが述べられている。

◇第 2 段落第 1 文 (But this observation ...) に "this observation" とあるが，この observation が「〈…に基づく〉見解［意見］」の意味であることに注意。第 1 段落のどこを中心にまとめるかを決めてくれるのは，まさにこの表現である。

◇第 1 段落第 6 文 (The loss of ...) に "of course" があるので，（段落を越えて）Of course ... But ～「もちろん…だが，しかし～」の流れができていると考えれば，この「言語の喪失は遺憾なことだ」という「考え方」が this observation に対応する内容だということになる。第 1 文～ 5 文の内容を細々と書く余裕はないので，ここまでを「多数の言語が消滅に向かうのは遺憾［残念］なことだという見解」という程度にまとめておく。

◇第 1 段落最終文 (As we lose ...) は，前文の "a pity"（遺憾なこと）に対する「理由」として読める部分であり，解答に含めておきたいが，これも解答字数との兼ね合いですべては書けないので，「歴史［過去］の喪失になる」という点に触れておけばよい。

◇第 2 段落第 1 文 (But this observation ...) の "one curious feature" については，この意味を明確にしておく必要がある。これはコロンの後の「新たな方言を生み出す傾向」を意味するという点が表現できていればよい。

◇以上をまとめると「多数の言語が消滅に向かうのは歴史の喪失になり遺憾なことだという見解は，新たな方言（dialect）を生み出すという人間の特性を見逃している」となり，これで大筋を表す解答になる。ただし，ここでの dialect が，一般の「方言」とは異なる意味で用いられていることに注意。"new dialects" → "many local dialects ... whose speakers can hardly understand each other" → "distinct

— 379 —

2003 年　　解答・解説

languages" という表現の連鎖を考えると，ここでの「方言」とは「個別言語と言ってよいもの」という意味だと思われるので，これを解答に含めておけば万全であろう。このように，特殊な意味で用いられた言葉の意味を明確にするのも，要約作成におけるポイントである。

解 答 例

> ［解答例１］　多数の言語が消滅に向かうのは歴史の喪失になり残念なことだという見解は，個別言語とも言える方言を生み出すという人間の特性を見逃している。(67 字)
>
> ［解答例２］　多数の言語が消滅するのを過去の喪失になると悲観する見方もあるが，これは新たな方言を個別言語として生み出すという人間の特徴を見逃している。(68 字)

1　**(B)**　**全訳**　長い硬材のサーフボード上で腹這いになったり立ち上がったりして波に乗るスポーツは，ヨーロッパ人には，18 世紀後半以降ハワイ諸島を連想させるものであった。当時ジェームス・クック船長の太平洋への第３次遠征隊の公式航海日誌には，サーフィンについて２ページにわたる記述があった。しかし，このスポーツの真の起源は，それよりはるか昔，ポリネシア人の古代の歴史にさかのぼることができる。(　　1　　)

しかし，タヒチ人もボード上で立ち上がることがたまにはあったと言われているが，長いボード上で直立してサーフィンをする技術が，発明とまではいかないにしても完成を見たのが，ハワイにおいてであったことは確かである。18 世紀末までには最初のヨーロッパ人がハワイを訪れていたのだが，その時すでに，サーフィンは何世紀にもわたるハワイの伝説と文化に深く根付いたものとなっていた。(　　2　　)

(　　3　　)「白い肌の人々」の到来以前，同島の生活のほとんどあらゆる側面は，サーフィンを含め，禁忌律によって規定されていた。禁忌律は，食事の場所，食糧栽培方法，天気予報の仕方，サーフボードの作り方，サーフィンに格好な時期の予測法，更には，神々を説得してサーフィンに格好な時期を作ってもらう方法まで定めていた。ハワイの社会は，王族と平民にはっきり分かれていて，首長たちがサーフィンをする浜辺と平民がサーフィンをする浜辺とがあった。平民のサーフィンは一般に最長 12 フィートのボード上で腹這いになったり立ったりするものであったが，首長たちは 24 フィートもあるボードでサーフィンをしていた。

(　　4　　)クック船長のハワイ島人との接触以来 50 年にも満たない 1819 年

— 380 —

2003年　　解答・解説

に，支配者カメハメハ1世の子息で後継者のリホリホが，母親を含む身分の高い女性たちと公に食事を共にした。男性が女性と食事を共にすることは，ハワイ時代の初めから禁忌であったが，リホリホはヨーロッパ文化の影響を受けていたのであった。彼が基本的禁忌を守らなかったことで，それまでの古い法制度をもはや遵守しなくてよいのだというメッセージがハワイ全土に送られたのであった。

（　　5　　）20世紀開始時点にはすでに，サーフィンはハワイ諸島からほとんど姿を消していた。サーフィンの大半は，オアフの南海岸で行われており，マウイ，カウアイなどの他の島々のいくつかの地点に少数のサーファーがいるだけであった。ホノルルがハワイの最大の都市となっており，ハワイ人の4人に1人がそこに住んでいたが，サーフィンは今やそこでは珍しいものとなっていた。ダイヤモンドヘッド近くの原住民サーファーの当時の有名な写真が何枚かあるが，そこに写っている男たちは，連れもおらず，ほとんどがカメラにポーズを取って，かつては数百人がサーフィンをしていたところに独りで立っていた。ハワイの人々にとってサーフィンの重要性は，ほぼ完全に消滅していたのである。

（　　6　　）その後，劇的な写真や著名なファンの力添えもあって，サーフィンは世界中に広まり始め，カリフォルニアの海岸とその先に至った。かつてはハワイという地域文化の活気に満ちた独特な一部分であったものが成長し始めて，世界文化の極めて大衆的な一部分という現在の地位を得るに至ったのである。古代ハワイ人の生活の他の多くの側面とは異なり，サーフィンは進化し現代に生き残っている。大衆化に伴う商業主義にもかかわらず，サーフィンは世界中の何百万もの人々に楽しみを与え続け，自然との特別な結びつきを与え続けているのである。

ア　サーフィンほど劇的でわくわくさせるスポーツはほとんどない。

イ　サーフィンはまたハワイ人の生活の社会制度に深く結びついてもいた。

ウ　禁忌律が衰退すると共に，ハワイ文化内でのサーフィンの儀式的意義も衰退した。

エ　サーフィンは，初期のハワイ人の生活のうちで，禁忌律による厳格な管理を受けていなかった唯一の側面の1つであった。

オ　しかし決定的な瞬間に，サーフィンは好奇心旺盛で影響力のある非ハワイ人の注目を引きつけた。

カ　「白い肌の人たち」の文化とハワイ人の文化が18世紀末に衝突した後，ハワイは永久に変わってしまった。

キ　短い「ボディ・ボード」に乗ってサーフィンをする慣習は，実際には，ポリネシア人がハワイにもたらしたもので，彼らはタヒチから4世紀にハワイ諸島にやって

― 381 ―

2003年　　解答・解説

来たのであった。

ク　例えば，地元ハワイの地名の中には，有名なサーフィンエピソードを記したもの
もあったし，サーフィンの熟練者たちは特別な歌を歌うことで，新しいサーフボー
ドの初めての使用を祝ったり，波を大きくしたり，大波に挑戦する男女を勇気づけ
たりしたものである。

【考え方】

(1)　正解は**キ**。

直前に「サーフィンの真の起源はそれ（＝18世紀後半）よりはるか昔，ポリネシ
ア人の古代史にさかのぼることができる」とあり，直後の第2段落第1文に "Tahitians"
（タヒチ人）が登場するので，キが正解。

(2)　正解は**ク**。

直前に「その時（＝18世紀末）すでに，サーフィンは何世紀にもわたるハワイの
伝説と文化に深く根付いていた」とあるので，「地名や歌の中にサーフィンが登場する」
ことが例として成立するクがふさわしい。

(3)　正解は**イ**。

段落冒頭の文は，その後に「逆転」の表現がない限り，その段落の Topic Sentence（主
題文）になると考えてよい。この段落は，ハワイの生活が禁忌律によって支配されて
いたことや，当時のハワイ社会に階級制度があったことが述べられているので，「サー
フィンは "the social system"（社会制度）とも深い関連があった」というイがふさ
わしい。この空所にイが入れば，第2段落の「伝説や文化」の面に「社会制度」を加
えるという点でイの also も正しく機能することになる。

(4)　正解は**カ**。

この空所に入る文も，この段落の Topic Sentence だと考えてよい。「白人到来か
ら50年も経たないうちに，王族がタブーを破り，古い制度に従う必要はないという
メッセージを送った」という内容を導き出す文としてカがふさわしい。

(5)　正解は**ウ**。

これも，この段落の Topic Sentence が入る。後続する部分で「サーフィンの衰退；
サーフィンの重要性の消滅」について述べているのでウが正解。

(6)　正解は**オ**。

これも，この段落の Topic Sentence が入る。「サーフィンが世界的に拡大していっ
た」という内容に合うのはオである。この空所にオが入れば，第5段落の「サーフィ
ン衰退」の内容との関連でオの however も正しく機能することになるし，直後の
Then で時系列に沿った内容が続く点も自然である。

— 382 —

2003 年　　解答・解説

※不要な選択肢

アは，選択肢の中でこれだけが現在形で書かれていることに注意。第 1 ～ 5 段落は
すべて「過去」の話であり，第 6 段落は「過去形→現在完了形→現在形」の流れで
書かれているので，どの空所にもふさわしくない。エは "not strictly controlled by
taboo rules" が第 3 段落と矛盾する。

解答

(1) キ	(2) ク	(3) イ	(4) カ	(5) ウ	(6) オ

2 **(A)** 2000 年以来のグラフ読み取り問題である。前回は円グラフが 3 つ与えられ
ていたが，今回は折れ線グラフ 2 つ。

考え方

＜語数について＞

「40 語程度」とあるから，30 または 40 語台で書くのがよいだろう。むろん，40
語近辺が理想。

＜内容のポイント＞

「グラフの読み取り」というのは，あまり細かい部分にとらわれることなく，グラ
フ全体が示していることを簡潔に書くことが重要である。一番目のグラフ（気温変化）
は見ての通り細かいギザギザ模様になっているが，このギザギザにとらわれては答案
が書けない。

答案に盛り込まれていなければならない内容は，「**地球の気温と二酸化炭素排出量
の相関関係**」すなわち「**二酸化炭素の排出量が増加するにつれて地球の気温も上がっ
ている**」ということである。具体的な数値や年代を取り上げても構わないが，それよ
りももっと全体的なことを書くべきだろう。

＜答案作成＞

［解答例 1］

まず冒頭で「2 つのグラフより，地球の気温変化と二酸化炭素排出量の間には相関
関係があることがわかる」とはっきり述べることが大切。そしてその関係性を具体的
に述べればよい。

［解答例 2］

「相関関係がある」と明言はしていないが，グラフが 1880 年から 2000 年という
120 年間を扱ったものであることに言及しつつ，関係性の具体化に徹した。

<u>2003 年　　解答・解説</u>

［解答例 3 ］

　［解答例 1 ］と同様，冒頭では相関関係があることを明示したが，その後は具体的
な年代や排出量に触れながら関係性を説明した。

解 答 例

［解答例 1 ］

　These two graphs show that changes in average global temperature are
closely related to the amount of carbon dioxide in the atmosphere; that is,
the more carbon dioxide that is emitted into the atmosphere, the higher
the global temperature. (39 words)

［解答例 2 ］

　The two graphs show that over a period of 120 years, both average
global temperature and the amount of carbon dioxide in the atmosphere
increased. This suggests that the amount of carbon dioxide in the
atmosphere is playing a role in global warming. (43 words)

［解答例 3 ］

　From these two graphs, we can see that global temperature increases
are caused by the increase in the emission of CO_2: the global temperature
changed from about 15 degrees in 1880 to about 16 degrees in 2000, while
CO_2 emissions increased from 290 ppm to 370 ppm. (47 words)

---

2 **(B)**　3 年連続となる「日本文英語要約」である。ただ，何を書けばよいのかは
問題文で細かく指示されているので，そういう意味では楽だろう。あとは英語にする
ことができればよいだけ。

考え方

＜語数について＞

　「60 語程度」とあるから，50 または 60 語台で書くのがよいだろう。むろん 60 語
近辺が理想。

＜内容のポイント＞

　問題文で指示されていることを，その順番で書く。書かなければならないことは以
下の 3 つ。

① 「『雨降って地固まる』の字義通りの意味」

② 「『雨降って地固まる』の諺としての一般的な意味」

— 384 —

2003年　　解答・解説

③　「与えられた文において『雨降って地固まる』が表している状況」

　上記3点を盛り込めば自然と60語近くになるので，これら以外の内容を盛り込もうとする必要はない。

＜答案作成＞

　ここでは①〜③をどのような英語にすればよいかについて解説する。

① 「『雨降って地固まる』の字義通りの意味」

☆ 「字義通り」とは，簡単に言えば「直訳」ということ。名詞で表現するなら "the literal translation"，動詞で表現するなら "translate literally" となる。

☆ 「雨降って」は「雨が降った後で」ということだから，"after it rain<u>s</u>" "after rain fall<u>s</u>" など。一般論なので時制は現在。

☆ 「地固まる」は「地面が固くなる」ということだが，液体が固体になるという意味ではないので注意。「固い」は firm / hard など。雨が降る前との比較なので，firm<u>er</u> / hard<u>er</u> と比較級にすること。

☆ 全体的には，「この諺の直訳は…である」という趣旨の英文でまとめる。

② 「『雨降って地固まる』の諺としての一般的な意味」

☆ 「雨降って地固まる」の直訳は①で終わっているから，ここで諺を引き合いに出すときは単に it でよい。

☆ 諺の一般的な意味だが，国語辞典には「変事があってかえって前より基礎が固まることのたとえ」「争いごとのあったあと，かえって前よりもうまくいく」とある。

☆ 「変事」「争いごと」ということだから，problem / trouble / difficulty / terrible accident などのような語（句）を用いる必要がある。単に「何らかの<u>出来事</u>の後」では不足。ちなみに，「論議」「論争」という意味の語句を使うのは ×。これは次の③で使うからである。

☆ 「基礎が固まる」「かえって前よりもうまくいく」とは，要するに「事態［状況］が好転する」ということ。「事態［状況］」は things（必ず複数形）/ situation など。「好転」は get better / improve など。

③ 「与えられた文において『雨降って地固まる』が表している状況」

　この部分は問題文のきちんとした読み取りが求められる。盛り込まなければならない内容は，「**監督は，（チームの運営の仕方に関する）論争の後で，チームの結束が固まった（と思う），という意味で使っている**」ということ（カッコの部分はなくても可）。

☆ 「監督」は単に the speaker でよいが，the coach などとしても構わない。

☆ 「…に関する論争」は "the argument<u>s</u> over [about] …"（論争は一度ではないので複数形）または動詞で "argue over [about] …" など。問題文には「やり合う」

— 385 —

2003 年　　解答・解説

とあるので，単に talk ではなく argue を使うべきだろう。

☆　「チームの運営」は "the management of the team"。ちなみに，論争の具体的な内容（マネージャー・補欠・実力主義）については英訳不要。与えられた語数の中で収まらなくなる。

☆　「結束が固まる」の部分の処理が一番難しい（unite / unify という語を思いつくことができれば簡単に書けるが）。「結束」に bond を使うなら "the bond between the members" とする必要がある。時制だが，問題文を読むと，過去ではなく現在完了を使うべきである（過去形だと終わったことになってしまって，現在と無関係になる。結束が固まって現在に至る，という解釈をしないとおかしい）。

解 答 例

[解答例1]
　The literal translation of this proverb is "After it rains, the ground becomes firmer." It is used when we want to say that things get better after some trouble. In this passage, the speaker uses it to mean that after the heated arguments over the management of the team, the members have become more strongly united. (56 words)

[解答例2]
　This saying can be literally translated as "After rain falls, the ground becomes firmer." Its actual meaning is that after some terrible incident, the situation improves. In the passage given here, the speaker uses this proverb to say he thinks that after arguing about the management of the team, the bond between the members has become all the stronger.

(59 words)

[解答例3]
　This expression literally means "After it rains, the ground becomes firmer", and it generally means that a situation improves after there have been some problems. In this context, it means that, in the coach's view, the large number of arguments they had last year has made the team more unified and better prepared for the coming season. (57 words)

— 386 —

2003 年　　解答・解説

4 (A) **［考え方］** (1) 「誰であれ，スーが説得しやすい人間だろうとどうして期待できるのか，私には想像できない。彼女は人の話に絶対耳を傾けない人だよ」

　　正解はエ・カ (can _expect_ Sue to be easy _to_ convince)。

　　① "how anyone ..." となっていることから，anyone は how 節中の主語と考えられる。述語動詞は動詞の現在形・過去形，および助動詞であるから，can に目をつける。can の後は動詞の原形が続くから，"can convince" か "can expect" のいずれか。

　　② easy は形容詞で，形容詞の用法は「名詞にかかる」「補語になる」のいずれか。"〈anyone〉easy" という英語は内容的に考えにくいので，補語になっていると考え，"to be easy" とする（expect / convince は第 2 文型も第 5 文型もとれない）。

　　③ Sue は固有名詞だから，S / O / C のいずれかになっていなければならない。①で見た構文を考えると，convince か expect の目的語と考えるのが適当。したがって "can convince [または expect] Sue" とする。

　　④ convince にも expect にも "V + O + to 原形" という語法があるので，②と③をまとめて "convince [expect] Sue to be easy" とする。

　　⑤ 残った選択肢は to のみ。ここで，"S be easy to V" という tough 構文を考える。この構文は S と V の間に意味上〈O − V〉の関係が成り立っていなければならない。さらに，④で述べた "V + O + to 原形" という形は O と原形の間に意味上〈O −V〉の関係がある。したがって，"convince Sue to be easy to expect" または "expect Sue to be easy to convince" のいずれかが正解だろう。前者は「スーに期待しやすくなるよう説得する」となって意味不明だから，後者が正解になる。

　(2) 「掲示を見てごらん。『いかなる時もこのドアには鍵をかけておくこと』と書いてあるよ。中に何があるんだろう」

　　正解はエ・ウ (time _must_ this door be _left_ unlocked)。

　　① "At no" となっていることから，no の後には名詞が続く。選択肢中の名詞は door / time だが，"〈At no〉door" というのは意味的に考えにくいので，とりあえず "〈At no〉time" としておく。

　　② 上記設問(1)①と同様，must は助動詞なので述語動詞。must の後は原形なので be。must の主語は door 以外なく，さらに this があることから this door とする。この段階でとりあえず "this door must be" とまとめておく。

　　③ 残りは left / unlocked で，さらに be があることから，"this door must be left unlocked" とする。これは must leave this door unlocked の受動態である。

　　④ これで正解が出来上がったように思えるが，文頭の "〈At no〉time" に注意。これは否定の副詞句である。否定の副詞句が文頭に出ている場合，その後は疑問文

— 387 —

2003年　解答・解説

の形の倒置にしなければならないというルールがある。したがって，"⟨At no⟩ time must this door be left unlocked" とするのが正しい。

⑶　「彼らが一番望まないのは，彼らがまもなく結婚することになっているのを新聞に知られることだった。結婚のことは友人にも親戚にも話してなかったのである」

　正解はカ・ア (The last *thing* they wanted was *for* the newspapers)。

　①　they は主格なので主語。述語動詞は wanted 以外ないので，"they wanted"。

　②　was は過去形なので述語動詞。主語は thing しかないが，これは可算名詞なので単数無冠詞では使えない。したがって "the thing was" または "the last thing was"。

　③　for は前置詞なので，その後には名詞が続く。したがって，"for the (last) thing" か "for the (last) newspapers" のいずれかだが，②で見たように "the (last) thing" は was の主語になっているため，"for the (last) newspapers" だろう。

　④　②③で明らかになった2つの文の存在をうまく処理しなければならない。want には want *that SV* という語法はないので，"*they wanted the (last) thing was*" はありえない。ここは関係代名詞の省略と考え，"the (last) thing they wanted was" とまとめる。

　⑤　ここで空所の後の部分の内容を見る。「彼らがまもなく結婚する」こと，および「その結婚について友人にも親戚にも明かしていない」ことがわかる。したがって，「彼ら」は自分たちの「結婚」のことを知られたくないのではと考え，"the last thing they wanted was" に決定する。このカタマリの中に for the newspapers を入れられる所はないので，"the last thing they wanted was for the newspapers ⟨to find out ...⟩" を正解だと判断する。last には least likely，つまり「最も可能性が低い」という意味があって，"The last 名詞 S V is ..." という形で「SがVする可能性が最も低い[名詞]は…だ」という意味合いになるのはよくあることだ。ちなみに "for the newspapers ⟨to find out⟩" の部分は，"for 名詞" が to 不定詞（ここでは名詞用法）の意味上の主語で，「新聞が知ること」という意味。

⑷　「ジョンがなぜあのような行動をとるのか，誰にもわからない。彼はとても変わっているからね」

　正解はア・ウ (has *any* idea why John *behaves* as he does)。

　①　No one が主語。述語動詞は has か behaves。

　②　has には本動詞と助動詞があるが，選択肢に過去分詞がないことから，ここでは本動詞。ならば目的語が必要になるため，"has any idea" とまとめる（設問⑶②で述べたように，可算名詞は単数無冠詞では使えないから）。

　③　疑問詞の why があることから，この文中には疑問詞節が存在することがわか

— 388 —

2003年　　解答・解説

る。疑問詞節は必ず名詞節として働くが，has も behaves も疑問詞節を目的語にすることはできない。したがって，"have no idea＋wh."（「wh. 以下のことがわからない」という意味）という慣用表現を考え，"has any idea why" とまとめる。さらに，No one が主語でないと any になっていることの説明がつかないので，No one の述語動詞は behaves ではなく has に決定する。ちなみに，これは本来 "have an idea of ＋名詞" という表現だが，"have no idea ＋ wh." という表現になった場合のみ of をつけないのである。

④　③の why 節の中にくる S V は，"John behaves" か "he does" で，この２つを接続詞 as がつなぐと考える。"why he does as John behaves" とすると，「なぜ彼はジョンがふるまうようにやるのか」が直訳となり，要領を得ない。"why John behaves as he does" は「なぜジョンはあのような行動をとるのか」という意味だから内容的に適切。したがって，"〈No one〉has any idea why John behaves as he does" が正解。ちなみにこの does は behaves の代用で，元々は "John behaves as he behaves" で，「ジョンが行動しているように行動する」が直訳。つまり，「普段あのような行動をとっている」ということ。

(5)　「綿密な調査の結果，その店はテロリストが所有しているものであることが明らかになり，客たちは衝撃を受けた」

正解はエ・ア (Close *investigation* revealed the store to *be* owned by).

①　owned / revealed を過去形と考えれば述語動詞の候補である。さらに，investigation は「調査」という意味だが，owned とは内容的につながらない。したがって，とりあえず "investigation revealed"（調査が明らかにした）とまとめておく。

②　reveal は他動詞だから目的語を必要とする。reveal の語法としては reveal that S V が代表的であること，選択肢の中に be / by / owned つまり be 動詞・過去分詞・by の３つが与えられていることから，「明らかにした」内容は「その店はテロリストたちが所有するものである」（という）ことではないかと考え，"investigation revealed the store be owned by〈terrorists〉" としてみる。ところが be 動詞が原形で与えられていることが問題。このままでは英語にならないので，ひょっとしたら reveal には "reveal O to –" という語法もあるのではと考え，とりあえず "investigation revealed the store to be owned by〈terrorists〉" とまとめておく。

③　残った選択肢は close のみで，この語には動詞と形容詞がある。前者は「閉まる；閉める」で後者は「近い；綿密な」という意味。内容的には形容詞ととらえて investigation を説明していると考えるのが妥当なので，"close investigation revealed the store to be owned by〈terrorists〉" とし，これを正解とする。ちなみに，

－ 389 －

<u>2003年　　解答・解説</u>

"reveal O to be C"（必ず to be）という語法はあまり一般的なものではない。

解答

(1)　エ・カ	(2)　エ・ウ	(3)　カ・ア
(4)　ア・ウ	(5)　エ・ア	

4　**(B)**　**全訳**　あらゆる出来事の裏側に，神の手の存在を探し出そうとする人がいる。私は，ある女性を見舞いに病院に行く。彼女の自動車は，赤信号を無視した飲酒運転者に衝突されたのだ。その女性の車は大破したが，奇跡的に彼女は足首を骨折しただけで済んだ。病院のベッドから私を見上げて，彼女は言う。「私，やっと分かったんです，神様がいるって。(1)私があのような事故から生きて無事に生還することができたとすれば，それは天国で神様が私を見守っていて下さるからに違いないわ。」私は微笑んで黙ったままでおり，(2)自分も同じように考えていると彼女に思わせてしまう危険を冒してしまうが，必ずしもそうではないのだ。私は2週間前に自分が執り行ったある葬儀のことを思い出す。それは同じような飲酒運転者が起こした衝突事故で亡くなった，妻子のいる若い男性の葬儀だった。私の目の前にいる女性は，神が自分に生き残ることを望んだゆえに自分は生きていると信じているのかもしれないし，(3)神様のご意志で生き残ったなどと思うのはやめなさい，と彼女を説得したいとは思わない。しかし，彼女なら，あるいは私なら，あのもう一方の家族にどんな言葉をかけるだろうか？

考え方　(1)　**If I could come out of that alive and in one piece**「私があのような事故から生きて無事に生還することができたとすれば」　that は，下線部以前の箇所で説明されていた「自動車事故」を指している。come out of ... で「…から出てくる，抜け出す」の意。alive と in one piece が，「どのような状態で事故から抜け出したのか」を説明している。直訳すれば「生きて無事な状態であのような事故から抜け出す」となるが，「生きて無事にあのような事故から生還する」といったようにまとめればよいであろう。in one piece が「無事で，無傷で」の意の熟語であることにも注意。

(2)　1．**running the risk of ...**「…という危険を冒して」　直前の smile and keep ... を修飾する分詞構文。run a risk は「危険を冒す」の意の決まり文句。of はいわゆる「同格の of」で，of 以下が「危険」の中身を説明している。

2．**letting her think that I agree with her**「自分も同じように考えている（彼女の考えに賛成だ）と彼女に思わせてしまう〈という危険〉」　let (V) her (O) think

－　390　－

2003 年　　解答・解説

(C) が動名詞化したもの。agree with ... は「〈人やその人の考え〉に賛成する」の意。

(3)　1．**I am not inclined to** −「−したいとは思わない」　be inclined to −で「したいと思っている，したい気がする」の意。(例) *I'm inclined to* believe her story.（彼女の話を信じてもいい気がしている）

2．**talk her out of it**「神様のご意志で生き残ったなどと思うのはやめなさい，と彼女を説得する」　talk 人 out of ... で「人を説得して…をやめさせる」の意。(例) Can't you *talk them out of* selling the house?（彼らを説き伏せて，その家を売るのをやめさせられませんか？）　it は直前の「神が自分に生き残ることを望んだゆえに自分は生きていると信じること」という内容を受けている。ここを指していることが分かるように訳せていれば，100％原文通りである必要はない。

解 答

(1)　私があのような事故から生きて無事に生還することができたとすれば

(2)　自分も同じように考えていると彼女に思わせてしまう危険を冒してしまうが

(3)　神様のご意志で生き残ったなどと思うのはやめなさい，と彼女を説得したいとは思わない

5　**全訳**　ケルマーンとヤズドの間の砂漠を通り抜けるバスに私が乗っていると，私たちのバスが検問所に停まる。検問所は，イランの幹線道路沿いにはよくあるもので，およそ 100 マイルごとに停車して，運転手が書類を手に車から降りていくのを眺めることに私は慣れてしまっている。ときには，深緑の制服を着た警備兵がバスの中に入ってきて，通路を歩いて行ったり来たりするのだが，目は左右へと機敏に動き，影がさした車内の明かりでピストルがキラリと光る。

今回も，そんな場面の一つである。若い衛兵が入ってくるとバスが静かになり，私たちは皆，決然と正面を向くのだが，それはあたかも，私たちが衛兵を無視するふりをすることによって，彼も私たちを無視することになるかのように行われる。通路に沿って敷いてあるペルシャ絨毯の上を彼の足音が鳴っていき，向きを変え，再び戻ってくるのに私たちは耳を傾ける。男はバスの先頭までたどり着き，ドアの方へと 90 度向きを変える。しかしそれから，ちょうど私たちが一斉に深呼吸をし始めると，彼は最後まで回転して通路を再び歩き始めることで私たちをびっくりさせる。そして今度は，いろいろな乗客の肩をたたいていく。肩をたたかれた乗客たちは，荷物をまとめ，ゆっくりとバスから降りて，コンクリートブロックの建物の階段を上がっていく。

私は凍ったように座っている。私にも，そしてまた，私のルサリ（という頭髪用の

— 391 —

スカーフ）から突き出ている金髪にも，衛兵が気づかないことを願いながら。衛兵が乗客をバスから引き降ろすのをこれまでにも見たことがあるし，必ず5分か10分以内に乗客たちが戻ってくるので，深刻なことのようには全然思えないのだが，私は自分の席に留まったままの方がよい。

　衛兵がバスから降り，私はほっとするが，それと同時に，彼が何かを探しているとしたらそれは何だろうと不思議に思う。こういう捜索が通常は麻薬や密輸に関するものだと聞かされているが，私には，権力の誇示の方が目的であるように思われる。

　衛兵が戻ってきて，直感的に，私にはその理由がわかる。彼は私を指さす。

　私？　私は身振りで尋ねるが，私に用があるということは，いまだに完全には確信が持てないままだ。イランに2ヵ月滞在してわかったことだが，予想していたこととは裏腹に，この国で外国人が厄介な目にあうことはめったにない。

　お前だ，と彼はうなずく。

　他の乗客たちのまねをして，私は持ち物をまとめて立ち上がる。誰もが私をじっと見ている。いつもどおり，バスに乗っている外国人は私だけなのである。

　自分の長い黒のレインコートを踏みつけて転びそうになりながら，私はバスから降りる。イランではすべての女性が，人前ではそれかそれに似た何かしらのものを着用していなくてはならないのである。心臓が激しく打ちつけている。衛兵と，同僚の1人が，衛兵所の階段で私を待っている。彼らの足元には私のバッグがある。彼らがバスの胴体から引き出しておいたのだ。そのバッグは丸々とした緑のスイカのような見た目をしている。

　「パスポート」と若い衛兵がペルシャ語で怒鳴る。

　私はパリパリした紺色の書類を彼に渡すが，そのとき突如として，「アメリカ合衆国」の文字が表面全体に，あまりにくっきりと印字されていると感じる。イランに入国する前にパスポートにカバーをつけておくようにと，母国で誰かが注意してくれたのを思い出す。もはや手遅れである。

　「ビザは？」

　私は彼にパスポートの該当ページを見せる。

　「やってきたのは，どこから？」

　彼のペルシャ語には，それまで聞いたことがない奇妙な訛りがある。

　「ケルマーンから」と私は言う。

　「行先は？」

　「ヤズド」

　「観光客？」

2003年　解答・解説

　私はうなずく。ペルシャ語で旅行談，直訳すると「旅行手紙」に相当する *safarnameh* を執筆するために，ここイランにいるのだと彼に伝えることによって事態を複雑にする必要はないと考えてのことだ。しかし，その後すぐに，自分の行ったことは正しかったのだろうかと思う。私のビザには「ジャーナリスト」と書いてある。

　ゆっくりと，その若い衛兵は私のパスポートのページをめくり，入国スタンプや，後ろの方に記載されている法律や規定に入念に目を通す。彼は私の写真を長い時間じっくりと調べてから，にこりともしない同僚にそのパスポートを渡すが，その男もまた，私が聞かれたばかりのものと同じ質問を私に尋ねる。

　「やってきたのは，どこから？」

　「ケルマーンから」

　「行先は？」

　「ヤズド」

　「観光客？」

　今度も私はうなずく。今さら答えを変えられない。

　２番目の衛兵がパスポートを最初の衛兵に手渡すと，彼は渋々それを私に手渡して戻す。彼の滑らかな少年のような顔を見て，ひげを剃る年齢に達しているのだろうかと私は思う。

　「これはお前のスーツケースか？」と私のバッグを見ながら彼は言う。

　「そうです」と私は言って，それを開けようと体を動かす。

　彼は首を横に振る。

　他の乗客たちは皆，もうバスに戻っていて，私はあとどれくらい衛兵たちに引き留められるのだろうかと思う。私を乗せずにバスが出発したらどうなるのだろう，と私は心配になる。私たちは町から離れた砂漠の真ん中にいて，他に建物は見えない。固くて灰白色の平地が四方八方に広がり，それを途切れさせるのは，まばらな草地だけである。空は，景色から色と湿度を吸い取っている，淡い色の金属製のドームのようである。

　咳払いをして，最初の衛兵が私をじっと見る。彼の目は，ふつうとちがう煙がかった青い色で，長い睫（まつげ）で縁どられている。少なからぬイラン人に以前見かけたことがあるのと同じ目だ。彼は同僚に目をやり，二人はひそひそと話し合う。汗が彼らの額から，そして私の額からもすべり落ちる。

　すると，最初の衛兵が肩をまっすぐにして，深呼吸をして，顔を赤らめる。「ありがとう。お目にかかれて何よりです」と彼はぎこちなく照れくさそうな英語で注意深く言う。

— 393 —

2003 年　　解答・解説

今度は 2 番目の衛兵が最初の衛兵と同じくらい激しく顔を赤らめて「こんにちは，ごきげんよう」と言う。彼はペルシャ語に戻り，私は彼の言うことの一部しか理解できない。「私たちは今日のことを決して忘れません。あなたは私たちが出会った最初のアメリカ人なのです。イラン・イスラム共和国へようこそ。アラーとともにありますように！」

(考え方)

　(1)　**just as we begin a collective deep breath**「ちょうど私たちが一斉に深呼吸をし始めると」

　この just as ... は「ちょうど…のとき」という意味。節内の動詞が begin なので，「ちょうど…し始めると」のように訳せばよい。begin a deep breath「深い呼吸を始める」→「深呼吸を（し）始める」。工夫が必要なのは collective の処理。「集団の深呼吸を始める」では要領を得ない日本語になってしまうので，内容をよく考え「一斉に」と副詞的に処理すると上手く訳せる。（参考）to give a quick answer「すばやい答えをする」→「すばやく答える」

　(2)　正解は**ア**。

　下線部の "d" は would で，would just as soon ... で「むしろ…したい」という表現（この soon は時間的な意味ではなく「進んで，喜んで，むしろ」といった心理的な意味で用いられている）。よって，I'd just as soon remain my in seat は「私は自分の席に留まったままの方がよい」という意味になる。したがって，ア「座ったままでいることを許されることを私は願う」が正解。この表現を知らなければ，下線の手前にある「必ず 5 分か 10 分以内に乗客たちが戻ってくるので，深刻なことのようには全然思えないのだが」という although 節の内容から，下線部は「できれば席にいるままがよい」という意味合いであることを理解して正解を選んでもよい。

　イ「まもなく私は席につき，そこに留まる」，ウ「席から離れる時間が長くないとよいなあと願う」，エ「即座に私は席に留まる決心をする」は，上記の説明からどれも不適。

　(3)　正解は**ウ**。

　空所の直後に anything があり，空所と合わせて 2 語で挿入表現になっていること，直前に what があることから if を入れて if anything とすれば，what, if anything, ...「（少しでも）あるとすれば何が／を …」という表現になり，「彼が何かを探しているとしたら，それは何だろうと不思議に思う」となり文意も通る。（例）I'd like to see *what, if anything,* is wrong.「（何も悪い所はないかもしれませんが）もし仮に何かが悪いとしたら，何が悪いのかを知りたいのです」

― 394 ―

2003 年　　解答・解説

他の選択肢はどれも意味が通らないので不適。ちなみに for anything は通例 would not と共に用いて「（どんなものと交換だとしても）絶対に…しない」という表現になる。（例）I wouldn't marry him *for anything*.「彼なんかとは絶対に結婚しない」

⑷　正解は**イ**。

空所を含む文は「こういう捜索が通常は麻薬や密輸に関するものだと聞かされているが，私には，権力の（　　）の方が目的であるように思われる」という意味であることから「権力の誇示」といった意味にすればよい。名詞の display には「（権力や能力の）誇示；見せびらかし」といった意味があるため，これが正解となる。

他の選択肢を入れると，ア「権力の否定」，ウ「権力の発見」，エ「権力の欠如」となり，どれも不適。

⑸　解答例「**（この国で）外国人が厄介な目にあうこと**」（17/13 字）。

contrary to ... で「…に反して」という意味の表現。contrary to what I had expected「予期していたことに反して」わかったことが foreigners are seldom bothered here であり，seldom が「めったにない」という意味なので，予期していたことは foreigners are bothered here となる。bother O で「O を困らせる；O に面倒をかける」なので are bothered は「厄介な目にあう；面倒なことに巻き込まれる；困らされる」のように処理すればよい。here は文章の最後の部分からわかるとおり「イラン」のことなので「この国で」のように処理するのがよいが，これは必ずしも解答に含めなくてもよいだろう。

⑹　正解は **"similar being required for all"**

整序英作文は空所の前後も考えることが重要であることが多いが，東大もそのような出題をすることが多い。まず，空所の手前に it or something とあることから，similar を続けそれが something にかかるようにすれば，〈it or something〉similar「それ，あるいはそれに似た何かしらのもの」となり，うまくまとまる。次に，be required for ... で「…に必要とされる」という表現なので，空所の後ろにある women の直前に all を置いて all women「全ての女性」とし，全体を it or something <u>similar being required for all</u> women ... とすれば，it or something similar が意味上の主語の分詞構文になり全体がまとまる。小説・物語では分詞構文が多用されることを知っておくと，問題に取り組みやすくなる。

⑺　正解は**ウ**。

直前の文にある「『アメリカ合衆国』の文字が表面全体に，あまりにくっきりと印字されていると感じる」とあることから，ウを入れ「〈イランに入国する〉前にパス

— 395 —

2003年　解答・解説

ポートにカバーをつけておくようにと，〈母国で誰かが〉注意してくれたのを思い出す」
とするのが適切だとわかる。また，これを入れれば，直後の文の「もはや手遅れであ
る」ともうまくつながる。

　ア「〈イランに入国〉後，衛兵たちに逆らわないよう警告する」だと直後の文の「も
はや手遅れである」と合わない。イ「〈イランに入国する〉前に基本的なペルシャ語
を学んでおくよう忠告する」だが，会話は英語で書かれてはいるものの，空所(7)の3
行上に barks in Persian，3行下に His Persian とあることや，文章の最後の部分で
「『ありがとう。お目にかかれて何よりです』と彼はぎこちなく照れくさそうな英語で
注意深く言う」と述べられていることから，最後の部分以外の会話はペルシャ語で行
われていることが読み取れるため不適。エ「〈イランに入国〉後，パスポートを携行
し忘れないよう警告する」だと，行っていたことなので，直後の文の「もはや手遅れ
である」と合わない。

　(8)　正解は**イ**。

　「『観光客？』という質問に対してうなずいた→（空所）→ 私のビザには『ジャー
ナリスト』と書いてある」という流れから，イ「自分の行ったことは正しかったのだ
ろうかと思う」を入れれば，自分は観光客だと嘘をついてやり過ごそうとしたが，ビ
ザに『ジャーナリスト』と書いてあるためその嘘がばれないか不安になっている，と
前後関係がうまくつながる。

　ア「自分がジャーナリストだったらよいのに，と私は思う」は，実際にジャーナリ
ストなので不適。ウ「自分があまりにも観光客に見えることに私は気づく」および
エ「英語で『観光客だ』と言うべきだったことに私は気づく」は，後ろとつながらな
いので不適。

　(9)　正解は**ウ**。

　「彼は私の写真を（　9　）する」の空所を埋める問題。正解のウ studies に「よく
調べる」の意味があることを知っていたか，および他の選択肢がどれも入らないとい
う消去的視点から正解を導き出せるかがポイント。ア detects「検出する」は意味的
におかしい。イ gazes「じっと見つめる」は gazes <u>at</u> my picture と前置詞 at が必要
なため不適。エ watches「見守る」は「動くもの，動きそうなもの」を目的語にと
るため不適。

　(10)　正解は**ア**。

　空所の手前に「他の乗客たちは皆，もうバスに戻っていて，私はあとどれくらい衛
兵たちに引き留められるのだろうかと思う」と述べられていることと，空所の直前に
「私は心配になる」という表現が挿入されていることから，この状況で心配するよう

― 396 ―

2003年　解答・解説

な内容になればよい。アを入れれば「私を乗せずにバスが出発したら〈どうなるのだろう〉」となるため文脈に合う。

上記の説明より，イ「天気が突然変わったら」，ウ「バスがガス欠になったり故障したりしたら」，エ「他の乗客の一部がバスを降りるよう求められたら」はどれも不適。

(11)　正解はア。

ア in sight「視野の中には」という意味の熟語が正解。イの on vision は定型表現ではないし，空所に入れて意味が通るものでもない。ウ in my eyes は「私の見るところ；私の意見では」という意味で，物事が人にどのような印象を与えたかを述べる表現なので不適。エ to the view「公然と」も文脈に合わない。

(12)　解答例：**has spoken in English to an American**

直後の文に「ぎこちなく照れくさそうな英語で注意深く言う」とあることや，後続箇所に「あなたは私たちが出会った最初のアメリカ人なのです」とあることから，「アメリカ人（またはネイティブ・スピーカー）と英語で話す〈のが初めてだから〉」といった内容にすればよい。

他の解答としては，has met an American / has spoken to an American (in English) / has spoken (in) English to a native speaker / has used English in real life などが考えられる。It is the first time に続く表現なので，現在完了形を使うのが自然である。

(補足)　本文に出てくるペルシャ語 safarnameh の前半の safar は，サファリと関連のあるアラビア語起源の言葉，後半の nameh は世界史に登場するペルシャの詩人フィルドゥーシーの作品の名前『王書（シャーナーメ）』の後半部分と同じ。

解答

(1)　ちょうど私たちが一斉に深呼吸をし始めると

(2)－ア　　　　(3)－ウ　　　　(4)－イ

(5)　（この国で）外国人が厄介な目にあうこと

(6)　similar being required for all

(7)－ウ　　　　(8)－イ　　　　(9)－ウ　　　　(10)－ア　　　　(11)－ア

(12)　has spoken in English to an American

解答・解説

1 (A) **[全訳]** 日本のテレビ番組では，小さな画面に解説者とアシスタントが並んで出てくる。解説者は通例男性で中年である。アシスタントは通例女性で，若くて美人であることが多い。男性の方が様々な話題について論評し，女性がそれを補佐する。しかし，補佐といってもたかが知れており，私たちの目には，女性はいなくてもまったく構わないのではないかと思われる。その女性は，解説者が様々な発言をする度にカメラに向かってうなずき，彼が重要な論点を述べると「そうですね」と言うだけである。彼女は自分の意見は決して述べないのだ。この両者を見ている多くのアメリカ人には，このような状況は確かに極めて奇妙に思えるかもしれない。もちろん私たちも解説者が2人いることに慣れてはいるが，たいていの場合それぞれの解説者が実際に論評するのであり，両者は対等である。日本のテレビでよく見られる上記の方式では，美人の女性はまったく不必要だと思われる。私たちにはこの女性の役割が理解できない。ところが，この女性は非常に重要な役割を担っているのである。

そもそも解説者とは持論を述べるものであり，欧米ではこれで十分である。しかし日本では，公に意見を述べることは自己中心的すぎるように見えるのであり，これは意見の一致が重要な価値を持つ社会においては欠陥である。魅力的でほとんど口を開かない若いアシスタントは，この価値を際立たせているのである。彼女のうなずきや同意の表現によって伝えられるのは，解説者の見解は本人だけのものではなく，したがって，彼は単に自己中心的なのではないということだ。それどころか，解説者の発言に同意している人間が少なくとも1人はいるのだから，彼は正しいことを述べていることになるのである。この女性は同時に，私たち皆が同意している（そもそも，彼女がうなずいているのは私たちに対してなのだ）と示すことによって調和を伝えている。そうすれば，意見の一致は望み通りすでに達成されたということになるのだ。

[考え方]

(1) 「外国人（この場合はアメリカ人）から見て日本の女性アシスタントはまったく不要」に思える理由を説明する。そのためには，アメリカのニュース番組との対比を明確に表している部分をまとめるとよい。直前に「もちろん私たち（＝アメリカ人）も解説者が2人いることに慣れてはいるのだが，たいていの場合それぞれの解説者が実際に論評する」という記述がある。これと対比を成すのは第1段落第7文 (She never presents ...) の "She never presents an idea of her own." である。5 〜 15

— 400 —

2002 年　解答・解説

字という指定なので,「自分の考え［意見］を言わない」という点が含まれていればよい。第 6 文 (She only nods ...) に「『そうですね』とは言う」とあるので,「まったく何も言わない；無言である」などは不可である。

(2)

◇「日本の文化の特質」に関係するのは第 2 段落第 3 文 (In Japan, however, ...) の "to give ... too self-centered ～ a society where ..." の部分である。「人前で意見を述べるのは自己中心的すぎるように見える。これは意見の一致が重要な価値を持つ社会では欠陥である」とあるので,「意見の一致が重視される［尊ばれる］；意見の一致に価値がある」が特質として含まれていればよい。

◇「役割」については,第 4 文 (The attractive, nearly ...) に "emphasizes this value" とある。this value は当然 unity of opinion を指すので,「意見の一致を強調する［際立たせる］」という程度にまとめておく。

◇第 5 文 (Her nods and ...) ～最終文 (At the same ...) は,emphasizes this value とはどういうことかをより明確にするために補強した部分だと考えてよい。「うなずきや同意の表現」は「解説者が自己中心的ではなく真実を述べていることを示す」と同時に「調和をもたらす」が大筋である。

◇第 3 文と第 4 文を中心に「意見の一致［統一；調和］が達成されたことを強調する役割」とまとめると 20 字になる（役割という言葉はなくても可であろう）。解答字数が 40 ～ 50 字しかないので,これに「日本の文化」「価値を置く［重視する］」「同意によって」といった言葉を加えてまとめたのが以下の解答例である。

解答

> (1)　自分の意見を言わないから。(13 字)
> (2)　意見の統一に価値を置く日本の文化において,それが達成されたことを同意によって強調する役割。(45 字) ／日本の文化は意見の一致を重視するものであり,同意によってこの一致が見られたことを強調する役割。(47 字)

1 (B) **(全訳)** 「雪」は,一見したところでは,文化史家とか社会史家の論題のようには思えない。むしろ,研究のテーマとしては,明らかに雪は地理学者や気象及び気候の専門家のものだと思えるかもしれない。雪について何が「文化的」でありえるのか。雪について何が「社会的」でありえるのか。最初は,これは答えにくく思える問いかもしれない。（　1　）

雪は確かに,人間が最初にそれを記述する語を作る前から存在していた。雪は自然

— 401 —

2002年　　解答・解説

現象である。しかしまた同時に，人間が共有してきた体験の一部でもある。だから，文化史家や社会史家が雪という論題に取り組む際に用いる問いの焦点は，雪についての「体験」であるということになろう。つまり，人々が雪に対してどのような名を与えてきたか，雪に関してどのような問いを投げかけてきたか，どのような象徴的な意味を見出したか，どのように雪を扱ってきたか，ということだ。この種の問いによって，有益な歴史的探究の広範囲な分野が開けるのである。

アメリカにおける社会的意味合いでの雪についての考え方や雪との共存の仕方は，歴史的にはっきりと変化している。アメリカの歴史において雪は不変なものであったが，その文化的意味合いはそうではなかった。ある歴史家によれば，アメリカにおける雪の歴史のこの変化は6期に分類できるとのことである。第1期には，アメリカ人は単に雪を切り抜けて生きてきた。その後，次の期では彼らは次第に，雪と一体となり，雪を自分たちの国民としての一体感の一部，きれいで純粋なものの象徴とみなし始めた。

（　2　）雪は，多様な意味合いと多くの側面で知られるようになった。雪はアメリカ人の生活の矛盾，相違，多様性を象徴し始めた。アメリカの雪が示す終わることのない変化の様相に新たな関心が寄せられた。雪は平和であると同時に危険であり，創造的であると同時に破壊的であり，消極的であると同時に積極的であり，冷たいが生き生きしており，無表情だが美しいものとなった。

（　3　）雪は計測し予測できるものであった。そして，雪は正確に制御できないにしても理解できるものだとみなすこのような傾向は，人々の雪の研究への取り組みを促進した。次のこの期には，アメリカの雪は，調査し，記述し，命名すべき対象となった。この期には，国家気象局が重要性を増し，南北両極への科学的関心は大衆の雪に対する意識を高めた。

第5期には，ウィンタースポーツ，とりわけスキーが主要な商業活動となり始めた。しかし，その当時雪は初めて娯楽の様相を帯びるようになってきたばかりであったが，人々は深刻な社会問題であるとして雪に注意を寄せ始めるようにもなった。（　4　）

最後に，今日の多くのアメリカ人にとっては，雪は失われた過去の安全を最も直接的に連想させるものかもしれない。この過去は，子供の頃の冬の記憶かもしれないし，想像上のかつてのアメリカ，つまり，生活がともかくも現在よりきれいで質素であった時空間なのかもしれない。このような雪の見方は，汚染，環境，地球規模の気象変化についての社会的関心の高まりと結びついていることはほぼ確かであろうし，アメリカの国家的一体感や世界の大国としてのその地位の変化とも奇妙に結びついているのかもしれない。

— 402 —

2002年　　解答・解説

（　5　）　個々の降雪の歴史を見れば，「4つのD」に彼らはおそらく目を向けるであろう。その発生と消滅の日付は？　どれほどの積雪であったか？　その密度ないしは水分含有量は？　それと，持続時間，つまりどれくらいの期間雪が降ったのか？　これらの問いに対する答えは，個々の地理的地域における雪の影響力についての基本情報を提供してくれるであろう。

しかし，文化史家にとっては，雪は米国の自然と文化の相互関係の歴史についての窓となってくれるのである。大半のアメリカ人は，毎年いくらかでも雪を体験している。毎年，何世紀にもわたって，雪はアメリカの景観を変えてきたし，その国民に肉体的にも精神的にも様々な課題を与えてきた。（　6　）

ア　しかし，もちろん，雪は常に概念や象徴にとどまるものではなかった。それは同時に気象でもあったのだ。

イ　天候と気候を研究する専門家の関心は，自然現象としての降雪にある。

ウ　次に，創造的な執筆家や創造的な科学者たちが雪を新たな目で見始めると，アメリカの雪についてさらに複雑な見解が現れ始めた。

エ　輸送革命の開始と共に，雪は，都市や道路や鉄道の責任を担う人々にとって大きな頭痛の種となった。

オ　第3期には，余暇が増え出して，人々は雪を娯楽として体験する方法を知った。雪は厄介なものであるだけでなく楽しいものともなった。

カ　アメリカ人が雪についての知識をどのようにして知るのかを検証すれば，雪自体についての真相よりもはるかに多くのことを理解できるようになる。アメリカの文化と社会についても多くのことを知ることになるだろう。

キ　しかし，文化史家にとっては，「雪は雪」，つまり，自然のもの，気象の一部，文化や社会とは無縁なもの，と言っているだけでは済まないのである。文化史家にとっては，雪にはそれをはるかに超える価値がある。

ク　しかし，アメリカにおける雪は，自然現象としてよりも思想として常に重要であったし，研究テーマとしては，科学者ではなく歴史家のものである。その要となるのは，アメリカの気候ではなく，アメリカ人の想像力なのである。

【考え方】

(1)　正解は**キ**。

「雪の『文化的・社会的』側面は何なのか」という問いかけがあり，直前の文に At first「最初は…」があるので，逆接を表す But で始まり「文化史家にとっては，雪は単なる自然現象ではない」という内容を持つキがふさわしい。

— 403 —

<u>2002 年</u>　　解答・解説

　なお，クについては，though（しかしながら）に続く「アメリカの雪は常に自然現象としてよりも思想として重要であり，研究テーマとしては科学者ではなく歴史家のものである」という内容がこの空所に入ると考えたかもしれないが，第2段落以降の「自然現象としての<u>みならず</u>社会的・文化的現象でもある」という内容に合わない。

　(2)　正解は**ウ**。

　後ろに話題の方向転換がない限り，段落冒頭の文はその段落の Topic Sentence（主題文）だと考えてよい。この段落では「雪の多様な意味合い；多面性」が紹介されているので，"a more complicated version of snow in America began to appear" という表現を含むウがふさわしい。なお，この version は「見解」の意味である。

　第3段落に「第1期と第2期の説明」があるので，当然(2)には「第3期の説明」が入るだろうと早合点してオを選んだ人は，「読まずに済まそうとして出題者の罠にかかった」ことになる。オの内容は "snow as entertainment" であり，この段落の内容とは無関係である。

　(3)　正解は**ア**。

　これも Topic Sentence が入ると考えてよい。measured（計測され），predicted（予測され），understood（理解され），organize the study of snow（雪の研究を組織的に行う），investigated（調査され），described（記述され），named（命名される）といった一連の表現との関連で，「雪は概念や象徴だけではなく気象でもあったのだ」という内容を持つアがふさわしい。もちろん snow を直後の It が受けるという代名詞の関係も成立する。

　(4)　正解は**エ**。

　第5期の説明に入り，第2文（But then just ...）で「雪は社会問題にもなった」とあるので，これとの関連でエが正解となる。なお，第6期については次の第7段落で説明があり，ここでアメリカにおける雪のとらえ方の変遷に関する話は終わる。

　(5)　正解は**イ**。

　空所の直後に，"four Ds"（4つのD），すなわち dates（発生と消滅の日付），depth（積雪の深さ），density（密度），duration（持続時間）に「彼らはおそらく目を向けるであろう」とある。そのような行動をとる人といえば，雪を自然現象として扱う人であろう。よって，この they の指示対象として Specialists studying weather and climate を含むイがふさわしい。

　(6)　正解は**カ**。

　第8段落で「自然現象としての雪」に触れた上で，この最終段落で「文化史」に戻るという構成になっている。「雪はアメリカの自然と文化の相互関係の歴史について

－　404　－

2002 年　　解答・解説

の窓になっている」といった表現や,「アメリカの景観を変えて,国民に肉体的にも精神的にも様々な課題を与えてきた」という表現との関連で,(6)に入れるのはカがふさわしい。

解 答

(1)－キ　　(2)－ウ　　(3)－ア　　(4)－エ　　(5)－イ　　(6)－カ

2 (A)　1999 年以来 4 年連続の会話文空所補充。

全訳 （便宜上 A を女性, B を男性のように訳をつけてある）

A：今度の休みはどんな計画を立ててるの？

B：やりたいことがいっぱいあるんだけど,たぶんほとんどバイトで過ごさなきゃいけないだろうな。

A：私も。ねえ,休みが 1 ヵ月あってお金も十分に持ってたら,どうする？ あなたの理想的な休暇って何かな？

B：こんなことがしたいな。(1)＿＿＿＿＿＿＿＿＿＿＿＿＿＿＿＿＿＿＿＿＿＿。

A：私はそんなこと絶対にしたくないわ！

B：なぜだい？

A：もし私がそんなことをしたら,(2)＿＿＿＿＿＿＿＿＿＿＿＿＿＿＿＿＿＿＿＿。

考え方

＜語数について＞

「それぞれ 10 ～ 20 語程度」とあるから,基本的には 10 語台だが,20 語を多少超えても構わない,ということ。10 語未満は減点対象になる。

＜内容のポイント＞

会話文は話の流れを的確にとらえる必要がある。文脈をおさえて,空所にどのような内容を盛り込むべきなのかを正しく判断すること。空所の前の部分だけを読んで判断するのではなく,その後空所に対してどのような受け方がなされているかも考慮に入れなければならない。

答案に盛り込まれていなければならない内容は以下の通り。

(1)「休みが 1 ヵ月あってお金も十分に持っていた場合に B がやりたいこと」

(2)「A が(1)のようなことを絶対にやりたくないと思っている理由」

空所(1)(2)は内容的に対立していなければならない。したがって,(1)で書くことを決める際には,必ず反論できるような内容にしないと(2)で困ることになる。そこがこの問題のむずかしい所である。

— 405 —

2002 年　　解答・解説

＜答案作成＞

　解答例に沿って答案の展開を眺めることにする。なお，空所(1)(2)とも「仮想状況」であるから，仮定法を使って英文を書かなければならない。正しく仮定法が使えているかどうかが大きな得点ポイントになる。

［解答例 1 ］

(1)　「日本一周旅行をする」→「一度も行ったことがない所がたくさんあるから」

(2)　「戻ってきたとき疲れ果ててしまって，家でゴロゴロする以外一切やりたくなくなってしまうだろう」

　(1)にはやりたいことの「理由」も付加した。ちなみに「一度も行ったことがない所がたくさんある」のは「事実」だから，この部分は直説法。

［解答例 2 ］

(1)　「フロリダに行って，浜辺で甲羅干しをしたり海で泳いだりする」

(2)　「日焼けしすぎてやけどをしてしまう」＋「泳げない」→「フロリダに行くのは時間とお金の無駄遣いになる」

　「泳げない」のは「事実」だから直説法を使う。ちなみに，「健康的な」日焼けは "a suntan" と言う。

［解答例 3 ］

(1)　「イタリアに行って，各地域で最高の料理を食べまわる」

(2)　「帰って来なくなる」→「イタリア料理が世界で一番好きだから」

　(2)だが，Ａもイタリアが好きなのだから，一見すると対立していないように思えるかもしれない。しかし「大好きだからこそ行きたくない」という論理である。

解 答 例

［解答例 1 ］

(1)　I'd travel around Japan.　There are a lot of places I've never been to.

(14 words)

(2)　I'd be tired out when I came back and wouldn't want to do anything but lie around at home.　(19 words)

［解答例 2 ］

(1)　I'd go to Florida and sunbathe on the beach and swim in the ocean.

(14 words)

(2)　I'd get a sunburn.　Moreover, I can't swim.　Going there would be a waste of time and money.　(18 words)

－ 406 －

2002 年　　解答・解説

［解答例3］

(1)　I'd like to go to Italy and travel around eating the best food in each region. (16 words)

(2)　I probably would never return. I love Italian food more than anything else in the world. (16 words)

---

2 **(B)**　2001 年に引き続き「日本文英語要約」である。

【考え方】

＜語数について＞

「40 ～ 50 語」とあるから，この範囲で収まっていなければならない。

＜内容のポイント＞

書かなければならないことは以下の4つ。

①　A先生の主張＝「能力別クラス編成に賛成」

②　①の根拠＝「生徒一人一人の能力に応じて指導ができるから」

③　B先生の主張＝「能力別クラス編成に反対」

④　③の根拠＝「民主主義の原則に反するものであり，差別である」

　問題文には「2人の主張とその根拠を明確に伝えるような形で」とあるが，この2人の意見の対立を示すことが重要である。したがって，①→②→③→④の順，つまり，まずA先生だけをまとめ，次にB先生をまとめる形で答案を展開するべき。①→③→②→④では，A先生とB先生を行ったり来たりすることになり，大変わかりにくいものとなる。

　ちなみに，A先生の発言中「本校には…」から「…中途半端になってしまいますからね」までは，要するに「生徒一人一人の能力に応じない大雑把な指導しかできない」という意味で，単に②の逆を述べただけであるから不要である。最後の「生徒主体の授業運営をする」だが，これを具体的に言えば「生徒一人一人の能力に応じたきめ細かい指導」ということだから，やはり不要。B先生だが，「だって…やさしくなるわけでしょう？」を一言で言い表したものが「差別」であるから，不要である。最後の「成績自体は…どうします？」の部分だが，自分の反対意見に説得力を持たせるために引き合いに出した具体例にすぎないので，これも不要。

＜答案作成＞

　ここでは①～④をどのような英語にすればよいかについて解説する。

①　「A先生は能力別クラス編成に賛成」

— 407 —

2002年　　解答・解説

☆　「A先生」は Ms. A であって *Mr.* A ではない（したがって，あとで代名詞で受ける場合は he でなく she）。問題文に与えられているにもかかわらず間違える答案が多いので注意しよう。

☆　「…に賛成する」は agree with ... / be for ... など。ただ，agree with の場合はその後に見解や行動を表す名詞が続く。a ranking system というのは 1 つの「システム」であるから，「システムを導入することに賛成」という内容にする必要がある。さらに，本問ではこのシステムを導入してはという「提案」だから，agree with the idea of introducing a ranking system とする。

②　「生徒一人一人の能力に応じて指導ができる」

☆　「一人一人」という感覚は "each ＋単数形" で表すのが最も簡単。

☆　「応じて」という日本語にとらわれると書けなくなる。「(生徒一人一人) に適した指導」と考えて，suited / suitable / appropriate などの形容詞を使うのがよいだろう。

☆　「指導」だが，ここでは教師が生徒に行う「指導」だから，「授業」「教授」ということ。したがって，instruction という名詞や teach という動詞を使って工夫する。ちなみに，本問では「能力別クラス編成の導入」が決まったわけではなく，導入したとしたらどのようになるかを話し合っている段階である。したがって「仮想状況」と考えて仮定法で書くのがよい。

※　［解答例 3］は内容を大胆に翻訳した英語で書き表しているので，書き方がかなり異なっている。また，「能力別クラス編成とはどのようなものか」という一般論として解釈しているため，全体的に直説法を使っている。

③　「B 先生は能力別クラス編成に反対」

☆　①と逆で，「B 先生」は Mr. B であって *Ms.* A ではない（したがって，あとで代名詞で受ける場合は he）。

☆　「…に反対する」は be against ... / be opposed to ... など。

④　「民主主義の原則に反するものであり，差別である」

☆　「民主主義の原則に反する」は直訳すると "be against the principles of democracy" だが，単に undemocratic という形容詞を使う手もある。

☆　「差別である」は，動詞ならば "discriminate against O"，形容詞なら discriminatory を使う。

— 408 —

2002 年　　解答・解説

解答例

［解答例1］
　　Ms. A agrees with the idea of introducing a ranking system. She
believes she would be able to teach her classes in a way that was suited
to each student. Mr. B disagrees with her. He thinks a ranking system
would be against the principles of democracy, and discriminatory.

(49 words)

［解答例2］
　　Ms. A is for a ranking system because she thinks that it would allow
her to give each student appropriate and effective instruction. On the
other hand, Mr. B is against one because he believes ranking students as
superior or inferior would be undemocratic and discriminatory.

(46 words)

［解答例3］
　　Ms. A thinks ranking systems are a good idea because they take into
account the fact that students with different levels of ability have different
needs. Mr. B thinks they are bad because they discriminate against some
students, and not discriminating against people is a basic principle of
democracy. (49 words)

4　(A)　全訳　思考と行動は2つの異なるものであると考えられる傾向にあるが，
必ずしもそうではないと示唆している研究者もいる。ジグソーパズルを考えてみよう。
そのようなパズルへの取り組み方として一番可能性が低いのは，断片をじっくり見て
から，思考だけによってそれが特定の場所にはまるかどうかを判断しようとすること
であろう。しかし，我々が実際に行っていることは，大まかに当たりをつけ，その後
その断片を実際にあててみて，それがはまるかどうかを確かめる，といった複合的な
やり方なのである。我々は一般的に，断片の詳細な形を十分に心に描いて，そのよう
なはめ込み作業を行う前にその断片がはまるかどうかを確信したりすることはない。
さらに，はまりそうな断片を，はめてみようとする前であっても実際に回転させてみ
ることもあるが，それはその断片がはまるかどうかを推測するという精神的作業を単
純化するためである。このように，ジグソーパズルの完成には複雑で反復的な動きが
関わっており，その中では「純粋思考」が行動へとつながり，今度はその行動が「純

－　409　－

<u>2002年　　解答・解説</u>

粋思考」に直面する問題を変化させたり単純化したりするのである。これはおそらく，思考と行動が必ずしも別々に機能しているわけではないことを示す最も単純な例だろう。

(考え方)

(2)　正解は **let**。let alone は必ず否定文で用いるのが決まりで，"not A, let alone B" という形でＡＢを比較し，「Ｂばかりでなく A も…ない」「A ではない。ましてＢでもない」と和訳する。本文はこれらの条件を一切満たしていないので誤り。let を取り除けば，"by thinking alone" で「思考だけで」（この alone は only の意味合い）という意味になり，要領を得る。

(3)　正解は **itself**。itself に続く which は関係代名詞と考えられるが，we make 以下は完全な英文となっているため，which 自身が節中で働く役割がない。itself を取り除いて in which とすれば，先行詞は a mixed method だから，関係代名詞でつなぐ前は "in the mixed method we make a rough guess" だったことがわかり，「その複合的方法において我々は大まかな当たりをつける」という意味になって要領を得る。

(5)　正解は **even**。even if は「条件を表す副詞節」なので，その後に続く is going to が問題になる。be going to が「心づもり」を表現する場合はともかく，ここでは「予測」である。「予測」の意味の be going to が「時・条件を表す副詞節」の節中で使われることはない。even を取り除いた if は「…かどうか」という意味で名詞節として働くこともある。even の前にある know for certain と合わせて「それがはまるかどうかを確実に知る」という内容になれば，文法的にも内容的にも問題はない（if 節が know の目的語）。

(6)　正解は **as**。"as ＋形容詞＋名詞" という形は英語として誤りである（数量詞 many / much / few / little は例外）。as を取り除けば，rotate possible pieces（可能性のある断片を回転させる）となり，文法的にも内容的にも問題はない。

(9)　正解は **to**。face（…に直面する）は他動詞であるから "face O" で，前置詞を必要としない。

解答

(2)− let	(3)− itself	(5)− even	(6)− as	(9)− to

4　(B)　(全訳)　私は一体どうやってその晩を乗り切ろうかと思いを巡らせていた。土曜日だった。土曜日の夜のことで，私は祖母と２人で置き去りにされたのだ。

— 410 —

<u>2002 年　　解答・解説</u>

　他の人たち（私の母親と姉）は，２人ともデートに出掛けていなくなってしまって
いた。当然ながら，もし最初に逃げ出せることができていたなら，私だって出掛けて
いただろう。そうすれば，あの老女が晩に必ずやるたくさんの決まりごとを耐え忍ん
で，彼女のことを気にしていなければならないということはなかっただろう。こっそ
りと立ち去って，母と姉にああだこうだと言わせておいただろう。母と姉が互いに言
い争うのではなくて，それぞれが別々に夜の外出の準備をしつつ，祖母との長期戦を
繰り広げながら言い争うように仕向けて。２人のうちどちらか１人が負けるだろうか
ら，敗れたほうが家に残ることになるだろう。土曜日の夜，すなわち，丸々１週間の
うちのただ一度のお楽しみの一夜に（まぁ，正確に言えば，お楽しみが得られる可能
性が多少はあったということだが）憤り不満を募らせながら，家に残ることになるだ
ろう。(1)<u>実際に希望が少しでも叶うなんてことはまずなかったけれど，少なくとも</u>
<u>外出するという行為は，一つの可能性をもたらすものであり，その可能性はそれを得</u>
<u>るために戦う価値のあるものだったのだ。</u>

　「どこに出かけるつもりなのよ？」　私の祖母は，46 歳で 15 年間未亡人の自分の娘
に問い詰めたものだ。

　「外出するのよ」という母の返事は冷静であり，(2)<u>母は決然たる表情をしていただ</u>
<u>ろうし，私が想像するに彼女は 16 歳のときにもそうであり，いつでもそうだったの</u>
<u>だろう。</u>

考え方　(1)　1．**There was hardly ever any real fulfillment of hopes**「実際
に希望が少しでも叶うなんてことはまずなかった」　hardly any ... で「…はほとんど
ない」の意。（例）There are *hardly any* stores nearby.（近くに店がほとんどない）
ever は「否定の強め」だが，あえて訳出する必要はない。real fulfillment of hopes
は really fulfill hopes（希望を実際に実現する；実際に希望が叶う）が名詞化された
もの。

　2．**but at least the act of going out brought with it a possibility**「しかし，
少なくとも外出するという行為は，一つの可能性をもたらすものであった」　the act
(S) ... brought (V) ... a possibility (O) が文の骨格。bring や take という動詞は，
しばしば with ... を伴って用いられるが，通常はあえてそれを訳出する必要はない。
（例）Take your umbrella *with you*.（傘を持っていきなさい）　The next time you
come, bring him *with you*!（今度来る時は彼を連れてきなさい）　問題文の it は主語
の the act of going out を受けている。of は「同格」を示し，「出かける<u>という</u>行為」
の意になる。

　3．**and that was something to fight for**「そしてそれは，そのために戦う価

－ 411 －

値のあるものだった」 that は possibility を受ける代名詞。to fight for は直前の something を修飾する形容詞用法の不定詞。「そのために戦うべきもの，戦ってでも手に入れるべきもの」といった訳出も可能。

（2）　1．**she would look determined**「母は決然たる表情をしていたものだ」would は「過去の習慣」を表す。determined は形容詞で「決然とした；意志の強い」の意。

　2．**as I imagine ...**「私が…と想像するように」　接続詞の as のまとめる副詞節は would look を修飾している。imagine の後ろに，後続のＳＶ ... を名詞節にまとめる接続詞の that が省略されている。副詞節がやや長いので，「全訳」のように，「私が想像するに，…」と前から訳し下してもよい。

　3．**she had done at sixteen and always would do**「16歳のときにもそうであり，その後もいつでもそうだった」　she had done = she had *looked determined* で，always would do = always would *look determined* であることに注意。and は had done ... と ... would do をつないでいる。この would は「過去から見た未来」を示し，「それから先の人生も常に（死ぬまで）決然とした表情をしていた」ことを示している。

解 答

---

(1)　実際に希望が少しでも叶うなんてことはまずなかったけれど，少なくとも外出するという行為は，一つの可能性をもたらすものであり，その可能性はそれを得るために戦う価値のあるものだったのだ。

(2)　母は決然たる表情をしていただろうし，私が想像するに彼女は16歳のときにもそうであり，いつでもそうだったのだろう。

---

5 【全訳】「神が世界に関してサイコロを振っているなどと私は決して信じない」とアインシュタインが語ったのは有名である。彼が一般相対性理論と宇宙について正しかったかどうかは別にして，この発言が，人々が日常生活でしているゲームに当てはまらないことは確かである。人生はチェスではなくバックギャモンゲームであって，サイコロが事あるごとに振られるのである。だから，予測を立てるのは難しい。しかし，少しでも何らかの規則性がある世界では，過去の情報に基づく判断は，無作為になされる判断よりもすぐれているものである。それはこれまで常に真実であったので，動物たち，とりわけ人間は，蓋然性（がいぜんせい）についての鋭敏な直感を発達させてきたと我々は予想するのだろう。

　しかし，人々は蓋然性について非論理的な判断をしていると思えることがよくある。

— 412 —

2002年　　解答・解説

その悪名高き一例が，「ギャンブラーの誤謬」である。「誤謬」とは，真であると広く信じられている誤った考えのことである。ギャンブラーの誤謬に陥っている場合とは，投げたコインが落ちて出た面が，まるでコインに記憶があって公平でありたいという願望があるかのように，例えば，立て続けに3回同じであれば，次回はもう一方の面が出る可能性が高くなるはずだと考える場合である。恥ずかしい話だが，今でも覚えているのは，自分が10代の頃家族で休暇を過ごしていた時のある出来事である。数日間も雨にたたられたからそろそろよい天気になるだろうと父が言った。私は，それは誤りだと指摘し，ギャンブラーの誤謬だと父を非難した。しかし，辛抱強い父が正しく，知ったかぶりのその息子が間違っていたのであった。雨をもたらす寒冷前線は，1日の終わりに地球から取り除かれて翌朝新しい前線と入れ替わるというものではない。雲には一定の平均的な大きさ，速度，方向が必ずあるものであって，一週間曇りが続いたことで，その雲の終わりが迫っており太陽が再び現れようとしていることが実際に予測できるとしても，今の私なら驚きはしないだろう。それはちょうど，通過中の列車のうち5両目よりも10両目の方が，最終車両の通過が迫っていることをより強く示唆するのと同様なのである。

多くの出来事はそのように動いている。出来事には特有の履歴があり，時の経過とともにそれらが起こる可能性が変化するのである。賢い観察者ならばギャンブラーの誤謬を犯して次に生じる出来事をこれまでの履歴から予想しようとするのが当然だ。例外が一つある。それはそれまで起こった事柄と無関係に出来事を生じさせるように設計された装置である。そんなことをするのはどういった装置だろうか。我々はそうした装置のことをギャンブルマシンと呼んでいる。それは規則性から予想を立てるのが好きな観察者を打ち負かすために存在する。不規則性は至る所に存在するのだから我々が規則性を好むのは賢くないのだとすれば，ギャンブルマシンは簡単に作れるし，ギャンブラーを打ち負かすのも簡単なはずだ。実際には，ルーレット盤やスロットマシン，そしてサイコロでさえ，不規則な結果を生み出すためには，極めて入念に高精度で作らなければならない。

したがって，カジノを除くどんな世界でも，ギャンブラーの誤謬が誤謬であることはめったにない。実際，我々の直感的な予想はギャンブルの装置に関して外れるからといって当てにならないと考えるのは合理的ではない。ギャンブルの装置は，定義上，我々の直感的な予想を打ち負かすよう仕組まれた，人工的に作り出された機械なのである。それはまるで，その形のせいで手錠から手を外しにくいという理由から，我々の手のデザインがひどいものだと考えるようなものなのだ。

— 413 —

2002年　　解答・解説

[考え方]

(1)　正解は**イ**。空所を含む文の冒頭の As a result（結果として）という表現から，直前の文 (Life is not ...) から判断すると，そこでは人生が毎回サイコロを振るバックギャモンというゲームに喩えられていることから，空所に predictions を入れれば「結果として，予想が立てにくい」という文脈に合った意味となる。ア，ウ，エを入れると，それぞれ make progress（進歩する），make random turns（不規則に旋回する），make probable moves（ありそうな動きをする）という表現を構成するが，いずれも文脈に合わない。

(2)　正解は**ア**。空所(2)を含む文は「しかし，（　2　）何らかの規則性がある世界では，過去の情報に基づく判定は，無作為になされる判定よりもすぐれているものである」という意味。文頭に But があることから，ここまでの記述と対比的な意味を有しているはずである。よって，空所に all を入れれば「ともかくも規則性のある世界」という意味となり，予想を立てにくいサイコロゲームに喩えられている Life と対比的な内容となる。any ... at all は肯定文では「…を少しでも」といった意味になる点に注意。

イ，ウ，エを入れると，それぞれ at large（逃亡中で；全体として），at length（詳細に），at most（せいぜい）という表現を構成するが，いずれも文脈に合わない。

(3)　正解は**イ**。直前の文 (But in a ...) で「規則性のある世界では過去の出来事を踏まえて予想を立てるのが賢明だ」といった内容が述べられており，そのあとで「そのことは常に真実であってきたのであり，そのため我々は動物たち，特に人間は…を発達させてきたと予想する」と続いている。この文脈を踏まえると，intuitions about probability とは「過去の経験→未来の予想」という趣旨に沿った内容であると推測できるが，この内容に合致しているのはイのみである。

ア，ウ，エは，いずれも後半部分が「未来を予想する」という意味になっておらず誤り。ちなみに，ここでは intuition に対応する訳語「直感」がすべての選択肢に共通であり，問(11)の和訳箇所の intuitive「直感的な」のヒントになっていることにも注意。

(4)　正解は**ア**。直前の部分 (when a tossed ... the next time) で「コインのトスで3回連続して同じ面が出ると，次は反対の面が出やすくなる」といった趣旨が述べられていることから，空所にアの be fair を入れれば as if 以下の部分が「まるでコインに記憶力があり公平でありたがっているかのように」という意味となり，文脈に沿った内容となる。

イの cheat us（我々を騙す），ウの amuse us（我々を喜ばす），エの be repetitive（反復的である）は，いずれも文脈に合わない。

— 414 —

2002 年　　解答・解説

(5)　正解は**ウ**。空所(5)を含む文は「（　5　）私は自分が 10 代の頃家族で休暇を過ごした時のある出来事を覚えている」という意味。続く第 2 段落第 5 文 (My father mentioned ...) から同段落第 7 文 (But long-suffering Dad ...) にかけて，幼い頃の筆者が，ギャンブラーの誤謬を犯していると言って父を誤って非難してしまった「ある出来事」が語られている。そのような自分の不名誉なエピソードが回想されていることを考えると，to my shame（恥ずかしいことに）という表現がもっともよく文脈に合う。よって，正解は**ウ**。

アの in pride（誇らしげに），イの in despair（絶望して），エの to my surprise（驚いたことに）は，いずれも文脈に合わず，不適切。

(6)　正解は**イ**「**いい天気になる可能性が高い**」。空所(6)を含む文は「数日間も雨を耐え忍んだのだから（　6　）と父が言った」という意味。続く第 2 段落第 6 文 (I corrected him ...) で「私は，それは誤りだと指摘し，ギャンブラーの誤謬だと父を非難した」と述べられていることから，父の発言内容は，一見すると「ギャンブラーの誤謬」（コインのトスで同じ面が続いたあとには反対の面が出やすくなる）と似たような意味内容を持ったものだと推測できる。そうした視点から見た場合，空所にイを入れると，父の発言は「雨が数日続いたのだから，次には天気が晴れる可能性が高くなる」といった論理となり，これがギャンブラーの誤謬と似たような意味構造となる。

アの「しかし晴れるのを願うことしかできない」，ウの「悪天候は続く可能性が高い」，エの「しかし雨がいつ止むのかわからなかった」は，いずれも文脈に合わず，不適切。

(7)　正解は**ウ**。空所(7)を含む just as ...という副詞節は「通過中の列車のうち 5 両目よりも（　7　）両目のほうが，最終車両の通過が迫っていることをより強く示唆するのとちょうど同様に」という意味で，雲の動きから天気の変化を予想できることを列車の走行に喩えたもの。5 両目よりも強く最終車両の接近を示唆するのだから，5 両目よりあとの車両のはずである。よって，正解は**ウ**の「10 番目の」となる。

アの first やイの fourth は，5 両目より前なので不適切。エの final は，「最終車両それ自体がその接近を示唆する」という意味になり，不自然である。

(8)　正解は**エ**。空所(8)を含む文は「多くの出来事はそのように（　8　）する？」という意味。この文は，直前の第 2 段落第 8 文 (Cold fronts, which ...) から同段落最終文 (A cloud must ...) で述べられている寒冷前線の具体例を受けて，「ある種の出来事は，そういう風に生じるのだ」と，発生の仕組みが一般化可能であることを指摘しようとする文である。その仕組みの具体的な内容は，続く第 3 段落第 2 文 (They have a ...) で「それらには特有の履歴があり，時の経過とともに起こる可能性

— 415 —

<u>2002 年　　解答・解説</u>

が変化する」と説明されているのだが，空所(8)を含む文それ自体は「多くの出来事はそういう生じ方をするのだ」と漠然とした一般論を述べるための文である。よって，エの work（機能する）が最も文脈に沿った表現である。

アの change（変化する）は，出来事それ自体が変化するという意味になり，不適切。変化するのはある時点で出来事が生じる確率であって，出来事それ自体が変化するわけではない。イの follow（続いて生じる）は，follow という語に「何らかの出来事のあとに，あるいは結果として，生じる」という意味が含まれており，不適切。筆者はここで，ある<u>一つ</u>の出来事の生じ方の話をしているのであって，ある出来事と他の出来事との間の関係性を論じようとしているのではない。follow という語を用いると，必然的に「他の出来事に続いてある出来事が生じる」という出来事間の関係性が含意されてしまい，ここで筆者が論じようとしていることからずれてしまう。ウの look（…に見える）は，文脈に合わず，不適切。

(9)　正解は **so [thus]**。空所(9)を含む文は「賢い観察者ならばギャンブラーの誤謬を犯して，（　9　）のその履歴からある出来事が次にどうなるかを予測しようとするはずだ」という意味。直前の第3段落第2文 (They have a ...) で「それら（＝多くの出来事）には特有の履歴があり，時の経過とともに起こる可能性が変化する」と述べられている。これはつまり，現実の世界においては，過去の状態がある出来事が生じる確率に影響を及ぼすことが多い，ということである。それゆえ，「賢い観察者」は，過去の状態を考慮に入れて未来を予測しようとするはずだ，ということになる。こうした文脈を考えると，空所に so [thus] を入れて so far [thus far]（これまでのところ）という表現になるようにすれば，predict the next occurrence of an event from its history so far [thus far]（これまでのその履歴から，ある出来事の次の発生を予測する）といった内容となり，文脈に合った適切な意味となる。

(10)　正解は**ア**。空所(10)を含む文は「それら（＝ギャンブルマシン）の存在理由は，（　10　）変えるのが好きな観察者を打ち負かすことだ」という意味。まずここでの「観察者」とは，第3段落第3文 (A clever observer ...) にある「賢明な観察者」を言い換えたものであるが，それは，**過去の出来事の履歴を踏まえて次に起こることを予測**する観察者のことである。また，ギャンブルマシンは第3段落第4文 (There is one ...) にあるように「それまで起こった事柄と無関係に出来事を生じさせるように設計された装置」であり，**過去の出来事に基づく予測が通用しない**ものである。これらを考え合わせて，空所にアを入れると「規則性を予測に変えるのが好きな観察者」という意味になり，「規則性」とは**過去において出来事が生じたパターン**を意味する表現と解せることから，文脈に合った適切な文意となる。よって，正解はア。

— 416 —

2002 年　　解答・解説

イ，ウ，エは，いずれも文脈に合わず，不適切。

⑾　正解は「**我々の直感に基づく予測を，ギャンブルの装置に対してはうまく機能しないからといって，当てにならないとみなすのは合理的ではない**」。文全体は，calling (S) is (V) unreasonable (C) という構造。call (V) our intuitive predictions (O) unreliable (C) で「我々の直感に基づく予測を当てにならないとみなす」という意味で，calling は動名詞主語。because they fail with gambling devices は（is unreasonable ではなくて）call ... unreliable を修飾する副詞節で，they は our intuitive predictions を指している。gambling devices とは第3段落最終文で述べられていた roulette wheels や slot machines などを意味している。

⑿　正解は**ウ**。空所⑿を含む文は「ギャンブルの装置は，定義上，（　12　）するように仕組まれた，人工的に発明された機械なのである」という意味。ここでの a gambling device とは，第3段落第4文 (There is one ...) から同段落第7文 (Their reason for ...) で描写されている gambling machine と同じものであるが，その「存在理由」は，過去の出来事の規則性に基づいて未来を予測するという我々人間の特性，すなわち，第1段落最終文 (That has always ...) で述べられている人間が進化させてきた蓋然性に関する直感を，打ち負かすことだと言われている。よって，空所にウを入れれば「我々の直感に基づく予測を打ち負かすように仕組まれた…機械」が「ギャンブルの装置」ということになり，文脈に合った適切な文意となる。よって，正解はウ。

アの「観察された規則性に従うように」，イの「ギャンブラーの要求を満たすように」，エの「自然界の規則性を我々に念押しするように」は，いずれも文脈に合わず不適切。

解 答

(1)—イ	(2)—ア	(3)—イ	(4)—ア	(5)—ウ	(6)—イ
(7)—ウ	(8)—エ	(9)　so [thus]	⑽—ア		

⑾　我々の直感に基づく予測を，ギャンブルの装置に対してはうまく機能しないからといって，当てにならないとみなすのは合理的ではない。

⑿—ウ

— 417 —

解答・解説

1 (A) **全訳** 先日たまたま初めて気がついたのだが，私が使っている電動歯ブラシは色が白で，柄には握りやすいように縦に青いゴムの筋が2本伸びていた。その電源を入れたり切ったりするボタンも，同じ青色のゴムでできていた。ブラシ自体にもつりあいのとれた青い部分まであって，ブラシの持ち手の底部にも色のついたゴムのリングがあった。これは私がかつて想像したことがないほどに実に周到に考え抜かれたデザインであった。これと同じことは，私が使っている使い捨てのプラスチック製カミソリについても言えた。それは優雅に湾曲していて，頭部が仕事をしようとしきりに身を乗り出しているように思えた。その歯ブラシもカミソリも，もし台座に乗っていたら，十分彫刻作品として成立したであろう。これらが仮に芸術作品として提示されていたら，物を超えている何かを，形がそれ自体の生命を得て永続的価値を生み出すという意味でより深い何かを，私は見て取ったであろう。トマス・カーライルはその著書『サーターリザータス（衣装哲学）』でこう述べた。「正しく見れば，どんな平凡な物も無意味ではない。物はすべて窓として在るのであり，それを通じて哲学の目は，無限そのものを覗き込むのである」

考え方

◇解答字数が30〜40字しかないので，解答は基本的に1文でまとめることになる。最終文に焦点があるのは明らかだが，これをそのまま訳すのではなく，前半の例に対応する言葉が出せたかどうかがポイントである。

◇前半第1〜第7文 (Had they been ...) までの「歯ブラシ」や「カミソリ」は，言うまでもなく「例」に相当する。これらを受ける言葉が最終文の "meanest object"（この mean は「卑しい→劣った；つまらない；平凡な」の意味）であり，この部分自体は「どんなに平凡な物でも無意味ではない」という意味である。歯ブラシやカミソリを一般化する言葉としては「平凡な物」が妥当であろう。

◇最終文冒頭の Rightly viewed「正しく見れば」は無視できない。第6文 (If either my ...) および第7文の「台座に乗っていたら；仮に芸術作品として提示されていたら」という内容が対応しているからである。普段何気なく目にしている物も「見せ方が変われば」芸術作品になる，というわけである。また，最終文の "the philosophic eye" がこれを受ける言葉になっている。

◇第7文の「形がそれ自体の生命を得て永続的価値を生み出す」の "enduring

— 420 —

2001年　　解答・解説

values" の部分が，最終文のカーライルの言葉にある Infinitude（無限）に対応している。

◇以上のことから，要約には以下の３点が含まれていればよいと思われる。

1．平凡な物〈も無意味ではない〉；どんなに些細な物〈でも意味はある〉

（この「無意味ではない；意味はある」とはどういうことかを明確にしたのがポイント２と３であるから，これらの表現は必須ではない）

2．正しい見方をすれば；正しく見れば；見方を変えれば

3．永続的価値（不変の価値；無限の価値）が見える。

解答例

［解答例１］　平凡な物でも無意味ではなく，正しく見れば不変の価値が見えてくる。(32字)

［解答例２］　どんなに些細な物でも，正しい見方をすれば，無限の価値を持つことがわかる。(36字)

1　(B)　全訳　(1)　成功の見込みがほとんどないのに闘う孤高の真理の探求者。これが「科学者」の従来像である。ガリレオを考えてみればよい。彼は独力で，なかなか秘密を明かそうとしない物質世界における物体の落下法則を発見し，望遠鏡を改良し，教会の怒りに対抗せざるをえなかったのだが，科学の真理に対する彼の献身的努力によって歴史は変わったのである。

(2)

(3)

(4)

(5)　この英雄モデルが，少々あまりにも性急に捨てられつつあると私は思う。個人個人が行政や大企業と対決して根深い国策を変更させることができるのと全く同様に，個々の科学者が科学上の確立した偏見に対峙して科学の進路を変更することもできるのだ。

(6)

— 421 —

2001 年　　解答・解説

(7)

(8)

(9)　したがって，成功の見込みがほとんどないのに闘う孤高の科学者が勝利し得るのである。パーディとフーパーはガリレオの現代版と見ることができる。しかし，この場合，教会は誰ということになるのであろうか。それは宗教の体制ではなくて，科学の体制である。自分の専門の研究をしている個々の科学者に関する限り，教会に取って代わったのは，科学の硬直した独断的な制度，つまり，大がかりな実験所，学術研究機構，政府の省庁なのである。

(10)

ア　もしかしたら，真の教訓は，あらゆる類の制度は不都合な真実を抑圧する傾向をもつということかもしれない。そして，真理で武装している孤高の科学者は，それでもなお，強大な力を発揮し得るのである。

イ　しかし，今日では，大発見が個々の科学者によってなされることはまれである。今日の科学の大部分は共同科学であって，個々の問題に大勢の科学者集団が取り組む巨大な実験設備を必要としている。

ウ　気の毒なことだ。パーディには，法律上必要とされる殺虫剤が原因であるという彼独自の説があったが，これは科学の体制には受け入れられなかった。10 年間にわたる孤独な研究によって，遂に，BSE と過剰な金属元素マンガンとの関連が明らかとなったが，この関係は最近になってケンブリッジの研究チームが追認するところとなった。

エ　そして，驚くにはあたらないことだが，科学にかかわる大半の哲学者や社会学者は，この英雄モデルを捨ててしまった。科学的真理の個々の探求者は，独りで研究していても，すい星の 1 つや 2 つはたまには発見できるかもしれないが，大体において，科学それ自体に対して貢献することはほとんどない，と言われている。

オ　一方，アイザック・ニュートンの『プリンキピア・マテマティカ』は，17 世紀の科学革命の頂点，体系的で秩序立った経験科学の偉大な出現と，一般には考えられている。しかし，生理学や天文学では偉大な成功がニュートンに先んじていたのである。

カ　もちろん，このロマンチックな図式には重大な問題がある。ガリレオは私たちが

2001 年　　解答・解説

考えるほど無邪気ではなかったし，彼の観察は厳密に科学的と言えるほどのものではないことが明らかになっている。しかしガリレオは，英雄である個々の科学者が独力で取り組んで重大な発見をするという，科学の英雄モデルを実際に与えてくれている。

キ　はるかな過去を振り返らなくても，この英雄モデルが機能している別の実例は見つかる。最近では，HIV はチンパンジーのウィルスが原因だとする説を否定しているエイズ研究者エドワード・フーパーがいる。代わりに彼が示しているのは，アフリカのエイズの大半の症例は，チャットと呼ばれる試験的経口ポリオワクチンが使われているのと同じ地域から発生しているということである。

ク　マーク・パーディは，どのようにしてこれがなされるかの実例を提示している。パーディは有機農家で，BSE（いわゆる狂牛病）の原因についての公認の説に疑いを抱いていた。彼は，自分の飼育している牛が，羊や牛の脳を粉末にしたものを含む「固形飼料」に全く触れたことがないのに，BSE に感染したことに注目した。パーディの詳細な記録を入手して点検することは可能であったのだが，一介の農夫に誰が耳を貸そうとしたであろうか。

[考え方]

◇空所(2)(3)(4)は，第1段落と第5段落の「挟み撃ち」で絞る。

第1段落で「孤独な科学者」としてガリレオが紹介され，第5段落で「英雄モデルが，あまりにも性急に捨てられつつあると思う」という筆者の視点が提示されているので，最初の3つの空所には，「ガリレオ以後，科学の英雄モデルが捨てられつつある」という話が入るはずである。これに該当する選択肢が，イ，エ，カの3つになる。

カにはガリレオが登場しており，this romantic picture が第1段落のガリレオ像を受ければ，文意もスムーズにつながる。さらに Of course .... But ～「もちろん…だ。しかし～」という「譲歩→逆接」の展開を用いて，「ガリレオは孤高の英雄モデルを提供している」という内容も記されているので，空所(2)にはカがふさわしい。

この後にイを置けば，however（しかしながら）が機能し，「今日では大発見が個々の科学者によってなされることはまれで，今日の科学の大部分は共同科学である」という内容が正しくつながることになる。

そして，エをこのブロックの最後に置けば，then（そして；それゆえ）が機能し，「哲学者や社会学者が英雄モデルを捨ててしまったのも驚くにはあたらない」という内容が正しくつながり，さらにエの "have given up the heroic model" と第5段落

― 423 ―

<u>2001 年　　解答・解説</u>

の "the heroic model is being abandoned" との密着感も生まれる。以上より，(2)
カ，(3)**イ**，(4)**エ**となる。

◇空所(6)(7)(8)は，第5段落と第9段落の「挟み撃ち」で絞る。

　　第5段落で「個々の科学者が単独で科学上の偏見に対峙して科学の流れを変える
ことができる」とあり，第9段落で So（したがって；だから）に続いて「孤高の
科学者が勝利し得る」とあるので，「1人の科学者が大きな改革をもたらした」とい
う意味の具体的な話がこのブロックには入るはずである。また，第9段落第2文
に Purdey と Hooper という人名があり，この両名がこのブロックで登場していな
ければならないことになる。以上より，このブロックに入る選択肢はウ，キ，クの
3つに絞られる。

　　固有名詞を持ち出す時は，最初はフルネームを提示して，その後はファミリーネー
ムのみにしたり頭文字を使って簡略化したりするのが通例である。そこで Purdey
の表記に着目すると，クは Mark Purdy でウは Purdey となっているので，ク→
ウの順になるはずである。また，このブロックの最初にクを入れれば，クの "how
this can be done" が第5段落最終文の so 以下を受けることになり，クの最後の「一
介の農夫に誰が耳を貸そうとしたであろうか→誰も一介の農夫の話に耳を貸さな
かった」とウの「殺虫剤が原因であるという科学の体制には受け入れられない自説
を持っていた」という内容が，Worse（さらに酷い）によってつながることにもなる。
さらに，キでは another example として Edward Hooper の事例が紹介されてい
るので，キはこのブロックの最後がふさわしい。以上より，(6)**ク**，(7)**ウ**，(8)**キ**となる。

◇最後の空所(10)は，第9段落との関連で決まる。

　　第9段落で述べられた「では現代において教会は誰ということになるのであろう
か。それは科学の硬直した独断的な制度である」という内容に続くものとして，ま
た，結語としてふさわしいのは，「真の教訓は，あらゆる制度は不都合な真実を抑
圧するということかもしれない。それでもなお，真理で武装した科学者は強大な力
となり得る」という内容の**ア**である。

※選択肢オは，以上で述べた「科学者 vs 体制」の流れとは無関係な内容である。

解 答

(2)-カ	(3)-イ	(4)-エ	(6)-ク	(7)-ウ	(8)-キ	(10)-ア

2　(A)　「日本文英語要約」は東大で自由英作文が初めて登場した1991年にその
ひな形のようなものが出題された。本問はそれをパワーアップしたもので，この後

－ 424 －

2001 年　　解答・解説

2005 年を除いて 2007 年まで毎年出題が続く。与えられた日本文の中から問題文で問われている部分だけを抽出し，それを英語に直していくという作業だから，その抽出には日本語の読解力が求められる。また，抽出部分も逐語訳をするのではなく，内容を大づかみにして英語に直す必要がある。

[考え方]

＜語数について＞

　「50 ～ 60 語程度」とあるから，基本的には 50 語台だが，60 語を多少超えても構わない，ということ。50 語未満は減点対象となる。

＜内容のポイント＞

　書かなければならないことは以下の 4 つ。

① 「人間はいつの日か自分が死ぬと考えただけで怖い」

② 「人間は，自分の持ち時間が永遠でないことを恐れる」

③ 「動物も死を避けようとする」

④ 「動物は目の前に迫った死の危険を恐れるだけ」

　問題文には「死に対して人間の抱く恐怖が動物の場合とどのように異なると論じているか」とあるので，「人間→動物」の順に述べた方がよいと思うが，本文通り「動物→人間」の順にしても構わない。また，本文冒頭にある「死の恐怖を知るのは人間だけである」の部分は入れても入れなくてもよいだろう。

＜答案作成＞

　ここでは①～④をどのような英語にすればよいかについて解説する。

① 「人間はいつの日か自分が死ぬと考えただけで怖い」

☆ 「人間」だが，本問では「動物」と対比されているので，humans / human beings がよいだろう。people / we でも構わないと思うが，*man / mankind* を使うのはやめよう。これは女性差別になる。

☆ 「いつの日か自分が死ぬ」は直訳して "they will [are going to] die someday [some day / one day]" でよい。未来の表現は必要。

☆ 「…と考えただけで怖い」だが，「だけで」という意味合いは抜かしても大丈夫だろう。直訳は "they are frightened by the mere thought that S V" であるが，単に "they fear that S V" とするのも OK。

② 「人間は，自分の持ち時間が永遠でないことを恐れる」

☆ 「自分の持ち時間が永遠ではない」は直訳できない。「永遠に生きることはできない」と意訳して，"they can't live forever" という簡単な英語にするべきである。

☆ この部分は①を言い換えただけで内容的には同じだが，動物との違い（動物は

— 425 —

<u>2001 年　　解答・解説</u>

このようなことを考えない) を際立たせるため，答案には入れた方がよい。

※　①②のようなことを考える［知っている］から人間は死を恐れるのである。したがって，"Humans fear death because ① and ②"（どちらか一方を because 節の中に入れ，もう一方は独立した英文にしてもよい）という形でまとめるべき。

③　「動物も死を避けようとする」

④　「動物は目の前に迫った死の危険を恐れるだけ」

☆　この2つは独立した英文にしてもよいが，接続詞でつないで1つにまとめる方がよいだろう。中心テーマは「人間」なので，「動物」の方は軽く済ませたい。

☆　「死を避けようとする」は "try to avoid death"。これを「死を恐れる」(fear death) と解釈してもよいが，人間は「恐れ」，動物は単に「避けるだけ」という趣旨なので，違いを際立たせるには「避ける」とした方がよい。

☆　「目の前に迫った死の危険」だが，これは「目の前に生命の危険が迫ったとき」と考え，"their lives are being threatened" とするか，あるいはもっと簡単に "they are facing death" と処理する。「自分が殺されそうになったとき」と考えて，"they are about to be killed" などもよいだろう。この2つを両方書く場合だが，「生命の危険が迫る」とは具体的には「他の動物に襲われる」ということで，「殺される」のはその後である。したがって，「生命の危険が迫る」→「殺される」の順にすること。

<u>解</u><u>答</u><u>例</u>

［解答例1］

　　Humans fear death because they know that their lives can't go on forever. In other words, they are frightened by the mere thought that they will die someday. In contrast, animals just try to avoid death when their lives are being threatened and they know they might soon be killed.

(50 words)

［解答例2］

　　Humans fear death because they fear the very fact that they are going to die some day, that they can't live forever. Wild animals, on the other hand, fear death only when they are facing it, when they are about to be killed. So we can say that it is only humans that really know the fear of death. (59 words)

— 426 —

2001 年　解答・解説

［解答例 3］

　　Only humans have a fear of death.　While animals want to avoid death, that is simply a natural reaction.　They run away when another animal wants to kill them, but otherwise don't think about death.　But humans are afraid of their own deaths far in the future.　Just knowing they will die someday makes humans feel fear.　(57 words)

2 **(B)**　1999 年以来 3 年連続の会話文空所補充。

全訳　（便宜上 A を女性，B を男性のように訳をつけてある）

A：ねえ，20 世紀最高の発明あるいは発見って何だったと思う？

B：それは難しい質問だな。いっぱいあったからね。でも 1 つだけ挙げなきゃいけないのなら，(1)＿＿＿＿＿＿かな。

A：なぜそれなの？

B：だって(2)＿＿＿＿＿＿＿＿＿＿＿＿＿＿＿＿＿＿＿＿＿＿＿。

A：変に思うかもしれないけど，私の考えは正反対なの。それって最悪のものだったんじゃないかしら。だって(3)＿＿＿＿＿＿＿＿＿＿＿＿＿＿＿＿＿。

考え方

＜語数について＞

　(2)(3)は「それぞれ 10 ～ 20 語程度」とあるから，基本的には 10 語台だが，20 語を多少超えても構わない，ということ。10 語未満は減点対象になる。

＜内容のポイント＞

　会話文は話の流れを的確にとらえる必要がある。文脈をおさえて，空所にどのような内容を盛り込むべきなのかを正しく判断すること。空所の前の部分だけを読んで判断するのではなく，その後空所に対してどのような受け方がなされているかも考慮に入れなければならない。

　答案に盛り込まれていなければならない内容は以下の通り。

(1)　「B が 20 世紀最高の発明あるいは発見と考えているものを具体的に 1 つ挙げる」

(2)　「B が(1)を最高の発明あるいは発見と考えている理由」

(3)　「A が(1)を最悪の発明あるいは発見と考えている理由」

　空所(2)(3)は内容的に対立していなければならない。したがって，(1)を決める際には，必ず反論できるような内容にしないと(3)で困ることになる。そこがこの問題のむずかしい所である。

— 427 —

2001 年　　解答・解説

　ちなみに,「20 世紀」であることにはこだわるべきだが, 本問は 2001 年の問題だからこのような設問が成り立つのである。だが, この本を読んでいる現時点から考えると, 2001 年自体が相当昔であり, 21 世紀を生きる諸君が 20 世紀のものだと思っていて実は 19 世紀のもの (電話や自動車など) ということもあるだろう。ただ, 東大がそこまで採点基準の中に含めているとは思えない (これは英語の試験であって常識の試験ではない)。むろんできるかぎり 20 世紀のものを選ぶべきだが, うっかり 19 世紀のものになってしまっても減点はないだろう。

＜答案作成＞

　解答例に沿って答案の展開を眺めることにする。

［解答例 1］

(1)　「インターネット」

(2)　「世界中の人とコミュニケーションをとるのがずっと容易になった」

(3)　「対面式の会話を避ける人が増えて, 人間関係が損なわれている」

　(2)は「発明以来今まで」ということなので現在完了, (3)は現状を表しているので現在進行形を使う。

［解答例 2］

(1)　「核エネルギー」

(2)　「環境にやさしくて, 地球の限りある資源の一部を使わずに済んでいる」

(3)　「恐ろしい軍事兵器を作り出すことに利用され, 原発事故は人類の生命を危険にさらすものだ」

　(2)は「発明以来今まで」ということなので現在完了, (3)の前半もやはり「発明以来今まで」ということなので現在完了, 後半は「今まで」というより「日常」の脅威だから現在形。

［解答例 3］

(1)　「遺伝子工学」

(2)　「あらゆる病気の治癒につながりうる新しい方法を医学にもたらしている」

(3)　「恩恵を受けられるのは金持ちだけで, 不公平な社会を作り出す」

　(2)は現在完了。(3)だが, 遺伝子工学を利用した治療法はまだこれからという部分が大きいので, 未来の表現を用いた。

解　答　例

> ［解答例 1］
>
> (1)　the Internet

— 428 —

2001 年　　解答・解説

(2)　it has made it far easier for us to communicate with people all over the world (16 words)

(3)　more and more people are avoiding talking face-to-face, and personal relationships are suffering (13 words)

［解答例 2 ］

(1)　nuclear energy

(2)　it is very eco-friendly and has allowed us to avoid using some of the earth's limited natural resources (18 words)

(3)　it has been used to create terrible military weapons, and accidents at nuclear power plants are a threat to human life (21 words)

［解答例 3 ］

(1)　genetic engineering

(2)　it has introduced a whole new approach to medicine which may allow us to defeat all diseases (17 words)

(3)　it is only rich people who will really benefit from it, so it will create an unfair society (18 words)

4　(A)　**全訳**　哲学の進歩というものは存在せず，哲学自体はその歴史に他ならないと結論づける哲学者もいる。このような見解を提唱している哲学者は一人だけではなく，それは「歴史主義」と呼ばれている。哲学はその歴史のみで構成されているというこの見解は奇妙なものであるが，一見すばらしい論で擁護されてきている。だが，我々はそのような見解をとらざるを得ないということはないだろう。私は全く異なる哲学観をとるつもりである。たとえば，誰でもプラトンの『対話』の一部を読んだことがあるだろう。その中で，ソクラテスは質問をし，さまざまな回答を得る。これらの回答によって何が意味されているのか，ある言葉がなぜこのように，またあのように使われているのかを彼は問う。要するに，ソクラテスの哲学は，表現の意味を分析することで思考を明快にしようとしているのだ。

考え方

(1)　正解は **of**。数量詞の後に of をつけるのは，その後に「特定」の名詞が続いている場合である。本問では "philosophers"，つまり「不特定」の名詞なので，単に "Some philosophers" でよく，of は不要。

(3)　正解は **not**。"philosophy consists not only of its history" の部分は「哲学は

— 429 —

2001年　　解答・解説

歴史だけで成り立っているわけではない」という意味だが，(1)の文の最後に「哲学自体はその歴史に他ならない」とある。つまり，「哲学を構成するものは歴史しかない」ということだから，内容的に矛盾する。not を取り除けば矛盾はなくなる。

(4) 正解は **are**。ourselves のような再帰代名詞は主語になることはできない。つまり，"find (that) ourselves⟨S⟩ are⟨V⟩" という解釈は不可能ということ。are を取り除けば，"find＋O＋過去分詞" という第5文型が成り立つ。

(5) 正解は **in**。"take an entirely different" の部分だが，different は形容詞である。したがって，an を受ける名詞が存在しない。in を取り除けば，"take an entirely different view" となり，構文的に正しくなる。

(8) 正解は **it**。"what it was meant" の部分だが，mean は第3文型をとる動詞なので，it was meant の部分は完全な英文である（能動態は "S meant it"）。したがって，疑問代名詞 what の果たす役割がなくなってしまうので，構文的に誤りである。it を取り除けば，what は was の主語となってつじつまが合う。ちなみに，"what was meant by these answers" は "S meant what by these answers" の受動態（"mean A by B" で「BによってAを意味［意図］する」という意味の慣用句）。

解 答

(1)− of	(3)− not	(4)− are	(5)− in	(8)− it

4 (B) **全訳** 実のところ，西暦1000年には消毒剤の概念はまったく存在しなかった。ひとかけらの食べ物が皿から落ちた場合，同時代のある書き物には，それを拾い上げ，その上で十字を切り，よく塩を振って，それから食べること，という助言があった。十字の印とは，いうなれば西暦1000年における消毒剤だったのだ。すなわち，自分の食べ物を床に落とした人は，それを拾い上げて口に入れる場合，ある種の危険を冒しているということを知ってはいたが，自分の信仰を疑わなかったということだ。今日では，私たちは現代の薬を信じているが，(1)実際に現代の薬がどのように働くのかについて個人的な知識が豊富にあると言える者は私たちの中にはほとんどいない。(2)私たちはまた，非常に深刻な病気と闘う能力は，私たちが「前向きな気持ち」と呼ぶものによって影響を受けることがあるということも知っている。そしてこの「前向きな気持ち」は中世が「信仰」として経験したものだったのだ。

考え方 (1) 1. **few of us can claim much personal knowledge of ...**「…について個人的な知識が豊富にあると言える者は私たちの中にはほとんどいない」few の前にaが置かれていないので，few は「ほとんどいない，少ない」と否定的

— 430 —

2001 年　　解答・解説

に処理することが必要。claim はここでは「…の所有権を主張する」の意。よって claim knowledge で「自分は知識を持っていると主張する」の意になる。

　２．**how it actually works**「実際に現代の薬がどのようにどのように働くかということ」it は modern medicine を受けている。設問の指示より，「それ」と訳したものは不可。

　⑵　１．**We also know that ...**「私たちはまた…ということも知っている」

　２．**the ability to combat quite major illnesses can be affected by ...**「非常に［かなり］深刻な［重大な］病気と闘う能力は，…によって影響を受けることがある」to combat ... illnesses は that 節の主語である the ability を修飾する形容詞用法の不定詞。can be affected が the ability に対応する動詞。can は「可能性」を示す。

　３．what we call "a positive state of mind"「私たちが『前向きな気持ち』と呼ぶもの」「いわゆる『前向きな精神状態』」といった訳出も可能。We call X "a positive state of mind."（我々は X を「前向きな精神状態」と呼ぶ）→ what we call φ "a positive state of mind"（我々が「前向きな精神状態」と呼ぶもの）と考えればよい。

　４．— **what the Middle Ages experienced as "faith"**「中世が『信仰』として経験したもの」３．の what 節と同格で働いている名詞節。「私たちが『前向きな気持ち』と呼ぶもの，すなわち中世が『信仰』として経験したもの」のような訳出も不可能ではないが，前の what 節の内容を受ける「これは」のような訳語を加えて，「（そして）これは，中世が『信仰』として経験したものである」などと処理した方が日本語としては分かりやすい。

解答

> ⑴　実際に現代の薬がどのように働くのかについて個人的な知識が豊富にあると言える者は私たちの中にはほとんどいない。
>
> ⑵　私たちはまた，非常に深刻な病気と闘う能力は，私たちが「前向きな気持ち」と呼ぶものによって影響を受けることがあるということも知っている。そしてこの「前向きな気持ち」は中世が「信仰」として経験したものだったのだ。

5　【全訳】　彼女が彼に言った。「マックリーディ，誕生日には何をしたいの」彼女はいつも彼のことをマックリーディと呼んでいた。長年彼の妻をやってきたのだから，彼女は彼のことをジョンと呼び始めてもいいはずだと，もうお考えのことだろうが，彼女は決してそう呼ばなかった。彼の方は彼女をヒルダと呼んでいた。彼女は彼のことをマックリーディと呼んでいた。まるで他人のように，まるでテレビで見たことの

— 431 —

2001 年　　解答・解説

あるフットボール選手のように。

「子供たちは何が望みかな」と彼は言った。

彼女はタバコの火をつけた。この日曜日の妻のタバコが 20 本目なのか 30 本目なのか，彼は数えるのをとうにやめていた。

「子供たちはどうでもいいのよ，マックリーディ」と彼女は言った。「自分の誕生日でしょ」

「アイルランドに戻る」と彼は言った。「それが僕の望みだ。戻ってそれっきり帰らないんだ」

彼女はタバコの火を消した。またか，と彼は思った。あらゆることについて，彼女は絶えず，刻一刻と気が変わるのだった。「まともな答えが見つかったら」と彼女は言った，「どんなものか教えてちょうだい」

彼が庭に出て行くと，9 歳になった娘のケーティが独りで遊んでいた。ケーティとその庭に共通するところがあった。共に小さく，誰がどう頑張ったとしても絶対に美しくはならないように見えた。ケーティが父親似だったからだ。残念ながら。

いま二人はほったらかされた庭に一緒にいて，北ロンドンの 9 月の日差しがとても温かく彼らの上に降り注いでいた。そしてマックリーディは自分が必死になって可愛がろうとしている娘に向かって言った，「じゃあ，パパの誕生日には何をしようかな，ケーティ」

娘はこれみよがしに見た目のよい小さな人形たちで遊んでいた。彼女は人形の形の良い脚の部分を握っており，その金髪が旗のように揺らめいていた。「分からないわ」と彼女は言った。

彼がプラスチックの庭椅子に座ると，彼女は美少女たちを並べて置いた。「シンディとバービーが刺されそうなの」と彼女は不平を漏らした。

「誰が刺しそうなのかな」

「もちろん，あの草よ。切ってくれないかしら」

「いや，無理だよ」と彼は，ヒルダが何年か前に植えたバラを押しのけて，その草が猛烈に茂っているあたりを見ながら言った，「あのね，あの草は残してあるんだよ」

「どうして」

「スープ用さ。イラクサスープだよ，お前をきれいにするためのね」

彼女は真剣な顔つきで父を見た。9 年間，父の言うことすべてを信じてきた。いま彼女は断崖の端にいて，ほとんど今にも飛び立とうとしているところだった。

「きれいになる？」

「きっとなるさ。そのうち分かるよ」

— 432 —

<u>2001 年　　解答・解説</u>

　その日，しばらくして，息子のマイケルが帰って来ると，マックリーディは息子が自分の部屋に上がって行く前に呼び止めた。息子は 13 歳であった。

　「パパの誕生日にみんなで何をしようかって，ママが迷っていたよ。お前に何か考えでもあるなら…」

　マイケルは肩をすくめた。まるで，自分が手の届かない，征服不可能な存在であることがわかっているかのようだった。彼は未来なのであった。現在には何の注意も払う必要がないのであった。「いや」と彼は言った。「特に何も。そもそも何歳なの」

　「45 だ。もう 1 つ上かもしれない。覚えていないな」

　「よしてよ，パパ。誰だって自分の歳ぐらい覚えているよ」

　「でも，覚えてないんだ。アイルランドを出てからは。当時は分かっていたんだけど，ずいぶん前のことだものな」

　「じゃ，ママに聞いたら。ママなら分かるよ」

　マイケルは，階段を上がっていった。履いている臭い靴でじゅうたんをこすりながら。息子は何も考えていなかった。何も浮かばなかった。特に何も。

　そしてまたマックリーディは独りになった。

【考え方】

　⑴　正解はエ。空所⑴を含む文は「彼女は彼のことをマックリーディと呼んでいた，まるで（　1　）のように，まるでテレビで見たことのあるフットボール選手のように」という意味。第 1 段落第 4 文 (You would have ...) に，長年の夫婦であるにもかかわらず妻 Hilda は夫のことを John という名前では決して呼ばなかったとあり，その代わりに McCreedy という苗字で呼んでいたということである。よって，空所にエの「他人」を入れれば，文脈に合った適切な文意となる。

　アの brother，イの father，ウの master は，いずれも文脈に合わず，不適切。

　⑵　正解は「この日曜日の妻の 20 本目なのか 30 本目なのか，彼は数えるのをやめていた」。この文は，He didn't know whether that was her twentieth or thirtieth cigarette that Sunday, because he had stopped counting（それが，その日曜日で，彼女の 20 本目のタバコなのか 30 本目なのか彼にはわからなかった，なぜなら彼は数えるのをやめていたからだ）といった意味であるが，He didn't know whether that was, cigarette, because は書かれていない。

　⑶　正解はウ。空所⑶を含む文は「（　3　）そこに戻るんだ」という意味。第 3 段落最終文 ('When you've got ...) で「まともな答えが見つかったら教えてちょうだい」と妻が述べていることから，ここでのマックリーディの発言は「まともな答え」とは言えない内容のものだと推測できる。よって，空所にウの good を入れ，for

— 433 —

2001 年　　解答・解説

good（永久に）という慣用的な副詞句になるようにすれば「永久にそこに戻るんだ」といった文意となり、妻ヒルダは単に夫の誕生日のささやかなお祝いを意図しているだけであるのに対して、マックリーディは故郷のアイルランドへ完全に引き上げるという、妻らからすれば非現実的な願いを吐露してしまった形となり、文脈に沿った内容となる。

アは、for all ...の形で「…にもかかわらず」という意味で用いるが、all の後に何もない形ではふつう用いない。イとエについては、それぞれ leave [give up] ... for dead（…を死んだものとして見捨てる［諦める］）、take ... for granted（…を当然のものとみなす）という言い方はするが、for dead や for granted を単独の副詞句として用いるのは一般的でなく、文脈に合わず不適切。

(4)　正解はイ。下線部(4)は「あらゆることについて、彼女は絶えず、刻一刻と気が変わるのだった」という意味。まず選択肢の要点を確認すると、ア「夫の驚嘆」イ「夫のいらだち」ウ「妻の不満」エ「妻の困惑」となる。下線部(4)は、直前文に続いて夫の心の内面を描いている描出話法（心内表現）と考えられる（このことは直前文の typical と下線部の always のつながりでもわかる）。この段階でアかイに絞られる。次に、下線部ではしばしば否定的な感情を示す進行形が使われている。（例）You *are* always *asking* for money.（君は金をいつもせびってばかりいるね）　よって正解はイとなる。

(5)　正解はウ。空所(5)を含む文は「どちらも共に小さく、誰がどう頑張ったとしても絶対に美しくはならないように見えた、なぜならケーティは父親（　5　）からだ」という意味。この文の前半で、ケーティと庭の外見についてその共通点が語られていることから、空所にウの resembled「…に似ていた」を入れれば、ケーティが美しくならない理由として外見が父親似である点が指摘されている形となり、文脈に合った意味内容となる。よって、正解はウ。

アの「…を認識した」、イの「…を表した」、エの「…を尊敬していた」は、いずれも文脈に合わず、不適切。

(6)　正解は**「あの草は残してあるんだよ」**。下線部(6)は We are saving them が簡略化されたものと考えられる。them は第 7 段落第 4 文 (Those plants, of ...) にある Those plants を指している。save は「…をとっておく；…を残しておく」といった意味。

(7)　正解は**「父の言葉を疑う気持ち」**（10 字）。比喩表現を文脈から理解できるかどうかの設問。直前の第 8 段落第 2 文 (For nine years ...) には「9 年間、彼女は父の言うことすべてを信じてきた」とあり、過去においてはケーティが父の言うことを鵜呑みにしてきた事実が語られているが、続く下線部(7)は、そうした過去と対比す

— 434 —

<u>2001 年　　解答・解説</u>

る形で現在におけるケーティの父への姿勢が語られたものだと考えられる。したがって，「いま彼女は断崖の端にいて，ほとんど今にも飛び立とうとしているところだった」という言葉は，父の発言を鵜呑みにせず批判的に吟味しようとする意識がケーティの心の中で芽生え始めていることを比喩的に描写したものだと推測できる。よって，「父の言葉を疑う気持ち」「父の発言への不信感」などといった内容が正解となる。

(8)　正解は **see**。第 7 段落最終文 (Nettle soup – ...) で，マックリーディは娘ケーティに向かって，庭のイラクサを切らずにとってあるのは彼女をきれいにするスープを作るためだと述べている。対するケーティは，半信半疑ながらも，第 8 段落第 4 文で Will it (make me beautiful)? (それ（＝スープ）は私をきれいにしてくれるの？) と父に聞き返している。それに対するマックリーディの返答は Sure it will (make you beautiful) であり，空所(8)を含む文はその内容をさらに念押しするような意味合いの表現になると推測できる。それゆえ，空所に see を入れれば，wait and see（様子を見る：成り行きを見守る）といった意味の慣用表現となり，文脈に合った適切な流れとなる。

(9)　正解は「**彼は，現在に対して，何の注意を払う必要もなかった**」。present は直前の the future と対比されており，「現在」という意味の名詞。文章全体が誕生日の話だからといって，うっかり「贈物」などとしないこと。attention は名詞で，「注意：関心」という意味。

(10)　正解は **ウ**。直前の第 10 段落第 13 文 (Well, I don't ...) は，Well, I don't (remember my age) という意味であるが，この文に続くものとして，アの Especially，イの Ever，エの Not を空所に入れると，それぞれ「特にアイルランドを離れて以来は（覚えていない）」「アイルランドを離れて以来ずっと（覚えていない）」「アイルランドを離れて以来覚えていない」という意味となり，すべて適切な文意となる。他方で，ウについては，lately（最近は）という副詞を「…以来」という意味の since とともに用いるのは一般的ではなく，意味的にも不自然である。よって，正解はウとなる。

解答

---

(1)－エ

(2)　この日曜日の妻の 20 本目なのか 30 本目なのか，彼は数えるのをやめていた。

(3)－ウ　　　(4)－イ　　　(5)－ウ

(6)　あの草は残してあるんだよ。

(7)　父の言葉を疑う気持ち

－　435　－

2001 年　　解答・解説

⑻　see

⑼　彼は，現在に対して，何の注意を払う必要もなかった。

⑽ － ウ

解答・解説

1 (A) **全訳** 人間をとりわけ人間たらしめているものは何であろうか。言語の複雑さだろうか。問題解決の戦略だろうか。ショックを受けるかもしれないが，私の考えでは，ある非常に深い意味合いで，言語も人間の問題解決の一部の側面も，その複雑さの点では他の生物種の行動様式と全く変わりはないのである。複雑さそれ自体は争点とはならない。クモは複雑な巣を作り，ハチは蜜の供給源と質について複雑な情報を伝達する。アリは複雑なコロニーの中で交流しており，ビーバーは複雑なダムを築き，チンパンジーは問題解決の複雑な戦略を持っている。これらは人間が複雑な言語を使いこなしているのと全く変わらない。また，人間の問題解決能力もそれほど優れたものではない。人間の中にも，完璧に正常な人間としての知能を備えていながら，それでもやはり，チンパンジーが解けるような問題を解くことができない人がいる。しかしながら，人間の知力と人間以外の生き物の知力の間にはきわめて重大な違いが，人間を他のすべての生物種と区別する違いが１つある。クモは巣を作ってしまえばそれで終わりであるが，それと違って，人間の子供には（しかも，これは人間の子供だけであると私は主張したいのだが）自分自身が表現したものを認識対象とみなす潜在能力が備わっている。通常，人間の子供は，言語を手際よく使うようになるだけではなく，同時に幼い文法学者になる素質を備えてもいる。これに対して，クモもアリもビーバーも，おそらくはチンパンジーでさえも，自分自身の知識を分析する潜在能力は持っていないのである。

考え方

◇典型的な「問題解決型」の文章構成

　　この文章は「問題提起をして，それに答えようとする」という Problem Solving タイプの典型である。文章そのものをただ訳すのではないので，「ＸはＡである」が解答の基本フォーマットになる。ただし，本問ではもう１つの要素が加わってくる。

◇一般によくある考え方を否定し，筆者自身の論点を出すという典型的な構造

　　第 2 文 (The complexity of ...) と 第 3 文 (Our problem-solving ...) で "complexity of our language"（言語の複雑さ）と "problem-solving strategies"（問題解決の戦略→これは後で problem-solving skills と言いかえられている）が紹介されているが，これらは一般に「人間と他の動物を区別する特徴としてよく引き合いに出されるもの」であり，第4文 (You may be ...) でそれを否定しようとしてい

— 438 —

ることがわかる。具体的には，第5文 (Complexity as such ...) と第6文 (Spiders weave complex ...) で complexity of our language を否定し，第7文 (Nor are our ...) で problem-solving skills を否定している。このように「世の中によくある視点をまず提示し，それを否定したり，別の面を紹介する」という構成は，非常によくある文章構成の仕方である。

　よってここまでの解答のフォーマットは「XはY⑴でもY⑵でもなく…」という形になり，まとめると，「人間の独自性は言語の複雑さでも問題解決能力でもなく，」となる（これで26字）。「X」に該当する部分は「人間の人間らしさ；人間と他の動物の違い」などでも可である。

◇言いかえを利用して表現の意味を明確にする

　第8文 (There is, however, ...) の however で文章が方向転換し，筆者自身の考えに持ち込もうとしていることは明らかであろう。よって，解答全体のフォーマットは「XはY⑴でもY⑵でもなくZである」となるはずである。ただし，「Zをすぐには言わない」という書き方になっていることに注意。

◇第8文の「きわめて重要な違い」ではあまりにも意味が曖昧なので，これに続く内容を見てみる。すると第9文 (Unlike the spider, ...) に "the potential to take ... attention" という表現があるが，これは認知心理学で用いられるような専門性の高い表現である。さらに次の第10文 (Normally, human children ...) を見ると "the capacity to become little grammarians" とあるが，この「幼い文法学者になる」というのはもちろん比喩である。さらに最終文 (By contrast, spiders, ...) を見ると "the potential to analyze their own knowledge" という表現がある。つまり，以下のように「言いかえ」の連鎖がなされていることになるので，解答の「Z」の部分には最後の「自分自身の知識を分析する潜在能力」を使ってまとめておけばよい。

　〈第8文〉one extremely important difference（きわめて曖昧）→〈第9文〉the potential to take its own representations as objects of cognitive attention（きわめて専門的）→〈第10文〉the capacity to become little grammarians（比喩）→〈最終文〉the potential to analyze their own knowledge（平易な表現）

解 答 例

　　［解答例1］　人間の独自性は，言語の複雑さでも問題解決能力でもなく，自分の
　　　　　　　　知識を分析できる潜在能力にある。(46字)
　　［解答例2］　人間と他の動物の違いは，言語の複雑さや問題解決能力ではなく，
　　　　　　　　自分の知識を分析する潜在能力である。(48字)

<u>2000 年　　解答・解説</u>

1 **(B)** **[全訳]** (1) 科学技術は，私たちの生活を過去 150 年にわたって改善して
くれた。そして，適正な規制の枠組みがあれば，同様な働きを今後 150 年にわたっ
てしてくれる可能性は十分ある。科学的知識の増大によって，私たちは生命の危険の
一部を制御したり，その最悪の弊害の一部を除去したりできるようになった。とりわ
け，医学面での前進によって，非常に多くの疾病の脅威が減少するに至っている。

(2)

(3)

(4) このように科学の恩恵は甚大なものであり，しかもそれは，平均余命と医療の
分野においてにとどまらない。現在，私たちが直面している最も深刻な問題の 1 つは，
環境破壊である。工業化への突進は，天然資源への無分別な接近という結果になった。
しかし，前工業社会への回帰を欲するなら別だが，環境保護も科学を用いずには可能
とはならないであろう。

(5)

(6)

(7) 人間の幸福に対するこのような脅威に備えるには，効果的な規制システムを適
所に設けて，将来の科学の前進が安全で，倫理にかない，環境面で健全であることを
保証するようにしなければならない。科学の進歩の持つ意味とそれがもたらす可能性
のある帰結の情報開示は，行政機関においても科学界においても，絶対に不可欠である。

(8)

ア　単純な例を 1 つ挙げるならば，CFC（例えば冷蔵庫や噴霧器に使われているフ
　ロンガス）が大気の上層に放出されるとオゾン層を破壊し得るということを最初に
　示したのは，米国とドイツの化学者の研究であった。さらに，1980 年代には，英
　国の科学者たちが，成層圏のオゾン層が南極上空で一部消滅しているとの証拠を提
　示した。このような観察がなされたことや化学構造が分かっていたことが決定的な
　証拠となって，1987 年に CFC の使用削減に関するモントリオール議定書が調印
　される運びとなったのである。CFC に代わる冷凍の手段を開発する点でも，頼り
　となったのは科学であった。

— 440 —

<u>2000 年　　解答・解説</u>

イ　英国では現在健康は当然視されがちであるが，前工業時代においては幼少期における死がいかにありふれたものであったかを，そして，それがもはやそうではなくなっている理由が主として科学の進歩のおかげであることを銘記すべきである。歴史家 J. H. プラムがかつて述べたように，「正気な人なら誰でも，前時代に生まれていた方がよかったとは思わないでしょう。裕福な家庭に生まれ，極めてよい健康に恵まれ，自分の子供の大半が死んでも平然と甘受することができていただろうと確信が持てない限りは」ということなのである。

ウ　情報技術は，すでに情報の入手可能性と伝達速度にけた外れの影響を与えてきた。それによって文字通り世界は，いや，少なくとも先進世界は，縮小したのである。しかし，科学技術が進歩し，コンピューターがさらに廉価になり，その結果として世界のあらゆる地域でますます多くの人の手に届くものとなるにつれて，情報に対するこの新たな世界的接近手段は，絶大なる，そして場合によっては遺憾な結末をもたらすこととなろう。

エ　私は，科学上の変化を思慮もなく探究せよと主張しているのではない。それに対して思慮もなく反対するなと言っているのである。次世紀の私たちの生活は，ほとんどすべての科学分野で起こっている大変革によって，必然的に変わることとなろう。しかし，科学の枠組みの適切な規制があって初めて，科学の発達が私たち皆の幸福のために利用されることが保証されるであろう。進歩を拒否することはできないが，進歩を促進し，あらゆる国の人がその利益を享受できるようにそれを導いていくことはできる。

オ　したがって，医療と環境の両分野において，運輸，メディア，情報工学，食料のような他の分野同様，科学の進歩は私たちの生活の質を改善している。しかし，科学の前進について傲慢であってはならない。サリドマイドのような恐ろしい医療悲劇や大量破壊兵器の開発などは，進歩に逆らうものと位置づけなければならない。

カ　その結果，この 50 年にわたって私たちの生活の質と長さは，途方もなく向上した。世界全体で見れば，誕生時点の平均余命は 1950 〜 1955 年には 46.4 年だったが，1990 〜 1995 年には 64.4 年に伸びた。そして，同様に意義深いことだが，先進国地域と途上国地域の間の平均余命の差は，1950 〜 55 年には 26 年だったものが，1990 〜 1995 年には 12 年へと減少した。

【考え方】

◇空所(2)(3)は，第 1 段落と第 4 段落の「挟み撃ち」で絞る。

　　第 1 段落で「科学技術は生活の質を向上させた。とくに医学の発達によって疾病の脅威が減った」とあり，第 4 段落で「このように科学の恩恵は甚大なものだ」(thus

— 441 —

<u>2000 年　　解答・解説</u>

が前の内容を受けることに注意）とあり，さらにその直後に not only in the areas
of life expectancy and health care（平均余命と医療の分野においてにとどまらな
い）とあるので，空所⑵⑶には寿命の延びや医療面の向上の話が入るはずである
から，このブロックに入る選択肢はイとカに絞られる。

　ここでカの冒頭に The result has ... という表現があり，イの内容の「結果」と
して「人生の質が向上し平均余命が伸びた」とは思えないので，イ→カの順は不適
切である。逆にカを⑵に入れれば，第1段落最終文の結果として，具体的な年度
や数値が含まれるカの内容が成立するので⑵カ，⑶イが正しいと判断できる。そ
うすれば，「カの内容→ life expectancy」で「イの内容→ health care」となり，
第4段落の表現との対応が順序通り成立することにもなる。

◇空所⑸⑹は，第4段落と第7段落の「挟み撃ち」で絞る。

　第4段落で，平均余命と医療だけではなく，「環境に対する脅威」が引き合いに
出され，「科学なしでは環境保護もなしえない」という記述がある。そして第7段
落第1文に "such threats to human well-being"（人間の幸福に対するこのような
脅威）という表現がある。そこで，このブロックには「環境面に触れたもの」とし
てアとオが入ると考える。

　アの冒頭に "To take ..."（単純な例を挙げれば）とあるので，これを⑸に入れれ
ば，第4段落最終文の内容を具体的に展開したものとして成立する。

　オには "both health care and the environment" とあるので，オは「医療面と
環境面」両方の話を出した後に置くものとして⑹にふさわしいものとなる。さら
に，オの後半の But 以下の「しかし，科学の前進について傲慢であってはならない。
サリドマイドのような恐ろしい医療悲劇や大量破壊兵器の開発などは…」という内
容が，第7段落の "To guard against such threats" という表現につながることに
もなる。以上の点から⑸ア，⑹オとなる。

◇空所⑻は第7段落の内容で決める。

　第7段落には "effective systems of regulation" という表現があり，「このよう
な脅威に備えるには，効果的な規制システムを適所に設けて，将来の科学の前進が
安全で，倫理にかない，環境面で健全であることを保証するようにしなければな
らない」とある。エの However 以下の強調構文にある "existence of a properly
regulated scientific framework" という表現が，上で述べた第7段落の記述と関
連することになるので，空所⑻にはエがふさわしい。

※ウの「情報技術の話」は，全体の論旨とは無関係である。

－ 442 －

2000年　　解答・解説

解 答

(2)－カ　　(3)－イ　　(5)－ア　　(6)－オ　　(8)－エ

2 (A)「グラフ読み取り」は新傾向の問題で，与えられたグラフを元に会話文の空所を埋めるという形式。ちなみにグラフの出題はこれ以降は2003年のみ（このときは完全な自由英作文となっている）。

全訳 場面は日本のある中学校における社会科の授業である。先生が生徒に前頁のグラフを見せている。

　　先生：大きく異なる2つのグラフをとりあげ，それらの地域の状況はどのように異なっていますか教えて下さい。

　　ミヤコ：(1)＿＿＿＿＿においては(2)＿＿＿＿＿＿＿＿＿＿です。一方，(3)＿＿＿＿＿においては(4)＿＿＿＿＿＿＿＿＿＿です。

　　先生：今自分が8歳だということにしましょう。グラフに示された地域の一つに住んでいるとしたら，どのタイプの学校に通いたいですか？　またそれはなぜですか？

　　カズユキ：もし(5)＿＿＿＿＿に住んでいるとしたら，僕は(6)＿＿＿＿＿＿＿＿＿＿＿したいです。なぜなら(7)＿＿＿＿＿＿＿＿＿＿＿＿＿＿＿＿＿＿だからです。

考え方

＜語数について＞

　(2)(4)(6)は「以内」となっているから，文字通り「以内」に収めること。(7)は「15〜25語で」だから，当然この範囲内で書き，1語たりとも不足またはオーバーのないように。

＜内容のポイント＞

　(1)(3)→「大きく異なっている2つのグラフ」とは，アジアと北米である。ヨーロッパは3種の子供たちが均等なので，その2つのどちらとも「大きく異なる」とは言えない。したがって，**この(1)(3)にはアジアと北米を選ぶ**。順番はどちらが先でもよい。

　(2)(4)→はなはだしく違う点は①の「日本人学校のみに通う子供」または②の「日本語補習学校に通いつつ現地校またはインターナショナルスクールに通う子供」の数である。したがって，**この(2)(4)ではアジアと北米における①または②の数の違いを述べる**。順番は(1)(3)に合わせること。ちなみに，具体的な数値や％を引用するよりも，それを別の英語で言い表すことが望ましい。

　(5)(6)(7)→(5)(6)はどの地域でも，どのタイプの学校でも構わない。(7)でどのような

－ 443 －

<u>2000 年　　解答・解説</u>

ことを書くか次第である。したがって，⑺が書きやすい内容になるよう，⑸⑹を選ぶこと。

＜答案作成＞

　⑴～⑷は解答例を読めばわかると思うので，解説は省略する。⑺だが，一番簡単なのは「言語ネタ」だろう。日本人学校・現地校・インターナショナルスクールの選択次第で最も大きく変わるのは「言語習得」である。日本語・現地語・英語のどれを習得したいかで⑸⑹を決めればよい（インターナショナルスクールはさまざまな人種・国籍を持つ生徒が集まるところだから，授業で用いられる言語は通常英語である）。むろん教育内容や学校生活の過ごし方などに言及してもよいが，あくまでも「答案の書きやすさ」を基準に考えるべきである。

解 答 例

［解答例1］

⑴　Asia

⑵　over eighty percent of Japanese children go to full-time Japanese schools (11 words)

⑶　North America

⑷　there are very few who are enrolled only in full-time Japanese schools
(12 words)

⑸　Asia

⑹　go to a full-time Japanese school (6 words)

⑺　it would be far easier to make friends with people who speak the same language (15 words)

［解答例2］

⑴　Asia

⑵　almost no one attends local or international schools while going to a part-time Japanese school (15 words)

⑶　North America

⑷　more than half go to local or international schools and a part-time Japanese school (14 words)

⑸　Europe

⑹　attend both a local school and a part-time Japanese school (10 words)

— 444 —

2000 年　　解答・解説

(7) then I'd be fluent in the local language and at the same time be able to improve my Japanese ability (20 words)

［解答例3］

※(1)〜(4)は省略。

(5) North America

(6) be enrolled only in an international school (7 words)

(7) English is the global language and I'd be able to communicate with anybody in the world if I learned it (20 words)

2 (B)　手紙文の空所補充は 1996 年以来である。

【全訳】

編集者様：

　「クローン技術：もはや羊だけではない」という記事を大きな関心を持って読ませていただきました。私は政府が人間のクローンを作成する研究を支持する(1)［ア　べきである　イ　べきではない］と思います。なぜなら(2)＿＿＿＿＿＿＿＿＿＿。さらに(3)＿＿＿＿＿＿＿＿＿＿。

敬具
タロウ・ヤマシタ

【考え方】

＜語数について＞

　(2)(3)は「それぞれ5〜10語」とあるから，この範囲内で収まっていなければならない。

＜内容のポイント＞

　2つの空所には，「政府が人間のクローンを作成する研究を支持するべき［支持するべきではない］」理由を2つ書くことになる。だが，語数が何分にも少ないので，具体的に詳しく書こうとするとすぐにオーバーしてしまうから，簡単で大雑把な内容で構わない。

＜答案作成＞

　解答例に沿って答案の展開を眺めることにする。

［解答例1］

(1) 「するべき」

(2) 「科学における大躍進になる」

— 445 —

<u>2000 年　　解答・解説</u>

(3)　「医療にも使用可能である」

　人間のクローンを作成することはまだ現実味がないこととととらえて, 仮定法で書いた。

［解答例 2］

(1)　「するべき」

(2)　「いつの日かさまざまな病気の治療に役立つだろう」

(3)　「自分のクローンを作ってほしい」

　［解答例 1］とは逆に, 大いに可能性のあることととらえて直説法にした。このように,「仮想状況」としても「可能性のあること」としても構わないだろう。

［解答例 3］

(1)　「するべきではない」

(2)　「今の世界は人口過剰に苦しんでいる」

(3)　「研究費を貧しい人々の救済にあてるべきだ」

　(2)は「ただでさえ現在人口過剰に苦しんでいるのに, 人工的に人間を作ってどうする」という意味合い。(3)はクローン技術の研究には膨大な費用がかかることを前提にしている。

［解答例 4］

(1)　「するべきではない」

(2)　「不自然であるし, 恐ろしいことだと思う」

(3)　「人々が気づいている以上にずっと危険なことだ」

　(2)(3)ともに非常に漠然としていて具体性がないが,「5 ～ 10 語」という短い語数なのでこのようなものでもよいのである。

解 答 例

　［解答例 1］

　(1)　ア [should]

　(2)　it would be the biggest breakthrough in science　(8 words)

　(3)　the technology could also be used for medical treatments　(9 words)

　［解答例 2］

　(1)　ア [should]

　(2)　someday it will help us to cure many diseases　(9 words)

　(3)　I want to have a copy of myself made　(9 words)

　［解答例 3］

　(1)　イ [should not]

— 446 —

2000 年　　解答・解説

(2)　our world is now suffering from overpopulation　(7 words)

(3)　the money should be spent helping poor people　(8 words)

［解答例 4 ］

(1)　イ [should not]

(2)　I think it is unnatural and frightening　(7 words)

(3)　it is much more dangerous than people realize　(8 words)

---

4 (A)　**考え方**　(1)「その誤りについて君がどのように感じているかはわかるが，それは大した問題ではない」

　正解は**イ・ア (not *much* of *a* problem)**。"S be not much of a 名詞 "で「S は大した〈名詞〉ではない」という意味の慣用表現。

　(2)「ジョンが第一試合に遅刻してくるだろうから，10 人の選手で間に合わせるしかないだろう」

　正解は**エ・ア (have *to* make *do* with)**。"make do with 名詞 "で「〈名詞〉で間に合わせる」という意味の慣用句。

　(3)「彼の公の立場には変更がないが，実際彼は我々の意思決定過程には以前ほど関わっていない」

　正解は**オ・ウ (as *involved* as *before* in)**。"be involved in 名詞 "で「〈名詞〉に関わっている」という意味の慣用句。"〈isn't〉 involved in our decision-making processes"という並びには間違いなく，involved に同等比較の as ... as をつければよいことも明らかだが，before の置き場所が重要。内容的に「今」と「以前」の比較であろうから，as involved as before とし，in 以下はその後に続けるのが正しい。

　(4)「彼女は電話に出られない。仕事の真っ最中なので」

　正解は**ア・イ (right *in* the *middle* of)**。"in the middle of 名詞 "で「〈名詞〉の真ん中に」という意味の慣用句。本問では「名詞」の部分が "her work" であるから，「仕事の真っ最中」という意味合い。残った right だが，名詞の「右」「権利」，形容詞の「右の」「正しい」では内容的に要領を得ない。副詞の right には前置詞句を強調する働きがあり，置く場所は前置詞句の直前。したがって，"right in the middle of 〈her work〉"とするのが正解。

　(5)「君の言うことは意味を成してないよ。何がほしいわけ？」

　正解は**ア・ウ (what *is* it *that* you)**。" 疑問詞＋is it that"（疑問詞節の場合は " 疑問詞＋it is that"）という形になった場合，この it is [is it] that は強調構文である。

— 447 —

<u>2000 年　　解答・解説</u>

したがって，この 3 語を抜いて考えれば一目瞭然となる。本問の場合，通常の疑問文なら "What do you want?" でよいのだが，これを強調構文を使って表現すれば正解の形になる。

解答

(1) イ・ア	(2) エ・ア	(3) オ・ウ
(4) ア・イ	(5) ア・ウ	

4 (B) 【全訳】 偶然はあまりにも頻繁に私たちの味方をしてくれていた。私たちはその忠実さに満足し，その忠実さを過信するようになってしまっていた。だから，偶然が初めて私たちを裏切ることに決めた瞬間は，偶然が裏切るかもしれないと私たちがもっとも思いそうにない瞬間でもあったのだ。

【考え方】 1．**the moment ... was also the moment**「〈…の〉瞬間は瞬間でもあったのだ」 the moment (S) ... was (V) also the moment (C) が文の骨格。

2．**when it first chose to betray us**「偶然が初めて私たちを裏切ることに決めた〈瞬間〉」 when は関係副詞で，この部分は直前の the moment を修飾する形容詞節として働いている。it は「偶然」を受ける代名詞であり，題意より「それ」と訳したものは×。to betray us は chose の目的語として働く名詞用法の不定詞。

3．**when we were least likely to suspect that it might**「偶然が裏切るかもしれないと私たちがもっとも思いそうにない〈瞬間〉」 この when も直前の the moment を先行詞とする関係副詞。least likely to suspect は「考える可能性が最も低い」ことを示している。that は suspect の目的語になる名詞節（…ということ）をまとめる接続詞。it might は it might betray us から betray us が落ちたもの。it はここも「偶然」を受けている。

解答

偶然が初めて私たちを裏切ることに決めた瞬間は，偶然が裏切るかもしれないと私たちがもっとも思いそうにない瞬間でもあったのだ。

5 【全訳】 ある日学校から帰宅すると，台所に見知らぬ男がいた。コンロで何か作っていて，鍋の中をじっと見ていた。

「あなたは誰？　ここで何してるの？」と私は聞いた。父が死んでから 1 週経ったところだった。

— 448 —

2000年　　解答・解説

　その男は「しっ。今はダメ。ちょっと待って」と言った。男には強い外国訛りがあった。彼が集中していることは分かったので私は言った。「一体何を作っているの？」

　今度は男は私をちらっと見た。「ポレンタだよ」と言った。

　私はコンロのところまで行って鍋の中を覗いた。中身は黄色っぽくねばねばして，どろどろしたセモリナ粉であった。「まずそうね」と彼に言ってから，私は母を探しに行った。

　母は庭にいた。「ママ，台所に男の人がいるわよ。料理しているの。ポレンタを作っているんだって」

　「え，なに？　ポレンタ？」と母は言った。母では助けにならないかもしれないと私は思い始めた。父がここにいてくれたらと思った。「どういうものなのかはっきりは分からないわ」と母はあいまいに言った。

　「ポレンタなんかどうでもいいのよ，ママ。あの人誰なの？　うちの台所で何しているの？」「ああ」と母は叫んだ。母は薄い花模様のサマードレスを着ており，私は突然，母がとても痩せていることに気づいた。ママったら，と私は思った。あらゆることが私の上にのしかかってくるように思われ，私は思わず泣き出していた。「ねえ，泣かないでちょうだい」と母は言った。「大丈夫よ。あの人は新しい下宿人なの」母は私を抱きしめた。

　私は鼻をすすりながら涙をぬぐった。「下宿人？」

　「パパが亡くなったので」と母は説明した，「空き部屋の一つを貸さなくちゃいけないと思うのよ」母は向きなおって家の方へ歩き始めた。台所にその下宿人がいて動き回っているのが見えた。私は母の腕をとって，中に入るのを引き止めようとした。

　「じゃ，ここに住むことになるの？」と私は聞いた。「一緒に？　食事や何から何まで一緒にってこと？」

　「ここはもう彼の家なのよ」と母は言った。「くつろいでもらわなくちゃね」母は後から思いついたかのようにこう付け足した。「彼の名前はコンスタンチンというのよ。ロシア人よ」それから母は中に入っていった。

　私は一瞬立ち止まって母が言ったことを理解しようとした。ロシア人だって。エキゾチックで興味をひかれる響きがあったので，彼の不作法も許してやろうかという気になった。私は母が台所に入っていくのを見ていた。コンスタンチンというロシア人は，目を上げると微笑んで顔を輝かせた。「マリア！」彼が両腕を広げると，母は彼に近づいた。2人は両頬にキスをした。母は振り返って，私を手招きした。

　「私の娘よ」と母は言った。彼女の声には私の聞いたことのない調子があった。母は私に手を伸ばした。

— 449 —

2000年　　解答・解説

「ああ，アンナちゃんだね」とそのロシア人は言った。

私はびっくりした。私の名前がそんなにさらりと彼の口から出てくるなんて思ってもいなかったから。私は母を見た。何も伺い知ることはできなかった。そのロシア人は，両手を差し出すと言った。「コンスタンチンだよ。会えてとても嬉しいよ。君のことはずいぶん聞いているよ」

私たちは握手をした。どうして私の話をずいぶん聞いていたことがあるのか知りたかったけれど，聞き方が思いつかなかった。少なくとも，母がそこにいるのでは思いつかなかった。

そのロシア人は料理に戻った。うちの台所に慣れているみたいだった。セモリナのようなものの塊の上に塩とコショウを振りかけて，それから居間までそれを持っていった。なんとなく，母と私は彼についていった。みんなで肘掛け椅子に座ると，互いに顔を見合わせた。少しでも落ち着かない気持ちになっているのは私だけだと思った。

翌日の夜，遅くに帰宅すると，コンスタンチンと母は夕食を食べながら夢中で話をしていた。テーブルにはロウソクが何本かついていた。

「どういうこと？」と私は聞いた。

「ねえ，おなか空いたでしょう」と母は言った。「あなたにもとってあるわ。台所にあるから」

私は腹ぺこだった。「いらない」と私はふくれて言った。「大丈夫」

まだ早かったけれども，私は2階に行ってベッドに入った。

しばらくすると母が階段を上ってくる足音が聞こえた。部屋に入ると，母は私の上にかがみこんだ。私は目をつぶったまま，深く息をしていた。「アンナ」と母は言った。「アンナ，起きてる？」

私は黙っていた。

「起きているのはわかってるわよ」と母は言った。

少しの間があった。降参しかけたまさにそのとき，母がまた口を開いた。「パパは一度だってママのことを愛してくれたことはなかったの。こんなこと，あなたは知らなくてもよかったんだけど。パパはママのことを愛してくれなかったの」と母は言った。彼女は一語一語を恐ろしくはっきりと口にした。まるで私の脳裏に焼き付けようとするかのように。私は目をきつく閉じていた。ベッドの中で硬直したまま，私は母が部屋を出ていくのを待っていた。時がたてば何もかも乗り越えられるのかしらと思いながら。

2000年　　解答・解説

【考え方】

(1)　正解は**イ**。下線部(1)は「彼女はあまり助けにならないかもしれないと私は思い始めた」という意味。suspect は「〈明確な根拠はないが〉…だろうと思う」という意味。学校から帰宅した筆者は台所で見知らぬ男性を発見し，第1段落第3文 ('Who are you ...) で「誰なのか？」と尋ねているが，男性自身から明確な返答をもらえなかったために，母親に男性のことを伝えようと第5段落最終文 ('That looks disgusting ...) で母親を探し始めている。そして第6段落第1文 (I found her ...) で母親を見つけた筆者は男性のことを伝えるが，母親は男性が台所にいること自体には動じず，その代わりに「『え，なに？　ポレンタ？』」と料理の内容に関して反応しているのである。つまり，見知らぬ男性が家の中にいることについて筆者は母親も自分と同様に驚くはずだと予想していたにもかかわらず，そうした反応の代わりに，(筆者から見れば) まことに見当違いな料理への反応をしている，ということになる。こうした文脈を辿るならば，下線部(1)に込められた意味として最も妥当なのは，イの「母親は驚いていないのではないかという懸念を表わしている」である。

アとエについては，前後の文脈に照らし合わせると，下線部(1)の内容から大きく外れており，誤り。ウについては，下線部(1)の時点で筆者は母親にまだ質問はしていないので，「自分の質問を理解できない」という内容は不適切である。

(2)　正解は**エ**の**「もう耐えられないと私は突然感じた」**。下線部(2)の pile は「〈困難な物事が〉積み重なる」といった意味の自動詞で，下線部全体は「あらゆることが私の上にのしかかってくるように思えた」といった意味で，痩せた母の姿を見て，父なき今，自分にあらゆることがのしかかってくると感じたことを表している。こうした内容に最も近いのはエで，直訳すると「事態は耐え忍ぶにはあまりにもひどすぎると私は突然感じた」といった意味になる。

things は「事態：状況」といった意味の名詞。too much は「〈行うには，あるいは耐えるには〉あまりに困難な」といった意味の慣用的な表現。

アの「私はまだ深い落胆のうちにあった」は，still という語があることから「父親の死に対する落胆から立ち直れていない」といった意味に解釈できるが，下線部(2)にある Everything (あらゆること) には，前後の文脈を考えると，父親の死に加えて，さらなる何らかの困難な事柄が含意されていると考えられる。その意味で，父親の死による落胆のみに言及しているアは不適切である。イの「彼女がいかに無防備か私は突然理解した」，ウの「母の腕は私の肩の上で重たく感じられた」は，いずれも文脈に合わず不適切。

(3)　正解は**エ**。空所(3)を含む文は「『パパが亡くなったので，あいにく空き部屋の

— 451 —

2000年　解答・解説

一つを（　3　）しなければならない』と母は説明した」という意味。let には「〈家や部屋など〉を賃貸しする」という用法があり，let を空所(3)に入れると，父が亡くなり経済的に苦しい状態になることから，その埋め合わせとして部屋を間貸しして収入の足しにする，といった自然な内容となる。よって，正解はエ。

アの close（…を閉める），イの decorate（…を飾りつける），ウの keep（…を維持する）は，いずれも文脈に合わず，不適切。

(4)　正解はイ。空所(4)を含む文は「あの人は私たちと一緒に食事や（　4　）をするってこと？」という意味。第7段落第7文 (Is he living ...) で，筆者は「じゃあ，あの人はここに住むってことなの？」と問いを発しており，I mean（つまり）という表現の後でその内容を言い換えたのが空所(4)を含む文である。... and everything は「…やその他あらゆること」といった意味の慣用表現で，空所にこの表現を入れれば，「一緒に暮らすこと＝すべてを共にすること」という言い換えを筆者が行った形となり，文脈に沿った自然な繋がりとなる。よって，正解はイ。

他の選択肢は，いずれも文脈に合わず，不適切。

(5)　正解はイ。空所(5)を含む文は「私はこの情報を（　5　）するために一瞬立ちどまった」という意味。「この情報」とは，直前の第7段落第12文 (She added, as ...) から第13文 (He's Russian ...) で述べられた「彼の名前はコンスタンチンよ。彼はロシア人なの」という母の言葉を指しているが，空所(5)を含む文に続く第8段落第2文 (A Russian ...) や第3文 (This sounded exotic ...) を見ると，「この情報」に関して筆者が思いを巡らしている様子が描かれている。以上の文脈を考え合わせると，空所(5)に副詞 in を入れて take in（…を頭の中に取り込む；…を理解する）という意味の熟語になるようにすれば，文脈に沿った自然な内容となる。よって，正解はイ。

他の選択肢を入れた場合，take down，take out，take over という句動詞ができる。これらの表現は文脈次第で様々な意味を帯びるが，いずれの意味もこの文脈には合わず，不適切。

(6)　正解はエの「**彼女の話し方には聞き覚えのない何かがあった**」。下線部(6)は「彼女の声には，私には特定できない調子があった」という意味。note は「調子」といった意味の名詞で，関係代名詞 that の先行詞になっている。また，ここでの identify は recognize とほぼ同義で，「〈すでに見聞きして知っているもの〉がそれだとわかる」という意味。よって，この文の実質的な意味は「彼女の口調は私には聞き覚えのないものだった」といった内容になる。こうした内容に最も近いのはエである。

アの「彼女が何故そんなに静かに話すのかが私にはわからなかった」，イの「どの

— 452 —

2000 年　　解答・解説

ようにして彼女が口調を変えたのか私にはわからなかった」，ウの「彼女の声の抑揚のせいで理解するのが難しかった」は，いずれも下線部(6)の意味内容としては不適切である。

(7)　正解はウの**「彼女の表情からは何もわからなかった」**。下線部(7)は「彼女は何も表に漏らしていなかった」という意味。give away は慣用表現で，「〈秘密や感情など〉を表に漏らす」という意味。この内容に最も近いのはウとなる。tell ... from ～は「～から…がわかる」という意味の慣用的な表現で，この tell は know とほぼ同義。

アの「彼女は自分の手を差し出してはいなかった」，イの「家からは何もなくなっていなかった」，エの「状況は完全に彼女の管理下にあった」は，いずれも下線部(7)の内容および文脈に合わず，不適切である。

(8)　正解は**「しかし（私には），少なくとも母がそこに居ては，尋ね方が思いつかなかった」**。think of ...で「…を思いつく」という意味。at least は「少なくとも」という慣用的な副詞句。at least の直後は could not think of a way of asking with my mother there という意味であるが，could と think of a way of asking は直前部分との共通要素として省略されている。with は付帯状況を表す用法で「母がそこにいる状態では」という意味。「しかし（私には），尋ね方が思いつかなかった，少なくとも母がそこに居ては思いつかなかった」などと訳し下す形も可能である。

(9)　正解はエ。空所(9)を含む文は「自分は（　9　）の気持ちをわずかでも感じている唯一の者だと思った」という意味。空所(9)を含む文の直前の数文では，ロシア人男性が作った料理を母と三人で居間のテーブルに着いて食べるに至った経緯が描かれているが，この第 11 段落に至るまでの文脈において，筆者はそもそもこのロシア人男性（および彼と母親との関係）について不信感を抱いていたのであり，そうした不信感が消えないまま三人で夕食を共にすることになったわけである。こうした文脈を踏まえると，空所(9)に unease（不安；当惑）を入れれば自然な繋がりが形成される。よって，正解はエ。

アの「方向」，イの「ユーモア」，ウの「目的」は，いずれも文脈に合わず，不適切。

(10)　正解は**ア**の「私は泣き出す寸前だった」。下線部の was on the point of －ing は，すべての選択肢に共通の was about to 不定詞と同義で「いまにも…しそうで」という意味（東大では，選択肢に共通部分があって読解の手助けとなる場合がしばしばある）。

下線部までの流れを確認すれば，「私」が 2 階に上がってベッドに入り，目をつぶっていると母親がやってきて「起きているのはわかっているのよ」と言う。少しして「私」が「今にも give in（降参）しかかった」ときが下線部である。すると，イ「話しかける」，

— 453 —

2000年　　解答・解説

ウ「目を開ける」，エ「自分が起きていることを認める」は，不自然ではないが，ア「泣く」は流れとして大げさで不自然であり，題意の「ふさわしくないもの」と言える。

　⑾　正解は**エ**。空所⑾を含む文は「ベッドの中で硬直したまま，時がたてば自分は何もかもを（　11　）するのだろうかと思いながら，私は母が部屋を出ていくのを待っていた」という意味。直前の第17段落第3文 (She said, 'Your ...) から同段落第5文 (He did not ...) を見ると，「お父さんは私を愛していなかった」というショッキングな内容が母によって告白されている。これは，筆者にとって，今後長期に渡って脳裏から離れないようなトラウマ的な経験であると言える。それゆえ，空所に前置詞 over を入れて get over ...（…を克服する；…を乗り越える）といった句動詞になる形にすれば，たったいま自分が何年も心の傷として残りそうな酷い経験をしたことに自覚的な筆者が，それでもいつの日か，時が経過してゆく中で，自分はそうした出来事を克服することになるのだろうかと思いを巡らしている形となり，文脈に合った適切な内容となる。よって，正解はエ。

　アからウの選択肢については，それぞれ get at，get in，get on という句動詞を形成するが，いずれも文脈に合った適切な意味内容にはならず，不適切である。

解答

---

(1)－イ　　　(2)－エ　　　(3)－エ　　　(4)－イ　　　(5)－イ

(6)－エ　　　(7)－ウ

(8)　しかし（私には），少なくとも母がそこに居ては，尋ね方が思いつかなかった。

(9)－エ　　　(10)－ア　　　(11)－エ

解答・解説

1 **(A)** **[全訳]** 20世紀後半，オーラル・ヒストリーは，多くの国で実践されている現代歴史学に多大な影響を及ぼしてきた。社会的政治的エリートたちへの面接取材によって既存の記録資料の幅は拡がったが，オーラル・ヒストリーを最も特徴づける貢献は，他の方法では「歴史に埋もれて」いたかもしれない人々の集団の経験と視点を歴史の記録に含めているということである。そのような人々は，かつては社会評論家によって，あるいは公式文書の中で，記録されることもあったかもしれないが，その生の声が保存されることはまれにしかなく，それもたいていは個人の書簡や自伝的記述の形で残っているくらいである。オーラル・ヒストリーの面接取材を通じて，労働者階級の男女や，中でも文化的マイノリティーに属する人々が，自らの経験を歴史記録に加え，彼ら自身の歴史解釈を提示していった。さらに，面接取材によって，他の資料源では抜け落ちてしまいがちな歴史的経験の特定の側面，たとえば個人の人間関係や家事，家庭生活などが記録され，それらは実体験の主観的あるいは個人的意味とも波長が合うものとなった。

　オーラル・ヒストリーは他の点でも，大いなる歴史学の仕事に挑んできた。オーラル・ヒストリーの歴史家は面接記録の作成に必要な技術を修得しなければならず，さらに，記憶に基づく話をより良く理解するために，社会学，人類学，心理学，言語学といった歴史以外の様々な学問分野からも学ばなければならなかった。最も重要なのは，オーラル・ヒストリーが歴史家と情報提供者との活発な人間関係に基づいており，そのために歴史学の実践はいくつかの点で様相を変えることになるという点である。語り手は過去を回想するだけではなく，その過去を自分なりに解釈したものを口にする。それゆえ，参加型のオーラル・ヒストリーの企画においては，取材される側が情報源であると同時に歴史家にもなりうるのである。さらに，それを実践する者にとっては，オーラル・ヒストリーは単なる歴史構築にとどまらないものになっている。ある企画においては，過去を回想し再解釈する過程を通じて，個人や社会集団に力を与えることが主たる目的になっていた。

［考え方］

　おおざっぱに言えば，第1段落にはオーラル・ヒストリーの「特徴」に該当する部分が多く，第2段落には「影響」に該当する部分が多いが，特にこの2つを明確に区別してまとめる必要はない。因果関係，逆接関係，対照関係，条件論理などを基に構

— 456 —

1999 年　　解答・解説

成された文章ではないので,該当する要素を順番に取り上げてまとめる「情報列挙型」
の要約である。

〈第1段落〉

　第1文 (In the second ...) は,全体の統括をする Topic Sentence (主題文) であり,
要約に含める必要はない。

１．誰を対象としたか

　第2文 (While interviews with ...) の the most distinctive contribution of oral
history is that ... の that 以下が最初のポイントで,これを「他の方法では歴史に埋
もれていた人の経験と視点を記録した」とまとめればよい。第3文 (Although such
people ...) と第4文 (Through oral history ...) は第2文の補強であることに注意。
"their own voices have only rarely been preserved" や "working-class men and
women ... cultural minorities" といった表現があるので,「歴史に埋もれていた人」
という部分を「〈労働者など〉文化的には少数派に属する人；無名の人」といった表
現でまとめてもよい。

２．何を記録したか

　第5文 (Moreover, interviews have ...) で,今度は「何を記録したか」に言及さ
れている。「生活の私的側面が記録された」という点が解答に含まれていればよい。

〈第2段落〉

１．しなければならないことが増えた

　第2文 (Oral historians have ...) に "Oral historians have had to develop ... and
to learn ... memory" とあるので,オーラル・ヒストリーに携わる者は「記録作成に
必要な技術を習得し,理解のために他の諸分野の勉強をしなければならない」という
点に触れておけばよいだろう。

２．被取材者が自らの解釈を主張する歴史家になり得る

　第3文 (Most significantly, oral ...) と第4文 (The narrator not ...) には,「オー
ラル・ヒストリーは歴史家と情報源の人間関係に基づくゆえ,歴史の実践の形を変え
うる」「語り手は自分の解釈を主張するので,語り手自身が歴史家にもなりうる」と
ある。これはオーラル・ヒストリーの特徴・影響と言えるので,「語り手自身が自ら
の解釈を加えるので情報源であると同時に歴史家になりうる」とまとめる。

３．単に歴史記述にとどまらない。

　第5文 (Moreover, for some ...) と第6文 (In certain projects ...) には「オーラル・
ヒストリーには歴史を作る以上の面がある。(…) 個人や社会集団に力を与えること
を目的とする企画もあった」という記述があり,これもオーラル・ヒストリーの特徴・

— 457 —

<u>1999年　　解答・解説</u>

影響と考えてよいので「個人や社会集団に力を与える面もある」という程度にまとめる。

解 答 例

> 面接取材により無名の人の経験と視点を取り込み, 生活の私的側面が記録された。記録用の技術修得や他分野の勉強が必要とされ, 語り手自身が歴史解釈を加えるので情報源であると同時に歴史家にもなりうる。さらに個人や社会集団に力を与えることもある。(117字)

1 **(B)** 【全訳】 彼がある朝, 表通りを渡って短い通りを下っていると, ケイト・カルドウェルが狭い脇道から彼の目の前に姿を現し, 通学かばんを腰で弾ませながら, 学校へ向かって歩いて行った。彼は胸躍らせて彼女の後ろについていき, 彼女を追い越すつもりだったのにそうする勇気が足りなかった。彼女に何を言えばいいのだろう?　彼は, 授業だとか天気だとかの退屈でつまらないことをつっかえながらしゃべっている自分の声を想像したが, 彼女がそれに応えてありきたりなことを言っている様子しか思い浮かべることができなかった。<u>ケイトはどうして振り向いて, 微笑み, そして「私と一緒に行かない?」と言って自分に声をかけてくれないのだろうか。彼女がそうしてくれたら, かすかに微笑んで, 「えっ, 僕?」という感じで眉を上げて近寄って行くのに。</u>しかし, 彼女は何もしなかった。そんなそぶりは少しも見せなかったのだ。

【考え方】 ※この下線部が「語り手」の思っていることを述べたものなら, If she did, he would smile ... の部分は, 仮定法過去完了形で書かれていないとおかしい。下線部以降の箇所から明らかなように, 語り手は実際には彼女が振り向かなかったことを知っており, If she did は事実に反することを仮定していることになるからである。そのあたりから, この下線部は「少年の心の中でのつぶやき」であると判断する。全体を直接話法で書き直すと, Why *doesn't* she turn and smile and call to *me*, saying, "Don't you like my company?" If she *does*, *I will* smile faintly and approach with eyebrows questioningly raised. となり, 本問ではこれを和訳することが求められているので, 以下の解説でも上のように言い換えたものについて説明していくことにする。

　1. **Why *doesn't* she turn and smile and call to *me*** 「ケイトはどうして振り向いて, 微笑み, そして自分に声をかけてくれないのだろうか」「現在時制」で訳していることが必要。"she" は, それが指す人物を明らかにするよう求められてはいな

— 458 —

いので，もちろん「彼女」と訳しても問題はない。

2．**saying, "Don't you like my company?"**「『私と一緒に行かない？』」と言って〈声をかける〉」 call を修飾する分詞構文（= turn and smile にはかからない）。「一緒に行かない？」と言いながら，振り向き，同時に微笑み，さらには同時に声をかけるとは思えないからである。company はここでは「同伴」の意。（例）I enjoy her *company.*（彼女が一緒にいると楽しい）

3．**If she *does***「もし彼女がそうしてくれれば」 does は「振り向いて，微笑んで，声をかけてくれること」を指している。

4．***I will* smile faintly and approach with eyebrows questioningly raised**「僕はかすかに微笑んで，『えっ，僕？』という感じで眉を上げて近寄って行くのに」and は smile と approach を接続している。with eyebrows ... raised は「付帯状況（= 状況説明）」を表している。付帯状況を示す with の後ろには目的語 (eyebrows) と補語 (raised) が続き，第 5 文型の場合と同様に，その両者の間には意味の上で「主語・述語」の関係が成立する。ここも「眉が上げられている状況で」→「眉を上げて」と考える。questioningly は「不審そうに」の意の副詞だが，文脈を考慮して上のように意訳しても良い。話に登場する少年はとてもシャイで，ケイトに声をかけてもらいたくて仕方がないのだが，いざ声をかけられると，「声をかけられるのを待っていたよ」と堂々と応ずることはできない。むしろ「全然予想していなかった」ふりをして「え？僕？ なんで？」と応ずることになるのである。「えっ？」と言うと眉毛が上がるのは，実際に言ってみればわかるだろう。

解 答

> ケイトはどうして振り向いて，微笑み，そして「私と一緒に行かない？」と言って自分に声をかけてくれないのだろうか。彼女がそうしてくれたら，かすかに微笑んで，「えっ，僕？」という感じで眉を上げて近寄って行くのに。

2 (A) 1998 年のものと似ているが，これは「論説型」ではない。ただ，しっかりとした論理構成が求められている点では同じ。なお，次にこの形式が出題されるのは少し先のことで，2004 年である。

（考え方）

＜語数について＞

「40 ～ 50 語程度」とあるから，基本的には 40 語台だが，50 語を多少超えても構わない，ということ。40 語未満は減点対象になる。

— 459 —

<u>1999 年　　解答・解説</u>

＜内容のポイント＞

　答案に盛り込まれていなければならない内容は以下の通り。

① 「どのようなボランティア活動に参加したいか」

② 「それはなぜか」

　答案の冒頭で参加したいボランティア活動を 1 つ挙げ，その後参加したい理由を述べる。また，1998 年同様，冒頭で述べた具体的なボランティア活動について，答案の最後でもう一度繰り返さないこと。

＜答案作成＞

　解答例に沿って答案の展開を眺めることにする。

［解答例 1 ］

　具体的な活動＝「老人介護」

　理由 1 ＝「現在日本は高齢化しつつあり，大きな問題になっている」

　理由 2 ＝「老老介護をしなければならない家庭が増えている」＋「我々若者はこの
　　　　　　事態を何とか食い止めなければならない」

　老人介護をテーマとし，今日本で問題になっている「高齢化」や「老老介護」についてスポットを当てた。なお，この解答例では理由を 2 つ挙げているが，むろん 1 つだけでも構わない。

［解答例 2 ］

　具体的な活動＝「自然災害の被害にあった人々を助ける」

　理由＝「台風や集中豪雨の被害にあう地域が最近増えている」＋「地球温暖化が原
　　　　　因か」→「このような地域ではボランティアはいくらいてもよい」

　大規模な自然災害に遭遇した地域ではボランティアの力が重要になることは今さら言うまでもない。よくあるテーマではあるが，このように誰もが考えつく内容を選ぶことが自由英作文では重要だ。

［解答例 3 ］

　具体的な活動＝「幼児の世話」

　理由＝「自分は子どもが好きだ」＋「出産後に職場へ復帰したいと思っている女性
　　　　　は，日中子どもの面倒を見てくれる人がいれば戻れるから」

　baby-sitter はアメリカなどではアルバイトとして定番である。ここではアルバイトではなく，ボランティアとして考えてみた。

1999 年　　解答・解説

解 答 例

［解答例１］

　I would like to help elderly people.　Their number has been increasing in Japan, and this is a big problem now.　Another problem that more and more families are experiencing is that elderly people have to help other elderly people.　We young people must do something to stop this.

(49 words)

［解答例２］

　I'd like to help people living in places that have suffered from a natural disaster.　More and more areas have recently been damaged by storms or torrential rain, probably because of global warming.　In those areas, there can't be too many volunteers.　(42 words)

［解答例３］

　I would do anything which involves looking after young children.　I really like children, but I also believe more young women who want to go back to work after they have their children would do so if they knew someone would look after the children during the day.　(48 words)

2　**(B)**　1992 年に会話文空所補充が初登場した後，少し間をおいてこの年出題された。ちなみに，会話に登場するのが女性のみというのはめずらしい。東大は基本的に性差別に配慮して，人物が２人の場合は男と女に設定するのが普通だからだ。

全訳　マイコとユリコは友人のカズコがテニスの試合で負けるのを目にしたばかりである。マイコは試合の結果に驚き，ユリコは驚いていない。家への帰り道，２人はその異なる意見を話し合っている。

マイコ：カズコが負けるなんて残念ね。いつもはすばらしい選手なんだけど，今日は
　　　　(1)　　　　　　　　　　　　　　　　　　　　　　　　　　　　　　　　　　。

ユリコ：あら，私は彼女が負けた本当の理由はそうじゃないと思うわ。つい先月，
　　　　(2)　　　　　　　　　　　　　　　　　　　　　　　　　　　　　　　　　　。
　　　　だから(3)　　　　　　　　　　　　　　　　　　　　　　　　　　　　　　　。
　　　　そりゃもちろん，テニスの選手がそうしなかったら，困ったことになるわよね。

— 461 —

1999 年　　解答・解説

[考え方]

＜語数について＞

　「それぞれ 5 ～ 10 語程度」とあるから，5 語未満は減点対象，10 語を多少超えても構わない，ということ。

＜内容のポイント＞

　会話文は話の流れを的確にとらえる必要がある。文脈をおさえて，空所にどのような内容を盛り込むべきなのかを正しく判断すること。空所の前の部分だけを読んで判断するのではなく，その後空所に対してどのような受け方がなされているかも考慮に入れなければならない。

　答案に盛り込まれていなければならない内容は以下の通り。

(1)　**「マイコが考える，カズコが試合に負けた理由」**

　直前に "Normally she's an excellent player, but today" とあるから，カズコがいつもと違っていたところを書く（むろんそれが敗退の原因になっていなくてはならない）。

(2)　**「先月発生した出来事」**

(3)　**「(2)の出来事がもたらした，テニス選手にとって望ましくない事態」**

　空所(2)(3)は(1)の反論になっていなければならないのだが，ただ反論すればよいわけではなく，"Just last month" から最後の "she's in trouble." まで全体でマイコとは異なる意見を述べなければならない。

　空所(2)の直前に "Just last month" とあるから，空所には「先月起こった出来事」を書くのは当然だが，空所(2)と(3)の間に "So" があり，さらに空所(3)の後では "And, of course, if a tennis player doesn't do that, she's in trouble." とあることに注目しなければならない。つまり，空所(2)の出来事が空所(3)に影響を与え，さらに空所(3)は「その影響のせいで，テニス選手としては必要なことをやらなかった」という意味合いの内容が盛り込まれていなければならない。したがって，空所(2)は出来事なら何でもよいというわけではないし，空所(3)はテニス選手に必要なこととは何かを考えて書く必要がある。このあたりがむずかしいところだろう。

＜答案作成＞

　解答例に沿って答案の展開を眺めることにする。

［解答例 1］

(1)　**「注意力散漫で集中できていないように見えた」**

(2)　**「雨の中を練習して，ひどい風邪をひいた」**

(3)　**「2 週間練習ができなかった」**

— 462 —

<u>1999 年　　解答・解説</u>

　カズコが負けた理由はマイコの言うような「単なる集中力の欠如」ではなく，「2
週間練習ができなかった」というのがユリコの言い分で，それぞれがちゃんと別の理
由を挙げている。また，「風邪」が「練習できない事態」を引き起こし，「練習しない」
ことは「テニス選手には致命的」，というように，正しい流れが出来ている。

［解答例2］

⑴　「カズコの足がまだ**痛む**ようだ」

⑵　「クラスの男子に**恋をした**」

⑶　「**練習しないでデート**していた」

　「足が痛む」原因を明示していないが，短い語数なのでそこは気にしなくてよい。「恋
に落ちデート」をし，「練習をサボっていた」ことが敗因，という流れ。ちなみに "if
a tennis player doesn't do that" の "do that" はここでは "practice" ということ。

［解答例3］

⑴　「ベストを尽くそうという**意欲が見えなかった**」

⑵　「**バイトを始めた**」

⑶　「**睡眠時間が足りなかった**」

　「意欲がなかった」のではなく，「（意欲があったとしても）寝ていなかったのでベ
ストが尽くせなかった」というのが対立点。また，⑵⑶は「バイトのせいであまり
寝ていない」という流れで，"if a tennis player doesn't do that" の "do that" はここ
では "have much time to sleep" ということ。

|解| |答| |例|

　［解答例1］

　⑴　she looked distracted and couldn't seem to concentrate　(8 words)

　⑵　she practiced in the rain and caught a bad cold　(10 words)

　⑶　she couldn't do any training for two weeks　(8 words)

　［解答例2］

　⑴　it seemed like her foot still hurt　(7 words)

　⑵　she fell in love with a boy in our class　(10 words)

　⑶　she's been spending time with him instead of practicing　(9 words)

　［解答例3］

　⑴　she didn't seem very interested in playing her best　(9 words)

　⑵　she started a part-time job　(5 words)

　⑶　she hasn't had much time to sleep　(7 words)

1999年　　解答・解説

4　考え方

(A)　「その問題に対処する方法の一つが委員会によって提案される予定になっていた」

正解は(6)。この文の主語は "One way" であるから，be 動詞は was でなければならない。ちなみに，"was to be" の部分だが，これは "be to −"（「予定」の意味）であって "One way(S) was(V) to be …(C)"（to be は名詞用法）という構文ではない。「方法の一つは提案されることだった」では意味を成さないからである。

(B)　「その機械を元通りに組み立てる方法を教えていただけるととてもありがたいのですが」

正解は(2)。"I would appreciate it if you could [would] …" で「…していただければありがたいのですが」という定型表現。強調するために very much をつけても構わないが，appreciate の後に it が必要。

(C)　「その使者が来るまでには，彼を中に入れるために門が開けられているだろう」

正解は(10)。"let in O" で「O を中に入れる」という意味の慣用句だが，O に人称代名詞がくるときは必ず "let O in" の順にしなければならない。したがって，let **him** in とするのが正しい。

(D)　「彼らが働く姿を見た人は皆，非常に多くのさまざまな機械を同時に使う彼らの能力に感銘を受けた」

正解は(6)。「…する能力」は ability *of − ing* ではなく ability to − である。したがって，their ability **to use** とするのが正しい。このような名詞の語法は難しいが，ability のような形容詞の名詞形の場合は，元の形容詞の語法を考えてみるとわかりやすい（be able to − である）。

(E)　「皆さんの中で定期的に運動していない人にとっては，30分以上走り続けるのはおそらく極めて大変でしょう」

正解は(8)。"keep *to* −" という語法はなく，"keep *− ing*" が正しい。したがって，keep **running** とするべき。

(F)　「メアリーが何とか火を消し止めた人間だったとは思えない。消防署に電話したというのなら別だが」

正解は(8)。"S *be possible to* −" という語法はない（it … to 構文で "It is possible to −" という並びになることはあるが）。どう直すかだが，(2)で Mary could have been と仮定法過去完了になっているので，この(8)も she **could** 〈have called〉とするのがよいだろう。仮定法が使われているのは，話者が極めて可能性が低いと考えているからである。

— 464 —

1999年　解答・解説

解答

(A)-(6)	(B)-(2)	(C)-(10)	(D)-(6)	(E)-(8)	(F)-(8)

5 【全訳】 (1)　地球上で最も環境上不安定な地域の一つにおいて有毒廃棄物が流出し，二つの大陸の野生生物を脅かしている。被害を受けた地域は，ドニャーナ国立公園で，セビリヤという南スペインの都市から南へ約100キロのびて海に至る湿地帯からなっている。

(2)　このドニャーナ国立公園は，野生生物にとっては非常に重要な場所である。ヨーロッパの北部，とりわけスカンジナビアで夏を過ごす多くの種の野鳥が，この湿地帯にやってきて，初秋から早春にかけて滞在し，北方の冬の厳しさを避けるのである。この公園はまた，珍しいイベリア・カタジロワシが見つかる最後の土地の一つでもある。その上，多くの種の鳥たちが，アフリカ南部とイギリスのような北ヨーロッパの国々との間を毎年渡る際にスペインを通過するのだが，公園とその周辺はそういう渡り鳥たちの主な休息地となっている。

(3)　惨事が起こったのは4月25日の早朝で，セビリヤの北西にある採掘施設で廃棄物貯蔵所の防壁が崩壊したのであった。重金属やその他の有毒物質を含む約15万8千トンの廃棄物が，グアディアマール川を下って同公園に流れついた。

(4)　しかしこの事件は，1週間かそこらも経たない内に新聞の一面から消えてしまったが，一つには廃棄物がセビリヤそのものに影響を与えることがなかったからであり（グアディアマール川は同市から西へやや離れたところを流れている），また一つには有毒な灰色の土壌が，大部分，ドニャーナ公園の心臓部に到達する前にせき止められたからであった。廃棄物をかぶったのは，同国立公園の地表の3パーセントだけであった。しかし，この事故の影響は，南スペインのあらゆる生活面に浸透しつつある。

(5)　影響の中には，比較的小さいものもある。例えば，エルロシオの町では毎年恒例の真夏の巡礼祭が今月行われるが，このために，伝統的な幌馬車とか馬に乗ってセビリヤから旅をしてきた巡礼者たちは，グアディアマール川を渡る通常のルートをとらないように警告を受けた。彼らは通常ルートに代わって，今なお川岸を覆っている有毒廃棄物の層を避けるため，幹線道路を通らざるを得なかった。

(6)　現在，この廃棄物の除去作業が進行中であり，この浄化作業を担当している公的機関の推定では，一日1万立方メートル弱という現在の速度なら，10月27日までに地表からの廃棄物除去を完了できるとしている。

1999年　　解答・解説

(7)　しかし英国王立野鳥保護協会の推定によれば，同地域が元通りになるには25年もかかりかねないとのことである。広報担当者は，「これが今世紀ヨーロッパでのこの種の事故で最悪の環境破壊になるのではないかと恐れている」と述べた。

(8)　[   ]

(9)　しかし，膨大な規模の惨事であったにもかかわらず，専門家の中には心配していない人もいる。同公園の園長の見るところでは，「すべてがこれまで同様に推移するのであれば，危険な影響が広範囲に及ぶ見込みは小さい」のである。しかし，彼は今では少数派である。事態はその尋常ならざる性質のために，地域や国の当局が主張するよりもはるかに劣悪であるとする声明文の発表に，周知のごとく分裂状態にあったスペインの複数の環境圧力団体が参加した。この災害は影響が遅れて現れる可能性が十二分にある，と彼らは語っている。

(10)　[   ]

(11)　有毒物質がグアディアマール川に流入して死んだ動物や鳥や魚は，従って，この事故がもたらす最終死亡総数のほんの一部に過ぎない可能性がある。というのも，この毒物は食物連鎖を上昇し始めたばかりに過ぎないからである。アジサシ，カイツブリ，鵜といった，同地域にやってきて魚や貝を餌としている鳥たちは，とりわけ危険にさらされている。

(12)　[   ]

(13)　他方で，亜鉛，鉛，銅，銀という泥の中の金属類は土壌中に浸透し，人間に対する目に見えない危険を生み出すことになるだろう。スペイン青年農民協会によれば，人間が消費する作物を栽培している数百エーカーの土地が危険にさらされている。廃棄物に覆われはしなかったが，その土地では汚染されている可能性のある井戸の水が使われているからである。

(14)　もし仮に廃棄物中の重金属物質が公園の地下の帯水層に浸透すれば，この災害は大惨事になるであろう。いわゆる帯水層27は，最大200メートルの深さに達し，5200平方キロメートルに及んでおり，この地域全体の健康状態は，この巨大な地底湖にかかっているのである。

(15)　初期検査が示唆するところでは，毒物はまだ帯水層までは浸透していない。しかし，確信を持てる人は誰もいない。スペイン科学研究協議会の会長の発言によれば，「帯水層は汚染されていないと最初の分析で示されているからといって，いつかそうならないということにはならない」ということである。

ア　現時点では，同公園内の鳥の数は比較的少ない。この流出が起こったときに，多

— 466 —

1999 年　　解答・解説

くの鳥は，春夏を北ヨーロッパで過ごすために，南スペインを飛び立ったばかりであった。しかし，恐らくは，アオサギを先頭に，鳥たちは 8 月には戻り始めることであろう。そして，当局でさえ，その頃までに泥を除去できるとは考えていない。

イ　「重金属の特徴は初めは目立たない」と言うのは，スペイン自然保護協会で働いているある科学者である。「重金属は体内に入ってからゆっくりと多くの種類の問題を引き起こす。発育，性的成長，大脳，免疫系に影響する。ある種のガンの原因にもなりうる」

ウ　彼の指摘によれば，鉱山の破壊された貯蔵所から流出した有毒物質の重量は，この種の単一事故としては世界最悪のものと広く見なされている事故，1989 年のエクソン・バルデズの石油タンカー事故で流出した量の 4 倍近くであった。

エ　広報担当者の言では，セビリヤ周辺地域は，野生動物にとって重要であるだけでなく，長い歴史と豊かな文化的伝統があり，近くのエルロシオでの宗教祭はその一例にすぎない。そのような伝統に対するこの事故の影響は，非常に遺憾なものである，と彼は語った。

【考え方】

　(1)　第 8 段落は，正解は**ウ**。直前の第 7 段落最終文の冒頭に A spokesman said ... とあり，ウを入れると，冒頭にある He が A spokesman を指示する形となり，自然な繋がりができる。また内容的に見ても，空所にウを入れると，第 7 段落最終文 (A spokesman said ...) で「これが今世紀ヨーロッパでのこの種の事故で最悪の環境破壊になるのではないか」という事故の規模について言及されたのに続けて，ウにおいてその内容が詳しく説明される形となり，さらには直後の第 9 段落冒頭に Despite the huge scale of the disaster ともあり，一連の自然な文脈が形成される。

　なおエは，The spokesman said という冒頭部分は第 7 段落最終文とつながるものの，その代表者の発言内容は，直前の第 7 段落および直後の第 9 段落いずれの内容ともつながらず，不適切であるとわかる。

　第 10 段落は，正解は**イ**。直前の第 9 段落最終文 (Spain's notoriously divided ...) の後半に，「この災害は影響が遅れて現れる可能性が十二分にある，と彼らは語っている」とあることから，空所にイを入れると「重金属の特徴は初めは目立たない」という内容が「遅延効果」を具体的に説明づける形となり，自然な繋がりになる。また，イで触れられている「スペイン自然保護協会」とは，おそらく第 9 段落最終文の前半で述べられている「複数の環境圧力団体」の一つだと考えられ，その意味でも適切なつながりを形成する。さらに，直後の第 11 段落 (The animals and ...) の内容を見ると，有害物質の食物連鎖への影響は始まったばかりで今後広がっていくといった内容

— 467 —

1999 年　　解答・解説

が述べられており，やはり「遅延効果」の具体的説明として自然な流れになる。

第 12 段落は，正解はア。空所にアを入れると，直前の第 11 段落最終文 (The birds －...) で公園に餌を求めてやってくる鳥たちについて言及されたあと，アで「現時点では，同公園内の鳥の数は比較的少ない」と鳥について説明が追加される形となり，自然なつながりとなる。また，アの最終文 (And not even ...) で「そして，当局でさえ，その頃までに泥を除去できるとは考えていない」と有害物質を含んだ泥の処理について述べられたあとで，直後の第 13 段落 (In the meantime ...) で再び泥の中に含まれている重金属について具体的な説明がなされており，その点でも適切な文脈を形成している。

(2)　正解は **toxic**。poisonous は「有毒な；有害な」という意味の形容詞で，これとほぼ同義の語は，第 3 段落や第 5 段落などにある toxic である。

(3)　正解はアの「そこで冬を過ごすために鳥がアフリカからやって来る」。第 2 段落第 2 文 (Many species of ...) に「ヨーロッパの北部，とりわけスカンジナビアで夏を過ごす多くの種の野鳥が，この湿地帯にやってきて，初秋から初春にかけて滞在し，北部の冬の厳しさを避ける」とあるが，これらの鳥はアフリカからやって来るのではない。また，同段落最終文 (In addition to ...) に「多くの種の鳥たちが，南アフリカとイギリスのような北ヨーロッパの国々との間を毎年渡る際にスペインを通過する」とあるが，公園で「冬を過ごすために」とは述べられていない。以上より，アが正解。

なお，イの「長距離を旅する鳥たちがそこで休息する」は，第 2 段落最終文 (In addition to ...) の内容と一致する。ウの「多くのスカンジナビアの鳥たちはそこで冬を過ごす」は，同段落第 2 文 (Many species of ...) の内容と一致する。エの「稀少な種の鳥がそこに生息している」は，同段落第 3 文 (The park is ...) の内容と一致する。それらの並列関係を also や In addition で明示していることにも注意。

(4)　正解はイ。第 1 段落最終文 (The area affected ...) に「被害を受けた地域は，ドニャーナ国立公園で，<u>セビリヤという南スペインの都市から南へ約 100 キロのびて海に至る湿地帯からなっている</u>」とあり，この記述からだけでも，セビリヤのすぐ下の辺りから大西洋に向かって国立公園が広がっているイが，最もよく該当しそうであることがわかる。加えて，第 3 段落第 1 文 (Disaster struck in ...) を見ると「惨事が起こったのは 4 月 25 日の早朝で，<u>セビリヤの北西にある採掘施設で廃棄物貯蔵所の障壁が崩壊した</u>」とあり，この時点でアが該当しないことがさらに明確になる。よって，正解はイ。

(5)　〔期間〕は，正解はイ。第 4 段落第 1 文 (But the event ...) に「しかしこの事件は，

－ 468 －

1999 年　　解答・解説

１週間かそこらも経たない内に新聞の一面から消えてしまった」とあることから，消去法で選択肢を選ぶと，イの「ほんの短期間」が正解となる。

　〔理由〕は，正解はキの「**有害廃棄物はセビリヤ市を通過することはなかった**」とクの「**有害物質が国立公園の中心部に到達することは阻止された**」。第４段落第１文 (But the event ...) の後半に，「一つには廃棄物がセビリヤそのものを襲うことがなかったからであり（ガジャマル川は同市から西へかなり離れたところを流れている），また一つには有毒な灰色の土壌が，大部分，ドニャーナ公園の心臓部に到達する前にさえぎられたからであった」とあることから，キとクの内容がこれらと一致する。本文では，partly because によって理由の並列を明示している。

　オの「有害廃棄物のすべての影響が比較的小さいものに過ぎなかった」は，第５段落第１文 (Some effects are ...) に「影響の中には，比較的小さいものもある」とあるが，「すべての影響」とは述べられていない。また，短期間で新聞の一面から消えてしまった理由としても明瞭ではない。カの「有害廃棄物は公園の大部分を覆うことはなかったものの，その影響は深刻だった」は，第４段落第２文 (Only 3 per ...) から最終文 (But the effects ...) の内容とほぼ一致するが，影響が深刻だったのだから短期間で報道が終わってしまうのは理不尽であり，よってその理由であるとは考えられない。ケの「有害廃棄物は南スペインのあらゆる生活面に影響を及ぼしている」は，第４段落最終文 (But the effects ...) の内容とほぼ一致するが，カと同様，これは短期間でニュースが消えてしまった理由とは考えられない。

　(6)　正解はエの「**彼らは通常は互いと意見が一致しないが，この災害に関しては意見が一致している**」。第９段落第４文 (Spain's notoriously divided ...) に「周知のごとく分裂状態にあったスペインの複数の環境圧力団体が参加した」とあり，この内容に一致するのはエである。

　アの「彼らは通常は意見が一致しており，この災害に関しても意見が一致している」，イの「彼らは通常は意見が一致しているが，この災害に関しては意見が一致していない」，ウの「彼らは通常は意見が一致せず，この災害に関しても意見が一致していない」は，いずれも本文にそのような内容は述べられておらず，不適切。

　(7)　正解は **underground lake**。第 14 段落第２文 (Aquifer 27, as ...) に「いわゆる帯水層 27 は，最大 200 メートルの深さに達し，５千２百万キロに及んでおり，この地域全体の健康状態は，この膨大な地底湖にかかっている」とある。文末にある this huge underground lake という語句の this という指示語に注目して，それが指す内容を辿っていくと，文の主語である Aquifer 27 だとわかる。よって，aquifer とは underground lake のことだと判明する。

— 469 —

1999 年　　解答・解説

(8)　正解はイの「ドニャーナ国立公園の園長」。第 9 段落第 2 文 (The park's director ...) に「同公園の園長の見るところでは,『すべてがこれまで同様に推移するのであれば,危険な影響が広範囲に及ぶ見込みは小さい』のである」とあることから,イが正解。

　ア の「王立野鳥保護協会の代表者」については第 7 段落最終文 (A spokesman said ...) に,ウの「スペインの環境圧力団体の成員」については第 9 段落最終文 (Spain's notoriously divided ...) に,エの「スペイン青年農民協会の会員」については第 13 段落最終文 (According to Spain's ...) に,それぞれ記述があるが,これらはみな,事故の被害を楽観視した内容とは言えず,不適切。

(9)　(a)は,正解はアの「人々はあるフェスティバルに伝統的なルートを通って行くことができなかった」。(b)は,正解はエの「公園の下にある帯水層は将来的に汚染される可能性がある」。(a)については,第 5 段落第 1 文 (Some effects are ...) に「影響の中には,比較的小さいものもある」とあり,その具体例として,同段落第 2 文 (For example, pilgrims ...) から最終文 (Instead they had ...) にかけて,フェスティバルに向かうルートが変更されたことが述べられている。よって,正解はアとなる。

　(b)については,第 14 段落第 1 文 (What would turn ...) に「廃棄物中の金属物質が公園の地下の帯水層に浸透すれば,この事故は大惨事になるであろう」とあり,それに続けて同段落最終文 (Aquifer 27, as ...) で 帯水層への影響について具体的な説明がなされている。よって,エが正解となる。なお,第 14 段落第 1 文は,What would turn the disaster into a catastrophe(S), would be(V), if the heavy metals in the waste were to penetrate the aquifer under the park(C) という構文で,直訳すれば「この事故を大惨事に変えるであろうものは,廃棄物中の重金属が公園の下にある帯水層に浸透するようなことがあった場合であろう」等となる。このように,副詞節がＳＶＣのＣになることも時折ある。

解 答

(1)　第 8 段落 - ウ　　第 10 段落 - イ　　第 12 段落 - ア
(2)　toxic
(3) - ア　　　(4) - イ
(5)　〔期間〕イ　　〔理由〕キ, ク
(6) - エ
(7)　underground lake
(8) - イ　　　(9)　(a) - ア　　(b) - エ

解答・解説

1 (A) **[全訳]** 環境を保護する最良の方法は何だろうか？ 基本的には，この問題に対して2つの異なる答えを持つ，2つのグループがある。両者の答えは，自然の価値がどのように決定できると考えるかによって決まる。1つのグループは，たとえば手つかずの熱帯雨林や汚染されていない河川の価値は金銭で計れるものでは決してないと主張する。したがって，これらの自然はいかなる産業上，経済上の使用からも保護しなければならないと彼らは論じている。それゆえ，環境を守る最良の方法は，汚染や自然の乱用に対する強力な法案を通過させることだと彼らは考える。

しかし，もう一方のグループは，同じ目的を達成するのに市場原理に頼る方が良いと言う。環境がどれくらいの価値を持つかは計算可能だと彼らは考えるのだ。たとえば，彼らの計算によれば，汚染によってヨーロッパにかかるのはその GNP の5％である。この費用は汚染を起こす側が支払うべきだと彼らは考える。言い換えれば，どれだけの汚染を引き起こしたかに応じて，企業に課税すべきだということであり，そうすれば企業はより汚染の少ない技術を使って汚染の少ない製品を作るよう促されるであろう。そうしないと，事業を続けていくことができなくなる。汚染を引き起こす製品の方が価格が高ければ，その製品は売れなくなるからだ。この種の汚染税は，企業や消費者に対して，汚染は経済的に引き合わないが汚染予防はそうではないのだと知らしめることとなるのである。

[考え方]

◇ 典型的な問題解決型（**Problem Solving** タイプ）と対照法（**Contrastive Argument**）の合成された文章構成である。対比［対立］する要素を網羅するよう心がけること。

◇「立場」と「方法」で対立要素を網羅する。

テーマである「環境保護の最良の方法は何か？」をめぐり，2つの立場が紹介されている。第1段落では「自然の価値は金に換算できない」という立場が紹介され，第2段落では「自然の価値は計算可能だ」という立場が紹介されている。

さらに，それぞれが異なる方法を提示していることに注意。第1段落最終文 (Thus, they think ...) に "the best way of saving the environment is to pass strong laws ..." とあるので，「〈汚染や乱用を禁止する〉強力な法律を作ること」を最初のグループの方法としてまとめておけばよい。

— 472 —

1998 年　　解答・解説

第2段落では，第2のグループの方法が述べられている。第1文 (The other group ...) の "rely upon market forces"，第4文 (In other words, ...) の "should be taxed"，最終文 (Pollution taxes of ...) の "Pollution taxes" といった内容から，「市場原理を利用し，汚染者に課税する」という点をまとめておけばよい。

解 答 例

［解答例1］　環境保護の方法には，自然の価値は金に換えることはできないから強い法規制で守るべきだという立場と，金に換算できるから，汚染を引き起こす企業に課税して市場原理を利用すべきだという立場がある。(93字)

［解答例2］　環境保護の方法には2つの立場がある。自然の価値は金で計算はできないから法律で守るべきだという立場と，自然の価値は計算可能だから市場原理を使って汚染者に課税し環境を守るべきだという立場である。(95字)

1 **(B)** 全訳　現代のコンピュータに関する最大の問題点のひとつは，あらゆる命令に機械的に従ってしまうということだ。コンピュータは行うように命じられたことを実行するが，これは人間がそれを意図したかどうかには関係がない。さらに，コンピュータは自分で自分の電源を入れることはできないし，何かまったく新しいことを自力で始めることも決してできないのである。

考え方　1．**Computers do what they are told to do**「コンピュータは行うように命じられたことを実行する」　関係代名詞 what がまとめる名詞節が最初の do の目的語で，what は節内で do の目的語として働いている。節内の構造は，tell O to −（O に−するよう命じる）の受動態で，they は computers をさしている。

2．**whether we meant it or not**「それを人間が意図したかどうかには関係がなく」　接続詞 whether が導く副詞節（whether ... or not「…であろうとなかろうと；…かどうかには関係なく」）で，〈Computers〉do を修飾している。it は what 節の内容を受けている。プログラムが間違っていて，我々の意図通りでない場合も，コンピュータはそのプログラム通りに動くので，「コンピュータは我々の意図とは関係なく，命じられたままに動く」と述べられているのである。

3．**Moreover, they cannot turn themselves on**「さらに，コンピュータは自分で自分の電源を入れることはできない」　turn ... on で「〈電気，ガス，エアコンなど〉をつける；…の電源を入れる」の意。

— 473 —

<u>1998 年　　解答・解説</u>

4．**nor can they ever begin something entirely new on their own**「また，何かまったく新しいことを自力で始めることも決してできない」 nor から文が始まっているため，それに続く主語・動詞が倒置形になっている。ここでは，and they can never begin ... と同義。entirely new は直前の something を修飾している。on one's own は「自力で，独力で」の意の熟語。（例）She cannot walk *on her own*.（彼女は一人では歩けない）

解 答

> コンピュータは行うように命じられたことを実行するが，これは人間がそれを意図したかどうかには関係がない。さらに，コンピュータは自分で自分の電源を入れることはできないし，何かまったく新しいことを自力で始めることも決してできないのである。

2 （A）　1991 年東大に自由英作文が導入されて以来，初めての「論説型」（ある事柄に対する是非を述べるもの）である。かなり本格的なもので，しっかりとした論理構成が求められる。

なお，問題文の最後に「内容よりも作文能力を問う問題であることに注意せよ」という文言がついている。最近はこの注意書きがつけられていないが，東大の基本姿勢は変わっていないと思う。内容を重視するのなら何も「自由英作文」という形式を取る必要はなく，日本語による「小論文」にすればよい。これはあくまでも英語の試験である，つまり，正しい英語で書かれ，かつ読み手にきちんと内容が伝わることが重要なのである，と東大は言いたいのではないか。

考え方

<語数について>

「40 ～ 50 語程度」とあるから，基本的には 40 語台だが，50 語を多少超えても構わない，ということ。40 語未満は減点対象になる。

<内容のポイント>

問題文は「日本の若者は 18 歳から選挙権を持つべきである」という意味（現在では実際選挙権が与えられているが，与えられていなかった時代を想像して書くこと）。答案に盛り込まれていなければならない内容は以下の通り。

① 「18 歳からの選挙権に賛成か反対か」

② 「それはなぜか」

①は問題文に指示されている内容で，しかも書き出しの英語まで与えられている

－ 474 －

<u>1998 年　　解答・解説</u>

ので問題ないだろう。注意してほしいことは，冒頭で書いた "I (dis)agree with this idea." を答案の最後でもう一度繰り返さないこと。すでに述べたことを繰り返す必要は全くないし，このような短い語数の中で同じことを2度も言えば，それは単なる語数稼ぎに過ぎず，採点者の印象を悪くするだけだ。

＜答案作成＞

　解答例に沿って答案の展開を眺めることにする。

［解答例1］

**　意見＝「賛成」**

**　理由＝「若者が責任を担うよい機会になるだろう」→「いまだ親に依存しているか
　　　　ら，通常は責任をほとんど負わなくて済んでいる」→「政治家を選ぶことは
　　　　初めての責任となるだろう」**

　政治家を選択することは，今後の社会の行く末を決める重要な行為である。普段親に依存している若者は自己責任に基づく行為をほとんど行っていない。このような観点から，選挙権があることは若者にとって有意義なこと，という趣旨である。

［解答例2］

**　意見＝「反対」**

**　理由＝「日本人はますます長命になり，80歳を超えても生きている人が多く存在
　　　　する」→「人生50年という時代には18歳はすでに大人だったであろうが，
　　　　現在は違う」→「政治に参加するにはまだ未熟である」**

　一番最後の「人間的に未熟」というのがメインの理由である。しかしこれだけでは説得力がないので，なぜ「未熟」なのかを平均寿命と関連づけながら論じてみた。自分の意見を読み手に納得させることが自由英作文では重要で，そのためにはきちんとした論の積み重ねが必要である。「内容よりも作文能力を問う」という注意書きがあるから，レベルの高い意見を述べる必要はないが，たとえ内容的には拙くとも，階段を一段一段上っていくように論理をしっかりと構成する力は求められる。

解 答 例

［解答例1］

　I agree with this idea. It would be a good opportunity for young people to take on some responsibility. Many of them are still dependent on their parents, so they have few responsibilities. Having to choose between one politician and another could be their first responsible act. (47 words)

— 475 —

1998年　解答・解説

[解答例2]

I disagree with this idea. Japanese people are living longer and longer, and there are many who live to over eighty! In the days when people only lived to fifty, eighteen-year-olds may have already been real adults, but now they aren't. They aren't mature enough to take part in politics.

(50 words)

2 (B)　本年の短文空所補充は前年（1997）と同一形式である。

全訳　(a)　騒音やその他の問題も存在するのに，なぜジョンと私は都会の中心近くに住みたいと思うのか。その理由は2つある。1つは，都会の中心に住めばほしいものが手に入りやすいからである。たとえば，家から歩いて行けるところにデパートや映画館がある。＿＿＿＿＿＿＿＿＿＿＿＿＿＿＿＿＿＿＿。もし郊外に住んでいたら，職場への往復に数時間かかることだろう。だが，今の場所に住んでいるおかげで，2人とも会社まで20分かからない。

(b)　多くの動物が人を欺こうとすることができることはわかっている。著名な科学者であるコンラッド・ローレンツは，視力がかなり悪くなっているペットの老犬ブリーについて，ある話を語ってくれた。ローレンツが帰宅すると，ブリーはときどき彼に誤って無愛想に吠えかかることがあった。自分の誤りに気づくと，ブリーはローレンツの前を勢いよく駆け抜けて，隣の家の門に向かって怒りながら吠えたものだった。それはまるで＿＿＿＿＿＿＿＿＿＿＿＿＿＿＿＿＿。このエピソードにより，ローレンツは，人を欺こうとするのは人間だけではないことに気づいたのである。

考え方

＜語数について＞

(a) は「それぞれ10～15語程度」とあるから，10語未満は減点対象，15語を多少超えても構わない，ということ。(b) は「5～10語程度」とあるから，5語未満は減点対象，10語を多少超えても構わない，ということ。

＜内容のポイント＞

答案に盛り込まれていなければならない内容は以下の通り。

(a)　**「筆者たちが都会の中心部に住みたいと思う第2の理由」**

　　第2文で "There are two reasons.", 第3文で "First, ..." とあるから，ここには筆者と "John"（パートナーか）が都会の中心部に住みたいと思う理由その2を書く。

(b)　**「ローレンツの犬が隣家の門に吠えかかった理由」**

— 476 —

1998 年　　解答・解説

書き出しが "as if" なので，むろん真の理由である必要はない（真の理由は「照れ隠し」であろう）。

＜答案作成＞

(a)→ "First" を受ける語は通常 "Second" である。空所に続く内容を考えると，「職場に近い」という理由以外は考えられない。ただし，あまり簡単に書いてしまうと（たとえば "we are close to work"）10 語未満になってしまうので注意すること。

(b)→「隣家の門に向かって吠える」理由としては，やはり「不審者がいる」というのが最も簡単だろう。ただ，［解答例 3］のように「何か他に理由があって」という簡単な答え方でも構わない。ちなみに as if 以下に続き，かつ「真の理由」ではないのだから，仮定法過去完了にする必要がある。

解 答 例

(a)

［解答例 1］

　　Second, we are close to work, so we don't have to waste much time commuting (15 words)

［解答例 2］

　　Second, it takes only a short time to get to work (11 words)

［解答例 3］

　　And second, we have more free time because we live close to work

　　　　　　　　　　　　　　　　　　　　　　　　　(13 words)

(b)

［解答例 1］

　　he had seen a stranger there trying to get in (10 words)

［解答例 2］

　　a complete stranger were standing there (6 words)

［解答例 3］

　　he had been barking for another reason (7 words)

---

4 【全訳】　世界の総人口は 50 億を超えている。常に増加しているので，正確な数字は誰にもわからない。世界の人口は今までになく早い速度で増えている。専門家による最近の計算によると，今後 40 年間で倍増するとのことだ。さらに，世界の人口は全世界にわたって均等に広がっているわけではなく，この人口密度における不均

— 477 —

<u>1998 年　　解答・解説</u>

衡もまた 1950 年以来増加しつつある。人口密度が最も高い国の多くはヨーロッパと
アジアに存在する。最も人口密度の高い地域の一つであるオランダでは，一平方キロ
メートル当たり平均 360 名の人が居住している。対照的に，オーストラリアにおけ
る一平方キロメートル当たりの居住者は平均たった 2 名である。

【考え方】　（解答は［直前にある語］／［入れるべき語］の順）

(1)　正解は **it / is**。進行形は "be + –ing" である。現在の内容であるから is を入
れる。

(2)　正解は **now / than**。faster という比較級があるのだから，何と何を比べてい
るのかを考えなければならない。本文は "now" と "ever before" の対比だから，now
の後に than をつける必要がある。

(3)　正解は **suggest / it**。suggest (that) に続くＳＶのＳが抜け落ちている。「倍
増する」(double) のは「世界の人口」で，それは(2)で既出しているため，代名詞の
it を使って補う。

(4)　正解は **is / not**。本文に文法上の誤りはない。前半部で "is spread <u>evenly</u>" と
あるのに，それを受けた後半部が "this <u>unevenness</u>" となっているのはおかしい。「一
語補充する」という設問なのだから，この unevenness は変更できない。したがって，
前半部を is not spread evenly とすればつじつまが合う。

(5)　正解は **are / in**。Europe / Asia は「地域名」であるから，countries とイコー
ル関係にはなれない。countries が Europe / Asia に「存在する」と考える必要がある。
したがって，場所を表す前置詞 in を加えて "in Europe and Asia" とすれば正しい。

(6)　正解は **Netherlands / which**。"In the Netherlands" は前置詞句だから続
く is の主語にはなれないし，まして is の前にカンマが打たれているのは変である。
また，本文は "an average of 360 people〈S〉 live〈V〉" という構造になっている。し
たがって "is one of the most crowded areas" の部分は "the Netherlands" に関す
る補足説明であると考え，関係代名詞の which を加えて "which is one of the most
crowded areas" とすれば構文的に正しく，また先行詞が the Netherlands という固
有名詞であるため非制限用法で使われていると考えれば，カンマが打たれているのも
頷ける。

【解】【答】

(1) it / is	(2) now / than	(3) suggest / it
(4) is / not	(5) are / in	(6) Netherlands / which

— 478 —

1998 年　　解答・解説

5　**【全訳】**　マヌケなピーターがある朝歩いて仕事場の畑に向かっていると，おば
あさんが道端に座っているのに出会いました。

「おばあちゃん，おはよう。どうしてそんなに悲しそうな顔をしているの」と彼は
聞きました。

「指輪をなくしてしまったんだよ」とおばあさんは言いました。「それも，世界中で
あんなのはひとつっきりしかない指輪なんだ」。

「捜すのを手伝ってあげるよ」とマヌケなピーターは言って，はいつくばってその
おばあさんの指輪を捜しました。

さて，長いこと捜しまわって，ようやく彼は葉っぱの陰にその指輪を見つけました。

「ありがとう」と言って，おばあさんは指輪を指にはめました。そしてエプロンか
ら鏡を取り出し，それをピーターに与えて言いました。「ご褒美にこれを持ってお行き」

「何でまたぼくに鏡が要るのかな」とピーターは尋ねました。

「それは普通の鏡なんかではないのだよ」とおばあさんは答えました。「魔法の鏡な
んだよ。誰でもこの鏡をのぞき込むと，自分のありのままの姿ではなく，他の人に見
える自分の姿が見えるのじゃよ」

マヌケなピーターはその鏡を自分の顔にかざして覗き込んでみました。まず一方を
向き，それから反対の方向に向いてみました。しまいに，彼は頭を振って言いました。
「うーん，魔法の鏡なのかもしれないけど，ぼくには全然役に立たないよ。自分の姿
が全然見えないんだもの」

おばあさんはにっこり笑って，「その鏡は決して嘘はつかないのだ。他の人の目
に見えるままの自分の本当の姿を教えてくれるのじゃよ」と言いました。そしてそう
言いながら例の指輪に触れると，彼女の姿は消えてしまいました。

さて，マヌケなピーターはとても驚いてそこに長い間立っていましたが，やがてま
たその鏡を覗いてみました。すると，鏡の真近まで鼻をくっつけてみても，やはり自
分の姿は見えませんでした。

ちょうどその時，農夫が馬に乗って通りかかりました。「すみませんが，鏡の中の
僕を見かけませんでしたか。この鏡に映らないものですから」とマヌケなピーターは
言いました。

「ああ」と農夫は言いました。「それなら，30分前に，この道を走っていくのを見たよ」

「ありがとう」とピーターは言いました。「捕まえられるかどうかやってみます」と
言うとその道を走って行きました。

農夫は笑って「あのマヌケなピーターは本物の間抜けだな！」とつぶやき，行って

— 479 —

1998年　解答・解説

しまいました。

　マヌケなピーターが走り続けていると，鍛冶屋に出くわしました。

　「そんなに急いでどこへ行くんだね，ピーター」と鍛冶屋は声をかけました。

　「鏡の中の僕を捕まえようと思ってね」とピーターは答えて言いました「こっちの方に走って行ったって，農夫のジョンが言っていたんだ。見なかったかい」

　この鍛冶屋は気の優しい人で，首を振るとこう言いました。「農夫のジョンは作り話をしていたんだよ。鏡の中の君が駆け出して行ってしまうなんてことはありっこないんだ。その鏡を見てごらん。ちゃんとそこに映っているよ」

　そこでピーターは魔法の鏡を覗き込んでみました。何が見えたかおわかりですか。見えたのは，くちばしが黄色で目が黒いガチョウが，こちらを真っ直ぐに見つめかえしているところでした。

　「ほら，鏡の中の自分が見えるだろう」と鍛冶屋が尋ねました。

　「ガチョウが見えるだけだよ」とピーターは言いました。「でもぼくはガチョウじゃない。みんないまに見ていろよ。出世してやるぞ。そうすれば，ぼくの本当の姿が見えるだろう」

　そこでピーターは，出世を目指して旅に出かけました。

　間もなく，木こりの一家が家財一式を背中にかついで，こちらに向かってやって来るのに出会いました。

　「どちらへ行くところですか」と彼は彼らに尋ねました。

　「この国を出るのさ」と木こりは言いました。「ここには竜がいるからね。人間の50倍の大きさだから，一口で喰われちゃうよ。今しがたこの国の王様の娘をさらっていったから，今晩のおかずにすることだろう。だから，お前さんもそっちの方へ行くのなら，気をつけた方がいいよ」。そう言いながら木こりの一家は急いで行ってしまいました。

　ピーターがさらに道を行くと，突然恐ろしい音が聞こえてきました。ある岩の向こうを見ると，そこに例の竜が見えました。まったく木こりが言っていたとおり，自分の50倍もの大きさで，石で歯を研いでいました。

　「おーい，お前が例の竜か」とピーターが言うと，竜は歯を研ぐのをやめて，大きなとても恐ろしい目でピーターを見ました。

　「そうだ！」と竜は言いました。

　「それじゃあ，ぼくはお前を殺さなきゃならないな」とピーターが言いました。

　「まさか」と竜は言って，火を吐きました。「それで，どうやってお前はわが輩を殺

— 480 —

1998年　　解答・解説

すつもりなのだ」

　そこでピーターは言いました。「ああ，殺すのはぼくではなくて，この岩の陰に一番恐ろしい生き物を隠してあるのさ。そいつはお前の50倍はあって，お前なんか一口で喰ってしまうぞ」

　「そんな馬鹿な！」竜は吠えるとその岩の陰に飛びかかりました。さてピーターは，あだ名とは違って結局のところそれほど間抜けではなく，そこに例の魔法の鏡を隠して置いたのです。ですから，竜がその岩かげに飛びかかって来たとき，竜はその鏡と真っ正面に向き合い，そこで，はじめて，他人の目に見える自分の姿を目にしたのです。50倍もの大きさで，一口で自分を飲み込むことが出来る姿でした。すると竜はすぐさま尻尾を巻いて，全速力で山を越えて逃げていき，再び姿を見せることはありませんでした。

　それからピーターは竜のいた洞窟に入っていき，王女様を見つけてお城に連れて帰りました。すると王様は彼に宝石や立派な衣服を与え，全国民が彼に喝采を送りました。そしてピーターがそこで例の鏡を覗き込んだとき，何が見えたかおわかりですか。見えたのは，勇敢でどう猛なライオンの姿の自分で，それが他のみんなの目に映った彼の姿なのでした。しかしピーターは心の中で思いました。「ぼくはライオンじゃない。ぼくはピーターだ」

　ちょうどその時，かの王女様がやってきましたので，ピーターは王女様にその鏡を見せて，そこに何が見えるかと尋ねました。

　「世界で一番美しい女性が見えるわ」と王女様は言いました。「でも私は世界で一番美しい女性じゃないわよ」

　「でもぼくにはそういう風に見えるのです」とピーターは言って，どのようにしてその鏡を手に入れたのか，そしてどのようにして竜をだましたのかについて，残らず王女様に語りました。

　「ですからお分かりでしょう。ぼくは本当はガチョウではありませんし，本当はライオンのように勇敢でもないのです。ぼくはただのマヌケなピーターなのです」

　彼の話を聞いて，王女様は正直な彼のことを気に入り始めました。彼女はたちまち彼を愛するようになり，王様は，ピーターが貧しい農夫の息子に過ぎないにもかかわらず，二人が結婚することを認めました。

　「でも，あなた！」と王妃は言いました。「あの子が本物の王子でないことで，国民は私たちを笑いものにしますよ」

　「ばかな！」と王様は答えました。「我々で，彼をこれまで見たこともない立派な王

— 481 —

<u>1998 年　　解答・解説</u>

子に仕立て上げるのだ！」しかし，王妃様のおっしゃることが正しかったのです。

　結婚式の日，ピーターは金と毛皮縁取りした最も立派な衣装を身にまといました。しかし，彼が例の魔法の鏡を覗き込んでみると，何が見えたかおわかりですか。裕福で堂々とした王子ではなく，見えたのはいつもの自分のボロ着を身にまとっている自分の姿，つまり，マヌケなピーターだったのです。しかしそれについて彼は気をもむことはありませんでした。彼はにっこり笑うと心の中で思いました，「やれやれ！ようやくみんながぼくの本当の姿を見てくれるようになったんだ」

（考え方）

　(1)　正解はエ。第3段落最終文 (I can't see ...) に，老婆から鏡をもらったピーターが最初にそれを覗き込んだ際の様子として「自分の姿が全然見えない」と述べられている。それから老婆が姿を消して空所(1)の場面へと続いているが，空所の直前にhe looked in the mirror again とあることから，空所には鏡を覗き込んだ際の結果が描写されていることが推測できる。ここでポイントになるのは，空所の直後にあるeven when he put his nose right up against it（鏡の真近まで鼻をくっつけてみても）という表現。even when ...（…の場合でさえ）という譲歩の意味を考えると，空所には「自分の姿は見えなかった」といった否定的な内容が入るとわかる。と同時に，この時点ではまだ一度も鏡の中に自分の姿を見ていないはずであるから，エの「やはり〈自分の姿は〉見えなかった」が文脈に合った適切な表現となる。

　アの「やがて〈自分の姿が〉見えはじめた」，ウの「今度は〈自分の姿が〉見えた」は，いずれも文脈に合わず，不適切。イの「今ではもはや〈自分の姿が〉見えなかった」は，これ以前には姿が見えていたことを示唆する表現であり，文脈に合わない。

　(2)　正解はエ。直前の第6段落第4文 ('Oh,' said the ...) で，鏡に映るはずの自分の姿を見かけなかったかとピーターに問われた農夫が「それなら，30分前に，この道を走っていくのを見たよ」と述べていることから，空所に see を入れれば「それを捕まえられるかどうかやってみます」という文脈に合った自然な応答となる。なお，see if ...は「…かどうか確かめる」という意味の表現で，接続詞 if は see の目的語となる名詞節を導いている。

　アの go やウの run を空所に入れると，if 節が条件を表す副詞節となり意味が通らなくなることから，不可。イの know を入れると，「それを捕まえられるかどうかを自分は知ることになるだろう」といった意味になるが，これは，自分の意志でこれからその姿のあとを追って捕まえに行こうとしている人物の発言としては，他人事のように聞こえ不自然である。

— 482 —

1998年　　解答・解説

(3)　正解はエ。goose は，口語表現で「間抜けな人物」を意味することから，正解はエの stupid（愚かな）となる。

なお，文脈から goose のそうした意味合いを推測することは十分に可能である。すなわち，直前の第6段落最終文 ('Thank you,' said ...) で農夫の言葉を真に受けてピーターが鏡に映る自分の姿を追いかけて行ってしまう様子が語られており，それに続く形で下線を含む文の冒頭で「農夫は笑って」と述べられていることから，農夫が内心でピーターを嘲笑していることが伺える。よって，下線部には嘲りの対象となるような意味合いが込められていると推測でき，選択肢の中でそうした意味合いとして最も適切なのは stupid（愚かな）だとわかる。

(4)　正解はエ。空所の直後の文 (Your reflection can't ...) に「自分の影が駆け出して行ってしまうなんてことはありえない」とあることから，鍛冶屋は農夫がピーターに言ったことは真実ではないと考えていることがわかる。それゆえ，stories（作り話）という語を空所に入れれば，「農夫のジョンは君に作り話を語っていたんだよ」といった文脈に合った自然なつながりとなる。

アの「事実」，イの「知らせ」，ウの「噂」は，いずれも文脈に合わず，不適切。

(5)　正解はエ。直前の第10段落最終文 (I'll seek my ...) で「出世してやるぞ。そうすれば，ぼくの本当の姿が見えるだろう」と述べられており，それに続く形で空所を含む文が「そこでピーターは（　5　）」と続いていることから，エの「出世を求めて旅に出かけた」を入れれば，文脈に合った適切なつながりとなる。なお，set off は「出発する；〈…し〉始める」という意味の慣用表現。seek ...'s fortune は「立身出世を求める；出世を目指す」という意味の慣用表現。

アの「自分の本当の姿が見えはじめた」，イの「間抜けな人物に見えないようにしようと決めた」，ウの「鏡を捨てようと決心した」は，いずれも文脈に合わず，不適切。

(6)　正解はア。第12段落第4文 (It's fifty times ...) で木こりがピーターに対して「その竜は人間の50倍の大きさだ」と述べたことを踏まえて，空所(6)にアの Just as ...（ちょうど…するのと同様に）を入れれば，「まったく木こりが言っていた通りに」という文脈に合った適切なつながりとなる。

イの Just that については，It is just that ...（単に…ということに過ぎない）という慣用的な表現が It is を省略した形で用いられることはあるが，ここでは文脈に合った意味にならないし，it was fifty ...という後続の節とも文法的につながらず，不適切。ウの Such as は，通例〈名詞 (,) such as ...〉（…のような〈名詞〉）という形で先行する名詞を修飾する表現であり，ここでは不可。エの Such that については，「…するような［に］」という意味を持って接続詞的に用いられることはあるが，文頭に置

— 483 —

1998年　解答・解説

いて主節に前置させる用法は存在せず，不可。

(7)　正解は **simple**。空所(7)を含む文の前半は「さてピーターは，あだ名とは違って結局のところそれほど（　7　）ではなく，そこに例の魔法の鏡を隠して置いた」という意味。空所の直後に despite his nickname（彼のあだ名に反して）とある点がポイント。彼のあだ名とは，すなわち Simple Peter（マヌケなピーター）である。よって，空所に simple を入れれば文脈に合った適切な表現となる。

(8)　正解は2番目で，**the (magic) mirror**。下線部(8)は「それ（＝竜）はそれ（＝その鏡）と真っ正面に向き合い，そこで，はじめて，それ（＝竜）は，それ（＝竜）が他人の目に見えるようにそれ自身を見た」という意味。一つだけ指すものが異なるのは2番目の it であり，それは the (magic) mirror を指している。

(9)　正解は **which was how everyone else saw him**。第4段落第2文 (It will show ...) で老婆が「その鏡は，他の人の目に見えるままの自分の本当の姿を示してくれる」と述べていたように，その鏡は，それを覗き込んだ人物の，他の人間の目に映った姿を映し出すことになっている。よって，ここでも同様の事柄が述べられていると推測でき，which was how everyone else saw him（それが，他のあらゆる人の彼の見え方だった）とすれば適切な意味内容となる。which は，as a brave, fierce lion の内容を先行詞とする非制限用法の関係代名詞。how は関係副詞で，was の補語となる名詞節を導いている。

(10)　正解は**ウ**。空所(10)を含む文は「『でもあなたはぼくにはそういう風に見えるのです』とピーターは言って，どのようにしてその鏡を（　10　）のか，そしてどのようにして竜を（　11　）のかについて，一部始終を王女様に語りました」という意味。空所(10)の直前に the whole story（一部始終）という表現があることからも，そもそも最初にどのようにしてその鏡を彼が入手したのかを王女に語ろうとしている，と考えると自然な流れになる。それに関しては，第2段落第3文 (Then she took ...) で，老婆に指輪を見つけてやった褒美として老婆から鏡を与えられたエピソードが述べられている。選択肢の中で，ウの get（手に入れる）が，人から物を与えられた場合も含み得る最も適切な語であり，これが正解となる。

アの changed（変えた）は，そのような内容は述べられておらず，不可。イの found（見つけた）は，人から与えられた物に対して用いるのは不自然であり，不適切。エの wanted（欲しかった）については，鏡は老婆から一方的に与えられた物であり，ピーター自身が欲していたとは言えないことから，不適切。

(11)　正解は**エ**。空所(10)に続いて，ピーターはここでは王女に対して竜にまつわるエピソードを語っているところである。それについては，第14段落第1文 (And

— 484 —

1998 年　　解答・解説

Peter said ...) に「そこでピーターは言いました。『ああ，殺すのはぼくではなくて，この岩の陰に一番恐ろしい生き物を隠してあるのさ。そいつはお前の 50 倍はあって，お前なんか一口で喰ってしまうぞ』」とあり，ピーターが鏡を使って竜をだましたことが述べられていた。よって，正解はエの tricked（だました）が正解。

アの「攻撃した」，イの「焼いた」，ウの「殺した」は，いずれも第 14 段落で語られている内容に合致しておらず，不適切。

⑿　正解はイ。空所⑿を含む文は「『あの子は本物の王子でないのですから，国民は（　12　）』という意味。第 17 段落第 2 文 (Pretty soon she ...) で王女がピーターを愛し始めたことが語られ，それに続けて「王様は，ピーターが貧しい農夫の息子に過ぎないにもかかわらず，二人が結婚することを認めた」と述べられている。そして続く同段落第 3 文 ('But, my dear ...') では「『しかし，王様』と王妃は言った」とあり，But によって逆接になっていることから，それに続く空所⑿を含む文では，二人の結婚を認める王様に対して王妃が否定的な事柄を述べようとしていることがわかる。それゆえ，空所にイの「我々を笑いものにする」を入れれば，直後に続く「彼は本物の王子ではないのだから」という内容が，高貴な王女と一般庶民との不釣り合いな結婚を国民が嘲笑の対象にするだろうという意味で，適切につながることになる。

アの「我々を無視する」は，身分不釣り合いな結婚を許した王室に対して国民が愛想を尽かして「我々を無視するだろう」という意味では，正解の可能性はあると言える。ただし，空所の直後の「彼は本物の王子ではないのだから」という表現との関係を考えると，イの「我々を笑いものにする」のほうが，アよりも原因と結果の意味関係が近い内容になっている（不適切な結婚→嘲笑→無視）。よって，イのほうがより文脈に合った内容であると言える。エの「我々に敬意を示す」は，文脈に合わず不可。

⒀　正解は **really am**。最終段落第 3 文 (Instead of a ...) を見ると「裕福で堂々とした王子ではなく，彼に見えたのは，いつもの自分のボロ着を身にまとっている自分の姿，つまり，マヌケなピーターだった」とあり，ついにピーターが周囲の人々の目に彼の本当の姿で映っていることが述べられている。それゆえ，空所に really am を入れれば，空所を含む文は「みんながぼくを，ぼくの本当の姿のままに見ている」といった意味合いとなり，文脈にあった適切な内容となる。なお，第 10 段落最終文 (I'll seek my ...) で，then you'll see me as I really am（そうすれば，ぼくの本当の姿が見えるだろう）と述べられている点も大きなヒントになるだろう。

⒁　a は **the Queen**，b は **the farmer**，c は **the woodcutter** が正解。a は「ピーターの社会的地位を懸念している人物」という意味。これについては，第 17 段落第 3 文 ('But, my dear ...') から第 4 文 ('People will ...') にかけて，王妃がピーターの身

－ 485 －

1998年　　解答・解説

分を気にかけている様子が語られている。よって，Queen が正解。

b は「ピーターを馬鹿にする人物」という意味。これについては，第7段落 (The farmer laughed ...) に「農夫は笑って『あのマヌケなピーターは本物の間抜けだな！』とつぶやき」とあることから，farmer が正解。

c は「ピーターに身の危険に注意を促す人物」という意味。これについては，第12段落第6文 (So, if you're ...) で「だから，お前さんもそっちの方へ行くのなら，気をつけた方がいいよ」と木こりがピーターに対して述べていることから，woodcutter が正解。

解 答

(1)－エ　　　(2)－エ　　　(3)－エ　　　(4)－エ　　　(5)－エ　　　(6)－ア		
(7)　simple		
(8)　2番目，the (magic) mirror		
(9)　which was how everyone else saw him		
(10)－ウ　　　(11)－エ　　　(12)－イ		
(13)　really am		
(14)　a. the Queen　　b. the farmer　　c. the woodcutter		

－ 486 －

解答・解説

1 (A) **［全訳］** 数年前まで考古学者一般の見解では，古代人が農業を始めたのはそうせざるをえなかったからだということになっていた。人口が増加したために仕方なく，狩猟や野生の食物の大量採取が楽な豊穣な土地から部族の一部を追い出したのだという説を，専門家は唱えていた。

そのような旧式の考え方によると，追い出された古代人は，豊饒な土地の周辺にある恵みの少ない所で生活するうちに，集めた野生植物の種子が，捨てた所や偶然落とした所で育ち始めることがよくあるのに気づいた。そして，そうした恵まれない土地に意図的に作物を植える方が，狩猟や食用野生植物の採集よりも豊かで信頼性のある食料源になることを知った。その結果，恵まれない土地での仮の住まいが永続的な居住地となっていった，というのが従来の考えである。しかし最近の研究では，どうやらそうではなかったらしいと言われている。

現在考古学者は，農業が始まったのは単なる偶然ではなく，古代人が何らかの科学的研究を行っていたからではないかと考えている。野生の食料を手に入れるのに苦労するようなひどい年月をいくたびか経験したために，常に十分な食料を確保する手だてを探すべきだと古代の人々は考え，特定の野生植物で実験をし，最終的に，一番適していると思えるものを育てることにした，というのが考古学者の見解である。「農業の発明の母は必ずしも必要性ではなかった。それは人間の創造力だったのだ」と，現在の考古学者は言っている。

［考え方］

◇典型的な対照法（Contrastive Argument）の文章構成である。

過去と現在のコントラストを明確に出すのが最も重要なポイントで，あとは字数の範囲内にそのプロセスを含めていく。

◇農業の起源に関する過去の見解（第1～2段落）

農業の起源に関する考古学者の過去の見解を最初の2段落で紹介し，第2段落最終文 (Recent research, however, ...) でそれを逆転させて，「現在の見解」を述べるという構成になっている（このように段落の最終文に「次の展開の予告」となる文を入れておくのは，段落構成でよくあることである）。

第3段落第1文 (Archaeologists now thinks ...) に "by accident"（偶然）という表現があるので，過去の視点としては「農業の起源は偶然の産物だ」という点をまず

— 488 —

<u>1997 年　　解答・解説</u>

入れておく。もちろん，これだけでは 100 字にも届かないので，それを「膨らませる」部分を第 1 〜 2 段落から拾っていくと以下のようになる。

a)　人口増加→豊かな土地から一部の集団を排除（第 1 段落第 2 文）

b)　移動した人が捨てたり偶然落としたりした種子が成育することに気づいた（第 2 段落第 1 文）

c)　作付けが狩猟採集より豊かで安定した食料源になると気づいた（第 2 段落第 2 文）

d)　そこが定住地になっていった

　もちろん，これらすべてを解答に含めることはできないので，「人口増加の結果追いやられた人のもとで農業は偶然生じた」という程度にまとめる。

◇現在の見解（第 3 段落）

　過去の見解を否定し新たな見解を紹介する部分で「偶然」と対比を成すのは，「科学的思考」や「創造性」である。これも「人間の科学的思考すなわち創造性によって生まれた」だけではなく，そのプロセスを使って内容を膨らませる必要がある。

a)　古代人は科学的調査を行っていた可能性がある（第 3 段落第 2 文）

b)　野生の食料が手に入りづらい年月を経験→食糧確保の方法を模索（第 3 段落第 3 文）

c)　特定の植物で実験→最適な植物を選んで栽培（第 3 段落第 4 文）

　以上の点をまとめたのが以下の解答例である。

|解| |答| |例|

> ［解答例 1］　考古学者は以前は，農業は人口増加により古代人の一部が追いやられた土地で偶然生じたと考えていた。しかし現在では，食料不足を経験したのちに十分な食料を確保する手段を得るための科学的研究を行い，最適なものを育てるに至ったという人間の創造性が農業を生んだと考えている。（130 字）
>
> ［解答例 2］　農業は，古代の狩猟採集民の一部が人口増加によって貧しい土地に追いやられた結果として偶然生まれたものだと昔は考えられていた。しかし今では，食料不足をきっかけとして食料の安定確保を目指した科学的な思考，すなわち人間の創造力によって農業は生まれたと考えられている。（129 字）

1　**(B)**　**【全訳】**　ある外国で 10 年暮らしてからマレーシアに戻ってきたとき，私は文化面で失っていた自己を取り戻そうと意識的に試みた。プロの文筆家であったか

－　489　－

<u>1997 年　　解答・解説</u>

ら，私特有のそのやり方は，母国語に可能な限り深く再び関わるように努めることであった。しかし，そういうことをしてみた者なら誰しも承知のごとく，そのような試みは，対象が言語であろうがなかろうが，せいぜい部分的にしか成功し得ないのである。私の試みもそうであった。それでも私はそのことを悔いてはいない。実をいえば，私は，自分の本来の文化的アイデンティティを完全にしかも純粋に取り戻したいと思ったわけではないのである。

(考え方)

⑴　この it は第 2 文 (Being a professional ...) の doing this を指し，さらに this は第 1 文 (When I came ...) の a conscious attempt to regain my lost cultural self を指すので，この部分の内容をまとめる。

⑵　この it は直前の So was mine の内容を受けるもので，この So が第 3 文 (But, as anyone ...) の only partly successful を受けるものであり，mine が my attempt の意味であることがつかめていればよい。my attempt の内容は問⑴で述べているので，具体化する必要はない。

解答

⑴　文化面で喪失した自我を回復しようという意識的な試み。(26 字)

⑵　筆者自身の試みも部分的にしか成功しなかったこと。(24 字)

2　(A)　「4 コマ漫画」という形式は後にも先にもこれ 1 回きりで，2000 年代に登場する「イラストの説明」の原形と考えられる。

(考え方)

＜語数について＞

　特に語数は指示されていないため，「解答欄に収まる範囲で」ということだろう。1 コマ目の解答がサンプルとして与えられているので，同じような語数で書けばよい。

＜内容のポイント＞

　与えられた注意書きを読むと，2 ～ 4 コマ目でしゃべっている人物について，セリフを含めて説明することが求められていることがわかる（セリフに関しては直接話法を用いてはならない）。また，あくまでも各コマの説明として妥当なものにしなければならないため，何を書いてもいいというわけではない。特に 4 コマ目につながるよう 2，3 コマ目の内容を考えなければならないのがむずかしい所。なお，1 コマ目の説明文より，漫画に登場する男女は父娘で，娘はどこかへ出かける所であるという設定にしなければならないことに注意。

— 490 —

<u>1997 年　　解答・解説</u>

以上のことを踏まえ, 答案を書く上で考慮しておかなければならないことは次の通り。

２コマ目 → 女性が着飾っていることから, 近所のコンビニなどに行くのではなく, 「お出かけ」という感じにする必要がある。

３コマ目 → 帰りが夜になっていること, 女性が暗い表情であることをきちんと示す必要がある。父親に関しては, 「娘にどうしたのかと聞いている」という設定以外ないだろう。

４コマ目 → この日にあった出来事を, 暗い表情の理由になるように説明する。

＜答案作成＞

解答例に沿って答案の展開を眺めることにする。

［解答例１］

２コマ目 → 「恋人とデートなので, 帰りが遅くなると言った」

３コマ目 → 「娘は夜も更けてから悲しげな顔つきで戻ってきたので, 父親はどうしたのかと聞いた」

４コマ目 → 「恋人とケンカし, 別れることにしたと言った」

　「デート」という設定で, 最終的に「恋人との別れ」という着地にした。陳腐な展開かもしれないが, これが一番簡単だろう。

［解答例２］

２コマ目 → 「友人と映画を見て, その帰りに高級レストランで食事をすると言った」

３コマ目 → 「娘が夜帰宅したとき落胆した顔をしていたので, 父親はどうしたのかと聞いた」

４コマ目 → 「つまらない映画で, 食事も高いばかりでまずかったと言った」

　「友人との外出」はいろいろなオチをつけられるが, あくまでも自分の英語力で書ける内容を選ぶこと。下手にウケねらいなどをしようとすると, 英語がついてこなくなる。

解 答 例

［解答例１］

2：She said she was going on a date with her boyfriend, so she wouldn't be back until late.

3：Late in the evening she came back, looking very unhappy, so her father asked her what the matter was.

4：She said she had had a quarrel with her boyfriend and decided to break up with him.

— 491 —

1997 年　　解答・解説

［解答例 2 ］

2 ：She said she was going to go to a movie with some friends and after
　　that, have dinner at a first-class restaurant.

3 ：When she came back that night, she looked upset, so her father asked
　　her if there was anything wrong.

4 ：She said the movie had been very boring, and the dinner had been not
　　only expensive but awful.

2 **(B)** 空所補充は 1990 年代・2000 年代は大変ポピュラーな形式で，毎年のよう
に出題されている。本年は短文が 2 つ与えられ，それぞれの空所を埋めるというもの。

全訳

(a)　この国では，人々は通常土曜の夜になると外食をし，日曜の夜は家でテレビの
前にすわり，自分たちがひいきにしているサッカーチームの応援をしたものだっ
た。ところが数年前から，試合が日曜だけでなく土曜にも放映されるようになった。

——。
このような理由で，レストランのオーナーたちは放映されている試合で宣伝されてい
る製品のボイコットをしようと決めたのである。

(b)　今日，平均的なアメリカの家庭は，洗濯機や皿洗い機のような労力を節約する機
械であふれている。——。
かくして，平均的主婦が現在家事に費やす時間は 50 年前（週 52 時間）と変わって
いない。数多くの機械の恩恵を受けているにもかかわらず，彼女たちが掃除しなけれ
ばならない家はもっと広くなり，要求される清潔さのレベルも上がり，生活様式の幅
も広がっているため，これらが合わさって彼女たちを忙しくさせているのである。

考え方

＜語数について＞

　「適切な 1 文をそれぞれ 8 〜 15 語」とあるから，ピリオドを打つのは 1 回だけで，
かつこの範囲内に収まっている必要がある。

＜内容のポイント＞

　答案に盛り込まれていなければならない内容は以下の通り。

(a)　「レストランのオーナーたちが，放映されている試合で宣伝されている製品のボ
　　イコットをしようと決めた理由」

　　空所の直後に "This is why ..." とあるから，書かなければならないことは明白。さ

— 492 —

<u>1997 年　　解答・解説</u>

らに具体的には, その「理由」とは「人々が土曜日にレストランで外食しなくなった」こと以外考えられない。

(b)　**「現在の主婦が家事に費やす時間が 50 年前と変わっていない原因」**

　やはり空所の直後に "Thus, ..." とあるから, 書かなければならないことは明白。ちなみに, 「50 年前」とは本文中にある "labor-saving devices" がまだ全く存在しなかった時代, ということだろう。注意してほしいのは, 「原因」の具体例 (「清潔さ」について) が本文の最後に挙げられていることだ。したがって空所には掃除・洗濯のような具体的なことではなく, 全体的なことを書く必要がある。

解 答 例

(a)

［解答例 1 ］

　　As a result, many people began to stay at home on Saturday nights, too

　　　　　　　　　　　　　　　　　　　　　　　　　　　　　　　　(14 words)

［解答例 2 ］

　　Now many people stay at home on Saturday nights and don't go to restaurants　(14 words)

［解答例 3 ］

　　People began staying home on Saturday nights and now a majority do

　　　　　　　　　　　　　　　　　　　　　　　　　　　　　　　　(12 words)

(b)

［解答例 1 ］

　　But even though they are labor-saving devices, they don't save time

　　　　　　　　　　　　　　　　　　　　　　　　　　　　　　　　(11 words)

［解答例 2 ］

　　However, housework these days isn't as simple as it used to be

　　　　　　　　　　　　　　　　　　　　　　　　　　　　　　　　(12 words)

［解答例 3 ］

　　Now, though, life is much more complicated than life in the past

　　　　　　　　　　　　　　　　　　　　　　　　　　　　　　　　(12 words)

— 493 —

<u>1997 年　　解答・解説</u>

4 (A) 【全訳】 いったい誰が新聞を隅から隅まで読むだろうか。言うまでもなく，そんな人はほとんどいない。忙しい日には時間がないし，すべての記事が同じように面白いわけではない。<u>読者は誰でも新聞を読む際の自分自身の個人的な好みや目的を持っており，そのため読者は，どの欄でも興味があるものへと直ちに新聞をめくることになり，残りは見向きもしないことになる。</u>それゆえ，新聞の大部分は読まれないままになるが，それでも 1 部丸ごと買わないわけにはいかないのだ。

【考え方】 1. **All readers have their own personal tastes and purposes for reading**「読者は誰でも新聞を読む際の自分自身の個人的な好みや目的を持っている」for reading は their ... tastes and purposes を修飾する形容詞句。reading はここでは「新聞を読むこと」を表しているので，「読書」のような訳語は不適切。

2. **which cause them to turn immediately to ...**「そのため読者は，…へと新聞を直ちにめくることになる」cause に「3 単現の s」がついていないことから，先行詞は their onw personal tastes and purposes for reading と判断する。cause (V) them (O) to turn (C) ... とつながる第 5 文型。turn to ... で「〈ページ〉を開く［めくる］」の意。(例) *Turn to* page ten, please.（10 ページを開いてください）

3. **whichever sections interest them**「どの欄でも興味があるもの」whichever は関係形容詞で，sections を修飾しながら全体を名詞節にまとめている。ここでは，any sections that interest them と同義。(例) I'll use *whichever treatment* the doctor recommends.（医者が勧めるどの治療も受けます）section は「新聞の欄」の意。「どの欄であれ読者に興味を抱かせる欄〈をめくる〉」や「読者の興味を引くどの欄でも〈めくる〉」ではややぎこちないので，「どの欄でも興味があるもの〈をめくる〉」などと処理すればよい。

4. **and to ignore the rest**「そして残りは見向きもしない［無視する］」and は to turn ... と to ignore ... を結ぶ等位接続詞。したがって，to ignore も cause の補語として働いていることに注意 (cause (V) them (O) ... to ignore (C) ...)。rest は「残り」の意の名詞。

【解】【答】

読者は誰でも新聞を読む際の自分自身の個人的な好みや目的を持っており，そのため読者は，どの欄でも興味があるものへと直ちに新聞をめくることになり，残りは見向きもしないことになる。

— 494 —

1997年　解答・解説

4 (B)　1997年は出題形式が少々変則で，大問2で自由英作文，4(B)で和文英訳となっている。

考え方　☆　「これは，他のいかなる動物にも見られないことである」

①　「見られる」は直訳で "be seen"，または "be found" でもよい。

②　「他のいかなる動物にも」は "in [among] (any) other animals" で，any は単なる強調であるから，つけなくてもよい。

☆　「二本足で立って歩くとか，言語を話すというのと同じような」

①　この2つは後で出てくる「基本的な人類の特徴」の具体例であるから，「同じような」は単に like でよい。

②　「二本足で立って歩く」とは「二足歩行」のことだが，"walk upright" 以外別解はない。

③　「言語を話す」とあるが，人間以外の動物は言語を話すだけでなく，読んだり書いたりすることもできない。したがって，これらすべてを包括する "use language" がベスト。むろん直訳しても減点はないだろう。

☆　「基本的な人類の特徴だろう」

①　この「だろう」は文字通り断言を避ける表現。動物には動物の言語があって，それを用いて相互にコミュニケーションしているとも言えるからだ。したがって may や probably / likely / perhaps のような語を使う必要がある。

②　「基本的な」は，ここでは「根本的」という意味合いだから，basic よりも fundamental の方が望ましい。

③　「特徴」は characteristic / feature / trait など。

解答例

［解答例1］

　This can't be seen in any other animals. Like walking upright or using language, it may be a fundamental characteristic of humans.

［解答例2］

　This is something that isn't seen among other animals. Like walking upright and our use of language, it is most likely one of humankind's most fundamental features.

［解答例3］

　This is something that is not found in other animals. It is probably a distinctive human trait, like walking upright or using language.

— 495 —

<u>1997年　　解答・解説</u>

4 (c) **[全訳]**　人は太古の昔から幽霊を想像してきた。肉体が滅びても霊魂は生き続けると信じている。一部の霊魂は霊魂の世界で満足している。しかし，落ち着かない霊魂もある。それらは元の人間生活に未練を残し，かつて暮らしていた場所に戻り続ける。たいていの幽霊は悲しんでいて，静かで，何の問題も起こさない。だが，それ以外のもの，特に殺人犯や犯罪者の幽霊は，みじめな気分である。それらは自分を目撃したいかなる人間をも怖がらせる。世界の一部の地域では，人々は特定の日に教会へ行き，死者が墓の中で静かにねむれるよう祈る。これらの祈りが唱えられないと，死者は起き上がって元の家へ再び戻ってこようとすると人々は信じているのだ。

[考え方]

(1)　正解は **it**。it の前に出てきている名詞は "our bodies" で，さらにその前にさかのぼっても "ancient times" "ghosts" "people" で，単数形のものは1つもない。つまり，この it が何を指しているかわからないのである。it を取り除くと "live on" で「生き続ける」（この on は副詞で「継続」を表す）という意味になり，内容的にも要領を得る。

(2)　正解は **were**。"be used to" という慣用句は確かに存在するが，この to は前置詞であって不定詞ではないため，その後に動詞が続く場合は動名詞形にしなければならない。ところが本文では "live" という原形になっている。were を取り除けば "used to" という助動詞だからその後には原形が続くし，「かつて暮らしていた場所」という意味になって内容的にも問題がなくなる。

(3)　正解は **among**。are の主語に "the ghosts" はなりえない。"especially" という語がついていること，およびカンマで囲まれていることから，"especially the ghosts of murderers or criminals" の部分は挿入語句と考えるべきである。したがって，among を取り除けば "others〈S〉 are〈V〉 miserable〈C〉" という構文になり，文法的に正しくなる。

(4)　正解は **more**。"They terrify any more human being who sees them" は「それらは自分を目撃したより多くの人間を怖がらせる」という意味だが，何よりも「多い」のかが全くわからない。more を取り除けば単に「自分を目撃した人間」となって，要領を得る。

(5)　正解は **never**。"S + V + that 節" という語法を持つ動詞は，単に "S + V" だけで挿入的に使われることがある。したがって本文の場合は "People never believe that unless these prayers are said, the dead will rise up ..." が元の形ということになるが，that 以下の内容を人々が「決して信じていない」というのは，ここまでの内容に反している。never を取り除いて単に "people believe" とすれば，問題文の趣

— 496 —

<u>1997 年　　解答・解説</u>

旨に合う。

解 答

(1)　it　　　(2)　were　　　(3)　among　　　(4)　more　　　(5)　never

5　**全訳**　ベンジーの姿が目に入った途端，エジーは立ち上がって言った。「ねぇ，どうしたの？　放課後，どこに行ってたんだよ？」

ベンジーは言った。「ハマーマンに追いかけられているんだ」

エジーのピンク色のくちびるが，完璧な O の形になった。エジーは何も言わなかったが，吐き出す息が，同情するような長いため息となってもれた。やっとのことで彼は「マーヴ・ハマーマンかい？」と言ったが，もっとも，ヒトラーと言えば1人しかいなかったように，ハマーマンと言えばこの世に1人しかいないことは分かっていた。

「うん」

「追いかけられてるの？」

ベンジーはしょげかえった様子でうなずいた。マーヴ・ハマーマンの姿が目に浮かんでいたのだ。怪物がホラー映画に現れるように，大きくて強くて，同じような冷たいこの世のものとも思えない目をして，ハマーマンがベンジーの脳裏に浮かんだのだった。ベンジーが本当に怖かったのは，この目だった。この目で少しでも見つめられたら最後，自分が次の彼の犠牲者であると分かるのだった。

「何をしたんだい？」とエジーは尋ねた。「いや，そもそも何かしたのかい？」

少なくともエジーは分かってくれている，とベンジーは思った。マーヴ・ハマーマンであれば，人を追いかけ回すことに理由など必要ないのだ。ベンジーは階段に座り込んで，足下に視線を落とした。「僕，やっちゃったんだ」と彼は言った。

「何を？」エジーは尋ねた。「一体何をしたんだよ？　彼にぶつかっちゃうとか何かそんなこと？」

ベンジーは首を横に振った。

「じゃあ，どんなこと？」

ベンジーが言った。「あのでかい図表を知ってる？　学校の2階の廊下の」

「何て言ったんだよ？　よく聞こえないよ，ベンジー。ぶつぶつ言ってたってわからないよ」エジーは身をかがめ顔を近づけた。「こっちを見てよ。ねぇ，何て言ったんだい？」

ベンジーは顔を上げて言った。「歴史の教室の外にあるあのでかい図表を知ってるだろ？　廊下にあるやつ」

— 497 —

1997年　　解答・解説

「図表？」エジーは，ぽかんとして言った。「どんな図表だい，ベンジー」

「壁一面を占めている図表のことだよ，エズ。わからないわけないよ。大昔の人間の図表で，猿から人間へ進化していくのを表していて，クロマニョン人とかピテカントロプスのような，先史時代のいろいろなあらゆる人間を横から見た姿が描かれている，あの図表だよ」

「あぁ，そうか。あれなら見たことあるよ。それで？」

エジーが話のいいところ，つまり暴力の部分に早く入ってもらいたがっていることが，ベンジーにはわかった。彼は肩を落として，くちびるを舐めた。そして言った。「ええと，歴史の教室を出てこの図表の脇を通り過ぎている時にね，――自分でもなんでそんなことしたかわからないんだけど――いや本当にわからないんだよ。この図表の脇を通り過ぎている時に，エズ，数学の教室に行く途中でさ」彼は何度か喉をごくりとさせた。「この図表の脇を通り過ぎている時にね，僕は鉛筆を取り出して，図表の下のところにマーヴ・ハマーマンの名前を書き込んで，それからネアンデルタール人の絵のところまで矢印を描いちゃったんだ」

「何だって？」エジーは叫んだ。「何だって？」エジーは話が飲み込めていないようだった。エジーが不慮の出来事には同情しようという気になっていたことは，ベンジーにはわかっていた。エジー自身もこうしたことの一つの犠牲者に危うくなりそうだったことがあるのだ。ある日学校で，エジーはマーヴ・ハマーマンよりも一瞬早く水飲み場の取っ手に手を伸ばしてしまったのだ。もしエジーがぎりぎりのところで上をちらっと見上げて，ハマーマンに気がついて，「お先にどうぞ。僕は喉は渇いていないから」と急いで言っていなかったら，今階段にうずくまっているこの哀れな人物はエジーだったかもしれないのだ。「一体何のためにそんなことしたんだよ，ベンジー」

「わかんないよ」

「頭がどうかしているんじゃない？」

「わかんないんだよ」

「マーヴ・ハマーマンか」エジーはため息をついた。ため息は悲しげに響いた。「ハマーマン以外なら学校の他の誰に追いかけられても，ましだったろうな。僕だったら，マーヴ・ハマーマンより校長先生に追いかけられる方がましなくらいだよ」

「そうだよね」

「でも，もしかしたらハマーマンは君がそんなことしたのを知らないんじゃないかい」とエジーは言った。「そうは考えてみなかったの？　つまりさ，一体誰がわざわざハマーマンのところまで行って，あいつの名前が先史時代の図表に書かれていることを言ったりするかい？」エジーは身体を前に乗り出した。「『おい，ハマーマン』」と，

－ 498 －

1997 年　　解答・解説

彼は実在しないバカな奴の口真似をして言った。「『先史時代の図表にお前のことで面白いことが書いてあったぞ！』　ほらね，正気な頭をしているなら誰がわざわざそんなこと――」

「奴はすぐ後ろにいたんだ，僕が書いている時に」とベンジーが言った。

「何だって？」

「奴はすぐ後ろにいたんだよ」ベンジーはこわばった表情で言った。振り向いて，ハマーマンと目が合ったことを思い出すことはできた。それはなんとも奇妙で不穏な瞬間だったので，ベンジーはそれについて考えることはできなかった。

(考え方)

(1)　正解は**ア as**・**エ the way**。空所の前後に注目する。He(＝Marv Hammerman) came up in Benjie's mind (　1　) monsters do in horror movies, …と，空所の前にも後にも S＋V があり，両者を結びつける接続詞が必要であることがわかる。そこで，まずアの従位接続詞 as「…するように」が適切である。また，エの the way は，(in) the way S＋V として，副詞的に「S が V するように」の意味で用いることができる。イの how は通例名詞節をまとめるものであり，ここでは不可（how が副詞節をまとめる場合があるが，「どのように…しても (＝in any way that ...)」という意味で用いられるもので，節内で用いられる動詞は通例 like, please, want などに限られる）。ウの just は副詞であるので，節をまとめることはできない。

(2)　正解は「**マーヴ・ハマーマンが人を追いかけ回す理由**」。下線部(2)を含む一文は，「マーヴ・ハマーマンであれば，理由など必要ないのだ」という内容なので，「誰が」にあたるのは，ハマーマンである。本文冒頭で「ハマーマンに追いかけられているんだ」と言ったベンジーに対して，下線部(2)の前の部分で，エジーは「何をしたんだい？」と尋ねたすぐ後に，「いや，そもそも何かしたのかい？」と問いかけ直している。この問いかけは，何もしなくても，つまり理由などなくても，ハマーマンがそのような行動をとる可能性があることを，エジーが知っていることを表している。したがって「何をする」の部分は「人を追いかけ回す」とすればよい。

(3)　正解は**イ I can't even hear you**。下線部(3)の前には「何て言ったんだよ？」，後ろには「ぶつぶつ言ってるんだもん」とあるので，「よく聞こえないよ」が適切である。その他の選択肢は，ア「よく見えないよ」，ウ「君を見てもいないよ」，エ「君の話に耳を傾けてもいないよ」である。

(4)　正解は**イ miss**。下線部(4)を含む文は「壁一面を占めている図表のことだよ，エズ。どうしてそれを（　　　　）ことができるだろうか [＝（　　　　）するわけない]」

― 499 ―

1997年　　解答・解説

という内容の修辞疑問文になっている。「壁一面の大きな図表を，見落とすはずがない」という文脈である。miss はここでは「…を見落とす；…に気づかない」という意味の他動詞。その他の選択肢は，ア「…を失う」，ウ「…に気づく」，エ「…を眺める」である。

(5)　正解は **was eager for him to get on to**。be eager for A to – 「しきりに A に – してほしいと思っている；A が – するのを強く願う」という表現。この for him はベンジーを指している。get on to ...は「（新しい話題など）に移る」という意味で，並べ替えた文は，「エジーが，ベンジーに話のいいところ，つまり暴力の部分に早く入ってほしいと思っている（とベンジーはわかった）」となる。

(6)　正解は (6a) **E**，(6b) **E**，(6c) **E**。(6a) は，前文と同じ主語。'What?' と 2 回繰り返しているのはエジー。(6b) を含む文は，「彼自身もこうしたことの一つの犠牲者に危うくなりそうだったことがある」という意味で，その後にエジーのエピソードで具体的に内容が説明されているので，これもエジー。(6c) を含む部分は「もしエジーが…していなかったとしたら，今階段にうずくまっているこの哀れな人物は (6c) 彼だったかもしれない」という内容であるので，彼とはエジーと判断できる。階段でうずくまっているこの人物とはベンジーのことで，エジーもベンジーのような状況になっていたかもしれないという意味を表している。

(7)　正解は**イ go**。Go ahead で「お先にどうぞ」と，相手に順番を譲る場合の言い方。

(8)　正解は**ウ Hammerman is the worst person in school that can be after you.**　各選択肢の意味は以下の通り。

ア　「他の誰かが，ハマーマンに追いかけられるべきだ」

イ　「ハマーマンを追いかけるのは，校長先生を追いかけるのと同じくらいひどいことだ」

ウ　「ハマーマンは，人を追いかけることにかけては学校内で最悪の人物である」

エ　「君は，ハマーマンが追いかけるのに学校内で最悪の人物だ」

下線部(8)の Anybody else は「ハマーマン以外のどんな人」を意味している。直後に「僕だったら，マーヴ・ハマーマンより校長先生に追いかけられる方がましなくらいだ」とあることから，下線部(8)は「ハマーマン以外なら学校の他の誰に追いかけられても，ましであっただろう」といった意味になることがわかる。よって正解はウ。

(9)　正解は**イ know**。直前の「僕だったら，マーヴ・ハマーマンより校長先生に追いかけられる方がましなくらいだ」というエジーの言葉に対するベンジーの返答の箇所。'I know.' として「そうですよね；ほんと，わかるよ」という相手への同意・共感を表すのが適切。'I see.' は，「なるほど；わかった」といった，相手の説明を理解

— 500 —

1997 年　　解答・解説

したことを伝える表現であることに注意。

⑽　正解は **tell**。下線部⑽の前で，エジーは「一体誰がわざわざハマーマンのところまで行って，あいつの名前が先史時代の図表に書かれていることを言ったりするかい？」と述べていて，下線部はこれと同様の内容を繰り返している。空所の後に，him that と目的語が２つあることから，tell が適切で say は不可である。

⑾　正解はイ **His turn came right after mine.**　下線部⑾の right は，「まさに；ちょうど」という意味の副詞で behind me を修飾したもの。各選択肢は以下の通り。

　　ア　「今度は正しくできただろうか」　right は「正しく；間違いなく」という意味
　　　　の副詞で動詞 do を修飾している。
　　イ　「彼の順番は，私の順番のすぐ後に訪れた」　right は「すぐに；ちょうど」の
　　　　意味の副詞で after mine を修飾しており，これが正解。
　　ウ　「次の信号で右に曲がりなさい」　right は「右へ」という意味の副詞。
　　エ　「今は事態を正常化することは不可能である」　right は「正常で」という意味
　　　　の形容詞。put A right で「A を正常にする」という意味を表す。

解答

⑴ − ア，エ
⑵　マーヴ・ハマーマンが人を追いかけ回す理由
⑶ − イ　　　　⑷ − イ
⑸ − was eager for him to get on to
⑹　(6a) − E　　(6b) − E　　(6c) − E
⑺ − イ　　　　⑻ − ウ　　　⑼ − イ
⑽　tell　　　⑾ − イ

— 501 —

解答・解説

1 (A) **全訳** 文明は，はじめから，その大部分が労働という概念を中心として築かれてきた。しかし現在，歴史上初めて，人間の労働が経済活動から組織的に排除されつつあり，近い将来，我々が知るところとなった雇用は姿を消す可能性が高まっている。新世代の高度情報通信技術が導入され，さらに，新たな形態の企業組織や経営が生まれて，何百万人もの労働者が臨時雇いの仕事に就かざるを得なくなったり，失業に追い込まれたりしている。失業率は，今はまだ比較的低いままだが，世界経済が全面的に情報化時代に入ると今後数十年にわたって上昇をつづけるものと予想される。我々は，大衆労働から高度な技術を有する「エリート労働」への長期にわたる移行の初期段階にいるわけだが，これには商品生産やサービス提供の自動化がますます伴ってくる。労働者のいない工場や会社が現れつつあるのだ。しかしながら，こうした展開は必ずしも暗い未来を意味するものではない。週労働時間を大幅に短縮し，市場経済に属さない社会的に有益なプロジェクトにとりくむという新たな機会を創り出すことによって，この新たな技術革命から得られる恩恵はすべての人々が広く共有できるであろう。

考え方

◇第7文の方向転換に注意せよ。

第1文 (From the outset ...) と第2文 (But now, for ...) で「従来文明の中心となっていた労働形態は消滅するだろう」と述べられている。多くの失業者が発生するので，これは「暗い」話になると一般には考えられる内容だが，第7文 (These developments, however, ...) で「しかし，未来は必ずしも暗くない」とこの内容が逆転されている。このように「一般によくある考えを紹介しておいて，それを逆転させて新たな視点を持ち出す」という展開は，よくある文章構成の仕方である。これを考慮して，全体の大筋をまとめるのが第1のポイントである。

第1文の「文明の中心概念」という内容は，ことによると解答には含めなくてもよいのかもしれないが，採点者にどう判断されるか分からないので，これも含めて内容をまとめると，「文明の中心概念であった従来の労働は消滅する可能性があるが，未来は必ずしも暗くない」（40字）となる。

◇言いかえに注意して反復を避ける。

第3文 (The introduction of ...) の主語は A together with B の形になっているが，

— 504 —

<u>1996 年　解答・解説</u>

このＡ（情報通信技術の発達）とＢ（新たな形の企業組織や経営）が「従来の労働が消滅する，すなわち失業者が増えることの原因」と考えられるので，このＡとＢは必須要因と考える。

　問題は第 4 文 (While unemployment is ...) 〜第 6 文 (Factories and companies ...) で，「世界経済が情報化時代に入ると失業が今後増加することが予測される」「生産やサービス提供の自動化に伴う，大衆労働から高度なエリート労働への移行の初期段階にいる」「従業員のいない工場や会社が現れつつある」といった内容は，先ほどのＡとＢの具体的な言いかえに過ぎない。よって，これらの内容は解答に含めないことに注意。

◇理由に該当する部分は含める。

　第 8 文 (The gains from ...) の文は，第 7 文の「理由」として成立するので，解答に含める。さらに by 以下はその「手段」として成立する内容なので，これも採点者にどう判断されるか分からないので，解答に含めておくのが安全だろう。この部分を「労働時間を減らし新たな社会参加の機会を作ることにより，万人がその恩恵を共有できるので」とまとめると 42 字になる。

　以上をまとめたのが以下の解答例である。

|解|答|例|

> 文明の中心概念だった従来の労働は高度情報通信技術と新形態の企業により消滅するだろうが，労働時間を減らし新たな社会参加の機会を作ることによって万人がその恩恵を共有できるので，未来は必ずしも暗くない。(98 字)

1 (B) **全訳**　たいていの子どもは，おもしろい物語を繰り返し聞くのが好きである。これは昔から変わらずそうである。困ったことに，たいていの大人は，子どもが聞きたがるほど頻繁に物語を話したいとは思わないのである。時にはただ退屈しのぎに，ないしはからかい気分で，親や祖父母は言葉を換えてしまうことがある。

　まだ小さい子どもたちにいつも同じ物語をせがまれると，私は彼らとの間でそれでちょっとしたゲームをした。物語の中に入ってからいろいろ細かい点が混乱したふりをする。そうすると子どもたちは，逆に，私がそんなに馬鹿だなんて，と怒ったふりをするのである。

　それから，ある日のこと，雑誌を読んでいて，赤ずきんちゃんの話を孫に話して聞かせながら私と同じことをした祖父の話を見つけた。

祖父：むかしむかし，青ずきんちゃんという名の小さな女の子がいました。

— 505 —

<u>1996年　　解答・解説</u>

孫：ちがうよ。赤ずきんちゃんだよ。

祖父：うん，そう，もちろん，赤ずきんちゃんだね。さて，ある日のことお母さんが
　　呼んで言いました。「青ずきんちゃん」

孫：赤だよ。

祖父：すまん。赤だったね。「ねぇ，いい子だから，メイおばさんのところに，このジャ
　　ガイモを持って行っておくれ」

孫：ちがうよ。そうじゃないよ。「おばあちゃんにこのケーキを持って行っておくれ」
　　だよ。

祖父：そうだ。そこで，少女は出かけました。そして森の中でキリンに出会いました。

孫：全く，めちゃくちゃなんだから。オオカミだったでしょ。

祖父：するとオオカミは言いました。「8の6倍はいくつかな」

孫：ちがう。ちがう。どちらへお出かけなのってオオカミは聞いたんだよ。

祖父：確かにオオカミはそう聞いたんだったね。そこで黒ずきんちゃんが答えました。

孫：赤！　赤！　赤でしょ！

祖父：少女は答えました。「トマトを買いに市場へ行くのよ」

孫：そうじゃないよ。こう言ったんだよ。「おばあちゃんが病気だからお見舞いに
　　行くの。でも道に迷っちゃったの」

祖父：もちろんそうだね。そこでオオカミはこう言いました。「75番のバスに乗って，
　　大広場で降りて右に曲がると，最初の戸口に階段が3段あるよ。そこにコイン
　　が落ちているからそれを拾って，チューインガムを買うといいよ」

孫：おじいちゃんは，お話がほんとに下手だなあ。まちがってばかりだもの。でも
　　ね，チューインガムなら悪くはないね。

祖父：よしきた。それじゃ，ほらお小遣いだよ。さあ，行っといで。

(考え方)

（1）「退屈しないように，あるいは，からかうために，親や祖父母は言葉を変える」
という意味になるはずである。from －ing が続くので **keep** が正解。keep from
－ing で「－しないようにする」の意味。to 不定詞なので原形のままでよい。

（2）「子どもたちが小さくて，いつも同じ物語をせがまれると，私は彼らとの間で
それでちょっとしたゲームをした」という意味にすればよい。直後に for があるので
ask for ...「…を求める［ねだる］」が思いついたかどうかがポイント。ただし過去形
asked にする必要がある。また，were と constantly があるので，**asking** を入れて
過去進行形にするのも可能である。

（3）「ちがう，話はそんな風に**進まない**よ」という意味になるはずなので，It

— 506 —

<u>1996年　　解答・解説</u>

doesn't **go** like that. とする。doesn't の後なので原形でよい。

(4)　オオカミであるべきところをキリンと言われたので，「話をメチャクチャにしてる」という意味になるように選ぶ。これは make a mess of ... で「…をメチャクチャにする；台無しにする；ぶちこわす」という意味になることを知っているかどうかがポイント。これをもとにして，you are の後なので – ing 形の **making** にする。

(5)　直前の「どちらへお出かけなのってオオカミは聞いたんだよ」を受けて「彼（オオカミ）はそう聞いたんだよね」という意味になるように，asked の代動詞である **did** を入れる。So ＋ S ＋ V は「（前文を受けて）たしかにその通りだ」という意味になる。ex. "I hear he is coming tonight." "So he is." 「今夜彼が来るのでしょう」「そうだったね」

(6)　「道に迷った」という意味になるはずである。lose one's way の完了形だから **lost** を入れる。

(7)　直後に up があるので，「コインを拾いなさい」という意味になるように **Pick** を入れる。命令文なので原形でよい。

(8)　冗談でわざと間違えているのに，孫はそれに気づかない状況での，「おじいちゃんは，お話がほんとに下手だなあ。まちがってばかりだもの。でもね，チューインガムなら…」という孫のセリフに入るものを考える。直後に祖父が，「よしきた。それじゃ，ほらお小遣いだよ。さあ，行っといで」と言っているので，この流れに合うものを考えると **mind** しかない。空所に mind（wouldn't の後なので原形）が入れば，「〈間違いだらけだけど〉チューインガムなら気にしない→チューインガムならまあいいか」という意味になる。

解 答

(1)– keep	(2)– asked [asking]	(3)– go	(4)– making
(5)– did	(6)– lost	(7)– Pick	(8) mind

2　(A)　手紙文空所補充の出題は東大ではまれで，類似するものは2000年（かなり短いが），2008年の「メール文空所補充」，2017年の「返信文完成」だけである。ただ，本年の出題は自由英作文というよりも，ほぼ和文英訳である。

全訳

7月3日

スーザンへ

　先日のお手紙ありがとう。元気そうでなにより。それに君からの知らせを聞いてよかったです。僕からの大ニュースは，僕のイギリスでの2週間の語学研修の詳細がつ

― 507 ―

1996年　解答・解説

いに決定したということです！

(1) _____

(2) _____

　君と君の家族に会う機会があるといいな。それに旅行全体がとても楽しみです。日本を出て旅行するのはこれが初めてになるでしょう。ご両親やお兄さんにもよろしくお伝えください。

　近々会いましょう！

　じゃあね

　ジュン

【考え方】

＜語数について＞

　「20 ～ 30 語程度」とあるから，基本的には 20 語台だが，30 語を多少超えても構わない，ということ。20 語未満は減点対象になる。

＜内容のポイント＞

　空所(1)は与えられた日本文から読み取って英語に直せばよい。

　(1)＝「イギリスでの日程」→「ヒースロウ空港に 8 月 2 日午後 3 時半に到着する」＋「レスターに 8 月 4 日午後 4 時までに到着しなければならない」

　「レスター」の話をする都合上，前もって「レスター大学で語学研修」についても触れておいた方がよいとは思うが，これは「日程」ではないので，なくてもよい。

　(2)

　(ｱ)「空港に迎えに来てもらえるか」

　「丁寧な表現でたずねる」と指示されているので，"Could [Would] you ...?" などを使う。「迎えに来る」は "(come to) meet me" が一般的で，もし車を使うなら "pick me up" とする。出迎えの場所は「空港」なので，"at the airport"。

　(ｲ)「レスターに行く前にスーザンの家に泊めてもらえるか」

　やはり「丁寧な表現」とあるので，"Could I ...?" "I'd like to −" などを使う。「スーザンの家に泊まる」は "stay at your house" "stay with you [your family]" など。

解答例

(1)

［解答例 1］

　I will be studying at Leicester University. I'll be arriving at Heathrow Airport at 3:30 p.m. on Friday, August 2, and I must get to Leicester by 4 p.m. on Sunday, August 4. (33 words)

— 508 —

1996年　　解答・解説

［解答例 2 ］

　　I'm scheduled to arrive at Heathrow Airport at 3:30 p.m. on August 2, and I must be in Leicester by 4:00 on August 4. (24 words)

(2)

［解答例 1 ］

　　Could you pick me up at the airport? And if possible, could I stay at your house before going to Leicester? (21 words)

［解答例 2 ］

　　I'm wondering if you could meet me at the airport, and if possible, I'd like to stay with your family before going to Leicester. (24 words)

2 (B) 考え方

(1) ☆ 「**彼女が死んでみてはじめて，やはりいい人だったと気がついた**」

① 「…してはじめて S が V する」は "It is not until [only after] ... that S V" が定型表現だが，直訳して "After ..., S V for the first time" とすることも可能。ちなみに，本問は死んだ後で気づいた内容だから，when ではなく after を用いること。

② 「気がつく」は realize がベスト。find / notice は「何かを見て［聞いて］気がつく」という意味合いなので，適当ではない。

③ 「やはり」は無視。

④ 「いい人だった」だが，単に "I realized that she was a good person" としても誤りではないが，"I realized what a good person she was" とした方が感情が込められていてよい（この場合 I realized *that* what ... とすると誤りになるので注意）。

☆ 「**もう少し親切にしてあげるのだった，と私は心から思った**」

① 後悔の気持ちを表現する方法は，"I thought I should have 過去分詞" "I wished I had 過去分詞" "I regretted – ing [または having 過去分詞]" の 3 つ。

② 「もう少し親切にしてあげる」は，「彼女に」と補って "be a little kinder to her"（生前以上に，ということだから，必ず比較級にすること）。ただ，「少し」という日本語は言葉のあやで，英語で a little とすると本当に「少し」でよいことになるので，つけない方が内容的には適当。

③ 「心から」は直訳して from the bottom of my heart としてもよいが，単なる強調にすぎないから，really くらいで十分。

(2) ☆ 「**日本人のふしぎなところは…ですね**」

— 509 —

1996年 解答・解説

「ふしぎな」は strange / curious など。「ふしぎなところ」が1つしかないのなら "What is strange" と関係代名詞 what を使い，他にもあるのなら "One strange thing" とする。本問はどちらでもよいだろう。「日本人の」の「の」は about であって，of は×。

☆ 「いなかを一段下に見ること」

① 実際に一段下に見ているのだから，接続詞の that を使って表現する。

② 「いなか」は直訳して the countryside としてもよい（単に *the country* だと「その国」に解釈されるので×）が，本問で言いたいことは「いなか暮らし」なので，"living in the country" がベスト（この場合は in the <u>country</u> とする）。

③ 「一段下に見る」は文字通り "look down on" だが，「劣っていると考える」「いなかに住みたくない」と解釈することもできる。

☆ 「アメリカ人はニューヨークに住むよりも，いなかに住みたがります」

現実にアメリカ人がニューヨークよりもいなかに住みたがっているわけではなく，どちらに住むかと言われればいなかを選ぶ，という仮想状況である。したがって，"would rather ... than～" "would prefer [choose] to‒ ... rather than～" を使う必要がある。ちなみに，「ニューヨーク」は厳密には New York City が正しいが，単に New York でも OK（New York は「ニューヨーク州」の場合もある）。

解答例

(1)

［解答例1］

　It was only after she died that I realized what a nice person she was. I really wished I had been kinder to her.

［解答例2］

　After she died, I realized for the first time that she was really a good person. I felt from the bottom of my heart that I should have been a little kinder to her.

［解答例3］

　I only realized what a good person she was after she died. I really regretted not having been kinder to her.

— 510 —

1996年　　解答・解説

(2)

［解答例1］

　　One strange thing about Japanese people is that they look down on the countryside. Americans would prefer to live in the country rather than in New York City.

［解答例2］

　　What is strange about Japanese people is that many of them don't want to live in the country. Americans would choose to live there rather than in New York City.

［解答例3］

　　An interesting thing about the Japanese is that they consider living in the country to be inferior. An American would rather live in the country than in New York City.

---

4 **(A)** **全訳**　フレッドとアンは，アンの健康診断のためにミネアポリスに向かって高速道路を走っていた。住んでいる町の医者は彼女に心配ないと言っていたが，新聞で癌についてたくさん読んでいたので，アンは自分が癌かもしれないと心配したのだ。寒々として雨が降っていた。車の流れは激しく，巨大なトレーラーが轟音をたてて彼らの横を通り過ぎて行った。フレッドは言った，(1)「ぼくが決めてもかまわないなら，むしろ U ターンして家に帰りたいんだけれど」

　そのときのアンの気持ちを考えれば，それは言ってはいけないことだった。(2)しかし，彼女は彼がそう言うのを予期していたし，彼が言った場合に備えて口にする言葉を心の中で用意していた。「そうね，もちろんよ。あなたが U ターンしたいのは分かり切っているわ。あなたにはどうでもいいのよ。ほんのこれっぽっちも気にかけないし，これまで気にかけてくれたことなんてないのよ。だから，今あなたが気にしてくれなくたって驚かないわ。私が死のうと生きようと，あなたにはどうでもいいことなのよ」

考え方

(1)　1. **If it was up to me**「ぼくが決めてもかまわないなら（もし僕次第なら）」be up to ... で「…次第だ」の意。（例）It is all *up to* you how you spend your time.（どう時間を使うかはすべて君次第だ）　It はここでは「この先どうするかという判断」を漠然と指している。

— 511 —

<u>1996 年　　解答・解説</u>

　2．**I'd just as soon turn around and go home**「むしろUターンして家に帰りたいんだけど」　would just as soon A (as B) は would rather A (than B) と同義で，「（B より）むしろ A したい」の意。（例）I *would just as soon* stay here (*as* go out). ((外出するよりは) むしろここにいたい)　問題文は「（このまま車を走らせるよりも）むしろUターンして帰りたい」の意。

　(2)　1．**But she had been expecting him to say it**「しかし，彼女は彼がそう言うのを予期していた」　expect (V) him (O) to say (C) ... とつながる第5文型。it は下線部(1)の Fred の発言内容を指している。

　2．**and had prepared a speech in her mind**「そして，口にする言葉を心の中で用意していた」　and は had been expecting ... と had prepare ... を結んでいる。a speech は，ここでは「せりふ，言葉」といった意味で「演説，講演，スピーチ」は不適切。

　3．**in case he did**「彼が言った場合に備えて」　in case は「…する場合に備えて；…するといけないので」の意の接続詞として働いている。（例）You should leave now *in case* traffic is heavy. (交通渋滞があるといけないので，もう出発した方がいい)　did は said it を受ける代動詞。

[解][答]

---
　(1)　「ぼくが決めてもかまわないなら，むしろ U ターンして家に帰りたいんだけれど」
　(2)　しかし，彼女は彼がそう言うのを予期していたし，彼が言った場合に備えて口にする言葉を心の中で用意していた。
---

4 (B)　[全訳]　権利とは何だろうか。権利とはまさにどのようなものかと普通の人々に尋ねたら，彼らはおそらく困ってしまって，返答することができないだろう。彼らは，誰かの権利を侵害するとはどういうことかは知っているかもしれない。(3)<u>彼らはまた，自分たちが持つあれこれの権利が，他人によって否定されたり，あるいは無視されたりすることがどういうことなのかも知っているかもしれない。</u>しかし侵害されていたり不当に否定されているものは，まさに何なのだろうか。それは人が後天的に獲得するものなのだろうか，それとも生まれたときに受け継ぐものなのだろうか。

[考え方]　1．**They may also know ...**「彼らはまた…も知っているかもしれない」

　2．**what it is to** -「－することがどういうことなのか」　it は形式主語で to - を指している。It is X to - (－することがX だ) という文が，what it is to - (－する

— 512 —

ことがどのようなことか）という what 節になったもの。

3．**have their own right to this or that denied or ignored by others**「自分たちの持つあれこれの権利が，他人によって否定されたり，無視される」 have (V) their own right (O) ... denied or ignored (C) ...（自分たちの権利が否定されたり無視される）という構造がつかめたかどうかがポイント。to this or that は right を修飾する形容詞句。（例）a right *to* privacy（プライバシーを保護される権利）　this or that は「あれこれ」の意を表すのに用いられる表現。（例）He looked *this* way *and that*.（彼はあちこち見回した）「あれこれに対する権利」とは「様々なことに対する権利」ということ。by others は denied and ignored 全体にかかる副詞句。

解答

> (3)　彼らはまた，自分たちが持つあれこれの権利が，他人によって否定されたり，あるいは無視されたりすることがどういうことなのかも知っているかもしれない。

5 【全訳】　ダゲレオタイプとは写真の初期の形態である。そのダゲレオタイプに写っている，パリの街並みの風景は非現実的な特性を帯びている。人が写っていないのである。撮影者は誰ひとりいなくなるまで待っていたのだろうか。あるいは，夜明けの誰も目覚めないうちにその写真を撮影したのだろうか。

このような初期のカメラで写真を撮るには何分も時間がかかったので，その間に人が行ったり来たりしただろうが，できあがった写真には何の痕跡も残さなかったのである。残っていたものは，街の中のどっしりとした動かない部分だけだった。写真に不変のものしか写らないことは，おそらくこのような初期の写真家には不思議に思われなかっただろう。彼らにとっては，不変のものだけが「現実」だったのである。ひょっとすると，人が足を一歩踏み出す途中のところがとらえられていたり，縄とびをしている子どもが奇跡のように空中に浮かんでいて再び地面に触れそうもないといった，街並みの風景を写した現代の写真を彼らが見たら，非現実的だと思ったかもしれない。その一方で，彼らの目に，現代の写真の方が彼ら自身の写真よりももっと現実的なものに写ったかもしれないという可能性も同様にありうる。というのも，その当時であっても画家は街並みの風景の中に，人が歩いている姿や子どもが遊んでいる姿を描いていたからである。

しかし，初期の写真家がどのように感じた可能性があろうと，画像のもつ「現実性」は，慣習の問題であるようだ。語られているところによれば，ある男が Les

— 513 —

<u>1996 年 解答・解説</u>

Demoiselles d' Avignon（アヴィニョンの娘たち）を見たあとで，ピカソに近づいていき，「なぜあなたは実際に見える通りに人々を描かないのですか」と質問したという。「そうですね」とピカソは言った。「実際にはどんなふうに見えるのですか」そこでその男は財布から自分の妻の写真を取り出した。「こんなふうですよ」と言うと，ピカソはその写真を見た。それから写真を返しながら，こう言った。「この人は小さいですね。それに平べったい」

　ある画像を認識できる光景にするために，私たちの脳がどれほどたくさんの情報をその画像に付け加えなければならないのか，私たちはわかっていない場合が多い。アメリカの画家マーク・タンゼイが描いた，*The Innocent Eye Test*（汚れなき視力検査）という表題の油絵には，1 頭の牛が等身大の複数の牛が描かれた 1 枚の絵を見せられているところが描かれている。科学者の集団がすぐそばにいて，その牛の反応を記録しようと準備している。まったく反応はないように見える。その牛が何も描かれていない塀を見ている可能性もあるだろう。

　その絵――ニューヨークのメトロポリタン美術館に掛かっている絵――も，またその絵の中に描かれている絵も，どちらも色鮮やかなものではない。それどころか，それらはどちらも昔の写真のような色である。これは，おそらく「本物の」牛，つまり牛の絵を見せられている牛そのものが絵であり，他の牛たちと同じくらい平べったく生気のないものだという事実を強調するためであろう。それらは皆描かれたものであり，同じ大きさ，同じ形であるのだが，私たちには一頭は本物の牛に見え，他のものは牛を描いた絵に見えるのである。その最初の一頭の牛は何の感銘も受けていない。牛には芸術という概念はなく，そのために絵を理解することはできないのである。

(考え方)

　(1)　正解は**エ out of the way**。ダゲレオタイプという初期の写真には，街並みの風景の中に人の姿が写っていないという内容に続いて，その理由を「撮影者は誰ひとり（　1　）まで待っていたのだろうか？」と問いかけた部分。(be) out of the way で「邪魔にならないとところに（いる）；（邪魔にならないように）その場をどく」という意味を表す。

　ア empty は「〈場所・乗り物などが〉人のいない；がらんとした」という意味の形容詞で，人を主語にした場合はその意味にならない。その他の選択肢は be 動詞のあとに置かれると，イ「適切な位置にある」，ウ「残されている」，オ「止められている；うんざりさせられている」である。

　(2)　正解は**ア**と**エ**。各選択肢の意味は以下の通り。

　ア　「彼らは現代の写真を現実的と思うかもしれないが，それは彼ら自身の時代の

－ 514 －

1996 年　　解答・解説

一部の絵画に似ているからである」

イ　「現代の写真は彼らに現実的であるという印象を与えるかもしれないが，それ
　　はその写真には不変のものしか写っていないからである」

ウ　「現代の写真は奇妙に見えるかもしれないが，それは不変のものは何も写って
　　いないからである」

エ　「現代の写真には人が写っているのを見て彼らは驚くかもしれない」

オ　「彼らは現代の人々のふるまいを奇妙なものと思うかもしれない」

　初期の写真家が現代の写真を見たとした場合に示しそうな反応については第2段落
に述べられている。初期の写真には人の姿は写らなかったが，彼らにとっては動かな
い不変のものだけが「現実」と思えていたので，それを不思議には思わなかっただろ
う，という内容に続いて，第4文 (Perhaps they would ...) に「ひょっとすると，人
が足を一歩踏み出す途中のところがとらえられていたり，縄とびをしている子どもが
奇跡のように空中に浮かんでいて再び地面に触れそうもないといった，街並みの風景
を写した現代の写真を彼らが見たら，非現実的だと思っただろう」とある。これに合
致するのがエ。続く第2段落最終文 (On the other ...) に「彼ら（初期の写真家たち）
には，現代の写真の方が彼ら自身の写真よりももっと現実的なものに写ったかもしれ
ない」とあり，その理由として「その当時であっても画家は街並みの風景の中に，人
が歩いている姿や子どもが遊んでいる姿を描いていたから」と述べている。これに合
致するのがア。

　イは理由の部分，ウは不変のものが写っていないという点が誤り。ここでは写真に
人の姿が写っているかどうかがポイントになっており，オは「人のふるまいが奇妙で
ある」の部分が誤りと言える。

　(3)　正解は**ア convention**。空所を含む部分の意味は「画像のもつ『現実性』は，
（　3　）の問題であるようだ」である。その後にあるピカソと男性のやりとりのエ
ピソードで述べられているのは，絵や写真の現実性は絶対的なものではなく，それを
見る人がもつ現実性の概念，捉え方によって変わるというもの。したがって「慣習［し
きたり］の問題」とするのが適切である。

　その他の選択肢は空所に入れた場合，イ「当然のこと；成り行きの問題」，ウ「事
実の問題」，エ「ほんの数分；時間の問題」といった意味である。

　(4)　正解は**「なぜあなたは実際に見える通りに人々を描かないのですか」**。ここで
の why don't you ...? は「なぜ，…しないのか」の意味であって，「…したらどうですか」
などの「勧誘」の意味は不適。(in) the way S＋V は「SがVするように［通りに］」
といった意味で，ここでは副詞的に用いられている。

— 515 —

1996 年　　解答・解説

(5)　正解はウ「あなたの奥さんが写っているこの写真は，現実の描き方のうちの一つにすぎない」。下線部(5)の意味は「この人は小さいですね。それに平べったい」であるが，これは男性が現実的な人の姿だとして写真を見せた時のピカソの言葉。写真に写っている人間は，実際の姿よりもはるかに小さく，実際と違って平面であることを指摘し，絵や写真がもつ現実性の捉え方はいろいろと存在し，絶対的なものはないことを述べたもの。

　その他の選択肢の意味は以下の通り。ア「その写真はあまりに現実的なので，私は興味がわかない」，イ「あなたの奥さんは十分興味深いわけではないので，私は描きたいと思わない」，エ「小さくて平べったい写真は，実物大の絵画に太刀打ちできない」

(6)　正解は **reaction**。「まったく<u>反応</u>はないように見える」という意味。直前の ready to record the cow's reaction を受けて，同じ名詞の反復を避けて省略したもの。doesn't seem とあるので，複数形は不可。

(7)　正解はエ「牛から見れば，絵も塀と変わりがなかった」。下線部(7)の意味は「その牛が何も描かれていない塀を見ている可能性もあるだろう」である。牛は絵の中で，牛の姿が描かれた絵を見せられているのであって，実際には塀を見ているわけではない。この点でア，イ，ウは誤り。最終段落最終文 (It has no ...) に「牛には芸術という概念はなく，そのために絵を理解することはできない」とある。牛の目には絵は見えていてもそれを理解できず，見せられている絵画に対してまったく反応をしていないように見えるので，その牛は実質的には何も描かれていない塀を見ているのと同じようなものだろうと表現したもの。

(8)　正解は **painting**。空所を含む部分は「私たちには一頭は本物の牛に見え，他のものは牛の（　8　）に見えるのである」という意味である。a real cow「本物の牛」と対照的な表現としては，a painting of cows「牛が描かれた絵」が適切。picture も可能であろうが，英文中の記述からは，painting の方が自然なつながり。

解答

(1)－エ	(2)－ア，エ	(3)－ア
(4)－なぜあなたは実際に見える通りに人々を描かないのですか。		
(5)－ウ　　(6) reaction　　(7)－エ　　(8) painting		

— 516 —

解答・解説

1 (A) **【全訳】** 伝統文法は，ギリシャ語・ラテン語を基礎に作り出された。そしてそれはその後，修正は最小限にとどめ，しかもしばしば無批判なまま，他の多くの言語の記述に適用された。しかし，少なくともある点では，構造上ラテン語・ギリシャ語だけではなくフランス語・英語・ドイツ語のようなより身近な西欧語とも著しく異なる言語が数多くある。したがって，現代言語学の主要な目的の一つは，伝統的な文法理論よりも一般性の高い文法理論，すなわち，人間のすべての言語を記述するにふさわしいと同時に，文法構造面でギリシャ語やラテン語に類似した言語に有利になる偏りを持たない文法理論を構築することであった。

[考え方]

本問は，But, therefore でつながった，たった3文から成る文章なので，以下の3点が盛り込まれていればよい。最終文は a theory of grammar which ... と one that ... が同格関係であり，どちらをとっても内容上は同じだが，解答字数を考えると，前半でまとめるのが無難である。

1．伝統文法はギリシャ語とラテン語を基礎として作られた。(26字)
2．しかし，構造が異なる言語が多数ある。(18字)
3．ゆえに，現代言語学はより一般性の高い文法理論の構築を目指してきた。(33字)

[解答]

> 伝統文法はギリシャ語とラテン語を基に作られたが，構造が異なる言語が多数あるため，現代言語学はより一般性の高い文法理論の構築を目指してきた。(69字)

1 (B) **【全訳】** 私の考えでは，可能な限り多くの時間を馴染みのある環境で過ごすことができるようにすれば，旅をずっと快適なものにできるだろうと最初に思いついたのはコンラッド・ヒルトンであった。遠隔の地で聞き慣れぬ響きの名前がついた土地だって全くかまわない。ただし，朝食にはスクランブルエッグが出て，エアコンがあり，トイレがちゃんと使えて，奇妙な訛りのしゃべり方であれ英語が話せる人間がいればの話である。外国人の中に終日どっぷり浸かってくたびれている旅行者に必要なのは，氷がたっぷり入った飲み物であり，通訳なしでも分かりやすい夕食のメニューであり，ちゃんとしたバスルームであり，キングサイズのベッドである。つま

— 518 —

1995年　　解答・解説

り，自分のところと全く変わらないということである。

　周知のように，ヒルトンのこの着想は，世界的成功を収めた。そして，その理由は至極単純なものであった。自分がどこにいるのかが分からないことはあっても，何があるのかは必ずわかる。想定外のことがない，ということであった。その土地らしい風情が少しは時に忍び込んでくることもある。オレンジジュースではなくマンゴージュースであるとか，スカートではなくサロンをまとったウェイトレスであるとか。しかし，ほとんどの場合は，寝るのが東京であろうがメキシコシティーであろうが，実は関係なかった。食事と宿泊施設がある程度規格化されており，そのため旅行者はどんなに風変わりな土地の真ん中にいても，快適さと安心と親しみを感じることができる。

　この着想がそこで，つまり多くの旅行のあり方の一つとして止まったのであれば，結構なことであったであろう。残念ながら，これが人気を博することとなったために，次から次へとホテルチェーンがこれを取り入れて，しかも，様々にその土地の趣向を凝らして多国籍方式に特徴を持たせようと図った。買収したホテルのそれぞれの特色は維持していると声高に主張してはいるが，新しいオーナーは，規格化できるものはすべて，バスルームの器具から部屋の配色まで規格化したため，ついには，旅行者は目が覚めて自分がどの町にいるのかを知りたかったら，起きてすぐそこの電話帳を見る以外に手はないということになってしまったのだ。

【選択肢全訳】

(a)　しかし，たいていの場合，寝るのが東京だろうがメキシコシティーであろうが，大した問題ではなかった

(b)　その一方で旅行者は，歴史と地理を特別に予習しておかない限り，初めての町を歩き回るのは難しいと感じる

(c)　ついには，自分がどの町で目を覚ましているのかを知る唯一の確実な方法は，ベッドを出てすぐに電話帳を調べることになってしまった

(d)　朝食にスクランブルエッグが出て，エアコンがあり，ちゃんと使えるトイレがあり，妙な訛りがあっても英語を話す人がいれば

【考え方】

　(1)　正解は(d)。

　第1文のヒルトンの発想に関連する内容が入るはずである。逆接や対比の関係を作る言葉がないので，「馴染みのある環境で過ごせるようにすれば旅はずっと改善される」という内容と同一方向に進むはずで，そうすると(d)が最もふさわしい。provided が「条件」を表す接続詞として使われており，この選択肢が副詞節のまと

― 519 ―

<u>1995 年　　解答・解説</u>

まりになっていることにも注意。

(2)　正解は(a)。

「ヒルトンの発想は世界的に成功したが，それは，どこにいるか分からなくても何を期待すべきかは分かる，想定外のことがないからだ」という「標準化・均質化」の話なので，「どうしても多少の地方色が入り込むことがあった」という内容の後に逆接で(a)の内容がつながるのが自然である。直後の文に standardization「規格化；標準化」という言葉があることにも注意。

(3)　正解は(c)。

ホテルチェーンが規格化を進め，なんでもかんでも同じにしてしまった結果どうなるかを考えると，(c)の皮肉っぽい内容がふさわしい。この until S V ... は「そしてついに S V …」（≒ and finally S V ...）のニュアンスで使われている。

解 答

(1)—(d)　　(2)—(a)　　(3)—(c)

2　(A)

1994 年に引き続き，物語文空所補充である。

【全訳】　雨が降っているとき，ジャッキーはどうしたらよいか決めることが一度もできなかった。一日中屋内に降り込められたが，彼女はすでに家中のあらゆる部屋を探索していた。ただ 1 つだけ，彼女が開ける勇気がなかったドアがあった。彼女はその老人が彼女に言ったことを覚えていた。(1)「＿＿＿＿＿＿＿＿＿＿＿＿＿＿＿」。

だが，ジャッキーは座って本を読むことに飽きていたので，自分で確かめようと決意した。階段を這うようにして上がると，彼女はそのドアに近づいた。慎重に把手を回すと，ドアがすっと開いた。すると彼女は見たのである。(2)＿＿＿＿＿＿＿＿＿。

【考え方】

＜語数について＞

「30 語程度」とあるから，基本的には 30 語前後。20 語未満は減点対象になるだろう。

＜内容のポイント＞

「物語」というのはフィクションだから，どのような奇想天外な内容でも構わない。ただ，必ず自分が英語で書ける内容にすること。アイデアばかり膨らんで，英語がついていかない答案は最悪。

空所に盛り込まなければならない内容は以下の通り。

(1) →「その老人がジャッキーに言った言葉」

— 520 —

1995 年　　解答・解説

"the old man" とは誰なのかわからないが，その正体をはっきりさせる必要はない（むろんさせてもよいが）。ジャッキーの祖父であろうが，どこかの見知らぬ老人であろうが，どうでもよいことだからである。とにかく，その老人がジャッキーに残した言葉を書けばよい。その言葉の内容だが，前文に "the one door she had never dared to open" とあるから，「開けてはいけない理由」を「警告」という雰囲気を出しながら書くべきだろう。

(2) → 「ジャッキーが目にしたもの」

(1)の「種明かし」に相当する部分。直前の文に "Then she saw it." とあるから，ジャッキーが目にしたものは何か 1 つの物でなければならない。ただ，解答例を見ればわかるように，必ずしもこの "it" の正体をはっきりさせなくてもよい。何らかの「あやしげなもの」としても構わないのである。

＜答案作成＞

解答例に沿って答案の展開を眺めることにする。

(1)

［解答例 1 ］

「ドアを開けるどころか，部屋に近づいてもいけない」→「何が起こるかわからないぞ」→「深く後悔することだけは間違いない」

全体的に警告となっているが，「後悔することになる」をその理由にしている。

［解答例 2 ］

「ドアを開けようとしてはいけない」→「私も入ったことがないから，中に何があるのかは知らない」→「父によると，開ければ不幸に見舞われるとのことだ」

警告で始め，「不幸に見舞われる」をその理由にしている。

［解答例 3 ］

「開けると，中にいる恐ろしい動物に殺されることになる」→「近所の子どもたちを守るため，何年も隔離している」

老人は部屋の中にあるものを知っているという設定で，かなり創作を加えて，具体的にしてある。

(2)

［解答例 1 ］

「部屋をいっぱいにふさぐほどの大きな象のぬいぐるみがあった」→「おそらく老人が子どものころから持っていたもので，孫娘に見られたくなかったのだろう」

老人とジャッキーは祖父と孫という設定。(1)の恐怖漂う雰囲気と対照的に，ほのぼのとした内容にしてある。

— 521 —

1995年　解答・解説

［解答例２］

「暗い部屋の片隅に黒い物が」→「家具ではなさそうである」→「じっとこちらを見つめていて，怖くなって部屋から逃げた」

(1)の恐ろしい雰囲気をそのまま維持して，恐ろしさの頂点を表現している。この解答例では結局 "it" の正体を明らかにしていない。

［解答例３］

「部屋の真ん中にすわってじっとこちらを見ていた」＋「ジャッキーは怖くなって顔をそむけた」→「恐ろしい叫び声を上げて彼女に飛びかかってきた」

［解答例２］と同様，全体的に「ホラー」にしてある。やはり "it" の正体は明らかにしていない。

解 答 例

(1)

［解答例１］

　　You must never get close to this room, let alone open the door. If you do that, there's no telling what will happen to you. There's just one thing I know: you will have deep regrets. (36 words)

［解答例２］

　　Don't try to open the door of this room. I've never entered the room, so I don't know what's inside, but my father said that if I did, I would have a series of misfortunes. (35 words)

［解答例３］

　　If you enter this room, you will be killed by the horrible animal that lives inside. I have kept it here for many years in order to protect the children in the neighborhood. (33 words)

(2)

［解答例１］

　　There was a huge stuffed elephant that filled the room! Perhaps the old man had had it since childhood and didn't want his granddaughter to know about it. (28 words)

［解答例２］

　　Though the room was dark, in a corner there was something darker. Somehow she knew it wasn't just furniture. It was looking at her! Scared, she went out immediately. (29 words)

<u>1995 年　　解答・解説</u>

［解答例 3］

　　It was sitting in the middle of the room, looking at her without moving.
Jackie was so frightened that she just looked back.　Suddenly it jumped
toward her, making a terrible sound!　(32 words)

2 (B) 【考え方】

(1)　☆　**「電気も使わないでどうして冷えるんだ」**

　①　「電気も使わないで」は直訳で without (using) electricity でよいが，「電気を
使わなければ」と解釈して "if you don't use electricity" としても構わない。

　②　「どうして」は how が正しく，*why* は×。why を使うと「冷える理由」とい
う意味になり，実際に冷えることになってしまう。子どもたちは電気を使わない冷蔵
庫では物が冷えないと思っているのだから，「どうすれば冷えるのか」という「手段」
として考えなければならない。

　③　「冷えるんだ」だが，冷蔵庫とは物を「冷やす」機械であるから，cool things /
keep things cool などとする必要がある。さらに，「電気を使わなければ物は冷やせ
ない」というのが子どもたちの考えだから，can を使う必要がある。ちなみに，この
部分の処理は直接話法でも間接話法でもよい。

　☆　**「と反論されてしまうに違いない」**

　①　「木でできた冷蔵庫があったのだと言っ」たらば「反論する」のであるから，
will が必要。「反論する」だが，「どうして冷えるの？」と質問してくるわけだから，
ask がよい。ただ，直接話法を使う（解答例 2），あるいは「冷えることなど不可能だ」
と言い切る（解答例 1）場合は say を使う。直訳は object だが，object *that S V* は「S
V と言って反論する」，つまり that 節中は反論する理由に相当するため，本文では ×。
［解答例 3］のように "they will object, <u>asking</u> ..." としなければならない。

　②　「違いない」は surely / no doubt / without a doubt のような副詞（句）を使
うか，"I'm sure that S V" "There is no doubt that S V" などの慣用表現を使う。

(2)　☆　**「A の方が B などより価値があるに決まっている」**

　"A is more worthwhile than B"（解答例 1），"A has more value than B"（解
答例 2），"A is of greater value than B"（解答例 3）など。「決まっている」は "It
goes without saying that S V" "Of course" などがよいが，内容的にこの日本語は無
視しても構わないだろう。

　☆　**「苦労のある読書」**

— 523 —

<u>1995 年　　解答・解説</u>

①　これは「苦労のある読書」と「苦労のない読書」に分類しているわけではない。「読書には苦労が必要だから，読書［の方が価値がある]」という意味合い。したがって，「苦労のある」の部分は because を使って処理するのがよい。ちなみに，関係代名詞の非制限用法を使って処理することも可能（解答例2）。

②　「苦労」だが，「苦難」「困難」という意味合いの語（*hardship / trouble / difficulty* など）はすべて×。これは最後まで本を読み通す「努力」または「忍耐」と解釈すべきだから，effort / perseverance など。

☆　「ぼんやり見ていられるテレビ」

①　「テレビ」と「読書」は比較できない。「テレビを見ること」と「読書をすること」，つまり2つの「行為」の比較と解釈しなければならない。したがって，"watching TV" と動名詞にすること。

②　「ぼんやり」は難しい。mindlessly / vacantly / blankly など。ちなみに，「読書」と違って「テレビを見ること」には「努力が必要ない」と考えて，［解答例2］のように "watching TV, which you can do without effort" と処理することもできる。

🈁🈁🈁

(1)
［解答例1］
　　They will surely say it's impossible to cool things without using electricity.
［解答例2］
　　I'm sure that they will say, "How can food be kept cold without using electricity?"
［解答例3］
　　Without a doubt they'll object, asking how it could be possible to keep things cool without electricity.
(2)
［解答例1］
　　It goes without saying that reading is far more worthwhile than watching TV mindlessly, because it takes perseverance.
［解答例2］
　　Reading, which takes energy and effort, has more value than watching TV, which you can do without effort.

— 524 —

1995 年　　解答・解説

［解答例 3 ］

Of course, reading is of greater value than vacantly watching TV, because it requires effort.

4 (A) **【全訳】** おそらく，創造的な思考というのは，これまで常に行われてきたように物事を行うことに特に利点があるわけではないと悟ることを単に意味するに過ぎないのだろう。

【考え方】 1. **Creative thinking may well mean simply the realization**「おそらく創造的な思考というのは，認識［悟ること］を単に意味するに過ぎないのだろう」Creative thinking (S) ... mean (V) ... the realization (O) が文の骨格。may well は「おそらく－だろう：十分に－する可能性がある」の意。(例) This *may well* be the last time we meet. (おそらく君に会うのもこれで最後だろう)　まれに，「－するのももっともだ」の意味になることもあるので注意が必要。(例) You *may well* be proud of your son. (君が息子を誇りに思うのももっともだ)

2. **that there's no particular virtue ...**「特に利点があるわけではないという〈認識〉」　節内が完全文なので，この that 節は the realization と同格であると判断する。realize that ... が名詞化されたものなので，「特に利点があるわけではないと悟ること」などと処理してもよい。

3. **in doing things the way they have always been done**「これまで常に行われてきたように物事を行うことに〈利点があるわけではない〉」　in doing ... は there's no ... virtue を修飾している副詞句。the way は，ここでは事実上 as と同義の接続詞（「…するように」）として働いている。(例) Just do it *the way* I did it. (ただ私がしたようにそれをしなさい)　they は things を受ける代名詞なので「彼ら」と訳してはならないことは言うまでもないが，the way ... を後ろから訳し上げる場合には they を「それら」としても不自然な訳文になってしまうので，(they を訳出しないなどの) 何らかの工夫が必要となる。

解答

おそらく，創造的な思考というのは，これまで常に行われてきたように物事を行うことに特に利点があるわけではないと悟ることを単に意味するに過ぎないのだろう。

— 525 —

<u>1995 年　　解答・解説</u>

4 (B) **全訳**　たいていの人は，時間とはほかの何ものにもまったく影響を受けることなく，おのずからいつまでも進み続けるので，仮にすべての活動がいきなり停止するようなことがあっても，それでも時間は途切れることなく続いていくのだろう，と直観的に感じている。多くの人々にとって，時計とカレンダーで時間を測る方法は絶対的なものであり，なかには，そのいずれかに手を加えることは災いを招くことだったと考えた人さえいる。

考え方　1. **if all activity were suddenly to cease**「仮にすべての活動がいきなり停止するようなことがあっても」　if S were to - は「仮に S が - するようなことがあれば」の意の仮定法で用いられるが（(例) *If you were to* die tomorrow, what would you do?（もし明日死ぬとすれば，あなたはどうしますか？）），if が even if の意味で用いられることも少なからずある（(例) *If* the sun *were to* rise in the west, I would never change my mind.（もし太陽が西から昇るようなことがあるとしても，私は絶対に自分の考えは変えない））。この問題文も if を even if の意味に解釈しないと意味が通らないことに注意。

2. **time would still continue without any interruption**「それでも時間は途切れることなく続いていくのだろう」　still は「それでもなお」の意の副詞。without any interruption は「なんの中断もなしに；途切れることなく」の意の副詞句で，continue を修飾している。

解答

> 仮にすべての活動がいきなり停止するようなことがあっても，それでも時間は途切れることなく続いていくのだろう

4 (C) **全訳**　太陽がすっかり昇りきる前に，私は家の庭に出ていったが，リッチーがまだそこにしゃがんでいて，花壇の中で本を読んでいるのを見てひどく驚いた。私は歩いていって，彼に話しかけた。ところがリッチーは本から目を離して私を見ることすらしなかった。その場にいれば，私の言うことが彼には聞こえていないように思われたことだろう。

考え方　1. **But he didn't so much as -**「しかし，彼は - さえしなかった」「not so much as ＋動詞」で「- さえしない (≒not even -)」の意。(例) He would *not so much as* (≒not even) look at me.（彼は私を見ようとさえしなかった）

2. **take his eyes off the book to look at me**「私を見るために本から目を離す〈ことさえしなかった〉」　off は前置詞で「…から離れて，外れて」の意。(例) take a

— 526 —

1995 年　　解答・解説

cap *off* the pen（ペンからふたを取る）「離陸する」あるいは「脱ぐ」という意味の take off の場合は off が副詞であることに注意。（例）The plane was about to take *off*.（飛行機は離陸せんばかりであった），She took her coat *off*.（彼女はコートを脱いだ）　to look at me は take を修飾する副詞用法の不定詞。前から訳し下して「本から目を離して私を見る」と処理しても良い。

　3．**you'd have thought he didn't hear me**「私の言うことが彼には聞こえていないように思われたことだろう」　you'd（＝would）have thought ... は仮定法過去完了。you は読者を含めた人一般を漠然とさしていると捉えれば良い。仮定法が使われているのは,「仮にその場にいたなら」という仮定条件が隠れているためなので,「全訳」のようにこの仮定条件を訳出しても良いだろう。

|解| |答|

> ところがリッチーは本から目を離して私を見ることすらしなかった。その場にいれば，私の言うことが彼には聞こえていないように思われたことだろう。

5　【全訳】　曖昧語法 (equivocation) とは，言葉を曖昧に用いることである。それは，人を欺こうという意図を持って行われることが多いが，その表現を用いている本人を欺くことさえありうる。論理的思考が正当であるためには，一貫して同じ用法が維持されなければならないのだが，2つ以上の意味を込めて言葉が用いられると，曖昧語法が生じるのである。

　「幸福は人生の目的 (end) である。
　　人生の終焉 (end) は死である。
　　したがって，幸福は死なのである」

　「パン半分でも何もない (nothing) よりはましである［パン半分は nothing よりも良い]。
　　健康よりも良いものは何もない (nothing)［nothing は健康よりも良い]。
　　したがって，パン半分は健康よりも良いのである」

曖昧な言葉づかいが誤解の元になるのは，それによって私たちは，ある概念にあてはまることを，たまたま同じ名称をもつ別の概念に転移させてしまうからである。論理というものは，概念同士の関係を扱うものであるので，概念そのものが変化してしま

— 527 —

1995年　解答・解説

うと役に立たなくなる。

> 「象は英国では見つからない［象は英国にはいない］，したがって，象を飼っているのならそれを失くしてはならない。さもないと，2度と見つけることはできないだろう」
> （'found' という言葉がここでは異なる2つの概念を表している）

言葉の曖昧な使い方の中には見抜きやすいものも多い。見抜きづらいもの方がさらに多い。占い師は，事態が自分が予想したものと反する結果になってしまう場合に備えて，自分の身を守るために曖昧な表現に精通している。曖昧語法を避けなければならないとしたら，政治はまったく異なる技巧を必要とするものになるだろう。また，ビジネスの書簡についても同様だろう。

> 「賜りましたお手紙には十分に相応の配慮をさせていただきますので，ご安心ください」
> （と同時に，その手紙はゴミ箱の方へ向かって，空中で緩やかな曲線を描くのである）

> 「スミス氏に働いてもらえる人は誰であれ，本当に幸運である」

だじゃれや演芸場のジョークは，曖昧語法に依存している場合が多い。

> 「うちの犬は鼻がないんだよ」
> 「どうやって匂いを嗅ぐの？［どんな匂いがするの？］」
> 「ひどいもんさ」

選考委員会に臨む政治家候補に対して与えられる助言は，「確信がない時には，曖昧表現を使え」である。単純な事実だが，常にすべての人を満足させることができるわけではないが，たいていの場合にたいていの人々をだますことができる可能性はかなり高いのである。候補者は，死刑賛成論者には，自分は殺人に対して「現実的な」刑罰を望むものであると言って安心させる。死刑反対論者に対しては，自分は「人道的配慮」を望むものであると言う。しかし，彼は現実的な軽い刑罰や人道的な死刑に賛成している可能性もあるのだ。

— 528 —

1995 年　　解答・解説

　曖昧語法は，国際的な紛争の亀裂に注ぎ込むためのものとしては特に強力な糊である。それは，滑らかで継ぎ目も特定できないような仕上げで，和解しがたい不和をつなぎ合わせるのである。多くの「十分にして率直な」協議は，共同の条約が出されることでめでたく終結となるが，その言葉づかいは，条約に調印したそれぞれの国にとってまったく異なることを意味するように入念に選ばれているのである。

　曖昧語法の語彙は，国会の傍聴席にいれば学べるだろう。国会に議席を持っている人であれば，それについて学ばなければならないことなどひとつもない。

考え方

　(1)　正解は(イ)「**自分が論理のわなにはまる**」。下線部(1)を含む 1 文の意味は「それ[曖昧語法]は，人を欺こうという意図を持って行われることが多いが，(1)<u>その表現を用いている本人を欺く</u>ことさえありうる」である。使っている本人が曖昧な表現によって欺かれることを論理のわなにはまると言い換えている。

　(2)　正解は (2a) (ア)**aim**「**目的**」，(2b) (エ)**termination**「**終結**」。the end of life がもちうる 2 つの意味を考えると，happiness と結びつくのが「人生の目的 [目標]」であり，death と結びつくのが「人生の終わり [終焉]」である。

　(ウ)の last day という表現は (2b) には不可。これをあてはめると，The <u>last day</u> of life is death となるが，「人生の最後の<u>日</u>が死である (day＝death)」とは言えないからである。

　(3)　正解は **Nothing**。空所の前後は「A は B(nothing) よりも良い。(　3　) は C よりも良い。したがって，A は C よりも良い」という三段論法になっていることに注目する。空所には Nothing を入れるのが適切。空所は文頭なので，頭文字を大文字にすること。

　(4)　正解は(ウ) **your letter will be considered carefully because it is important**「あなたの手紙は重要なものなので，慎重に考慮されるだろう」

　(オ) **your letter will not be taken seriously because it is not worth bothering about**「あなたの手紙はわざわざ配慮する価値がないので，真剣に受けとめられないだろう」

　下線部(4)は「あなたの手紙は，それが十分に受けるにふさわしい配慮を受けるだろう [賜りましたお手紙には十分に相応の配慮をさせていただきます]」という意味。手紙が受けるにふさわしい配慮とは，「手紙に価値があれば配慮する」し，「価値がなければ配慮しない」という 2 通りの意味に解することができる。前者に一致するのが(ウ)，後者に一致するのが(オ)。下線部(4)の後にある「その手紙はゴミ箱の方へ向かって，空中で緩やかな曲線を描く」のは後者の場合。

— 529 —

1995 年　　解答・解説

その他の選択肢の意味は以下の通り。㋐「私たちは，あなたの手紙に誠実にお返事します」，㋑「あなたの手紙への返信として，有益な助言を提供しましょう」，㋓「あなたの手紙は何らかの面倒を起こしかねないので，慎重に取り扱われるだろう」

⑸　正解〈話し手〉「その犬はどうやって匂いを嗅ぐの？」

　　　　〈聞き手〉「その犬はどんな匂いがするの？」

下線部⑸How does he smell? は，話し手は，相手が「うちの犬には鼻がない」と言ったことを受けて疑問を返しているので，"How does your dog smell without a nose?"「鼻がなくてどうやって匂いをかぐのか」という意味が妥当である。この際の smell は「〈動物などが〉匂いをかぐ」という意味。一方，相手の疑問に対して「ひどいもんだ」と答えた聞き手は，"How does your dog smell?" / "What kind of smell does your dog have?"「あなたの犬はどんな匂いなのか」と解釈したと考える。この場合の smell は「…の匂いがする」という意味。

⑹　正解は㋐ if you are not sure what to say「何を言うべきか確信がない場合には」。下線部⑹を含む文は，When (you are) in doubt, equivocate.「確信がない時には，曖昧表現を使え」という意味を表している。(be) in doubt は「確信がない；不確かである」という表現。選考委員会に臨む政治家候補に対する助言としてここで述べられているのは「発言すべき内容に確信がもてない場合には，曖昧な表現を使っておけ」ということ。

その他の選択肢の意味は，㋑「不誠実であると疑われている場合には」，㋒「欺かれることが怖い場合には」，㋓「自分は選出されないと思っている場合には」である。

⑺　正解は「死刑反対論者に対しては［死刑に反対している人々には］」。下線部⑺は，直前の文の those in favor of the death penalty「死刑制度に賛成の人々」と対比をなしており，To those (who are) against (the death penalty) と補って考える。

⑻　正解は㋑ entirely different「まったく異なった」。空所⑻を含む部分は「その言葉づかいは，条約に調印したそれぞれの国にとって（　8　）ことを意味するように入念に選ばれている」である。下線部の前では，曖昧表現が国家間の和解しがたい不和をつなぎ合わせる働きをすることが述べられているが，本文冒頭で述べられているような，2つ以上の意味を込めて言葉を用いる曖昧語法の表現が，共同の条約の中で用いられると，それぞれの国にとってまったく異なったことを意味すると考えられる。

その他の選択肢の意味は，㋐「かなりあやふやな」，㋒「まったく同じ」，㋓「まったく理不尽な」である。

— 530 —

1995 年　　解答・解説

(9)　正解は(ア) **If you are a politician, you must already be good at equivocation.**
「政治家であるならば，その人はすでに曖昧語法が得意であるにちがいない」。下線
部(9)の意味は，「国会に議席を持っている人ならば，それ［曖昧語法］について学ば
なければならないことなどひとつもない」である。第2段落の後ろから2文目 (Politics
would be …) の「曖昧語法を避けなければならないとしたら，政治はまったく異な
る技巧を必要とするものになるだろう」にもある通り，政治家は曖昧語法を技巧とし
てうまく用いる人々であり，下線部(9)はそれを皮肉った表現である。国会に議席を
持っているとは，国会議員であるということ。

その他の選択肢の意味は以下の通り。(イ)「政治の世界では，曖昧語法の技巧を知っ
ておく必要はない」，(ウ)「国会に足を踏み入れる前に，曖昧語法の技巧を研究すべき
だった」，(エ)「政治家になるほど利口な人ならば，曖昧語法に頼る必要性はない」

解 答

(1)－(イ)	(2) (2a)－(ア)	(2b)－(エ)	(3)　Nothing	(4)　(ウ), (オ)

(5)　〈話し手〉その犬はどうやって匂いを嗅ぐの？

　　　〈聞き手〉その犬はどんな匂いがするの？

(6)－(ア)

(7)－死刑反対論者に対しては［死刑に反対している人々には］

(8)－(イ)　　　　(9)－(ア)

— 531 —

"The farther backward you can look,
the farther forward you can see."

—— Winston Churchill

振り返り，はるかかなたに目をやれば，さらにいっそう前が見える。

とうだいにゅうししょうかい ねん えいご だいはん
東大入試詳解25年　英語〈第2版〉

編　　者	駿 台 予 備 学 校
発 行 者	山 﨑 良 子
印刷・製本	日経印刷株式会社
発 行 所	駿台文庫株式会社

〒101-0062　東京都千代田区神田駿河台1-7-4
　　　　　　　　　　　　　　　　小畑ビル内
　　　　　　　　TEL. 編集 03 (5259) 3302
　　　　　　　　　　　販売 03 (5259) 3301
　　　　　　　　　　　《第2版①-880pp.》

©Sundai preparatory school 2018
落丁・乱丁がございましたら，送料小社負担にて
お取替えいたします。
ISBN978-4-7961-2357-0　　Printed in Japan

駿台文庫Webサイト
https://www.sundaibunko.jp